Not Authorized
For Sale

POLICE LEADERSHIP
IN AMERICA

DATE DUE

APR 15 2011		
NOV 16 2012		

POLICE LEADERSHIP
IN AMERICA
Crisis and Opportunity

edited by

William A. Geller

 American
Bar Foundation

PRAEGER

PRAEGER SPECIAL STUDIES • PRAEGER SCIENTIFIC

New York • Westport, Connecticut • London

Library of Congress Cataloging in Publication Data
Main entry under title:

Police leadership in America.

 Bibliography: p.
 Includes indexes.
 1. Police administration—United States—Addresses,.
essays, lectures. 2. Police chiefs—United States—
Addresses, essays, lectures. 3. Police—United States—
Addresses, essays, lectures. 4. Public relations—
Police—Addresses, essays, lectures. 1. Geller,
William A.
HV8141.P58 1985 352.2'0973 85-6284
ISBN 0-275-90205-6 (alk. paper)
ISBN 0-275-91672-3 (pbk. : alk. paper)

Library of Congress Catalog Card Number: 85-6284
ISBN: 0-275-91672-3

First published in 1985 by American Bar Foundation
750 North Lake Shore Drive, Chicago Illinois 60611, and
Praeger Publishers, 521 Fifth Avenue, New York, NY 10175
A division of Greenwood Press, Inc.

Printed in the United States of America

The paper used in this book complies with the Permanent
Paper Standard issued by the National Information Standards
Organization (Z39.48-1984).

10 9 8 7 6 5 4

To my wife—my muse and my music;
and to my mother, whose *nachus* over
this publication I would have enjoyed very much.

Foreword

William Geller's introduction to this book, and his lead comments on each of its main parts, well describe its contents; and those who are at all informed on the police in the United States will know and esteem many of the authors. Words of mine are not necessary to attract you to it. But, in brief, I would affirm that it is an *informed* book on a topic usually covered by barnyard effluvia.

The case for the importance and interest of this book being thus made and confirmed, let me address the general issue, rather than this particular instance, and try to state why I think a collection of essays by senior administrators and reflective scholars of the police is now important.

The public, including those members of the public who are usually well-informed on matters of community and political significance, remain vacuously ignorant of the work of the police. They see the police as controlling the faucet of crime; if crime increases, they have failed; if crime reduces, they have succeeded. If this were so, then the sweeps of increase and decrease in crime would be related, at least to a degree, to the extent and efficiency of policing in different regions of America; but no responsible scholar suggests any such thing. There would appear to be little correlation between variations in crime and variations in policing in this country or elsewhere.

Yet it is common at public meetings of police boards throughout the United States to act out this absurd ritual: The chief reads out the figures for index crime in the city for the past month. If they have decreased as compared to the preceding month and the same month last year, he expresses pride in the efficiency of his force; if they have increased, he castigates the public or sections of it — the "gangs" are the current scapegoat in some locales — for the decline in moral values in the community.

The reality of communal security, of whatever level of internal safety and sense of security is achieved in any place at any time, is to be found in the extent of consent to governmental authority, in the broad acceptance of mutual collaboration and tolerance to achieve a relatively safe and unthreatened life, by the avoidance of violence, predation, and insult by most people most of the time. To this over-arching social climate the police can contribute only marginally. And further, they may be able to contribute more to the minimization of the fear of crime than to the minimization of crime itself, though the two are obviously interwoven. But the myth is that they control crime; and the myth corrupts them and us.

Am I suggesting, then, that the police are the inconsequential acolytes of a ritualistic criminal law — the rain dancers against crime? Not at all. Quite the contrary: I see the police as centrally important to the social fabric, giving the citizen a sense of security in his person and property, reducing the disorder and the anarchy of urban life, holding steady that difficult balance, determinative of democratic values, between individual autonomy and state authority. And, in the United States, this must be done in a social setting more generative of crime than that of other Western democracies and at the same time more protective of individual autonomy than any other country.

The key figure in this difficult task is the police chief executive, who must provide leadership, set standards, define policy, and compromise the conflicting pressures of public expectations and political interference. He must do these things in a peculiarly difficult setting, a setting in which his tenure is likely to be transient, in which unions and politicians greatly restrict his freedom of action, and in which there is no well-established body of professional standards and practices on which he may rely.

In sum: The community expects too much of the police. The point was excellently made by August Vollmer, a former police chief who in 1929 became America's first professor of police administration at, of all unlikely places, the University of Chicago:

> The policeman is denounced by the public, criticized by preachers, ridiculed in the movies, berated by the newspapers and unsupported by prosecuting officers and judges. He is shunned by the respectables, hated by criminals, deceived by everyone, kicked around like a football by brainless or crooked politicians. . . . He is supposed to possess the qualifications of a soldier, doctor, lawyer, diplomat and educator. . . .

The passage of the years has not changed these high and unrealistic expectations. I have been interested in police policy and practice for 20 years in Chicago and, to a lesser degree, elsewhere in the United States and in other countries. Over that period it is clear that policing has dramatically improved here as elsewhere. There is much less police brutality, much less corruption, much less venality, much less political interference — though there are damaging residues of all these problems. Police leadership is better informed; the police better trained and better equipped. Yet here, as in most other places, the problems of crime have grown worse than they were 20 years ago.

There is no paradox in those apparently conflicting developments. Nor should they be productive of despair. There are encouraging signs of the reduction of serious street crime, encouraging experiments in better policing, increasing understanding of the sources and stimuli of predatory crime. We have begun to learn how to do much better; and the leadership to that end will come, if it indeed does come, from senior administrators of the police and thoughtful scholars of the police like those who have contributed to this book.

Yet how many students from this law school have, over these same 20 years, responded to these high flown sentiments of mine about the need for police leadership and decided to make their careers either in police service or as scholars of the police? Two! Truth is not always quickly perceived.

If the public cares about crime and its control to the extent that the opinion polls tell us it does, this is a book that merits the close attention of every concerned citizen, and — I wish it were true — a politician neglects it at his or her peril.

Norval Morris
Julius Kreeger Professor of Law
University of Chicago
January 1985

Acknowledgments

As somebody (I forget who) once said, "'Originality' is remembering what you heard but forgetting where you heard it." In those terms, what writer is skilled enough to produce a totally unoriginal piece of work? Surely not I. I do remember, however, with gratitude and affection, the assistance I have received from many people in the preparation of this volume.

The American Bar Foundation supported my work from the conception of the book through its publication, and I am indebted to the Foundation's board of directors for their belief in my efforts and to the staff for their guidance. Among the staff, affiliated scholar Wayne Kerstetter, with his rare blend of the practitioner's and the scholar's insights into the complexities of policing, provided a beacon for me at nearly every stage of this project; ABF Executive Director John Heinz, his predecessor Spencer Kimball, and my colleagues Lori Andrews, Samuel Jan Brakel, Thomas Davies, Fredric DuBow, Terrence Halliday, Richard Maas, Joanne Martin, Bette Sikes, and Anne Tatalovich supplied a sonorous sounding board on a number of occasions; research assistant Tim Bell, with able and affable assistance from Technical Services Director Katherine Rosich and editorial department whiz Susan Messer, turned in his typically tenacious effort in preparing the indexes; editorial consultant Louise Kaegi graced several of the contributions with her copyediting talents; and my secretary Janet Atkins, my former secretary Eddie Clark, and clerical wonder Susie Allen performed with such skill and infectious good cheer that I hesitate to name them for fear that a competitor will entice them away from the ABF.

This volume's themes and structure bear the imprint of a remarkable ad hoc advisory committee that convened at the Bar Foundation when the project was only a gleam in my eye. The group, chaired with goodwill, good humor, and good sense by criminologist Norval Morris, included Peoria Public Safety Director Allen Andrews, former Chicago Police Superintendent Richard Brzeczek, Houston Police Chief and IACP Vice-President Lee Brown, law and public administration professor Herman Goldstein, Police Executive Research Forum Executive Director Gary Hayes, criminal justice professor and former police executive Wayne Kerstetter, former ABF Associate Executive Director Donald McIntyre, sociologist Albert Reiss, Jr., and criminologist Jerome Skolnick.

Others whose consultation was invaluable at critical junctures include Chicago Police Superintendent Fred Rice, Deputy Superintendents Dennis Nowicki and Matt Rodriguez, and Captain Ray Risley; labor specialist Murray Geller (one of whose early "cases" involved the labor at my birth!); police historian Samuel Walker; Chicago Police Board member and political sage Marshall Korshak; former IACP Executive Director Norman Darwick and Acting Executive Director James Sterling; Police Executive Research Forum President Sheriff John Duffy; and National Organization of Black Law Enforcement Executives President Ira Harris.

The National Institute of Justice helped to underwrite the research for this book, but my greatest debt to the NIJ is for the generosity of its director, James Stewart, and its staff — particularly Robert Burkhart, Mary Graham, Louis Mayo, and Annesly Schmidt — who shared their enormous expertise on policing whenever I issued an SOS.

Finally, my wife, Julie, as always, provided love and belief to sustain my spirit, a sharp eye to avert my editorial mistakes (the reader will doubtless discover the instances where I've outwitted her), and a model of excellence in her field of music that sets a standard for me to pursue in my own work.

Contents

Introduction

Policing is criminal justice alfresco. For the most part, other criminal justice practitioners — prosecutors, defense attorneys, judges, and jailers — do their challenging work in relatively controllable indoor settings; but police are mainly street workers. In serving up justice alfresco, the police do not, of course, have the luxury of closing the café on a seasonal basis, during inclement weather, or in the pitch-black of night. They dispense their notably varied and ambitious menu not in a central, easily supervised locale but in hundreds or thousands of disjointed places, many seedy. Moreover, they cater to an enormous diversity of clientele, a substantial segment of which, with some justification, hates the service and detests the food. Police are, in Elizabeth Barrett Browning's phrase, "sunburnt by the glare of life."

If a food service were encumbered by the obstacles that confront policing, the restaurateur very likely would close the enterprise. Yet police chiefs do not have this option. The public must be served; and for many, the police department is the only shop in town. Although citizen demands for service have continued to rise, the spigot on the police world's traditional human and material resources has been slowly closing (see Chabotar 1982). Individual police practitioners may decide to walk away from their burdensome mission, but someone else will have to keep the store open.

Given the realities of American policing, who will answer the want ad when a vacancy opens for top central management? Who should? And how can the applicant, or the incumbent, do a creditable job of ensuring that his employees provide reasonably effective, efficient, and equitable service? This volume attempts to look at the varied practical challenges confronting those who will hold leadership positions in the police field during the next several decades. It does so from a considerable array of perspectives. The contributors attempting to articulate these challenges and to fashion solutions include 16 current or former police chief executives, 7 other criminal justice practitioners (including the director of the National Institute of Justice, a national police union president, the executive director of Americans for Effective Law Enforcement, and a staff counsel of the American Civil Liberties Union), 2 mayors, 16 academics (most of whom have at least one foot in the practitioner world), a newspaper executive, and a network television news reporter. They come from 19 states and 29 cities — from Seattle to Fort Lauderdale, from Newark to Honolulu, from Chicago to Houston. During their careers the police authors have headed 22 law enforcement agencies, many of them the nation's largest and most challenging; and they represent a wide range of professional viewpoints, having occupied positions of authority in the International Association of Chiefs of Police, the Police Executive Research Forum, the National Organization of Black Law Enforcement Executives, the Police Foundation, and countless other professional and public service organizations.

The nonpolice executive authors represent the enormous expertise that sympathetic but tough-minded outsiders can offer, in harness with police leadership, to advance the quality of American policing. Still, the presentation of insiders' perspectives interacting with other practitioners' and scholars' viewpoints is perhaps this book's most important contribution. The 16 police administrators were selected as contributors because they exemplify an important national resource for governmental and private sector urban policy planners. A comprehensive list of the talented, but grossly underconsulted, police executives of this country would be hundreds of times longer than this volume's contributor list.

Two themes have guided the organization of this book: first, the questions, Who runs the police, and who should?; and, second, the perception that, despite significant advances, policing in America today in some ways remains in a state of crisis — but a crisis pregnant with opportunity for progress due to the emergence of a strong cadre of police leaders. The introductions preceding each of the eight major sections of the book will touch on these themes as they relate to the particular subject matter to follow, but some additional general discussion at this point may help clarify what the chapters in this volume aim to accomplish.

In addressing the questions of who runs the police and who should be running them, the contributors attempt to identify most of the key constituencies and forces that push and pull the police leader. If the questions sound rhetorical (the implicit answers being that the chief does and should run the police), that only underscores the popularity of the misperception that the American police chief enjoys unfettered autonomy. In reality, the pressures on chiefs' policy and operational decisions are plentiful and powerful and, in many cases, interdependent. Those explored in the pages of this volume are exerted from within police departments by unions and officer review units (staffed by sworn and civilian personnel) and from without by a host of forces. The latter include political chief executives (mayors and city managers); city councils; community leaders; business executives, merchant associations, and other components of the economic power structure; the private security industry; the media; prosecutors; courts; bar associations; civilian review boards, ombudsmen, and other external oversight bodies; public and private blue-ribbon commissions; researchers; and governmental support bodies such as the National Institute of Justice. Some of the contributors to this volume examine the impact not of individuals or groups but of ideas or movements, such as "police professionalism" and the "crimefighter" conception of the police role. The interdependence of many of these pressures means that isolated discussion of any given one is neither possible nor desirable. Hence, for example, the reader will find consideration of the increasingly important role of police unions in constraining police executive decisions throughout the book, not only in the section that focuses intensively on unions. The introductory notes to sections and parenthetical references within each chapter will attempt to alert the reader to helpful discussions of particular topics that appear elsewhere in the book.

This volume touches on, but does not asssess in any detail, a large number of other constituencies or forces, not mentioned above, that in varying degrees may limit or enhance police leaders' abilities to "make a difference" in the quality of public safety. These include middle managers and lower level supervisors within police departments; the individual line police officer, who has received considerable attention in the literature and who a number of practitioners and scholars argue really runs the police department (see, for example, Muir 1977; Ruchelman 1973, p. 11); state legislatures, which play a part in prescribing police duties (by passage of criminal codes and statutes affecting municipal finance) and in structuring police working relationships (by authorizing or prohibiting collective bargaining); civil service boards, which may control most of a department's hiring and promotion; and police boards or commissions, which have received scant scholarly attention in this country even though they possess enormous potential powers over police chief selection, police budgets, policymaking, and discipline (see Goldstein 1977; Stenning 1981).

Still other possibly significant influences on the manner and quality of police service are exerted by city law, finance, personnel, fire, housing, public works, and other departments; special interest groups, such as civil liberties and civil rights organizations, the National Rifle Association, crime victim advocates (see Bard and Sangrey 1979; Morris 1983; Hillenbrand 1984), the elderly, and women's advocates—particularly those focusing on domestic violence and sexual assault control; businesses (nightclubs, taxi companies, and the construction industry) that may operate only when licensed and inspected by the police; police professional associations, including the International Association of Chiefs of Police, the Police Executive Research Forum, the National Organization of Black Law Enforcement Executives, the National Black Police Association, the Mexican-American Command Officers Association, the National Sheriffs Association, the Police Management Association, and so forth; nongovernmental police chief screening services, such as the International Association of Chiefs of Police's or other agencies' "assessment centers" or any of the executive search firms increasingly being hired by city managers and mayors; police executive training institutes, such as the FBI's National Academy at Quantico, Virginia, the Kennedy School of Government at Harvard University, the Traffic Institute at Northwestern University, and the Southern Police Institute in Louisville, Kentucky; independent police research and advocacy organizations, such as the Police Foundation and Americans for Effective Law Enforcement; mayors' and city managers' professional groups, including the National League of Cities, the U.S. Conference of Mayors, and the International City Management Association (see Goldstein 1977, p. 318; ICMA 1977, 1982); governmental entities, including the U.S. Commission on Civil Rights, congressional committees (which over the years have held hearings on alleged constitutional violations by major police departments), state and county criminal justice planning agencies, and the U.S. Justice Department's Community Relations Service; the FBI's voluntary Uniform Crime Reporting system; illicit sources of influence, such as those documented by the Knapp Commission and racketeer organizations; and the ever-present depictions of police and their world in fiction, especially those generated in Hollywood, which have done much to make the American public armchair experts on the police and to foster unreasonable citizen expectations of the police.

Among two of the more interesting nominees for who runs the police elicited from police practitioners are "911" and "no one." The suggestions are that calls to the emergency phone number in many cities are permitted to structure excessively officer work time and that many police department areas, precincts, and beats run themselves without meaningful direction or control. In a sense, these two nominees are directly related, for if, by dialing 911, *everyone* runs the police, then, in practical effect, *no one* runs them. The dispersion of power in too many directions can produce a power vacuum. In reading the contributions in this volume for guidance on who runs the police, it is advisable to keep in mind the distinction between influencing something and actually controlling it. In a more literal concern with who actually *runs* the police, the preceding lists of relevant constituencies and forces would doubtless be shorter. This volume is more directed, however, at identifying the predominant social, political, economic, and professional *influences* on the direction of American policing and at helping police executives enlarge their expertise in how to deal with them. Thus the net of concern is cast broadly.

One of the underlying assumptions in asking who *should* run the police is, of course, that some forms of pressure on the police chief are quite proper. How much pressure is proper, from what sources, and on what issues clearly are questions of great complexity and practical importance. The answers, if any, are not timeless. Herman Goldstein (1977, p. 145) has observed that over the years society's ideas have changed about the police matters on which it is appropriate for the citizenry to have a say. The reforms recommended by the contributors to this volume are in many respects different from those found in the literature several decades ago and very likely will be out of step with the prescriptions of the coming century.

At any point in history, making constructive changes in some of policing's more tradition-bound practices can be enormously difficult. Dorothy Guyot (1979) likened the task to "bending granite." Psychologist Havelock Ellis captured the loneliness of leadership a century ago when he observed that "to be a leader of men one must turn one's back on men." In providing leadership in policing, as in most other endeavors, forging good solutions depends heavily on an ability to ask the right questions. When novelist Gertrude Stein was asked on her deathbed, "What is the answer?" her whispered reply is said to have been: "What is the question?" In the introductions preceding each section of this volume, I will indicate the two or three questions that I posed for the authors' consideration in commissioning their contributions. I hope they were some of the "right" questions.

As editor, part of one's job is to establish accurate expectations on the part of both the contributors and the readers. Playwright Arthur Miller (1963) once described the fiction writer's objective as telling the truth about life. But, he cautioned, "life is like a fist clenched around the truth. The playwright, if he is successful, has the ability for one moment to lift back one finger for a glimpse of what lies beneath." If a glimpse of the truth is the fiction writer's objective, so, I suppose, should it be the objective of the nonfiction writers in this book. In wielding the editor's blue pencil, if I have been of any assistance I would like to think it has been to insist on clarity of communication without loss of subtlety. Steiner (1979) stated the objective more elegantly: "Everything should be made as simple as possible, but no simpler."

PART 1

THE CHIEF AS A MAJOR MUNICIPAL POLICYMAKER

Introduction

The chapters in this section address some of the most delicate power issues faced by a police executive. They describe, and prescribe, both the constraints imposed on police chiefs by mayors and city managers and the police executive's role in civic policymaking. Ironically, as the authors make clear, to avoid being swallowed by politics, the chief must be among the city's most adept politicians. If he does not enter office with a hearty respect for diplomatic skills, he will surely exit with one — and with an appreciation of the sardonic definition of diplomacy as "the art of saying 'Nice doggie!' till you can find a rock" (Peter 1977, p. 152).

The contributors — three chiefs and two mayors — have focused on three central concerns: (1) What are the appropriate limits on the authority of the *political* chief executive (mayor, city manager) on police matters? (2) How do these limits change depending on the issue (personnel decisions, general enforcement policymaking, specific enforcement decisions, and so forth)? and (3) What should be the role of the police chief on matters (education, public health and welfare, zoning, and the like) that do not have immediate consequences for the police but may have longer term consequences for law enforcement and order maintenance? How would an enhanced role for the police chief on these matters affect the balance of political power between the chief and the mayor or other public officials?

Traditional politician-police chief relationships plunged policing into a crisis of legitimacy. The crisis was rooted partly in too much meddling by mayors in police decisions and partly in not enough intervention. The taproot of the problem, however, was that many police chiefs *tolerated* either the politicization of their department or the unbridled discretion that came from a laissez-faire stance by their mayor or city manager. The opportunity for striking an appropriate balance between police managers' professional

3

autonomy and their political responsiveness and for taking full advantage of the depth and breadth of police expertise on a wide range of urban problems comes from the growing awareness by mayors, city managers, and police chiefs of one another's responsibilities and needs (see, for example, ICMA 1977, 1982). This awareness may be greatly advanced by the fledgling National Institute of Policing, which is discussed by Patrick Murphy.

Murphy's chapter and the others in this section are notable for their candor about and their principled reaction to the meshing of the political and police worlds. (Other contributors to this volume who touch helpfully on the political aspects of police administration are Anthony Bouza, Raymond Davis, George Kelling (in the chapter on order maintenance), Wayne Kerstetter, Carl Klockars, and Albert Reiss.) These discussions stand in marked contrast to traditional statements on the subject. For example, when, following the 1968 Democratic National Convention in Chicago, Hubert Humphrey criticized Mayor Richard Daley for having presided over a deplorable misuse of the police, the mayor's response was: "I had nothing to do with . . . running the police department. . . . Daley gave no orders to the police department. I defy you or anyone else to show that I did. No one runs the police department but [the superintendent]" (*Chicago Daily News* 1969; see also *Chicago Tribune* 1969 and Richard Brzeczek's chapter). Even today, it is not unusual for mayors and police chiefs in public statements to assert flatly that (under their administration) the police are nonpolitical and the politicians are removed from police decision making (see Robinson 1975). Another tradition in the public administration field is to distinguish between policymaking and administration (for instance, the city council would make policy and the city manager or police chief would implement it as an administrator). But, as Goldstein (1977, p. 145) observed, it has become clear that this is an unrealistic distinction; today, "much of administration is policymaking."

Thus the starting place for the discussions that follow is that police administration is an inherently political (although, hopefully, nonpartisan) activity and that the chief's municipal superior needs to play a significant role in assuring quality policing. Neither the mayor nor the chief can afford to remain aloof from the other's concerns, for a serious mistake by either one could cost both their jobs, to the public's detriment. These treatments of the police chief's and mayor's roles in law enforcement are, in some respects, inconsistent with the civics class lessons that have shaped public opinion about proper conduct by public officials. These chapters are not much of a contribution to the literature that explores how angels should behave in paradise (Klockars 1979, p. 265). They are, instead, sincere efforts by seasoned practitioners to articulate how those working in the crucible of urban government can provide police services without abandoning democratic ideals. Their messages will provide a backdrop for the discussions in the remainder of the volume.

1

Structuring the Political
Independence of the Police Chief

Allen H. Andrews, Jr.

Many, if not most, police chief executives express serious concerns with the authority a political chief executive (mayor or city manager) exerts or attempts to exert over their responsibilities. The suggestion is that the political officials are involved in matters that should not fall within their purview. Is there a real issue here, or are the police chief executives succumbing to the typical human desire to be independent, to chafe at and resent external pressures? Why should society at large be concerned?

Few municipal functions are simultaneously as sensitive and as seemingly insensitive to the citizenry, as routine and as unpredictable, as rule-bound and as discretionary, as supervised by external oversight and as unsupervisable (even invisible) in daily detail as is policing. And no other city function is so likely to touch the lives of any citizen as unexpectedly or in such unpleasant circumstances. The turbulence of crime and the cloud of fear it spreads over the land, combined with the shrinking social services available to those of few means in a society that has created public expectations of cradle-to-grave governmental assistance, make policing, in even its smallest details, of enormous interest and concern to the community at large, the news media, and politicians.

A matter of such pressing concern as policing can hardly be expected to escape the squeeze of conflicting public agendas. It is the purpose of the political process to effect compromise between such conflicting desires and opinions, and it is in the nature of the political process to accomplish that compromise through persuasion and the trading of favors. It is also in its nature to take administrative issues into the partisan political arena, either for political initiatives or to respond to the media or citizen-generated issues. Within proper bounds these tendencies underpin our successful system of government; unregulated, they can destroy it. In providing political oversight to the application of law and coercive force, to the resolution of conflict and preservation of peace, to the regulation of conduct, to the response to calls for and provision of emergency assistance, and to most of the other duties and services expected of the municipal police, we must guard against the inherent pressures of the partisan political process that lead those within it to expand their influence and authority beyond proper bounds and to create controversy where none exists. In the nature of things, political representatives are subjected to a steady stream of pressures by the citizenry, their staff, various interest groups, and the news media. The politicians are peppered by such "political considerations" as "bad publicity," "he can do us a good turn," "they could have raised hell on that last occasion—we owe them one," and similar bromides.

Police chiefs often confide in one another how they have resisted improper political pressures, running the gamut from demands to clamp down unlawfully on teenagers to pressures for differential enforcement policies in different neighborhoods in order to adapt to varying customs and traditions to requests to fix tickets or reduce drunk driving charges for friends and relatives to pleas to overlook "privileged" taverns and gambling spots or parking violations at certain locations (see Brown, 1984). Political interference in duty assignments, promotions, transfers, hiring, and especially discipline is not uncommon, and it is increasing in other management areas through the door opened by collective bargaining laws. The various versions of civil service provide uneven protection at best because mayors appoint the members of the civil service commissions, and many communities observe a custom in which members of overlapping term commissions "resign" on election of new mayors. This interference subverts justice, weakens and divides police command authority, demoralizes police officers, and leads the police into politics and, consequently, temptations. Just as police are made more cynical by such interference, citizens lose faith in the objectivity, the integrity, and the trustworthiness of the police and of justice. Ultimately, this undermines the trust of the people in their government and in the rule of law—of which the police are the most visible emblem.

NEED FOR FORMAL ESTABLISHMENT
OF POLICE INDEPENDENCE

Conversations with and writings by city managers and mayors (the political chief executives, for the purpose of this discussion), seminars on police-city hall relations, interdepartment team-building efforts within cities and discussions with those who conduct such efforts, and meetings involving mayors and city managers at municipal league gatherings all produce strong evidence of a widely and firmly held belief among city officials that the police are excessively independent of city hall. In my opinion, the belief is factually based: The police do not see themselves as part of city hall or city government. Most heads of other municipal departments would unhesitatingly agree that the police chief is given far more autonomy and independence than they are. Most police chiefs probably would concur privately, while urging that political restrictions and interferences are still excessive in too many localities.

Assuming that when the antagonists and protagonists agree there is at least a reasonably good chance that they are correct, any serious discussion of the bounds between political and police chief executives in the administration of the policing function must take account of this phenomenon of police autonomy from civic government. This independence seems to originate primarily from the great misconception that the police are concerned mainly with crime and the law, from the political chief executive's unwillingness (and vulnerability) to being perceived by the public as injecting politics into law enforcement, and from the fact that the police, and therefore the police chief, in most communities are involved with so many people and receive so much continuing publicity as to become "politically" powerful without trying. Our constitutional and political philosophy of balancing power requires that the chief's activities be kept "nonpolitical" as defined by the community and be confined to "appropriate" professional spheres of effort and that the chief's image and public activities be approved by the public. In many communities a public leadership position for the police chief is not acceptable to his political boss. For example, speaking publicly on municipal policy issues is discouraged or even forbidden to many police chiefs, especially in the case of issues embroiled in political controversy or on which the police chief and the political chief executive hold conflicting opinions.

If, as it appears, the police often do enjoy de facto independence in police operational matters, why the concern with improper political interference? The answer may lie with the unwritten, informal, extralegal nature of the independence. Without clear bounds of legally established authority, clear day-to-day relationships cannot be established, and consequently much personal and organizational energy must be expended on each issue or event as it develops to define the power and the working and the authority relationships. Such continuing uncertainty does not improve either city government or police organization stability or success.

My thesis is that this independence is appropriate, probably needs to be expanded, and must be formally established. This conclusion follows from the observation that mayoral and city manager dissatisfaction with police autonomy is prompted by the de facto, political, informal, and therefore invisible nature of this independence. This allows police chiefs to build and use power yet escape public accountability without, in fact, providing the police chief executive with the legal power and authority actually needed. This state of affairs may be useful to some police chiefs and to many political chief executives who like to exercise power under these ambiguous conditions, but it does not promote good government or proper law enforcement independence.

Advantages and Parameters of Independence

If the police chief executive function were legally endowed with independence from certain political processes in professional matters — an independence that was accompanied by a visible and effective structure for political accountability to the local legislative body (as opposed to a mayor or other single elected official) — and if the independence of the chief were combined with as full responsibility and authority over the police function and its organization as our system could constitutionally permit, then issues of police management and policy would readily surface and would be addressed by the political body representing the citizenry.

The chief's responsibility and authority should include complete control over the personnel system, subject to appeal to an independent body in disciplinary matters but with the appeal limited to due process and sufficiency of the evidence. Appropriations to the police department should permit the chief to depart from the line items and should, as much as practicable, be structured to fund police officers and support personnel by building the direct and indirect costs of supporting each position into the personnel line according to a cost analysis justified to the appropriating authority. Too often the traditional line item appropriations process succumbs to the political pressure to both maintain police officer numbers and balance the budget by retaining personnel but reducing the line items for training, quality control, supplies, and equipment and its replacement — often weakening the organization more than if the number of officers were reduced with the remainder supported by an adequate budget.

The deployment of police officers and other resource allocation decisions should be exclusively the province of the chief, as should be the choice of tactics to cope with specific situations and problems. Strategies for the long-range approach to problems should be developed by the chief with the community's policymaking body or its chief executive, according to the customs of the community and within the law.

With adequate legal and public authority and responsibility for policing and the police organization, the police chief executive could properly be held accountable by society without engaging in the sacrifice of a political scapegoat, as happens so often now in our cities because of the informality and invisibility of police independence from the political process. This accountability should rest not only on visibility but on some legal requirements and duties.

The chief must be required to provide written policy guidance and regulation of the discretion exercised by police officers in effecting arrests, in deciding between custodial and noncustodial arrests, in using force, and in establishing tolerances for enforcement of traffic and parking laws and other regulatory offenses, including gambling and prostitution. In most states this will require revision of statutes and county and city charters and ordinances defining the duties and responsibilities of the police. The "arrest *all* offenders" language usually found must be replaced by specific recognition of police discretion and by a grant of authority and responsibility to the police chief to regulate the exercise of that discretion. The chief also should be required to maintain sufficient quality control and training programs and have authority to expend the funds necessary for these vital functions.

Following an inevitable transition period from informal independence to independence formalized by law, charter, and ordinance, the constant behind-the-scenes testing and friction inherent to informal power relationships could be substantially eliminated; and political chief executives would be relieved of the charges, suspicions, and *expectations* that they interfere politically (see Reiss's chapter in this book). With proper, public recognition of the police chief's independence, political figures will hesitate to imply to citizens (voters) that they will take care of "problems" with the police because formal, legal definition of police administrative independence will allow police chiefs to resist publicly improper pressures and, consequently, political figures will know that the chief could, and would, make a public issue of transgressions over proper boundaries.

Formal definition would encourage public debate and legislative setting of boundaries and amendment of those boundaries rather than interpersonal jockeying behind the scenes. Most important, this formalization would shove the police chief out front as the major public figure he really is and ought to be, with the attendant authority, responsibility, and accountability that the responsibilities of the office merit.

Models for Formalized Independence

The city management form of city government offers an instructive model for implementation of this formalized independence from improper political interference or influence. Some of the balancing mechanisms developed and tested over years of experience include the following six: (1) The chief executive officer (CEO) or city manager is accountable to the elected members of the city council *as a body* rather than to any individual council member; (2) individual council members are prevented (by law or council rules) from giving administrative, operational, or policy direction to the city manager; (3) the council as a body may not give specific administrative direction to the CEO, who generally has exclusive executive authority over the city employees; (4) the CEO, consistent with civil service statutes and subject to employee appeal rights, has full authority to hire, promote, and discipline city personnel; (5) the CEO, consistent with state municipal finance statutes, has broad authority to manage the budget and to depart from line item appropriations to meet unanticipated needs; and (6) the council as a body hires the CEO and may dismiss him in its discretion without stating cause. The city manager model is significant because it clearly has been successful in the American local political milieu and because the necessary separation between the political policymaking body and the independent chief executive is realistically defined.

Another useful model is the British structure for insulating the chief constable from improper political influence, yet assuring reasonable responsiveness to local concerns. Seven of the most significant features are the following: (1) The local police authority (two-thirds local government elected councilmen and one-third government-appointed magistrates) appoints the chief constable with concurrence of the home office as to qualifications (the local police authorities were created to provide representation for the local governments in the region served by each police force); (2) the police authority may remove the chief constable only for cause and with approval of the home office (personality differences do not justify a chief constable's removal); (3) the police authority provides the local funds and facilities for the police force through its budget but cannot direct its activities or the chief constable or make rules or regulations for the force or its operations; (4) the police authority may request reports from the chief constable (a serious, public matter in Great Britain), who may appeal the request to the home secretary and need not comply unless directed to do so); (5) through the Police Act of 1964, all personnel matters were transferred from the police authority to the chief constable, who recruits, hires, trains, assigns, promotes, and disciplines all police employees (unlike most U.S. chiefs); (6) the chief constable has sole authority over the operations, operating policies, deployment, enforcement policies, and methods of the police force (no official government body at any level of government is able to exercise that authority or give direction in such matters to the chief constable); and (7) to establish public confidence in the quality and integrity of police discipline investigations and actions, a Police Complaints Board of citizens appointed by the prime minister oversees the investigation of citizen complaints against the police by reviewing the investigations, by requesting reconsideration of its disciplinary decisions, or even (although rarely, in fact) directing specific action (see Police Act 1976; Police Complaints Board 1983; Goldstein 1977, p. 320; Holdaway 1979).

Defining the role of the police chief executive in the United States confronts us with several questions. Is the police chief executive a mere minion, who faithfully executes the policy of the political and legal systems, or a major community leader and public policymaker in his own right as chief executive of the city's most complex, sensitive, and conspicuous function and organization? If American policing really is becoming more professional, more educated, and more honest a career rather than a political reward, why do police chiefs have such short tenure in office, frequently losing their positions almost as often as the political leadership changes (except, generally, in city manager cities)? With municipal resources decreasing, taxpayers in revolt, and other problems emerging, should the police continue to follow the example of the political process and only react to changing social problems and conditions, or should the police devote resources to effective research and development for problem solving and planning for the future (see Goldstein 1979; Reiss's chapter)? If we really expect the police chief to exercise effective direction and control over the police organization, can we increasingly follow the confrontational private sector collective bargaining model and deny the police chief control of the bargaining on noneconomic issues (see Bouza's chapter)? Can we afford to subject the operations of our law enforcement agencies to control on a broad spectrum of matters by the collective bargaining process, labor arbitrators, and police unions? The answers to these questions suggest the kinds of structures needed to ensure the police chief's independence from the political superior.

LEADER OR MINION?

If the de facto independence of the police were legally formalized, the role of the police chief executive as a significant community leader would quickly become apparent. But is the police chief executive actually a significant community leader, or would the restructuring be creating rather than confirming the role? What characteristics of the police chief executive position point to his role as a significant community leader?

First, the chief is responsible for controlling the great discretionary power that police exert over the lives of individuals and groups. Although the police are the primary source of justice in the community and should be so regarded by the citizenry and the government, they can do more harm and injustice in a day than the courts could remedy in a month. Despite thoughtful discussions in scholarly writings over the past two decades, the public and their political leaders still do not fully appreciate the very great amount of discretion that the police do and must exercise and the fact that this discretion must necessarily be exercised by the relatively low ranks, who are far removed from the police chief in the large departments. Controlling such discretion to the satisfaction of citizens, community organizations, courts, police unions, and all those others who are or suddenly can become interested in police conduct or activities is the most difficult responsibility in city government. The processes of control are delicate, frustrating, and subject to resistance and conflicting pressures and, consequently, require an unusual level of authority and power over the organization on the part of the police chief executive. For practical purposes, it can be safely generalized that the United States is almost alone among nations in restricting the chief's authority over his organization.

For a variety of historical and other, but primarily political, reasons, such authority is more notable for its absence than its presence. This has serious consequences in this era of archaic civil service laws, police unions and collective bargaining agreements, federal, state, and local police regulatory legislation, and the constant tussle of local politics. Further complications stem from the courts' traditional view of the role of the police and police practices as society rapidly evolves in untraditional directions. To the extent that rapid and dramatic change produces instability, dissension, disruptive behavior, and social pathology, the police are immediately involved — with or without an informed view of policing on the part of the law.

Second, the chief's importance as a community leader stems from the extraordinarily important but rarely discussed role the police play in resolving conflict before the need to suppress it develops. Police should be society's experts in conflict prevention and resolution, whether the problems be the daily "small" conflicts between persons or within families, neighborhood youth in conflict with the elderly, or the racial and ethnic tensions simmering in many of our cities. The police executive should be the city's chief peacekeeper. To that end, he must be a major civic figure, since the conflicts that concern the police are epidemic and require solutions throughout the community. Implementing a policy of early intervention requires public respect, power, and influence. Merely following past police practices and tidy administrative procedures in courteous reaction to complaints and pressures, even in the best style of the enlightened and dedicated administrative minion, will not suffice for the task of conflict resolution.

Third, the chief inevitably attains community prominence by virtue of the fact that the police touch the lives of an extraordinary number of citizens, exerting many different (often unpleasant) influences. The police, as George Bean sagely advised me before he became my first city manager, are the primary influence on the public's views of local government, law, and justice. The number of citizens having direct and indirect contact with the police exceeds in number and public relations importance the citizens who interact with all other city departments. In Peoria, a city of 124,000 population, the citizen Advisory Committee on Police-Community Relations polled adult citizens in 1982 and found that 39.4 percent of the adult residents sampled reported direct contact with the police in one year. Clearly, the leader of any city department whose employees have face-to-face contact with so many of the city's voters and taxpayers each year bears a heavy, occasionally decisive, responsibility for the public's opinion of its government. Logically and practically, the leader of employees with such unusual public impact should have the ability and authority to direct the affairs and control the performance of those employees. Perhaps nothing is more important to our system of law and government than that its citizens believe that it serves their interests in a just, objective, and effective but civil manner.

POLICE CHIEF TENURE

A business leader in Peoria asked me a few years ago how the $80,000 salary proposed at that time for the superintendent of police of Chicago could be justified. I asked him what he would have to pay to hire a chief executive officer without a contract for a $400 million corporation with 15,000 employees while assuring the prospective CEO that he would probably lose his position in approximately two years. The prospective CEO would also know that whatever his experience or ability, he would most likely never again be employed as a chief executive officer in that industry but would have to abandon his career and take up a new one. His response was, "A lot more than $80,000."

Chicago's turnover of seven superintendents and almost as many acting superintendents in the past two dozen years is not too far off the average of 2.8 years of service by chiefs in cities with more than 1,000 officers found in a 1975 survey (NAC 1976, p. 10). Our municipal leaders, in sharp contrast to the consensus of police chief executives, apparently seem to believe that these complex, sensitive, large police agencies can be effectively managed — including the development of objectives, the acquisition of necessary resources, the compilation of teams, and the implementation of innovative programs — with a new chief executive officer and a new top staff every few years (NAC 1976, p. 7). At least that is the way the large cities' police forces are being operated, with the exception of most of the city manager cities.

Although some of the short tenure results from the up-from-the-ranks selection system used in many locations and consequent quick retirement of very senior career officers promoted to chief, the greatest amount of the short tenure problem is clearly due to early termination of police chiefs. And it is obvious that if the appointing authorities were concerned with long tenure and the opportunity to effect significant improvement, they would not appoint early retirement individuals as police chief executives. Significantly, the International Association of Chiefs of Police (IACP) study conducted for the National Advisory Commission on Criminal Justice Standards and Goals (NAC 1976, p. 147) showed that only 52 percent of the political chief executives agreed with the concept of fixed-term appointments of police chiefs; and only 67 percent agreed that police chiefs should have protection from arbitrary removal through some form of due process.

It appears reasonable to suspect that many political superiors of police chief executives prefer a dutiful minion to having an independent community leader in their administration. Although "chief for life" clearly is not a workable or desirable concept in our culture and times, several alternatives offer practical possibilities to ensure the professional rather than political character of the position. A multiyear contract with early severance indemnity, such as many business CEOs and city managers secure, would make dismissing a police chief executive too costly (and, therefore, visible) to be done for other than good reasons, publicly explained. The IACP study recommended some form of due process protection to formalize and make public the removal of a police chief executive, thus reducing the incidence of arbitrary (or corrupt) removal.

Short-term police chief executives may be able to hold things together, and the unusually good ones can make some of the structural and organizational changes that are frequently accepted in police management and politics in the United States as symbols of successful police management. But there is good reason to question whether the internal agency improvements such executives have made, however considerable, have produced concomitant benefits in the life of the communities they serve. The matter of tenure should be considered in recognizing that police have been essentially reactively oriented, focusing on citizen calls for service and preoccupied with the effectiveness of their response to those calls and the individual incidents they represent. By contrast, some in the police world and many outside it (for example, Goldstein 1979, 1981, 1982c) have been concerned with the output of the police organization — What effect are police efforts and investments having on the problems faced by the community? This, of course, immediately goes to a whole series of issues: What are the community problems? What alternative approaches can "solve" them? How should one choose among the alternatives? How can one determine whether or what success is being achieved? Approaching these questions requires an effective research and development capability, which is essential to the chief seeking an alternative to political pressure in dealing with community issues.

RESEARCH AND DEVELOPMENT

Rare is the law enforcement agency that has been able to develop a research and development capability that proceeds systematically to identify needs, develop new and more productive techniques, and measure objectively the accomplishments of the resources expended. The existing body of information that could help determine the efficacy of police operational decisions and deployment strategies and tactics is appallingly slim, although policing is one of the primary and oldest functions of the municipality. This is true, at least partly, because "everyone" knows how to do police work (particularly since the advent of television) and because cities and states have rarely funded valid research of any consequence, let alone rigorously evaluated the various operational strategies and tactics developed over the years. The typical police administrative response to a street problem is to throw police officers at it — and this invariably pleases those citizens concerned with the problem because it is their opinion of the most appropriate response.

Much was accomplished in police research during the years of Law Enforcement Assistance Administration/National Institute of Justice financing, particularly in the study of police resource allocation, community relations, crime prevention, police tactics, and technology (see Stewart's chapter). But police research and development has not really become institutionalized in police forces, and that which has is primarily focused on operational procedures and orders, equipment and hardware, paperwork, and information processing. The academic researchers who are doing very promising work are finding it increasingly difficult to keep themselves within police research, as federal research funding has been cut and cut again; at the same time, the state and local government fiscal situations have become so desperate that the struggle in the face of major reductions in police appropriations is to preserve even the little R&D capability that has developed — and that has been shifted almost totally to coping with the effects of radical budget cuts. It is unrealistic under these circumstances to expect that we will see any significant increase in appropriations for research and development by the local political leadership.

Yet the problems of policing and the problems that require policing in our cities are legion, growing and changing at an increasing rate. If we are to convert police executive decision making to a strategic, proactive, and continuing process focused on community problems, then clearly there is a desperate need for even greater resources for research and development unless we are willing to sacrifice essential activity now being performed.

Adopting a problem-oriented (Goldstein 1979) management style based on research and evaluation offers great potential to fiscally pinched cities given the wide diversity of municipal problems that the police are expected to solve or at least keep the lid on. The fact is that most of these problems involve dynamics and mechanisms much larger than the resources or capabilities of the police. True crime prevention in the old sense of preventing and remedying juvenile delinquency may more likely be found in better parenting than in policing strategies. Crime prevention considered in those terms might also result in concomitant benefits for society such as reduced family breakup, less child and spouse abuse, fewer family disputes, a higher rate of school achievement for more children, and so forth. Systematic analysis of the complex problems of our urbanized society (for example, alcohol and substance abuse, deinstitutionalization of mental health services, wholesale early parole releases due to prison overcrowding) would reveal as many "solutions" outside the purview and capability of the police as it would reveal actions appropriate for the police system. And, if costed out carefully, the nonpolice remedies might be more economical and socially productive than approaches relying primarily on the police.

Already possessing a great wealth of information about a community's problems, the police could assemble even more if provided with sufficient resources and talent, and the results could be surprising. One community used federal funds granted for violent crime reduction to fund a 24-hour, radio-dispatched social worker service to respond to family trouble calls. The beneficial end results included a leveling off of the increase in violent crime known to the police, a reduction in calls to the police concerning family trouble, diversion of those calls to the social service system, a decrease in complaints against the police by citizens, greater success in having mentally disturbed individuals accepted by the mental health facility, and a consolidated and more cost-efficient handling of street drunks. These results were far more impressive than those that would have been obtained by investing the same sum of money in police officers or other police efforts.

A police chief who paid the same fee to an alcohol treatment center for accepting drunks that had been paid to the jail for accepting drunks salvaged an alcohol treatment program, relieved the jail of a serious and complex work load and the courts of great frustration, brought several portions of the community together (around the money) to cooperate and improve the alcohol treatment resources of the community, and, because the monies were under the chief's control, was able to exercise considerable influence on many community agencies to take an interest in and work on the alcoholism problem. When a state chose to enact a street intoxication decriminalization law and belatedly realized that the impact on local medical and other treatment facilities was unknown, only a police department was able to provide good data, not only on the number of drunkenness arrests but also on the use of alcohol by persons arrested for a wide range of crimes.

The fact is that most policing and police tactics are based on usage and "that's the way it's done" experience, as well as the intuition of very talented people. But much of this conventional wisdom has been called into serious question by research, which has improved some police management, particularly in patrol officer allocation and deployment and in predicting the likelihood of solving burglary cases. Far, far more remains to be done in providing managerially useful research to police chief executives (see Stewart's chapter).

A police chief more independent of the community political process and needing practical approaches to lighten his burdens would certainly allocate a portion of his resources to researching his problems and developing potential solutions. It is the political process, which prefers to alleviate the pressures by applying the remedies of those who "know" how the problems of policing can be "solved," that is largely to blame for the fact that policing is based so much on intuition and what "everybody knows" and so little on hard information and measured results. Research will never be popular with local voters, but a determined and independent but accountable police chief executive would be able to allocate more funds from the police budget than the political process now permits.

Managing from factually based, research-developed strategies would require at the outset that the police persuade numerous governmental and private agencies to allocate some of their resources to achieving police strategies aimed at reducing community problems. Clearly, the community leadership style this calls for is not that of an administrative minion but that of an effective, innovative, and pioneering community leader.

COLLECTIVE BARGAINING

Although the advent of collective bargaining rights for police officers was long overdue, unfortunately it has not generally brought with it a thoughtful consideration of the nature and implications of collective bargaining in government. The inapposite analogy to private sector collective bargaining, so often advanced during legislative consideration, has resulted in uncritical acceptance of the notion that denial of the right to strike to "essential" public employees must be counterbalanced by the grant of compulsory binding arbitration to the police union (see, generally, Rynecki and Morse 1981; Bouza's chapter).

Failure to think critically about the requisites of police collective bargaining has permitted abuses by police unions that threaten the police chief's ability to be a major policymaker on police matters, let alone on major municipal concerns. These unions have made strides virtually unheard of in the private sector. For example, what private sector unions can cause a recall election among the stockholders to remove the CEO? Or contribute funds (or withhold contributions) for the CEO's continuance in office? Or elect union members to the corporate board of directors? Or have its union member on the board of directors appointed to the bargaining committee? Or secure corporate agreement that its management be members of the union? Or, having management in its union, refuse to bargain for appropriate benefits for those members? Or, not able to achieve a goal through collective bargaining with management's bargaining team, take the negotiations to the individual members of the corporate board of directors or to the meetings of the entire board of directors? Or, unable to achieve a bargaining objective with management and the board of directors, change the bargaining arena to the legislature or take the issue in a referendum to the stockholders? Or bargain with the board of directors or a stockholder elected from among the stockholders instead of with the management? Such practices show why public employee collective bargaining raises fundamental issues of how public decisions should be made and make a strong case for the view that the major decisions in the collective bargaining process are political.

It is imperative not only that some suitable and truly public sector model of bargaining be developed for the police but that the police chief executive be in control of the bargaining as it relates to management prerogatives and control of the police. The elected political chief executive will leave, usually soon, for another career beyond any practical accountability for what his collective bargaining has left behind. But the police chief must live with bargaining's daily effects and be held publicly accountable for the management results. Formal independence and accountability would correct the perception, currently widely held by political chief executives, that police chiefs are likely to "side with the men" and are not "management oriented." Any remaining chiefs of that type would be either reoriented or eliminated under a system of full formal responsibility and public accountability.

In order to confer major influence over the collective bargaining process on the police chief, perhaps labor laws could separate authority to bargain by subject matter, giving jurisdiction over the cash salary and benefits to the political chief executive and jurisdiction over working conditions to the police chief executive. This structure might more effectively insulate working conditions and management control from budgetary pressures. An alternative to making the police chief executive responsible for working conditions bargaining (which has its disadvantages in the political process) might be to require the assent of the police executive to the working conditions terms before an agreement was reached. This would assure control by the mayor or city manager and still require that the bargaining process include the police chief. It is the unfortunate truth that even in cities placing bargaining in the hands of professional city managers, police chiefs are still often excluded from the bargaining process.

CONCLUSION

I have argued that the police have de facto a measure of the autonomy they are perceived to possess by their political superiors and that this independence should be increased and, most important, formally established to eliminate the harmful effects of invisible power and ambiguous boundaries of authority and to enhance public accountability. An exploration of approaches to implement a formalized independence from politics suggests that the city management form of government and the British chief constable model may be particularly promising. Whatever structural arrangements are chosen will have to satisfy four requirements for the truly independent police chief to carry out his work: He must assume the role of a major policymaker as opposed to an administrative minion, he must have protection against arbitrary or corrupt dismissal, he must have and provide adequate resources for research and development to guide the multifaceted work of his department, and he must have substantial influence over the collective bargaining positions taken by the management team with respect to "working conditions." In a country sorely lacking in leadership at all levels of government, we can ill afford to forego structural changes that will reveal a great pool of talent among our more than 17,000 police chief executives.

2

The Police and the Polis:
A Mayor's Perspective

William H. Hudnut III

In discussing the relationship between the mayor and the police department, it is important to distinguish between "Politics" and "politics." In my opinion, the former is unhealthy, the latter very sensible and productive. By "Politics" I mean attempting to impose external partisan political influence on the operation of the department. People are promoted because they know precinct committeemen and ward chairmen who have influence with the party in power. The department is manipulated for partisan political advantage and forced to make financial contributions. Justice is not enforced evenhandedly. This is bad. However, "politics" means governance of the city. In Aristotle's original understanding of the word, politics meant "the science of the polis." It sought the good for both the citizen and the city-state. The "police" are its practitioners, as are politicians at their best. In Muir's (1977) phrase, the police are "streetcorner politicians." Politics with a small "p" eschews political leveraging. It believes in merit and job performance, and this is good.

The art of governing a local community requires a commitment to take bad politics out of the police department while putting the right kind back in. Meeting this commitment demands a shared philosophy between mayor and police chief and a mutual respect for their roles in shaping a professional and politically responsive police department. The mayor is not an expert in law enforcement and cannot be the super police chief; but taking a hands-off approach to the police chief does not guarantee desirable kinds of political immunity for the police department, either. The police chief can be effective as a major municipal policymaker only if he is integrated into the policymaking structure.

As in most cities, Indianapolis's first law enforcement agency took the form of an elected town marshal. With my election in 1975, I inherited a politicized animal in the throes of evolution and under investigation by the

U.S. Justice Department for illegal hiring and promotional practices. While the police chief himself was no longer an elected official, and a statutory merit system was in place, decades of partisan political influence peddling had nurtured a self-sustaining patronage system. Political clearance could be a prerequisite to being promoted or transferred to a prestigious assignment, and the chief was expected to run a department in which the highest ranking officers had the immunity of being hand picked by the political party in power.

Political powerbrokers make even worse police chiefs than mayors, particularly when they are allowed to dictate the transfer — based on political allegiance rather than merit — of officers to such sensitive areas as vice and narcotics. The inevitable problems created by political interference in normal police policies and procedures attracted media attention in the years preceding my election, culminating in a Pulitzer Prize-winning newspaper series exposing corruption and selective enforcement.[1] Although those charges may have been exaggerated, political interference in normal police policies and procedures was a widespread problem.

The strongest police chief cannot single-handedly take on politically rooted problems. He will be undermined by those anxious to maintain business as usual, creating confusion when the rank and file have to choose between answering to the chief or those with more political influence. At bottom, a law enforcement professional can only refuse to serve as chief of a politically influenced department. But a mayor's political clout can buffer the chief from internal and external attacks and facilitate such a system's overhaul.

In Indianapolis the existing state merit law,[2] clearly contemplating civilian involvement in the department, was a good foundation for building a more professional police department. By law, the mayor appoints a public safety director, who serves at his pleasure and is a member of his cabinet. In turn, the director appoints a police chief, subject to the mayor's approval, who serves at the director's pleasure. With some minor amendments, the law was refined to give the chief more authority over his highest ranking subordinates. The chief is now the sole appointing authority for his top deputies and assistants, recommends officers for promotion, and continues to have authority for the day-to-day operations of the department. Separate civilian merit and safety boards oversee the operations and management of the police department. With strong mayoral support, the chief now has a relatively free hand in running his department, and political abuses are a thing of the past.

But a "clean" police department does not guarantee a department responsive to the polis. There are no clear-cut guidelines for achieving the delicate balance between mayor and police chief, and perhaps there never will be. While a mayor recognizes the police department as part of the executive branch of government, often law enforcement agencies see themselves as straddling the lines between the executive, legislative, and judicial branches of government, occupying a satellite known as the criminal justice system. That perception impedes accountability to the executive branch. There can be an "us against them" mentality ("them" being all nonpolice), born in the turbulent 1960s, in which the police become modern-day cowboys keeping peace at any price on an urban frontier. Adding to the confusion are the constantly shifting priorities of a modern community. Inner-city law enforcement problems are not always the same as suburban problems. Communities change through growth, economic shifts, and demographic trends. Their public safety problems and priorities change too. Besides all these comparatively gradual influences on lines of authority and responsibility between the police chief and the political chief executive the picture is further complicated by the political reality that a single incident can make what is the police chief's sole responsibility this week the mayor's business the next.

Working together, the mayor and police chief of Seattle are responding to a shifting national economy and changing demographics, including the problems inherent in the growing presence of a large, close-knit, and insular international district. National attention focused on Seattle after a mass murder-robbery at an Asian social club reputed to be a center for gambling in the district. Unfounded rumors that an organized youth gang was responsible raised community fears that immigrants were linked to organized crime rings in their native countries. Investigation of the murders was hampered by language and cultural barriers, as well as the natural mistrust of persons who had learned to fear police in their home countries. The mayor realized that the link between his administration and the international district needed to be strengthened[3] and that the impact of a single, major criminal incident had created the erroneous perception that crime was rampant in the international district. The response, designed by the mayor and his police chief, was to hire a bilingual civilian officer to accompany beefed-up patrols in the area, acting immediately before fear closed the door of the international district to the administration and police and before isolated troublemakers could make the perception of crime a reality in that area. It was a response to the polis.

Economic growth, resulting in an increase in vehicular traffic, provided the backdrop against which a single dramatic encounter pushed onto my desk a simple police policy of strictly enforcing the law against double parking on Monument Circle, the circular street that is the heart of the downtown area in Indianapolis. In 1981, a motorist who was double-parked became belligerent with a police officer and attempted to drive away. When the police officer reached into the car to remove the car keys, the motorist rolled up the window, trapping the officer's arm, and gunned the car into drive. As he was dragged along the street toward a concrete retaining post, the officer drew his gun with his free hand and fired, fatally wounding the motorist. The headline stories in the media (see "FBI Launches Probe of Slaying on Circle" 1981) were that deadly force had been used against a double-parker, and the community was outraged. Immediate mayoral intervention was necessary to assure the public that there would be a thorough investigation of the incident and to involve the Department of Transportation in devising a traffic control program that would ease the parking problem on the Circle.

In adapting the mayor-police chief relationship to changing times, it is important to recognize the expanding role of the police in resolving social as well as traditional law enforcement problems. Today's police officer is more than a cowboy. He or she is a sociologist, an ambassador for the city, and a community relations expert. Research has documented that the average police officer spends less time making arrests and issuing citations than in performing social and public services (see Wycoff 1982). Despite a tendency for police officers to see themselves as part of an independent satellite of government, this increasing role in public and social services places the police department firmly within the executive branch of government. If an appointed police chief does not answer to the executive branch, administratively and politically, he answers to no one at all. And I see no reason why he should be any less accountable than the public servant who oversees street repair or sanitary sewer operations. A mayor who does not feel that his police chief is trying to help him achieve his legitimate public policy goals should find a new chief who will.

I have replaced two chiefs during my ten years in office, and I would not hesitate to do so again to ensure a responsive police department. In a break from tradition, my predecessor had appointed an outsider—a former secret service agent—as police chief. His status as an outsider, coupled with the problem of political influence in the department, seriously damaged morale among the rank and file, who questioned whether there was any professional career path for moving through the ranks to the chief's office. Appointing a chief from within the department was a keystone of my campaign promise to professionalize the department and restore morale and was enthusiastically received by the department members.

I replaced the chief with an outstanding member of the police department. His residency in a community outside the consolidated city-county—established before enactment of an ordinance requiring new members of the department to live within the county—was the major drawback to selecting him as chief. Even though his residency was legal under the ordinance, the administration's policy is that executives within the administration live in the community they serve. The chief never made good on his promise, given during the interview process, to move back into the county. In retrospect, it seems apparent that my decision not to hold him to that promise and insist that he be a responsive member of the administration, coupled with my administration's zealous effort to depoliticize the department, probably signaled that he could operate with nearly complete independence from the executive branch. The pendulum was swinging from overpoliticization to political unresponsiveness. Administration priorities, such as development of a strong neighborhood crime watch program and open dialogue with concerned elements of the community, were pushed to the back burner. The chief made it clear that he was the law enforcement professional and was not required to be answerable to or responsive to the mayor. Finally, acting without my prior approval or knowledge, the chief publicly announced at roll call sites throughout the city that he would resign within three months. Facing the possibility that the police chief and his department would drift further away from the administration, I accepted the chief's resignation, and his tenure ended not in three months but in two weeks. In neither instance where I replaced chiefs was I confronted with charges of political meddling in police matters. The problems with both chiefs were widely enough known that replacing them was accepted as a legitimate management decision. I believe that a mayor must have the authority, directly or through one of his cabinet members, to replace the chief at will if he is to have a responsive police department.

But that authority must be exercised with wisdom and restraint. Until recently one major midwestern city operated under a system that gave the mayor, who was elected to a two-year term, complete control over the hiring and firing of the police chief. The system became so politicized that in a ten-year period the city had nine police chiefs. The police union and the rank and file actively campaigned for selected mayoral candidates, collecting political IOUs from their successful candidates. In essence, a vote for a particular mayoral candidate was also a vote for a police chief, and issues best left to contract negotiations were resolved through political trade-offs. The number of high-level ranks in the police department was increased at the whim of the police chief and bloated with political appointees and former police chiefs, who were invulnerable to demotion by a weak civil service system. A campaign promise to retain two-man patrol cars further diminished available line personnel for routine patrols. Politics and the police force became so intertwined that a police chief used his power base as a springboard to the mayor's office. The resulting political manipulations of the police department convinced the citizenry that reform was needed. The reform gave the next mayor a four-year term, instituted a formal selection and testing procedure for police chief candidates, and established a three-year term for police chief. Although the chief is selected by the mayor, the appointment must be ratified by the city council. Except in a case of dismissal for cause, the only question before the council at the expiration of the chief's term is whether the chief should be retained. This safeguard against capricious removal has given the police chief the protection he needs to professionalize the department.

There are those who would go one step more, arguing that a police chief should be given an employment contract that provides him with tenure for a set period of years in order to enhance stability, provide an incentive for long-range planning, and place a protective distance between policing and greedy politicians. I agree that the mayor should not try to be a super police chief, but he is the chief executive officer. His policies are as easily thwarted by benign neglect as by intentional sabotage. A mayor who gives his police chief a contract runs the risk of being a public safety eunuch. No one at the cabinet level in my administration has an employment contract. The only contract is the personal relationship between mayor and administrator — it is my handshake when I swear him or her in. Confidence and responsiveness are not instilled on paper.

At the same time, neither reform movements nor replacement of the police chief will change attitudes overnight. A police chief has to have the space and time to come around to the political chief executive's point of view and bring the rank and file with him. There is a tremendous inertia and resistance to change, and often a police executive's vision is limited to his own police department, although police chiefs' organizations, such as the International Association of Chiefs of Police, the Police Executive Research Forum, and the National Organization of Black Law Enforcement Executives, have made some headway against the traditional isolation of law enforcement agencies and their heads. Forcing change too fast may drive a wedge between the chief and the police force, making it impossible for the rank and file to feel that the chief is one of them and not a political pawn.

In August 1977, 20 months into my first term, Indianapolis was a vivid example of a change made too fast. During budget preparations for the coming year, it was obvious that there would be insufficient money to offer the city's firefighters anything comparable to the take-home cars that constituted a fringe benefit worth up to $2,000 a year for the police (see Kelling's "experimentation" chapter, p. 432). The police chief proposed that the take-home car program be eliminated, which precipitated a debate among the chief, the mayor, and other executive branch members whether to announce the end of the program in August, before negotiations on a new police contract were completed, or to wait and avoid making the cars an issue in negotiations. I backed the chief's decision to announce an end to the program immediately, agreeing with him that the issue should be aired in contract negotiations. The dramatic response by police officers to this local announcement catapulted the issue into the bright spotlight of national network television news. Dozens of police officers drove their take-home cars to city hall on a Sunday afternoon, turned on the red lights and sirens, locked the car doors, and threw the keys in a heap. The mass confusion while keys were sorted and the traffic jam of police cars was removed was one of the day's most colorful and best played news stories.

Changing police attitudes and policies generally requires a cooperative effort by the mayor and the police chief and effective communication of the rationale behind the change to the rank and file officers. There are other times when the mayor — absent some overwhelming policy consideration — should defer to his police chief and change his own attitudes if necessary. Generally, these involve specific law enforcement decisions, the day-to-day supervision of the department, and personnel decisions.

I do not always agree, for example, with the disciplinary decisions made by the police chief. There are times when I feel he has gone too far and other times when I think stronger disciplinary actions are called for. When the decision attracts public attention and stirs public emotion, it can be difficult not to get involved. When a city police officer was publicly identified as a member of the Nazi party, I agreed with the segment of the community that demanded the officer in question be fired. A police officer has a responsibility to enforce the law fairly, and it was difficult to believe that this officer could be true to his political views and still be equitable in carrying out his duties, particularly in the minority community. But I deferred to my police chief, who brought the officer in off the streets but did not fire him, because it was impossible to prove a connection between the officer's beliefs and poor job performance — and absent that kind of proof, an appeal of the discharge would have been successful.

Moreover, a municipal chief executive must recognize when his personal political preferences are dictating his decisions and, where there is a conflict, often defer to his chief. In the summer of 1982, a community in an adjoining county called for K-9 assistance from the Indianapolis police department to patrol an area hit by strike-related violence. The lives of those on both sides of the dispute were in danger. I would never have authorized the use of police dogs in a situation where union members might perceive that the dogs were being used against them in a flashback to the early days of union-busting. But the chief, as a law enforcement professional, provided the assistance because his priority was to help a community restore peace and order. Likewise, my own political instincts dictated that leaders in the Catholic community should have been contacted before the police chaplain, a Catholic priest, was fired. But the firing was strictly a personnel decision, handled by the chief, and my role was limited to supporting his action in the subsequent backlash from the Catholic community.

While deferring to his chief on specific decisions, the mayor has a role in reviewing the general policy that the chief applies in making those decisions. The point can be illustrated by reference to shootings by police, which frequently are controversial (see, generally, Geller 1982). The use of deadly force — and, indeed, the *capacity* to use coercive force to overcome resistance to orders (see Bittner 1970; Kerstetter's chapter) — is one factor that sharply distinguishes the police department from other local governmental agencies. In November 1980, a young black male was shot and killed by a police officer in Indianapolis when, fleeing from the scene of an armed robbery, he failed to heed the officer's order to halt. This incident, coupled with other police action shootings around that time, sparked sharp protest in the minority community ("Mayor Names 25 to Study Police Deadly-Force Use" 1980). It became clear that the public was concerned about being safe *from* the police department and that minority mistrust of the police department had reached dangerous proportions. There were calls for the mayor to intervene directly in the investigation of these shootings and take disciplinary action against the officers involved. That is not the mayor's role. But a chief executive cannot ignore fundamental human rights.

While the police chief dealt with individual incidents, I created a special task force, which included representatives of local law enforcement agencies as well as a broad cross section of the community, to review the state laws and local regulations governing police use of deadly force as well as the system in which these laws and regulations were operating. My intervention served two purposes: first, to defuse the community's emotional response and buffer the police chief against demands for hasty decision; and second, to provide a thoughtful review of existing general policies. The task force held several meetings and took public testimony. Their recommendations some six months later ("Report of the Tanselle-Adams Commission" 1981) included not only changes in local firearms training and community relations policies but also a proposed amendment to the state deadly force statute limiting the circumstances in which deadly force could be used.

Initially, the chief and his department members resisted any change. Rather than dictating changes, I won the chief's support, and ultimately that of most of his department, by working through the proposals and discussing their implementation with the chief prior to any modifications. Most of the changes recommended by the task force were adopted. But the state legislature was unwilling to restrict further a police officer's ability to use deadly force. As a result, the Indianapolis police chief enacted a local policy— the most restrictive in the state—governing the use of deadly force by members of his department. Unlike the state statute, this policy, still in effect, specifies that deadly force is a last resort and limits its use to situations where necessary to prevent bodily harm or the commission of a forcible felony, or to arrest those suspected of forcible felonies or crimes that endanger other persons. It is unlikely that this change in policy, so controversial with law enforcement officers initially and with the chief himself, would have been enacted without the mayor's intervention. But it is equally unlikely that the police force would have accepted it without the police chief's commitment to the mayor and his philosophy.

A police chief who makes this commitment and expands his vision beyond the narrow confines of the internal workings of the police department is a functioning component of the executive team. He becomes politically responsive and, consequently, comes to understand that public perception can be as damaging to the mayor's goals and to public safety as actual crime. Dealing with these perceptions gives the police chief a proactive rather than a merely reactive role in law enforcement. For instance, the public may perceive a particular government housing project as negatively affecting the surrounding neighborhood. Or a particular area of the city may be perceived as a high-crime area, even though the statistics show few law enforcement problems. Or economic development may be stymied by a citizenry fearing new pressures on already overtaxed municipal services. By responding to these and similar perceptions rather than dismissing them as invalid, police leaders can help change attitudes and foster progress.

The kind of proactive police stance I am encouraging can also be illustrated by reference to a local example concerning one of Indianapolis's largest public swimming pools. For years this facility was located in the heart of a predominantly white, middle-class neighborhood grappling with the effects of court-ordered busing in the nearby high school. Citizens in the area mounted vigorous opposition to a neighborhood development program that included a revitalized public park with a new pool to replace the large one closed because of age and maintenance problems. The neighborhood perception was that a new pool would attract large numbers of young blacks and that crime would increase. Working with the police chief, we were able to counter opposition, not by pointing out the invalidity of the perception, but by responding to it and relocating a police roll call site to the park. The public had visible evidence that the police would respond to problems if and when they occurred, with the result that the tension that breeds conflict and law enforcement problems dissipated and neighborhood development moved forward with a minimal investment of public safety resources.

Another invalid but widely held perception threatened to block the Indianapolis Symphony's move from its quarters in a university setting on the north side of town to a downtown location targeted for revitalization. The perception that the downtown is a high-crime area, particularly strong among older symphony goers, was not changed by statistics showing otherwise. But the police chief clinched the deal by committing mounted police patrols downtown on performance nights. A police chief looking only at the narrow public safety issues would not have made that decision. But it was a creative response by a police chief who appreciates his role as a member of the executive team and assumes a proactive posture.

When possible, a proactive chief should be involved in the earliest planning stages of a project. The police chief was actively involved in strategy planning for the desegregation of Indianapolis schools in 1981 under a court-ordered busing program. Disturbances and calls for police assistance were inevitable. Responding to the experience of other communities, the police chief determined that a visible police presence promoted rather than forestalled violence. Working with religious and community leaders, the chief adopted a plan for civilians to negotiate problems unless police intervention was necessary to prevent violence. A sophisticated communications system was established to keep the police department in contact with potential trouble spots. Indianapolis is now considered a model for the peaceful implementation of court-ordered desegregation of public schools, in part because a proactive police chief was involved in the initial planning stages of the project.

The police chief in another major American city assumed a proactive posture in planning for the construction of a domed stadium. Under constraints that prevented the expenditure of general tax revenues for stadium functions, the chief was asked to devise a traffic control plan without using police officers. His solution was to expand the police reserve program and use these volunteers for traffic control duty on stadium event days. By designing and coordinating this component of a major municipal project, the chief helped convince the public that a domed stadium could be constructed and operated without reducing the level of existing services or increasing taxes.

The police chief's role, with his department members, with the political chief executive, and ultimately with the community, is one of a major municipal policymaker. The mayor's recognition of that role and his efforts to integrate the chief into the executive policymaking structure ensure that the mayor will benefit from the chief's expertise in a wide range of policy matters. By the same token, only full integration into the executive policymaking structure can give the police chief the support he needs to function effectively and without partisan political interference and ensure that he is politically responsive.

NOTES

1. The series included several hundred stories for more than a year in the *Indianapolis Star* by reporters William E. Anderson, Harley R. Bierce, Richard E. Cady, and Myrta J. Pulliam (see the "wrap-up" story when the Pulitzer was awarded, "Star Wins Pulitzer Prize for Police Probe" [1975]).

2. The merit law was Indiana Code sections 18–4–12–17 through 18–4–12–27. As a result of home rule legislation, the state statute has been repealed and adopted without change as Appendix B III of the Code of Indianapolis and Marion County (our local ordinances).

3. Santa Ana Police Chief Raymond Davis (see his chapter) proposes an affirmative responsibility of the police to help immigrants acclimate to their new community.

3

The Prospective Chief's Negotiation of Authority with the Mayor

Patrick V. Murphy

THE NEED FOR ENLIGHTENED POLICE LEADERSHIP

After the encouraging success of our civil rights "revolution," in a relatively short period of time we are faced with an urban crisis caused by white middle-class flight and larger poor minority populations. Higher rates of crime and violence have accompanied demographic changes. They, in turn, increase racial tensions. The problems are exacerbated in proportion to the size of the city,[1] for anonymity is the seedbed of crime. Sensational news reporting and political demagoguery often distort the facts. Exaggerated fears are generated. Not only the media but (with notable exceptions) many police chiefs place the blame for the urban plight not on historic injustices that have spawned the problems but on leaders who have worked to correct those injustices (see Panel on the Future of Policing 1984). The litany of scapegoats includes "soft" judges, "plea bargaining" prosecutors, "obstructionist" public defenders, "country-club prison" administrators and their parole board allies, "buck-passing" legislators, and other "permissive" leaders many of whom actually have been in the forefront for overdue change.[2]

The police, for better or worse, play a critical role in shaping the urban environment. The more successful they are in preventing and controlling crime, the more they contribute to progress in racial harmony as well as social and economic justice. By the same token, the weaker the police are in preventing inner-city crime, due to their alienation from the community and other factors, the more they perpetuate the majority population's identification of crime with blacks and Hispanics and the more they generate resistance to, and delay, integration in education, housing, and employment (including police employment). Enlightened public positions by chiefs and police union leaders who recognize the socioeconomic roots of crime and avoid the use of law and order rhetoric (which often constitutes a coded effort to slow the pace of racial justice) will expedite solutions to racial and other urban problems.

The predicament confronting many of our large cities cries out for the best police leadership we can get. Seventeen years after the President's Commission on Law Enforcement and Administration of Justice issued its reports, considerable improvement has occurred (see Walker's chapter). Chiefs and officers are better educated. Research is beginning to provide a body of knowledge. The number of minority and women officers has grown. Community relationships are better. Force is used with greater restraint. There is less corruption. Expertise is more freely exchanged. Yet few city departments are well run, organized, or managed — a goal whose attainment will require greatly improved executive development programs and a much expanded body of knowledge in urban police management. Cutbacks in the federal law enforcement assistance program, premised on the absurd argument that it failed because crime increased during its existence, will retard the police world's gradual climb toward professionalization.

What can the prospective police leader, interviewing with his potential employer, do to contribute to progress? In this chapter I will attempt to share a few insights I have gained over a career in running and watching police departments. While political as well as union and community pressures are frequently asserted at a precinct or division level rather than at headquarters in a large police department (for example, a councilman gets an officer a favorable work schedule by calling the sergeant or captain), nevertheless a mayor or city manager, by direct action and by setting a tone, can have an enormous positive — or negative — influence on the quality of urban policing. Although the formal lines of authority and the informal working relationship between a police chief and his mayor frequently are difficult to define with any precision even *during* the chief's incumbency, it is possible to suggest some kinds of matters the candidate for police chief should attempt to clarify with his prospective boss prior to his selection.

ASSESSING THE NEGOTIATING MILIEU

The reality is that most police chief candidates do not negotiate; they are up-through-the-ranks aspirants on the verge of attaining the pinnacle of success in a law enforcement career and are not about to upset the applecart by making demands or even asking critical questions of their benefactor. Indeed, most of those who have reached the chief's chair head departments in which they began as young officers 20 or more years ago. They have not had the benefit of experience in the private sector or other branches of government. Their police experience has been narrowly confined to one agency, limiting the beneficial cross-fertilization that characterizes any true profession. If they have had higher education it has usually been as part-time students in low quality programs. They have not come from society's leadership class nor attended the universities that educate its members. They have not moved in the circles of power of either national or local elites (see Potter and Blackmore 1980). They often are politically unsophisticated and inept in their news media relationships.[3] They know that when the city administration changes, they may well be returned to a lower rank to serve under their current subordinates.

Set against this tradition, the prospective chief's reluctance or inability to negotiate is understandable, which of course does not make it right — or helpful in addressing pressing community needs for better policing. Given the practice in most cities of turning to outsider police chief candidates only when, due to corruption or brutality or other scandals, the department develops a bad reputation and does not appear to have the strength within to clean things up, it will be inherently easier for the outsider to take a firm stance on certain issues. Indeed, the conditions that usually lead to appointment of an outsider frequently obviate tough bargaining positions by the candidate; the mayor willingly gives the chief a free hand in exchange for restored police credibility.[4] But the imaginative and dedicated *insider* can also do much to help himself, the department, and the public during his early encounters with the hiring authority.

In thinking about the many diverse factors that constitute the negotiating milieu, the police chief candidate must remember that, as Fogelson (1977, pp. 111–12) noted, the police executive's job is inherently political. Many mayors have told me that the police chief is protected from the rough and tumble of politics. But the reality is that politics is our way of life. J. Edgar Hoover always said that law enforcement and politics don't mix, and yet he was one of the shrewdest politicians ever to appear. If the politics of a municipality is such that it serves the mayor's interest to give the chief a free hand (that is, if the mayor wants or needs to communicate to the public that the police department is independent and the chief is at liberty to do the best job he can), I would suggest strongly that the police chief seize the opportunity. For example, Robert Wagner, when he was mayor of New York City for 12 years, said many times — and I think all the evidence supported him — that he did give independence to the chiefs. That was also true of John Lindsay when I served in New York. Many other mayors want as good a police department as they can get, and they support the chief, letting him put together the team he wants and make the changes he needs to bring improvement. But it is still the exception rather than the rule in this nation's 17,000 police agencies that the incoming chief will automatically be given the kind of independence he should have. Usually the challenge for the prospective chief is to set and communicate the minimal conditions below which he will not take the job and to seek constructive compromise with his employer on many other matters.

Among the factors I would want to have accurate information about before deciding whether to take a police administrative position are the chief's access to the mayor — Does the chief need to go through the mayor's staff or can he go directly to the mayor even when the matter is not an emergency?; the roles of the mayor and chief on such matters as media relations; the city's financial situation; the lines of authority between the police chief and the city's budget office concerning the police budget; the department's organization and style; the power of the police union, if one exists; the city council's and the public's understanding and support of greater civilianization of the department; the popularity of the mayor and his attitude toward reform of city government and reduction of waste and inefficiency; the city administration's enforcement policies, especially any that concern activities in which there is a danger of such conduct as fixing tickets; the department's history and recent experiences — whether there have been corruption, brutality, crime reporting, or other serious difficulties; the department's and your predecessor's general reputation and the kind of media coverage the agency has been receiving; whether police personnel have civil service tenure and if so how far up the ranks it extends; and whether the chief has a free hand in making appointments (especially at the high levels), assignments, transfers, and promotions and in meting out rewards and punishments (and what the opportunities are for favoritism to intrude).

The insider candidate will know the answers to many of these questions, but the outsider needs to do his homework as quickly and accurately as possible prior to his three- or four-day site visit. During the visit, he should attempt to confirm his impressions and find out whatever else he can — and then pray that the skeletons in the closet that local contacts haven't told him about don't start to dance after he raises his right hand. In suggesting that all these factors are part of the negotiating milieu, I do not mean to imply that the prospective chief must have finely detailed information about every one of them or should take inflexible positions on each with the municipal chief executive and his staff. There are, however, some issues that it seems to me require fortitude on the applicant's part.

NON-NEGOTIABLE ISSUES

Although the candidate's general goal should be to obtain as much independence in running the department as he can get, what should be his "deal breakers" — the minimal conditions without which he simply will not accept the job?[5] One such condition is that the chief must have a free hand in personnel matters — as free as possible within a structured civil service system.

While many departments, such as New York's and Chicago's, have "exempt" positions at the top that the chief can fill at his discretion, others have very little leeway: Everyone except the chief has tenure and cannot be replaced. This is why so many chiefs get gray hair and ulcers; they feel they can't do the job if they can't assemble their own team. Especially if he is brought in as an outsider, and it's he against everybody who has been there, the situation is impossible. Even when the top positions are civil service, it is still essential for the chief to achieve some flexibility, as Chief Lee Brown and his mayor have done in Houston by securing a change that permits the chief to select civilians for a few top-level positions. Even five or six such people give the chief a team he can work with. Otherwise, it's very lonesome at the top.

Although the mayor should not be making *decisions* about appointments, promotions, transfers, or assignments, this is not to suggest he should be deprived of a right to *input*. The key is for the chief to have some *standards* for personnel decisions and to be the one who determines when they have been met. If there is an excess of people who meet the standards, there can be some flexibility in determining which ones to select. I do not think as chief one has to be alarmed if the mayor says, "Well, if he's qualified, I'd really appreciate it if Joe Blow was one of the people who was advanced to second grade detective." Fortunately, that was not a problem for me in New York under Mayor Lindsay[6] nor in the other departments I headed. But I do not think serious harm would be done in my hypothetical example if the chief, in advancing 20 people to second grade detective, included Joe Blow, so long as he was otherwise qualified and promotable.

Even with positions above lieutenant or captain, which many mayors (Lindsay included) *do* express some interest in, the point is not to deprive the mayor of an advisory role but to set minimal standards. For instance, I would not want the councilman's ignorant brother-in-law walking around in a deputy chief's uniform; a patrolman could not be made a deputy chief (which has happened); the appointee must operate within departmental policies and guidelines; the chief must have the opportunity to evaluate the person's performance; and if the person turns out to be performing unsatisfactorily, there must be some resolution of the problem — possibly that the political official could select someone else who otherwise meets the chief's criteria. The chief has to realize that, as a practical matter, the mayor sees appointments to desirable city jobs as opportunities to pay some rewards — rewards that may help him build a political coalition so that both he and the chief can survive in office. By the same token, the mayor must recognize the importance of allowing the chief to preserve ultimate control over personnel matters: It gives the chief the ability to motivate his people to work for him because they know he can reward them.

Another, closely related, power that I believe the chief candidate could not afford to bargain away is ultimate control over discipline. Who has the final administrative authority in disciplinary matters varies from city to city these days (see Kerstetter's chapter), but within the existing legal structure, the chief rather than the mayor or city manager should have the principal responsibility and commensurate authority. In matters of integrity, brutality, and misconduct the chief has to have the power to discipline, and the mayor should not override those decisions.

Also non-negotiable is the subject of partisan political activity by the chief or other members of the department. Without encroaching on First Amendment rights, I believe it would be a serious mistake for a chief to become involved in making political endorsements during civic campaigns, and if that were made a condition of employment I think it should be a deal breaker. A chief cannot be foolishly rigid about such matters, however. If the media ask me as chief what I think of the mayor, who is running for reelection, I would say, "I have the highest regard for this mayor, he's been an excellent administrator, he's been fair to me, he's lived up to the agreement we made when I was hired." If they ask, "Do you endorse him?" my answer would be, "I don't think it's appropriate for me to endorse anyone for election, so I won't endorse him."

Other matters that may not merit quite the same insistence on independence by the chief candidate but on which I would certainly try to avoid yielding ground include the chief's flexibility in being able to use his resources to best advantage, which often is related to budget authority; control over media relations; and the existence of an in-house departmental legal adviser.

NEGOTIABLE ISSUES

Clearly, the issues that are, in varying degrees, "negotiable" are too numerous to list, let alone discuss. But some of the more important ones merit brief mention. It would be highly desirable but, I'm sorry to say, highly unlikely, for the prospective chief to secure some sort of tenure — not "chief for life" as existed until a recent change in the law in Milwaukee, but a contract for a term of, say, three to five years, during which he could only be removed for cause or by being compensated for the remainder of his contract. Among the terms some contracts cover are "severance pay, work hours, moving expenses, professional expenses and travel, vacation and leave, pension, retirement, and other fringe benefits" (Kelly 1975, p. 50). Where city ordinances provide that the chief serves at the pleasure of the mayor or city council, the candidate will not, of course, be able to secure tenure by contract. The few instances where the chief has been given reasonable job security typically involve an outsider candidate; the insiders usually have civil service protection of some sort. By contrast, it is not uncommon for city managers to have contracts of employment (Kelly 1975), and in that regard it is worth considering

Andrews's (see his chapter in this volume) recommendation that police chief independence be structured somewhat in the way a city manager's autonomy from partisan politics is structured.

Another matter that the realistic candidate has to be flexible about, within reason, is whether he has his own in-house news affairs office or handles media relations through the mayor's staff. In some cities, chiefs cannot make a speech or hold a press conference without calling city hall to get briefed by the mayor or the mayor's press person as to how to handle the situation. By contrast, the mayors of some of the smaller cities often complain at leadership institutes and other conferences that their chief is *reluctant* to talk to the media. That is not particularly surprising when one realizes that everything during the chief's police career has made him suspicious of the press and that, except in recent years, he probably has had no media relations training and little or no contact with the press on policy questions. Then there are large cities, like Minneapolis, where the mayor (Donald Fraser), although very competent, by nature is the quiet, retiring sort, and he has no problem with the chief (Tony Bouza) being out front all the time and saying flamboyant, insightful things in the media. The New York department has had its own press office for many years, so that was not much of an issue when I discussed my appointment with John Lindsay.

But where it is not clear who will handle the media, I think the chief candidate should attempt to negotiate. If the mayor says during the interview, "Look, I want the news. I want releases done through here, and I want inquiries to come through here," the applicant might respond: "Oh, is that what the *news media* expect too? Will they believe that I'm independent if I can't give an interview to one of them without saying, 'I have to call the mayor'? Will the media think I'm independent if they know, when they call the mayor, he'll tell me to give them an interview?" I think the argument the candidate needs to make is that, while arrangements should be devised to avoid substantially conflicting policy statements coming out of city hall and police headquarters, the department's image and the chief's image are very important, and the chief needs the capacity to get out the word and define the department's positions and seek citizen cooperation—all of which require that he have his own press office and not appear to be the mayor's puppet.

The mayor might say, "That's fine, except I can visualize an incident of one kind or another a few times a year where I'd like to be informed, where I'd like to know what you're planning to do." That would be fine. I think a chief can let the mayor know in advance so he doesn't hear a major story on the six o'clock news without any prior knowledge. There are ways to negotiate those arrangements and reach understandings so that if the matter to be announced is the kind of thing the mayor should know about—such as a major personnel change, a new policy on use of deadly force, a criminal investigation involving one of the mayor's staff, or long-awaited findings in a highly controversial disciplinary investigation—he is told perhaps 24 hours before releasing a statement or making an announcement. This helps the mayor because when reporters come to him it will not look like the chief is keeping him in the dark. Occasionally the chief saves himself some real headaches as well by alerting the mayor to impending announcements. For example, an outsider recently appointed as chief may learn, by virtue of sending a list of intended promotees to city hall, that his proposed deputy chief had a bloody battle with the mayor over some issue four years ago.

Yet another area that could be negotiated is the chief's role in municipal policymaking on subjects that are only indirectly related to law enforcement and order maintenance, such as zoning matters, the management of school integration, other educational issues, public health and welfare planning, traffic engineering, public works, and so forth. Chiefs could also be useful in designing buildings to improve their safety features. I think it is good practice for a mayor to have some input from the chief or one of his people early on during the planning phase on these kinds of issues.

Even on policymaking bearing directly on policing, the mayor has an appropriate role, and the prospective chief must be open to finding suitable arrangements. As an elected representative of the people, the mayor is responsible for the proper and efficient performance of the police department and has the right and the duty[7] to oversee its policies and methods. (Although city managers are not elected officials, in my view they should be governed by the same principles as mayors because they function for the elected officials and are responsible for the performance of the police.) How much a mayor is involved in police policymaking may be determined by the size of the mayoral staff or the amount of staff time dedicated to police matters.[8] Among the steps a mayor might properly take in performing his oversight function is the creation of a citizen committee to look into the department's conduct in some particularly controversial incident, such as a highly questionable shooting. This is not to invite city hall review in routine cases, but it is to acknowledge that sometimes the department makes mistakes in explaining its position or dealing with the community in other ways that can best be remedied by external oversight.

A final specific example of a negotiable issue might be the mayor's role in guiding the chief's deployment of personnel and organization of the agency. Ideally, the chief should retain complete control over the strategies, tactics, and management techniques for implementing the public's and the mayor's mandates concerning enforcement and service priorities. I could envision exceptions, however, such as where a senior citizens' group creates such a political clamor for establishment of a specialized departmental unit on crime against the elderly that the chief should yield to the mayor's intervention in organizational matters and create the unit. The chief should indicate to the mayor his strong feeling that in order to have credibility in directing and controlling the department he should have authority over organizational matters of that kind and should indicate that he is always happy to discuss the pros and cons of departmental reorganization but does not feel it should be imposed on the agency when he believes it would be a mistake. The chief should understand, of course, that it may be in the *department's* interest to create the unit so as to relieve the constant source of pressure from seniors and encourage them to be the allies of the police one would naturally expect them to be.

When mayoral pressure or intervention does impose a new bureau or division on the police department, however, it is essential that the personnel in the new unit report and answer to the chief, not, as occasionally happens, directly to the mayor. It may be tempting, especially for a new mayor, to place an informer or two inside the department to keep tabs on the chief's loyalty to city hall. But the mayor would be far wiser to find a way to assess the chief's performance that does not run the serious risk of undermining the chief's ability to perform well. The chief needs power not only to use himself but to delegate to his commanders so he can fairly hold them accountable for their subordinates' conduct.

Although, as suggested earlier, it may not be possible to negotiate or even discuss a great number of issues prior to one's appointment as police chief, I think what is essential is for the candidate to put the mayor on notice that he wants independence, that he is not taking the job just to have the job. The prospective chief needs to say, not as a threat but in order to create clear expectations, that if he finds out down the road that he cannot have the promised independence, he would not want to stay. If the chief has some stature, a good reputation in the community and in the police world, the mayor will realize the potential embarrassment of trying to interfere in the department in a political way. For example, Mayor Richard Daley in Chicago would have been hurt politically if O. W. Wilson, after his appointment in 1960 as superintendent in the wake of a police corruption scandal, had resigned saying he had not been given the free hand the mayor promised him.

In urging prospective chiefs to come to the mayoral interview with their own set of questions and a few fairly inflexible conditions of employment, I do not mean to imply that any of these matters are susceptible to easy answers. While idealism and ultimate objectives are essential in running a police department, the prospective chief has to be realistic and not expect his employer to make commitments involving the municipal budget or other matters that are unreasonable.

Besides all the specific items I have mentioned that could bear on the candidate's decision whether to take the job, he needs to calculate the career risks, if he takes the chief's job and *fails*. Even with some cities open to outsiders, a chief in a major city who fails may have a hard time going elsewhere; a smaller department would be too much of a step down and a comparable or larger department will not be available. Private sector jobs for retired police chiefs often have many letters in their titles but few of the challenges of public service that presumably lead people to aspire to chief's positions.

At the conclusion of the negotiations, the chief candidate will end up saying, "I sure as hell wish *this* were different, but I can live with it, as long as *that* is OK. And I got more than I thought I would on that other matter." It's like a balance sheet. The candidate will add it all up and ask, "Well, will I take it?" Conceivably — although this is unlikely — the circumstances will be such that the response is, "I can't lose. This is heaven." Realistically, if he is lucky, the potential chief will be able to say, "It's never going to be heaven. There's a good chance to go here, do a job, and come out pleased with what's happened." Given the imposing constraints on police management in modern America, if that forecast can become a reality, the new chief will have done well indeed.

NOTES

1. The most difficult challenges of policing are in the large cities, which have much more than their proportionate share of crime and related problems. The 58 cities with over a quarter million population serve 20 percent of the population, employ 24 percent of all police, experience 31 percent of the index crime, 47 percent of the violent crime, and 61 percent of the robberies, the bellwether crime of stranger violence.

2. The conventional wisdom that courts are the weakest link in crime control is fallacious. While judges can do better and courts can be better managed, prevention, which requires close citizen-police cooperation, is the key to control. It has broken down in many inner cities because the police are not well run. Among the many unproductive practices that persist are random patrol that does not prevent crime, mismanagement of criminal investigators, costly arrests that cannot survive a first court hearing in cases that should be processed without arrest or by diversion, clogging the criminal justice system with minor arrests while failing to track violent career criminals, and neglecting to obtain citizen assistance in monitoring criminals residing in beats.

3. Lack of political sophistication and ineptitude in media relations are by no means limited to those from smaller agencies. I could cite a number of managers from New York City who went out of town to see another department and came back very critical, saying, "Gee, they don't do this, they don't do that." I would tell them, "Look, because we did it in New York doesn't mean it's the only way." A lot of police officials return from such visits and before you know it they are quoted in the gossip column saying, "Such and such a department is run like an old folks' home." They come off as not very astute politically.

4. In the four cities where I served as top police administrator the mayor saw fit to give me a relatively free hand without difficult negotiations. It has not been so much any magic on my part but rather the circumstances under which I was asked to come in each time. In Syracuse (where I served during 1963-64) there was a scandal involving gambling graft; a state investigation commission came into the city, and the chief and the first deputy chief resigned. In Washington, D.C. (1967-68), when I took the job the government was being reorganized anyhow, although there were some tensions about police-community relations. In Detroit (1970) a new mayor, Ray Gribbs, was coming into office, and the fellow who was police commissioner was sending up signals that he was almost going to be beyond the mayor's control. That put the mayor on the spot. In New York (1970-73), I arrived in the wake of the corruption and graft scandal

investigated by the Knapp Commission. The incumbent commissioner, Howard Leary, could not seem to get ahead of the problem, got a lot of bad publicity, and resigned.

5. I do not suggest that the several issues discussed below are an exhaustive list of non-negotiable matters. The particular circumstances of each job and jurisdiction may permit flexibility on some matters in some places and not in others.

6. At one point in New York I found that something was going on where council members would call from city hall recommending someone for advancement. In a big department like New York's, things like this can go on without the chief administrator's knowledge. But I happened to get evidence of this, and I made sure it was closed down.

7. Despite everything I have said about the importance of the chief's independence, nevertheless, I think most mayors permit their police department too much autonomy. They do not use experts in the complexities of police administration on their staffs. They do not know how to hold their departments accountable. During the Wagner era in New York (1954–65), arguably the limited progress in policing could be partly attributed not to Bob Wagner's interference (he hired as commissioners men of good will — all, incidentally, lawyers — and gave them a free hand) but to his lack of positive interference in holding the department accountable. The fledgling National Institute of Policing, created in 1983 by the United States Conference of Mayors with some support from the Police Foundation for the purpose of bringing mayors and chiefs together to discuss policy and exchange ideas, is attempting to help mayors and chiefs achieve better working relationships that ensure better police services for the public. In part the impetus for the National Institute was a series of very useful seminars to which the U.S. attorney general brought the mayors and chiefs from the nation's 100 largest cities in the wake of the tragic Newark and Detroit riots of 1967. Mayoral prodding during and following those meetings brought about improvements that helped reduce urban disorders — improvements the chiefs alone would have implemented much more slowly.

8. Regrettably, how much the *police chief* is involved in *police* policymaking may also be dependent on staff capabilities. It is all well and good to talk about the desirability of the chief becoming a major municipal policymaker on a broad spectrum of issues. It would be a momentous development, however, if the chief emerged as a major policymaker in the law enforcement/ criminal justice system production line. The agencies in the criminal justice "system" do not coordinate well or mesh their policies in many urban jurisdictions, and the chief's leadership could be a positive force for change.

4
Politics and Police Leadership: The View from City Hall

Donald M. Fraser

The late theologian Reinhold Niebuhr was fond of saying, "The purpose of politics is to establish justice in a sinful world." Although one can hardly disagree with such a worthy dictum, the longer I serve as mayor of a large city the more I become aware of its ambiguities. Irate citizens can differ volubly as to both the meaning and application of "justice." Similarly, "politics" is often seen as exalting personal loyalty or partisan interests above the public good rather than as the democratic political process that provides needed governance in our daily lives. My point is that even simple truths can become complex in application, as every municipal policymaker quickly discovers. This has been particularly true in the Minneapolis Police Department, which only recently extricated itself from a decade of politically inspired turmoil.

To most of the nation, Minneapolis is a uniquely endowed city at or near the top of almost every national "quality of life" study. The *National Geographic* characterized this metropolis as a thriving area where "there still is hope for the American city: an urban landscape [that] can still nurture the human species." The city, heavily Scandinavian in heritage, has a hardworking, mostly law-abiding population. An outsider examining this seemingly model American city would be hard-pressed to understand why its police department could have been embroiled in such difficulty throughout most of the 1970s.

In that decade alone the department changed police chiefs seven times, with an equal number of turnovers at the command level. My own first campaign for mayor in 1979 was dominated by the issue of who should run the police and how best to professionalize the department. The conflict within the department began in 1969, when the head of the police union was elected mayor of Minneapolis on a strong law and order platform. He was reelected two years later but lost the third election to a Democrat. His fourth try found him back in office, but on his fifth attempt, the public returned the Democratic mayor whom he had defeated.

This seemingly endless round of musical chairs in the mayor's office kept the department in a high pitch of political ferment. Each new shift in administration brought new shifts in departmental fortunes. Those who had pounded political signs for a losing candidate found themselves pounding remote pavements on graveyard shifts. Choice assignments were regarded strictly as political plums (see Potter and Blackmore 1980, p. 44). Such cronyism exacted a heavy toll in morale. A psychologist's study of stress in the department conducted partly through interviews with officers' wives revealed that this kind of political influence in assignments added to the discouragement and strain police officers were experiencing. I found this especially troubling since there is already considerable evidence that more law enforcement officers are killed or maimed by job-induced pressures than by criminals.

My defeat in 1979 of the former union president, who was then in his sixth campaign for the mayoralty, brought an end to the "boom and bust" cycle within our police department. The cycle was broken partly by strong voter approval during that election of a charter amendment that sets a three-year term for police chief, ensuring that the police chief's term usually does not expire in the same year as the mayor's. When a chief's term ends, the city council, not the mayor, decides by vote whether the chief shall continue for another term. The mayor may still act to remove the chief at any time, but that can only be done for appropriate cause, rather than capricious whim.

In the five years I have now been in office, no one in the police department has been retained, transferred, promoted, demoted, rewarded, or punished on the basis of instructions from the mayor's office. This is consistent with my pledge to "remove the police from politics and politics from the police department." As I saw it, achieving this goal also required finding a competent police chief through a process that minimized political considerations, with the new appointee given full authority to run the department within the framework for law enforcement set by the mayor.

This was not intended to exempt a mayor from maintaining a watchful interest in the department's operations, policies, and priorities. I have found that periodic meetings with the chief are important. In these meetings we go over a written statement prepared each month in which our jointly established goals for the year are listed along with a progress report from the chief on the current status of each.

Underlying all of this is the chemistry between a police chief and his supervisor that rarely receives the attention it deserves. The chief can be likened to the head of a company and the mayor to the chairperson of the board. The relationship is complex and requires tact, subtlety, trust, and the courage to do what is right rather than expedient. Together, the mayor and the police chief can set a tone for the department, including standards of professional conduct and service to the community. A mayor may call for a policy on appropriate behavior of police toward the citizenry, such as prohibiting the use of racial or other epithets by officers, or a policy on the proper sphere of activities for a vice squad, but the chief has the responsibility to formulate and enforce that policy.

If the chief and the mayor are on the same general wavelength in understanding and commitment, the chief should be able to proceed with a minimum of involvement by the mayor. My views, admittedly, may be shaped somewhat by the fact that when I took office I was able to choose a new chief. Thus I determined beforehand that he and I were committed to similar goals and values in the general area of law enforcement. Future Minneapolis mayors may find themselves at considerable philosophical odds with a holdover chief. Should this create constant friction between them, clearly the mayor, as the chief's superior, must prevail, with the holdover chief remaining for as short a time as contractual obligations allow. The more likely scenario, however, is that most of the time a chief and a mayor will work reasonably well together through a mutually agreed-upon framework for the general conduct of the department. This should include identifying the criteria the mayor will apply in deciding whether to override the chief's actions or opinions if substantial differences between the mayor and the chief arise.

A chief who seeks longevity in his post would do well to become familiar with the mayor's priorities for the administration of law enforcement in his city. He should also be aware of the mayor's personal convictions regarding the general manner in which the city's business is conducted and apprise himself of the mayor's position in sensitive policy areas, particularly if the mayor has made public commitments on such issues during his campaign for office. Although a mayor and a chief may differ as to whether the chief has overreached his authority in a specific matter, my feeling is that when a reasonably cooperative chief appears to step out of line, it is probably due more to a remediable failure of communication between the chief and the mayor than to an intended act of insubordination. Of course if the chief willfully strays too far from the mayor on key issues of public policy, that would certainly be reflected in the mayor's assessment of the chief when his contract is to be renewed or, in a city without police chief contracts, sooner.

At the same time, I firmly believe that within these broad boundaries the mayor must give full assurance that the chief is in complete charge of managing his department, that he possesses full authority to administer the agency without constant mayoral interference.

Perhaps the most extensive point of collaboration and consultation between city hall and the police administration in Minneapolis occurs during preparation of the city budget for submission to the council. The budget process entails review of previous policy decisions, the chief's general management and allocation of police resources, and future priorities. Because resources are becoming increasingly scarce, city programs to respond to even the most basic community needs must be subject to careful scrutiny. In Minneapolis, the joint mayoral–police chief response has been to reduce the number of sworn personnel while maintaining police service by increasing the number of civilian employees, reducing the size of the supervisory staff, and deploying a mix of one-officer and two-officer patrol cars.

In these days of "cutback management," an urban police department needs to concentrate its efforts on the service and enforcement priorities set by the chief and mayor. These priorities may and probably should differ from city to city, an important point to remember when the topic of national standards for policing arises. In Minneapolis, a top priority is community crime prevention. In many sections of the city, "neighborhood watches," "operation identification," and "block clubs" have become familiar phrases. We have also successfully emphasized traffic enforcement, concentrating on drunken driving and other moving violations in areas with the most accidents.

One of our more difficult budget considerations has involved wage negotiations. Since this is an area in which police unions are becoming especially skilled (see Bouza's chapter), mayors increasingly find they must deal with tough and talented groups. In recent negotiations many matters that would impinge on the police chief's authority to run his department, including discipline, seniority, and job assignments, have been added to the bargaining. A knowledgable mayor and city council will do well to limit their role to setting the outside limits for wage and benefit packages, leaving other negotiations to the city's professional labor staff.

An area of police administration with which I remain actively concerned is police-community relations and the related subject of affirmative action in the department — both matters in which failures can produce volatile civic consequences. Police-community relations these days, like citizens' relationships with many other governmental institutions, are often affected by the public's enhanced perception of their civil and political rights. Well-publicized court decisions set limits on permissible police conduct; aroused community groups monitor police policies and tactics. Arrested persons are more vocal in calling for due process and equal treatment. Concerns are vigorously expressed about the use of dogs in crowd control, police harassment, and the inadequacy of law enforcement in low-income neighborhoods. Confrontations may begin on the streets but often end in the mayor's office with an angry group demanding that the mayor "make" the police do something or stop what they are already doing.

Often a zealous chief can be caught in the middle in such conflicts. The mayor expects the chief to be sensitive, fair, and firm. The police expect their chief to back them in their actions. If he sides with his officers he is accused of being unresponsive and even hostile to citizens. If he sides too frequently with citizen complaints, he is cited for running a complaint-ridden department. Moreover, he can quickly become a target of the police union and lose rapport with his subordinates. Little wonder that the position of police chief is increasingly viewed as a "high profile job of uncomfortable circumstances."

Perhaps the most difficult problem of all with which the chief and the mayor must contend is the manner in which allegations of police brutality are handled. One has only to mention the phrase "civilian review" to ignite a premixed package into combustion. Yet it has been difficult for the public — especially the minority community — to have confidence in a review process in which the only scrutiny is applied by police officers (see Kerstetter's chapter). I remember once, in a dispute with a plumber over a bill, being outraged to learn that the resolution of the matter was to be handled by a board consisting solely of other plumbers.

To provide the kind of initiative I believe a mayor should take to assure the public credibility of internal police misconduct investigations, I asked our county bar association a few years ago to appoint a panel to study the previous ten years' case files on alleged police brutality. This seven-member panel of local attorneys objectively and independently examined the department's internal affairs unit to see how it had been functioning and whether the self-policing process needed any changes. The committee's report was submitted to me in December 1982 and was made public. No cases were reopened, and no dispositions were altered. We were concerned only with the efficacy and equity of the process. Our Minneapolis police chief has been outspoken in his endorsement of this kind of review and has been instrumental in the development of municipal policies designed to institutionalize good police-community relations. To support his good efforts, on July 1, 1983, I created the Minneapolis Police Review Panel, which includes two civilians (one of whom headed the Hennepin County Bar Association study) and a police officer. The panel reviews every internal investigation after the chief disposes of it and semiannually issues reports that have been constructively critical and whose recommendations have been adopted (for example, issuance to the public of an informational brochure explaining the complaint process, and greater feedback to complainants on the status of investigations).

In considering the limits of a police chief's role as a municipal policy-maker, it should be recognized that there are few formal constraints on a chief as a public spokesperson. He can work with business and philanthropic foundation leadership to urge cooperation with the police on specific projects or to provide grants for new programs. Moreover, he can make an important contribution on a variety of municipal matters that relate to law enforcement — and not only law enforcement in its narrowest sense. A chief who demonstrates an understanding of and sensitivity to societal problems that contribute to crime, such as unemployment, poor housing, and inadequate education, has a tremendous advantage in dealing with minority leaders on police-community relations. At the same time, a chief should be sensitive to the tensions that even his most casual remarks may inadvertently provoke within various segments of the community. For example, while gun control is an appropriate issue on which a chief may be expected to express his views, a prudent chief will be aware of the potentially inflammatory nature of this highly politicized subject.

Although a chief should not be expected to avoid public controversy, he should consider how to express his views in a manner that will not impair his effectiveness as the head of his department. In that sense, the chief must be extremely politic. If he frequently utters controversial views that are at variance with the prevailing sentiments or practices within the community, he may engender such public hostility as ultimately to undermine the good will and public support he has built. Carried to extremes, such outspokenness can make the successful conduct of his office extremely difficult.

The chief must be sensitive not only to the community's sentiments but also to the city council members' sense of "turf." A police chief who strays from police-related matters, such as by offering specific comments on zoning proposals, liquor licenses, and other concerns, might well be regarded by city council members as trespassing on their areas of responsibility. Moreover, if the chief espouses views that run counter to those held by members of the council, the public may find it confusing to hear conflicting voices coming from city hall. These dynamics leave even the most tactful chief in a somewhat unenviable role vis-à-vis the mayor and council. In Minneapolis, as I have indicated, the administrative authority for the police department lies with the mayor, yet the council controls the department's purse strings and ultimately renews the chief's contract.

A knowledgeable chief must therefore keep a watchful eye on his relations with the council without either impairing the professional management of his department or deviating from policy commitments to the mayor. As in all check-and-balance systems, this requires the chief both to make delicate compromises from time to time and to develop political skills (that is, to develop proficiency in "the art of the possible").

Finally, in thinking about the lines of authority between the chief and the mayor, one must never forget that ultimate control over the police resides in the citizenry, without whose support the best police professionals will not achieve effective peace and safety. Common sense tells us that our police can no longer afford to maintain a stance of isolation and removal from community concerns. Similarly, the public they serve must recognize that their law enforcement officials are not a breed apart but come out of the ranks of the general population. As one astute observer noted, "The public are the police, and the police are the public."

I sometimes think the ideal way to ensure this interdependence among the police and the community would be to have the police live in the neighborhood to which they are assigned. This would facilitate greater understanding of the goals and aspirations that citizens and the police share for themselves and their families and aid in reducing antagonisms and needless friction. The concept of neighborhood-based policing is not far from the role of police in small communities or the cop on the beat in larger cities who used to know everyone on the block. In any event, by fostering a joint police-citizen effort rooted in acceptance, knowledge, and trust, a solid foundation is laid for the police chief—in collaboration with his mayor—to exercise leadership on a wide range of policies significantly affecting the well-being of the entire community.

5

Chief-Mayor Relations:
The View from the Chief's Chair

Richard J. Brzeczek

"Politics," according to Noah Webster, is "the art or science of government: a science dealing with the regulation and control of men living in society." One of the definitions offered for "police" is "the control and regulation of a political unit (such as a nation or state) through the exercise of governmental powers." Both words derive from the Greek terms for "citizen" and "citizenship"; and "police" also comes from the Greek word for city — *polis*. It is no wonder, then, linguistically or pragmatically, that police and politics are intertwined in many ways. The objective for the mayor and the police chief, in my opinion, should not be to deny this interdependence but to clarify its proper scope. Policing and police administration should avoid party or partisan politics but should embrace politics and political action in the highest sense of those terms.

The difficulty, of course, stems largely from the fact that nonpartisan political governance in the United States is, generally speaking, left to the tender mercies of political partisans. These politicians, whether mayors, judges, prosecutors, sheriffs, dogcatchers, or the president of the nation, unavoidably must operate with one eye on the rights and requirements of the citizenry and the other on the implications of their decisions and conduct for survival in office. The statesman sees and seizes the opportunities for marriage between personal aspirations and the public interest. The average politician misses the mark by a country mile, contributes to the largely deserved bad image of governmental leadership, and stimulates an alarming rate of divorce between the leaders and the led in this country, with the result that, on a rather routine basis, the ballot card becomes a "Dear John" letter to the incumbents at all levels of government.

The fact that the police chief executive typically is not elected does not, except in the most basic, civics class view of the world, mean that the chief is, or should be, removed from nonpartisan politics – or, unfortunately, that he is exempt from partisan political pressures. The chief would be irresponsible in the extreme to attempt to run the police department without a healthy respect for the needs and preferences of the polis. This is not to say that a chief should abrogate his authority or pretend he possesses less expertise than he does in law enforcement, disorder prevention and control, and the provision of an almost countless array of emergency social services. ("Getting along" with the usually and necessarily publicity-hungry mayor will, however, have practical implications for the style and visibility with which the chief handles and shares this expertise.)

In attempting to strike a proper balance between the chief's political responsiveness (congruence between the chief's objectives and those of the public and the public's elected representatives), on the one hand, and his professional autonomy from the world of party politics, on the other, what should be the proper lines of authority between the chief and his elected superior(s)? How might the answer vary, depending on the particular issue (general law enforcement priorities, specific enforcement and tactical decisions, police department personnel matters, municipal policymaking questions only indirectly related to peacekeeping and law enforcement)? These obviously are enormous questions. This chapter takes a brief look at some of them based on my own experience and the experience of other police chief executive officers around the nation.

BRIGHT LINES AND GRAY AREAS

The sort of "bright-line" distinctions and "black letter law" that beleaguered first year law students tend to long for are, for better or worse, quite hard to find or articulate concerning the police chief-mayor relationship. A few points, however, seem to me to be incontestable. First, the mayor (or city manager) is the boss. He or she can, in most cities, either legally or by virtue of raw political power toss or force the police chief out of office almost at whim. There are a few notable exceptions, such as the recently eliminated "chief-for-life" arrangement in Milwaukee and a few police executives around the country who have organized their communities so effectively that they enjoy greater de facto job security than their elected superior.

Second, the mayor has an essential role to play in assuring the electorate that the police are performing as well as can be expected in light of fiscal realities (and resultant staffing and other problems), the state of the art of policing, various complexities of urban life, and so forth.

Third, the police executive, if chosen on merit (a large "if" in many locales), has considerable knowledge about the problems of the community and the efficacy of a wide array of possible palliatives – an expertise that will

be drawn on by the resourceful mayor in making policy decisions about policing and otherwise in governing the city. It is not only the police executive's
knowledge but his perspective on the world that the mayor may find very
useful — as one among several perspectives — as the mayor strives to improve
the urban environment. What the police careerist can offer his mayor perhaps
better than most other municipal advisers is his pragmatism, his take-charge
approach, and his appreciation of the volatile ambivalence that characterizes
the urban poor's attitude toward the police and city government — an ambivalence best expressed by Morris and Hawkins (1970, p. 88): "There is no
lack of logic in the ghetto dweller's statement: 'I hate the police and we need
more police here.'"

Fourth, the chief must have authority commensurate with his responsibility for running the police department day to day. Thus the police CEO
should have an autonomy, perhaps *guided* by the mayor's input, in a range
of matters of the sort that Pat Murphy (see his chapter) describes as "deal
breakers" in a prospective chief's negotiation of authority with his potential
employer. These matters include personnel decisions, integrity control within
the police department, determination of whether a proposed use of the police
oversteps the bounds between nonpartisan and partisan political purposes,
and the like. A mayor should not emasculate the chief's authority by such
steps as reserving the right to appoint the majority of a department's "exempt"-
rank personnel, publicly criticizing the agency, or announcing police programs
without consulting the chief.

Many areas are gray. There is not, and probably never will be, a clear
set of principles to guide the chief and the mayor in surveying the boundaries
of their adjoining "turf." In part, this is because these property lines are
necessarily transient, depending on the personal characteristics of the individuals and on the issue and the context in which it arises. As Mayor William
Hudnut observes in this volume, the clamor of public controversy (surrounding a questionable police shooting, for instance) sometimes requires mayoral
intervention (again, hopefully in an advisory rather than autocratic way) in
matters that would be handled entirely by the chief under quieter circumstances. Not all public controversy concerning the police merits mayoral
intercession, of course. The wise new police chief will make a top priority
assuring himself that the mayor has some sophistication in differentiating real
political liabilities (such as questions of integrity in the police department)
from apparent political liabilities (such as fluctuations in burglary rates criticized by an isolated foe of the mayor or the chief). Even when the issue does
warrant city hall's involvement, the mayor should realize that *particularly*
when pressures mount — due to a persistent city hall press corps, an arm-
twisting police union, political power grabs by rival politicians, and so on —
that is a time to *seek* the chief's counsel and work collaboratively with him
rather than a time to shut him out of key planning and policymaking discus-

sions. A few specific examples may help to illustrate my thinking about these topics.

MAYORAL INVOLVEMENT IN POLICE MATTERS

Historically, mayors abused their power over the police department, placing inept cronies on its payroll and using its members as footsoldiers in political skirmishes. Remnants of such inappropriate mayoral meddling can be found in modern times in a number of cities. For example, Minneapolis, during the 1970s, suffered from mayoral abuse of the police personnel structure (see Fraser's chapter), and Chicago only within the past decade ceased unconstitutional use of the police for surveillance of the mayor's political enemies. For the most part, however, the "reform" movement that swept American policing during this century (see Walker 1977) left mayors reticent to exercise strong, visible, and *proper* power over policing (see Goldstein 1977, pp. 132-35).

Today, the issues on which mayors most commonly attempt to influence the police, usually after a controversy has arisen, are the form of police response to a disturbance, use of deadly force, and the manner of enforcing particular laws. Increasingly, city halls across the nation have also taken a cautious but keen renewed interest in the recruitment and selection of police officers — now, however, motivated by concern about the psychological fitness of officers for jobs that unavoidably entail coercive force (Bittner 1970) and interest in rectifying past employment discrimination based on race, ethnicity, gender, and other factors. Moreover, mayors are starting to look intently at the *form* of patrol and the strength of deployment of officers from neighborhood to neighborhood. Traditional notions that such matters are routine tasks for police administrative personnel have given way to a perception that the citizenry and their elected officials have vital interests at stake in the outcomes (Goldstein 1977, pp. 139, 145-46).

When these vital interests are tempered by proper regard for police expertise, the citizen/elected official/police collaboration can be a genuinely successful one. When, however, politicians' self-aggrandizing solutions are substituted for professional police methods, the likely result will be to waste taxpayers' money and, at worst, to aggravate public fear of crime and actual criminality. Both extremes of mayoral involvement can be illustrated briefly.

First, the negative. Mayor Richard Daley's "shoot to kill" histrionics during Chicago police attempts to suppress rioters at the 1968 Democratic National Convention can be fairly said to have contributed to injury on both sides of the "thin blue line." He — with considerable help from network television's ability to bring instant fame to its subjects — egged on the protesters to feats of daring and stupidity for which many of them were ill-suited. A

similar example, at the level of state law enforcement, is Governor Nelson
Rockefeller's bloody solution on September 13, 1971, to the stand-off between
rebellious prisoners and nervous state police at Attica Penitentiary in upstate
New York (see Silberman 1978, p. 508). A less dramatic but equally pernicious
problem in municipal policing is some mayors' tendency to foist top command
staff on the police chief — not only without consulting him but without ceding
to him effective power over the new subordinates.

On the positive side, mayors have exemplified proper involvement in
policy decisions (setting priorities, choosing among alternative policies, and
so forth) while leaving to the police chief executive a monopoly, or at least
a corner, on review of individual police actions. They have also shown a sensitivity to Goldstein's (1977, p. 150; see also pp. 142 and 151) prescription
that they — and the public — should provide

> guidance on direction and priorities, but they ought not become involved
> in developing detailed instructions on how policies are to be implement-
> ed. A chief's day-to-day control over personnel, equipment, and resources
> cannot be reduced without seriously detracting from his ability to manage.

Creatively using his considerable power, the mayor does not actually *run* the
police department; rather, he ensures police department compliance with
obligations imposed by authorities higher than the municipality (federal constitution, state law), as well as police department receptivity to input from
more localized interests (neighborhood groups and the like).

Mayor Jane Byrne, during my superintendency in Chicago, illustrated
what I believe to be a proper role for the municipal chief executive when she
dramatically called attention to rampant crime and civic neglect in public
housing projects by taking an apartment in the Cabrini Green housing complex. Although political adversaries questioned her motives, there can be little
doubt that, at least during her residency there in March 1981, Cabrini Green's
residents benefited from a saturation of city services of every type — from
policing to sanitation; that some of the benefits lingered after her eventual
and inevitable move out of the complex; and that, because of the media attention she focused on conditions in Chicago public housing during her fact-
finding mission, she raised public and political consciousness about the need
for reform in public housing not just in Chicago but throughout the nation.

When the mayor announced her bold decision to move in, she hardly
needed to tell me or the other cabinet members explicitly that beefed up services to Cabrini Green were in order. Importantly, however, at least in my case,
which is all I can speak about with firsthand knowledge, she did not purport
to tell the police *how* to improve the policing of Cabrini Green.

Another example from my own experience of what I regard as a proper mayor-chief relationship under trying circumstances was Mayor Byrne's courage in letting me have a free hand to react to media disclosures concerning underreporting and downgrading of crime by the Chicago Police Department in its periodic counts for the FBI's voluntary Uniform Crime Reporting system. The investigative media reports on "killing crime" were a political threat to the Byrne administration, even though the phenomenon they addressed had existed at least as far back as the beginning of Daley's dynasty. Yet Jane Byrne allowed me, through a rigorous internal audit, to look considerably deeper than the media's allegations, and to identify, publicly disclose, and correct long-standing department practices (I dare say not unique to Chicago) that made our crime tallies even more unreliable than the media thought they were. Perhaps the stringency of the constructive self-criticism the city administration engaged in on this issue can best and most briefly be conveyed by indicating that the media's incessant calls during the several-month pendency of my audit for "outside" scrutiny (based on the belief that an internal investigation would be a whitewash) were quieted instantly when my auditors' findings were released at a news conference.

THE CHIEF AS A MAJOR MUNICIPAL POLICYMAKER

Just as the mayor has an entirely appropriate role in governing the police, the talented police chief executive can make substantial contributions to civic well-being by asserting, with the support of an enlightened mayor, a strong leadership role in criminal justice matters generally and even in other areas that only "tangentially" bear on policing. (The fact is that virtually any civic matter of major consequence could have some important effect on the police, who have, by a process frequently beyond their control, become municipal America's utility infielders — its 24-hour helpers, healers, social workers, tough guys, travelers' aides, mediators, educators, community organizers, and what have you.) As I said in an extended interview some time ago with *Crime Control Digest* (Borsage 1982, p. 5), most chiefs fail to realize that they have a very important function as a municipal policymaker. Unaware of their opportunity to be a policy *initiator*, they seem to feel their policymaking role is subordinate to that of the mayor. In my view, the chief's policymaking role should be supportive of, not subordinate to, that of the mayor. The ideal mayor, I believe, looks for a police chief who will complement him, not compliment him — in terms of philosophy concerning the appropriate quality and quantity of municipal services and other key matters.

One example of my own efforts to be proactive in policymaking was my establishment shortly after becoming superintendent of a part-time Chicago Police Department liaison to the Illinois legislature. We maintained a high profile in Springfield, the state capital, on matters of interest to policing.

Besides making our opinions known on pending legislation, when we saw a need that legislative drafters had not addressed after a reasonable opportunity to do so, we drafted the legislation in-house, took it to Springfield, and lobbied until we got it passed. In this way, for instance, we plugged a gap in the state statute indemnifying police officers for damages assessed against them by courts for good faith but legally deficient conduct (Borsage 1982, p. 5).

Another example of what I believe a police chief owes to his troops and his community by way of leadership was my own rather scathing public attack on a Cook County Circuit Court judge who, sitting in *divorce* court and lacking jurisdiction in the matter, on July 29, 1982, released from prison on personal recognizance a man who had been convicted of cold-bloodedly murdering a police officer — and bragging about it — in 1972. The inmate was ill but was receiving competent medical treatment — possibly better than he could get outside of prison — from the State Department of Corrections. A police chief takes a calculated risk on such occasions, but I was gratified that my public criticisms were quickly echoed by other criminal justice officials and by editorial writers and led to the convict's reincarceration the next day, followed two weeks later by an appellate court decision approving that temporary result and entering a final order overturning the lower court's release decision (see Borsage 1982 for a detailed account of the episode).

A chief's possible role in criminal justice matters can also be illustrated by a media campaign I waged in 1980 to pressure the Illinois Department of Corrections to stop parolling large groups of inmates, primarily sex offenders, to the Cabrini Green housing project. That ultimately successful campaign was not responsive to a city hall initiative (it preceded the mayor's consideration of moving to Cabrini Green by many months), but it was supportive of the municipal administration's overall goals and objectives.

The police chief can add valuable perspective and leadership to mayoral cabinet deliberations on various matters, much as the municipal attorney traditionally has done. One illustration concerns the announcement by Chicago-based Operation PUSH, then headed by Jesse Jackson, that it planned a week hence to mount a boycott and set up mass pickets in front of the 1982 ChicagoFest, at the time a popular and important annual summer fair on the city's lakefront. ChicagoFest was not the principal target — it was to be the hostage in a larger drama Jackson was playing concerning alleged racial discrimination (some of the allegations no doubt were true) in the awarding of city contracts. Against some serious advice to cancel ChicagoFest lest there be confrontations reminiscent of the Democratic convention, I urged the mayor during a cabinet meeting to proceed with the festival.

My argument, which prevailed, was that canceling the Fest would fuel the issue and invite Jackson and others to attempt to exert extralegal control over municipal decision making in Chicago by dangling the threat of racial boycotts and racial unrest over the mayor's head. My advice was to let the Fest start and give the pickets a prominent location by the front ticket gates as well as various conveniences, such as portable toilets, a canopy, and picnic tables and benches. I suggested that if everything went well, the mayor could, of course, take all the credit; and that, if something went wrong, she could shut down the festival, blaming me for her reluctant decision to open it in the first place and saying the festival was being closed because the police reported they were unable to preserve the order necessary for a successful event.

As a brand new superintendent in 1980 (two weeks into the job) I had the opportunity to play a similar role in formulating the city's contingency plans for a possible firefighters' strike. I counseled a wait-and-see approach concerning pending labor negotiations with the firefighters. This suggestion ran counter to what I considered precipitous calls by the mayor's other advisers for her to issue an emergency executive order imposing a citywide curfew and banning the sale of gasoline and alcohol. The recommendation for that executive order came from some fear adviser's paranoia that, if the firefighters went on strike, they would all go out and get drunk, buy gasoline, and start torching the city. My view was that such drastic actions by the mayor before the conclusion of negotiations would be used by the firefighters to accuse her of precipitating a strike and that, in any event, existing city ordinances gave the mayor full authority to take these steps in due time if the negotiations broke down and the firefighters' mood proved ugly. I offered the further observation that the presumption by some of the mayor's advisers that such an executive order could be prepared and distributed to the necessary city agencies without the fire union leaders finding out about it was utterly unrealistic. The success of my advice, which, because I was the "new kid on the block," was given only after each of the other two dozen or so top mayoral advisers sitting in her office had finished supporting her announced intention to issue the proposed emergency executive order, set a tone for my relationship with the mayor over the next several years. The mayor solicited and was willing to listen to unsolicited advice from me on major municipal matters, ranging from imminent transportation crises to long-term planning for a Chicago World's Fair, and I did my best to rise to the challenge.

In the end, the chief's ability to serve as a major municipal policymaker — and even his ability to run a police department free from the most outrageous kinds of partisan political incursions — is largely dependent on local idiosyncracies rather than on the scientific application of immutable principles concerning the police chief-mayor relationship. As Goldstein (1977, p. 152) observed, "In the long run the potential for minimizing improper influences depends on the local situation and, most especially, upon the operating philosophy, commitments, and integrity of the individuals involved." This may sound like a rather hopeless note on which to conclude. I view it as uplifting, however, for it may help mayors, police chiefs, and interested others begin to cut away a lot of the rhetorical underbrush that historically has been used by mayors and chiefs to conceal their inability or unwillingness to accept personal leadership responsibility for improving American policing.

PART 2

THE CHIEF AND THE COMMUNITY

Introduction

Egon Bittner (1984, p. 208) observed in a recent book review that a dramatic change has occurred in the relationship between police executives and the public. While at one time the police "institution was hermetically sealed and nonresponsive to outside influence," today management "has opened somewhat to outside pressure and is far more responsive to the demands of those segments of the community who in the past received no recognition at all." The three contributors to this section, Professor Albert Reiss, Jr., and chiefs Lee Brown and Raymond Davis, are united in their approval of this trend toward more open communication between the chief and the community. Indeed, they see it—and many of its programmatic implications—as possibly the single greatest opportunity for improved policing in the coming decades. They hail the way policing is, more and more, broadening its goals from domestic tranquillity to community vitality and extending a hand of cooperation to new constituencies while strengthening existing collaborations (also see Hubert Williams's chapter in this volume).

But coupled with their praise of police executives who welcome interaction with new groups is a clarion warning to chiefs to take care lest they be struck by the pendulum as it swings back toward public influence over policing. As Davis puts it eloquently, "a blind pilgrimage to the temples of community control will not solve the chief's problems and may well prove disastrous." Some new alliances, such as that between police and the Guardian Angels, are extremely delicate—a fragility captured in Woody Allen's homily that "the lion and the calf shall lie down together, but the calf won't get much sleep" (Shapiro 1984, p. 33).

While they call in bold—and, to some, politically threatening—terms for police leaders to "shape" or "organize" the community and to "share power" with it, Reiss, Davis, and Brown recognize that traditional, and still pervasive, "police-community relations" programs bear little resemblance to their ideal. Indeed, much of what has been done over the past two decades to overcome police-community alienation shows little more sophistication than the attempt by some restaurants to make up for poor service and food by instructing the waiters to greet customers with a gosh-and-golly grin and a personal introduction.

In assessing the crises and opportunities presented by community pressures on police chiefs, the three authors in this section have addressed the following central questions: What are the legitimate incentives and disincentives for greater interaction between the chief and the community? Should the police chief assume a leadership role in fostering community crime prevention and in addressing broader community social service needs? If so, what are the political implications of police chiefs' organizing community crime prevention efforts? And what are the appropriate limitations on community crime prevention activities?

The reader will note that these questions are similar to those asked of the contributors who wrote about the chief as a major municipal policymaker. The principal difference is that the focus there was on the chief-mayor relationship; here it is on the chief-community relationship. The importance of considering the impact of the community separately from the impact of its elected leadership lies in the view of some careful observers that, in the end, it will not be the police administrator or legislature or other government agencies that will determine the nature and rate of police changes — it will be the community (Goldstein 1977, p. 329). If the prospect of the public "running" the police seems fraught with risks, one may well respond, as Winston Churchill did about democracy, that it is, admittedly, the worst possible system, except for all the others.

6

Shaping and Serving the Community: The Role of the Police Chief Executive

Albert J. Reiss, Jr.

POLICE AND COMMUNITY

Police executives of the past decades have listened to a great deal of rhetoric on "police and community," on police and community *relations*, on policing *the* community, and on *community-oriented policing*. Each of these designations cloaked problems that police departments were experiencing in carrying out what was regarded as their mandate to enforce the law *by* police work and a concern that all was not well with the citizenry they policed. Each also implied that there was some particular organizational solution to these problems.

Police and Community Relations

Conceptualizations concerning police and community relations assumed that the solution to problems with minority citizens lay in improving relationships between police officers and minorities by creating human relations or community relations units in police departments whose responsibility was a community relations program and community relations training of police officers. These units were established in the aftermath of investigations following rioting in minority communities and a growing political awareness in municipalities that failure to respond to these pressures and complaints threatened the traditional power and authority of both political officeholders and their police executives.

What was cloudy at the beginning became transparent with time—that police-community relationships could not be manufactured by assigning responsibility for them to a group of officers in a specialized public relations unit. Nor did it help much to put minority officers in such specialized units

61

when most policing is done by a traditional police cadre. The lesson to be gained from those ventures in police-community relations was that a chief cannot affect relationships between the citizenry and police personnel by bureaucratically specializing responsibility for them. Nor is officer behavior changed by training unless the department ensures the behavior is carried out. Making significant changes in citizen satisfaction and cooperation with police, rather, requires substantial reorganization and restructuring of who does what to whom, how, when, and where. More fundamental transformations are required in organization, recruitment, training, and control of behavior in policing if these objectives are to be reached.

Policing the Community

Continuing concerns on the part of police managers to do something about their mandate to enforce the law and keep the peace, to affect the level of crime in a community, and to respond to public demands for local policing in ways that are sensitive to citizens as persons caused police executives and their command staffs to rethink the consequences of the shift to a rapid response deployment of a motorized patrol to citizen calls for service. Their concerns were fed by a growing body of research that undermined traditional beliefs about the effectiveness of preventive patrol, of foot patrol, of detective investigation, of specialized vice units, and, indeed, of most traditional police practices thought to affect what came to be called the "crime problem."

Partly because of and partly in spite of these research findings and police executives' concerns, some major departments were led to search for specific solutions that addressed the pressures to reduce crime, often by focusing on strategies and tactics for policing community life. Although there were and there continue to be a large number of different strategies and tactics aimed at policing *the* community, perhaps the concepts of team policing (Schwartz and Clamen 1977) and of community profile policing (Boydstun and Sherry 1975) illustrate well the core ideas in strategies for policing the community. The community sector team policing model held that consistent assignment of the same officers to the same neighborhood to work as generalists under a unified but simplified control structure that improved communication with members and representatives of a community would achieve the main goals of policing. The community profile model assumed that individual officers rather than a police team are the core of community public safety planning. The effectiveness of individual beat officers could be enhanced if they were consistently assigned to the same beat and given responsibility for developing their personal profile of their working community.

Although none of these attempts at reorganizing patrol on a community basis was the panacea sought, there were certain lessons gained for police executives to ponder about how to reorganize the mission and work of police patrol. One is that most team efforts to involve members of the community *directly* in policing programs were not very effective. This is related in part to the stability of residence in many communities. The more transient the community, the less one can depend on enduring relationships with residents. The organizational patterns chosen to involve residents, moreover, failed to address problems of continuing organization and division of labor between police and citizens. But failure also seemed to be due to the resistance of trained police officers to altering their behavior. A second lesson is that piecemeal strategies for reorganizing patrol work that fail to make clear the nature of the organizational task being revamped will produce highly variable results. Success depended unduly on unusually talented and dedicated individual officers and the leadership given to a team. What seemed less obvious, but worthy of consideration, is that police cannot do very much to a community without finding ways of involving its members in a common concern. "Working with" strategies may be more effective than "doing to" strategies.

Community-Oriented Policing

Community-oriented policing has its roots in both community relations and policing the community programs. Often it incorporates elements from earlier programs such as team policing and community service units that were established to improve police-community relations. What distinguishes community-oriented policing, however, is that it represents a substantial shift in the organizational model of policing, one where police strategy and tactics are adapted to fit the needs and requirements of the different communities the department serves, where there is a diversification of the kinds of programs and services on the basis of community needs and demands for police services, and where there is considerable involvement of the community with the police in reaching their objectives.

Where community-oriented policing is highly developed, it is reflected in a fundamental reorganization of police management, work roles, and the locus of police work. Among the more fundamental changes are the creation of a variety of community service and police service officer roles that are occupied by civilian rather than sworn personnel, the organization of neighborhood service centers that have victim assistance, crime investigation, and crime prevention jobs, and the development of opportunities for citizen participation (see Davis's chapter).

Community-oriented policing has led to a rich variety of efforts to deal with some common crimes and the fear of crime in communities and to a great deal of experimentation with new ways for dealing with victims and preventing crimes. In a few cases it has altered dramatically the ratio of civilian to sworn personnel. Yet community-oriented policing in and of itself has not had a dramatic effect on common crime rates. Such effects as it has appear largely as increased cooperation between citizens and the police and a stabilization of residence and business activity in local communities.

Police executives can gain much from the experiences of different police departments in developing community-oriented policing.[1] Community-oriented policing is, in its nature, a dynamic rather than a static enterprise. It is a model for solving problems rather than a fixed strategy for policing. To implement that model requires several things of police executives. First, it requires a *commitment* by the chief and his top executives to developing a community-oriented policing system over a period of years. It is a strategy for long- rather than short-run change, which must cope with the reality that the average tenure of a major city police chief is short. Second, police executives must be committed to a *style* of policing characterized by receptivity to community involvement. This means a continuing search for ways that the community can be involved in attaining police objectives and a continuing reinforcement of community efforts. And, third, police executives must develop a style of policing characterized by an *openness to change* rather than implementation of a program with fixed solutions. That style must characterize the department's orientation at all levels of function — from training to operations — and at all levels of staff and command.

To implement a community-oriented policing model also requires substantial changes in the structure of the organization and its operations. Among the most important is a change in the basic reward system of the department so that at least a substantial part of the work force is rewarded for cooperative rather than individual effort and for the promotion of community objectives in policing. Likewise, the department must be engaged in a continuing program of experimentation and of trying different ways to solve its policing problems. One of the great lessons of the Kansas City Preventive Patrol Experiment (Kelling et al. 1974a, 1974b; see also Kelling's chapters) was that it demonstrated the possibility of making substantial changes in the way patrol and other departmental resources are used without any substantial effect on the crime rate. Police commanders are thus free to experiment with the allocation of police resources without having to be overly concerned about trade-offs. Where returns on current effort are low, gains are potentially much greater when trying new ideas.

There are some other lessons from community-oriented policing for structuring and operating police departments. The most difficult problems in community-oriented policing are how to involve communities in policing or to sustain that involvement once gained. It seems clear that a centralized command and a reactive mobilization system are insufficient for doing so. Both a decentralized command, at least for part of the operations, and local community centers, where police and community work together, are essential. But essential as these are, the wherewithal to cope with many of the problems of policing lies beyond the residents and the police of a local community;

it lies with the government of the city and beyond. For police executives and for community residents, this raises issues of how one solves the problems of crime and public safety in local communities. It also raises questions about how one deals with the problems of changing communities and their shifting requirements for policing. These problems, in turn, raise issues for police executives about their role in social change.

AN EXPANDED ROLE FOR THE POLICE IN SOCIAL CHANGE

A central issue in modern policing is the role that police executives and their organizations shall have in responding to, and in shaping, social change, given its ubiquity and accelerating rate. Historically the police served status quo interests. But, is it possible that conditions are now so altered that the police may be regarded as agents of social change in communities? Can they actively plan for changes in society and participate in planning the future of society, as well as responding to what takes place?

Designing and carrying out the future course of policing raise questions about the criteria to be used in developing and implementing that design. Were police to follow their historic sense of duty, they would think primarily in terms of reactive strategies and tactics, looking to what police organizations did in the past rather than to what other organizations accomplish in other ways. There would be a tendency to look to the future in terms of what it tells them about their proactive and reactive capabilities rather than in terms of what those capabilities might become. They would think in terms of adopting and adapting technology developed by other organizations for other purposes rather than of developing technologies for their new purposes. And they would see material rather than nonmaterial technologies as needed to meet their requirements. They would be unlikely to think that the critical strategies in designing and implementing a planned future are research and development.

Were police organizations to rely more on research and development than they have in the past, many of their problems would be far more tractable. Research would become a core technology of policing (Goldstein 1979; Reiss 1982; see also Stewart's chapter). Law enforcement agencies where research is a core technology will do research on the communities they police. The problems those communities and their residents present, rather than what the police "can do about the crime problem," might come to determine the tasks of police agencies. The solution to vandalism, for example, as Goldstein (1979, p. 250) notes, may not be more or better policing in the sense of patrol and arrest, but attention to the causes of vandalism and the role that the police may have in dealing with those root causes. Were police organizations to shift their concerns to the problems of their communities in all their diversity, the role of research in police work could change dramatically. The police no longer would be consumers of research but producers of it, and research would not be done primarily by outsiders but as a management operation. Moreover, research and development within a police organization might become as critical to its future as research and development is to other modern industrial and government agencies (see Shanahan's chapter). A modern military organization would not survive long if it had to depend, as does a modern police department, on its past.

Police administrators and their municipal employers seem reluctant to think of an expanded role for the police in policing community life, one where the police are concerned with the quality of life in a community and the effect that social change has on that community. Police executives likewise seem unwilling to view the police as responsible agents in ensuring minimal properties for community life and in helping residents shape and control their future. But above all, they seem unwilling to reshape radically the role that *they* might play in shaping the communities they have the responsibility to police.

Imagine the public police having a strong voice in denying a zoning permit, in identifying the public order requirements for a planned public facility, in assessing the traffic and security control essential for a privately developed shopping center, or in developing and enforcing all municipal codes. Indeed, with few exceptions (see Hudnut's and Fraser's chapters), if the police are consulted in these matters at all, it is more likely to be with respect to the movement of traffic than for what maintaining order may cost the public or what may enhance the quality of life in a community. Consider the following proposals and whether and in what ways the police must be involved in their coming about, and evaluate the consequences for the police when they do come about: A decision is made to bus many students to schools that are distant from their place of residence; pornography shops are concentrated in a single neighborhood of the city by the action of a common council; a decision is made to close a park or public playground in a community; a decision is made to build high-rise public housing units by demolishing local housing (and thereby increasing the density of settlement).

As a further example, consider the effects on policing when public drunkenness is decriminalized. Then, instead of using the means of arrest and jail as they once did when encountering drunken persons, the police must relate to new means — services such as detoxification centers — and to new views — that drunkenness is an illness. Decriminalization changes the use the police can make of the law. The problems that originally gave rise to the law used against public intoxication, and the use of control by police enforcement of the law, do not go away, however, with this single change in the law. Decriminalization often may exacerbate the public order problem for the police. With detoxification, ordinary citizens may continue to demand that intoxicated persons be removed from public streets and public view, but both the police and the residents may be powerless to do so by traditional means.

To press the matter further, how active a role are we to give the police in working with communities in planning their quality of life over and beyond their role in preventing crime? Shall the police work with the community in changing the traditional patterns of enforcement of housing, building, and sanitation codes that progressively deteriorate communities and launch them on community crime careers? Shall the police be permitted to see to it not only that the laws protecting the integrity of communities as organizations be enforced but that they be strengthened in the interest of the quality of life of their residents? Such questions pose quite pointedly the issue of whether we are prepared to have a more activist police executive and an ever-changing police organization – an organization that does more than respond to change, one that helps to shape the future of the communities of which it is a part.

Very real dilemmas arise whenever the police come to participate in social change, particularly where they become responsive to the demands for change in local communities. Local communities make demands about the quality and quantity of law enforcement; in particular, they often demand that the police respond to *their* problems as *they* define them. But how responsive should the police be to local community demands for law enforcement when meeting those demands conflicts with the rights of others? If one grants autonomy to local policing and local determination and control of policing, how does one guarantee the rights of everyone in that local community? These are not simple matters. A complex society can ill afford law enforcement where its substance changes considerably from community to community, as what is plainly at stake are the rights of everyone to move about without undue constraint by the law and without the necessity of having to know what is required locally. In a free society we cannot afford local diversity in substantive and procedural law that infringes the rights of others. But, correspondingly, we can afford great diversity where no such infringement is involved. Ultimately, a sensible policy may be to maximize diversity in community life rather than conformity, a position that is not congenial to conventional policing.

A closely related issue is how accountable the police should be to the local constituency that is being policed. This is a difficult matter to resolve because there are no obvious trade-offs. On the whole, a democratic police requires some insulation from local political influence if it is to be nonpartisan in its attention to problems[2]; on the other hand, there must be ways that local constituencies can make the police responsive to their needs and problems if we are to have *their* as well as *our* respect for the rule of law. Under our system of local government and policing, the police chief must share the role of policymaker with the community that is to be policed.

The insulation of the police from partisan political influence should not absolve political leadership of responsibility for setting and overseeing the implementation by police of public policy on police matters. The appropriateness of limits on authority over police matters of both the municipal chief executive and the police chief executive will depend in large measure on what problems are considered police matters in a given community. Do they include not only tasks given to police departments by law, such as enforcement of the state criminal and municipal codes, but also licensing investigations, inspections of various kinds, granting licenses, informally mandated provision of a host of social and other services — from undertaking accident investigations to advising on family problems — and even the prevention of harm and maintenance of the quality of life in a community? Police organizations are given largely to deterrence rather than compliance law enforcement and to attending to "serious" rather than to "soft" crime matters. Yet what may matter most in the communities the police are policing are matters of compliance with the law and control of soft crime. For the major victims of crime in our major cities are not only people but their communities. Failure to comply with regulations governing the health, welfare, and safety of communities may be far more consequential to collective life than are major crimes by offenders called criminals. Failure to deal with crimes that destroy property, that subject residents to harassment and intimidation, and that bring undesirable communal situations often is far more destructive of community life than are the major crimes within it.

What seems clear is that the broader the definition given to what constitutes a police matter, the broader the mandate given to police organizations to serve their communities, and the more public controversy surrounding any police matter, the more likely it is that chief executives of municipalities and a host of public and private agencies will insist on involvement in defining police authority and responsibility for these matters.

There are, of course, no simple answers to the role of police executives in shaping the welfare of the communities that they police. Yet participation in communities may well require the police to be more active in shaping them than they have been in the past, for a community-oriented policing model means that one cannot treat law enforcement as a problem isolated from the problems of a community and its residents and from their quality of life. All too often public policy on policing is set in the cauldron of scandal, allegations of police misconduct, and the postmortem surrounding public disorder where the police are somehow held responsible. All too rarely are there ways that controversy can surface, issues can be defined, and policies set in an atmosphere devoid of rancor. The emergence of community policing with its community police specialists and of community organization to assist police in cities such as Santa Ana, California, appear to be ways to deal successfully with issues surrounding the policing of conventional crime. To meet the challenges ahead, one cannot simply react to community changes as they occur, for many of the problems of policing may be prevented by shaping the community's future. Ultimately, a dynamic view of the police executive is a view of the police leader and of the police department as one that shapes its environment as well as responds to it.

NOTES

1. The experiences of different departments is about all an executive has to draw on for innovative ideas and standards, for, at the present time, police occupational practice lacks both consensus on standards and a machinery of enforcement — both key to professionalization. These deficiencies are attributable partly to the fact that police policies and practice are considered the exclusive domain of *each* police organization rather than the domain of a profession of policing. This localism is enforced by the vulnerability of police leadership to local political forces. A police officer's practice and career are tied to an employing organization rather than to a profession. Unlike school superintendents, who are itinerants among organizations, the lateral mobility of police chiefs in most cities is restricted to retirement from an organization. The vulnerability of police chiefs and their officer cadre to their municipal employers means that when external political pressure concerning police policy and practice is deemed unwarranted, the chief or his members cannot resort easily to professional standards and cannot call on a professional organization to represent those standards and insist on conformity to them. A police chief who seeks to restrict the political authority of municipal executives cannot now resort to an argument about violation of professional standards of policing and make it stick. Some organized professions can do so.

2. The reality of American municipal politics is such that the police are not very insulated from the political pressures of the moment precisely because political figures are not insulated from those pressures. The process has a cyclical quality. Lacking the capacity to insulate municipal officials from political pressures in their environment by being able to treat police matters as professional rather than political matters, the police organization leaves municipal officials vulnerable to public pressures and caprice.

7
Police-Community Power Sharing

Lee P. Brown

The changing social order of the 1980s calls for a new type of police leadership. In many instances, police administrators are rising to the challenge, questioning many of the traditional concepts that have determined how the police deliver services and redefining the police mission itself. Historically, the police have adhered to a single mission — enforcement of the law. Today, however, police administrators are realizing that the battle against crime and for community security engages the police as problem solvers and multipurpose service providers. Belatedly, they are recognizing something that was common knowledge in this country 200 years ago — that crime is a community problem, not just a problem for the police.

Armed with the perception of crime fighting as a community responsibility, police administrators are now realizing that they cannot accomplish their mission without the understanding, support, and cooperation of the people they serve. This recognition of the importance of citizens' involvement is a great advance for police chiefs, who have not been in the forefront of the trend of government and business to encourage collaborative undertakings and community involvement (compare Shanahan's chapter). Instead of adopting a "we versus they" defensive posture, as they have in the past, police executives are coming to see how citizens' rage and frustration over crime and the fear it creates can become a vital resource to police agencies in effective crime prevention and control.

In his emerging leadership role, the police chief has a primary responsibility for educating the public not only about the problem of crime in general but in particular about the limited capacity of police to control it. That limitation arises largely from the inability of the police to control the factors that cause crime. Although debate continues over precisely what factors or mix of factors promote law breaking, few social scientists would exclude the possibility that crime is rooted in the socioeconomic problems of the community, and few criminologists would dismiss the fact that most persons arrested come from areas manifesting high levels of unemployment or underemployment, poor schools, substandard housing, high rates of alcohol and drug addiction, and poor delivery of services. If one accepts the proposition that negative environmental conditions do, indeed, influence criminality, then one might expect society to place a premium on police capacity to control those conditions. However, the police have been organized not so much to prevent crime but to react after it has occurred, and they find themselves charged with managing a phenomenon created in an arena they have little power to change or shape. It is this very limitation, however, that provides the basis for the development of police-community collaboration.

Right or wrong, like it or not, however, police continue to be regarded by the public as society's vanguard in the battle against crime. Historically, police have contributed to the myth that they, in fact, control crime by claiming that they represent a "thin blue line" between community chaos and community order and by publicly taking credit when crime decreases. There is ample evidence to suggest that their historical isolation from the public has been detrimental to the communities they serve. Such isolation, common to all occupational groups to a certain degree, is more pronounced in police agencies because of their position of authority, the danger of the work, high visibility, and the great public stake in efficient delivery of service. Unfortunately, society's almost total reliance on the police for protection complicates a community's capacity for effectively managing its crime problem.

Not only must a police chief assume leadership in fostering his community's sense of responsibility for crime prevention, he must also take the lead in addressing broadened local social service needs that could, if neglected, produce greater crime problems. He must articulate the principles that define the public's involvement, establish processes and structures to ensure appropriate police-community collaboration, and recognize both the limits and the possibilities of that interaction. In my experience as former public safety commissioner in Atlanta and now as chief of the Houston Police Department, I have attempted to abide by the following three principles: (1) The police department must collaborate with the community in planning, operations, and performance evaluation. (2) All segments of the police department must be involved in improving the department's relationship with the community. (3) The police department must share its power with the community. The chief should begin with a full understanding of his role as both educator and motivator in involving citizens in the search for a safer community.

THE CHIEF AS EDUCATOR AND MOTIVATOR

The informed police chief knows that the idea of community crime prevention is not new in our culture or in many others. As the National Advisory Commission on Criminal Justice Standards and Goals (1973f, p.7) has noted, in "the early days of law enforcement, well over a thousand years ago, the peace-keeping system encouraged the concept of mutual responsibility to rouse . . . neighbors and pursue the criminal. Peace was kept, for the most part, not by officials, but by the whole community" (p. 7). Over the years, as suggested earlier, that notion was lost and came to be replaced by the belief that crime prevention and control are the responsibility of paid professionals.

The informed chief realizes also that, in the emerging collaborative relationship between the police and the community, both partners have distinct contributions to make. I attempted to sum up the community's potential contribution and immediate stake in the control of crime in a departmental statement of philosophy when I was public safety commissioner in Atlanta:

> It is from their neighborhoods that the offender is spawned, often known to them as their friend, neighbor, or child. They know intimately what conditions in their neighborhood perpetuate crime, and to some extent, how to best respond to them. It is they who most often shoulder the full brunt of crime—from personal property losses to insult, injury, and even death to themselves, their families, and friends. That they respond with apathy, a sense of powerlessness, and pathetic individual attempts to isolate and protect themselves by hiding behind fortress-like homes and offices, is to some extent a measure of how much they have been excluded from active participation in crime control efforts. (Brown 1979)

Thus the major incentive for the police chief's greater involvement with the community is the prospect of effectively managing the problem of crime. To that end, active citizen involvement potentially holds out the following specific benefits: greater public awareness of the crime problem; an increased sense of citizens' individual responsibility for dealing with the causes of crime; a reduction in passivity and isolation; increased cooperation between police and community; enhanced collective action to prevent crime; a greater sense of shared responsibility for crime control; less likelihood of the public's singling out the police department and/or the chief for blame; and expansion of resources in times of budget cutbacks. An understanding of how these benefits are interrelated will suggest some of the processes, structures, and programs that might be developed for realizing them.

Because to a large degree the public's knowledge about crime comes from secondary sources, such as the news media and rumors, what knowledge citizens do have of crime is often inaccurate and lacking in what they need to know to initiate preventive action. By actively involving citizens in their community's crime control efforts, the police should have an opportunity to provide them with accurate information about the type and frequency of crime at the neighborhood level. Greater public awareness will lead to citizens' personal commitment to be a part of the process for the management of crime, just as involved businesspersons who come to understand the relationship between crime and unemployment are more likely to develop a personal commitment to addressing the problem of unemployment. Although crime is affecting more and more Americans, uninvolved citizens often regard crime as an arbitrary given and themselves as unlucky victims. Involved and informed citizens, on the contrary, come to see that crime must be addressed by all segments of the community and that apathy and isolation contribute to the sense of a deteriorating civil order. Houston is now testing a variety of strategies in its Fear Reduction Study (English and Fowler 1983), including "directed" citizen contact and a neighborhood information network, to determine the best modes of police-community collaboration to reduce fear of crime in given types of neighborhoods.[1]

Citizens coming together will recognize that they are not alone in their concern about burglaries and other crimes committed in their neighborhood. And, realizing that their involvement with other residents in the neighborhood could, indeed, make a difference, they are in a better position to cooperate actively with police. Crimes are often prevented by citizens' efforts, which traditionally have been channeled through the many programs developed by police crime prevention units such as "target hardening" techniques, "operation identification," neighborhood watch projects, citizen alert programs, and crime prevention education. Equally important, crimes that have not been prevented are often solved by citizens assisting the police—in fact, information provided to the police by victims or witnesses of crimes is the primary method by which crimes are ultimately solved (Eck 1983; Greenwood and Petersilia 1975). Although in any given community only a small percentage of the people create the crime problem, they can intimidate the entire populace. But collective action on the part of the law abiding, who constitute the overwhelming majority of the people, creates an atmosphere that communicates clearly to the rest that they cannot offend with impunity.

The involvement of the whole community leads to a collective sense of responsibility for the control of crime, and this leads the way to the sharing of both credit and blame with the police. In the process of accepting responsibility for containing crime—and of taking bows when crime figures decline—the police have also left themselves vulnerable to becoming a scapegoat in public concern over crime. It is not unheard of for elected officials to demand the dismissal of the police chief because of the incidence of crime. Many elected officials, who have little substantive knowledge about crime and are therefore numbers-oriented, react out of political considerations to public reports of an increase in the crime rate or a poor showing in comparison with other cities. Thus, for example, the FBI's annual *Uniform Crime Reports*, once established to help the police, now serve as a noose around the necks of some chiefs. Informed and involved communities are less likely to single out the police chief or the department for blame and are more likely to demand the adoption by their law enforcement agency of more meaningful crime reporting systems (see, for example, Police Executive Research Forum 1982).

Cooperation with the community must go beyond the kinds of consultations and police-community relations mechanisms of the past where the police and the community merely talked to each other. The chief must recognize that each party to the dialogue possesses a unique power that the other lacks, and that both must be brought to bear on the problem of crime if success is to be achieved. Citizens have that piece of the crime puzzle—intimate knowledge about their neighborhood—that cannot be provided by the police, whereas the police are the professionals with special knowledge and skills on how best to harness the available resources for improved public safety.

By involving citizens in the operation of the police department, police chiefs also expand the resources of the department. Until recently (see Shanahan's chapter), knowledge, skills, and expertise from the community have remained virtually untapped by police agencies throughout the United States, which is unfortunate in these times of shrinking departmental resources because the public has been and remains quite willing to assist if only asked. The Houston Police Department's experience in this regard has been very positive. For example, teams of loaned business executives (see Shanahan's chapter), communications and training experts at various times have analyzed the sufficiency of our helicopter and fleet maintenance operations, internal and external communications systems, budgeting process, recruit training programs, and physical police complex.

PROCESS AND STRUCTURES RECOGNIZING IMPORTANCE OF COMMUNITY INVOLVEMENT IN PLANNING AND OPERATIONS

If police chiefs' efforts in fostering community crime prevention are to be effective, there must be specific processes and structures that clearly indicate to both the public and police officers that the community has input in the operation of the police agency. There are many ways this can be done. The most important is by example. The chief should be accessible to the community, which can be achieved by his participating, and by requiring command staff, supervisors, and beat officers to participate, in community meetings. The police chief can also explicitly recognize the importance of community involvement through the official set of value statements he establishes for the department.[2]

Formal programs can be developed to ensure continuing community involvement. Two examples of such efforts are operating in Houston. In one, the Houston Police Department has instituted a Police-Community Positive Interaction program, having as its primary goal the development of police and citizen awareness of their respective roles and responsibilities in maintaining order. Under this initiative, each district commander is required to organize representatives of the geographic area for which he is responsible to serve as his advisers, and he is expected to provide the leadership needed to involve organizations as well as individuals in addressing crime problems and the quality of life in his district. An important element of this program is its decentralization — it is operated by those who actually deliver police services at the neighborhood level rather than by headquarters personnel.

The other project is the department's Police Advisory Committee, composed of representatives of such citywide organizations as the Chamber of Commerce and the National Association for the Advancement of Colored People and six members appointed by the mayor. The committee is responsible for providing the police chief with "support and advice" regarding programs, policies, and procedures that affect police-community relations. One accomplishment of this committee has been helping the police develop a procedure for handling mentally ill persons.

Structures involving the public in actually writing policy collaboratively with the police have been instituted in a number of cities, including Battle Creek, Michigan, Madison, Wisconsin, and Dayton, Ohio. Such efforts have resulted in departmental policy statements guiding police operations that have a direct impact on the community.

The process and structures for involving the community must encourage *real* collaboration in planning and implementation of crime prevention programs — which is to say, something beyond what has passed for community programs in the past. The traditional crime control planning programs developed solely by the police were viewed by the public as just that — "police" programs — and they resulted in limited citizen participation. In reviewing the rise and demise of police-community relations programs during the 1960s, one sees the negative effect of failing to provide for community input (Brown 1973). Such programs included asking citizens to "Wave at a Cop," police lectures to the community about *police* problems, and other efforts to educate the public about the police (for an inventory of such programs, see Johnson et al. 1981). Because the community was not involved from the start in these programs, they all ended up as one-way communication from the police without ever securing real citizen participation.

While police-initiated activities are necessary and important, typically the more substantial programs are designed through collective planning by both the police and the community. Such planning can be either proactive or reactive, and it can issue from work with existing community organizations or from programs involving police in organizing the community.

Proactive Planning

Proactive planning is planning before something occurs — that is, preventing a crime problem from developing in a neighborhood. Implicit in the concept of such planning is a determination of community needs, which to be effective must be undertaken in concert with community groups and relevant government agencies.

One example of proactive planning on a citywide basis is the Houston Police Department's recent self-assessment, which provided for input from all segments of the community and focused attention on understanding the environmental context in which the police must work. The ultimate objective was to enable the police to involve citizens in departmental efforts to address crime and, at the same time, to improve the department's efficiency in delivering services. Citizens provided key input in identifying problems and issues and in developing a course of action to address those problems. The plan of improvement serves as the department's road map for the future delivery of police services to the city.

Reactive Planning

Reactive planning, on the other hand, occurs when a neighborhood or community already has a major crime or service delivery problem. This planning, which also must involve joint police-community efforts to describe the problem and identify responsive strategies, is often called "contract writing" because police, neighborhood residents, and businesspersons agree to assume responsibility for certain activities. For example, community residents may agree to identify persons selling stolen goods or dealing in drugs, and the police may commit themselves to increased foot patrol, or both may agree to implement a joint neighborhood watch program.

A formalized reactive planning program was initiated in Atlanta while I was public safety commissioner. Called Police-Community Action Agreements (PCAA), the concept germinated at a meeting of a public housing tenant association where residents forcefully voiced their complaints about crime, disorder, and inadequate police service. Not having answers to the problems, I requested another meeting, to which I brought the relevant command staff to hear the complaints firsthand. The command staff was then directed to reduce the complaints to writing and develop an action plan to address the problems. A third meeting was held with the tenant association to present the plan of action, which outlined not only what the police could do (for example, foot patrol, more frequent beat patrol, and assignment of a police official as a liaison to the tenant association) but also what the residents could do (such as reporting suspicious circumstances, calling the liaison when they knew people were committing crimes, and supporting the housing authority administration when, at police request, it evicted residents who repeatedly created problems). After several months, the police were called back to a meeting of the tenant association. This time, however, they were welcomed with a dinner prepared by the residents to express their appreciation for what had been accomplished. The residents reported that there was more police presence, the police were more responsive to their calls, some of the known troublemakers were gone, and they no longer feared living in their community (see Lindsey's chapter in this volume concerning a similar experience in Fort Lauderdale, Florida). On the other hand, the police were able to tell of greater citizen concern and participation, evidenced by information provided to the department on criminal activities. In one such instance, a citizen's report on the identity of a homicide suspect enabled the police to solve a murder case.

The success of this effort resulted in the formalization of the process. Now the police may either initiate or respond to a request for a meeting with residents or businesspersons to hear complaints and put the expressed concerns in writing. After the meeting, the police gather data from crime statistics, surveys, and the like to clarify the problems further. Then the collective expertise of the department in the areas of patrol, investigation, crime analysis, and crime prevention is brought to bear on developing a two-part plan of action, detailing what the police commit themselves to do and what it is recommended that the community do. In some cases, other government agencies are brought in with their commitments also outlined in the agreement. Finally, a meeting is convened to present the plan of action to the citizens. The plans are then signed by the police chief, officially committing the police department to do certain things. Because the police serve the community, the community is not asked to sign anything; its commitments are moral ones. Because the commitments on both sides are specific, they can be monitored, and each group can hold the other accountable at ongoing meetings.

Other communities have experimented with variations of this contract process, ranging from having the community group and the police jointly brainstorm problem solutions to having all participants sign the agreement. The key in all these cases is joint agreement to share responsibility for action. Without exception, the PCAA process has worked in every area in which it has been used in Atlanta. The Houston Police Department has now developed a similar program as part of its crime analysis efforts. In the future, police managers will be provided with a format for drawing up such "contractual" agreements identifying the specific tasks of police and community members.

Working with Preexisting Community Organizations

Some of the most vital sources of potential community support at the grass-roots level, historically neglected by police chiefs, are existing community-based organizations. (To be sure, the police cannot and should not give support and cooperation to every group that requests it, about which more will be said later.) An example of how police departments can work with community groups, drawn again from my own experience, is the Houston Police Department's ongoing collaboration with the Metropolitan Organization (TMO). TMO represents more than 65 churches whose stated purpose is "to strengthen the family by reducing the pressures on family life that result from such problems as crime, lack of adequate public service, and other problems in the neighborhoods in which TMO members live." One of TMO's first projects, after its founding in 1979, was creation of a security task force that conducted research on the Houston Police Department over a three-year period. Among the major recommendations of its report, which was prepared without formal input from the department, was the suggestion that the department should implement an experimental project involving neighborhood police patrol. Ironically, the police had also been developing plans for a similar project, called Directed Area Responsibility Team (DART). Both concepts had as their goal the intensification of community and police cooperation in crime prevention. There were, however, some significant differences in how the programs were proposed to operate (for example, the location and size of the experimental areas differed).

After a series of meetings with TMO leaders, I participated in a meeting attended by almost 2,000 citizens in which I initiated a process to design a plan for neighborhood-oriented policing. A task force of TMO and department members, after more than four months of planning, designed two programs. One, the Neighborhood Response Team Program, provides for the selection of two beats in high-crime areas to be staffed by patrol officers who volunteer to be part of the program. These officers' responsibility is to *organize the community* (a fairly unusual role definition for police personnel; see Davis's chapter) in the interest of crime prevention. One church (with a designated liaison person) in each area serves as the focal point for hearing citizens' concerns and conveying them to the beat officer at his regular visits. The second program, the Directed Area Responsibility Team, is broader in the scope of its concerns and geographic coverage in that it serves an entire police district. Working under a team supervisor, a group of officers, who are "permanently" assigned to a given area, are responsible for profiling the area, knowing the people, their leaders, and the neighborhood's problems.[3] The objective is to get the entire community — residents and businesses alike — involved in crime prevention, crime solution, and other efforts designed to improve the quality of life in the area. Equally important, the program allows the police to serve as problem solvers (see Goldstein 1979, 1981, 1982c), thereby making them an integral part of the community and not an agency imposed on the community.

Both programs are currently in operation, and it is anticipated that after trial and evaluation, the concepts will be implemented citywide. As a side benefit, TMO, through its individual member churches throughout the city, will also be working with the police on other crime prevention programs at the neighborhood level, such as neighborhood or business watch programs.

Even more effective than work with citywide organizations is cooperation with groups at the neighborhood level, which is where the police can make noticeable differences in the quality of life experienced by the residents. In fact, most neighborhoods have some form of organization existing solely to address local issues. Ideally, the police should work with those organizations that already exist rather than create new groups. Cooperation with the Atlanta public housing tenant association in the PCAA effort discussed earlier is a good example of how positive differences can be made in the quality of life in a given neighborhood as a result of police and community efforts.

Besides working with neighborhood organizations, police chiefs should give serious consideration to designing precinct and beat boundaries around natural neighborhoods and then assigning police officers to those areas on a long-term basis, which would make the police true partners with the people. Unfortunately, however, this is rarely the case, with district and beat boundaries often drawn only to serve the administrative and technical needs of the police, as, for instance, according to work load distribution and geographic dividing lines. Houston has redrawn its beat and district boundaries to keep natural neighborhoods intact.[4]

Organizing the Community

In certain new and rapidly growing cities, particularly in the Sunbelt, the police chief may face a lack of organization at the neighborhood level, which exacerbates the fear of crime and disorder and the sense of a deteriorating quality of life common to many large urban neighborhoods. Under such conditions, police chiefs can take the initiative in helping neighborhoods organize around their own needs. This is what Houston's Community Organizing Response Team (CORT) program is designed to do. The CORT program is one of several mounted as part of Houston's Fear Reduction experiment. The accompanying chart (p. 80) depicts the various programs being used in this experiment and their community-improvement objectives.

The basic premise of the CORT strategy is that police can become an integral part of the community by becoming agents of positive change. That is, the police can work to organize the neighborhood around specific crime-related issues and quality of life issues, such as public disorder, vandalism, and litter. The CORT strategy has five phases, each focused on specific tasks: (1) presentations within the Houston Police Department to explain the Fear Reduction experiment in general and CORT's place in it and to solicit input from all staff before implementing the strategy; (2) neighborhood background information gathering to prepare for community organizing; (3) Community Organizing Response Team task force formation, open to the community; (4) CORT planning meetings to provide a forum for identifying and assessing specific community problems that may be a source of fear or public disorder—these meetings are intended to allow the officers and the community to develop collaboratively strategies to resolve those problems, to give police a chance to provide accurate information to citizens and control rumors, and

Strategies to Improve the Quality of Life
and Reduce Fear in Houston

Program	Involve Police in the Community	Increase Citizen-Police Efficacy	Increase Accurate Information	Demonstrate Police Caring and Police Presence	Increase Personal Police-Citizen Contact
Community Organizing Response Team	x	x	o	o	o
Neighborhood Information Network		o	x	o	o
Houston Police Community Station	x	o	o	o	x
Victim Follow-Up		o	o	x	o
Police Service Response		o		x	
Directed Citizen Contact	o	o	o	o	x

Key: x = primary objective; o = secondary objective.

to bring the community and the police closer together; and (5) contractual agreements, which become the agenda for each meeting until the initially identified problems have been resolved.

INVOLVING THE WHOLE POLICE DEPARTMENT

As suggested, the second of the three general principles I have attempted to operationalize in my administration of police agencies requires the entire police department to be involved in efforts to involve the community in crime prevention. Many of the outreach programs and efforts discussed earlier engage the whole department. It is important, however, to see such programs as only one way of encouraging the entire agency's involvement. There must also be internal initiatives and procedures to reinforce the principle that every member of the police department has a role to play. There is a saying that "the speed of the boss is the speed of the crew." Stated differently, the police chief must set the example and create the atmosphere for departmental interest in developing police-community relationships. All officers should be given an orientation concerning ongoing departmental crime prevention resources, programs, and policies and should be encouraged to participate in crime prevention activities consistent with assigned duties. Special training programs, in-service training, roll call training bulletins, newsletters, management reports, and departmental policy statements are ways of involving police officers.

Equally important, police personnel should be taught that citizens' perceptions of crime in a neighborhood extend beyond what crime statistics indicate. To the extent the police assigned to neighborhoods are aware of the problems and involved in finding solutions, their roles as crime preventers are enhanced. Beat integrity, the concept requiring officers to remain on their beat except in emergency situations, helps achieve this objective.

SHARING POWER

The final principle, requiring the police chief to share power with the community, encompasses the first two principles and adds another dimension. The concept of power sharing is premised on the assumption that it is difficult for one person to serve another when the "servant" possesses all the power, which is exactly the case in traditional police work: An inverse power relationship exists between the servants and those served. Power sharing may be the most difficult issue confronting police agencies, but it is also critical to the new kinds of policing required in our contemporary social order, in which police ultimately are servants of the community.

The underlying proposition, elaborated earlier in the discussion of shared responsibility as a benefit of community involvement, is that the police lack the essential piece of the crime puzzle that only the community can furnish. It should be recognized that the legal and political constraints on a police chief's performance of his duties obviously require that he not abdicate his rightful control of the police department. Nevertheless, the chief must allow the community to provide input into the development of police operational policies that affect the quality of life in the neighborhood. The chief remains the ultimate decision maker, but he makes a costly mistake when he forgets that his mandate is supplied by free and powerful people. To ignore this fact and, in effect, to strip the people of the community of *their* power is to nullify the benefits of shared responsibility.

The police chief will have to work at ensuring continuous citizen input in police policymaking. In some ways this will be difficult, as it goes against the grain of normal procedures to base police decisions about day-to-day operations on anything but assessments by police personnel. But unless day-to-day administrative decision making on such matters as personnel allocation, selective enforcement, and levels of patrol is expanded to incorporate community concerns about unique problems of the neighborhoods, barriers will continue to thwart solid police-community collaboration. The police-community Positive Interaction program operated by the Houston Police Department is an example of one way to break down unneeded barriers. Houston's practice of involving citizens in the development and implementation of programs, procedures, and policies is another example of power sharing.

Pitfalls in Interaction with the Community

Even the strongest advocates of active police involvement in the community are aware of pitfalls inherent in the practice. Most police chiefs serve at the pleasure of an elected official. To the extent that the police chief becomes a community leader, he receives extensive public exposure, and it is not unheard of for an elected official to become concerned about the chief's popularity.[5] This is, indeed, always a potential problem and can best be addressed by the police chief's keeping his superior informed on what he is doing and why he is doing it. Equally important, the police chief must never forget that he is an appointed official, not an elected official. Using the office of the police chief for partisan political purposes is not only unprofessional but unethical. Professional considerations clearly dictate that one of the chief's very important functions is to protect the operational integrity of the police department from political interference. To the extent that the police chief becomes involved in local partisan politics, he is unable to carry out this important responsibility.

It should also be remembered that there are those people who will attempt to use the police department's outreach for their own benefit. The police chief must be aware of such possibilities and not allow the prestige of the department to be used for unsavory purposes. To say, as I have, that police should work as much as possible with the community is not to say that every group claiming to represent legitimate community interests does in fact represent such interests, and there clearly need to be some restrictions on the types of groups with which the police chief should work. But while drawing the line at organizations that are secret, subversive, or criminal (such as the Ku Klux Klan), the police should be more inclusive than exclusive in their outreach efforts. Among other traditional restrictions that I think need to be abandoned is the reluctance of police leaders to work with organizations that are critical of the police.

In considering cooperation with any group having an overt crime control agenda, such as the Guardian Angels, the police should operate under the basic principle that anyone who takes to the streets to render law enforcement services should be accountable ultimately to an elected body. If groups such as the Guardian Angels adhere to that principle by operating under the auspices of the police and in accordance with police guidelines, their services should be used as part of an overall crime control effort. The chief, of course, is ultimately responsible for the total operation of the department and must expect to be held accountable for all decisions made. Experience has shown that when decisions are based on the principles of whether the decision is right, moral, ethical, legal, and in the best interest of the community, and not on what is politically expedient, the chief has little to worry about. Those programs, those requests, and those decisions that do not meet these criteria present predictable sorts of problems for the chief.

THE FUTURE ROLE OF THE POLICE CHIEF

The police chief can no longer isolate himself from the people he serves, but the role he must play as community leader has yet to be fully realized (see the chapters in Part 1, "The Chief as a Major Municipal Policymaker"). The old, narrow view of policing as lights, locks, and alarms must be enlarged to encompass all activities affecting the quality of life in the community threatened with crime and disorder. Just as presidents of corporations, the clergy, and others routinely involve themselves in community affairs and come to be regarded as community leaders, so must the police chief. His particular contribution to community betterment can be enormous – a secure and civil community order. The public deserves no less, and the conscientious police administrator sets his sights no lower.

NOTES

1. The Fear Reduction experiment, conducted simultaneously in Houston and Newark, New Jersey, applies various techniques in an attempt to minimize public anxiety about crime that is out of proportion to the actual crime threat. Under a grant from the National Institute of Justice, the Police Foundation has carefully monitored and assessed the experience in both cities (see note 3).

2. In Houston, for example, a specific set of values that emphasizes citizen involvement has been developed. Those values are reinforced in a variety of ways: recruit and in-service training, policy statements, training bulletins, and public statements by the chief and other members of the department.

3. The DART program is conceptually similar to the full service model of "team policing" (Sherman et al. 1973) but designed uniquely for Houston.

4. In Houston, citizens generally consider their "natural" neighborhood to consist of a housing tract or housing development.

5. A police chief who is tuned in will be able to tell when his boss is concerned about his popularity. He can tell from statements or comments made, often in a joking manner, by the superior or the superior's immediate staff. The signs will be more indirect than direct, unless, however, the chief is required to discuss his public comments with his superior before making them. Then the signs are very direct.

8
Organizing the Community for Improved Policing

Raymond C. Davis

For many cities, this chapter might more appropriately be titled "The Police versus the Community." We have seen the image of the police change dramatically over the past 15 years. In the 1960s they were portrayed on the television screens of America as the oppressive tools of the political machine, suppressing dissent and controlling divergent views in our society. The 1970s saw the emergence of strong public scrutiny of police practices, including but not limited to use of force and measures of restraint, racial- and gender-based employment practices, and violations of rights. Throughout all this, portions of our communities have held blindly to unconditional support of the police. Such groups proudly proclaim through their bumper stickers "Support Your Local Police," "If You Don't Like the Police, Next Time You Need Help Call a Hippie," and so forth. Somewhere between these poles of opinion may be found the legitimate role of law enforcement in a free society.

Questions of community involvement, community participation, community-oriented policing, and service roles for the police have prompted some police chiefs to attempt to define with some precision what the role of law enforcement should be. Today police administrators across the nation find themselves faced with substantial budget cuts and beleaguered by activist groups demanding change and by militant police organizations wanting a "piece of the action" in the management of police services (see Bouza's chapter). In past years some police chiefs have jealously guarded what they perceived to be their role as champion of the downtrodden and defender of community morals. Some police chiefs have assumed command of departments with firm ideas of what the community needs and should get in law enforcement. All too frequently such chiefs have decided "what this city needs" with little if any consultation with the community.

Fortunately in many communities, however, we are beginning to find police administrators who willingly relinquish much of what they formerly perceived as their controlling role and who recognize that a police department exists for the community—no more, no less. Some police chiefs have come to realize that they can achieve many of the things they have been seeking, including job satisfaction, recognition, progress, or material advancement, simply by recognizing and understanding their new role in the community (see Dodenhoff 1983).

DISCOVERING THE BENEFITS OF COMMUNITY SUPPORT

The police chief will find that initiating positive interaction with the community generally results in increased citizen support, higher morale in the work force, protection against or insulation from many hostile external forces, and increased resources. And these positive results interact with one another. In many cities where a "we versus they" climate used to prevail in community meetings, a feeling by police that they have community support—and particularly an appreciation of that support by previously suspicious or defensive police officers—can completely turn around a department's siege mentality. In cases where a major problem originates in a particular sector of the community, it does not take long for the officers assigned to interact with the community to recognize the value of strong community support. We have seen officers return from community meetings and remark how happy they were to see supporters in the audience, an experience that minimizes the impact on these and other officers of previous attacks. But change will not necessarily be dramatic, and there will always be some officers who simply will not adapt. As the benefits of community support become apparent, however, those who steadfastly resist positive change generally will be suppressed or weeded out by peer and administrative pressure and leadership.

POLITICAL OPPOSITION AROUSED
IN BUILDING COMMUNITY SUPPORT

Just as predictably as the chief's involvement with the community can prompt desirable police-community collaborations, it can elicit accusations that the chief is empire building, seeking political control, and going on an "ego trip." Many times a police administrator enjoying positive public opinion has come to be seen as a threat by a political power structure. In Boston, for instance, there were strong indications that Police Commissioner Bob diGrazia was perceived as a political threat by virtue of his popularity and community support. In Cleveland some of the problems that existed between former Mayor Dennis Kucinich and former Chief of Police Richard Hongisto exemplify a mayor fearing political popularity for anyone other than himself. Even while his relationship with the mayor was disintegrating, Chief Hongisto tried to initiate programs, which ultimately led to his termination. Kucinich so wanted to restrict personnel below him that he even designed their business cards to ensure that his name appeared more prominently than theirs. In many communities positive police programs have been disbanded merely because they gave a power base to someone viewed as jeopardizing the political establishment. In Santa Ana, three councilmen resented and feared my department's Community Oriented Policing program and made unsuccessful attempts to disband it. (Subsequently, this program became the subject of a major public television documentary, "Forces of Order" [Public Broadcasting System 1984], which compares Japanese and American policing.) In some communities it is my distinct impression that the police chief did not want to start such a program because doing so would place him too much in the limelight with regard to his mayor. In Beverly Hills, Chief Joseph Paul Kimble's runaway popularity and considerable visibility were rewarded by attempts to eject him from his own professional police associations and the eventual loss of his chief's position. Elsewhere police administrators have been able to weather such a storm. Drawing on their base of community support, they have maintained programs while dealing with the politicians' fears.

Community elements, the strengths and weaknesses of the police department, and the political system are all tools that a police administrator must be able to use in seeking the support necessary to sustain programs needed by the citizenry. He must constantly attend to "stroking" the politicians, within acceptable boundaries. Building a foundation or balance of power in the political field unquestionably exposes a police chief to risks, including the accusation that he is playing a political game. But if a police chief clearly analyzes the benefits of community interaction and the value of organizing the community, he may wonder why he missed these insights earlier in his career. Strong crime prevention programs, implemented as a broad community social service, will thrust the chief into a leadership position and place him in a stronger position to accomplish his goals.

ASSESSING THE EXISTING PROGRAM AND EDUCATING THE POLICE DEPARTMENT

To enable him to even start to build a positive community relationship, the chief must take firm control of his department with an in-depth assessment of how the agency is meeting public needs and of what changes are needed in the department's attitude and philosophy. The chief should begin this assessment before he reaches the community or assumes his position.

His first steps may include a review of police-related and community concerns expressed in the media and outreach to identifiable formal and informal power centers in both the community and the department. The various existing groups, supportive and hostile, will give early indications to the chief of how the department's service is perceived, and these same groups can serve as sounding boards for future changes.

Once deficiencies have been recognized, they should not be kept secret. The head of the law enforcement agency must be on the "speaker circuit" discussing the department and frankly admitting the need for improvement. Clearly, the chief must demonstrate that he is making changes and why and what these changes are before he can expect any credibility before members of the community. Advertising the failings of a police agency as strongly as its accomplishments will display the chief's commitment to positive reform.

Only the chief can successfully initiate and implement these reforms. Over the past years we have seen little progress in attempts to effect change within police agencies through the medium of an external assault on those agencies. The end result of such endeavors has been the emergence of a "circle the wagons" mentality within the police department – in other words, a "we versus they" stance before the community.

Certainly, a new police chief must expect that his strong departure from what was an accepted, established direction may alienate a portion of the police personnel. A less than effective police department can exist only because there are those within the organization who allow it to exist. Thus the chief must be prepared for a long period of education and discipline before he can demonstrate to his subordinates the advantages of supporting strong community service and the disadvantages of resisting it.

Once he recognizes the deficiencies of the police agency, the chief must carefully plan evolutionary change in order to have a base within the department on which to build positive interaction between the police and the community, interaction that ultimately will lead the police to a recognition of their new role. The chief will have to place "carrot-and-stick" incentives along the way to secure employee compliance with his new direction. Community leaders as well as authority figures within the department who are willing to identify and accept change within the police department might be used to supply positive reinforcement for the reforms within the community.

The chief may be accused of using a "two by four to the head" approach, and to get the attention of some people unsubtle methods may indeed be necessary. This is an extremely hazardous but nonetheless unavoidable enterprise for the chief. The chief can possess the highest ideals and most carefully articulated objectives, but unless he can secure the department's support he will fail. I believe firmly that the majority of police officers want to be respected and liked and want to serve the public. The chief must demonstrate that this is the only acceptable attitude and that there will be rewards for manifesting it and punishments for defying it. If, as often happens, internal peer pressure is putting the police department on a collision course with the community, the chief must immediately take measures to channel the peer pressure in a positive direction. It is not realistic to expect to change an individual officer's personality and prejudices acquired over a number of years. But a police administrator has a right to demand that traits inconsistent with departmental programs not be displayed in an individual's capacity as a police employee.

IDENTIFYING THE NEEDS AND SOURCES OF SUPPORT IN A COMMUNITY

The improvements a chief should seek will be suggested by his cautious yet concerted efforts to interact with those forces that reflect the community's needs. But a blind pilgrimage to the temples of community control will not solve the chief's problems and may well prove disastrous. The chief's objectives should be governed by respect for democratic principles and the need to generate strong police-community collaboration.

There will be a testing time for a new chief during which he can search deeply within the community to learn its articulated and unarticulated needs and identify the groups that really serve to express its standards and directions. One most certainly could not enter a strongly liberal city, such as Berkeley, California, and expect to achieve anything by seeking or accepting support from the American Nazi party or the Ku Klux Klan. In any city the chief will find fringe groups that really do not reflect the majority of the populace. This is not to imply, however, that the police should allow themselves to be used to suppress minority views — no matter what the majority view of the community is. Some groups that depart from the true needs of the community must nevertheless be tolerated by the police as an expression of our national freedoms. But I do not believe a free society demands wholehearted interaction by the police with a group that works counter to community purposes. The successful chief adopts a tempered approach toward every force or group within his service area.

The chief must approach his involvement in community organizations as he would a chess game, and the players and stakes in that game will vary according to the particular locale. In Santa Ana, the police leadership has been condemned by the white power structure because of our strong move to secure Hispanic community support, including the protection of undocumented workers from improper enforcement efforts by the federal Immigration and Naturalization Service (INS). In a few short years the population of our city of nearly 204,000 (1980 census) has changed from 25 to 30 percent minority (predominantly Hispanic) to 60 to 70 percent minority (still mostly Hispanic). The school district has a minority population of more than 80 percent. Not surprisingly, with this large Hispanic population has come a sizable undocumented population, estimated at more than 50,000 (but not reflected in the preceding population figures).

Recognizing that our primary role is community protection and service, we have clearly indicated to the community that local police are not associated with the INS and will not be involved in immigration enforcement. This position is based on the fact that California law does not authorize municipal police to arrest people for being illegal residents and on the police department's need to build confidence and trust in individuals, whether or not they are documented, so they will report previously unreported crimes, serve as witnesses, and assist in prosecutions. We have even gone so far as to monitor INS enforcement efforts in Santa Ana to ensure that the rights of all individuals are protected. This posture is not taken without hazard, and there are many in our agency and in the ranks of police administration around the nation who do not support this position. In my view, our somewhat controversial stance is necessary if we are to serve the *total* community.

In his cultivation of public support, a chief should not abandon any element of the community, even one that criticizes him, but he must necessarily make the most of his resources to reach the largest, most positive segments of the community. He also must take particular care not to allow himself to be used by marginal groups seeking enhancement of their own political power. When the chief finds a group working for objectives inconsistent with his own, as so often happens, he has to find a supportive countergroup to work with that will ultimately overshadow the attacks from the dissident faction.

At the same time, the chief should not write off an antipolice group too quickly. I have seen many initially antipolice groups moderate their hostility and even begin to offer grudging support for the police.

The guiding principle in determining which groups to work with should be whether, regardless of their attitudes toward police, they are interested in the betterment of the community. Assuming an antagonistic posture toward organizations such as the Guardian Angels until they have proven themselves does not help the community. For too long police have lolled in a vacuum of isolationism and cut themselves off from vital components of the community merely because they did not conform to police beliefs of what was proper. It is too easy for a police officer to retreat into a defensive posture when facing a group that holds values different from his own. The challenge is to see how one can channel those values for good.

Having referred repeatedly to the existence of both positive and negative community forces, I must hasten to admit that I know of no formula for identifying which is which and no sure-fire antidote to prevent a negative group from poisoning a community. It takes a broad, intelligent, comprehensive, and enlightened effort by the police chief — aided by all the public and private resources he can muster — to discover and refine the right balance of forces.

In my experience, once a proper base is built in the police department and the potentially supportive community power structure is identified, then organizing the community can be relatively simple and increasingly satisfy both the police and the citizenry as a whole.

TAILORING THE LAW ENFORCEMENT PROGRAM
TO THE COMMUNITY

As adverted to earlier, the chief's recognition of the nature of a community and its problems is far different from his simply deciding what should be the law enforcement service and then imposing his standards unilaterally. The department's crime prevention, public service, and other programs must be tailored to the community's particular needs and socioeconomic, cultural, and ethnic composition. And the impact of those programs and of law enforcement in general will differ widely, depending on the structure of the community.

Clearly a predominantly low-income area with mixed ethnic composition and an affluent WASP community with different problems must be considered from different points of view. An extensive crime prevention campaign or a "target hardening" security program, for instance, must be implemented differently in low-income and high-income areas. You cannot enter into a program of planned community meetings expecting large turnouts when the people are striving to make a living, work at varied hours, and have little funds to devote to crime prevention projects. In an affluent community it is very easy to use homeowner associations, service clubs, Boy Scouts, the PTA, and similar groups to reach the bulk of the residents. In a predominantly low-income community with many language barriers, those avenues are not available. Instead, the chief must begin a program of bringing people together to break down distrust and to demonstrate how they can affect the government's influence on their lives. In a low-income Hispanic community, for example, he will find that labor unions, Catholic churches, and Hispanic organizations provide good access to the public.

Cultural differences will dictate much in the manner of enforcement, in the management of police discretion, and in the hiring and assignment of officers. Many officers would be uncomfortable working in a low-income neighborhood and might show their negative feelings, which would of course have an adverse impact on the target population. In training and deploying officers, a chief serving a Hispanic community must consider the public reaction that would come from a "macho" male being ordered about by a female police officer.

Care should be taken in selecting an approach for controlling activity associated with particular cultural subgroups. Well-meaning efforts often destroy a relationship because we have ignored the fact that people's backgrounds lead them to perceive actions in different ways. One might employ an educational effort to gain willing compliance with laws against cockfighting, for instance, instead of mounting an undercover investigation to arrest as many people as possible. In fashioning enforcement programs, the chief must be mindful of different levels of visibility of certain vice activities in upper-income sectors of the community and in lower-income and certain ethnic sectors. Police in America continue to close their eyes to the "friendly card games" in politically powerful fraternal clubs and direct crackdowns on gambling in social clubs of poor ethnic communities. Such enforcement patterns, of course, are not difficult to understand. An arrest quota for the vice squad many times can misdirect police energies to the most easily attainable areas of enforcement, areas that lack political muscle. The chief and vice unit commander should recognize, however, that avoiding the "heat" in the short run will contribute to long-term problems for both the chief and the agency. This type of "tailoring" the police response announces to the community that the police are serving the power structure and not the people. Similarly, when police take action against individuals gathering in public parks or meeting in drive-ins because powerful people see such behavior as suspicious, if not dangerous, the police typically achieve nothing but a further rift within the community. One must understand that in certain ethnic groups social gathering in public places is part of the cultural heritage.

Differential application of laws to respect cultural or ethnic differences must be understood and recognized as appropriate and not a dereliction of duty. This is not to say the chief should tolerate open prostitution in one neighborhood while he spends his time fighting illegal church bingo in another neighborhood. Balanced methods of enforcement and publicity concerning enforcement efforts can clearly communicate that the police role is one of fair enforcement with respect to all citizens. The chief must certainly expect pressure from the political and economic elements of the community that have previously been untouchable because of their stature, but he should be able to identify those elements in advance and develop sufficient power before he makes his move against them. The chief must also have the wisdom to keep his department from becoming entangled in local frays, such as debates over minor regulatory ordinances dealing with improper parking, ice cream truck vending, political signs, and so forth, unless such entanglements will achieve something positive without damaging community relations. The chief's ability to withstand political onslaughts is really no different than his ability to manage those pressures and walk those lines in day-to-day enforcement activities. It is not an easy role, and it carries many perils, but it is the only way I know to present balanced enforcement to the citizenry.

The role of community organizer for the police chief is similarly fraught with promise and risk. But it can and must be done. The police executive will find his work considerably easier if he always remembers that along with popularity and the perception of power comes real power, which must be handled in a professional, judicious manner. Doing so in a multicultural community carries added challenges. There, the chief's obligation is to provide leadership both within and outside the department in understanding and positively responding to culturally based differences. The goal should be willing compliance and change rather than merely enforcement of the laws.

SETTING THE TONE OF LAW ENFORCEMENT

The tone the chief sets in launching his programs is critical. Recently in Signal Hill, California, a community in turmoil over the death of an individual while in police custody, an interim reform police chief made the following statement to the department personnel: "Up to this date the Signal Hill Police Department existed for the police employees. From this date forward it will exist for the benefit of the community." This apparently simple statement is probably one of the most important that can be made. It established a direction for tremendous change within the Signal Hill Police Department.

One must never underestimate the impact a chief can have on a community. In all candor, there are few public figures in any locality who can have a greater impact — positively or negatively — than a new police chief. A positive or negative tone clearly can be set not only by a police administrator's personal style but by the agency's style — for example, does it attempt to control rather than serve society? The strong enforcement stances taken by former Police Commissioner and former Mayor Frank Rizzo of Philadelphia, for instance, stand as a sorry monument to the negative impact a police administrator can have on the style of law enforcement and on a community in general. As long as they were not on the receiving end of Rizzo-style law enforcement, certain segments of the Philadelphia community appeared to welcome the approach. But I wonder if a more reasoned strategy, instilling a greater empathy within the police department for the entire community it served, would not have been more beneficial for the city of brotherly love.

Simple matters of agency style, such as wearing helmets or not wearing hats, can be used to advantage by the police administrator. A chief's relaxing standards in removing helmets can be seen by the police officer as a supportive move and by the public as a demilitarizing gesture. Much progress was made within our department by simply changing the color of our cars from black and white to solid white and by moving shotguns from a visible, upright position to a position out of sight in front of the front seat. Allowing police officers to design a new badge and shoulder patch helped them to willingly accept name tags, which had been a very controversial issue in earlier years. Participation by officers in uniform committees set the stage for their involvement in establishing shooting regulations, shooting review boards, and internal investigations processes. A feeling of participation leads to acceptance with a minimum of dissension.

COMMUNITY-WIDE SCOPE AND DEPTH OF THE LAW ENFORCEMENT PROGRAM

Once a chief determines the strengths and weaknesses of his community and his department, he can initiate programs dealing with the community's needs. He must not remain confined by traditional views of the police role. People problems are community problems and ultimately police problems; the chief must be in the forefront of positive efforts to resolve them. Police crime prevention activities must address the spectrum of problems affecting the quality of life of a community. Overcrowded housing, health problems, traffic problems, summer jobs for youth, and nearly every determinant of public stability can affect the crime rate and the role of the police. Programs dealing with crimes against the elderly, victim assistance programs, youth employment programs, crisis intervention centers, school programs, and juvenile diversion and counseling programs are just some of the community activities needing the involvement, aid, and support of the police. Some cities have community centers staffed and operated by nonsworn police employees, supplemented with citizen volunteers. These are multipurpose centers that can help a citizen, whether the problem be street sweeping, street lighting, tree trimming, health, or insect control. In Santa Ana, we place great importance on "civilianization" of the police force, and we employ substantial numbers of civilians to do work that does not require the particular talents of a sworn officer.

Certainly, as suggested above, one must expect the broad approach to community service I am recommending to appear threatening to many other public services and government agencies, including organizations within the city structure. I am not saying the police should take active primary responsibility for all matters that affect the community's quality of life, but rather that they cannot turn a deaf ear to citizens' expressed needs for service if they want a first-rate department. Concerns will be expressed about duplication of services and defining the primary role of the police. In my view, the primary role of the police does not prevent them from serving as a multiservice provider or referral agency to citizens, particularly when the public's quality of life is at stake. A school resource officer should be capable of making referrals for jobs, psychological services, and counseling regarding domestic problems, venereal disease, pregnancy, and academic matters. The real question is what degree of activity and involvement on the part of the police is important at a given point. Generally the level I have in mind is referral; however, there may be a need for a stronger involvement on the part of an officer or a civilian police employee in a given situation. The staffing of police service centers with nonsworn police employees can provide opportunities for making referrals on a wider range of matters than has been possible in the past. The benefits arising from collaborating with or assisting police multiservice centers must be pointed out and sold to other agencies both within and outside the city.

When police can resolve or help resolve people's pressing problems, rather than dismiss requests for assistance with the bromide "That's not our area of responsibility," they start building the image of caring and concern that is needed for community strengthening. For instance, in a jurisdiction like Santa Ana, which has a large non-English-speaking population, the police should take direct responsibility for bilingual educational campaigns on the citizen's responsibilities and rights and the government and private services available to him or her. In a city that has recently experienced a large influx of refugees from Southeast Asia or Cuba the police need to take a proactive role in seeking conflict resolutions during the turbulent period of adjustment to the community. The police cannot stand idly by in this early stage when immigrants form attitudes toward government and then bemoan the problems that stem from antipolice attitudes among the public.

A new philosophy on police interaction with the business sector of the community should be encouraged (see Shanahan's chapter). Years ago any cooperation between the department and the business world was frowned on, and crime prevention brochures with commercial advertising were taboo. "We cannot become involved in endorsement or recommendation" was the standard explanation. Today, in the more progressive locales, we see newspapers, pamphlets, and other crime prevention material published by citizen groups with the aid of the police department under funding provided by the community, with a clear statement of the contribution by the individual businesses. Allowing a beer company to underwrite openly a community newspaper would still be shocking in the eyes of some chiefs, but in today's economy it is part of an expedient, necessary, and proactive approach to delivering police services. Billboards and bus-bench ads can be donated through local commercial activities and through public service efforts on the part of the billboard companies. The only thing the police have to sell is their role as a service entity. Police must use modern merchandising techniques to introduce the public to new concepts of the police role. This is not to say that a police department is merely a public relations effort. Rather, there must be a strong union between an open, community-conscious police department and professional law enforcement. Directed patrol efforts to deal with major crimes that are creating an unfavorable community environment will be aided considerably by a new citizen-police cooperation.

MAINTAINING PROFESSIONAL CONTROL OF POLICING

The police department's desire for strong community involvement should never deteriorate to an abdication of responsibility, however. The police should be constantly alert to the emergence of vigilantism. Groups, well meaning or with selfish motivation, may attempt to interject themselves into many troubled communities in a form that clearly indicates loss of control by the police. The guiding philosophy that seems to me to work best is that the police should work with any community organization that operates in a legal, positive manner. By that criterion, law enforcement agencies may begin to work with groups that will be shocked to receive a positive reception from the police. The police must never forget that they need all the assistance they can get.

In sum, the direction of law enforcement today must emerge from within the community and be grounded on a recognition that the mission of police is public service. There are hazards in the police role of community organizer, but there are also tremendous benefits. The spectrum of areas needing police attention differs from locale to locale, but the only limiting principle I would advocate is that police efforts must be aimed at improving the quality of life within the community. In setting priorities, police should not overlook the simple truth that people are safer if they feel safer. Clearly, the police are facing a complex task that becomes even more difficult with the constant change in our society. But through the storm of challenges we ask our police to enter shines a beacon to guide them toward their proper role. It consists of the notion that, in a democracy, the police should be accountable to and accountable for the people they serve.

PART 3
THE CHIEF AND THE MEDIA

Introduction

Given Jerome Skolnick's classic critique of the police in *Justice Without Trial* (1966), one might have expected his and Candace McCoy's assessment of police accountability and the media to highlight the unresponsiveness of police executives to probing questions asked by news reporters. Instead, Skolnick-McCoy aim their barbs mostly at the media, which they see as generally failing to ask the *right* probing questions. Rather than exploring the "institutional" or systemic factors that affect the quality of policing, they argue, reporters inquire about isolated and sensational crime "events" (see also Jacob and Lineberry 1982, pp. 77–117; Dominick 1978; Graber 1980). Skolnick-McCoy suggest further that if a reporter *does* ask the kind of questions that can help the citizenry improve policing, too often the editor fulfills Adlai Stevenson's dismal expectations and "separates the wheat from the chaff and prints the chaff" (Shapiro 1984, p. 76). If the police chiefs Skolnick-McCoy interviewed for their chapter were critical of newspaper coverage of policing, they were outright contemptuous of television reportage. TV news operations, unfortunately, have not yet figured out how to cover such apparently "nonvisual" subjects as police personnel policies and budgets. As one media critic put it (Barry 1983, p. 34):

> On local TV news shows, "news" means "anything you can take a picture of, especially if a local TV News Personality can stand in front of it." This is why they are so fond of car accidents, burning buildings, and crowds. These are good for standing in front of. On the other hand, local TV news shows tend to avoid stories about things that local TV News Personalities cannot stand in front of, such as budgets and taxes and the economy. If you want to get a local TV news show to do a story on the budget, your best bet is to involve it in a car crash.

Another detractor fired an even more lethal broadside at the medium: "The vast wasteland of TV is not interested in producing a better mousetrap but in producing a worse mouse" (Peter 1977, p. 331).

If such characterizations of news business coverage of policing are generally valid (a point hotly contested in reporter Carl Stern's response), they threaten self-government in a society like ours, where most of the public depends on the print and electronic media for information about the strengths and weaknesses of our social-political institutions. Ironically, even if Stern is right, that the media do report a great deal about the "institutional" obstacles to better policing, the public may be only slightly better equipped to reach important policy decisions than they are in the Skolnick-McCoy portrait. Whereas 50 years ago the "concerned citizen" was stymied by a lack of useful information, today he or she is immobilized by an avalanche of facts— coming from dozens of free or pay TV stations, numerous radio outlets, and myriad newspapers, magazines, and specialized journals and newsletters. Hence, simply adding "institutional" stories to the existing diet of crime stories may bloat the citizenry rather than provide better nourishment. What our nation needs, increasingly, is people who can tell us which pieces of available information are useful and which are not for given purposes.

In calling for reporters to ask the kinds of questions that social scientists ask about such organizations as police departments, Skolnick-McCoy prompt objections from editor Jack Fuller to the implication that the First Amendment may *prefer* rather than merely *permit* such news coverage. In worrying about unintended consequences of such a view of media obligations, Fuller is in harmony with a related concern raised by Reiss (1979, pp. 93–94) in a discussion of governmental regulation of human behavioral research: "As investigative reporting merges into behavioral inquiry, it encounters mounting curbs from the judiciary. Other possibilities of regulation loom. Any claim to a privileged status may be less easily defended in our future."

It may be that the best defense against external regulation is self-regulation. Just as policing has moved with its fledgling accreditation program (see Walker's chapter in this volume) toward self-imposed standards that exceed legal requirements, so the news business, through the New York–based National News Council, is beginning to respond to long-standing police objections to such practices as the publication of names and addresses of crime victims and witnesses (Washington Crime News Services 1984d).

One question not touched by the Skolnick-McCoy discussion or the responses to it that, in my view, needs greater attention from media and police representatives, is the extent to which Hollywood "runs" the police by disseminating, through TV shows and movies, images of policing that create public expectations about law enforcement's capacities (see Fogelson 1977). Unfortunately, most of the examples that come readily to mind are negative in that they involve the media misleading the public (for some opposite examples, see Clark 1984, which discusses recent television shows raising the public's consciousness about missing children, sexual abuse of children by family members, and the costs of drunk driving). One of the more tenacious myths generated by screen writers is that police officers are able to shoot "to wound" a fleeing suspect. In truth, the revolver, a weapon that has not changed much since its introduction around the time of the Civil War, does not permit that level of marksmanship under typical street conditions. As another example, one would think from watching investigations by many TV cops that police academies teach an expurgated version of the Bill of Rights, missing the Fourth and Fifth Amendments (Arons and Katsh 1977). A media observer (Mankiewicz 1983) cited yet another harmful product of TV police stories:

> The audience knows precisely who committed the crime and how, so the violent encounter between the police and the suspect in the last two minutes does not jar the implicit assurance that justice has been done. The real world result, however, is that when people see on the news that a person alleged to have committed a crime is free on bail or was acquitted because of a "technicality," they assume that the real system of justice is malfunctioning — because every crime on TV has a clear offender.

As a final illustration of the media misguiding the citizenry, TV has led the public to think that police crime labs are capable of extraordinary forensic feats (see Peterson 1983) — a belief that undercuts the citizen's incentive to volunteer information that may aid in the solution of crimes. As one police officer put it, "We really don't solve burglaries in a half hour, not counting the commercials" (Saffold 1984). Another aspect of Hollywood influence is that fictitious images may well influence police behavior. After all, police, like the rest of us, are creatures of their environment. A police patrol commander in a major city commented: "The troops are affected to some extent by whatever films are being shown at the time. When 'Dirty Harry' was popular, a lot of the guys ran out and bought a big gun, and they were drawing a little faster. On the other hand, when 'On Golden Pond' was showing, we all fell into a more melancholy mood because we realized we were going to get old someday."

The chapters in this section do, however, address some of the most important and difficult issues facing news business executives and police executives today (see also the chapters elsewhere in this volume by Murphy, Kerstetter, Brown, and Bouza). The police chiefs quoted by Skolnick-McCoy admirably call for more informed and thus more effective media criticism of policing. The chiefs are, in turn, openly critical of most current reporting. They take this posture with full awareness of the old adage that it's never wise to argue with anybody who buys ink by the barrel. Yet their courage is steeled by the perception that if American policing is to be measurably upgraded, the media must play a more helpful role than they have to date.

9

Police Accountability and the Media

Jerome H. Skolnick and Candace McCoy

> Those who won our independence believed . . . that public discussion
> is a political duty; and that this should be a fundamental principle of
> American government. They recognized the risks to which all human
> institutions are subject.
> — Justice Louis D. Brandeis, *Whitney* v. *California* (1927)

Any theory of the police in a constitutional democracy must engage the
issue of police accountability. Of course, American police are accountable
to the courts and the Constitution. One need only refer to Fourth and Fifth
Amendment law to perceive the depth of legal accountability regarding arrest, search, seizure, and interrogation. Assuming that police in a democratic
society should serve the public and not their own interests, we draw boundaries around police activities and engrain limitations into the political structure itself in an effort to prevent abuse of the public trust.

What institutions or political forces can hold police accountable? Influenced by the public debates of the past two decades, most Americans would
probably reply that courts are the primary reviewers of police activities. In
practice, other political actors such as city administrators and budget planners are probably equally potent. In addition, several cities have organized
citizen complaint boards that investigate particular incidents of misconduct,
applying sanctions and — perhaps most important — circumscribing police behavior by insistent reminders that public opinion is the final measure of police
accountability.

An expanded version of this chapter was prepared subsequently for and appears in *American
Bar Foundation Research Journal* 1984, no. 3. Readers wishing further explication and references
are invited to consider that article.

Considering the variety of institutional checks on police functioning, and mindful especially of the influence of public opinion, inquiry naturally turns to the role of the media in shaping public awareness about police and crime. The media, in their daily scrutiny of public agencies, can be a powerful force for police accountability.

This chapter addresses the risks and responsibilities of these two American institutions, the police and the media. We shall conclude that a theory of free speech can go beyond the question of speech abridgement by government to the broader issue of the moral and civic responsibilities of print and broadcast media functioning under the system of freedom of expression offered by the First Amendment.

As a complex governmental institution responsible for sustaining the civil order, police generate considerable media and public interest. Only a part of the police "product" involves sensational crime news, but by and large, the media's focus on that aspect of a police department's productivity vastly overshadows coverage of its complex governmental side. Thus inquiry into one of our most fundamental public institutions is less varied, thoughtful, and searching than is desirable. Further, considering the robust state of our major media, it is surprising that their reportage on policing is less complete than their strength would suggest is possible.

THE IDEA OF POLICE ACCOUNTABILITY

That police are ultimately accountable to the citizenry is hardly a new idea. Indeed, before the establishment of the police in 1829 in England, the police *were* the citizenry. At that time, intense public debate focused on whether England should retain what was essentially a watchman system. The Bow Street Runners and Patrol aside, individual community members were responsible for patrolling and apprehending criminals, but this was ineffective. How, then, in the absence of an organized police, was order to be enforced and life and property protected? Evidently, the English trusted the supposed deterrent effect of a rigorous penal code as their first line of defense, and they were not prepared to accept an organized police. To many people, Wilbur Miller (1977, p. 4) writes, the cop on the beat was an ominous intrusion on civil liberty. The English were very apprehensive about importing France's secret political police — "the Continental spy system" — and about the creation of a more formidable variety of England's own network of informers and agents provocateurs. Crime was indeed rising at an alarming rate, but a quite surprising consensus of political opinion resisted establishing an organized police force. As E. P. Thompson writes: "Tories feared the overruling of parochial and chartered rights and the powers of the local Justices of the Peace; Whigs feared an increase in the powers of the Crown or Government; Radicals . . . preferred the notion of voluntary associations of citizens" (1966, p. 82).

As a result, it was not until 1829, in response to major social dislocations engendered by the Industrial Revolution, by war, and by poverty and economic depression, that a police department could be established to maintain public order and to fight crime.

To respond to public fear of police, Sir Robert Peel had incorporated two central, related innovations before introducing the Police Bill to Parliament: abolition of the death penalty for more than 100 serious offenses and the disarming of the police.[1] Authority was to derive from confidence in the police, with their accountability to the citizenry through the rule of law and not from the capacity to employ deadly force. Indeed, special uniforms were designed to make police appear taller than but not socially distant from the average citizen. The uniforms were blue, after Peel and his associates abandoned the idea of scarlet and gold, since that might make them resemble the army (Miller 1973, p. 33). Eventually, most citizens began to call the police "bobbies," an affectionate nickname for Sir Robert Peel. Thus, in response to earlier mistrust of law-enforcing authority, the British police were developed according to a well-considered plan.

By contrast, the American police, although presumably modeled on the British innovation, were much more influenced by short-term crises, ethnic rivalries, and local politics. Like the growth of America itself, the growth of its police departments was rapid and haphazard, with the most striking developments being made in the nineteenth century.[2]

American police institutions largely reflected the qualities of local governments, and it cannot be said that either offered much justification for civic pride. The police were not responsive so much to a rule of law as they were to a rule of politics. While arguably this may have made them more acceptable to the community, it also made them more corrupt, more inefficient, and scarcely professional in any sense. According to historian Robert Fogelson (1977), police were accountable neither to the courts nor to their fellow citizens but to the political machines that dominated (and in some places continue to dominate) urban America (see Lane 1967; Richardson 1970).

Yet machine politics is not the primary mode of American city government today. And, in general, political machines can no longer control American police departments, nor can they protect police departments from public scrutiny. During the 1960s the propriety of police policies and activities came under intense public scrutiny and broad-based criticism at the local government level, emerging as perhaps the most controversial of all local government services. Major questions were raised, particularly by minority groups, about the structure and functions of police organization, the quality and direction of police training, and the proper use of police discretion.

Later, studies from several national crime commissions (President's Commission 1968; National Commission on the Causes and Prevention of Violence

1968; see also U.S. Commission on Civil Rights 1981) challenged the assumption that police always act with strict adherence to the law. A committee of the American Bar Association (1973), acknowledging that existing methods of review and control of the police were inadequate, suggested that public misunderstanding concerning the actual nature of police work, the amount of discretion exercised by police, and the opportunities for abuse inherent in the vagueness of criminal statutes limited the capacity of the public to imagine how police might be made accountable to the community (see also Walker's chapter). More clearly explaining to the public the complexities of criminal procedure and policing, it was thought, would encourage police accountability to legal norms.

The ABA committee, recognizing that the most deep-seated and powerful restraint on the police is self-control, also highlighted the importance of strengthening the contribution of police administrators in guiding and controlling police conduct. Public attention is often drawn to the role of nonpolice institutions in controlling police functions, but, to stretch the old phrase, accountability begins at home.

When internal controls over police conduct prove ineffective, however, citizens may demand extrinsic controls. Several cities have constituted citizen review boards, in which citizens who are either elected or appointed engage in fact finding and discipline officers they determine have acted outside the law (Chevigny 1969; Reiss 1971; concerning the questionable success of these boards, see Littlejohn 1981; "Complaint Review Boards in Florida" 1983; and Kerstetter's chapter). In other cases, citizens have initiated court proceedings to redress police misconduct and, incidentally, to require that internal police procedures be redesigned or better enforced. By suing the police in civil court, they demand police accountability not only to constitutional law but also to civil tort law (Antieau 1980; National Lawyers Guild 1981). Responsibility for holding police accountable broadens from a "checks and balances among political institutions" model — with courts as part of their general enterprise of criminal litigation incidentally checking the police — to a "citizen cooperation with powerful institutions" ideal — with citizens directly urging courts or other institutions to investigate and redress police abuse.

If the public has the capacity to review police behavior and to elicit the aid of powerful institutions (which could involve media organizations as well as courts) to do so, citizens must have knowledge about what police departments are like and how police officers carry out their duties. The media in their various forms can supply the information from which such knowledge grows.

Even citizen review boards are useless unless participants draw on a well-informed and realistic base of public opinion about proper police standards. Surely accountability is fostered when one powerful branch of government exerts power over another in an effort to uphold democratic values, as the traditional conception of separation of powers would prescribe. But accountability is even more carefully preserved when the political structure encourages more than governmental checks and balances. That is, accountability is most carefully guarded when citizens themselves are involved in the police oversight process.

Accountability-inducing actions such as filing complaints or lawsuits are important, but few citizens challenge police actions directly, and then only when they are most grievously harmed.[3] For most of us, monitoring police accountability simply requires that we be aware of the quality of police performance in our communities, that we be competent to evaluate it, and that we urge scrupulous adherence to high public service standards. Though the force of an informed citizenry is less obvious in the political arena than, for example, in dramatic litigation, ultimately it is the base on which other police accountability devices must build. Little of this is possible without the aid of a powerful private institution: the media. Here is the prime example of the "citizen cooperation with a powerful institution" model of police accountability.

As many police studies have hinted, the institution of policing involves a network of arrangements and processes that may not be understandable to the police themselves or to the courts, to say nothing of the general public (Bittner 1970; K. C. Davis 1973; Goldstein 1960). How, then, is the public to learn the realities of this complex institution so that police accountability will be premised on realistic and well-understood guidelines? Some of that understanding can come about through scholarly research, and indeed, starting in the 1960s, a substantial literature has emerged, from both scholarly and task force inquiries (for example, see Davis 1975; Goldstein 1977; Muir 1977; Neiderhoffer 1967; Rubenstein 1973; Skolnick 1966; J. Q. Wilson 1968). But common citizens are scarcely conversant with this literature, and they draw their perceptions of police, aside from direct citizen-police contact, from the mass media.

How well do the media report on the police? A proper answer would require first systematically sampling and examining media coverage of police and crime, analyzing its content, and developing measures for evaluating its quality and estimating its impact. But nobody has figured out exactly how to measure that impact.

We cannot claim to have undertaken a systematic study of media impact here. Neither have we enjoyed the opportunity to explore as participant observers the complex relationship between the police and the media in the depth that it deserves. Instead, we have conducted an exploratory analysis of the adequacy of media coverage of police by systematically interviewing a limited sample of articulate police chiefs and several carefully chosen journalists. We have also considered the role the media might fill according to different versions of First Amendment theory.

On the basis of this exploration, we arrive at a scarcely surprising, perhaps inevitable, conclusion: The public is too often exposed to reportage about *events* associated with policing and too little introduced to the *institution* of policing and the administrative issues implicit in the policing process. In short, we argue that were the media to report more carefully about policing as process and institution and less about disjointed and sensational events, citizens would be better equipped to hold police accountable and fulfill the values justifying freedom of expression as projected by First Amendment theorists. An examination of how police departments as public institutions do and could interact with print and broadcast media may be illuminated by first considering certain central arguments of these First Amendment scholars.

POLICE ACCOUNTABILITY AND FREE EXPRESSION

The First Amendment protects a vigorous free press (and since the 1930s a powerful broadcast industry)[4] for much the same reasons that the Fourth, Fifth, and Sixth Amendments protect the criminally accused: Government should not be too intrusive in the daily lives — here, the intellectual lives — of citizens. If we move from Fourth and Fifth Amendment controls on police to the idea of accountability implied by the First Amendment, we see police accountability in a broader, arguably murkier, but perhaps more fundamental sense. It involves the capacity of a free people to hold institutions accountable because they know the nature of the work those institutions do. It thus involves self-government itself.

Commentators have offered several theories of the values that the First Amendment must uphold. Checking and self-government are two. Checking implies that one powerful institution or branch of government can monitor and hold accountable to the public trust other powerful institutions; the assumption is that abuse of authority will probably occur but for this watchdog. Usually, the concept is applied to checks and balances among the branches of government, but under First Amendment theory it can also apply to media organizations. The media are seen as a powerful institution; indeed a common euphemism for them is the fourth estate.[5]

In contrast, according to the self-government conception, the First Amendment protects media to ensure citizens of the wide range of information they need to make informed, educated judgments about public affairs. This is a facilitative function of the First Amendment, not a restrictive one. It assumes not only that one branch of government or private institution will serve to check others but that ultimately all branches of government are accountable to the people themselves. In this light, individual citizens depend on a free press to assist them in formulating opinions and making decisions about government.

A closer look at the elaboration of these two theories by their proponents, Vincent Blasi and Alexander Meiklejohn, will suggest complementary ways of formulating the media's role in achieving police accountability.

The Checking Theory

In a historical survey of the various values embraced in First Amendment jurisprudence, concentrating especially on freedom of the press, Vincent Blasi distinguishes three sets of values that have provided the theoretical underpinnings of First Amendment case law in the twentieth century: individual autonomy, cultural and political diversity, and vigorous self-government (Blasi 1977, p. 544). From these values, Blasi carves out a rationale for a fourth, which he claims was probably the most important to the Founders: the checking value. "This is the value that free speech, a free press, and free assembly can serve in checking the abuse of power by public officials," Blasi asserts (p. 527). Arguing that these values are not mutually exclusive, but rather supplement and amplify one another, Blasi urges the contemporary Supreme Court to give primary weight to the checking value in light of both its central place in the adoption of the First Amendment and its recent impact on society.

Police chiefs offer a prime example of the type of public official to whom the checking function of the media could be addressed. Indeed, the premises justifying the checking value evoke the image of a police chief as the quintessential public official whose actions should be "checked" by print and broadcast media.

"The central premise of the checking value is that the abuse of official power is an especially serious evil," asserts Blasi; "the potential impact of government on the lives of individuals is unique because of its capacity to employ legitimized violence" (p. 538). Public officials at the top of bureaucratic hierarchies, who hold considerably more power than most private citizens, should accordingly be more carefully monitored to prevent abuse of power. Clearly, this observation applies well to police of all ranks, the only state agents permitted daily to employ coercion and even deadly force against the citizenry. One reason for protecting media inquiry into officialdom is that there are no other institutions able to do this monitoring job. Although theoretically governmental entities are checked and balanced by those sitting on other governmental branches and ultimately by public opinion, intragovernmental checking is often sporadic and, Blasi argues, is particularly likely to break down at the local level, where government is compact enough to become, in effect, monolithic. Again, this idea would seem to have particular relevance to the police, perhaps the most decentralized American public service system, other than local public education.

Finally, "the moral quality of official power" is accompanied by a need for a checking institution. Because "the investiture of public power represents a form of moral approval, public servants are probably more likely than those who wield private power to lose their humility and acquire an inflated sense of self-importance, often a critical first step on the road to misconduct," observes Blasi (1977, pp. 538-40). Police departments and individual officers are especially likely to adopt norms of aggressiveness and to lack a sense of public service. The checking function rests on the requirement that there be an institution as well organized and powerful as the government to serve as its counterforce; on the local level, often the only institution that meets this description is the media.

If the ultimate checking in a democratic state is grounded in the force of public opinion, that opinion must be stirred and nurtured. The free press is expected to do this. However, the idea that public awareness and opinion are tools to hold police accountable to their public missions may go deeper than merely encouraging checking by the media. The concept goes to the broader idea of the nature of self-government.

The Self-Government Theory

Before citizens "check" the police, they must know what the police department does, and why. Under a self-government analysis, the checking function is important, but it is checking done by citizens after they have absorbed the product of a free press. Ultimately, checking is done by the media as intermediaries, as carriers of information, not as political actors. The media alert the citizenry to misconduct, while the citizens act on the information. The media's first responsibility, therefore, is simply to describe governmental processes and institutions. Using that information, citizens can debate and agree among themselves as to what their "good government" should be, what conduct they consider proper. Then the public will be in a stronger position to interpret and use media and other critiques to ascertain whether public officials have acted improperly.

The self-government value was articulated by Alexander Meiklejohn in *Political Freedom* (1965). Blasi and Meiklejohn both compete and overlap in their visions of the role or significance of the First Amendment in contemporary America. Blasi's checking value focuses especially on the misconduct of government officials, while Meiklejohn's self-government value is concerned with and thus supports special protections for a much wider range of communications.

Meiklejohn's vision of American society embraces the concept of an informed, participatory, active citizenry enlightened by the press and other forms of communication[6] and applying that enlightenment to an interest in the day-to-day affairs of state. His vision of democratic participation is rooted in social contract theory as symbolized by the New England town meeting; it is a community of people assembling "to discuss and act on matters of public interest — roads, schools, poorhouses, health, external defense, and the like" (1965, p. 24). By contrast, Blasi's citizen is more apathetic and self-indulgent, almost an apotheosis of the disenchantment and narcissism of the 1970s. "I choose to spend little of my time," Blasi writes, worrying "about the general welfare writ large or even about discrete political issues. I would rather think about Mozart, or Jane Austen, or the White Mountains or the Michigan football team" (1977, p. 562). The luxury of this blasé attitude toward participation in government must be abandoned, the author concedes, in exceptional times (for example, during the advent of irreversible totalitarianism or when specific abuses of government power become evident).

Blasi argues in favor of a republic in preference to a pure democracy, quoting favorably James Madison's contention that a republican form of government will result in the refinement and enlargement of public views "by passing them through the medium of a chosen body of citizens, whose wisdom may best discern the true interest of their country, and with patriotism and love of justice will be least likely to sacrifice a too temporary or partial consideration" (1977, p. 561, quoting Madison). By contrast, Meiklejohn's visions are derived from the social contract theories prominent in the thought of Locke and Rousseau. There is among citizens "a pledge of comradeship, of responsible cooperation in a joint undertaking" (1965, p. 18). Meiklejohn's entire thesis rests on the assumption that "at the bottom of the American plan of government there is, as Thomas Jefferson has firmly told us, a 'compact'" (p. 17).

In this aspect of the debate that Blasi has framed to contrast himself with Meiklejohn, Meiklejohn's position seems better in formulating the more general relationship that should obtain between police and the media. This is largely because Meiklejohn's political theory is closer to the reality of the influence of the media on the political agenda. Gaye Tuchman's study of news making concludes that news organizations both circulate and shape knowledge by disseminating information that "people want, need, and should know." Citing other studies as well as her own, she finds that "the news media play an important role in the news consumers' setting of a political agenda. Those topics given the most coverage by the news media are likely to be the topics audiences identify as the most pressing issues of the day" (1978, p. 2). This observation fits nicely with Meiklejohn's conception that the most important public official in a democracy is "the citizen as ruler" (p. 38). Free speech ought to be protected to afford the citizen the most information and, by implication, information of the highest quality.

When considered as an affirmative, facilitative theory of free expression rather than as a nonabridgement theory, Meiklejohn's ideas are suggestive of how to evaluate whether the media are living up to obligations implicit in the First Amendment. Since government rests on an informed citizenry, the media under a Meiklejohnian view have a civic obligation to provide the relevant and necessary information for self-government.

THE CONTEMPORARY POLICE-MEDIA RELATIONSHIP

Do the media fulfill their obligation to inform the citizenry about the police as a public, bureaucratic organization? What can be done to aid them when and if they do not?

Interviews of PERF Chiefs

To begin our inquiry, we wanted to ground our theoretical interests in some empirical findings, that is, to know how modern American police and news media representatives interact, and we wanted to assess the quality of that relationship. Ideally, one should undertake a major research study with a sample of police chiefs and media operatives stratified according to standard demographic variables. Such a study would have included participant observation of the reactions of chiefs and rank-and-file officers as they handled media relations in different situations.

We were unable to undertake any such massive study. We did, however, elicit cooperation from the Police Executive Research Forum (PERF) to interview chiefs associated with that organization. Based on a series of prepared questions, we interviewed 25 police chiefs, asking them to describe their relations with news media and to give us their opinions of how well the media were reporting about police. We assumed this information would prove useful because, although individual officers may or may not have had frequent direct business with reporters for crime stories, the police chief is continually and routinely involved with the media.

Who are these PERF chiefs? To qualify for PERF membership, a chief must be a college graduate, committed to researching the police role in society, and willing to develop and implement standards to improve police performance. Members must subscribe to the idea that "the principles embodied in the Constitution are the foundation of policing." Each member also must be the chief of a police department in a city with a population over 100,000. Thus, PERF chiefs, although scarcely typical of police chiefs in the United States, are especially involved on a daily basis with most of the urban crime issues facing contemporary American police. All the police chiefs in this sample had substantial experience in police management, and most had worked through the ranks from patrol officer to chief of either their home departments or departments in different cities. Nevertheless, these chiefs seem to be somewhat out of the ordinary.

When we asked each of them what characteristics he possessed that resulted in his being offered the chief's position, several major themes ran through the answers. One was responsiveness to community needs and aspirations. "I was more community-oriented," answered one chief. "The city officials who were hiring a new chief knew that I was tuned into communicating with the Asian and Hispanic communities and that I was able to balance proactive with reactive policing." Another commented that he was well experienced and had a reputation for "people-oriented public service," while a third commented on his ability "to communicate with all neighborhood groups."

PERF chiefs also emphasized their administrative skills. Some focused on management ability, while others stressed their capacity to work with department personnel and particularly with the unions. "I was picked," said one, "because the chief who was here before me was a political liability. He had had lots of union trouble, and it was thought that I would calm things down and introduce progressive management." A third and minor theme involved prior scandal in the department and the need to reform an organization that had been publicly revealed as corrupt.

It is not surprising that in an organization such as PERF virtually all the chiefs interviewed pointed to superior attainment in education as one of the qualities that had made them attractive to the selecting authorities. Several of the chiefs objected to being labeled as "reformers" (see Kliesmet's chapter), instead viewing themselves and the PERF organization as oriented toward high-quality police services with an opportunity for collegial discussion of major police problems and changes. "PERF chiefs," said one, "are exploratory and willing to take risks. I am traditional and conservative, but a risk taker." Most of the chiefs interviewed stressed the importance of innovation in policing and related innovation to informed research on the policing process. One of them characterized the typical PERF chief as "someone interested in informed research who is also willing to use it as a guideline for policy change."

In summary, PERF chiefs were atypical of police administrators generally in that they enjoyed more years of formal education and were influenced by that education to maintain a greater commitment to research, innovation, and management skills. At the same time, expressions such as "compassion," "community responsiveness," and "openness" dotted their responses to our questions. For these chiefs, the police are not so much a paramilitary organization as an urban service agency that needs constantly to develop and expand its professional skills.

It is unlikely that PERF chiefs represent the usual police attitude toward outside observers, such as the media or social researchers, who seek entry into the departments for nonpolicing reasons. In fact, several mentioned that, in contrast to themselves, rank-and-file officers commonly were hostile to the media. They offered various explanations of rank-and-file hostility (as well as hostility from some chiefs), but most mentioned as one common explanatory factor that police perceive the media to be "too liberal." We tried to press for the source of this perception, asking how political liberalism manifested itself in actual reporting. One chief offered an interesting interpretation. "The press," he said, "are usually reporting incidents involving low-income people—

but of course that's the area that gets the most police activity and protection. There's not much you can do about it. But the rank and file see this as a liberal bias." Gary Hayes, executive director of PERF and himself a former police officer, elaborated on rank-and-file hostility as follows:

> Part of it, I guess, is the perceived liberal bent of the press and the more conservative nature of policing. But also the media will report about the blemishes, and that's resented by the rank and file, who want to retain the idea of "my department right or wrong." They want respect in the department and of the department. After all, policing is their profession, and we all want respect for the work we spend our lives doing.

The remarks of police chiefs, then, may not represent rank-and-file attitudes. By the time a police officer rises to the level of chief, especially of a major urban police department, he has necessarily developed political acumen and sophistication. He very likely has enhanced his earlier appreciation of the media's role and acquired greater sensitivity to its significance.

PERF Chiefs' Perceptions of Media Relations

When questioned, the chiefs we interviewed stressed the importance of good media relations. When asked to rank on a scale of 1 to 10 the importance of communication with the media as compared with other features of the police chief job, the median score given by the 25 chiefs was 8.5, with six giving media communication a top rank of 10. No chief responded with a ranking below 7. To test police chiefs' responsiveness to media, we asked the following: If three office phones were ringing and their secretary told them that the calls were from the mayor, a member of city council, and a reporter, which call would they answer first? One chief chuckled at the question and gave an answer that expressed the consensus of the group. "I'd pick up the mayor's call first," he said. "But I'd also figure that the mayor was calling me about what I was going to say to the reporter."

Police chiefs we interviewed saw the media as conduits for communication between the police and the community. Accountability was never far from their minds. Although chiefs are not politicians who run for office, they occupy a community position that demands the support of various interest groups, including elected officials, community leaders (particularly from varied ethnic groups), and other high-ranking public administrators. Asked what other interest groups could have an effect on police policies, they mentioned unions of public workers (including, of course, the police unions and fraternal organizations) and the internal organization of the police department itself. Favorable media coverage of police activity can smooth relations within the department.

Asked what bothered them most about media reportage, the chiefs responded with stories of interference with ongoing investigations and of insensitivity to the legitimate privacy interests of victims. Thus several chiefs were critical of reporters who had investigated crime stories and then published the facts without considering the effect on the police department's investigation. One chief ruefully recounted the tale of a rape/murder suspect whose name was released to the local media because the department believed local townspeople should beware of him. The department thought it a good possibility that this suspect had fled to another state but that he would return. The department made a specific request to the national wire services that they not broadcast the local information so that the suspect would not change his behavior in response to the knowledge that the investigation had focused on him as a prime suspect. The wire services broadcast anyway; as a result, the chief believes, the suspect was not apprehended. "They had a bureaucratic response to a human issue," the chief said. "They followed their procedures without looking at the individual facts of this case. When police make bureaucratic decisions in that way, it's wrong. It's wrong from the wire services, too."

Most of the chiefs felt that in the interest of victim privacy, names of youth arrestees and rape victims and addresses of witnesses should be withheld from the media. Most chiefs also reported that their departments had worked out arrangements with local media management representatives to retain confidentiality in such situations. But others mentioned that if the crime being covered lent itself to sensationalism, reporters would press for information and grisly details that the police wanted to withhold.

Chief Mack Vines of Charlotte, North Carolina, noted that television stations, especially, were pressured to report ugly details of crime stories because "they have to show the smoke coming out of the gun and the lady screaming" for visual impact. Vines summarized the attitudes of most of the chiefs when he said that the general media policy of his department is to release any information requested, but that occasionally the media's relentless push for sensational facts — those appearing to invade privacy needlessly or to be in bad taste — created friction between line officers and reporters.

> The cameramen want pictures of the bodies, and the officers on the scene say the family doesn't want to see that on TV or on the front page. I say wait, it's up to the media to be professional and in good taste here. The police don't have to shoulder all that responsibility. But sometimes we really do have darned good reasons to keep information private, at least for a few days. The media people yell and say the public has a right to know. I say, "Bring me one public who absolutely must see this right now."

The theme of friction between the media and the police surely is not new. Police chiefs themselves, as well as rank-and-file officers, often have shown marked hostility to the media, at least where they perceive the media as out-siders bent on destroying the social fabric of the local community. Indeed, some of our most important First Amendment law developed as a result of cases involving police and the media. The most famous case, of course, is *New York Times* v. *Sullivan* (1964), which constitutionalized the law of libel. That case held that the First Amendment protects media criticism of local police activity, shielding media organizations and personnel from defama-tion actions brought by public officials, so long as the defendant media or-ganization did not engage in a "reckless disregard of the truth" when it pub-lished the story.

The famous outcome of *New York Times* v. *Sullivan* aside, the case can be interpreted from a different perspective as the high-water mark of hostility between southern officials — notably police — and northern media that were reporting on impediments to the civil rights movement. Justice Hugo Black's concurring opinion highlights the political and social realities behind this libel suit.

> In fact, briefs before us show that in Alabama there are now pending eleven libel suits by local and state officials against the *Times* seeking $5,600,000, and five such suits against the Columbia Broadcasting System seeking $1,700,000. Moreover, this technique for harassing and punishing a free press — now that it has been shown to be possible — is by no means limited to cases with racial overtones; it can be used in other fields where public feelings may make local as well as out-of-state newspapers easy prey for libel verdict seekers. (p. 295)

Given the commitments of the PERF chiefs to research, education, and community responsiveness, it is scarcely necessary, but nevertheless interest-ing, to note the startling contrast between these chiefs and the 1960s southern police chiefs and other officials who sued the media as part of a political battle over desegregation. However unrepresentative southern police of the 1960s or PERF chiefs of the 1980s may be, times have changed for the better. One would expect PERF chiefs not only to avoid overt hostility to the media but to display special responsiveness to communication regarding police organiza-tion and process.

PERF Chiefs' Assessment of Media Coverage of Police

When asked whether television and newspaper reporters in their cities spent too much time reporting about crime, a clear majority of the 25 chiefs felt that the coverage was appropriate and accurate. Whatever criticisms they had were limited and fairly directed. Various chiefs criticized certain features of press coverage of crime; they also made distinctions between newspaper and television reportage.

Chief Jim Keane of Santa Monica, California, for example, averred that the Los Angeles newspapers rarely took a serious interest in crime and policing in his city. There is no local television station in Santa Monica, and, he added, "it takes an atrocious murder to get the Los Angeles TV people out here." Chief Ray Davis of Santa Ana, California, made a somewhat different reference to the Los Angeles media. He thought that the suburbs or the smaller cities surrounding large cities were overly influenced by the large city television news operations and newspapers. He was especially concerned that residents of his city were subjected to a distorted image of crime news that, in turn, increased their fear of crime. That fear of street crime tended to reduce pedestrian traffic and thus activated a kind of self-fulfilling negative cycle: The emptier the streets, the more frightening they are; the more frightening they are, the emptier they get. The cycle continues until the streets are desolate and forbidding (and perhaps genuinely subject to serious criminality) even though originally they may not have been very dangerous.

Former commissioner Charles P. Connolly of Yonkers, New York, echoed these observations as follows: "We don't have any local television. We get New York City television in Yonkers, and people in our city think that the sensational crime is happening in Yonkers, when it is really taking place in New York City." Former Newark, New Jersey Police Director, now Police Foundation president, Hubert Williams offered a similar observation about New York City television's impact on his city: "They report as many tragic and sensational events as they can, which adds to the fear of violence by the public. The image of Newark is seriously distorted by the media."

The chiefs as a group seemed to criticize television more than the press, even though they recognized that local news programs generally cannot report as completely as do newspapers because their format offers little time to analyze news. Nevertheless, chiefs were not reluctant to praise broadcast media when they thought it deserved it.

We tried to elicit some notions of what chiefs felt were particularly meritorious sorts of media coverage and then also asked for examples of coverage they felt was inferior or had even made them angry. Television shows received both high and low marks. For example, one city had experienced a police strike during which the chief became a focus of media coverage by approximately nine television reporters. The chief singled out one reporter as having behaved in an exemplary fashion.

He came in to talk to me, discussed the problems, developed questions, and then brought the camera in. He understood which questions were pertinent. The others just walked in cold. They asked questions cold, and I gave answers cold. I got the feeling that they didn't even know why they were there. There's nothing worse than having reporters fail to do their homework before interviewing.

Several of the chiefs complained that TV reporters did little homework. "They are not reporters," complained one chief, "they are personalities."

On the other hand, when asked to describe any particularly positive features of television reporting in their cities, several chiefs praised local "Crimestopper" programs they had instituted with the cooperation of local television affiliates. Crimestopper programs, which run for a few minutes once a week or even daily (depending on the city), have local actors vividly reenact on television serious unsolved crimes selected by the police department. Crimestopper efforts invite public participation in developing leads, clues, or other information that might help the department solve the crime or apprehend suspects. However, these programs are not reports about crime or policing; they are collaborative police-media projects and, while certainly interesting and praiseworthy, represent a noncontroversial and noncritical example of local television programming about crime. We would expect chiefs to approve of them and to hold more interpretive reportage in less esteem.

In offering harsher criticism of television than of newspaper news coverage, the chiefs recognized that these different media experienced different pressures, constraints, and opportunities. Those chiefs whose smaller cities were served by larger cities' TV outlets perceived the local press as doing a better job in reporting the realities of crime and policing in their cities than did broadcasters. For example, Chief Keane of Santa Monica, who criticized Los Angeles television's coverage of his city, praised his local newspaper's crime reportage. "Our local paper," he said, "even prints maps of crime patterns, and these are very informational to the public. The public has really taken to it."

Chiefs who believed newspapers were more accurate than television broadcasts attributed the difference to assignment policies of the two media. They thought newspapers assigned more experienced reporters to cover police matters or at least trained the rookies more carefully. Reporters who are stationed in the police department building or near it, they thought, tend to develop "good police sense." Thus, several chiefs agreed, television reporters based in studios, with no training in police reporting, were not as adept at digging for facts or interpreting them for viewers. Richard Brzeczek, former superintendent of the Chicago police, asserted: "TV reporters can't handle substance. Print media people, if they stay on the police beat, develop incisive minds. But TV people don't know the logical questions to ask or how to respond to an answer with the next logical point."

A few chiefs attributed the print media's superiority to their relative lack of pressure. The newspaper reporter seems to be somewhat less hassled to get a story out than is the television reporter with a six o'clock videotape deadline. One chief seemed to speak for the group when he ranked television reportage as being about 70 percent accurate and newspaper reportage 90 percent. Other chiefs, however, felt that newspapers seemed to need to sensationalize crime as much as broadcasters did. Reporters focus on crime, and particularly the violence involved with it, in order to sell newspapers. One police chief was particularly sarcastic about a leading New York tabloid. "If the United States had just dropped an atomic bomb on the Falkland Islands," he commented, "this publication would have a headline reading 'SEXUALLY ABUSED CHILD THROWN DOWN STAIRS; POLICE DO NOTHING.'"

Another police chief described the following incident to illustrate how the media's propensity to sensationalize distorts the realities of crime and the criminal justice process:

> We had a burglary ring situation. One of the suspects was being held in jail, but he was being harassed because he had agreed to testify against his crime partners. So we took him out of the jail and kept him in a room in the police department building. About six months later, when the case came to court, it turned out that his wife had been permitted to visit him, and they had had sex while he was locked up in the police station. Instead of focusing on the burglary investigation, the media sensationalized this story into a big sex scandal. If you'd just read the headlines screaming "SEX IN THE POLICE DEPARTMENT," you'd think it was the officers who were involved.

Interestingly, the chiefs rarely criticized media outlets for being politically or ideologically partisan. When chiefs were asked whether they regarded the media in their cities as politically partisan, most responded that television stations were not, although newspapers generally supported Democratic or Republican candidates for office. When asked if the media subscribed to any particular ideological (as opposed to partisan) political positions, there was no consensus. Ideology, most chiefs said, could be inferred from editorial positions, which varied from city to city and from newspaper to newspaper.

Nor was there a strict correlation between ideology and support of the local police department. Indeed, police in cities with conservatively oriented newspapers (actually *very* conservatively oriented) seemed to elicit more editorial criticism (or to feel that they did) than did chiefs in cities with liberal or middle-of-the-road newspapers. A truly professional newspaper would not permit political allegiance to penetrate the reporting of any news, including crime and police news. Some of the police felt that their local newspapers did not, however, always draw a scrupulously bright line between news and politics. By contrast, the chiefs rarely perceived television stations to be partisan. Distortion of news reported by television was attributed to other causes, such as competition for audiences and advertising dollars.

On the surface, then, there seemed to be little hostility between police and media when police chiefs were asked to describe particular facets of their interchanges with media representatives. But in the course of these interviews, several chiefs alluded to an annoying "Watergate mentality" that supposedly characterized the media. It was clear that there was an underlying distrust and tension between media institutions and police professionals that was not necessarily illuminated by discussing "accuracy" or "ideology." When these chiefs were asked to explain more fully what they meant by "Watergate mentality," they usually prefaced their remarks with a disclaimer that they indeed understood the reasons that a free press should be vigorous and unhampered in its reportage, even when sometimes overzealous reporters would "get out of line." They asserted that this was the cost of democracy and the price we pay for free institutions. But many chiefs said that their rank-and-file officers saw the media as carping critics seeking out "warts" that did not really exist.

Rank-and-File Officers' Hostility to the "Watergate Mentality"

Media representatives who probed for scandal or misconduct stories, the chiefs said, were regarded not as responsible journalists but as outsiders who did not understand policing as an institution. Officers had personal visions of their own job performances and of their own professionalism. Media critics would pick one particular part of the job, examine it, and splash it across the newspapers or the TV screens with no explanation of the constraints or institutional pressures that led officers to perform their jobs in certain ways. The chiefs thought that rank-and-file officers disliked the media because the media reported they did a bad job, and the officers themselves wanted to take pride in their jobs and policing handiwork.

Most of the chiefs said that police regarded reporters with hostility until a reporter "proved himself" by writing stories that officers thought were fair. The chiefs often remarked that rookie reporters begin work with a "Watergate mentality," which annoys officers because the reporter seldom has any understanding of how policing is done or what can realistically be accomplished. The reporter assumes that the department is inefficient or corrupt but does not know what this means in the context of a police institution. One chief said, "They think that we are covering up, that we are not giving them the whole story. But after a while, they learn that we have an open department, and they begin to accept us. We just have to break in the new reporters."

Journalists' Perspectives on Police Hostility to Media

David Burnham, a *New York Times* reporter covering police in New York City and, lately, federal administrative agencies in Washington, D.C., explains police hostility to the media as "a natural human instinct." "It's not just cops," he says. "It's any institution. We all want to protect our own jobs from outside criticism. If you came in here telling me how the *New York Times* does a really bad job, I'd dislike you. It's O.K. for an insider to criticize, but everyone guards against an outsider." Burnham also thinks, however, that police officers tend to remember the "bad" stories and forget the "good" ones:

> I've talked to a lot of police, and they think they get negative press. But they don't remember all the positive stories about the arrests and good services the police provide and that the media cover. "NYPD CLEANS UP TEENAGE DRUG RING, POLICE HELICOPTER RESCUES STRANDED HIKERS. . . . " Police are so used to seeing this, they don't even remember it.

Moreover, Burnham believes that the professionalism concept is the key to understanding police hostility toward the media. "Everybody wants to think he's doing a good job. It's your life; it's *you*. So a reporter can't come in and say, 'I know you cops are all corrupt and brutal and I'm here to get the facts proving it.' But if the reporter appeals to their professionalism," explains Burnham, "the cops will tell him about their jobs and what's wrong with them because they see the reporter as helping them do what they want to do—a good job." Burnham added:

> Officers don't like to see graft or brutality or whatever in the department, even though they themselves might be part of it. I'm the reporter who broke the Serpico story, and even Serpico would never answer the question "What percentage of cops do you think are corrupt?" If he'd have answered honestly, he'd have had to say, "Well, most of them." But he'd never answer directly. He'd say, "I know that most of them want to do a good job." Which is very true. A reporter must appeal to that, and then he'll get a lot of cooperation, not hostility.

"Event Reporting"

In general, the chiefs seemed to understand that it is the job of the media to find news. They did not object to reporters' aggressiveness, but they cited incidents where it was transformed into such overaggressiveness that the significant meaning of the event was lost. Police Foundation president Hubert Williams summarized this common criticism when he said that "the media's mistake is to look at *events*, not at a *progression* of events." Williams added:

> The news media usually report all the facts one time only, when the event first happens. They are not there at arraignment. They don't follow through to the trial to assess the quality of the police evidence. They don't know the budgetary implications or the personnel problems — the whole series of

things to know if you are going to talk about the efficiency of a police department.

Clearly, these police chiefs were not distrustful or hostile to the media out of a blind antagonism to any institution that would try to evaluate police performance. What tension there was could be attributed to the chiefs' own criticisms of how well the media performed the job that media representatives themselves said they were going to do. That is, if media oversight of police functioning is one important way to hold police accountable to the public, the chiefs thought that the media were reporting too superficially to accomplish this. Rather than extensively reporting isolated facts dredged up for one particular story about some crime-related event, the media should engage in more careful analysis of trends and policies, the chiefs hinted.

The police chiefs we interviewed, then, were not necessarily hostile to reportage about department policies; the media could tie that reportage to controversial or sensational events as particular illustrations of the larger issues involved. In fact, they seemed to invite more careful media coverage of policing as an institution. For example, several cited racial confrontations and police use of deadly force as incidents that were most likely to spark a media blitz. "The press keeps the pot boiling; they never let it simmer down," one chief said. "But things seem to have been getting better lately; even though there have been shootings and there has been a lot of press looking at them, the reports have not been as one-sided. Before, the reports were all tied into racism, police review boards, and so forth."

On the other hand, another chief said that "the news media are not as sensitive to racial incidents and their consequences as they used to be." He added, "I get worried about that. The black community gets worried about that. I'm not sure whether the press is simply getting careless or whether new reporters no longer sense the import or meaning that a given incident might have in different parts of the community." Thus, although the chiefs clearly believed that event reporting was justifiable and sometimes even important, they were concerned that the media fit such reporting into a larger picture.

This observation was echoed by the journalists we interviewed. For instance, in addition to reportage about the individual events of violent crimes or police-citizen confrontations, discussion of police-related issues by public officials may also often be characterized merely as "event reporting." Both David Burnham of the *New York Times* and David Johnston of the *Los Angeles Times* called this high-class stenography: It simply reports what public figures say. Such "quote" reporting neither examines the major institutions of society nor explains the process of government. (Burnham [1974] discusses police organization and management and police corruption in a collection of essays on police corruption.)

Problem of Sources in Police Reporting: The Public Information Officer and the Inexperienced Reporter

Although the chiefs and journalists agreed on many of their criticisms of how the media reported on the police, they naturally diverged on a key issue—the police department as a credible news source. While the interviewed chiefs deplored emphasis on crime stories, they nevertheless sought to manage crime news so as to make the performance of their departments appear in its most favorable light. Police chiefs are both *sources* and *critics* of crime news. Even though the interviewed chiefs were not enamored of crime news, their departments often employ specialists, known as public information officers, to help the media produce it. These press officers, expected to be accessible to the media at all times, collect facts about fast-breaking crime stories and make them available to reporters who need facts quickly (see Garner 1984).

Of the chiefs we interviewed, 60 percent reported that they employed full-time public information officers in their departments; 40 percent did not. The absence of a public information officer could be justified by two seemingly inconsistent theories. Under one theory, the chief himself was the public information officer. "I prefer to keep my fingers on the press relations," said the chief of a 315-member department. "I take the calls from the media and assign them out if necessary. This also keeps people from running off at the mouth about department policy." This might be designated the "direct chief control" theory of media relations. By contrast, we also encountered what might be called the "multiple spokesmen" theory. The Oakland Police Department, for example, according to Chief George Hart, used to have a press officer, but changed:

> We broke out of that single-spokesman mold. All employees of the police department are expected to cooperate fully with the press and to provide all the information requested. If anyone has a question about whether information should be divulged, they are supposed to refer it to their superior officer. Since we have had this policy, I have held my breath every day, but we have had it for several years and it seems to work.

A third model is also discernible. Here the chief serves as the media relations officer and in addition permits anyone in the department to talk to the press at any time about anything. Nevertheless, most chiefs prefer to employ designated public information officers. Usually, the public information officer is a sworn officer assigned exclusively to press relations. For example, the Santa Ana, California, department has developed an unusually expansive media relations capability as part of its general theory of the relation between effective policing and communication with the public, stressing crime prevention and fear reduction (see Davis's chapter). The community relations office works closely with the media, business, and various community groups. In conjunction with a local businessmen's support group, the department has mounted an outdoor billboard campaign, portraying the police as both humane and accessible. An Hispanic affairs office writes a weekly column explaining the law in the most widely read Spanish newspaper in southern California. The chief is also actively involved with the press and appears regularly on TV news shows. This department has even been favorably featured by national television, being praised as a model department on a segment of "60 Minutes." A Philadelphia station spent 14 days filming and reporting the department's success story.

Rarely do police departments have such a highly developed public relations program. Most do not blend the media informational role with a community relations role, for example. In the absence of a community effort on the scale of Santa Ana's, accepted wisdom is that the public information officer's distinct journalistic skills set him apart from community relations personnel (Brake 1978, p. 23). But the duties of a public information officer are varied. Many police departments have developed standard media policies, often designed in consultation with local media representatives. They define the public information officer as the main departmental conduit of facts about criminal incidents. The press gets its "who, what, when, and where" from that officer. He or she also is a ready resource when feature or documentary items are being prepared.

Also, though it was clear that the chiefs did not perceive that their public information officers were mere press agents for the chief's office, several mentioned that the media officer's job was to make the department look good. Chief Cornelius Behan of Baltimore County, Maryland, said: "It is the responsibility of the press officer to work with the troops and to get *them* on TV. We are open, and we want the lower ranks to talk, not just the bosses. It comes across as much more human. It reflects and builds the department better." Other chiefs mentioned that the public information officer was expected constantly to present a good image of the department to the media. Apparently, fullest cooperation between the media specialist and reporters builds that image. Some media officers accommodated the needs of television crews by arranging to have cameras present when police made major arrests. Andy Goodman, former public information officer for the Berkeley, California, department, said that "often the criteria the TV stations use in deciding whether something is newsworthy is whether they have pictures of it." Film footage and print columns describing the culmination of investigations or other successful police work bolster the public image of the department.

Building goodwill through harmonious media relations requires media officers to discuss departmental operations in depth. "I spend about 60 percent of the time with a reporter educating him about the subject he's writing on," said Andy Goodman. "The problem is that the news media are not expert enough to cover policing well because they don't know enough about how the department works." By contrast, public information officers know very well how media institutions work. Many have professional experience in news gathering and writing. Their counterparts on the reporting staffs of local newspaper and broadcast outlets are often young and inexperienced. Goodman notes:

> Over the last thirty years, the most seasoned reporters were put on the crime beat. Now that journalism has changed its focus — toward economics and politics — the more mature reporters are given up to those areas. The people who replaced them are the rookie reporters. And at the same time this process was happening, the criminal justice system got more complicated. So between these two developments, the quality of police reporting was lowered.

Several of the chiefs interviewed indicated that the reporters assigned to police beats in their cities were comparatively inexperienced, though they believed that these reporters were generally well qualified for their jobs. Several chiefs remarked that a green reporter "doesn't know the right questions to ask," and there was a consensus that a reporter should be kept on the police beat for a long period of time so that he or she could become throughly familiar with issues and problems in the criminal justice area.

The combination of inexperienced reporters and full-time police media specialists raises a serious question of whether reporters can become too dependent on the police department itself for a view of the criminal justice system. For example, a highly qualified and thoroughly engaging public information officer understands the deadlines and audience requirements of different media personnel and provides them with information as he or she feels they need it. Crime stories, of course, are always reasonably newsworthy, and a public information officer is frequently a useful conduit of information about such stories. The question becomes: Does this usefulness shade over into an undermining of the reporter's capacity to engage in objective and skeptical inquiry? Or, at least, Does the public information officer's ready storehouse of facts about particular crimes subtly divert inquiry away from the processes and procedures of policing?

In this respect, we find something of an irony. The more qualified the police media specialist, the less the reporter may exert his or her independence. As the reporter becomes dependent on the police department, the reporter may lose the capacity to dig independently. There is a fine line here between the reporter who can make use of the police knowledge and information in order to undertake deeper reportage of the policing process and the reporter whose emphasis on fast-breaking crime stories leads to dependence on the police department as the primary source of information.

Inadequate Understanding and Use of Statistics

However, some chiefs intimated that even when reporters were not content simply to report a significant fact or event and a quote or two from police officials in response to it, media coverage of the "bigger picture" nevertheless often seemed misguided. Several chiefs cited as an example of media inadequacy reporters' naivete regarding crime statistics. A segment of the press, these chiefs pointed out, through mistake, inertia, habit, or sheer laziness, confuses the description of the policing process with reportage of crime statistics. Though it certainly is not event reporting, description of crime rates and their fluctuations was not considered to be incisive reportage. It can become an easy substitute for in-depth reporting of the policing process. Chief William Swing of Greensboro, North Carolina, criticized the repetition of such simplistic crime rate announcements:

> Every year our department publishes crime rates. Three months later the state police information network will publish the same reports, and the press print it all again. In the middle of the year, the FBI issues a preliminary report. The press print that. Then they print the final report, so they therefore have printed the same set of figures on four different occasions. It's confusing. I always tell the media people, don't look at the crime *rates*, look at crime per capita. That doesn't mean anything to the press. It sounds better to show a crime increase. It gets attention.

It would, of course, come as no surprise to criminologists that reporters are confused about both the accuracy and the significance of crime rates. Students of crime statistics have observed that although few of our social problems command as much public attention or evoke as much public concern as crime does, it is extremely difficult to produce crime statistics that provide definitive answers to questions that the public and policymakers reasonably would like to see answered.[7] Crime statistics ought to be able to tell us whether we have more criminality and more criminals than usual, how effective our machinery of social control is, and what we can estimate the risk of becoming a victim to be. More generally, they can gauge the moral health of our society. Even radical criminologists have argued for using crime statistics to examine the class relationships in a particular society (Taylor, Walton, and Young 1973, pp. 11–14). Unfortunately, we do not systematically collect and report crimes well enough to facilitate definitive treatments of any of these issues.

Reporters who are not well informed about the limitations of crime statistics will often perceive the police chief as an almost oracular figure for interpreting numerical changes. The chiefs themselves are more sophisticated and are well aware of the limitations both of the statistics and of their capacities to interpret them. For example, one chief described his discussion with a local reporter as follows:

> There used to be a phone call every month that I dreaded. The reporter would say, "Crime is up 6 percent or down 3 percent. To what do you attribute this?" I felt like saying, "How the hell do I know?" But then I wouldn't be a professional law enforcement leader, would I? So I had to make up answers. "I think it's because of this; I think it's because of that." But I'm guessing. I don't really know why the hell crime is down. I feel like saying, "There are 20 factors out there that have an effect on crime. The police department is only one." But the reporter doesn't call me anymore, and I'm thrilled.

Chief Ray Davis of Santa Ana, California, suggested a distinction between the real crime rate and the symbolic crime rate as interpreted by the media. "The crime rate," he said, "is only a matter of publicity. The media can make people afraid, even when there is no change in the crime rate." The reporting of violent criminal events does not actually make people less safe, he contended, but it does make them *feel* less safe. Chief Davis's observation is supported by a sizable literature on fear of crime that suggests that crime "waves" do not necessarily reflect real increases in crime but rather may result from media or police crime reporting practices. A recent study of a Phoenix, Arizona, crime wave confirms the role of the Phoenix press in needlessly heightening fear of crime by exaggerating its rise through reporting and editorials (Baker et al. 1983).

Several of the police chiefs reacted negatively to media portraits of police as society's principal crime reducers. Former Commissioner Charles Connolly of Yonkers remarked that "we now have to inform the public of the limitations of our role. Many people seem to think that the police are solely responsible for crime reduction. They don't want to hear about social or economic factors."

In sum, our interviews with these chiefs revealed a persistent connection between the superficiality of reporting on the police as an organization and the media's (particularly broadcasters') reluctance to undertake institutional reporting. The media emphasize crime event stories, especially crime event stories containing drama and violence. Here, again, the chiefs did not complain so much about the accuracy of the media reportage of these stories as about their superficiality. Several of the chiefs connected shallow reporting to an unwarranted, or at least unnecessarily inflated, fear of crime by the public. On this score, Chief George Hart of Oakland commented: "The media don't look behind what leads to particular incidents. As a result, the public can get paranoid. There is no real counterbalancing; there is no real discussion about the limitations of public safety agencies, their parameters, and their mission. So public knowledge of our capacity to affect these incidents as they are reported, or indeed about the whole criminal justice system, is abysmal."

ORGANIZATIONAL THEORY AND
INSTITUTIONAL REPORTING

The interviewed chiefs' primary criticism of the media may be summarized as follows. The media are only superficially informed about the institutions and processes of criminal justice. They respond to the public's least laudable concerns for lurid details of crime and victimization. As regards First Amendment theory, we speculate that although such crime or disorder event reporting sells commercials and newspapers, it neither educates for self-government in the Meiklejohnian sense nor checks abusive governmental power in the Blasian. It would seem to follow that to educate more broadly or to check properly, journalists must develop some comprehension of the police as a complex bureaucratic organization. They must break out of the prevailing style of police and crime reporting, or at least supplement it with reporting about the process and structures of policing.[8]

To say that the majority of reportage about police is concerned with events (such as crime stories or accounts of crisis in the department itself) and not discussion of ongoing institutional processes is not to imply that event reporting is worthless. News of crime is and should be a matter of genuine public concern. Moreover, when unusual incidents occur within the police department itself, they are newsworthy because they break the pattern of daily organizational functioning—and reporting on them sheds light on the quality of routine operations. Our interviews with the chiefs, however, suggest that the media should supplement crime news and "Watergate" stories of corruption or misconduct with more thorough explanations of how policing institutions are designed and how they are expected to work. It is only with such a background understanding that the public can evaluate the significance of singular events as they are reported.

Of course, this prescription may reflect our own biases. After all, we are sociologists and legal critics; we would naturally want to have available to us daily news coverage that would give us information about American social characteristics and analysis of government agencies from organizational perspectives. Sociologist Herbert Gans faced this problem when he researched the social dynamics of four powerful national media organizations as a participant observer. He concluded:

> I have tried to avoid the temptation . . . of measuring journalism against [and recommending that we transform it into] sociology. . . . If I could design my own national news media, electronic or print, they would be considerably more liberal versions of newspapers like *The New York Times* or *The Washington Post*, but far stronger on news analysis and explanation. . . . Personal preferences, however, cannot be used to justify public policies. These must be based on public values: in this case, the values of those who participate in and are touched by the news. (1979, p. 303)

We do not say, and Gans would not say, that news about policing should exclusively involve searching analysis of police organization, function, and actual impact on the population policed. What we do say is that, if the public value of accountability is to be upheld, more reportage should fulfill this mission.

Theory of Bureaucracy as a Framework for Police Reporting

The public needs an intellectual framework for critically reviewing the bits of information that event reporting offers. The media can help citizens form their own full and adequate picture of policing, thereby fostering democratic self-government.

If reporters were to undertake a program of more comprehensive reporting about police departments as complex bureaucratic organizations, they could draw on a well-developed organizational theory literature. In fact, police departments almost perfectly illustrate "bureaucracy" as an ideal type, as described, for instance, by Max Weber (1957). Police departments are hierarchically organized, even according to rank, as befits a paramilitary organization. Assignment to higher ranks presumably results from formal procedures such as examinations or impersonal appointment by superiors. The authority of police is generally defined and externally regulated by a body of abstract and identifiable laws, and the police are internally governed by rules and guidelines that arrange authority within the organization and define the responsibility of different categories of police service. As with the pure type of bureaucratic official, police are not elected but are appointed through an impartial competitive process. Police chiefs will enjoy varying degrees of independence from elected officials but are never themselves elected (although sheriffs are).

We do not intend to assert that knowledge of the as yet partially developed theory of bureaucratic organization in itself will present a finely drawn agenda for in-depth reporting about police organizations, but it does offer contours of analysis for news gathering and reporting. Any functioning bureaucracy will be divided into specified activities that are both integrated with one another and regarded as duties. A social scientist or a journalist can inquire into whether the allocation of duties in a police department generally makes sense or makes sense in any particular application.

Examples and Possibilities of Institutional Reporting

David Johnston's analysis of police expenditures in Los Angeles offers a prime example of this sort of reporting. Johnston, who describes himself as "a police institution and politics reporter," not a police reporter, argues that police costs often consume one-third of a city's operating budget, yet many news organizations continue to devote more time and attention to covering decisions by the local planning commission than they do budgetary decisions by the police. Johnston further points out that budgetary decisions get little attention from mayors, city managers, or whichever officials are responsible for spending the taxpayers' money. The Los Angeles Police Department, Johnston (1982, pp. 1–3) found, spends more money ($6.7 million) annually responding to "false" burglar alarms than it does investigating murders ($5.5 million). Johnston sees this as a major reason why the Los Angeles police solve, in the 1980s, about the same number of murders they did in the mid-1970s, although the percentage of murders solved is lower. Johnston concludes:

> To understand the police and examine how well they are spending the taxpayers' money is not all that hard. Plenty of sources of reliable information exist, including each police department's budget and statistical reports. For reporters used to covering the bureaucracies of city hall, there is an easy rule to remember. The police are basically bureaucrats with guns. (1983)

Note that Johnston's reporting is not about events in which police were participants; his sort of "police story" is different, a type rarely undertaken by journalists.

The theory of bureaucracy further suggests any number of "organizational" or "institutional" stories that might be written involving the internal violation of police rules that have impact on police personnel budgets. David Burnham recalls his first story along these lines:

> Well, the first police process story I did for the *Times* was about "cooping." That's when on-duty police officers sleep on duty. When I first heard of it, I said, "Aw, bullshit." But a friend, a whistleblower type, said: "Come on, I'll show you." We drove around; I got the story on my own time. The *Times* wasn't interested.

But "cooping," it turned out, was totally institutionalized. Officers routinely kept alarm clocks in their cars. Sergeants knew about one "coop" in Brooklyn where a phone was installed so someone could be called if needed. "The whole department knew," says Burnham. "So I wrote the story on my own time and got pictures, and *then* the *Times* loved it."

Burnham's observation underscores a more general tenet of the theory of bureaucracy, or, more properly, the theory of organization. Organization theory suggests that a dry and literal reading of legal rules and agency pronouncements explains relatively little about the behavior of such legal officials as police and other bureaucrats. In their study of the Occupational Safety and Health Administration, for example, Bardach and Kagan (1982) found that the interpretation and application of rules on the factory floor were far more influential in determining OSHA's activist behavior as an agency than the formal process by which the Administrative Procedure Act structures the regulations. Students of organization repeatedly stress the significance of informal suborganizational entities and their associated norms. "No agency," writes Schuck (1983, p. 15) in his discussion of organization theory and administrative law, "illustrates this better than a police department." "Numerous studies," he continues, "have shown that the norms that pervade the peer subculture of police officers on the beat not only constrain but sometimes overwhelm the impact of the legal rules with which agency supervisors and courts seek to control their behavior."

The theory of organizations also suggests that police accountability will be heightened by public appreciation of the significance of a sense of purpose in police organizations. Purpose involves the organizational actors' philosophy of the organization's overriding goals and place in the community (Barnard 1938; Selznick 1957; Nonet and Selznick 1978, pp. 110–12; Nonet 1980). Serious police journalism is necessarily attuned to institutional goals, as is journalism about any public organization. David Burnham nicely summarizes his institutional approach to journalism along these lines:

> My job as a reporter is to describe what happens when procedures prevent whatever institution I'm looking at from achieving its stated goals. The stated goals may be fabulous. Now what is it that gets in the way of achieving them? Corruption? Difficulty of the problem? Or whatever? That goal examining approach fits whatever institution you're covering.

Finally, it is also possible to go beyond an assessment of goal achievement to a more comprehensive and comparative view of police as an institution. Not all police departments share the same vision of the police role in society. Such differences in philosophies of policing do not necessarily signify misconduct. Nevertheless, a philosophy might be misguided or counterproductive or anachronistic. The philosophy of a police department involves a conception of the goals of policing and an awareness of the reasons particular police departments are organized the way they are. Do police leaders regard their departments as service organizations with expansive conceptions of the police role (see the chapters by Davis and Brown) or primarily as repressive enforcement agencies with narrowly legalistic conceptions? Do some departments aim for a "middle ground," attempting to serve multiple, antagonistic constituencies and affecting a mixed, often conflicting policing style? What are the results of these approaches in actual public contact and service (see J. Q. Wilson 1968)? For example, to what extent does a police department rely on aggressive, preventive patrol as its principal crime prevention technique? Are such techniques outmoded (see Kelling's chapter; see also Kelling et al. 1974a)? Have others been tried?

All of these observations—involving questions of organizational philosophy, of the resulting organizational structure, of the impediments to fulfilling an institution's stated goals — should enrich public understanding of the police. Searching and reporting about some answers to these questions can thus heighten police accountability to the public.

CONCLUSION: THE PROSPECTS FOR IMPROVING POLICE REPORTING

Summarizing the views of the police chiefs we interviewed, Gary Hayes, executive director of PERF, asserted that the public misses the complexities of major criminal justice policy issues because newspapers adhere to a practice of simplistic crime reporting. "The criminal justice system," he avers, "ought to be reported like economics has been in the past few years. The level of sophistication of public knowledge about economics has been raised phenomenally since the Reagan administration took office. Now the press reports in a much more sophisticated, informative way, and the public knows much more."

Yet fast-breaking crime stories remain the staple of the police reporter's beat. Known in the trade as "bang-bang" reportage, crime stories are high interest, factual, and stereotyped. Every crime story is a "whodunit." There is always a victim with whom the public can identify and an alleged perpetrator to be feared and/or reviled.

Police news is transformed into crime news; crime news reflects the most traditional assumptions about the treatment of news. These are spelled out neatly by sociologist Todd Gitlin: "News concerns the *event*, not the underlying condition; the *person*, not the group; *conflict*, not consensus; the fact that *advances the story*, not the one that explains it. . . . In general, the archetypical news story is a crime story" (1980, p. 28). In this context, the police department offers the reporter the fundamental facts to write the story, as well as suggestions and opportunities for their visual presentation. To the extent that any analysis of the facts is appropriate, the department or public information officer can offer that to the reporter as well. Finally, the department can provide statements by police and prosecutorial officials concerning the development of the case. This sort of reporting necessarily lends itself to dependence on public relations professionals as the *source* of news.

For the average newspaper or TV reporter, then, "bang-bang" event reporting may be his or her primary, if not sole, responsibility. Few newspapers or television stations encourage reporters who are so inclined to delve more deeply into the structures and processes of policing. If the reporter wants to write more than crime event stories, there is little encouragement either from media management or from the reporter's own educational background.

Why editors seldom assign "institutional process stories" is too complex a question for a study of the relation between police accountability and the media to explore fully. But on a very general level, the same organizational theory that enhances our understanding of police bureaucracies can also go far in explaining why media organizations produce certain types of news. For instance, Gans sketched an "ideal type" of news bureaucracy after he worked as a participant observer in several media organizations. Like other bureaucracies, he says, news-producing organizations strive for "power and efficiency" (1979, p. 282). By "power," he means that media organizations crave association with persons and organizations that can significantly influence public life. Reporters gravitate to these power sources in order to obtain reportable information quickly; a source is also preferred if it is associated with a public official or organization that is powerful and lively enough to produce a constant stream of potential story material.[9]

Reporters operate under time constraints imposed by strict editorial deadlines. They therefore naturally rely on those sources that produce the most information for the least reportorial effort and those that are likely to be most influential in affecting the events the story describes. Though Gans studied news gathering by national media organs, his observations also nicely describe the interaction between reporters and local police department public information officers. Reporters need the police; conversely, the police chiefs we interviewed knew they needed the reporters.

Police officials are well aware of the media's hunger for readily available information, and they understand the importance of communication with citizens. The chiefs know that self-government is at stake in media relations, and they want the public to have a favorable picture of the quality of service the police department is offering. If reporters regularly use the police department as the primary source of news, crime-fighting stories and occasionally police reform stories will be the norm.

Since most news "concerns the routine activities (and routine conflicts) of public officials" (Gans 1979, p. 282) and reporters turn to the public officials themselves as sources of information, it is tempting to conclude that the media cannot effectively check officialdom until they diversify their sources. Though this is one important implication of Gans's work, he is careful to note that it is not a comprehensive prescription: "Journalists [first] choose stories rather than sources," he says, "and their stories are hardly limited to handouts from the powerful."

Once reporters set out to write about crime events or discrete incidents of police misconduct, an obvious source of information is the police department itself. But the initial choice of story shapes the news more than sources do. Were editors to assign stories that require explanation of public institutions—in the "self-government, institutional reporting" mold—reporters would probably seek out a wider variety of informational sources than they would for event reporting. For example, a story about police recruit selection procedures would involve information and opinion from police administrators, psychologists, educators, and community representatives concerned about affirmative action. A story about deterring drunk driving would discuss police department arrest procedures, but only by explaining the local jurisdiction's sentencing patterns could the police data be interpreted adequately. Necessarily, courthouse sources would supplement police sources.

It is not altogether clear that pure event reporting is the only efficient media approach to criminal justice issues. If some reporters specialized in writing about public institutions from an organizational perspective, they could become quite proficient indeed at producing concise, meaty stories explaining police and crime—a welcome supplement to—and even a partial replacement for—the steady diet of crime "whodunits." (The notion that well-written institutional reporting "won't sell papers" may be based on little other than "old editors' tales.") Perhaps the demand for organizational efficiency in news outlets could be met by training at least one reporter to be the criminal justice specialist. This could also lessen problems associated with rapidly finding a wide variety of sources once the editor assigns a story. Such a reporter could cultivate many sources, become educated about the policing bureaucracy, and produce a steady stream of stories that explain crime-related events in much more depth than is usual in most contemporary reporting. But other institutional constraints prevent news organizations from developing this talent.

Partly the problem is specialization itself. Rarely do newspaper or broadcast editors encourage reporter specialization, perhaps because it is expensive, but also because specialists may get to know more about their subjects than the editors do, thus diminishing the authority of those in charge. It is evident, however, that whatever the media's responsibility for heightening police accountability, that result will not be achieved unless further specialization is encouraged. Undergraduate journalism curricula, institutes and seminars for working reporters, and, of course, encouragement of editors to use knowledgeable reporters could all be helpful.

While such models for institutional reporting as David Burnham and David Johnston are working hard and well, they are rare. Although it can be argued that few newspapers enjoy the resources to train criminal justice specialists,[10] surely there must be more than the very few media outlets currently encouraging institutional reporting that could develop an appreciation for police organizational complexity and a capacity to explain it to the public.

Ironically, perhaps, the police chiefs we interviewed seemed more sophisticated in their understanding of the media than most editors and reporters apparently are about the institutional implications and processes of policing. Perhaps it is time for those who write and speak to catch up with their subjects. Not only does nothing in the First Amendment prohibit them from doing so, but the values behind protecting freedom of the press, particularly the self-government value, invite active media exploration of the policing process to inform the citizens, who must judge its quality.

NOTES

1. The early English penal laws were written in blood — offenses were punishable by death, without benefit of clergy, and as many as 40 people might be hanged in a day. Concerning the well-armed Bow Street patrols, see Lee (1901, p. 156).

2. For a comparison of the histories of English and American police, see Miller (1977).

3. This may perhaps be attributed to the fact that few citizens will undertake the time and expense of litigation in order to challenge simple routine police misconduct. It is difficult to estimate compensatory damages appropriate for redressing constitutional violations that may be real but nevertheless of short duration, difficult to prove, and likely to be compensated by only small monetary awards even if the plaintiff prevails. Illegal detentions for short periods of time, misdemeanor arrests made with less than probable cause, petty harassment of minority group members — these and other police practices may be degrading and unconstitutional, yet challenging them is seldom worth the costs of bringing suit unless a class action can be organized. Though civil litigation against police has increased markedly in the last ten years, most reported cases involve improper use of deadly force, brutal beatings, or false arrests and imprisonment causing plaintiffs to lose jobs and wages. Virtually all cases resulting in large damage awards against police officers reported over the past three years by a national law enforcement support group, for example, have involved death or severe physical harm to the plaintiffs (see, generally, Americans for Effective Law Enforcement 1979–82 and Schmidt's chapter).

4. In this discussion we use the term *media* to refer both to broadcast and to print outlets. Where distinctions between them are important for the themes discussed, we note these in the text.

5. Sociologist Gaye Tuchman (1978, p. 157) claims that "both newsworkers and news organizations insistently present themselves as the fourth branch of government [in the sense that they believe] . . . they act as gadflies to ensure that government serves the people." Media can check the police as they do other powerful public organizations; this "checking value" is an important rationale in First Amendment commentary.

6. The notion that the First Amendment is an admonition to the media to explore the broadest range of public concerns and topics permeates case law and is expressed in the fairness doctrine of the Federal Communications Commission, which requires that television and radio stations investigate and report on important public issues and cover as many contrasting viewpoints as possible regarding those issues (for the application of this doctrine and the First Amendment to broadcasting, see Center for the Study of Democratic Institutions 1973, especially the interchange between Harry Kalven, Jr., and Anthony Scalia). The media's obligation to cast their nets broadly in hunting for subject matter undoubtedly can be traced to Meiklejohn's metaphor for the mission of the press: Media must offer the public "a marketplace of ideas" from which a self-governing citizenry may "buy" the most compelling, reasoned, and true arguments. (The metaphor was originally formulated by Oliver Wendell Holmes, who said that free speech resulted in "the power of a thought to get itself accepted in the competition of the marketplace" [*Abrams* v. *United States* 1919].) Note that Meiklejohn's analysis of the marketplace was not a pluralistic assertion that each citizen should stubbornly hold his or her own opinions and that the "marketplace" of political decision making would establish a homeostatic balance among all the opinions. Rather, each citizen would debate and reason with others; the "market" is manifest when together citizens agree that one idea of police is preferable to others (Meiklejohn 1948, pp. 86–87). Meiklejohn said that "the welfare of the community requires that those who decide issues shall understand them," and in the modern era the media are powerful providers of the raw material necessary for achieving understanding (1948, p. 25).

7. An example of a news article that reported a change in the crime rate and then explained statistical interpretation, also advancing possible reasons for what caused the change in rates, is Basler's (1980, p. B1); it includes quotes from former New York Police Department Commissioner Robert McGuire and criminologists Alfred Blumstein and Marvin Wolfgang. Another quick and lively explanation of current crime statistics is in Jencks' review of Hacker (1983) in *The New York Times Book Review* (1983, p. 7).

8. Of course, some reporting does indeed do this. Our argument here is that it is scarce. We should note in passing two series we thought exemplary of process reporting: the Weiser-Knight seven-part series in the *Washington Post* (1983) and the Linn-Ross-Winokur five-part series in the *San Francisco Examiner* (1983). The American Bar Association recognizes such reporting in its yearly Silver Gavel Awards, given to those newspapers and television stations that presented the best justice-related reportage for that year. WBBM-TV in Chicago, for example, delved deeply into the crime rate question in "Killing Crime: A Police Cop-Out," revealing that the police department there regularly masked the true crime rate by labeling many cases as unfounded, or classifying a crime as a lesser offense than the offense for which the defendant was prosecuted. A list of the 1983 awards is found in 69 *American Bar Association Journal* 1775 (November 1983).

9. Because these power sources regularly offer news items related to highly visible individuals involved in public events, the news media often interpret public organizational behavior in terms of the individual officials who are the symbolic leaders of the organizations. This in turn evolves into an unspoken assumption that policies of complex organizations are the results of individual leaders' wishes, not of a process of achieving organizational performance by group effort. "The news tends to treat group members as followers," says Gans (1979, p. 63). But a deeper analysis of public organizations would require an explanation of how policies are generated and implemented through group decision making and interaction.

10. A few institutes train working reporters to specialize in legal matters. For example, Columbia University's Graduate School of Journalism offers a year-long program for reporters from major metropolitan dailies to hone their legal reporting skills, including criminal justice reporting. Other universities offer specialized training for reporters to learn other fields. The Bagehot Fellowships are offered to reporters who want to improve their knowledge of economics. Perhaps similar training could be more widely offered for reporters concerned with criminal justice matters.

10
Media Accountability and the Police: A Response to Jerome Skolnick and Candace McCoy

Jack Fuller

I could not agree more with Jerome Skolnick and Candace McCoy's conclusion that communities would be well served by more intelligent, broad-gauged, "institutional" reporting about police matters. But the way the authors get to the conclusion is curious, and it reveals a certain misunderstanding, I think, about the constitutional idea of free expression and about the concept of "accountability" in our system of government.

The first difficulty, it seems to me, comes of trying to derive a standard of evaluation of the media's performance from the Constitution. The First Amendment is a rule of limitation on government. If it says anything at all about the expression it protects, it only says that rambunctious speech — much of it out of accord with prevailing views of good government or even good sense — ought to be tolerated. Free expression is, as Skolnick and McCoy suggest, supposed to be a check on institutions of government. But the regime of tolerance guaranteed by the First Amendment does not envision that all expression will be uniformly helpful or even safe. And it does not provide any basis for deciding what speech will be useful and what speech will not. That simply isn't its purpose.

The idea was and is that out of a cacophony of speech, out of boisterous public debate, the people will be able to come to an informed opinion. It will be informed, not because all of what they read or hear will be well informed and responsible, not because all the perspectives on government conduct expressed will be thoughtful, but only because all viewpoints will have an opportunity to be represented.

Further, the constitutional idea was simply that government is a bad device to use to check expression. And this relates to another source of confusion in the chapter by Skolnick and McCoy: What is meant by the notion that the media serve as a check on government? The word "check" has a

136

number of meanings. And often the authors seem to use it as if the media ought to provide the same sort of check served by the provisions of the Bill of Rights applying to police conduct. That is, there seems to be an assumption that the media should be expected to buttress the limitations on abuse of police power embodied in the Bill of Rights.

If one believes, as I do, that those limitations are of surpassing value to our society, then of course one would hope for the help of the media in enforcing them just as one would hope that other institutions would share this constitutional faith. But I think that one has to expect expression that attempts to ameliorate those limitations. One way in which free expression might serve as a check on the police is to argue that the police are insufficiently aggressive, that they have been hamstrung by legal rules derived from the Bill of Rights. The sensational coverage of crime news decried by Skolnick and McCoy can be seen in this light as a goad to the police. The nettlesome attention paid by the media to investigations that have not yet come to fruition can be seen as simply a way of checking to make sure that the investigations are being pursued with vigor. Thus the very kind of coverage — of "crime, protest, or scandal" — that disappoints Skolnick and McCoy can theoretically be justified on the basis of the checking function they endorse. If it is less desirable than other kinds of reporting, it is because there are practical reasons why its significance is limited, reasons that are based not on the values embedded in the idea of free expression but on notions of where police behavior in these times can most fruitfully be reformed.

This leads to another source of confusion: the idea that accountability to the public — by which I suppose the authors must mean to the popular majority — is synonymous with a proper sense of constitutional restraint. This turns the idea of the Bill of Rights upside down. The restrictions on official conduct were made explicit in the Constitution precisely out of fear that a government accountable to the majority sentiment of the moment might behave in a way inimical to the freedom that ought to be guaranteed to every individual. The authors point out that until the nineteenth century independent police institutions were largely unknown. "Prior to this, the police *were* the citizenry." But the rule of the posse is hardly the model, I think, that Skolnick and McCoy would take for the rule of law that they so strongly believe in and that I share.

It is not that I disagree with the preference of Skolnick and McCoy for media coverage that is more analytical, that recognizes the bureaucratic nature of police institutions, that looks beyond the day-to-day occurrences. This kind of reporting is useful and, we in the media often like to say, professional. It is also, as Skolnick and McCoy rightly argue, too rare. Newspapers and broadcast news operations all too often swing wildly from crisis to crisis without examining the underlying forces that create them or impede government efforts to respond to them.

But this preference derives not from the system of free expression but rather from what has come to be thought of as an enlightened view of the way government institutions should work and the way the media can serve to help. The constitutional ideal of tolerance of free expression spreads much further to embrace both the enlightened and the benighted. And confusing what we think of as good and constructive expression with what we think of as protected expression concerning government behavior is a mistake as serious as confusing accountability to public opinion and accountability to the transcendent values of individual autonomy embodied in the Bill of Rights.

11
Media Coverage of Police Departments: A Response to the Skolnick-McCoy Critique

Carl Stern

It didn't take me long to realize what was wrong with the Skolnick-McCoy depiction of news reporting.

The local TV news came on as I finished reading a draft of the Skolnick-McCoy chapter. The first broadcast item was a live "minicam" report from a Washington suburb where a Vietnam war veteran was talked into surrendering by police after he kept them at bay for four hours while he sprayed the housing development where he was barricaded with semiautomatic weapon fire. After describing the event, the reporter's principal point was that *no* shots were fired by police, who were following a policy of restraint. A police official was interviewed about the no-shoot policy. Interviews followed with the gunman's wife, a former army buddy, and a hospital psychiatrist concerning the man's previous aberrational conduct and post-Vietnam stress syndrome.

Live coverage from a shooting scene: that sounds like sensationalism, in the Skolnick-McCoy sense. A "disjointed and sensational event," they would call it. Hardly the sort of "institutional analysis" of how police agencies work that Skolnick and McCoy would prefer. But in the real world, coarse and violent events often are the fuel that ignites our interest in the condition and circumstances of other human beings and the manner in which our institutions respond. "Event" coverage, which is the essence of news, is the *engine* for many things to follow.

Analysis need not be part of *every* crime report. As citizens we respond to an *aggregate* sense of what is going on. Coverage of the Vietnam veteran's barricade and shooting spree was typical. It included an evaluation of police handling of the incident and a reasonably complete picture of the man's illness. No editor I have encountered would have been satisfied with less. In fact, the other TV stations in Washington gave the incident similar coverage.

It is misleading and an oversimplification for Skolnick-McCoy to assert repeatedly that the "average" newspaper or TV reporter is engaging in "bang-bang" reporting.

Skolnick and McCoy are not alone in reflecting an elitist view of what they believe *should be* news. I recall vividly the efforts of a judge to exclude the press and public from the Connie Francis trial (*Connie Francis* v. *Howard Johnson, Inc.* 1976), which he believed was being covered only for its sensational aspects. The entertainer's successful negligence lawsuit against the operators of a motel where she was raped stands today as the leading case in the law of vicarious liability. It is true that some newspapers, and a few television stations, are notorious for the exaggerated treatment they give crime stories. But the very fact that they *are* notorious identifies them as *exceptions* to the rule. Many of the police-chief comments quoted by Skolnick-McCoy do not fit most newspapers or broadcasts. A systematic study, perhaps of one month's crime reporting in selected cities, would have been far more valuable than a few hyperbolic remarks of police officials who don't like occasionally unflattering or inaccurate news coverage any more than the rest of us would.

Not only have Skolnick-McCoy understated the amount of institutional coverage of police departments that is part of daily "event" coverage. They also seem unaware of the large amount of purely institutional reporting that *is* done (see, for example, Cohen 1984a, 1984b, 1984c). Recently, I was a judge in the national awards competition of the Newspaper Guild. The greatest number of entries were articles dealing with nuclear proliferation and nuclear safety and wastes. But the second largest group, including the winning entry, consisted of probes of police practices. Such reporting has become almost de rigueur, a required ritual for any news agency worth its printing presses or its microphones. If anything, I suspect police are becoming weary (if not wary) of too much "investigative" reporting.

Skolnick's view, that news organizations focus too little on police departments as complex governmental bureaucracies, was noted in a recent *Columbia Journalism Review* article (Johnston 1983) describing major behind-the-scenes investigations of police operations by newspapers and broadcasters in Chicago, New York, Philadelphia, Los Angeles, Miami, Long Beach, California, and Washington, D.C. The stories mentioned in the article concerned unpleasant activities: alleged manipulation of crime statistics, racial insensitivity, coerced confessions, misuse of weapons, sleeping on the job, and cover-ups of police misconduct. Complimentary stories generally involve new techniques or new equipment. Either way, it is likely that more journalistic resources go into covering the police beat than any other, and that the public gets a clearer picture of the policing process from the totality of what is reported than it gets of any other commonplace activity.

It would be wonderful if each television station could place an experienced reporter in the police department of every town within its signal. But

Skolnick-McCoy know that is impossible. To suggest that editors are reluctant to hire specialists because their greater knowledge might diminish the authority of the editors is so ludicrous (I never knew an editor who didn't pray for a reporter who knew more about the story than he or she did) that it discredits an otherwise appropriate call, heard daily within the industry, for more and better reporters.

Occasionally, newspeople are wrong. Occasionally, newspeople are ill-prepared. Occasionally, newspeople are inadequate to the task, or their copy too shallow, or their memories too short. But how often? Skolnick-McCoy have devised no method for finding out. Unless we know the proportions of the problem, it is difficult to argue that the present commitment is unreasonable.

Should every station offer the same deep level of coverage? Do people rely on only one news source, or is it sufficient that some news organizations cover the news well, while others do not? Is it meaningful that the TV stations don't have a police reporter all the time in Yonkers or Santa Monica when they probably have access to a regional wire service or a stringer or a local newspaper that is on the scene?

Skolnick-McCoy wish to impose priorities on the news media that are out of touch with common experience. They implore newspeople to report less about "disjointed and sensational events" and more about policing "as process and institution." But news events *are* disjointed. They consist of deviations from the normal and the ordinary. That is what makes them news. David Brinkley put it: "We report the cats that are lost, not the cats that aren't."

Of course, some lost cats are tigers escaped from the zoo. And others are mere pussycats, of lesser concern. News items vary in importance. But for every story of a shootout, there probably has been one about the use of women in police departments, or the new 911 numbers, or one-officer patrols, or response time, or burglar alarms that go off too easily. For every story on a bank stickup, there may have been one on walking the beat, or deadly force, or multiagency cooperation, or processing citizen complaints, or the purchase of bullet-proof vests, or budgets, or overtime, or promotions, or service-connected disability, or retirements, or pensions — funded and unfunded. The problems of *managing* police departments are well known to the faithful follower of news accounts.

Reporters are mindful of the desirability of going deeper into a story, of linking one event to another, of following up, of determining responsibility, of measuring official conduct, and so on, so that the public may hold its officials accountable. But that follows from the *reporting* of events, not the *non*reporting of them.

It may be that what Skolnick and McCoy sense about TV news is that relatively little time — or none at all — is spent sometimes on giving background or context to an event, or in suggesting reforms or better ways of handling a problem, which may occur to an experienced reporter. The plain fact is that reporters are schooled to keep their opinions, and their suggestions, to themselves — although they may seek relevant suggestions as part of reaction coverage. Would Skolnick and McCoy prefer a more activist, interventionist press corps? Or should suggestions for reform be left, as they are now, to interview programs and editorials?

As for the fact that news reports only occasionally place an event inside the "big picture," to see where it fits in some wider pattern, reporters and editors strive unceasingly to give an analytical (although not editorial) dimension to what they do. But such use of limited air time must be reserved for the stories that truly deserve it. Few happenings, even if worth reporting, have the global significance their advocates want us to believe they have.

Skolnick and McCoy are mistaken in believing that event coverage is being done at the expense of institutional reporting. Reporters savor a good, inside story. I still remember my first: a story about a village police chief who had a lucrative newspaper route — by having his officers deliver the daily newspaper on their morning patrol!

Most reporters have done their share of stories about the politics or bureaucracy or alleged mismanagement of local agencies, including the police department. The Skolnick-McCoy thesis is interesting to read, but I am certain that a fair-minded jury, familiar with the evidence, would acquit the news media on all counts.

12

Rejoinder to Carl Stern's and Jack Fuller's Criticisms of "Police Accountability and the Media"

Jerome H. Skolnick and Candace McCoy

One thing is clear: Carl Stern and Jack Fuller, our distinguished and articulate media critics, are in substantial disagreement about what is wrong with our essay. Stern vigorously defends event reporting as an "engine" to bigger things, while Fuller objects to our broader vision of the First Amendment.

It did not take us long to find evidence reaffirming our thesis that event stories about crime and policing are often shallow, so one-dimensional, in fact, that citizens receive little substantive information to use as a basis for their democratic decision making. We watched the San Francisco local news programs.

Stern apparently has the good fortune of living in a city that enjoys exemplary media outlets and whose citizens are exceptionally attuned and receptive to analysis of governmental functioning. Further, in his duties as a renowned journalist he has the opportunity to judge news stories offered as examples of the year's best. The police chiefs we interviewed told us they need more of this in *their* hometowns. Now who, exactly, is the elitist here?

We do agree with Stern that a systematic study of crime reporting would be a good thing. Still, we note that editorialist Fuller does not disagree with that part of our thesis. "Newspapers and broadcast news operations," he writes, "all too often swing wildly from crisis to crisis without examining underlying forces . . . or government efforts."

We do not abandon the "tolerance of free expression" idea; we would in no way censor "bang-bang" reporting. But why do media outlets expend their resources this way? Where we differ from Fuller is that we believe the First Amendment implies an affirmative duty on media outlets to supplement this reporting. It is a civic duty, not a contractual, enforceable one—but it is a duty that underscores what we take to be an important message of the First Amendment.

We also agree with Carl Stern that event reporting is inevitable, and may even be important. But we maintain that the real "engine" here is the background institutional reporting that pulls the train of events.

A man biting a dog (or a cat getting lost) is bizarre and newsworthy precisely because it is atypical. But it is not disjointed from the larger picture. We all know that dogs often bite, so media need not explain the phenomenon. Sadly, the same cannot be said for knowledge of how public organizations work, so media organizations must take pains to explain how police bureaucracies normally function. Only by absorbing a steady stream of information about typical policing can we understand an atypical — but not disjointed — event such as a corruption scandal.

We also agree with Fuller that the First Amendment was intended to keep government out of the city room and the broadcast booth. We maintain, however, that it also means more. It is a profoundly democratic principle: Public institutions like police departments are ultimately accountable to citizens. Citizens must know how these organizations work in order to evaluate them. The most powerful medium for learning about public bureaucracies is the printed and spoken word, disseminated widely, which today means through the media in their various forms.

PART 4

WHO DISCIPLINES THE POLICE?

Introduction

More than 2,000 years ago the Roman lawyer Juvenal asked, "But who would guard the guards themselves?" The answer is complex, at least in an avowedly free society, where the governed are the ultimate governors and yet they have, of necessity, delegated to full-time police specialists authority to order about and even use irreversible force against members of society. The friction between public rule and professional expertise in law enforcement has ignited the embers of police-community distrust from time to time in America's recent history, notably in battles over the creation of civilian review boards (see Bouza's, Jacobs's, and Murphy's chapters in this volume).

Exacerbating the problem of who should discipline the police is the preliminary finding, discussed by Wayne Kerstetter in this section, that civilian review systems seem to be weaker than police internal affairs units in identifying and punishing police misconduct. Still, substantial segments of the public doubt that police, any more than other workers, can impartially judge disputes about the quality and propriety of their own work. Neither this public perception nor police intolerance for lay control can be ignored because both can undermine effective police-community collaborations for neighborhood safety.

In order to explore suitable structures for reviewing police conduct and the police chief's proper role in those structures, Kerstetter examines the realities of adversarial police-citizen encounters — realities about which any reviewer must be well informed to avoid being duped into overly lenient or overly harsh judgments. Of central importance is the fact that the police officer is unique among municipal agents in his or her capacity ultimately to secure compliance with lawful orders. As Al Capone observed in a different context, "You can get much further with a kind word and a gun than you can with a kind word alone" (Singer 1984).

Kerstetter does not deny that effective and desirable police work often depends on the latent threat of force and occasionally on its actual use. Nor does he dispute the existence of police brutality — as aberrant behavior by the normally good officer or as routine conduct by the officer who is a genuine debit to his profession. Rather, Kerstetter attempts to take all these phenomena into account and to fashion a police conduct review system that maximizes both officers' incentives to perform well and citizen confidence in that performance. The key to a successful and fair administrative review system, he argues, is to acknowledge forthrightly the inevitability of police discretion, to assign to police administrators the primary responsibility for reviewing the exercise of that discretion, and to provide civilian oversight with adequate resources to ensure that the police administrators patrol the boundaries of that discretion with diligence and integrity.

In Kerstetter's view, the rehabilitation of errant police officers would be preferable to their removal from the force in most cases because many of the failures are the product of systemic rather than individual defects. He recognizes, however, that a company is known by the people it keeps and, accordingly, that some officers simply must be fired. By strengthening the police administrator's ability to make an effective case for dismissing really bad officers, Kerstetter's proposal can assist in addressing an emerging crisis in policing: that civil service restrictions, judicial decisions, and unions' political clout are making it increasingly difficult for police chiefs to remove the "rotten apples" from their forces (see Schmidt's, McDonald's, and McNamara's chapters in this volume).

Of the responses to Kerstetter's paper, the two voices from within policing (George Napper's and Wesley Pomeroy's) provide some firsthand evidence that his combined internal-external review system can work well in practice. Amitai Schwartz's response challenges the capacity of Kerstetter's proposed external ombudsman to review *systemic* abuses and, as such, provokes some helpful clarification in the rejoinder (regarding the ombudsman approach to police review, see Morris and Hawkins 1970, pp. 98–100). The relatively few points of genuine disagreement among the contributors to this section are a microcosm of the inevitable and healthy clash of societal concerns from which police and community leaders have the opportunity in the years ahead to forge constructive compromises that will serve everyone's interest in more successful and just policing.

13
Who Disciplines the Police?
Who Should?

Wayne A. Kerstetter

The inappropriate use of coercive force is the central problem of contemporary police misconduct because the *appropriate* use of coercive force is the distinguishing feature of the modern municipal police function. Bittner (1970, pp. 36–47) made the classic observation that the police role "is best understood as a mechanism for the distribution of non-negotiably coercive force employed in accordance with the dictates of an intuitive grasp of situational exigencies." Elaborating, he pointed out that a small amount of police time is devoted to arrests and other invocations of the criminal law and that most of police work involves providing a range of services, many of which fall loosely under the heading of maintaining the peace. All that police do, Bittner notes, is colored by their capacity to coerce:

> [W]hatever the substance of the task at hand, whether it involves protection against an undesired imposition, caring for those who cannot care for themselves, attempting to solve a crime, helping to save a life, abating a nuisance, or settling an explosive dispute, police intervention means above all making use of the capacity and authority to overpower resistance to an attempted solution in the native habitat of the problem. (1970, p. 40)

Brown (1981, p. 4) captures these notions when he characterizes the police role as "the coercive regulation of social behavior among the members of the community in the interest of the protection of life and the preservation of order"—a broad and open-ended charge.

At least two problems for the review of police conduct follow from these definitions. First, to assess the appropriateness of action taken "in accordance with the dictates of an intuitive grasp of situational exigencies" arguably requires the reviewer to have experienced the situation in question or at least similar ones. The difficulties in identifying and articulating the elements of a controverted police-civilian encounter to a nonparticipant have continually vexed judicial review of police activity. Second, police, if they are to succeed in their role as agents of coercion, unavoidably encounter what Muir (1977, p. 101) calls the "paradoxes of coercion" and particularly the "paradox of face" ("the nastier one's reputation, the less nasty one has to be"). Trying to deal with the "paradox of face" substantially motivates much of what is often alleged to be police misconduct and contributes to the difficulties in making a retrospective judgment about the questioned conduct.

Other types of police misconduct besides excessive use of nondeadly force obviously require some mention under the broad inquiry of "Who disciplines the police? Who should?" However, the review of alleged harassment, incivility (including racial and ethnic slurs), and corruption for the most part can be accomplished within the principles that will be articulated for the review of use or threatened use of physical force by police. Moreover, the problems of reviewing these other forms of alleged misconduct are not as complex as those attending review of excessive force complaints. I will not focus directly on the review of police use of deadly force. These incidents, by comparison to nondeadly force encounters between police and citizens, are less frequent and, by and large, receive closer administrative, prosecutorial, and media review as a result of both their gravity and their infrequency (see, generally, Geller 1982).

This chapter begins with a discussion of the dynamics of police conduct and conceptual problems inherent in any attempt to review that conduct, particularly for the purpose of assessing its appropriateness as measured against some standard. I then examine contemporary experience with various organizational structures created to review police conduct and identify four elements of the central dilemma inherent in the review of complaints regarding police conduct. The chapter concludes by articulating principles for the review of police activity.

THE DYNAMICS OF POLICE USE OF NONDEADLY FORCE

This section explores aspects of the police role and function that appear to be specifically relevant to the question of who should discipline the police. The police, by and large, have steadfastly maintained that the appropriateness of police conduct can be judged only by those who have experienced the problems and difficulties of being a police officer — other police officers. Concerned, and sometimes enraged, members of the community argue that the police cannot be trusted with that task. They assert that the obvious pressures on police to protect their own and not to embarrass the agency by admitting to wrongdoing work both to impede an evenhanded review and to undermine the credibility of their review in the community.

The Ambiguities of Police Use of Force: Three Anecdotes

In an attempt to sort out these conflicting viewpoints, I turn first to three recent Chicago newspaper articles that capture aspects of the problem. Roger Simon (1982, p. 7) wrote:

> Two OPS [Chicago Police Department Office of Professional Standards] veterans, whom I'll call Pat and Mike, agreed to talk. . . . So I asked Pat and Mike what they would do if stopped by police. "I would not get in an argument with them," Pat said. "Never argue. There are some policemen out there — a very small percentage — who just like to hit people." "I would be very respectful," Mike said. "Police who beat people fall into two categories: those under enormous pressure and those on ego trips — they just love that gun. Some cops are real jerks, but few start the day by saying, 'Hey, I'm going to beat somebody up.' You have to realize that cops get hit and bit and kicked. And if you are going to be an authority figure in Cabrini Green or the Robert Taylor homes, then the people there have got to be afraid of you. I'm sure some cops overdo it. But I don't know the solution. When a cop's authority is being questioned, being tough is sometimes the only tool he has."

In another article, Mike Royko (1982a) touches similar themes:

> My first reaction, when Big Raymond Hicks walked into my office, was to almost bust out laughing. "You say that a policeman was brutal to you?" I asked Big Raymond. "That's right," he said, in a soft voice. "Just one policeman beat you up?" "Yes sir, just one policeman." "Raymond, how tall are you." "Oh, I guess I'm about 6 feet 2." "And what do you weigh?" Big Raymond, 21, chuckled. "Tell you the truth, I don't know how much I weigh. Most scales don't show."
>
> I'm sure that's true. If I had to guess Big Raymond's weight, it would be a minimum of 300 pounds. So I think most people would be skeptical, and amused, to hear sombody who is the size of a small house talk about how one cop beat hell out of him. On the other hand, one side of Big Raymond's face was swollen. It looked like somebody might have recently pounded on it. And he had a hospital report that said he had been injured. And Big Raymond, who is black, does live in a part of town where policemen have been known to be less than courteous.
>
> Anyway, Big Raymond says he had just finished work in a restaurant near Belmont Harbor. He's a broiler cook. He had taken a CTA train to 62nd St. and was walking toward his home, where he lives with his mother. It was about 1 A.M.
>
> "A buddy from the neighborhood was with me. I ran into him on the train. He just got off work, too. We're goin' down the street when this squad car pulls up and this policeman yells out the window, 'Hey, you, come here.' I hadn't done anything wrong, so I say, 'What for?' Man, he jumps out and starts shoving me toward the squad and started hitting me with his fist.

He weighed about 215 pounds and was about 5 feet 11. He looked to be about 50 years old. And he kept punching me in the face. Man, he punched hard."

"Big Raymond, a 50-year-old cop was punching you and you didn't do anything to defend yourself? You didn't hit him back?"

"Huh! Where do you think I grew up? I know not to touch a cop. That's all they'd need is for me to hit one of them back. He might shoot me. Anyway, I never resisted. Soon I was bleeding from my nose to my lip. I could feel the blood flowing. I said, 'Hey, why you hitting me? I never seen you before.' He snarled at me and say he knew I didn't work, that I was a bum. I said, 'I been working since I been 15 years old. I worked in George Diamond's restaurant until it closed. That's where I learned cooking. And I went to school. I'm no bum. I work and I work hard. And I never been arrested except once for sneaking on a bus.'

"But he just said something about us being all alike and then bam! He socked me again. He was beating me real bad. I guess he was trying to knock me out. He was swinging both hands together in an uppercut motion. They were steady punches. I tried to cover my face, but it didn't do much good. Right after he stopped me, he talked on his radio. I guess he called other cops because it wasn't too long and there was nearly 10 more cops there. . . . Those other cops just stood there and watched him hit me. One cop told my buddy to get lost or they'd do the same to him, so he took off. I don't blame him. Then the cop handcuffed me and put me in the front seat of his car and you know what he did? He drove with his left hand and wham! He keep popping me with his right hand while I sat next to him in cuffs. I couldn't protect myself. When we got to the station, he said, 'I did what I wanted to you.' And he told me if he ever saw me on that street again he was gonna do the same thing to me. I told him he didn't own the street. Then he got nasty and punched me again. He said next time I see him I better give him some respect because he may be old, but he's got it right here, meaning his fist.

"He put me in the station and I talked with a guy at the desk. I told him what the cop had done to me. I was still bleeding. The guy at the desk told me to make a complaint to the Office of Professional Standards. He said they had lots of complaints about this cop but nobody ever followed up on them. They didn't question me at all. Then they charged me with disorderly conduct. That's all. I mean, if I had done something bad enough for a cop to beat me bloody, I would have been charged with something more than disorderly conduct, right? Then my mother came and got me out on bond. She almost fainted when she saw my face. I just don't know why he did that to me. I'm a working man. And he beat on me like I was some sort of criminal."

"Maybe he is a racial bigot, Raymond." "Heck, he was just as black as me. Except for his hair. It was gettin' a little gray. But he didn't hit like an old man." No, if what Raymond says is true, I don't suppose the cop hit like an old man. It happens that the cop, Antonio Francis, is an ex-fighter and about nine years ago he was indicted on charges that he beat an auto worker into unconsciousness just because the man made a remark about a traffic ticket. The court case was dropped on a technicality, but the Police Department found enough evidence against Officer Francis to suspend him for awhile.

"Big Raymond, are you going to stay off the street like he said?" "Nope. That's the way I go home after work, so I have to walk on that street. I'm too big to fly."

These two excerpts suggest explanations for problematic police use of force that recur throughout the popular, professional, and academic literature: the strongly felt need to maintain "respect" or "face," the dependence of expectations about police conduct on widely differing social contexts, the effect of job-related stress as well as tensions and problems in the officer's personal life, and the occasional appearance of an individual with a pattern of excessive use of force (see Friedrich 1983; Van Maanen 1980; Toch, Grant, and Galvin 1975).

Another Royko column (1982b) suggests an additional element to consider in police use of force:

The shaggy young man came padding up Navy Pier, a beer glass in his hand and a belligerent look in his eye. "Hey, man," he said, "you ought to write about the police brutality. They just took my buddy in, and they treated him rough. I mean, they knocked him around, you know?" "What was your buddy doing?" "Doin'? He was doin' nothin' man, he was just sittin' there doin' nothin' and they jumped all over him." "Your buddy did nothing — absolutely nothing?" "Uh, well, you know," he stammered, starting to sound a little unsure of himself. But he quickly regained his air of innocence and injured virtue and said, "Yeah, nothin', man. I mean they're just pigs the way they knock people around. You should write about it." "And exactly where was your buddy doing his nothing?" "We were at the rock stage, just sittin' there, takin' in the show, you know?" . . .

As a refugee who fled the rock stage had told me earlier, "Oh, they're nuts. The heavy-metal rockers. They're crazy." I don't know much about this form of rock, but I'm told that its loyalists are single-minded in their devotion. They are so devoted that while they wait for the heavy-metal rock group to appear, they like to throw things at the warmup bands. Bottles, nuts, bolts, firecrackers, rocks, vegetables — just about any kind of missile will do. And that night, with objects flying toward the stage, the police dashed in and began plucking some of the more ardent fans from the audience and stuffing them into paddy wagons. As can be expected, some of the heavy-metal rock fans weren't eager to ride in paddy wagons, and the police had to encourage them to come along. So it's possible that to some eyes, the police might have looked like they were being a bit rough, even — as the angry young man said — brutal. Now, brutality by policemen is wrong. There's no arguing with that. . . .

But while I disapprove of police brutality, I probably disapprove of it least when it involves somebody whose idea of music criticism is to throw a blunt object at a musician. In fact, my disapproval is strictly in principle — under those conditions I viscerally enjoy it. Chances are, those who are arrested for throwing things at the performers will be charged with disorderly conduct, a mere misdemeanor. The punishment will be a small fine, or the charges might be dropped. That's really not adequate punishment. So a punch to the offender's chops by a policeman might not be within the strict framework of the law, but it does help balance the books.

This column stands as an example that in some circumstances the public, even people with a substantial history of denouncing what they perceive as police misconduct, support the police in use of force that exceeds what the law allows. It also shows that what the public considers appropriate police behavior is significantly affected by the social milieu (see also Cordner's chapter, p. 390). In lower socioeconomic areas the police are expected to respond much more diréctly and forcefully than in wealthier neighborhoods. The tensions between these expectations often place the police in difficult situations.

Perspectives on Police Need to Maintain Respect and the Roles of Law and Custom

Scholars are at odds over the extent to which the need of the police to maintain "respect" helps to justify questionable uses of force by officers. Representing the predominant view, Bittner (1970, p. 103) belittles the importance of this need, attributing excessive force to "an exacerbated sense of masculine pride and soldierly prowess according to which insults and attacks must be met in kind, in the hope that fear will inspire respect, and in ignorance of the fact that it causes only hatred." But other scholars, and even Bittner in other writings (for example, 1967), have developed a contrasting perspective, holding that the police officer serves as an important mediator in neighborhoods suffering from social disorganization and that his success in this role depends on his effectively using the powers of coercion without invoking official mechanisms. The implications and problems of that role have been elaborated by Muir in *Police: Streetcorner Politicians*, in which he characterizes policemen as "powerful persons" who share with "political figures" "unique agonies and special dilemmas" (1977, p. 1). He finds inherent in the exercise of coercive power the four paradoxes of "dispossession," "detachment," "irrationality," and "face" (p. 60). The last is central to our considerations, and of it Muir says:

In roughneck politics no task exceeds the difficulty of managing the paradox of face: "The nastier one's reputation, the less nasty one has to be!" It involves the politician in preserving his opportunities to employ purposeful threats. He has to defend something of great value to him: his reputation for firmness, remorselessness, nastiness — in short, his honor. What is at stake is his entitlement to control others through intimidation. . . .

The paradox of face requires that the politician, anticipating future tests of strength, cannot allow his bluff to be called. "Not only does the statesman have to win the war," Muir explains, but "he also has to win it with honor. To gain an objective momentarily and yet sacrifice his credibility at the same time is to win a Pyrrhic victory." In certain situations in brutish and fear-ridden parts of our cities, the formal authority of the law as represented by the police officer is not sufficient to compel obedience even to reasonable orders (Muir 1977, p. 101; see also Muir 1980, pp. 50–51). Muir explores the dynamics of the police role by considering one officer's inept handling of a crowd scene:

Nor did he [the police officer — Garfield] see the psychology of the situation — the play between the antagonists and the crowd. He failed to grasp the necessity of face-saving and the importance of "respect" in a fear-ridden neighborhood. Therefore, he could not use the crowd to affect the behavior and the incentives of the two antagonists.

Having squandered the potential utility of the crowd to quell the dispute, he had to rely on making himself fearsome when he had no jurisdiction to be fearsome. He had no legal right to resort to threats. He was without authority to injure anyone. The crowd had done nothing to warrant being sent to jail. When he uttered the threat, Garfield was without probable cause to arrest the recreation aide, nor had he seen "the guy with the baseball bat" take a swipe at the aide. Garfield had made a phony bluff, and if any person there challenged it, if anyone refused to "get along with each other" despite the command to do so, either Garfield would have to back down from his threat or "hum" them in by resorting to some wobbly legal basis for arrest — refusing to identify oneself or resisting arrest (policemen called these the "chickenshit sections"). Or he might bend the truth a little, doctoring his version of what happened to justify an arrest.

Not having a lawful basis for arrest was just one aspect of a larger measure of phoniness. The fact was, the crowd was not convinced that Garfield had the fortitude to execute his threat. He had made a threat, but he had no reputation among the onlookers for ever having mixed it. The threat lacked personal authority (and the public was terribly perceptive in detecting those little hesitations and awkwardnesses which betrayed a policeman's bluff). So long as the crowd felt skeptical about Garfield's firmness, the exasperated brother was left in a position where he had to defy the policeman. The crowd expected him to live up to his responsibility to avenge his sister and his family. If this crowd felt he had not behaved sufficiently aggressively in accordance with the neighborhood law of revenge, he would be dishonored.

The short of the matter was that Garfield was not a sufficiently respected policeman to exonerate the brother from criticism for obeying a cop. In the crowd's mind, a man dishonored himself if he retreated before the ultimatum of an unworthy adversary. The blue uniform, the badge, the gun provided a presumption of respectability, but in the 1970s it was a presumption rebuttable by evidence of worthlessness or incompetence. (1977, pp. 104-05)

Unfortunately, the crowd's definition of being a "worthy adversary" in these situations is not necessarily congruent with the mandates of law.

Buckner (1967) also grappled with the tension between law (a societal control) and custom (a group control), arguing that custom has greater significance in street situations. Thus Buckner observes that the police officer often resolves the tension as to whether he should "act as a man or as a legal officer" in favor of the former — by imposing "informal control rather than invoking the legal process" (p. 450). He does so because "he is expected to deal with many situations which are violations of custom or morality but not of law" and because these public expectations, far more than "any formally granted legal mandate," largely control the police (pp. 2, 444-50).

It is widely accepted that the conception of the police as serving a ministerial function in enforcing the law is grossly inadequate (see Bittner 1967; Davis 1969; Goldstein 1977). What Muir and Buckner help us to do is to understand more clearly the complex relationship between the police and public and the role that law plays in that relationship.

Administrative Accountability

Understanding another concept, administrative accountability, will further instruct our conclusions regarding the appropriate ways in which to structure the review of police performance.

In his study of police accountability, Perez (1978) argues that policemen are administrators and thus subject to administrative accountability, which has features of both judicial accountability and legislative accountability. Like the judge, who is accountable to the principles of law as embodied in statutes, prior judicial decisions, and ultimately the Constitution, "the administrator must be held accountable to formal legal standards of competence." But, like the legislator, who is accountable to the wishes of the populace, "the administrator must react to his constituency," explains Perez. "He must consider the will of those citizens whom he contacts." In seeking to be responsive to public sentiment, administrators "may often be put in a position where they feel compelled to act illegally (or at least non-legally) in order to accomplish their functions," Perez asserts. Perez summarizes his analysis in a way that poses the issue clearly for us: "The problem of administrative accountability then becomes one of allowing the administrator freedom of action, while making sure that he does not abuse that leeway" (pp. 8-10).

INCIDENCE OF COMPLAINTS ABOUT POLICE CONDUCT

Table 1, drawn from Perez (1978), provides an indication of the incidence of complaints filed against police in four cities. One of these cities, Berkeley, experienced roughly one complaint for every officer. A university community, Berkeley enjoyed substantial citizen concern and participation in governmental affairs *and* it had a civilian review board, created by referendum in April 1973. The tumultuous and politically heated campaign for the review agency in Berkeley may well have created a sensitivity to police "misconduct" that accounts for the unusually high number of complaints against police.

Perez (1978, pp. xxvii–xxx) provides a breakdown of complaints by type, which will prove helpful in considering the available avenues for reviewing police activity. Aggregating across the five cities that he studied in depth, he found that the largest category of complaints (35 percent of all) was allegations that the police failed to take action in a situation in which it was required or appropriate. Brutality complaints were the next most frequent (25 percent), followed by complaints concerning illegal arrests (15 percent).

An earlier study suggests a somewhat different picture. Sampling citizens in 15 cities for the National Advisory Commission on Civil Disorders, Campbell and Schuman (1969, table IV) found that 22 percent of all black and 6 percent of all white interviewees reported being frisked or searched without (in their opinion) good reason, 20 percent of all blacks and 9 percent of all whites said police had been disrespectful or insulting to them in language or behavior, and 7 percent of the blacks and 2 percent of the whites indicated that they had been roughed up by police at some time. Yet another perspective comes from Reiss's (1971, p. 142) seminal study of 5,012 police-citizen interactions (involving 13,939 citizens) in the 1963–66 period. He found police

TABLE 1.   Ratio of Complaints to Number of Officers, 1976

City	Population	Size of Police Dept.	Number of Complaints	Ratio of Complaints/ Officers
Kansas City	500,000	1,200	623	.52 : 1
Oakland	340,000	650	335	.52 : 1
Berkeley	120,000	240	229	.95 : 1
Chicago	3,500,000	13,363	6,898	.52 : 1

Note: The numbers from all cities except Chicago are based on Perez (1978). The Chicago figures are drawn from Chicago Police Department (1976) and include nonexcessive force complaints that were forwarded by the police department's Office of Professional Standards to its Internal Affairs Division. Taken together, these Chicago complaints are roughly comparable in type to the citizen complaint experience of the other cities.

openly ridiculing or belittling only 5 percent of the citizens and behaving brusquely or in an authoritarian manner in another 5 percent of the interactions. Reiss's observers discerned excessive use of force in only 3 out of every 1,000 encounters. Police were found to treat citizens in an uncivil manner in 13 percent of all encounters and in a "personal" manner 15 percent of the time, whereas citizens treated police incivilly in only 8 percent of the interactions. All the openly hostile or provocative conduct by police was directed toward citizens whom the police viewed as offenders, but the police did act toward other citizens in ways that Reiss's observers characterized as personal, demeaning, authoritarian, or threatening. Reiss further reports that while more than three-fourths of all white police officers made prejudiced statements about blacks, the police did not treat blacks with incivility in actual encounters any more frequently than they treated whites in that manner (pp. 144–48).

Reiss suggests that police use of excessive force depends more on the circumstances of the police-citizen encounter than on racial prejudice. Suspects or charged offenders, young, lower-class males from any racial and ethnic group, persons in police-controlled settings or situations devoid of witnesses who could support the citizens' complaints, and individuals who defied the officers' authority were the most likely victims of excessive force. The latter element—citizen failure to defer to police authority—appears to be a particularly significant factor (pp. 147–50).

INSTITUTIONS FOR THE REVIEW OF COMPLAINTS AGAINST THE POLICE

External Social Institutions

Complaints about police conduct are reviewed from time to time by three social institutions: prosecutors, judges, and the news media. Each in its own way can be very effective, but each has substantial limitations that affect its impact.

Prosecutors, who have access to subpoena power and grand juries and often command their own investigators, have all the necessary tools for fact finding. Police conduct comes to prosecutorial attention in essentially two ways. By far the most frequent is prosecutorial review of cases in which the police have charged, or wish to charge, a person with a crime. But while our crowded criminal court dockets attest to the frequency of such prosecutorial contact with police, these cases reflect only a small portion of total police activity. Most of the interactions between police and citizens involve officers providing various services to citizens or general order-maintenance activity that does not result in criminal charges being filed. A small percentage of these interactions comes to prosecutorial attention, either on the state or the federal level, via citizen complaints. But even in these circumstances there are limitations on the prosecutorial response. Often the incident is not of a type or magnitude that makes criminal charges an appropriate redress. And even if it is, prosecutors do not lightly bring charges against police officers because they rely on police cooperation in a wide variety of ways. An irate police rank and file can and often will find effective means for retaliating against a prosecutor considered overly active in the area of police misconduct investigations.

Although judges may be somewhat less vulnerable than prosecutors to police retaliation, they are not totally insulated from its effects. Moreover, the judiciary sees an even narrower range of police activity than do prosecutors. And they have fewer resources with which to exercise an ongoing oversight of police practices. Unlike their practice in prisoner abuse cases, courts have almost totally abstained from using receivership or similar legal authority to intervene in the day-to-day operational affairs of the police.[1]

Civil suits in state and especially federal courts provide opportunities to review and redress police misconduct that have grown increasingly significant during the past 15 years (see Schmidt's chapter). Federal civil rights suits, by extending liability to the superiors of the officers who have been directly involved in the questioned activity, have made a substantial impact on policing. However, even these suits share some of the limitations of litigation-based remedies discussed above. They are not particularly well tailored either for providing ongoing oversight of police practices or for redressing low-level but nevertheless alienating police misconduct. They also require private funding for initiation.

From time to time in many cities the news media have been effective in precipitating changes in complaint review systems by highlighting actual or apparent deficiencies in these systems, but this effectiveness is limited by the internal dynamics of the news trade. First, it is difficult for the media to provide sustained attention to the issue because it becomes stale and thus loses reader/viewer/listener appeal. Further, at some point, the resources used to investigate the issue must be transferred to other matters simply by virtue of the need to cover more recent events and issues. Second, the news is also a competitive business. If at some point in continuing coverage of an issue such as police misconduct, a particular paper or TV or radio station is perceived by the police to be "out to get them," the police department may retaliate by playing favorites among the media when it comes to cooperating on important day-to-day stories. Thus, again, potential institutional constraints are limited in effectiveness because of their interdependency with the police.

Internal Administrative Review

Whereas all three of these external social institutions are limited, the most systematic and pervasive review of police conduct is provided by the police administrative structure, which includes routine supervisory and managerial review as well as specific incident investigations initiated, among other ways, on the basis of citizen complaints. A 1977 survey indicated that more than 80 percent of the police departments in the United States centralize the response to citizen complaints in a specialized unit. With a few notable exceptions these units are staffed by sworn police officers and report to senior police management (Cancilla 1977, p. 56). The adequacy of these arrangements has been the subject of chronic and intermittently acute controversy (for example, in Chicago in 1973 and in Miami in 1979), the core of which concerns the intense personal and organizational pressures, acknowledged by all parties, to protect the accused officer.

The police have, for the most part, weathered these controversies and repulsed attempts to wrest control of the administrative review process from their hands and vest it in external agencies. They have argued that inexperienced, politicized review of police conduct would seriously jeopardize public safety by creating an overly cautious police department more concerned with avoiding complaints than with protecting the public. The most notable success of the street police officers and their union in resisting outside review came in 1966 when the New York City administration attempted to establish a civilian review board. Arguing, among other things, that such a board would result in the "handcuffing" of police and reduce their ability to control crime, the police won an overwhelming defeat of the proposal in a citywide referendum (see Bouza's chapter).

MODEL COMPLAINT REVIEW STRUCTURES

A variety of complaint review structures have been proposed, many of which attempt to define a middle ground in the controversy described above. These proposals can be organized into three models: civilian review, civilian input, and civilian monitor (Kerstetter 1970).

The strongest form of the civilian review model vests authority to investigate, adjudicate, and recommend punishment in the external agency. The more common structure provides for the external agency to provide advisory opinions to the police chief.

The civilian input model places only the complaint reception and investigative functions with a civilian agency. That body acts as an independent source of facts for the police chief executive. As with the civilian review model, numerous variations are possible. Chicago has adopted a structure that employs civilian staff for complaint reception and investigation but places them within the police organization, reporting directly to the superintendent of police. In Chicago, the adjudication and discipline functions are discharged by sworn officers.

The civilian monitor model leaves the investigation, adjudication, and discipline functions within the police department but provides external civilian review safeguards. The external review directs its attention not so much to the officer's conduct as to the question of how well the police department discharged its responsibilities to provide an adequate and unbiased investigation and hearing of the citizen's complaint, an appropriate response to the citizen, and discipline of the officer when required. The monitor model is based on the Scandinavian concept of the ombudsman, which is oriented toward systemic issues and negotiation and conciliation between citizens and public officials.

Civilian Review Model

Of the three models, the most controversial is civilian review, which has been tried in Washington, D.C. in 1948, Philadelphia in 1958, Rochester (N.Y.) in 1963, New York City in 1966, and Berkeley (Calif.) in 1972. The fundamental argument against this model, adverted to earlier, is that review by people without police experience would cause morale and performance problems among the police, who would become so concerned about possible disciplinary action that they would be ineffective in their assigned duties.

The experience of Berkeley with civilian review was examined by Perez (1978), whose study encompassed the police misconduct review systems in six jurisdictions. These systems ranged in structure and degree of citizen involvement from decentralized police internal review to external civilian review. Perez collected data on the number and types of complaints and dispositions and used interviews with officers and surveys of citizen complainants (except in Chicago) to determine police and public attitudes toward their own review system. Created in 1973, the Berkeley Police Review Commission (PRC) investigates (through an independent civilian investigative capacity) and holds hearings on civilian complaints against police. It also monitors the overall operation of the police department as reflected in its policies and practices. The PRC's findings are made in the form of advisory recommendations to the city manager. The Berkeley Police Department, considered to be one of the most progressive in the nation, maintains its own internal affairs system so that citizens have the option to pursue redress of their grievance using either avenue. The relationship between the police department and the PRC, particularly in the early years, was tense and full of conflict, with each suing the other over issues of practice and authority (Perez 1978, pp. 264–75). Of the six systems studied, reports Perez, the PRC received the most favorable citizen evaluation in terms of its objectivity, thoroughness, and fairness (see Table 2).

Significantly, this survey disclosed that with all systems, except the PRC, there is a high correlation between the outcome of the review and citizen satisfaction with the integrity of the system (see Tables 4–9). While the number of cases involved in these surveys is so low that these results must be inter-

TABLE 2. Complainant Satisfaction with Investigation

Agency	Impartial	Thorough (very or fairly)	Fair (completely or mostly)
San Jose ombudsman	21.6%	28.1%	13.6%
Kansas City*	17.9	21.9	15.7
Berkeley Police Review Commission	64.9	85.7	73.3
Berkeley Police Department†	29.4	47.0	35.3
Oakland Police Department†	9.5	23.1	11.5
Contra Costa Sheriff's Office	31.8	21.7	39.1

These data, provided by Perez (1978), are based on surveys he conducted as part of his dissertation research but are not contained in this form in his dissertation.

*Kansas City's is one of the systems Perez calls "hybrid review systems" in that they represent a combination of police and citizen involvement in the review process.

†The Berkeley and Oakland police departments have centralized all police units that handle citizen complaints.

preted with great caution, it is striking that the PRC is the only review system to retain a substantial level of satisfaction among citizens whose complaints were not found to be justified.

Despite the almost universal opposition by police officers to the notion of civilian review, the evidence does not suggest that these agencies are unduly harsh in their review of police conduct. The experience in Philadelphia, New York, and Berkeley suggests that civilian review is less likely than police internal review to find officers guilty of misconduct and is more lenient in its disciplinary recommendations when it does find them guilty (Perez 1978, pp. 278–79; see also Hudson 1972). Hudson provides the data in Table 3 on the experience of the Philadelphia Police Advisory Board during the later 1950s and 1960s. The PAB was a civilian board; the Police Board of Inquiry (PBI) was the department review mechanism. Perez reports that a study by the California Peace Officer's Association found that "the Berkeley Police Review Commission has assigned blame in a far lower percentage of citizen charges against the police than has the Berkeley Police Department's internal complaint mechanism" (1978, p. 25).

Drawing on his study of Berkeley's PRC, Perez attributes relative leniency of the civilian review agencies to problems that the reviewers have in obtaining access to information, the relatively substantial procedural safeguards the civilian system offers to the accused officer, and civilian investigators' generally poor understanding of police subcultural norms and police processes (pp. 279–81). On balance, it appears that the Berkeley civilian review system may enhance procedural fairness for the officers at the cost of some loss in substantive fairness for citizens. Nevertheless, this model appears to enjoy great credibility with the community.

One police objection to civilian review has been borne out by the experience in Berkeley, where the PRC has tended to confound its complaint review and policy review functions, with the result that the disposition of individual complaints is sometimes drawn into a conflict about policy in inappropriate ways (p. 298). The concern that a civilian review system would prove to be irresistibly tempting for individuals with larger political agendas was also given credence by the Berkeley experience. Perez reports:

> There is a danger that civilian systems may be captured by vociferous, radical elements of the community. Indeed, over time some individuals in the Berkeley community have utilized Board of Inquiry hearings and policy hearings as platforms to expose political rhetoric aimed at the police department. It is apparent from monitoring such hearings that a very small, vocal segment of the Berkeley community is interested and involved in the "open" and "public" processes of the Commission. The danger that the PRC may be captured by such vociferous minorities is even greater given the Commission's [tendency to use] citizen "volunteers" from the audience when formulating panels to look into police procedures. (p. 295)

TABLE 3. PAB and PBI Hearing Recommendations

| | | PBI (1960–68) | |
| | PAB* | Civilian | Noncivilian |
Recommendations	(1958–68)	Complaints	Complaints
Suspensions	14%	52%	76%
Dismissals	1	14	5
Reprimands	16	6	9
Other negative action	6	†	†
Other action (letter of apology, expungement of record, etc.)	20	†	†
Not guilty	†	28	10
No recommendation	40	†	†
Not ascertained	3	—	—
Totals: %	100	100	100
N	145	458	2214

*Includes only principal complainants to eliminate double counting on recommendations.
†No comparable category.
Source: Hudson (1972, pp. 427–33).

Despite these problems, the often-heard prediction that civilian review would cause poor morale and hamper aggressive policing does not appear to have been fulfilled in Berkeley, based on Perez's interviews with rank-and-file police officers (p. 299). This finding confirms the conclusions of the Lohman and Misner study (1966, p. 262) in Philadelphia. By contrast, the police administrators in Berkeley have been more affected than street officers by the abuses that Perez found. The administrators feel the most direct encroachment on their prerogatives by the PRC stems from its policy review function, which challenges an expertise they have spent a career developing. Unless done with great sensitivity, outside review of policy may be perceived as insulting the police executives' intelligence, competence, and integrity. Moreover, even if well motivated, the individuals who become involved in police policymaking in this way enjoy the luxury of not being accountable for the consequences of their decisions. And civilian involvement in this manner raises the specter of the police becoming even more of a political football.

Further, the civilian review model is arguably less effective than internal review in deterring police misconduct, for reasons beyond any weakness in the investigations. First, for a variety of cultural, social, and experiential reasons police across the country tend to develop a marked sense of group identity and cohesion. As a result, peer pressure and socialization processes are particularly potent factors in behavior control. By contrast, the civilian review process is a weak socialization device because it creates a we-they dichotomy between the reviewers and the reviewed. By contrast, police internal review, if it avoids the unscrupulous and overzealous tactics to which it is prone, can gain legitimacy, and thereby effectiveness, as peer review. Second, removing the unpleasant responsibility for deterring and punishing misconduct from the police supervisory and administrative staff often has the result of encouraging them to abdicate all responsibility for controlling misconduct. The attitude becomes "leave it to them" — "them" being the civilian review system or a headquarters unit or whoever has stepped in. Allowing police managers to withdraw from the fray means at least the loss of their effective, nonprocedurally encumbered techniques of inquiry and disposition in the fight against police malpractice. Often it also means that first-line and more senior supervisors end up aligning with their nominal subordinates in a conspiracy to resist the resented "others." The result is precisely the problems that Perez reports with the Berkeley PRC: difficulty in obtaining the necessary information and the diminished effectiveness of a more judicialized system.

The strongest argument for the civilian review concept is its potential enhancement of the legitimacy of the review process and, indeed, the legitimacy of the police themselves in the eyes of the community. Even in the absence of evidence of past police cover-ups, a few moments of honest introspection makes clear the basis for concern about the integrity of an internal review process totally hidden from outside scrutiny. Clearly, what is needed is a system to provide credible reassurance that the substantial discretion inherent in any review process is being appropriately exercised. The question is whether we can meet that need without the losses in substantive justice and behavior control that the civilian review model apparently imposes.

Civilian Input Model

While it is a slight variation on the theme, the Chicago Office of Professional Standards (OPS) is, nevertheless, the clearest example of the civilian input model. The variation is that the OPS, while staffed by nonsworn personnel, is formally a part of the Chicago Police Department instead of an external agency. The OPS handles all complaints of excessive force, deadly and nondeadly, made by citizens against police officers. A parallel Internal Affairs Division (IAD), staffed by police officers, investigates all other allegations. Perez reports that street police officers view the OPS as more objective, fairer, and more lenient (its sustention rate is 7.5 percent) than the IAD, believing that IAD investigators come to assume that the accused officer is guilty of some sort of misconduct even if not of the particular allegation. Further, street officers in Chicago do not argue that OPS investigators, because they are civilians, fail to understand the policeman's role and lack a sense of the reality of police work. Contrary to expectations, Perez observes, "the civilian investigators of OPS identify directly with the police organization. They are defensive of policemen and the organization in a way that IA people never are. OPS civilians give great deference to police officers and are extremely cynical about complainants" (1978, pp. 343, 345). While rank-and-file officers in Chicago have accepted civilian participation in the review process, important parts of the local academic and political communities do not consider the OPS to be genuinely independent of the police department. Indeed, they claim it is a sham that fools the public into trusting internal review systems (pp. 346, 352–53, 412).

Kansas City employs another variation of the civilian input model. There the Office of Citizen Complaints (OCC) serves as a central clearinghouse for all citizens' complaints, whether made directly to the OCC or to the police department. The OCC reviews the complaint and, if it appears to be both nonfrivolous and not amenable to informal resolution, assigns it to the police department's internal affairs unit for investigation. After this investigation, the complete file is returned to the OCC for review. Perez characterized these files as the most thorough and complete of those he examined in the course of his study, and he reported that the OCC is pleased with the quality of the investigations. The OCC review is conducted by civilian analysts, who may require that additional work be done by police investigators. When these analysts are satisfied with the investigation they prepare a report recommending a disposition and giving supporting reasons, which is then reviewed by the OCC director. If he agrees with the proposal, it is forwarded to the chief of police. The police supervisory staff is then given an opportunity to review the report and recommend disciplinary action. Perez reports (pp. 319–24) that the chief of police has rarely disagreed with the OCC report. The OCC system has been accepted by the street police officers in Kansas City, but a survey of citizens found that a majority of the respondents questioned the thoroughness, fairness, and objectivity of the review process (see Table 2). One problem that undermines the credibility of the Kansas City system is that because the OCC does no direct investigation, the possibility of a police cover-up still exists.

An additional point is worth making here about the consequences of adopting either the civilian review or civilian input model. Both models entail the establishment of a separate agency. An organization of almost any size will tend to take on a life of its own in which serving the needs of the organization's members begins to compete in importance with serving the needs of its ostensible clients.

Civilian Monitor Model

Of the three models, the most widely acclaimed is the civilian monitor. Based on the Scandinavian ombudsman concept, it has achieved both theoretical and practical acceptance nationally and worldwide (see Gellhorn 1966, 1967; Carden 1983a, 1983b). The essence of the ombudsman concept is the capacity to provide an ongoing, objective evaluation of the delivery of government services with a specific focus on mediating disputes between citizens complaining about government services and the agency that provided those services.[2]

The ombudsman can play this role effectively only if the office and its incumbent have formal and informal authority. Formal powers are required to obtain the information necessary for an adequate review of the complaint. Traditionally lacking the authority to order an administrator to take any particular action, however, the ombudsman also needs substantial informal authority, based on an earned reputation for fairness and good judgment, which will give his findings and recommendations credibility with the agency under review, with the relevant administrator's peers and superiors, and with the public at large.

While the San Jose ombudsman's office was created in 1971 as a result of community pressure for external review of police conduct, the agency, in accordance with the original Scandivanian model, reviews complaints about all municipal government agencies. The office is staffed by civilian investigators. All complaints the ombudsman receives about police officers are investigated by both the ombudsman's investigators and the internal affairs unit of the San Jose Police Department. The police department also accepts complaints about police conduct; in these instances the ombudsman's office does not conduct its own investigation but does monitor the department's internal investigation. Thus the ombudsman's office investigates roughly half of the citizen complaints filed in San Jose (Perez 1978, pp. 367–71).

This ombudsman-civilian monitor system remedies the defect in the Kansas City civilian input approach created by the latter's lack of any direct investigative activity to safeguard against cover-ups. But it does so in a costly and inefficient way. To investigate fully all complaints it receives when they are also being investigated by the police department is unnecessary – a contention reinforced by the fact that the parallel investigations reach the same conclusions in 95 percent of the cases (p. 375). The integrity of the police department's investigative process can be ensured more effectively and efficiently by employing any one of a variety of alternative case selection methods for parallel investigations or reinvestigations.

The San Jose ombudsman has made only limited use of the traditional capacity of ombudsmen to mediate complaints. A substantial portion of citizen complaints against police result from the citizens' lack of information or understanding about the legitimate basis of the police action.[3] Providing this information or perspective in an appropriate, nonhostile manner and setting can satisfactorily resolve many of these complaints – an accomplishment of substantial importance.

Line police officers in San Jose appear to accept the ombudsman system and are not unduly concerned about its functioning, but the police administration has resisted the ombudsman's attempts to obtain departmental information, and the city council has had to impose directives ordering police cooperation (Perez 1978, pp. 377–78). Moreover, despite its formal independence of the police department, the ombudsman in San Jose has not overcome the problem of community skepticism about the legitimacy of its review system. Perez reports: "The San Jose respondents to our questionnaire indicate a lack of faith in the thoroughness, objectivity, and fairness of this system" (p. 382; see also Table 2). Three factors may contribute to such failures. First, sometimes the ombudsman is seen as part of the government even though it is external to the police. Second, the ombudsman depends heavily on the status of the office and its incumbent, especially in the United States, where the concept does not have an extensive history. Third, when, as in San Jose, the significant mediation function is not fully employed, the agency may be perceived as ineffective.

Such inadequacies feed the underlying problem that, for most review systems (see Tables 4 through 9), complainant satisfaction with the process is apparently highly correlated with the outcome of the complaint. A system limited to investigating complaints – and, in the vast majority of the cases, concluding that the officers were technically correct in their behavior – misses

TABLE 4. Comparison of Outcome of Complaint with Citizen Satisfaction in San Jose

	Satisfied with Final Decision	Not Sure	Dissatisfied with Final Decision
Citizen complaint found to be justified	80% (4)	—	20% (1)
Citizen complaint found to be not justified	0 (0)	—	100% (17)

Numbers in parentheses indicate number of cases.
Source: Perez (1978).

TABLE 5. Comparison of Outcome of Complaint with Citizen Satisfaction in Kansas City

	Satisfied with Final Decision	Not Sure	Dissatisfied with Final Decision
Citizen complaint found to be justified	50% (1)	—	50% (1)
Citizen complaint found to be not justified	—	5.9% (1)	94.1% (16)

Numbers in parentheses indicate number of cases.
Source: Perez (1978).

TABLE 6. Comparison of Outcome of Complaint with Citizen Satisfaction in Berkeley (Police Department Internal Review)

	Satisfied with Final Decision	Not Sure	Dissatisfied with Final Decision
Citizen complaint found to be justified	66.7% (4)	16.7% (1)	16.7% (1)
Citizen complaint found to be not justified	—	—	100% (1)

Numbers in parentheses indicate number of cases.
Source: Perez (1978).

TABLE 7.   Comparison of Outcome of Complaint with Citizen Satisfaction in Berkeley (Berkeley Police Review Commission)

	Satisfied with Final Decision	Not Sure	Dissatisfied with Final Decision
Citizen complaint found to be justified	60% (3)	–	40% (2)
Citizen complaint found to be not justified	66.7% (4)	16.7% (1)	16.7% (1)

Numbers in parentheses indicate number of cases.
Source: Perez (1978).

TABLE 8.   Comparison of Outcome of Complaint with Citizen Satisfaction in Oakland

	Satisfied with Final Decision	Not Sure	Dissatisfied with Final Decision
Citizen complaint found to be justified	60% (3)	20% (1)	20% (1)
Citizen complaint found to be not justified	–	6.7% (1)	93.3% (14)

Numbers in parentheses indicate number of cases.
Source: Perez (1978).

TABLE 9.   Comparison of Outcome of Complaint with Citizen Satisfaction in Contra Costa (Sheriff's Office)

	Satisfied with Final Decision	Not Sure	Dissatisfied with Final Decision
Citizen complaint found to be justified	100% (4)	–	–
Citizen complaint found to be not justified	–	–	100% (7)

Numbers in parentheses indicate number of cases.
Source: Perez (1978).

important opportunities to show citizens respect by responding to their needs for information, perspective, compensation (which may be justified even if the officer was not wrong), and an apology for being inconvenienced by legitimate police activity. An analogy can be drawn here from a much more violent citizen complaint situation—terrorist demands in hostage situations. We have learned that what the complainant demands in these situations is often different from what he needs and will satisfy him (Knutson 1980). It is the appropriate and successful use of the opportunity that this difference affords that is one cornerstone of an effective complaint review system.

The Dade County (Florida) Independent Review Panel (IRP), also patterned after the ombudsman or monitor model, has placed considerable emphasis on its conciliation and mediation powers with substantial success. The IRP has jurisdiction to receive and investigate complaints against any county employee or agency and to issue advisory findings as a result of its inquiries. The IRP decided that it would defer any action on a complaint until the agency whose action was complained of completed its own review (provided that that was accomplished in a timely manner). Thus the IRP views itself primarily as a "watchdog agency" or "oversight appeals" board but retains authority to conduct fact-finding investigations when appropriate. The IRP, in the ombudsman tradition, also addresses systemic problems that transcend the facts of particular complaints. Created in early 1980, the IRP during its first three years of operation has received and considered more than 500 complaints, 35 percent of them related to allegations of police misconduct (see, generally, Dade-Miami Criminal Justice Council 1981; Metropolitan Dade County Independent Review Panel 1983). At the end of the IRP's first year of operation, an outside evaluation concluded:

> [T]he Independent Review Panel has developed effective working relationships with almost every individual and/or organization with which the Panel, its members and its staff have been involved. It is through these relationships that this group of appointed, community organizational representative volunteers have been able to establish a sound and substantial citizen complaint/grievance review process. . . . (Dade-Miami Criminal Justice Council 1981, p. 54)

As evidence of continuing success, at the end of three years the county implemented the recommendation of the part-time executive director, who wished to return to the private practice of law, to convert to a full-time executive directorship.

A follow-up evaluation was conducted in September 1983 (Metropolitan Dade County Independent Review Panel 1983) based on interviews with key Dade County officials, including the county manager, county mayor, county prosecutor, director of the county public safety (police) department, head of the police union, senior representatives of the county community relations board, and IRP members and staff. With varying emphases, all the interviewees identified as chief functions of the IRP responding to community concerns about alleged police misconduct and ensuring the integrity of the public safety department's internal review process. They all agreed, moreover, that the IRP has been successful both in enhancing the credibility of governmental misconduct review processes and in improving the internal investigations of the public safety department.

Based on her observations of the nature and intensity of public dialogue, the state's attorney (county prosecutor) believed that the IRP had improved the credibility of the internal review process both among criminal justice officials and with the general community. The county mayor agreed with this assessment and added that he believed the IRP had been accepted by the police as well because he gets few complaints about it from either the police or the community. The county manager, who would of necessity become directly involved if the relationship between the IRP and the various county agencies became acrimonious, sees the IRP as providing a significant safety valve for community tensions and at the same time working productively with the police and other county agencies.

The director of the Dade County Department of Public Safety indicated that while initially he had reservations about civilian participation in the review process, he was confident at the time, based on his prior experience as commanding officer of the department's internal affairs unit, that outside scrutiny would not disclose major shortcomings. He credited his acquiescence in the creation of the IRP to a serious credibility crisis in 1979–80, in which even those parts of the community usually supportive of the public safety department were questioning its capacity to police itself. The IRP experience, having failed to discover systemic cover-ups, has borne out the director's confidence in his agency. The IRP has, however, contributed substantively to the improvement of the department's handling of complaints by identifying systemic problems and by virtue of the salutary effect on the department's internal investigators of knowing their work would be reviewed by outsiders.

The director, who by all accounts is an able, responsive, and responsible administrator, believes that the existence of the IRP and its interaction with the department have markedly improved the credibility in the community of the government's review of complaints. By being even-handed and fair, the IRP has also achieved at least grudging acceptance from some of the street police officers who were most suspicious of it.

The police union president relates essentially the same history, although his conclusions and recommendations for the future differ. He acknowledges that at the time the IRP was created it helped both in repairing a serious problem of community lack of confidence in the department of public safety and in improving that department's handling of citizens' complaints. However, he argues that, having accomplished these goals and in effect validating the integrity of the internal review process, the IRP is now superfluous because civil and criminal legal remedies at both state and federal levels and the media provide adequate safeguards that the department will continue to provide an appropriate review process. None of the other interviewees shared this view, and in expressing it the union president acknowledged that the IRP's abolition is politically unlikely. He also raised the troublesome issue of low-level complaints that he believes receive undue attention, being reviewed first by the public safety department and then again by the IRP. Although the IRP attempts to minimize this problem by screening out these cases early on, nevertheless they draw on its time and attention and on police resources. The possibility of articulating a *de minimis* standard or a more stringent screening process appears to deserve consideration.

On the other end of the opinion spectrum is the Dade County Community Relations Board, a public agency mandated to provide communication links with the county's various minority communities. Over the years it has been one of the most vigorous proponents of civilian review of police conduct. In the view of two senior representatives of the board whom I interviewed in September 1983, the minority communities' general knowledge of the IRP's existence, even without any detailed information about its operation, has provided important reassurances of the public safety department's fairness.

Nevertheless, these interviewees expressed some dissatisfaction with the current authority and practices of the IRP, citing a number of defects: the lack of subpoena power (although as a practical matter most police officers have been voluntarily cooperating); a jurisdiction limited to county agencies instead of covering all municipal agencies located in the county (seen less as a flaw in the current structure than as a failure to carry the reform to its logical conclusion); the scheduling of IRP meetings during weekdays instead of evening hours, when many more working people could participate; undue delay in investigations—and in their calming effect on community concern about incidents—resulting from the IRP's practice of deferring its investigation until after the subject agency's own internal inquiry has been completed; and failure to provide an adequate mechanism for community participation in planning and reviewing police activities. What is envisioned by this last criticism goes beyond the IRP's review of individual allegations of misconduct and even beyond its examinations of systemic problems and recommendations for their alleviation. Instead, the extensive police-community interaction envisioned by this criticism is of the sort that has occurred at times under the team policing concept, which entails regularly scheduled meetings between the officers policing a particular area and the residents of that area (see Brown's chapter and Sherman, Milton, and Kelly 1973).

The evaluation identified other issues and themes that are relevant to our inquiry. The IRP, as currently structured, depends significantly on the in-

formal personal authority of the executive director and the voluntary cooperation of the county director of public safety. The competence and charisma
of the first executive director and his staff created a credibility that has permitted this structure to function well. Key figures have been willing to grant
the IRP informal authority because of these personal attributes and, several
interviews appeared to suggest, because they perceived that they could withdraw that authority if an executive director did not appear to be deserving
of it. The structure, while successful in this context, is tenuous, and some
knowledgeable observers are concerned about the future of the agency if, for
example, a less cooperative director was appointed to head the department
of public safety.

The state's attorney identified these potential difficulties in the current
structure of the IRP and also indicated that an important underlying issue
was the limitations that had been placed on the public safety director's authority to direct and discipline the department. Some of these limitations arose
from court decisions and legislative enactments and others from union activities. These comments underline the need to ensure that the chief executive
of the public safety department has adequate authority to administer effectively, which complicates the already delicate task of striking the proper balance in the complaint review mechanism.

We turn now to an examination of those difficulties.

PROBLEMS INHERENT IN THE REVIEW
OF POLICE CONDUCT COMPLAINTS

Four Dilemmas

In my view, an adequate system for the review of police conduct will need
to resolve four key dilemmas: the inability to articulate objective standards
for police conduct, the inherent lack of credibility of internal review, the frequent inaccuracy of citizen perceptions regarding the fairness of the review
process, and the apparent costs of external review for substantive fairness.

The first consists of the problems inherent in rendering judgments about
the activity of police understood as administrators whose defining function
is the situationally appropriate distribution of coercive force. I have explored
the ambiguities inherent in the administrator's role: the tension between
judicial responsibility to adhere to the law and the legislative responsibility
to act in ways that are responsive to the needs of his or her constituency. This
balance must be struck by all governmental administrators. The task becomes
substantially more complex when the administrator is asked to assume responsibility for the distribution of coercive force. In that context he or she must
struggle particularly with the paradox of face and in doing so must respond
to the dictates of the secondary control system (custom and practice), which

at times are inconsistent with the simplicities of the law. In these situations, among other dilemmas, what Klockars (1980, p. 33) calls the "Dirty Harry" problem emerges: the dilemma of using bad means for good ends as against allowing injustice to prevail. These decisions must be made in the context in which the use of force against the officer, including but not only deadly force, is an ever present potential.

Bittner's definition of the police function, with which I began, suggests the appropriateness of peer review when it speaks of "the dictates of an intuitive grasp of situational exigencies." My discussion about the difficulties of defining appropriate standards against which to measure administrative discretion adds further support. If we have a situation in which intuition is an important cognitive tool and in which standards are shifting and hard to define, the judgment of peers who have experienced similar situations seems the most reliable guide.

Two general social organization considerations bolster this view. A wealth of both theory and experience suggests that organizational effectiveness requires that the managerial hierarchy control the disciplinary processes. Without this control, the motivational structure of the organization is fragmented, and employees begin responding to different messages in ways that undermine accountability at all levels of the organization. For example, Edward M. Davis, a former police chief, has stated:

> The right to discipline carries with it the power to control the conduct, action and attitudes of the employees of an organization. When the right to discipline is vested with management, management has the essential tool with which to attain the desired behavior from employees . . . when employees are subject to disciplinary action from outside the organization, a fundamental rule of organization has been breached and the employee becomes confused, diffident and inefficient. (Berkely 1969, p. 146)

See also Gerth and Mills (1948).

Another consideration is the efficacy of the socialization process in behavior modification. This is particularly true of peer pressure in a police organization. While peer pressure in these circumstances is certainly a two-edged sword,[4] to the extent that we wish to mobilize it in the interest of encouraging a higher quality of police performance that will be best accomplished by using the peer review of an internal system (Kerstetter 1979). Placing the review external to the agency inevitably creates a "we-they" polarization that solidifies peer support against the review function. These arguments, taken together with the comments below on the effect of judicialization of the review process, represent a strong case for an internal review system.

The second problem (or element in the dilemma of review of police conduct) is that internal review, despite its potential superiority as suggested by these arguments, by the dictates of both common sense and experience is inherently incredible to its central audience: the citizens whose law the police enforce and order they maintain and on whose acquiescence in its claims of legitimacy the civilian police system is premised. Internal review has a great capacity for effective control of police conduct but suffers from the equally great potential of human frailty.

Related to this dilemma is the third difficulty: The fairness of the review process will be assessed by most citizens almost completely as a function of their satisfaction with the result in their particular case. Perez found this satisfaction pattern in all the systems he reviewed except the civilian review board in Berkeley. Thus, if we accept Perez's conclusion that "policemen act legally and properly in the vast majority of their interactions with citizens and a majority of alleged cases of abuse" (1978, pp. 24, 346, 352-53, 412), our options are severely constrained because citizen dissatisfaction with the system is virtually guaranteed by the predictable outcomes.

The final problem relates to the consequences of moving the review system to an external agency. Perez suggests that one of the reasons the civilian review system in Berkeley exonerated higher percentages of officers than did the police department's internal affairs unit was that it afforded accused officers greater procedural protections. This tendency is inevitable as a system moves from a broad administrative function to one that focuses on adjudication of factual guilt for the purpose of disciplinary action. If a generalized sense of procedural due process does not cause this, judicial review – whether under state civil service law or federal civil rights litigation – will require it. Included in this trend will be a tendency toward the establishment of a higher standard of proof. This tendency will exacerbate the current problem of the legitimately aggrieved citizen whose grievance is not redressed because the standard of proof required for disciplinary action cannot be met.

Administrative, as opposed to judicial, control of behavior is informal and therefore more effective both in inquiry and in capacity to tailor an appropriate disposition. It also has the advantage of being both continuous and ubiquitous. Thus the likely cost of external review pursued to gain enhanced community legitimacy is greater procedural protections for the officer with reduced substantive justice for the citizen. External review with its judicialization of the review process may create the basis for treating the few officers convicted more severely, but does that really meet the needs either of the individual citizen or of the community as a whole in its search for adequate and appropriate police protection?

Interested Parties and Their Legitimate Needs

The quest for a satisfactory resolution of these four dilemmas should be aided by identifying the interested parties and their respective legitimate needs with regard to a review system. The parties are the complainant and those either directly or derivatively associated with him, the accused police officer and those concerned about his situation, other public officials who have responsibilities in this area, and the general public.

The complainant has the right to expect that the review system will listen courteously to his complaint, consider seriously what attention it merits, and reach decisions concerning its processing that are neither arbitrary nor discriminatory. The formulation and publication of decision rules defining thresholds for various kinds of actions by the review system provide a mechanism that helps reduce both the fact and the appearance of arbitrary or discriminatory responses. At the same time decision rules afford some flexibility in responding to complaints ranging from the obviously frivolous to those that appear on their face to allow informal resolution to those that require the most careful criminal investigation.

If an investigation of the facts underlying the complaint is warranted, then the complainant deserves a fair, objective inquiry and some measure of reassurance that it was fair. Depending on the outcome of the investigation the citizen may be entitled to an explanation of any police action taken and why it was appropriate, an informal apology from the police officer or a formal one from the department, and/or compensation, even in cases where the officer acted reasonably (for example, where officers made a mistake because they had been given inaccurate information and the error caused a loss to the citizen).

Another party with an interest in the matter is that segment of the community of which the complainant is an identifiable representative. This group needs to be reassured that the governmental structure respects their claims as citizens and treats those claims as it would the grievances of other citizens. Moreover, the community as a whole needs to know that the police are operating in a proper way, neither abusing their authority nor being unduly hindered in the exercise of that authority by an overreaching review, whatever its motivation might be. The community at large needs to be assured that there are adequate mechanisms to handle, and redress when appropriate, citizen grievances. And the community's media need balanced, accurate information in order to play a responsible role in reassuring the public on these points.

What legitimate claims can the accused officer make of the review system? First, he has a right not to be harrassed by patently frivolous accusations. Second, when an investigation of his conduct is appropriate, it should be objective and impartial and adequately insulated from pressure to make him a scapegoat. Third, he has a right not to be held to an unreasonable standard. Allowances must be made for the inherent ambiguities, uncertainties, time constraints, and psychological pressures of being a police officer. Attention must be paid to the realities of his role: an administrator exercising coercive power in the context of potential physical danger, with all that entails regarding the tensions between law and custom. Further, the officer's concern for his job, his professional reputation, and peace of mind requires the specification of appropriate procedural rights for his protection during the course of an investigation of alleged misconduct, including the right to have a reasonably prompt disposition of the accusation.

The review system should also provide protections against overly zealous investigative tactics and the "head-hunting" mentality that Perez (1978, pp. 348–50) noted in police internal affairs units. Just as all concerned need protection against cover-ups of police misconduct, the membership of the police force in particular need to be reassured that the review system provides appropriate protection, in both policy and practice, of their legitimate interests. The police department's supervisors and managers (considered in those roles rather than as potential targets of citizen complaints) need a system by which they can both constrain inappropriate police activities and—often the greater, less publicly visible, problem—motivate officers to perform the services for which they are employed.

The chief executive officer of the police department is a central figure not only because he stands in the bright sunlight at the apex of the hierarchical pyramid but also because he is the main boundary-spanning person between the department, on one hand, and the political structure and the community, particularly the organized community, on the other. His primary need is a review mechanism that does not undermine his capacity to run the department—as we have argued, the administrative structure provides the most efficient and effective way to control police conduct. The chief's control, which has always been shared with the political chief executive, the legislature, and to a lesser extent the courts, is currently being challenged further by union militancy (see Bouza's chapter) and a much more aggressive media stance (see Skolnick and McCoy's chapter).

The chief's secondary need is to maintain personal and organizational credibility with the community at large and its influential parts, such as political and governmental elites. To do so he needs to know and to be able to convince these others that his officers are not abusing their powers. Counterbalancing this need is a concern that the officers not be unduly hampered in their enforcement activities or demoralized by a review system that unfairly second-guesses them or abuses their rights and self-respect.

The political chief executive bears the ultimate responsibility for the administration of the jurisdiction and thus needs to be reassured that all administrative functions, including policing, are being performed without undue impediments or serious misconduct. The relevant legislative bodies also need accurate, balanced information regarding the discharge of administrative functions on which to base both their oversight activities and new legislation.

Finally, both state and federal prosecutors have law enforcement responsibilities with regard to the police. These responsibilities have, in the past, caused difficulties particularly for the state prosecutors because they depend on a daily basis on the goodwill and cooperation of police officers. They have found that the discharge of their prosecutorial oversight responsibilities has caused the police to retaliate against them. This problem is less severe for federal prosecutors, but even for them the local police can find numerous ways to withhold useful cooperation if they choose. Both state and federal prosecutors, then, need a way of monitoring police activity that will minimize the disruptions to normal working relationships with the police.

PRINCIPLES FOR THE REVIEW OF POLICE CONDUCT

Three principles for the review of alleged police misconduct seem to emerge from the preceding considerations: On balance, it is preferable to leave the work of complaint processing and decision making with the police department; a meaningful external monitoring of the police review is essential; and both the internal and external systems should, whenever possible, move from a judicialized, punitive model toward an emphasis on reconciliation and compensation for the citizen and training and assistance, when required, for the officer.

Why should the police department be given the authority to be the primary mechanism for complaint review? The departmental administrative structure has by far the greatest potential for efficient, effective action to prevent, to investigate, to adjudicate, or to punish police misconduct. Ultimately, the major purpose of any system should be to prevent inappropriate conduct by police officers. The department has great capacities to contribute to this goal by the actions it takes in hiring, training, and supervising employees and by the care it exercises in adopting policies and procedures that minimize the likelihood of misconduct. The first-line supervisor is the person who can contribute the most—in informal but extremely effective ways—in discouraging inappropriate conduct.

The actions that the department and its managerial and supervisory personnel must take in discharging this function are sometimes costly and often unpleasant. The effect of removing the responsibility for dealing with instances of misconduct from the department is to reduce substantially its motivation to address problem areas and individuals before they get out of control. It allows the administrative structure to evade responsibility by pointing to some other agency. It also allows them to be "good guys" and implicitly or explicitly side with their nominal charges. It encourages a "we-they" mentality and a conspiracy of silence to impede misconduct investigations.

Placing primary misconduct review responsibility outside the department also fragments an administrative authority in significant ways. With the police this authority is inevitably fragmented already by several factors: the agency's position as a subordinate part of a larger administrative structure that itself is situated in a governmental system involving explicit legislative review authority; the department's role as part of a criminal charge processing system in which important activities on its part are subject to prosecutorial and judicial review; and, increasingly, aggressive community, media, and union challenges to its claims of expertise and managerial prerogatives.

It might be argued that this decentralization of authority is a desirable trend that should be encouraged. Historically, the American experience with municipal police in the nineteenth century does not support the notion that decentralization enhances the likelihood of controlled police conduct. Indeed, a principal strategy of police reformers for the first half of the twentieth century was the centralization of administrative authority as a way of establishing greater accountability (Fogelson 1977; Walker 1977; Kelling's chapter on order maintenance; Klockars's chapter). Even the most radical proposals for restructuring police organizations (Angel 1971; Munro 1974), which have been criticized by some for overly optimistic assumptions about behavior control mechanisms (for example, Kerstetter 1979), retain in their new organizational structures a centralized misconduct review unit.

The police department is better situated to assume the primary review responsibility because it is a repository of the administrative and investigative expertise necessary to conduct thorough investigations and make sound decisions about the appropriateness of particular conduct. Perez concluded that the internal affairs investigators were more thorough and tenacious in their search for evidence than the civilian investigators. The fact that the investigators are experienced police officers will aid the investigation in at least two ways. They will be less susceptible to being confused by misleading statements or lack of understanding of police procedures. Further, the ability to think oneself into a situation and understand the dynamics of it is of crucial importance in ferreting out evidence. Their prior experience as police officers will enhance the capacity of internal investigators for this task.[5]

This same base of experience will provide a foundation for making sound decisions on the appropriateness of challenged officer conduct. I have argued that a central difficulty in the review of police use of coercive power lies in the fact that the use of coercion is essential to their function, that the legal limitations on its use are imprecise, and that the realities of the police role create further ambiguities by virtue of the tension between judicial and legislative accountabilities and by virtue of being existentially situated between custom and law (as control mechanisms) and needing to respond effectively on both levels. Sorting out this tangle is best done by those who have been there, provided that the discretion they must exercise is not open-ended.

Administrative processes also have an advantage by virtue of their superior flexibility, capacity for subtle responses, procedural freedom, and ability to pursue and modify quickly when necessary a course of action. These advantages allow responses to problems to be tailored to the needs of specific situations.

A final consideration is governmental efficiency. To create an external agency, particularly in a sizable city, that has the capacity to accept and process numerous complaints is to establish yet another large bureaucracy that inevitably will experience various institutional problems, including a tendency to become focused on the needs of its staff rather than its clients. The bittersweet benefits of civil service and public employee unionization undoubtedly will be bestowed on it as well. And over time it will face the substantial danger, encountered by all regulatory bodies, of being co-opted by those that it ostensibly regulates.

But what is to prevent those who operate this internal review mechanism from succumbing to the temptation to protect fellow officers and the department's reputation by covering up instances of misconduct? The answer, of course, is meaningful external review, premised not so much on the actuality of cover-ups as on the inherent lack of credibility of any internal review system that is not open to outside scrutiny. That lack of credibility cuts deeply into the police legitimacy in the community. Paradoxically, the review of misconduct allegations is so important that it should use police expertise, but it is also too important to be left solely to police administrative discretion.

What principles should govern the structure and operation of this external review? The central principle is that external review should be focused on the adequacy and integrity of the police department's response to complaints—that is, on the system rather than on individual cases. Individual cases should be addressed (in fact, a sample, varying in size depending on the perceived need, should routinely be reinvestigated to ensure the integrity of the police investigations), but they should be examined primarily in order to make judgments about the police department's discharge of its responsibility to provide a fair, objective, and credible review of allegations of police misconduct. The external review should be sensitive to overzealous "headhunting" tendencies on the part of the internal affairs unit and, indeed, should accept complaints from police officers on these matters.

Preferably, the external review should include allegations involving any of the administrative agencies in the jurisdiction, not just the police. This broad scope makes sense both because other agencies provide important services and in order to avoid the implication that only the police engage in misconduct. There is justification for singling out the police because of their extraordinary authority, but it is poor judgment to do so.

The external review mechanism so structured need not be large, but it must have the authority required to ensure access to necessary information. The power to compel production of records and testimony from police and others is essential.[6] While the staff may be small, it must have the capacity to conduct investigations, consider systemic issues concerning police policy and practice, deal effectively with individual citizens to facilitate conciliatory solutions, and work with community groups, political and social elites, and the media in order to build confidence and to mobilize opinion in support of any necessary change.

The monitor model, based on the ombudsman concept, provides the prototype for this external review system. Where and how it should be located in the governmental structure is problematic. Clearly, it should not be part of the police department, but can it be part of the municipal administration and still effectively address the credibility issue? Can it be outside the administration without becoming a political football? In part these questions must be answered by the political traditions and structures of the particular community. In part they will be answered by the performance of the personnel of the review agency, particularly its leader. Historically, the ombudsman's effectiveness has depended largely on his individual stature.

Whatever structure may be selected for an external system, both the internal and external processes should move away from heavy dependence on a judicialized, all-or-nothing, culpability-fixing, punitive model, except in the most severe cases. The emphasis in all other nonfrivolous cases should be on reconciliation and compensation, when appropriate, for citizens and on assistance and education for officers. A corollary of this emphasis is a lower standard of proof of misconduct combined with nonderogatory findings. The reviewer's attitude toward complaints should be less one of pointing a finger of blame and more one that says: "Here is a complaint. Let's determine what caused it and find a way to learn from it on both the individual and the systemic levels." One likely criticism of this approach is that it will occasionally allow an officer who has acted with malice to escape deserved punishment. That is true, but the system will be able to identify him as a potential disciplinary problem, and if the misconduct continues the department will be on notice that it needs to find a solution to this problem. My proposal intentionally relinquishes the opportunity to establish administrative or legal culpability in every possible case in order to enhance administrative control of behavior, to be more broadly responsive to citizen complaints, and to facilitate systemic problem solving.

CONCLUSION

I have attempted to respond to the several dilemmas attending police conduct review by creating a balanced system that defers substantially to police expertise in judging the appropriateness of police conduct but at the same time creates a capacity for informed outside critique of the exercise of that judgment. Further, by moving the review system, in both its internal and external elements, away from an either-or, guilty–not guilty, formal adjudication orientation, the resulting structure is more responsive to, and thus more likely to satisfy, the underlying needs of both police and citizens. The system nevertheless retains the capacity to deal with serious incidents or persistent malicious misconduct with formal rigor and severity. In my view, this system for the review of police conduct gives up very little in return for substantial gains in effective behavior control and increased community acceptance.

NOTES

1. In Chicago at times the courts have been more actively involved in controlling such activities as police spying and unwarranted disorderly conduct arrests.

2. While not necessarily limited in its usefulness to the review of government agencies and the services they deliver, that has been the ombudsman's primary use.

3. In all systems, the citizen's complaint is sustained in only a small percentage of cases (usually from 7 to 15 percent). In another, larger portion of the cases, insufficient evidence exists to either prove or disprove the allegations. Perez reports that 16.4 percent of the cases investigated by the Berkeley Police Department and 38.4 percent of the cases handled by the Chicago Office of Professional Standards were "not sustained" in this manner. He concludes: "Put bluntly, the police are usually legally and procedurally correct in their actions. A fair and objective system will therefore find 'for' the policeman much more often than for the citizen. And it *should* do so" (1978, pp. 402–03).

4. The literature on police and particularly police subcultural influences has documented fully the negative impact of peer pressure in police organizations. See Westley (1970); Skolnick (1966); Banton (1964); Van Maanen (1974); Harris (1973); and Goldstein (1977).

5. Chief Anthony Bouza of Minneapolis has commented (1983) that "internal investigators are like tapioca—they will be whatever flavor the chief wants." He means that if the chief demands fair, objective, and impartial investigations, he will get them.

6. Granting subpoena power has proven to be a nettlesome issue. Many community groups view a review mechanism without this power as a paper tiger. This issue has been raised in Dade County, where the response of the IRP's executive director has been to point out that without the additional power to compel testimony by granting immunity from prosecution, the subpoena is of little value. A police agency can partially avoid this problem by virtue of its power to compel testimony as a condition of employment, but such testimony cannot be used against the officer in a subsequent criminal proceeding.

14

The Sources of Police Legitimacy and a Model for Police Misconduct Review: A Response to Wayne Kerstetter

Wesley A. Carroll Pomeroy

The observations and proposals presented in Wayne Kerstetter's fine chapter deserve full and serious discussion. Having considered them from a variety of perspectives shaped by more than 40 years in local, state, and federal law enforcement, mental health and corrections administration, conflict management, police oversight, and law, I have chosen two on which to enlarge. One has my support; the other needs further critical discussion.

On the one hand, I endorse and support the bifurcated internal-external proposal, which is similar in many ways to the Dade County program that I currently administer. On the other hand, I am concerned that Kerstetter, whose views I have come to know and respect over the years, could be read as endorsing the position, as could Wilson and Kelling (1982), that a democracy can tolerate extralegal or even illegal behavior by its police.

In discussing the realities of street policing, of which a police conduct reviewer obviously must be aware to do a competent job, Kerstetter might be seen as endorsing some of the bleaker aspects of those realities. In recognizing that police respond not only to "the law" but also to sources of extralegal influences (for example, community customs), and proposing that those sources be used as standards in addition to those prescribed by law in judging police behavior, Kerstetter could be read as disparaging the rule of law.

One's reaction to the notion of police behavior being justified on extralegal grounds should be that police simply cannot be allowed to use *any* means, under *any* circumstances, that are outside the law. Men and women who are police officers have absolutely no identity or power as police officers outside the law. Police officers are creatures of law, their powers are described and limited by law, and if they operate outside the law, they become criminals just as everyone else and should be punished. It can be argued, additionally, that they are more deserving of punishment than others because they assume a higher level of responsibility to operate within the law by joining a profession charged with enforcing the law.

There is a very real problem in preserving the integrity of the absolute need to constrain the police within legal limits when one perceives both the inherent ambiguities in much of "the law" that guides police work and the police officer's — and police reviewer's — consequent need to apply an equitable standard to resolve those ambiguities. A typical state law authorizing police use of force to effect an arrest will help illustrate the point: "A police officer is . . . justified in the use of any force which he *reasonably believes* to be necessary to effect the arrest and of any force which he *reasonably believes* to be necessary to defend himself or another from bodily harm while making the arrest" (Ill. Rev. Stat., ch. 38, para. 7-5; emphasis added). The police officer must follow the law, but its requirement that the officer behave with a reasonable (although possibly mistaken) belief in the necessity of using physical force is so lacking in specificity that the temptation is strong for even the best intentioned and best led police officer to rely on social mores and other extralegal sources to determine the propriety of some of his conduct rather than on standards of conduct defined by law and administrative policy specifically developed through open and established processes to give more clarity to what is reasonable and what is not.

By contrast, some laws are relatively straightforward, and here it is much easier to avoid the tendency to be guided by extralegal or illegal factors. For example, the wiretapping laws in some states leave no question that police may not, regardless of the cirumstances or their "intuitive grasp of situational exigencies" (Bittner 1970), overhear or record a phone conversation unless one of the parties consents — and even then a judicial warrant is unambiguously required. If one feels the police are being too tightly constrained by existing legal restrictions as they attempt "to deal with many situations which are violations of custom or morality but not of law" (Buckner 1967), the response should not be to accept and endorse police deviance from the law. Rather, if society believes strongly enough that certain legal restraints on police activity should be removed or liberalized, its members have the clear responsibility to legislate changes. Any other approach makes a charade and a mockery of the democratic process.

Kerstetter is also open to harmful misinterpretation, it seems to me, by citing without explicit rebuttal the view of an experienced civilian reviewer of police misconduct allegations in Chicago, that "if you are going to be an authority figure in Cabrini Green or the Robert Taylor homes, then the people there have got to be afraid of you." It is a statement that needs to be challenged. A fair assumption is that there are authority figures in those projects such as parents, priests, and teachers who *are* effective even though they are not feared. Although the tough world in which police work may require that they inspire fear when other techniques fail, clearly one does not have to be feared to be respected, even in an inner-city housing project.

It is true, as Kerstetter says, that some people with a substantial history of denouncing what they perceive as police misconduct, such as Mike Royko, occasionally support and even expect the police to use force that clearly exceeds what the law allows, but the issue of individual civil rights has never been determined by popular gut reaction, and it never should be. If the police are, as a matter of conscious policy, allowed to use force that exceeds what the law allows, the physical safety and freedom of each one of us will depend only on the sense of fairness, the political philosophy, the goodwill, and the whim of the person or group that controls the police. The danger inherent in that should strike dread into the heart of anyone who "games out" the probable consequences, and I would have preferred Kerstetter to be explicit in whether or not he approves or disapproves of any review mechanism that condones deliberately excessive force by police.

On the supportive side, I would note that the Dade County Independent Review Panel (IRP), which I serve as staff director, is very much like the model proposed by Kerstetter. He has described the IRP's operations and the largely positive reception it has had from a broad base of governmental and private constituencies. Where these constituencies have reservations, they are essentially in the nature of wanting more of the same (Kerstetter notes the desire of community relations board representatives to see IRP jurisdiction expanded to include municipal services within Dade County) or overly optimistic assessments that higher levels of police accountability to the community, achieved through the IRP's intervention and mediation over the past few years, would be self-maintaining even if the IRP were now disbanded (for example, the police unionist's comments).

The difficulty of appropriately placing an ombudsman function such as the IRP within a governmental structure, as it is in Dade County, is, as Kerstetter observes, that it must be perceived as independent in order to be credible. This concern has been answered in part in Dade County by the way the panel members and the executive director are selected and appointed. Five of the six panel members are nominated by community organizations for appointment by the board of county commissioners. The sixth member is designated by the county manager. Panel members are paid no salaries or honoraria, and they are required to report to no one as panel members. The executive director is appointed by the chief judge of the county, and his or her salary is set by the county board of commissioners. Although obliged to manage the county-provided budget responsibly, the executive director is otherwise independent. The county ordinance establishing the IRP does not require the executive director to report to anyone, but implicit in the ombudsman nature of the position is the requirement that he or she must be accountable to everyone: the panel members, the county commissioners, the county manager, and, most importantly, all the people in Dade County.

Kerstetter points out that the IRP's effectiveness is somewhat tenuous because it depends heavily on the police director's voluntarily turning over investigative files for IRP review; if the director were a less responsible individual than the incumbent, the IRP could be severely hampered in fulfilling its oversight function. A strong argument could be made, however, that reliance on informal authority is precisely the IRP's strength because it creates a constant awareness that the success of the ombudsman function depends on all who are involved in that function performing with absolute honesty and integrity. If the IRP conducted itself with honor and the police director still refused to submit to its review and the county manager refused to order him to do so, then the ombudsman tradition would suggest an appeal to public opinion as a prod to the resistant public officials. Having observed a considerable variety of public and private institutions over the years, it seems to me that any system, no matter how carefully conceived and crafted, ultimately stands or falls on the integrity, goodwill, and goal consensus of those exercising power within it.[1] Nevertheless, the choice of structures within which well-motivated, talented individuals will attempt to prevent and ameliorate police misconduct *does* make a difference, and I believe the inside-outside arrangement Kerstetter recommends has the greatest potential for striking an appropriate balance among the strong, sometimes competing interests that are implicated by the delivery of police services in America.

NOTE

1. The Detroit Board of Police Commissioners, composed of five mayoral appointees and a legal, investigative, and clerical staff of twelve, has a great deal of apparent power. It receives and investigates citizen complaints of police misconduct, monitors police internal disciplinary investigations, and serves a final appellate function (unless the defendant officers choose arbitration) when the department seeks to punish police misconduct. The board also reviews and approves the departmental budget, all policies, and all promotions. This board works well for Detroit at this time, with the incumbent police chief and the incumbent mayor, because the present members of the board reflect the policies of the mayor and make no decisions contrary to them. If that were to change, the board would not be nearly as effective because the charter allows the mayor to remove a commissioner at any time for any reason, even though it sets commissioners' terms at five years. The members of the Detroit Board of Police Commissioners are not independent because they can make no decision of any consequence with which the mayor disagrees.

15

Reaching Systemic Police Abuses — The Need for Civilian Investigation of Misconduct: A Response to Wayne Kerstetter

Amitai Schwartz

At one time, several years ago, the San Francisco Police Department's self-investigations unit, known as the Internal Affairs Bureau (IAB), had pieces of one-inch-square paper displayed at the front counter where complaints of misconduct were received. A sign over the scraps said: "Write your complaint here."[1] The police department did not appear to investigate seriously complaints from the public. In 1980, a year before a campaign for civilian review of the police began to heat up in San Francisco, the department did not sustain a single complaint of excessive force, out of 301 received (*San Francisco Examiner* 1981). In 1982, a voter initiative turned the responsibility of investigating complaints over to civilian employees of the department under the control and supervision of the San Francisco Police Commission rather than the police chief (*San Francisco Examiner* 1982; see also the San Francisco Charter, sections 3.530 and 3.530–2).

In my experience working as an ACLU attorney in connection with police misconduct issues in the San Francisco Bay area, I have found that police self-investigation has rarely worked to protect constitutional rights. While some enlightened police administrators will impose self-discipline by promulgating police policies that limit police discretion on the streets and will enforce those policies through command supervision, most police departments fail to make a fair evaluation of alleged misconduct and rarely sustain a serious complaint of wrongdoing.

Ironically, most self-investigative units, like the IAB in San Francisco, are called internal affairs bureaus or similar names, denoting internal concerns that do not involve the public. But police misconduct is not an internal affair; it is the public's business.

Since police officers on street patrol are not routinely supervised as they work alone or in pairs, a primary source of information about the officers' street conduct must come from the public, often in the form of complaints. Unless the police are prepared to accept the feedback that comes from the complaint process and fairly evaluate the information given to them, they will deprive themselves of an important means of assuring self-discipline and management. Self-investigation, however, frequently yields distorted findings and deprives police management of important information because the police investigations are biased and inadequate. Several factors produce these results.

First, there is a constant tension between the observance of constitutional rules and the necessity to catch criminals and keep order. When the courts suppress evidence or award citizens damages because of illegal search and seizure, illegal entry and restraint, or mishandling of evidence, it is rare for police departments to discipline the responsible officers. Police internal investigations are unlikely to put as much emphasis on constitutional rules of behavior as on the exigencies facing an officer who had been attempting to fight crime and generated a complaint of misconduct in the process. In fact, police departments rarely impose discipline for conduct that courts have found to be illegal.

Second, many police administrators and street officers fail to recognize various sorts of constitutional violations as abusive. As was the case with warrantless (but probable cause) entries of suspects' homes, for example, the police frequently will engage in questionable practices until such time as the courts call them to task and declare the practices unconstitutional (see *Payton* v. *New York* 1980). As a practical matter the police have little incentive to impose restraints on themselves.

Third, it is difficult to discipline a hero (Fyfe 1978, p. 37). In my experience the most abusive officers frequently tend to be the most aggressive. Their ability to generate complaints is matched by their ability to make arrests. Interorganizational pressures and the maintenance of morale make the thorough investigation of these officers a difficult and unlikely prospect. Their aggressiveness is usually condoned by higher ranking officials, and police investigators have a tendency to forgive their behavior or look the other way. Of course there are occasions where constitutional violations will not be excused; but in my experience this is usually due to external political pressure that requires that some action be taken to root out blatant examples of misconduct, such as abuses by a highly visible SWAT team.

Kerstetter suggests a system of external checks on the fairness of police self-investigation coupled with a conciliation-mediation function. Although the idea is appealing in theory, and is probably inexpensive since it does not require a large staff to implement, I doubt that the system is much of an improvement over police self-investigation. So long as the police themselves gather, assemble, present, interpret, and then judge the facts related to misconduct complaints, few serious complaints are likely to be sustained. As evidence gatherers and assemblers, the police will act as a fraternal brotherhood, protecting their own whenever possible against negative feedback.[2]

I do not suggest that outside civilian review boards are the only answer to the age-old question of "Who shall watch the watchmen?" However, I do believe that civilian investigation of complaints is essential so that police management can make supervisory and disciplinary decisions on the basis of facts that have been fairly gathered and evaluated. There are simply too many ways in which the fact-finding process can be distorted to trust this function solely to police investigators, even with Kerstetter's ombudsman looking over their shoulders from time to time.

Part of the value of civilian investigation is that civilians may find abusive and unnecessary certain types of conduct to which a police administration has become insensitive because "that's the way it's done." Tight handcuffing, which can leave welts and bruises on suspect's wrists, is an example (see Goldstein 1977, p. 163). Police investigators may not think such injuries are important — or they may attempt to cover up the offending officers' uncaring or punitive behavior by routinely accepting the claim that the marks and wounds resulted from the suspects' attempts to wriggle free of the restraints. I have not heard of a case in the San Francisco Bay area in which an investigating police officer found excessive force solely in the misuse of handcuffs.[3]

Kerstetter's assumption that police can be depended on "to make sound decisions about the appropriateness of particular conduct" is illusory because the criterion police are most likely to use to determine the propriety of behavior is habitual operating practice. Although a new police chief with fresh ideas might have progressive opinions about "appropriate conduct" that differ from the habits of the rank and file, the complaint process is not likely to provide many new recommendations for changes in policy so long as veteran officers are in charge of investigating complaints and spotting troublesome departmental practices in need of review and change. The ombudsman favored by Kerstetter is not likely to be in any better position to comment on ongoing styles of police behavior. The ombudsman would be concerned with the procedural fairness of the complaint process itself, rather than underlying police practices generating those complaints. He would also, as I understand it, provide a mechanism for conciliation for disputes between police and citizens. But the ombudsman would leave the assessment of underlying police conduct to the police. This process is then ultimately devoid of civilian restraint.

Even Kerstetter's idea that spotchecking a handful of investigations would put controls on the investigators is not likely to have much of an impact because the spot checks could not comprehensively evaluate the ongoing investigative judgments and biases of the police investigators. It is easy enough for a spot check to point out that a police investigation missed a useful witness; it is quite another matter for the ombudsman to second-guess the police evaluation of the witness or the police assessment of the evidence gathered by the investigators.

As most trial lawyers know, the identity of the fact finder or judge can make an enormous difference in the way evidence is treated and interpreted and ultimately in the final outcome of a factual dispute. In San Francisco, the police would not seriously investigate a complaint unless there were "independent" witnesses or other evidence.[4] Although the term "independent" was not defined explicitly in police rules, in common practice it meant that a complainant's word was never good enough to find wrongdoing on the part of an officer and that some uninvolved bystander, neither a friend nor a relative of the complainant, had to be present to refute an accused officer's version of events. In contrast, the police officers present at the scene were considered reliable because they were under a departmentally imposed obligation to tell the truth to the police investigators.

Another reason complaints are rarely sustained by police investigators is that they require the complainant to meet an enormous burden of proof. While the standard of proof in an ordinary civil lawsuit is proof by a preponderance of evidence (that is, the claim is more likely true than false), the police in the California jurisdictions that I have seen require uncontradicted or overwhelming proof of misconduct; otherwise, the departments fail to sustain the complaints. This is one of the reasons one frequently encounters jury awards of money damages in situations where a police self-investigation previously found no wrongdoing at all.

In the long run, the police would be far better off to lower the burden of proof they require to something more akin to that used by the courts. Then they would find misconduct in their ranks, impose discipline or other corrective remedies, and hopefully avoid future civil liability. Under the present system, the police are simply hiding their heads in sand.

It is difficult to see how Kerstetter's ombudsman would remedy the burden of proof problem. The ombudsman would not routinely evaluate the nuances in the way the police investigators treat and present evidence relating to complaints. While Kerstetter assumes a "small staff is sufficient" to carry out the ombudsman's task, the small staff is not likely to have an impact on the vast majority of complaints about police street practices. Obviously, the capacity to oversee the police investigation process will depend in large part on the ratio between the ombudsman's staff and the number of complaints received by the police department. Where the ratio is a small one the ombudsman could probably correct many biases and distortions produced by police self-investigations. But if the ratio becomes small enough, the civilian ombudsman's staff might as well be doing the investigations in the first place, under the sort of civilian-run process I am suggesting here. On the other hand, if the ratio is a large one, it is unlikely that the ombudsman's staff is going to have much oversight capacity at all.

Essentially the principal difference between Kerstetter's proposal and the approach suggested by my own experience is that Kerstetter's model is an adjudicatory one and mine would be more regulatory in character. Kerstetter's system looks to the fairness of the investigations, that is, the fairness of the decision-making process, but not at the decisions that come out of the process. The conciliation role of the ombudsman is meant to reconcile disputes between individuals — police officers and civilians. But conciliation is a means of resolving a dispute short of adjudication; it does not look to systemic factors or serve as a means of regulating ongoing police conduct by assessing police policies and practices. The complaint process must be a source of feedback that leads to a fair assessment of police practices.

The regulatory role I advocate could best be carried out by an outside civilian review board with competent investigative staff. Less desirable but still acceptable would be civilian investigation from within a police agency. While the ombudsman may make the process appear fair to the complainants, he is not likely to provide the sort of detection of systemic problems that will come when civilians gather and evaluate complaints and then present the result as feedback to police administrators.

The police view all too often is that civilian reviewers, insensitive to the difficulties of police work, will handcuff the police (too tightly) and unreasonably restrain them. But measured restraint is precisely the role of civilian review; more importantly, it is a value at the core of our constitutional system, under which civilians decide what sort of police conduct is consistent with democratic ideals. Unfortunately, too few police departments have been capable of setting their own restraints and taking seriously the feedback that comes through the complaint process. Civilians then are called to the task as much by default as by constitutional imperative.

NOTES

1. The square-inch complaint form — and the tendency in most police departments to become defensive about citizen complaints — can be contrasted to the practice in many service industries of eliciting consumer responses as an aid in providing services. Hotel rooms, restaurants, and transportation services frequently include satisfaction questionnaires. Perhaps the police service would benefit significantly by bumper stickers on police cars inviting civilians to comment about the conduct of the police by calling the appropriate complaint unit. If police around the nation were to ask regularly for feedback, and heed the response, substantial improvements might come to all levels of police work.

2. It is commonplace to find persons belonging to organizations confronted by outside danger, such as armies and police, forming fraternal protective bonds. In the case of the police this frequently results in a "code of silence" that prevents officers from testifying about the wrongdoing of fellow officers; that is, one officer covers for another (see Goldstein 1977, pp. 165-66). Under the circumstances, it is difficult to believe police can be objective in investigating and criticizing the conduct of brother officers. Recently, San Francisco Police Chief Cornelius P. Murphy sent a memorandum to members of the department attempting to break the code of silence with regard to the investigation of a sex-related scandal. The memorandum stated in part:

Code of Ethics or Code of Silence? The choice is yours. . . . Who are you? Why did you join the Police Department? Where are your loyalties? What do you want out of life? It's so easy to remain silent, to say nothing; and by that silence to tacitly approve misconduct. Peer pressure can be enormous and overwhelming, and seemingly only the strongest of wills can overcome it. The code of silence is pervasive and forces one to compromise. Before long, the compromise leads to a lack of self-respect and a lack of respect for our chosen profession—law enforcement. When you compromise your pride and integrity and that of your department there is little left. (1984)

3. Meaningful San Francisco statistics showing percentages of complaints sustained are not generally available to the public, in part because many allegations of misconduct were not counted for statistical purposes. Moreover, complaints that were sustained were broken down into very general categories, such as "neglect of duty" or "excessive force."

4. In October 1981, San Francisco departmental orders provided:

Adjudication of the complaint [beyond initial screening] is mandated after the preliminary investigation, when based upon the information provided by the complainant and if, in the opinion of the investigator, further investigation would not influence the complaint disposition. The lack of independent witnesses, evidence, medical reports and a positive identification of the officer against whom the complaint is made, are sufficient cause for closing out the complaint as undocumented.

Undocumented complaints are closed without contacting the member against whom the complaint is made and no entry is made in the member's IAB or personnel file. . . . When a case is closed out as undocumented, the complaint is not counted for statistical purposes as a complaint but is included in the logbook tally of citizen's contacts. (San Francisco Police Department 1981)

16
Who Disciplines the Police? I Do!
A Response to Wayne Kerstetter

George Napper

Kerstetter's chapter is a good review of the conceptually complicated problem of disciplining police officers. Despite the complexities, however, and while others may disagree with me, the answer to the question "Who should discipline the police?" is straightforward: Discipline should be imposed by the person who is ultimately and legally responsible for an officer's behavior—the police chief executive. Since legally, politically, and morally the police leader can and will be held accountable for both the vast majority of proper conduct and the small but inescapable minority of misconduct by police officers, it would be both unfair to the police chief executive and ultimately against the public's interest to fail to give this executive authority commensurate with his accountability.

This is not to deny that there is an appropriate role for civilians in reviewing police conduct and encouraging the good police work and discouraging the bad. The language used to describe this civilian role, it seems to me, is critically important in terms of creating the proper expectations on all sides so that police morale and effectiveness are enhanced in the interests of providing high-quality public service and, concomitantly, public confidence in the integrity and quality of the law enforcement agency is maintained and elevated to the point where the community eagerly helps the police department fulfill its various and difficult missions.

The terminology we have adopted in Atlanta to structure and describe the positive role of citizens and police in working together to review police conduct is the phrase "interactive nonadversarial model." By this wording we seek constantly to remind all parties—police and community members, media, prosecutors, judges, and our civilian reviewers of police conduct—of the commonality of their interests and the importance of their putting their heads together in informal and formal efforts to solve difficult public safety problems. What we explicitly want to avoid with our phrasing is any implication that an "internal-external" police conduct review system, such as Kerstetter proposes and we have recently adopted in Atlanta, permits a polarization of the review process resulting from an "us versus them" mentality.

The approach we are currently using to review police conduct in Atlanta went through key formative stages this year (1984). Early this year, Atlanta police were called to deal with an armed, mentally disturbed citizen barricaded in a residence. During the incident, a number of officers were injured, and the residence caught fire, presumably from the use of tear gas cannisters, killing the deranged man. In the aftermath of a similar incident in Seattle, the police chief in that city convened an external expert review panel. In Atlanta, the mayor, whose values and fairness are unquestioned by the citizenry, felt that for "one time only" a panel of noteworthy citizens should review our barricade incident to enhance the community's perception of the appropriateness of the police response. The panel vindicated the police, providing needed education to the community about police functioning, although leaving both the police and the public with mixed reactions to its findings.

In mid-1984, at a city council meeting, the issue of impaneling a police civilian review board was brought up. The motion was defeated. The general tenor was that the existing internal review process was fair and that an outside civilian review board might undermine police morale by imposing what Kerstetter refers to as the public's "inexperienced, politicized review of police conduct." The very real cost of such demoralization could be serious jeopardy of the public safety by creating an overly cautious police department that is more concerned with avoiding complaints than with protecting the public. The wisdom that prevailed in Atlanta was to leave the police chief executive's ability to motivate and encourage officers to do their best work unhampered by counterproductive outside intervention.

In August 1984, we had an incident in which an officer shot and killed a 16-year-old, later discovered to be under the influence of a number of chemical substances, as the adolescent advanced on the officer with a knife. The community response to this incident, together with the city's recent history recited above, caused the mayor to establish, through his office, a permanent ombudsman civilian review panel. This panel, after completion of an internal investigation of questioned police conduct, is to review complicated cases and those in which the citizen is not satisfied with the police responses. Its goal, like Kerstetter's proposed ombudsman model, is to provide "an ongoing, objective evaluation of the delivery of government services with a specific focus on mediating disputes between citizens complaining about government services and the agency that provided those services." Importantly, this panel leaves the primary investigation, adjudication, and disciplining to the police (our supervisors, management, and Office of Professional Standards), while providing civilian safeguards and impact.

The panel consists of 25 citizens (with an additional two co-chairs) chosen by the mayor, whose occupations cover the spectrum, including business executives, students, and civic leaders. The co-chairs have universal community respect. All panelists serve without remuneration and at the pleasure of the mayor. The 25 appointees work, on a rotating basis, in panels of five, with the possibility that more than one panel could be operating simultaneously.

Monthly, the two co-chairs meet with my representative (the captain of our Office of Professional Standards) to review all cases handled by the OPS, whether or not officers were charged. The cases the co-chairs will choose to review typically will involve questions about the use of deadly force or serious bodily harm, although occasionally the cases will entail issues related to poor judgment (for example, failure to take action or illegal arrest), ethnics, maltreatment, and bias. Both cases that have received considerable media attention and low-visibility cases will be reviewed, except that cases with pending litigation are excluded until they are adjudicated. When a case is selected for review, the police will allow the panel to review the investigations related to the specific case. The mayor's staff will provide administrative support.

As of this writing (September 1984) we are undergoing our first review under the new system. Accordingly, it is too early to examine actual strengths and weaknesses of the process, although it may be worth noting that at the outset there is some sentiment among both the police and the community that the process is redundant, primarily because neither group feels the internal police review process entails cover-ups, inadequate or unfair investigations, and adjudications. The probable benefit of the process will be that recommendations by the panelists can be incorporated into revisions of department policies, training, and procedures where needed. Our "interactive nonadversarial model" combines positively diverse constituency viewpoints to establish a fair and equitable process — one in which it is widely understood and accepted that community input is extremely valuable and that the responsibility for disciplining the police belongs ultimately to the accountable body: the police chief executive.

17

Controlling the Police—
The Art of the Possible:
A Rejoinder to Napper, Pomeroy,
and Schwartz

Wayne A. Kerstetter

The issue that we are addressing here is the control of a central societal relationship—that between society's agents of coercion and the people over whom they exercise coercive authority. That relationship and the review of it are inherently and inevitably adversarial. To the extent that labeling that process as "interactive nonadversarial" (see Napper's response) denys that character, it misleads us. To the extent that on a deeper level it reflects a perception of the commonality of social interests in appropriate policing and a commitment on an operational level to use the opportunities available to resolve many problems between the police and citizens by discussion, mediation, conciliation, and other joint problem solving methods, it is immensely useful (see my discussion).

Wes Pomeroy's concept of the law appears to be that of a template that can be easily and clearly applied in all situations rather than a flexible mold the extension limits of which are determined ultimately by a jury of citizens reflecting on the circumstances of a particular situation. It seems to me that what the law really does is to create a zone of discretion rather loosely bounded by a reasonableness standard (see the Illinois statute quoted by Pomeroy). The model that I propose adopts and extends this structure to the administrative review of police conduct. It allocates to the police administration the primary responsibility for assessing the reasonableness of police conduct in particular situations. Buckner, Muir, Perez, Simon, and Royko's "heavy-metal rock" story are cited to suggest the complexity and conflicting pressures that bear on the exercise of that discretion and that need to be taken into account in making this judgment (see also Andrews's chapter). Instead of a jury, this model proposes civilian review with the necessary authority and competent staff to ensure that the police administrators patrol the boundaries of the discretion allowed to police officers with diligence and integrity.

I believe that by acknowledging forthrightly the reality of the inevitable police discretion in these situations, and the tensions and complexities involved in its exercise, we free ourselves and the police to deal effectively with police conduct that falls outside the reasonable limits of this discretion.

It strikes me that Amitai Schwartz and I have one apparent and one real disagreement. The former probably reflects a lack of sufficient elaboration in the underlying essay. Let me attempt to correct that. While the essay states that the civilian monitor must have the capacity to consider systemic issues concerning police policy and practice, I should indicate that that is one of four central functions of the model that I propose. These functions are:

• Ensuring the effectiveness and integrity of the complaint reception, investigation, and resolution process

• Ensuring that the police response, even in cases where the police are not "at fault," uses the opportunities available to enhance community acceptance of the police function by means of education, compensation (when appropriate), and reconciliation

• Reviewing police policies and practices to identify systemic problems and, when possible, suggest corrective action

• Providing the necessary public information to assure the community of the adequacy of police performance in these matters

Thus Schwartz and I share a belief in the central importance of a civilian oversight that extends beyond the right and wrong of a particular incident to include a systemic review of police policies and practices. We do differ on the best structure to carry out these functions. Schwartz opts for either the civilian review or civilian input models. I believe that the civilian monitor model is superior. Schwartz believes that this model has three defects:

• An inability to identify complaint investigation *policy* problems such as an unduly high burden of proof or an independent evidence rule

• An inability to identify complaint investigative *practice* problems such as "the nuances in the way police investigators treat and present evidence relating to complaints" and the fairness of "police evaluation of witnesses or the police assessment of evidence gathered by investigators"

• A failure to address systemic issues relating to general police policy and practices

I would argue, to the contrary, that civilian oversight that focuses on adequacy and appropriateness of the police complaint processing, using the routine reinvestigation or parallel investigation of cases as one of its sources of information, will efficiently disclose problems both of policy and practice in the police's handling of citizens' complaints. The civilian oversight that

I envision will continually ask: Is the outcome of this complaint appropriate? If not, why not? The latter question encompasses issues relating to general police policy and practices as well as to complaint investigative policy and practices. (In situations where there is a serious question regarding the integrity of the police investigative process, extensive and intensive reinvestigations and parallel investigations of complaints could be conducted.)

I would also argue that the capacity to look at these more fundamental issues, to see the larger picture, if you will, is markedly enhanced by not having to deal with the day-to-day pressures and problems of processing all civilian complaints and inquiries. In addition, charging the police administration with the primary responsibility for reviewing allegations of misconduct — and providing a means by which to hold them accountable for the exercise of that responsibility — create an incentive for them to take the necessary steps to prevent misconduct. Having served as a police administrator, I have observed firsthand the pressures on police executives to evade these responsibilities and believe that those pressures must be vigorously resisted.

The appropriate exercise of the police function is central to a civilized society. Particularly in a democratic society, its inherently coercive nature will and should be viewed with concern and with a tendency to challenge its authority. The police, in order to function effectively in such an environment, need to be assured that the discretion necessary to discharge their responsibilities will not be inappropriately curtailed. The public, having granted this discretion, needs to be reassured that it is properly constrained. The civilian monitor model attempts to achieve the *possible* in balancing these needs.

PART 5

THE CHIEF, THE LAW, AND LAWYERS

Introduction

If it is true that police and lawyers make strange bedfellows, then imagine the restless nights of Wayne Kerstetter, Richard Brzeczek, Wesley Pomeroy, and Hubert Williams — all attorney-chiefs represented in this volume. Traditional tensions between lawyers and police are, as William McDonald points out in his discussion of the prosecutor-police executive relationship in this section, due partly to personal value differences but primarily to institutional dissonance that is necessary in our governmental system of checks and balances. Such tensions (for example, over case attrition) also sometimes result from police misperceiving the law and courts as obstacles to be overcome in pursuit of justice.

Although some tensions are inevitable, as Joseph McNamara and Albert Alschuler contend in reply to McDonald, there is ample room for improved communication among police, attorneys, and judges. For example, steps could be taken to improve the educative function of judicial rulings, such as having the police officer who is assigned to a given courtroom report its decisions back to the officers whose investigative work is under review. McNamara emphasizes as well the importance of expediting justice to avoid what another critic termed the "overdue process of law" (Vaughan 1977). Ignorance by criminal justice officials of one another's legitimate needs, whether blatant or masquerading as professional independence, poorly serves the public's interest in an efficient and fair criminal justice system. For instance, in some jurisdictions prosecutors criticized police executives' attempts to institute team policing (see Sherman et al. 1973), a decentralized approach designed to bolster police-community rapport. Prosecutors disliked the concept because it meant they had to deal with less experienced, neighborhood-based police officers rather than downtown detective division veterans. But it is unlikely that many prosecutors gave due weight to the community relations importance of team policing before issuing their complaints.

To be sure, police executives, lawyers, and judges have worked constructively and in proper balance in many ways — from the routine daily consultation that occurs in almost any large city between the chief and his legal adviser to much more ambitious collaborations, such as the American Bar Association's development with the International Association of Chiefs of Police of the "Urban Police Function Standards" (discussed in Samuel Walker's chapter for this volume). This latter initiative addressed pressing police problems — and continues to do so through updates to the standards — from the unique perspectives of police administrators, prosecutors, defense attorneys, judges, legal scholars, and social scientists.

One of the growing areas of interaction between police administrators and the legal system, addressed by Wayne Schmidt in this section, is federal civil rights lawsuits against the chief. They are filed nowadays by everyone, from the crime suspect to the crime victim to the arresting officer. Arrestees use them to allege police brutality; victims and victims' relatives, to charge police ineptness in averting a crime; and officers, to seek affirmative action in hiring and promotions or to defeat it as reverse discrimination. Managing the flurry of lawsuits has become a time-consuming enterprise for large police departments, nearly all of which have adapted by hiring in-house counsel and some of which have employed professional "risk managers" to help identify ways of preventing agency conduct that gives rise to suits. While Schmidt strikes a pessimistic note concerning any imminent reduction in the level of suits, including frivolous ones, his review of the impact of legal pressures on police management carries hope for the future, for it is clear that numerous police leaders across the nation are not succumbing to what would be an understandable inclination to pull the wagons into a circle against the onslaught of legal attacks. Instead, they are seizing the initiative to forge new and more effective collaborations with the community, in all its frightening and exciting diversity, so as to root out injustice and fashion a safer, more vital urban environment. Such leaders have the vision to see, as Ramsey Clark once said, that ultimately "there is no conflict between liberty and safety. We will have both or neither."

18

Prosecutors, Courts, and Police: Some Constraints on the Police Chief Executive

William F. McDonald

When police chief executives were asked to rate the severity of problems confronting them, they ranked the "processing of cases by the courts" as their most serious problem — even higher than the crime problem. Problems with "prosecutors' offices" also ranked in the "serious" range.[1] Behind these ratings lies a history of frustration and antagonism between police agencies on the one hand and courts and prosecutors on the other. Numerous aspects of police administration and police interests are affected by the policies of local prosecutors and judges, including police budgets, morale, prestige, scheduling, organization, political accountability, and crime control effectiveness. In the past, frustrations with prosecutors and courts caused the police to rationalize an attitude of insularity from the court system. They believed they should do their job and not care about what the rest of the justice system did (National Advisory Commission 1976, p. 117). However, given the functional interdependencies of the police, prosecutorial, and judicial functions, this attitude only exacerbated the problem. Similarly, the other common posture, namely, open attacks in the press, did little to alleviate the "traditional antagonism" between these components of the justice system.

These self-defeating practices are beginning to change. The National Advisory Commission (1976, p. 116) deplored the old attitude of insularity and

Grateful acknowledgment is made to the Georgetown University Law Center and the American Bar Foundation for support in preparing this chapter and to the National Institute of Justice for support of the research on which this chapter relies, particularly for Grant No. 78-NI-AX-0025 awarded the Institute of Criminal Law and Procedure. Points of view or opinions stated in this document are those of the author and do not necessarily represent the official position or policies of the U.S. Department of Justice, the American Bar Foundation, or Georgetown University.

exhorted police chiefs to initiate communication with prosecutors, judges, and others. Such initiatives have occurred (McDonald et al. 1981), but even with better communication, some of the antagonism among police, prosecutors, and courts cannot be eliminated because it arises from structural conditions beyond their power to control.

This chapter examines the major constraints on the police chief executive arising from courts and prosecutors. It will consider both those things that are within and those beyond the power of police chiefs to modify. I will argue that, given our social order and legal ideals, that relationship must ultimately be an antagonistic one, but the basis for the antagonism should be structural inefficiencies and conflicts rather than personal politics or inefficiencies due to inadequate technology.

LENIENCY AND PLEA BARGAINING

When the police discuss their problem with the courts and the prosecutors' offices, they frequently reduce it to two things: leniency by judges and too much plea bargaining by prosecutors. For instance, Reiss (1967, p. 101) found that the majority of police officers surveyed in three cities believed the criminal court judges were too lenient. Arcuri (1973, p. 93) found that 60 percent of his sample of police officers felt that plea bargaining was "unfair to the arresting officer" in the sense that it was "disheartening" and "makes a police officer go sour." In a study of rape law enforcement, the Battelle Memorial Institute (1977) found that almost two-thirds of the police surveyed felt that "plea bargaining should be either changed or eliminated." A typical newspaper article reads: "70% OF CASES DECIDED BEFORE TRIAL.*** [P]olice detectives . . . charged that [plea bargaining] is too widespread. . . . State's Attorney defended the amount of bargaining . . . " (Cummings 1979).

The common police analysis of their problem with prosecutors and the courts seems to be a case of hyperbole and misunderstanding. In his analysis of the police demand for more punitive sentencing, McIntyre (1975) noted that "[t]he extreme impression police sometimes leave is unfortunate because when they are pinned down it becomes clear that most of them do not feel that strongly . . . that all criminals should be put in jail." More recently, McDonald et al. (1981, p. 77) pinned down a sample of police with a hypothetical armed robbery case and asked them to decide how the case should be disposed and sentenced. Their decisions were then compared to those of prosecutors who had been given the same case. The police recommendations were more "lenient" than those of prosecutors along all five dimensions of the decisions. Contrary to expectations, the police were not more likely than prosecutors to take the case to trial; rather, they were much more likely to dismiss it. In contrast, the prosecutors were more likely to seek a plea bargain.

Also contrary to expectations, when the police and prosecutors who recommended the case be plea bargained were compared, the police were twice as likely to recommend that the charges be reduced, twice as likely to recommend straight probation, and almost half as likely as the prosecutors to recommend a severe sentence (five years or more).[2]

On the other hand, studies indicate that for crimes against morality per se, the police are of a different mind than prosecutors. The police more strongly favor enforcing laws against gambling (Fowler et al. 1977; Clark 1969),[3] pornography and obscenity (Smith and Lock 1971; Clark 1969), marijuana possession,[4] and prostitution (Clark 1969, p. 139; Chambliss 1976). Taken together, the findings of these studies suggest that the police criticism of sentence leniency, plea bargaining, and, by extension, of courts and prosecutors is, at a minimum, overstated. While prosecutors appear to take a less repressive attitude toward sumptuary offenses than do the police, they are not less punitive (and in fact are more so) when it comes to serious predatory crime like armed robbery.

The really unfortunate thing about the strident police dissatisfaction regarding case dispositions is that the police have used them as an explanation rather than a thing to be explained. The police do not see the dispositions as an opportunity to examine their responsibility for case attrition and sentence leniency or to establish reasonable expectations for case outcomes. Instead they typically use these results as a way of accounting for their inability to control crime, which serves only to perpetuate a set of erroneous beliefs related to the old attitude of insularity.

One such belief is that the police responsibility for a case ends with arrest. Preparing a case beyond what is necessary to get it filed in court is "doing the prosecutor's job." A second is that most cases should be disposed of by trials. Thus high rates of case rejection or plea bargaining are necessarily wrong. The "proper" rate is never specified but is always believed to be lower than the prevailing rate in the local jurisdiction. How one determines what the "proper" rate should be is not even considered, much less made explicit. Nevertheless, the failure of prosecutors and courts to maintain this mythical rate, together with sentencing leniency, is regarded by the police as the primary reason they are unable to control crime.

A third belief is that case attrition and sentence leniency are due to factors that are largely beyond the control of the police and frequently "improper," such as "liberal" or "unrealistic" attitudes of judges and prosecutors, laziness, ineptitude, favoritism, politics, and mismanagement among prosecutors and judges (McDonald et al. 1981, pp. 25 ff.).

The police chief intent on overcoming the obstacle to police effectiveness that prosecutors and courts supposedly represent must begin by liberating his department from these erroneous beliefs and inappropriate standards of performance. For almost a century it has been beyond the capacity of urban court systems to give every case its day in court. Faced with the prospect of an ever-increasing discrepancy between caseloads and trial capacity, crime commissions since the 1920s have repeatedly recommended that prosecutors' offices inaugurate vigorous early screening programs (McDonald 1979). The probable cause standard is to be replaced by a "winnable" case standard. Cases not meeting that standard are to be dropped from the system as early as possible. In those jurisdictions where these recommendations have been instituted the police have sometimes been displaced by the prosecutor in controlling the initial stages of the court process, and case rejection rates have usually increased dramatically.[5] Rather than adjusting to this inevitable change the police have resisted, criticized, and tried to compromise it.[6] The new screening programs have not been seen by the police as long overdue responses to the recommendations of prominent crime commissions. Rather they have been viewed provincially as self-serving policies of politically ambitious prosecutors intent on establishing good track records by prosecuting only convictable cases.

Fortunately, in a few places progressive police administrations have prevailed. They have begun to explore their responsibility for case attrition and to develop realistic expectations of court dispositions. The Dallas Police Department operated a project that determined the extent to which felonies were "no-billed" by the grand jury or dismissed by the courts because of "police error." Using city attorneys to review cases for legal sufficiency and to advise officers as to the need for additional evidence, the project reduced those rates from 13.8 to 4.3 percent and from 6.4 to 2.6 percent, respectively (National Institute of Law Enforcement and Criminal Justice 1978, p. 9). In Tucson, Arizona, the prosecutor's office has agreed to give the police copies of the report form it uses when cases are dismissed or reduced. Police lieutenants review these cases with their officers to determine the general appropriateness of the decisions and whether there was something more the police might have done. In New Orleans the police department has begun reviewing cases before sending them to the prosecutor. The review is to determine the disposition that the police want in the particular cases given the facts of those specific cases. A record of these desired outcomes is kept and later compared with the actual outcomes. The police review unit has been surprised at the very high agreement between their wishes and actual outcomes.

These and similar efforts are needed if the police are to overcome that part of their frustration with courts and prosecutors stemming from their erroneous beliefs about the reasons for case attrition and their unrealistic standards for case outcomes. These false expectations become self-fulfilling sources of demoralization. Complaints about plea bargaining or dismissed rates being too high[7] are meaningless. There is no consensus as to what the appropriate rates for these outcomes should be. If anything, the consensus seems to be that these rates must be allowed to vary according to local needs and preferences (Jacoby 1977; National District Attorneys' Association 1977). If the police want to know whether their local rates deserve criticism they will need to construct a standard for comparison. In the absence of a national standard the only meaningful alternative would be one they construct themselves by recording their own estimates of what their cases are worth and how they would want them disposed and then comparing these expected rates with the actual rates. They may find as in New Orleans that they have less of a complaint than they thought, or they may identify specific policy differences that can then become the basis for reasonable discussions with the prosecutors and judges.

POLICE-PROSECUTION TECHNOLOGY

Police chief executives need a clear recognition of the underlying technology involved in case processing, the function of the police in that technology, and the degree to which police chiefs can influence its operation and impact on case attrition and sentencing patterns.

The criminal justice process involves two broad sets of technologies (that is, skills, activities, knowledge, and related apparatuses): people processing and information processing. Much of what police and correctional personnel do involves people processing: directing traffic, settling disputes, housing inmates. But prosecutors and judges are not people processors. They process files that contain information with which disposition and sentencing decisions are made. The police relationship to prosecutors, judges, and juries is that of information supplier to information consumer. The decisions of prosecutors, judges, and juries are determined by the information available to them plus their own personal attributes. Breakdowns in the communication process result in less than optimal decisions (regardless of the personal attributes of the decision maker). The information that is most essential for the charging and plea bargaining decisions is information about the strength of the case, the seriousness of the offender, and the seriousness of the offense (McDonald et al. 1979; Jacoby et al. 1982). The police influence the patterns of case attrition and sentencing by virtue of their performance as information obtainers and transmitters. Chiefs of police influence this process by the relative emphasis they place on thorough investigation and good report writing and by their policies affecting the transmission of information to the prosecutor (for example, whether each officer brings over his own cases or whether they are batch-processed, and whether reports are reviewed and enhanced by someone familiar with the prosecutor before being transmitted to court).

As a result of the insularity between police and prosecutors, and for other reasons as well, the police do not always do as much follow-up investigation as they might and do not always transmit all the information they actually possess. Both tendencies are subject to remedial action by police chiefs. The police reward structure is not presently linked to an officer's ability to get convictions.[8] Strengthening cases beyond what is necessary to get them filed in court has not been given as high a priority as returning to patrol or making additional arrests. This could be changed. While it would not be appropriate to measure an individual police officer's performance in terms of his conviction rates (because of the many contingencies involved beyond his control), a surrogate measure could be used. The officer's reports could be graded for their thoroughness from the point of view of the prosecutor.[9]

The failure to transmit all of the information they have is due to several additional considerations. Because of their lack of experience with the subtleties of evaluating cases for prosecution, the police significantly underestimate the amount of information prosecutors need in order to make their disposition decisions.[10] Unfamiliar with the dynamics of the plea negotiation process, the police do not appreciate that small differences in the degree of detail in a police report can translate into added concessions in plea bargaining. The difference between a report indicating that witness A had an unobstructed view of the crime and one that merely says witness A was present may be enough to assure the prosecutor that the case is strong and (all other things being equal) that he or she can hold out for a plea to a three-year sentence rather than a one-year term. Sometimes information, such as false exculpatory statements, is not transmitted because it is not recognized as having any evidentiary value. Other times officers withhold information to try to prevent the defense from getting it. Also, there is the practical consideration that lengthier reports are more work.

In many jurisdictions officers simply file their reports with the court and wait to be called to a hearing or possibly to a discussion with the prosecutor just before he or she pleads the case out. In other places the police departments employ a variety of organization strategies to enhance the information transmission process. One such strategy is to have all cases reviewed by someone familiar with the prosecutor's needs in the case.[11] Another is to have each officer meet directly with the prosecutor and review his cases. When the prosecutor involved in this intake review is experienced (in many locales the least experienced prosecutor does the work), this face-to-face review is probably the best method of transmission.[12] But this method is also labor-intensive. With union contracts calling for overtime pay, the cost of court overtime work has become one of the largest items in police budgets, and police administrators are being forced to make compromises.[13]

SCHEDULING, INPUT, AND FEEDBACK

Beyond their complaint about outcomes the police are antagonized by certain aspects of the process of case dispositions. Three are worth special mention: scheduling problems, police input into disposition decisions, and the lack of feedback on outcomes.

The efficient scheduling of police time for court has become a pressing concern primarily because of the dramatic increase in the cost of this work. But there has also been a concern for the lifestyle and morale of police officers, who frequently are subpoenaed into court on days off or continue on duty from the graveyard shift to a full day in court. Although many officers are happy to have the overtime pay, they also want the freedom to choose when to give up a leave day. Certain aspects of the scheduling problem are of common concern, including large amounts of police time spent in the prosecutor's office waiting for a case review, the ubiquitous court practice of scheduling more cases than can be disposed of and then continuing the balance to another day,[14] the calling of more police officers than is necessary (for example, nonessential witnesses), the failure to notify police officers when their cases have been settled and they are no longer needed, and the real and apparent disregard among prosecutors and judges for these legitimate police interests in the scheduling of cases. This last concern has another dimension to it, namely, the status of the police relative to that of the other actors in the court system. Police resentment of their sense of subordinate status is piqued by the appearance (or reality) of a double standard for scheduling. While attorneys seem to be able to get continuances for their personal convenience, police officers feel they are not accorded equal "professional consideration."

There is no simple answer here. To some extent it is a logistics problem. Police officers are not notified that their cases were settled because prosecutors may have found it difficult to reach individual officers and message systems have been unreliable. Courts overbook themselves because there is no way of predicting what cases will have problems (such as sick witnesses). Also, overbooking and related problems are linked in some places to plea bargaining tactics. Defendants (and their attorneys) will not negotiate until they reach "the steps of the courthouse" and know that the state is really ready to prosecute them. There may also be some misperception here. For instance, in response to police complaints about long waiting time for case review the Pima County, Arizona, District Attorney's Office analyzed waiting times and found the great majority of police officers waited only a few minutes.[15] Finally, there are political dimensions to the problem. Judges and prosecutors can be sensitized to police needs and persuaded to cooperate in special programs and policies to alleviate problems if the police chief executives exert appropriate leadership and influence. Partial solutions are possible in an atmosphere of mutual cooperation.[16]

The police complaint about input into disposition decisions refers to the fact that cases are often dismissed or negotiated without the officer being consulted. Officers do not expect to be given veto power over these decisions (a fear that prosecutors often voice when this topic is broached). Rather their manifest concern is with the inadequacy of the court system's method of communication by written report. The police believe they may have additional information that did not get into the report but should be considered, such as reliable tips that the defendant is responsible for more crime than the evidence supports.[17] The strength of the police feeling about this matter is attested to by the fact that it has been the focus of organized action. In Detroit, in 1978, for instance, the police detective association prevailed upon the local judges to refuse to accept guilty pleas unless the police have been consulted.[18]

The police concern about being consulted seems again to be a latent concern about their relative status among criminal justice actors. The police develop a proprietary interest in their cases, especially ones in which they have invested special efforts (as, for example, dangerous arrests or long stake outs). They feel this entitles them as much as the lawyers to have some influence on the disposition decision, but they perceive themselves to be the least influential of all the actors. When they are consulted they are more satisfied with the case disposition process even though they often have little to say (Kerstetter 1981b).

The police concern about feedback on case outcomes and the reasons for them stems from several factors. Besides personal interest, police officers are expected by victims and the general public to know this information. They serve as boundary spanners between the community and the court system. This is demonstrated most clearly by the example of the small town police chief searching the courthouse files to learn the disposition of the case that was his town's serious crime. To the prosecutor's office and the judges whose jurisdiction also includes a major city such a case may be just another burglary. But to the small town's citizens it will be viewed more seriously, and they will hold their chief responsible for knowing the outcome and being able to explain it.

Police administrators say they would like disposition feedback for use as a managerial tool. They complain that prosecutors will not cooperate and suspect that this is out of fear that the information could be used against them. Undoubtedly such refusals have occurred. But a large part of the fault lies with the police. Prosecutors have been willing to give disposition feedback. One of the new computerized information systems being widely adopted by prosecutors' offices (PROMIS) has the capability of feeding dispositions back to the police (INSLAW undated). Surprisingly, however, where feedback systems do exist, they are usually ignored by police administrators.[19]

COOPERATION AND CONFLICT

Many of the police problems with courts and prosecutors can be ameliorated. However, solutions usually depend on the willingness of prosecutors and judges to cooperate. Contrary to the belief of many police executives, such cooperation can be obtained, but it must be deliberately cultivated and constantly protected. Some police executives, such as a former chief in St. Lucie County, Florida, have succeeded in securing the trust of their chief prosecutors by dropping the customary defensive posture and indicating a strong interest in knowing what their officers might do better. District attorneys like Sandra O'Connor of Baltimore County, Maryland, have established agreements with their police counterparts regarding ground rules for criticizing each other.[20] Elsewhere the police executives have established "law enforcement councils" to which the prosecutor and sometimes judges and others are invited, less for the purpose of resolving specific issues than simply to open lines of communication (McDonald et al. 1981). For instance, police executives formed the San Mateo County, California, Police Chiefs Association and extended membership to the local district attorney.

In seeking better cooperation with courts and prosecutors, police executives should not lose sight of the structural antagonisms and inefficiencies that are either built into or surround the police-prosecutor-court relationship and that are not subject to technological improvements or administrative remedies. Two dimensions of this systemic conflict are noteworthy: the social and the legal.

American law enforcement occurs within the context of a pluralistic society in which there are deep divisions over morals and over the role of government intervention in the lives of citizens. The enforcement of law is inescapably a political and moral act. It is the use of state power to impose somebody's normative ideals on somebody else. When enforcing the laws against serious personal and property crime, police action is supported by a broad normative consensus. But when enforcing laws against morality per se the same consensus does not exist even within the justice system (see Fowler et al. 1977; Clark 1969; Smith and Lock 1971; Chambliss 1976; and notes 3 and 4). Rather than seeking philosophical unity within the system as some advocates of better cooperation have suggested (see National Advisory Commission 1976; Fowler et al. 1977), police executives should recognize that these philosophical discontinuities are one of the system's strengths. They reflect the normative inconsistencies of the larger society and mitigate the power of any group to impose its special morality on others. The police themselves are not above this normative conflict. Contrary to the civic book image of the legal system as an impartial framework for settling social conflicts, the police, prosecutors, and judges are committed to normative positions and are therefore part of the conflict.

The police are in a different relationship to the public and serve a different social function than prosecutors and judges. The police are closer to the public, more visible, and under greater pressure to take immediate action, to be productive, to solve crimes, and to keep the streets safe and free of nuisances. They are the guardians of the street and the engine that drives the justice system. Prosecutors are guardians of the court's resources and, together with judges and the defense bar, are guardians of the legal order. As such, they are the brakes on the system. Most of what the police do with their time involves order maintenance rather than law enforcement (Shelden 1982, p. 107). When the police do enforce the law it is usually not against serious crime.[21] When serious crimes are involved the cases freqently lack the evidentiary strength necessary for conviction or are treated relatively leniently because they involve persons who know each other rather than strangers (Brosi 1979; Vera Institute 1977; McDonald et al. 1981). Prosecutors and judges must dispose of this mass of cases by allowing only a few to go to trial and assuring that all others wherein penalties are imposed meet existing legal standards of arrest and processing. As with any braking mechanism, some friction is generated.

The law recognizes and condones the difference between police and court functions in two ways: in the difference between the standard of proof controlling police actions on the street and the standaid governing court decisions and in the doctrine of the separation of powers. The "probable cause" requirement for arrest allows the police to be more responsive to the social need for immediate action to secure public safety than would a more stringent restraint on police intervention. But once the urgency of the moment has passed, the concern for public safety must be balanced against the concern for a free society. The latter is served both by the "beyond a reasonable doubt" standard of proof and by the separation of powers. These checks on the power of the executive are built-in obstacles to the effective enforcement of law, but they also represent the difference between ordered liberty and totalitarianism.

CONCLUSION

The traditional antagonism between the police and the court system derives from both real and imagined sources. Police dissatisfaction with plea bargaining and sentence leniency is more a product of misperception and concern for professional status than of real differences in desired outcomes for specific cases. When the police have input into these decisions they are more satisfied. When they recommended dispositions in a hypothetical case they were even more lenient than prosecutors.

The real constraints on the police arising from the court system are of two different kinds: technological inadequacies in case (information) processing and structural constraints deriving from the legal and social order. The former can and should be remedied. The latter cannot be overcome, and attempts to do so threaten our national liberties. The challenge of police leadership on these matters is to minimize the problem of misperceptions and lack of input, to find acceptable solutions to the technological weak links, and to recognize when the incompatibility of police and prosecutor-court values reflects the pluralism of the social order and a desirable check on state executive power.

NOTES

1. "Prosecutors' offices" were rated as a more serious problem than each of the following problems (listed in descending order of perceived seriousness): "obtaining public support," "excessive involvement of appointed or elected officials in police agency management," "coverage by the news media," "employee labor organizations," "administration of internal discipline," "special interest groups," "community indifference to corruption," "civil service systems," "corruption inside local political systems," and "corruption inside police agencies" (National Advisory Commission 1976, p. 96).

2. These surprising results are based on limited samples of police and prosecutors responding to one hypothetical case of serious crime. Thus caution against overgeneralizing their implications is in order. But another study using a somewhat different simulation methodology has also found that the police are not that different from prosecutors in what disposition they want from specific cases (Jacoby 1981).

3. Sometimes the issue that splits police and prosecutors over the enforcement of sumptuary laws is not differences in judgments about the moral value protected by the law but the discriminatory enforcement of the law. For instance, in Milwaukee, Wisconsin, the district attorney's office refused to prosecute gambling cases as state crimes because the office had found gross inequities in the enforcement of the law. It was being more stringently applied in the black community than anywhere else (U.S. Commission on Civil Rights 1972, p. 53).

4. A survey of state prosecutors found that 31 percent of them said they would not prosecute anyone arrested at a private social gathering of marijuana users who were sharing a cigarette, 20 percent favored a policy of total decriminalization of marijuana possession, and 55 percent doubted the deterrent value of marijuana laws and would be lenient in applying them but believed the laws should remain on the books (see National Commission on Marihuana and Drug Abuse 1972, p. 103). In contrast, the International Association of Chiefs of Police has strongly and repeatedly opposed decriminalization, and a survey of chiefs of police in Maine found all 130 chiefs opposed to decriminalization. The police are convinced of the law's deterrent value (see Davis 1977, p. 82).

5. In the 1970s rigorous early prosecutorial screening programs were inaugurated in several jurisdictions. In Chicago the prosecutor's new Felony Review Unit declined charges in 21 percent of the 1,984 felony cases brought by the police (McIntyre and Nimmer 1972). In Philadelphia an experimental review project found that 41 percent of 20,000 arrests could be quickly eliminated from the system (Savitz 1975). In New Orleans there was a 20 percent decrease in the total number of cases accepted for prosecution during the first two years of a new screening policy (McDonald 1984, p. 38).

6. The Chicago Police Department insisted on retaining the right to override the prosecutor's decision to not file a case (McIntyre and Nimmer 1972). When the funds for the experimental screening unit ran out in Philadelphia, the program was abandoned, and the police department resisted the district attorney's effort to establish a permanent early review unit. Ultimately, the DA obtained a rule of court from the Pennsylvania Supreme Court giving Pennsylvania DAs the option of requiring any or all criminal cases to be filed in court only with their approval. In New Orleans the police department went to the press stating there must be something wrong with the high (46 percent) case rejection rate because they refused to believe they were "wrong" in almost half the arrests they make (Wheeler and Whitcomb 1977, p. 198).

In Alaska when the attorney general's no plea bargaining policy was inaugurated he was amazed to find strong police protests against it (Gross 1978). Their complaint was about the vigorous new screening policy that accompanied the no plea bargaining policy. They disliked that cases that used to be accepted even though they were weak were no longer being accepted, and they feared that certain categories of petty crime (for example, shoplifting) would not be accepted at all.

In some jurisdictions the anticipated police resistance to more vigorous screening systems has kept prosecutors from instituting the reforms they deem necessary. Curiously, in some places the police themselves are split over the desirability of these changes. In one county in New York (where prosecutors' offices historically have not controlled the initial filing decision) the principal police department in the jurisdiction does support the prosecutor's desire to assume control of the initial charging decision. But the prosecutor has not moved to do so because of anticipated objections from the smaller, "out-county" police departments. In other places such as Madison County, Illinois, prosecutors have plunged ahead and informed the police that either they obtain prosecutorial approval before filing cases or the cases would be nol prossed.

7. See the illustrative rates cited in note 5.

8. In the opinion of 180 officers from New York City and Washington, D.C., the number of arrests that result in conviction is the least important to their supervisors of 16 criteria that their supervisors might use to rate individual officer performance (Forst et al. 1982; see also McDonald et al. 1981).

9. The details of such a grading system remain to be worked out and would require some careful consideration. Nevertheless, I make this recommendation because I believe it is feasible and, more importantly, because it highlights both the fundamental technology involved and a concrete means by which police executives can influence that technology. It should be noted that my specification that this evaluation should be made from the point of view of the prosecutor is intended to distinguish it from the kind of pro forma review for probable cause that many police departments now exercise over all reports. The difference is made clearer in the text that follows.

10. When police and prosecutors were presented with the same hypothetical situation and asked to decide what disposition a case should receive, police officers reached their decisions after consulting significantly fewer items of information than did prosecutors — 9.2 items of information compared to 12.9 (McDonald et al. 1981, p. 372).

11. Typically this is done by a court liaison officer or a detective. But in Dallas city attorneys were assigned to the police department (National Institute of Law Enforcement and Criminal Justice 1978). In Nashville-Davidson, Tennessee, the prosecutor's office prepared a set of interrogatories for each type of offense. Police officers would then give their reports by answering these questions. The secretaries hired to type the reports eventually memorized the interrogatories and began taking reports directly from the police (McDonald et al. 1981).

12. Omitted and unrecognized evidence and detail can be probed for, immediate feedback on reasons for rejection or need for follow-up investigation can be given, and a better judgment about the credibility of the witnesses can be made.

13. In 1979 the officers of the District of Columbia Metropolitan Police Department spent 249,485 hours in court at a cost of $1.4 million. In the same year the 710-member Montgomery County, Maryland, force spent $197,000 in overtime at the courthouse. And the Philadelphia Police Department reported spending $4 million in court overtime pay (Knight 1980). Such costs have been trimmed in Detroit, where each officer used to review all his cases with a prosecutor, by batching together and delivering by couriers all but the most serious cases from each precinct (see also note 16).

14. This overbooking shifts certain costs of the case disposition process from the court system to the police. The court is able to ensure that its capacity does not go unused by forcing the police (and civilian witnesses) to bear the cost of being available in the event the court does get to their

cases. The police suspect that a careful analysis might show that it would be more cost-effective (overall) to let some court capacity go unused and eliminate the standby policy. As police budgets get even tighter, this issue may be forced to the surface.

15. In a 1977 sample of 1,978 cases, 66 percent of the police officers waited 5 minutes or less. Another 17 percent waited from 5 to 20 minutes (personal communication from Dave Dingledine, Chief Deputy County Attorney, Tucson, Arizona, July 25, 1979).

16. In Baltimore County, Maryland, the prosecutor's office agreed to operate its case review unit during the evening shift once a week in addition to its normal hours. This meant that most police officers working evening or late night shifts could have their case review sessions scheduled while they were on duty (thus minimizing overtime pay). In addition, the police and prosecutor agreed that henceforth only the principal officer(s) in the case rather than all officers named in any case report would be required to attend the review. All that was needed to effect this major cost saving was for the police to name the principal officer(s) in their report (personal communication from Mark Kolman, Chief Assistant State's Attorney, Baltimore, Maryland, September 26, 1979). In other jurisdictions the police have benefited serendipitously from victim/witness programs aimed originally at minimizing the civilian witness's burden of court attendance. Telephone alert programs operated by victim/witness units have allowed the police officer to attend to other responsibilities until it is certain that his case will be heard, at which point he is called. The one requirement is that he be immediately accessible and can reach the courthouse within an hour. In Delaware County, Pennsylvania, such a program produced substantial savings for the police (personal communication from Wendell Clark, Director of the Victim/Witness Assistance Unit, Delaware County, Pennsylvania, District Attorney's Office, May 2, 1977).

17. When the police were allowed to participate in an experimental plea bargaining project, their main contribution was to supply additional information about the crime or the criminal. However, they did not participate in the plea discussions as much as one might expect, given their strong sentiment about the importance of their being consulted (Kerstetter 1981a).

18. In some jurisdictions, such as Norfolk, Virginia, the police have worked out an agreement with the prosecutor to consult them before dismissing or negotiating a case. In other jurisdictions individual judges make it their personal policy to be informed of the police opinion of the disposition agreement. But one also finds fairly prevalent among judges and prosecutors the attitude that the police should not concern themselves with disposition decisions. It may be more politically expedient for the police not to give official opinions of preferred disposition decisions because they then share in the responsibility for what could become an embarrassing decision.

19. The reason police fail to use this resource seems to be twofold: First, police performance in making strong cases for prosecution is not rewarded under the all-important civil service system. Second, even if it were, the feedback received from prosecutors is an ambiguous indication of police performance because as yet no one has developed a meaningful framework for interpreting this information. The only effective use of feedback I have seen was limited to a supervisor's review of dismissed cases for signs of police error. That feedback system was established when the chief of police in Tucson, Arizona, simply asked the prosecutor's office to send a copy of a form it was already using when cases were rejected or dismissed.

20. They have agreed, for example, that all criticisms must be specific—there will be no generalized griping—and must be directed to the appropriate supervisor, with adequate time allowed for resolution. Moreover, airing complaints in the news media before honest efforts to resolve them can be made is prohibited.

21. In 1965, arrests for drunkenness, disorderly conduct, violation of liquor laws, vagrancy, and gambling accounted for 51 percent of all arrests reported to the FBI (excluding traffic offenses). An additional 19 percent of all arrests were for somewhat more serious matters, including driving under the influence, simple assault, larceny, and motor vehicle theft (President's Commission on Law Enforcement and Administration of Justice 1967a, p. 20).

19

Blighted Trees in a Benighted Forest: The Police Officer's Cases, the Prosecutor's Screening and Bargaining Practices, and the Social Scientist's Numbers

Albert W. Alschuler

The marriage between police departments and prosecutors' offices has sometimes been troubled; and in many respects, William McDonald provides the advice that a good marriage counselor ought to provide. Pouting and snarling about the relationship are unlikely to prove constructive; both parties should learn to communicate their concerns openly. When they do, they are likely to discover, first, that some problems are illusory — the product only of misunderstanding;[1] second, that other problems can be remedied in simple and mutually beneficial ways;[2] and third, that even serious disagreements need not always be incompatible with respect and cooperation.[3] Like spouses, police officers and prosecutors owe each other straightforward statements of their grievances, not whispers or mutterings; both are entitled to a dialogue in terms of specific cases, not generalities or invective; and both are entitled to explanations of challenged actions, not high-handed declarations of the prerogatives of one's office. McDonald's chapter underlines these points and makes a valuable contribution.

Sometimes, however, one spouse has a powerful and valid grievance against another; and in an effort to be Olympian, neutral, dispassionate, and detached, a marriage counselor may overlook the strength of this spouse's moral claims. Similarly, social scientists can strive too hard to rise above the battle and to attribute patterns of conflict to immutable principles of organizational interaction, to "structural antagonisms and inefficiencies . . . which are not subject to technological improvements or administrative remedies," or to "antagonism [that] cannot be eliminated because it arises from structural conditions beyond [anyone's] power to control" (McDonald's chapter). Detached social scientists, like detached marriage counselors, may disregard the merits of conflicting claims and treat these claims merely as manifestations of a claimant's position in the maze of life. Indeed, by dismissing these claims without serious consideration some social scientists may forsake neutrality and chastise people who assert moral claims for failing to think in the same organizational terms as the social scientists themselves. McDonald's treatment of police contentions that prosecutors negotiate "too much" and decline to prosecute "too often" provides an illustration.

Although McDonald's allegation that police criticisms of prosecutors often manifest "hyperbole and misunderstanding" is probably justified, his characterization of police criticisms may reflect some hyperbole and misunderstanding itself. I know very few police officers who must be "pinned down" before revealing that they "do not feel strongly . . . that all criminals should be put in jail." To the contrary, most of the officers I know do not suggest (even weakly) that every award of probation and every dismissal are unjustified. I also know few police officers who believe that "most cases should be disposed of by trials." To the contrary, most of the officers I know regard an offender's voluntary acknowledgment of guilt as admirable and desirable; they object only to the routine award of substantial charge and sentence concessions to induce pleas of guilty. Similarly, I know few officers who object to the bona fide use of a "winnable case standard" in screening cases for prosecution. Most officers whose views I have heard would be content if prosecutors would merely prosecute and win their "winnable" cases. I have, however, encountered police officers — lots of them — who criticize prosecutorial charging and plea negotiation practices.

McDonald observes that many jurisdictions have followed the recommendations of "crime commissions since the 1920s . . . that prosecutors' offices inaugurate vigorous early screening programs."[4] Noting that "case rejection rates have usually increased dramatically" following this change, he adds:

> Rather than adjusting to this inevitable change the police have resisted, criticized, and tried to compromise it. The new screening programs have not been viewed by the police as long overdue responses to the recommendations of prominent crime commissions. Rather they have been viewed provincially and seen as self-serving policies of politically ambitious prosecutors intent on establishing good track records. . . .

Later McDonald comments:

> Complaints about plea bargaining or dismissed rates being too high are meaningless. There is no consensus as to what the appropriate rates for these outcomes should be. If anything, the consensus seems to be that these rates must be allowed to vary according to local needs and preferences. If

the police want to know whether their local rates deserve criticism they will need to consult a standard for comparison. In the absence of a national standard the only meaningful alternative would be one they construct themselves by recording their own estimates of what their cases are worth and how they would want them disposed and then comparing these expected rates with the actual rates.

Should all police complaints about plea bargaining or dismissed rates being "too high" be regarded as "meaningless"? In New York City, 40 percent of all cases initially filed as felonies are dismissed altogether, and another 46 percent end in bargained guilty pleas to misdemeanors or to even less serious infractions. Only 12 percent of the cases that begin as felony prosecutions lead to felony convictions. Moreover, 89 percent of the felony convictions are by guilty plea rather than trial (Vera Institute of Justice 1981, p. 143), and most felony guilty pleas appear to be the product of substantial bargaining concessions (Kuh 1975; Zeisel 1982, pp. 42–43, 127–41).

The situation in New York City seems unusual; that in Washington, D.C., is more typical of urban jurisdictions. There 21 percent of all felony cases in which the police make arrests are rejected by prosecutors at the initial case screening, 29 percent are dismissed later, and 13 percent end in guilty pleas to misdemeanors. Thus 50 percent of all felony arrests ultimately are not prosecuted, and nearly two-thirds either are not prosecuted or are reduced to misdemeanors through plea bargaining (Forst, Lucianovic, and Cox 1977, p. 17).

Should one "adjust" to the "inevitable change" that these figures reflect? Should one view this change as a "long overdue response to the recommendations of prominent crime commissions"? Should one also refuse to listen to any criticism of a declination rate until the critic can point to "a national standard" or a "consensus as to what the appropriate rates for these outcomes should be" or his own estimate of an appropriate "expected rate"? Or should one begin to complain—and to complain louder than many police officers have in fact been complaining?[5]

Raw statistical measures of dismissal and guilty plea rates are undoubtedly subject to a variety of interpretations. In dangerous, threatening situations, it may be appropriate for police officers to make arrests on probable cause simply to "clear the streets" and for prosecutors then to decline to prosecute because the available evidence would not establish guilt beyond a reasonable doubt. It also may be appropriate to arrest on probable cause when evidence justifying prosecution is likely to emerge with further investigation although this evidence is not currently available. Nevertheless, it would strain credulity to suppose that all or most dismissals have occurred in cases in which police officers have made appropriate arrests but in which prosecutors have lacked sufficient evidence to go further.

Instead, today's very high attrition rates appear to bespeak a serious failure of the criminal justice system. Of course one cannot know on the basis of the statistics alone where blame for the failure may lie. Perhaps, for example, police officers are arresting scores of people whose guilt cannot be proven, and perhaps prosecutors are merely remedying the unjust detention of possibly innocent suspects when they decline to prosecute half or more of the felony cases presented to them.

Although the statistics leave open the possibility of police failure, the officers whose cases are rejected may know better, and the failure might not in fact be theirs. It might instead be that of the legislature. Many of the declined cases might be "winnable," and prosecutors might want to win them. Nevertheless, the legislature might have failed to provide adequate resources to do the job. When the citizenry becomes concerned about crime, legislative bodies tend to "support their local police." They may not support their local courts, prosecutors' offices, defender agencies, and correctional facilities to the same extent. The result is likely to be an imbalance in the criminal justice system, one that police officers who criticize current disposition patterns have not always rushed to protest. The police may generate more "winnable" cases than prosecutors can win, and high declination and plea bargaining rates may follow. In this situation, the legislature, by failing to treat the criminal justice system as a system, has ensured that a portion of the resources devoted to the police will essentially be wasted.

Or the failure indicated by current dismissal and plea bargaining rates may be that of the victims of crime. It has been common in academic circles to attribute these rates to "victim noncooperation" and other "difficulties of proof" that prosecutors encounter. The reason has been that prosecutors themselves have attributed their decisions to these circumstances in interviews and on hundreds of computerized forms.[6] Nevertheless, when the Institute for Law and Social Research (INSLAW) approached victims to learn the reasons for their reticence, 202 of 215 witnesses labeled "noncooperative" by prosecutors gave responses that were inconsistent with this designation. Some of these witnesses might have forgotten the facts or might have colored the circumstances deliberately in an attempt to "save face" with the interviewers, but the INSLAW study reported that "in cases where the witnesses knew the defendants, prosecutors were observed labeling witnesses as noncooperative not on the basis of observed noncooperation . . . but in anticipation of it" and that "[s]ome prosecutors acknowledged over-using the noncooperator label because such a designation reduced the probability of a challenge from the supervising attorney who reviewed case-screening decisions" (Cannavale and Falcon 1978, pp. 75–84, 87, 88).

Some case attrition is undoubtedly attributable to police failure, some to inadequate resources, and some to witness noncooperation. Yet some is probably attributable to another cause. The general failure indicated by high dismissal and plea bargaining rates may be in part the prosecutors'. Perhaps these rates sometimes do reflect the "self-serving policies of politically ambitious prosecutors intent on establishing good track records," (see McDonald's chapter). Or perhaps they reflect norms of "reasonableness" established in courthouse interchanges with trial judges and defense attorneys. Or perhaps they reflect bureaucratic cynicism and callousness toward crime, or even a little bit of laziness.

McDonald dismisses these possibilities and disparages police views of prosecutorial screening and plea bargaining practices without offering any evidence that the police views are unjustified. Certainly it is not difficult to find dedicated and energetic prosecutors in American courthouses; it also is not difficult to find some overzealous prosecutors who fail to abandon unprovable allegations when they should. Nevertheless, one need not spend very much time in the criminal courts to encounter some prosecutors who appear to consider routine law enforcement beneath their dignity. When a felony case does not involve political corruption, consumer fraud, "career" crime, homicide, or violence against a "stranger," some prosecutors seem to seize on almost any excuse to "wash it out" or bargain it to a misdemeanor. Some seem to discover evidentiary weaknesses whenever a defense attorney shakes a rattle, and some seem even to view high declination rates as a mark of professionalism (especially when they can give their wash-outs a cosmetic front and call them by a fancy name like "diversion," "pretrial probation," or "accelerated rehabilitative disposition").[7] The basic dilemma suggested by the rates seems inescapable: Either the police are making arrests in many doubtful cases, or, as one prominent crime commission of the 1920s remarked, "The force of law administration [is being whittled down] to a mere fragment of its basic seriousness" (Illinois Association for Criminal Justice 1929, p. 310).

When a police officer suggests that current declination and plea bargaining rates are "too high," his point is not that these rates should match a national norm or some preconceived percentage figure. Indeed, his goal is not a "rate" or a "magic number" at all; it is a sense that criminal cases are taken seriously and resolved on their merits. That sense frequently eludes him in American courthouses, just as it eludes defendants, the victims of crime, corrections officers, and members of the public. The police officer is talking about cases, not rates. He is talking about *his* cases, and only someone accustomed to thinking of law enforcement problems in impersonal numerical terms could miss his point.

NOTES

1. For example, stories of prosecutorial insensitivity to police concerns sometimes have grown with every telling, and police officers sometimes have become indignant about things that never happened. Similarly, when prosecutors have perceived police failures, they often have not bothered

to express their concerns but have responded by dismissing cases or entering plea agreements and then waiting resignedly for those incorrigible Keystone Cops to make the same mistakes again.

2. For example, police administrators ought to seek the prosecutors' help in improving the sometimes dismal quality of police offense reports; in response, prosecutors ought at a minimum to flag the weaknesses of particular reports and return them with comments. And face-to-face screening conferences should be held in serious cases even when resources are not adequate to permit the regular use of these conferences.

3. McDonald is probably correct, for example, that honest disagreement concerning the priority to be afforded the prosecution of "morals" offenses is likely to persist and that becoming indignant about this disagreement is unlikely to be helpful.

4. Although this statement is accurate, it may be somewhat misleading. Most crime commissions of the 1920s were highly critical of prosecutorial plea negotiation and dismissal rates, and their criticisms of prosecutors' offices were similar in both content and tone to those that police officers voice today (see, for example, Fosdick 1920; Illinois Association for Criminal Justice 1929; New York State Crime Commission 1927; Fuller 1931).

5. I am sometimes surprised by the restraint that police officers exhibit in their criticisms of prosecutors. In Boulder County, Colorado, the district attorney once instituted a "no plea bargaining" policy with great fanfare. The policy generated considerable favorable local and national publicity (as well as complaints to the press by the head of the local public defender office, who protested that the work generated by the policy had kept him from seeing his family even on weekends). Several years later, local police departments conducted a statistical survey of case disposition patterns, a survey that indicated widespread plea bargaining. The district attorney did not deny the plea bargaining, nor did he defend in principle the award of "deferred sentences" to serious felony offenders. Instead he pleaded a lack of adequate resources. The concerned police officials who had conducted the survey refrained from asking pointed questions about when the no plea bargaining policy had been abandoned and whether its abandonment had been announced. Instead they merely pledged their cooperation to the district attorney in his renewed efforts to secure adequate funding for his office.

McDonald emphasizes the "structural antagonisms" that sometimes prompt police officers and prosecutors to disagree; but in any ongoing working relationship (or marriage), powerful structural factors prompt cooperation and restraint as well. Consider, for example, agreements between prosecutors and police officers not to "blow the whistle" on one another without trying to work things out quietly—agreements to keep the public unaware of the failures of our criminal justice system that McDonald discusses with seeming approval.

6. Academic observers also have been sympathetic to the claims of criminal court regulars that almost all "nonstranger" or "prior relationship" crimes are "trash."

7. I do not suggest that all cases of diversion are essentially wash-outs, only that most of them are.

20
Overkilling the Police: A Response to McDonald on Police and the Legal Profession

Joseph D. McNamara

Although anachronistically impossible, it almost seems as though William McDonald would have the reader believe it was some parochial police chief whose social reform priorities were reflected in the Shakespearian exhortation: "The first thing we do, let's kill all the lawyers." To be sure, police and their administrators are no more immune to demagoguery than are prosecutors, academics, or most of the rest of us. But McDonald's view of the balance of fault and remedial responsibility for the state of police chief-prosecutor relations is mostly out of focus. This is not to say that some of his suggestions for improvement are without merit. Who would disagree that police chiefs and prosecutors should meet with each other? Who would deny the value of getting police, prosecutors, and courts to speed up the legal process so that the necessary evil of plea bargaining is not necessary quite so often?

McDonald implies, however, that police chiefs are the main obstacles blocking improvements in the criminal justice system. He contends that chiefs are more interested in attacking plea bargaining and judicial leniency than joining in cooperative efforts to improve the system. (The thinly veiled charge is that chiefs are not "innovative"; these days the only worse accusation is that a chief is felonious!) While some police chiefs may be recalcitrant, in my experience it is generally the case that the courts, prosecutors, and defense attorneys have actually been more resistant to analysis and change than the police. The police *are* on the subordinate end of the judicial system, whatever one's social-psychological assessment may be of the police self-image and sense of professional status vis-à-vis other justice system actors. Prosecutors decide which cases to prosecute, and when. Defense attorneys ask for continuances. Courts set calendars, subpoena police at will, and make rulings that institutionalize delay.

When McDonald places the blame predominantly on the police for inadequacies in the system, I remember my own frustrations over efforts to get better information and cooperation from courts and prosecutors so that we could jointly improve the system. Moreover, in the 12 years I have been attending meetings of big city police chiefs, it has become clear to me that, while chiefs' opinions of local district attorneys and courts vary, a common complaint is that judges and prosecutors rebuff periodic police requests for instruction on why cases are rejected and on how police can modify their conduct to facilitate successful prosecutions.

In some cities, such as San Jose, New York, and Kansas City, prosecuting attorneys nod in the direction of indicating their reasons for case rejections by routinely filling out a simple form (in many other jurisdictions prosecutors do not even keep written records on case attrition). But on closer examination one learns that the prosecutors all too often casually check off the caption "insufficient evidence" on the case rejection forms. When police administrators seek more information they often find that the term "insufficient evidence" is a catch-all. It could mean that witnesses had moved or died, or that the assistant prosecutor felt a key witness might not stand up to strenuous cross-examination. The same caption would be checked in some towns if the prosecutor thought a motion to suppress might succeed. Such vagueness or misinformation inhibits a well-intentioned police chief from improving his agency's collaboration with the rest of the justice system. At the same time it leaves the prosecutor free to talk about police incompetence and inadequacy — and politicians such as prosecutors may feel more comfortable when they have a convenient whipping boy. Another harmful result of prosecutors' inaccuracy in recording reasons for case attrition is that police chiefs are inhibited from serving a watchdog function with respect to prosecutorial decisions. If a prosecutor drops a case because he does not consider it important enough in light of his overall caseload, the police need to know the real reason for rejection if they are to be any help to the crime victim(s) in the particular case who feel a sense of injustice.

Proposing any sort of national model to guide the amelioration of poor police-prosecutor communication is clearly beyond the scope of a comment such as this. At best, one can note that all concerned must work toward a better balance of responsibility for solutions and a better acceptance of certain structural tensions, such as differences in the standards of proof of criminality that justify police and prosecutorial intervention, which lead each institution to make decisions that would be inappropriate for the other. One can also call attention to ongoing examples of effective police-prosecutor cooperation for emulation, with appropriate adjustments for local idiosyncracies, by other jurisdictions. For example, the county prosecutor in Alameda County, California, prepares videotapes concerning legal developments of importance to the police, which are regularly shown in area police stations.

In San Jose, a case enhancement program, prepared jointly by the police department and the district attorney, resulted in a 42 percent increase in the cases presented by the police and a 60 percent increase in the cases actually filed by the prosecutor. McDonald cites the Dallas Police Department's assessment of prosecutors' and grand juries' reasons for rejecting cases. Other examples could be offered.

Besides getting better information about such programmatic responses to police-prosecutor friction, it strikes me that progress would also come if prosecutors realized that, for better *and* worse, they are seen by police not only as fellow operatives in the criminal justice system but also as representatives of the American legal profession. As a result, prosecutors become the focus of some admiration but mostly a great deal of suspicion and hostility that police feel toward lawyers. The pique stems from behavior that may be only tangentially related to the criminal justice system but that sets a tone concerning the state of justice in our society generally. Thus criticisms of lawyer incompetency and the explosion of litigation, voiced by Chief Justice Warren Burger, the question whether our society is more just since the litigation explosion, asked by Harvard University President and former Harvard Law School Dean Derek Bok, and the characterization of litigation, in light of its expense, as "the sport of kings," proffered by Justice Sandra Day O'Connor — all form a social backdrop against which police, reflecting public attitudes, think about what is wrong with and how to repair police-prosecutor cooperation. I am sure my friends in the legal profession could prepare no less a litany about lawyers' perceptions of cops.

McDonald's thesis that cooperative efforts for reform are needed from all components of the system is correct. It seems to me counterproductive to play one institution against another. Each of the organizations that make up the criminal justice system has room to improve. Yet the ability of each to do so depends on the actions of the others. A free and open exchange of ideas is essential to that process. It is unlikely to occur when the ideas of police executives are denigrated as attacks, while similar contentions by prosecuting attorneys are viewed as deserving of study.

21
Of Overkill and Blighted Trees: A Rejoinder to McNamara and Alschuler

William F. McDonald

Most points made by Joseph McNamara and Albert Alschuler are not criticisms but validations of my argument. The underlying theme of their comments, namely, that I have placed too much blame on the police for breakdowns in the police-prosecutor-court relationships, ignores the scope of my assignment. I focused on what police executives have within *their* power to do about their relationship with the court system. This does not mean I hold them primarily responsible for the areas of breakdown I identify; nor do I suggest that we should "refuse to listen to any critic of a declination rate until this critic can point to 'a national standard' or a 'consensus as to what the appropriate rates for these outcomes should be' or his own estimate of an appropriate 'expected rate.'" The police have a legitimate watchdog function to play with respect to prosecutorial discretion. But in order to perform it effectively they must be able to do better than McNamara's vague statement that "prosecutors all too often casually check off the caption 'insufficient evidence' on the case rejection forms." Indeed, case attrition statistics are subject to a wide range of interpretations. Therefore, police executives must be able to say how often is "too often," and why. Since no standards exist as to what constitutes "too often," they will have to create their own based on assessments of their cases.

22
Section 1983 and the Changing Face of Police Management

Wayne W. Schmidt

THE SCOPE AND AMOUNT OF SECTION 1983 LITIGATION

When Congress passed the "Ku Klux Klan" Act of 1871 it had no intention of including police misconduct litigation. The plaintiff's bar largely ignored what is now 42 U.S. Code section 1983 until the seminal Supreme Court case of *Monroe* v. *Pape* (1961). In the next decade only a few police misconduct suits were filed in the federal courts, where this federal statute could be utilized. The New York City Police Department, for example, led the country in lawsuits during the five-year period from 1967 to 1972, but only 5 percent of those cases were brought to the federal forum. Although the federal percentage in other departments was somewhat higher, most of the litigation against police remained in the state courts. This is no longer true, and this chapter briefly looks at the recent history of section 1983 and the implications of its expanded use for police leadership in America.

Section 1983 encompasses "civil rights violations" under color of state law. When maintained by citizens, lawsuits attacking such violations are also cognizable in the state courts as actions concerning traditional torts. The Supreme Court noted in *Monroe* that section 1983 "should be read against the background of tort liability that makes man responsible for the natural consequences of his actions." The police misconduct torts recognized at common law that also constitute a civil rights violation include false arrest or imprisonment, malicious prosecution, battery (brutality), trespass (illegal entry and searches), property conversion (illegal seizure), and, in many states, the intentional infliction of emotional distress (harassment). A number of state statutory torts may also form the basis of a federal civil rights violation, including wrongful death and unlawful eavesdropping. And violations of certain rights secured by federal statute or international treaty are also covered by section 1983.

Besides these common law and statutory bases for federal jurisdiction, section 1983 can also be used against a police administrator to redress purely constitutional violations, such as infringement of the rights of free speech (for example, disciplining a sergeant for criticizing the chief of police) or assembly (denying a parade permit to a controversial group); improper license revocations (to such businesses as X-rated entertainment centers and bookstores); due process violations (depriving officers of certain rights in police disciplinary proceedings); denial of access to the courts (interfering with the attorney-client relationship, as in inmate mail censorship); and inadequate medical care of those incarcerated in facilities controlled by police or sheriffs' departments.

Only a few claims that are cognizable in state courts fail to rise to the level of a federal civil rights violation. For example, injuries to reputation are not encompassed within section 1983 unless accompanied by another claim, such as loss of employment; similarly, inmates do not have a cause of action for property losses when the incarcerating jurisdiction has adopted adequate administrative remedies.

There are several reasons why plaintiffs increasingly are choosing to bring suit in federal court. Some lawyers believe you get a "higher grade" of juror on the panel and a more erudite judge, though there is little evidence for such a conclusion. Also, federal judges, who are appointed for life, theoretically are less susceptible to political pressures than those state judges who must run for election or retention. Who would choose to sue the Adams County sheriff in the Adams County Court and argue to a jury that elected the defendant? A federal jury is selected from a multicounty area, and fewer of the jurors may be electors or taxpayers in the jurisdiction that employs the defendant officer.

Another reason for plaintiff preference of the federal forum is that the federal rules of pleading and evidence are uniform and straightforward compared to many state codes. Discovery procedures are liberal, and process can be served on a statewide and sometimes national basis. Additionally, lawyers may have easier access to the published case law required to prepare a federal suit than they would to the materials necessary for state court litigation. The *Federal Supplement*, reporting the growing body of federal district opinions on police misconduct, is more readily available, particularly in small towns, than the regional state court reporters. Besides access to necessary written materials, federal plaintiffs, when seeking injunctive relief, are assured of the competence and professionalism of the Federal Marshal Service to serve show cause citations and to enforce decrees, thereby avoiding reliance on elected sheriffs and their often partisan political deputies.

More importantly, Congress passed section 1988 of the Civil Rights Act of 1976, which allows attorney's fees to the "prevailing party" over and above the award for compensatory and punitive damages. This provision in the federal law has done more to move police litigation to the federal forum and to stimulate its growth than any other factor (see Nader and Schultz 1985). Attorneys who specialize in personal injury litigation usually accept cases on a contingency basis of one-third of the recovery. Thus a plaintiff's verdict in a shooting case can be quite profitable for the lawyer, as the award may be in six figures. Compare that with one-third share of a recovery of $2,500 for verbal abuse, a hostile shove, overly tight handcuffs, or an illegal frisk. In contrast to the contingent-fee approach, section 1988 bases the award for legal services on the time necessarily and customarily spent on the client interview, the drafting of pleadings, pretrial discovery, research, preparation, and trial. For example, one lawyer received $6,000 for a half-day trial; the client was awarded $600 because an officer had slapped his face. What would have been a "garbage" case ten years ago might, between 1983 and 1988, pay the office rent for a whole year.

Despite all the incentives to choose the federal forum, it should be noted that in cases involving minority-race, inner-city plaintiffs, lawyers may want to avoid federal court for strategic reasons concerning racial preference. Counsel may feel that a county jury in a large urban area will have a greater number of minority members and will adopt a more favorable attitude toward the minority clients than would be the case in the federal system.

In an attempt to measure the consequences of the various incentives for enhanced police misconduct litigation, Americans for Effective Law Enforcement (AELE) has conducted two five-year studies of such cases in both federal and state courts. The studies covered the period from 1967 through 1976. Police misconduct suits in state courts rose from 1,556 in 1967 to 8,007 in 1976 (an increase of more than 400 percent); during the same ten-year period, federal civil rights actions alleging police wrongdoing rose from 167 to 2,226 (more than a twelvefold jump). Combining jurisdictions, misconduct suits grew from 5.5 per 1,000 officers to 19.6 per 1,000 in the ten-year interval. In the second five-year period, 32 percent of all actions were arrest-related, and a similar portion primarily alleged excessive nondeadly force (see Blodgett 1985). Firearms-related suits accounted for 6.8 percent of the total, with half of these for bodily injury and half for wrongful death. Injuries to reputation constituted 2.1 percent of all actions, poor conditions in police- or sheriff-run jails 3.7 percent, illegal searches 3.6 percent, invasions of privacy 1.8 percent, actions seeking injunctive relief 3.7 percent, and other miscellaneous actions 14.6 percent.

Of all actions filed between 1972 and 1976, 41 percent were still pending as of 1977, 22 percent were settled, 23 percent were dropped by the plaintiff or dismissed on a defense motion, and 14.6 percent were tried. Plaintiffs won only 3.5 percent of all suits filed and lost 10.1 percent; viewing only those cases that actually went to trial, plaintiffs won 24 percent and lost 76 percent of the time. The AELE estimates that in 1983 about 25,000 police misconduct suits were filed in the United States.

IMPACT ON THE POLICE ADMINISTRATOR

Twenty years ago it would have been impossible to get more than a handful of police executives to a free seminar on police liability. Today such programs typically last three days and cost more than $300 in tuition and hundreds more in time, travel, and lodging expenses. In recent years more than 3,000 senior police officials have attended such three-day programs, and a greater number of them have attended shorter programs. The FBI National Academy has incorporated civil liability into its curricula, and the International Association of Chiefs of Police has an annual conference session devoted to this topic. The explanation for these developments is not only the availability of the federal forum and all its real and perceived benefits but also a greater willingness of jurors to give substantial verdicts against police officials and governmental entities and the personal liability of the police executive for "administrative negligence."

The police chief's personal exposure to litigation is large and growing steadily. Frequently a simple brutality suit will name senior police executives as codefendants. The allegation is that they breached their managerial duty at some point, prior in time to the event giving rise to the particular suit, and that that breach was the proximate cause of the later injury to the plaintiff. Typical allegations of administrative negligence include improper appointment of an unqualified applicant, insufficient training, retention of a known unfit subordinate, negligent entrustment of a firearm, inadequate supervision, and failure of the administration to properly direct personnel and limit subordinates' individual discretion. Such allegations serve three purposes in a damage suit. First, they ensure that a judgment will be paid by the employing entity because the chief executive, although jointly liable for the judgment, did not personally participate in the alleged misconduct. Second, allegations of administrative deficiencies widen the scope of discovery. Third, proof that the department or its senior executives could have prevented the instant occurrence will prejudice the jury against the named principal officer and encourage jurors to return a larger verdict.

One of the observable effects of section 1983 litigation is that some governmental agencies now employ risk managers and loss prevention consultants. Together with public entity attorneys and budget directors, they have brought steady pressure on police administrators to reduce their risks and minimize losses. The reason for such pressure is economic, not political. This is a new trend for the police executive, who previously had only to respond to occasional verbal criticism from small, but vocal, political action groups.

The economic stimuli for better risk reduction are not hard to discern. For example, police departments' and municipalities' annual costs of legal defense have risen dramatically. A typical false arrest insurance policy cost $12.50 per officer 20 years ago; it now costs about $300. The average suit consumes 96 hours of police time to investigate and 117 hours of a lawyer's time to defend (AELE 1974). The sheer volume of suits has encouraged many cities to settle frivolous claims for their nuisance value, and several actions have been lost by default due to oversight on the part of overworked governmental counsel. The new importance of economic pressures on police chiefs has an interesting practical consequence for these administrators: Now, for the first time, and for better or worse, there is an objective, nonpolitical criterion to measure police performance and misconduct, namely, the number of suits or claims and the amount of verdicts or settlements. The implications of this new yardstick for either lengthening or shortening police executive tenure could be substantial.

It is not surprising, therefore, that in small or medium-sized departments, police chiefs have become liability-conscious, sometimes overly so. They have initiated stronger administrative controls and increased the severity of disciplinary punishment of subordinates. A recent example of this occurred in Arlington, Virginia. The American Civil Liberties Union (ACLU) in 1980 and 1981 filed a series of suits against the sheriff alleging improper strip searches of persons arrested. Prior to 1981, the sheriff had persistently defended his strip search policy, both locally and on national television. But under the pressure of the lawsuits and heavy criticism, the sheriff adopted a more restrictive policy on searching persons booked into the county jail. Following the sheriff's policy change, an injunction was issued in one of the suits (*Logan v. Shealy* 1981), and the Virginia legislature enacted a restrictive jail search statute (Va. Code section 19.2–59.1 [1981]). Subsequently, a woman arrested in Arlington for driving on a suspended license was booked and strip searched, without supervisory approval and against the new department policy, which limited searches for such offenses to a "pat down" and metal detector scan. The department's three-person disciplinary board recommended that the deputy receive a written reprimand, to be removed from her file after 90 days of satisfactory service. Cognizant of the civil liability implications, the sheriff disregarded the recommendations of his own board and imposed a five-day suspension from pay and duty and ordered the forfeiture of 40 hours of accrued vacation leave. In addition, an official reprimand will remain in her file permanently. In spite of this administrative action, the ACLU indicated it would sue the sheriff and his deputy over the incident.

The Arlington example is indicative of the way section 1983 has caused administrators to change their policies and to enforce those new policies by the discipline of errant subordinates. A suit is filed against an intransigent law enforcement official, and an injunction is granted or damages are awarded. Departmental policies are revised, and subordinates are thereafter disciplined for violations. Administrative punishment is imposed, consistent with the gravity of the misconduct.

Another example of the policy impact of section 1983 is in the area of use of deadly force. In a number of cases, state law permits the shooting of a fleeing felon (see Geller and Karales 1981b). Cognizant of the facts that many felonies are committed by juveniles, and that felonies differ in gravity, a number of chiefs and sheriffs have administratively restricted the instances where officers can use deadly force. In some of these cases the prohibited class of shootings was permitted by state law. In every state except Florida plaintiff's counsel can seek to prove that the officer was guilty of negligence for violating his department's "work rules." A departmental finding of propriety is not admissible and will not exonerate a shooter from liability. A jury, often persuaded by so-called experts, may find that a shooting exceeded internal regulations and that the officer was therefore negligent in using deadly force. But a chief cannot avoid such liability merely by failing to adopt a restrictive firearms use policy because, as suggested earlier, plaintiffs can probably establish that failure to adhere to the "state of the art" by upgrading departmental policies is itself administrative negligence. Moreover, the awesome threat of punitive damages discourages leniency in shooting policies (see Baker 1976).

While section 1983 litigation has been effective against small and medium-sized agencies, it may be having far less of a direct impact on major city police administrators. These chiefs may not notice particular pending lawsuits, which may number in the thousands, or even specific judgments or settlements, of which there could have been hundreds in recent years. Large city police administrators often are unaware which cases are lost and why. The reason for this ignorance is partly political and partly institutional.

In the largest cities, suits against the police are defended by *assistant* city attorneys, who have little contact with the chief except to question him on the witness stand from time to time. They do not offer policy advice to him because their superior, the city attorney, is the policymaking lawyer in their office. But the city attorney, as a legal administrator, may be unaware of problems in the police department. For their part, chiefs in large departments too frequently fail to seek policymaking advice from lawyers. The chief may not seek advice from the assistants who litigate police cases because he perceives these lawyers in a lower status on the political scale.

Reliance by chiefs on publicly employed attorneys for legal advice concerning policing is somewhat problematic. There are many institutional differences between public lawyers and those in private firms. Private lawyers bill clients on an hourly basis and thus have an incentive to spend more time with their clients. To an assistant city attorney, extra time spent on one case means less time for other cases, more time away from his or her family, and no additional compensation. Moreover, private firms offer better salaries to their associates and the opportunity to become a partner. It is only natural that private firms get the best law school graduates, and assistant city attorneys who prove themselves in court get attractive offers from private firms.

A partial solution to this problem has been the employment of additional risk managers and legal advisers who can work together to minimize liability by the improvement of training, the reexamination of departmental policies, and the reassignment of officers who generate an abnormal number of complaints.

Police chiefs can learn from the practice of good military commanders, especially general officers, who debrief and analyze their battle losses. In large police agencies at this time, the debriefing analysis is often confined to cases where police officers are shot. As a result, the large city chief of police may be unaware of litigation trends, common exposures, and risk reduction options available to him.

RISK REDUCTION TECHNIQUES

Because of the bureaucratic shuffle and breakdown in communications in the largest departments, major city police chiefs would find it helpful to implement controls to assist them in curbing the increase in litigation and judgments. Civil liability exposure is not the only reason such controls are adopted, but it certainly is a primary factor.

One such control is to administer a battery of psychological tests to ferret out sadists, depressives, and other unqualified police applicants. Moreover, civil liability can be reduced by periodic testing of incumbent subordinates (*Bonsignore* v. *City of New York* 1981). Additionally, officers suspected of having psychological problems can be singled out for specific evaluation, particularly when an incident in question produced a disciplinary investigation (see *Nolan* v. *Police Com'r of Boston* 1981 and *Conte* v. *Horscher* 1977).

A number of departments have attempted to minimize liability by enhancing recruit training programs beyond state-mandated minimum levels. Sensitivity awareness, hostility control, conflict avoidance, and the use of nonlethal restraint methods are principal features of such training. Training directed at experienced police officers has also been used by police chiefs to manage their legal risks. Twenty years ago many administrators considered the sergeant position a mere step in the career ladder, and promotions were often based on considerations of seniority. Moreover, a sergeant who adversely affected the morale of his subordinates by initiating disciplinary action might be passed over in the selection process for lieutenant. Today there is a reverse tendency to hold sergeants accountable for the neglects and omissions of their subordinates. Sergeants are invariably referred to as supervisors and routinely receive specialized management training in the larger departments shortly after their promotion to that rank.

At the same time that chiefs increasingly are holding first-line supervisors and middle managers accountable for the conduct of their subordinates, departments are moving to protect themselves by centralizing disciplinary investigations and the authority to order punishment. This reduces favoritism or bias and cover-ups and promotes certainty in the disciplinary process. Previously, many chiefs left disciplinary matters to the concerned station commander.

Although, as indicated, firearms-related civil suits are not an enormous percentage of all cases filed against the police, losing such a suit can prove extremely costly in light of the typical gravity of the plaintiff's injury. Accordingly, better management of use of weapons is a prime focus of risk reduction efforts. Cognizant of the liability that can arise from poor marksmanship, most departments now require officers periodically to qualify on the range with their service and off-duty weapons. In some cases, officers with physical or mental impairments have been disarmed and assigned to administrative or correction duties. A growing number of departments have modified their firearms range to provide for moving and pop-up targets that realistically simulate combat shooting situations.

In addition, some agencies are repealing regulations that require an officer to carry his weapon when off duty and to take appropriate enforcement action when confronted by criminal activity while off duty (see Geller 1982, p. 171). This relaxation is intended to avoid shootings in cocktail lounges and other places of leisure, where an officer might escalate a private altercation into a police confrontation.

As a final example of risk management initiatives, it is worth noting the growing use of police legal advisers, who were employed in less than 20 departments in 1968 and now work for more than 300 departments. Although legal advisers provide counsel to chiefs on a variety of subjects, civil liability is an area of major concern, and department directives and training are under constant scrutiny by department house counsel for their civil liability implications.

POLICE PERCEPTIONS OF SECTION 1983 LITIGATION

Essentially two kinds of suits are brought against the police community. One is for intentionally wrong or simply sloppy police work. It might involve a false arrest, brutality, or a "bad" shooting. Police officers and administrators understand that liability should and will attach to an intentional tort or serious carelessness. They object, however, to the fact that so many cases are without merit and drain the resources of internal affairs and departmental counsel. They are upset when a damage judgment for a nightstick-inflicted lost eye is two or three times higher than the award in a suit for a similar injury caused by a slip-and-fall. The chief of police of Piedmont, California, recently shared a perception of other consequences that result from the litigation explosion:

> Piedmont, like numerous other local municipal jurisdictions, faces the potential of lawsuits filed based on the actions of our police officers. The suits we face most often are based on harassment, excessive force, and false arrest. Usually, the bottom line is the statement of the complainant versus that of the officer, and seldom are there independent witnesses to substantiate the claims of either individual.*** Our problem is further complicated by the fact that a claim is filed, and denied by the City, then a lawsuit is settled because it is cheaper than prolonged litigation. This process, although less expensive to the City, still leaves us with a disgruntled officer since he feels that any settlement leaves him with some type of taint of guilt. (Steckler 1984)

The other kind of lawsuit is where a police officer took the only action he could at the time of the injury, but liability is predicated on a lack of specialized training. There are more than 150 self-appointed "experts" in police liability who specialize in testifying that a particular procedure was deficient or improper. For example, one city paid $225,000 to the estate of a man who was killed just as he was about to plunge a knife into one of the several officers at the scene. A plaintiff's expert testified that the police had inadequate training on how to deal with mentally unstable persons and could have deescalated the incident to the point of preventing the decedent's aggression (*Edward H. Dent* v. *City of New Orleans* 1980).

In this example, an officer on the scene had but two choices at the point where the decedent raised the knife in his hand and stood over a sergeant who had fallen to the floor: shoot the armed aggressor and save the life of the sergeant (that decision cost the city $225,000 for "inadequate" training) or not shoot and watch the mental defective kill the sergeant. That decision would have cost the city for job-related death benefits paid to the sergeant's family. Of course, neither of the financial consequences was in the mind of the shootist at the time the aggressor was felled. He surely acted with common sense and prevented a homicide. The "good guys" were saved from harm from the "bad guy." Years later a jury would determine whether the session on handling mentally disturbed persons taught at the police academy was sufficient to prepare officers to intervene in domestic disputes, fights between neighbors, or barroom brawls.

Contrast that case to one several years ago in another city where a distraught father called police and said his daughter's ex-boyfriend was in the front yard and was armed with a knife. Four officers attempted to dissuade the young man's aggression. Even after the youth cut one of the officers, they remained cool and did not fire. The youth managed to break away, enter the house, lock the door, and then went on a bloody rampage. The daughter was stabbed to death; her mother and two other children were cut and injured. The parents then sued the officers for wrongful death and for the injuries inflicted on the mother and their minor children. They alleged the police should have shot the aggressor the moment they saw him with a knife and that their negligent failure to do so was the proximate cause of their grievous loss of kin (*Selensky* v. *City of Dubuque* 1979).

Although it is not hard to find negative police perceptions of the impact of section 1983, progressive police leaders will enumerate the positive aspects of increased liability:

1. More departments are placing greater emphasis on comprehensive background investigations — including psychological screening — to eliminate applicants with a propensity for violence or other misbehavior.
2. Officers accused of serious misconduct often are placed on administrative leave or assigned to cloistered settings pending disposition of any disciplinary proceedings and civil litigation; unfortunately, however, a suit may drag on for years.
3. Police administrators, anxious to avoid allegations of "negligent retention of a known unfit," are apt to act more promptly to charge an errant officer and to seek the ultimate sanction of termination.
4. Sergeants and watch commanders are given specialized training that emphasizes the attendant liability for their negligent failure to supervise subordinates adequately.
5. Cities and counties are noting that under *Monell* v. *Department of Social Services* (1978) a city can be sued in federal court for inadequate training of its officers, and that under *Owen* v. *City of Independence* (1980) the defense of good faith is no longer available to the government entity.

CONCLUSION

Police malpractice litigation will continue to impact on the profession the same way medical malpractice litigation has affected physicians. Officers, like family doctors, will practice "defensively" and assume that they will be sued on a regular basis. Reports will be written from the perspective that a jury will eventually read them in an effort to find possible negligence. Officers will be noncommittal but more thorough. They will be reticient to volunteer their opinion that a particular incident could have been better handled by themselves or their colleagues. Just as the cost of a doctor's visit goes up with increased physician-patient contact time and unneeded lab tests, police departments, facing new costs, will either lose personnel or have to hire more officers who will be out of service longer in an effort to justify every action or inaction in their notes and reports.

As the number of lawyers and judges increases, and as the public uses legal services with greater frequency, the number of suits, settlements, and verdicts will grow. Presumably, the trend toward litigation will someday level off and perhaps drop back, but it may not be due to increased police training or better applicant selection techniques. It more likely will be because the police, like physicians, become more proficient in defending their suits, or because the plaintiff's bar has agreed to the mediation of disputes without resort to the courts. I have little faith that either event will come quickly or painlessly.

PART 6

THE CHIEF
AND THE UNION

Introduction

In May 1980 Douglas A. Fraser, then president of the United Automobile Workers (UAW), was elected to the Chrysler Corporation's board of directors, "becoming the first leader of a national labor union to sit on the board of a national corporation." In October 1984, his successor as union head was named to the board ("UAW President" 1984), at which time UAW members owned more than 12 percent of Chrysler's stock, according to the *Wall Street Journal* ("Chrysler Corp." 1984). A number of years before these significant events in American private sector labor history occurred, rank-and-file police officers had attained the ability to dictate management policies in the public law enforcement field (see Allen Andrews's, Donald Fraser's, and William Hudnut's chapters, as well as Anthony Bouza's contribution in this section), and a private sector quipster opined: "My mistake was buying stock in the company. Now I worry about the lousy work I'm turning out" (Peter 1977, p. 282). Teetering precariously on that quip's thin line between truth and jest is much of today's police labor-management relations.

Bouza's chapter traces the historical ebb and flow and the current surge of the labor movement in American policing. He examines the dynamics of four major twentieth-century police strikes. Bouza writes of crises and opportunities confronting the police leader, the former at this point in history seeming to outnumber the latter. Having run out of the revenue needed to make monetary concessions in most cities, police and municipal management representatives have begun to bargain away prerogatives long considered the province of the chief and his political superior, such as policymaking authority concerning the use of force and the deployment of one- or two-officer squad cars. As one administrator put it at a recent chiefs' convention, "Collective bargaining today consists of the two sides dividing *my* side of the table." The specific concessions yielded to the unions, sometimes by city labor lawyers who lack even basic familiarity with the complexities of urban policing (see

239

James Jacobs's chapter in this section), occasionally reverse hard-won reforms of prior generations of police executives. Sometimes, despite acknowledged understaffing of the department, a union bars management from making innovative use of part-time or volunteer workers, such as the Los Angeles sheriff's "reserve" officers (Gold 1983; also see Caruso and Walinsky 1984 on the recently proposed "police corps"). Bouza's portrait is one of an occasionally responsible but frequently malevolent usurpation of control over policing by unions that, if pressed, go so far as to walk off the job, leaving the innocent citizenry at the mercy of the "vandals and visigoths" (for an interesting series of arguments supporting the right of police unions to strike, see *Harvard Law Review* 1984, pp. 1712–718).

In sharp contrast to Bouza's outlook, police union president Robert Kliesmet takes the view that one of the greatest obstacles to improved policing has been the antiprofessional, politicized, elitist treatment of the industry by its top managers, in which the line police officer is not given the recognition or support he needs to exercise the vast discretionary powers necessarily entrusted to him (see also Dodenhoff 1985). Kliesmet's portrait is one of an enlightened rank and file that brings some modicum of stability to a municipal service plagued by executive turnover every three or four years. All these factors, coupled with the line officer's expertise in the department's main business—street policing—not surprisingly lead Kliesmet to the conclusion that the rank and file should play a larger role in running the police (the hygenic term is "participative management"). My own observations of police organizations suggest that in many instances beleaguered police managers do tend to overlook the vast in-house talent pool represented by the rank and file in their search for innovations to meet the public's legitimate demands.

Jacobs, drawing on his extensive expertise with public employee unions in the corrections field, predicts that Kliesmet will, for better or worse, eventually have his way on the distribution of power to run the police—at least in sections of the country where unionism has taken hold in the private sector. (Quizzed on the presence of a union in his agency, one southern police chief joked: "Are you kidding? Down here they don't even believe in *the* Union.") The very existence of unions, Jacobs argues, tends to undermine the traditional chain of command and lays the foundation for union operatives to acquire greater de facto authority than the department's middle managers. Jacobs also helpfully targets the areas in which the currently "skimpy" scholarship on labor relations within the criminal justice system needs to be expanded, including assessments of the actual impact of collective bargaining and strikes on the agency, its policies, its lobbying power, and its service to the public. While, as Samuel Walker points out in his chapter in this volume, police labor unions were barely conceived of as a major influence on the future of policing 20 years ago, today they are likely to be the first item on many a police administrator's list of major challenges.

23
Police Unions:
Paper Tigers or Roaring Lions?

Anthony V. Bouza

"The only inherent rights of management are those labor does not bar-gain away from them." If any police chief continues to harbor any illusions about the impetus for the pendulum's swing from managerial prerogatives to union muscle flexing, these words of a Florida police labor leader should disabuse him of any notion that the shift has occurred haphazardly or ac-cidentally. Labor-management relations are adversarial processes that by their very nature become struggles for ascendancy. That the combatants sometimes enter inappropriate arenas, and perhaps even score unexpected victories there, should not surprise us. Battlers tumbling in the mud take their victories where they find them.

A discussion of police labor-management relations would be academic were it not for the fact that contemporary American society has discovered that police union militancy can ultimately pinch everyone's foot. To under-stand the potential impact of such miltancy, it may be useful to consider brief-ly the nature of our national response to pervasive crime and fear of crime.

THE CENTRALITY OF POLICING
AS A RESPONSE TO CRIME

Whatever some pundits may hold, the plain fact is that violence and criminality have been escalating at a terrifying pace for the past three decades or so. The increase in crime is not a statistical quirk or the product of im-proved data collection techniques; it is a stark and terrifying reality. America is responding to the fears engendered by this escalating violence in a number of ways, typically complex and even contradictory. Two contradictions are central: first, we suffer the effects of crime but are largely unwilling to attack its root causes; second, we are cutting back police resources at the same time that we are demanding better police protection.

As our underclass grows, mostly because its meager skills are no longer needed by an industrial nation whose jobs have been automated out of existence, the crime levels rise. The nation responds by avoiding its downtowns, changing its living patterns, bolting its doors, and demanding that something be done. The "something" we apparently have in mind, however, is not to cut the growth of criminogenic conditions but to call a cop to deal with their nearly inevitable results. In this approach, crime is seen as the core problem that must be attacked, and an increasingly restive populace is in no mood to talk about the social and economic causes of crime or about the painful readjustments that might be needed to correct the situation. The underclass in the urban ghetto—the principal but by no means only victims of crime, and of course the source that creates the predators—continues to be ignored. Citizen amateurs contribute to the carnage with the panicky buildup of personal arsenals, recently estimated to include 50 to 60 million handguns nationwide.

The growth of crime, and our almost exclusive reliance on the criminal justice system to deal with it, have thrust the police world onto center stage, with all the discomforts and joys that such prominence affords. But while our nation turns with an expectant heart toward the police, it withdraws its hand of support. The citizen demands better police protection but votes for propositions that have the inevitable effect of slashing the police—and the criminal justice system's—budget. This second key contradiction in America's response to its fear of crime is a classic example of trying to have one's cake and eat it too. Most large city police departments today are at strength levels not seen since the 1950s, their forces depleted by layoffs, budget crises, and voter initiatives to reduce taxes. The bureaucracy, especially the police establishment, is responding to the heat by becoming more efficient. Anticrime forces, tactical patrol units, hostage negotiators, sting operations, decoys, and technological advances—all attest to the response that the cops are offering to the pressure. This response also takes the form of managerial reforms and emphasis on productivity—innovations that are finally beginning to emerge from a police establishment traditionally far more comfortable with its ease, privileges, power, and other hidden blessings.

The rest of the system also responded, although the conventional wisdom perhaps holds otherwise. In this connection, it is instructive to note how successful the police have been at shifting the public's attention to the judiciary as a possible source of the problem—despite the fact that we have, over the past decade, about doubled the prison population in this country. And as America changes its living patterns to accommodate the fear of being mugged or worse, the system is creakily and disjointedly moving to respond to the public's pressure. Since the system, and the police in particular, is being asked to accomplish more with fewer resources than in previous decades, police managers must be especially sensitive to any source of influence, including police unions, that has the potential to disrupt the delivery of law enforcement and peacekeeping services.

The rise of police unionism, as an expression of a complex mix of forces, becomes a matter of real concern for the citizen who fears, and rightly, the wrath of the Vandals and Visigoths within our walls. Sporadic outbursts of urban violence, mostly centering in or pouring out of the ghettos, serve as periodic reminders of the beast being kept at bay by the "thin blue line." Granting the imperfections of the system and even granting that we are largely dealing with only the symptoms of a deep societal malaise, we are still forced to acknowledge the critical importance of the police in preserving the peace in our cities and towns. The prospect of an interruption of this service becomes unthinkable in direct proportion to the growth of the threat to that peace. In its approaching extremis, Rome was forced deeper into the arms of its men of arms.

America, in the 1980s, faces a very strong, and growing, police militance, mainly expressed in an indigenous, distinct, and peculiar union movement that must be understood both historically and in its current form if it is to be dealt with intelligently. Given the setting in which police unionism is currently operating, the movement's considerable energy must be channelled into positive lanes.

HISTORY OF THE POLICE AND THEIR UNIONS

The formal police establishment is not, contrary to popular myth, one of the oldest professions. It has its roots in Home Secretary Sir Robert Peel's "Act for Improving the Police In and Near the Metropolis" in 1829. The Statute of Winchester, in 1285, had set up the organized watch of constables who patrolled the street. This was the first attempt at organizing what we now recognize as the modern police force, with its familiar military accoutrements, such as ranks, salutes, forms of address, organizational structure, and point of view. Peel's reforms had sought a break with the military tradition, but the affinity of the police for the authority and power inherent in the military model made his effort seem more a dream than a reality.

The innovation easily hurdled the seas to land, as an abortive experiment, in Philadelphia in 1833. Nevertheless, Boston took up the organizational cudgels in 1838 and formed its constabulary. New York followed six years later, and by the 1870s all the nation's largest cities had full-time police departments.

It is a measure of the homogeneous nature of the institutions that, despite historical insularity and a pronounced absence of mobility – or even much communication – most of America's police establishment looks remarkably alike in all of its parts and regions. Cops and chiefs from different agencies have no trouble discussing their local problems in shorthand terms and in commonly accepted jargon.

Police unionism would not, however, experience such an uneventful, and seemingly inevitable, development and growth. Police unions grew spasmodically, suffered traumas, died, and emerged phoenix-like and, currently, wax hot. Police unions, like all other employee groups, have their roots in the common soil that produced the trade unions. The guilds that in post-Revolutionary War America grew along skill and apprentice lines ultimately evolved into the unions we know today. The later eighteenth- and nineteenth-century guilds were self-help organizations patterned after the European models. Their development followed the ebb and flow of battle with a resistant and willful management. Police unions began as fraternal organizations in the latter half of the nineteenth century, offering social activities and such benefits as life insurance, sick payments, burial allowances, scholarships, and charitable activities.

The dawn of the twentieth century precipitated America's bumptious entry into large-scale industrialization, rapid urbanization, and speedy economic growth. Police unions, like many other institutions that were not in the advance guard of the movement, were drawn forward in the speeding ship's wake.

The St. Louis Police Relief Association

The St. Louis Police Department's experience probably has general validity. The St. Louis Police Relief Association (PRA) was formed in 1867 to provide relief for members who became sick, disabled, or incapacitated, as well as to assist the families of deceased officers, adding life insurance in 1873 and funeral and hospitalization aid in 1894. (It should not be assumed that the early police fraternities took no interest in wages and benefits—they were mainly relegated to a hortatory and lobbying role that was both informal and, for lack of muscle, pretty ineffectual.) The St. Louis PRA continued to evolve over many decades, and on October 20, 1945, it applied for and received an AFL charter that included a no-strike clause. The parent organization would allow the police only the right to petition for redress of grievances, a pretty tenuous right. This application and approval transpired despite the fact that the state legislature had, in 1920, in response to the seminal Boston strike, forbidden any police membership in a union.

The St. Louis effort to unionize precipitated a crisis that resulted in the dismissal of the two officers serving as the organizers. A court suit followed in which management was upheld. The union issue was closed in St. Louis for another two decades as the PRA surrendered its AFL charter. (The Milwaukee Police Department is currently one of the few agencies holding the sort of AFL-CIO charter that was so tentatively offered, and hastily withdrawn, in St. Louis four decades ago.) The union question surfaced again in St. Louis in America's watershed year of 1968. In September of that year, another effort to organize into a legitimate union gained momentum. This one was energized by threats of a "blue flu" epidemic, sick calls, and such. The state legislature resolved the crisis by allowing the creation of a benevolent, social, fraternal association that would be recognized by management in return for the association's surrender of any right to withhold police services. By this stroke the lawmakers ensured the creation of an unaffiliated and independent union that would not be enmeshed in such problems as having to police a labor dispute in which its allies might be engaged.

This development—the attempt to keep police unions out of the orbit of organized labor—was to characterize scores of similar efforts at organizing the police in other cities. The police unions grew as local, independent organizations frequently linked with larger groups at the county, state, or national level but rarely tied to organized labor. One such national organization, the Fraternal Order of Police (FOP), was founded in 1915, making it the oldest professional service organization in existence. The FOP from its inception specifically eschewed collective bargaining at the national level, leaving this central issue to its local affiliates. National organizations like the FOP have not, despite vigorous recent efforts, taken hold.

As the St. Louis experience over nearly 80 years illustrates, in a world of finite power most movements of any consequence have grown by fits and starts. To understand better the background of police organizations, it is important to back up to the early twentieth century, when the unfocused search for labor's share slowly gained speed. Even the Cincinnati Police Department, an uncommon candidate for militancy, struck briefly in 1918. But it was to be Boston's experience, a year later, that would cast the shape of police unionism for the following 50 years.

The Boston Police Strike

Following America's emergence as a world power after World War I, the police happily joined the parade of workers seeking the better things of life. The American Federation of Labor, a slowly growing conglomerate of craftsmen, had stoutly resisted the temptation to include cops in its councils and was on record as early as 1897 in rejecting their overtures. In June 1919 it reversed this stand, with fateful consequences. Two months later a union charter, one of 37 granted to police groups, was extended to the Boston Organization of Policemen. AFL President Samuel Gompers accepted the cops on the understanding that they would not strike. The police function was, and generally still is, viewed as an uninterruptible service, like the military, on which society's safety depends.

The newly organized Boston officers soon found themselves in a thorny dispute over wages and working conditions. Neither labor nor management was much experienced in the complex business of negotiating an agreement, and the cops were experiencing the heady sense of power that seemed to emanate from their just-won association with a powerful national labor organization. Both legal and administrative restrictions barred union organizing, not to mention striking, but they were disregarded. Administrative response to organizing efforts was swift: Commissioner Edwin Curtis suspended 19 officers for union activity. The disaffected cops, unified by a common sense of outrage over the suspensions, voted to strike, 1,134 of the 1,544 patrolmen voting affirmatively.

The Boston police strike thus began at 5:45 P.M., Tuesday, September 8, 1919. The events of the few days that followed would alter the nation's history and stop the nascent police union movement dead in its tracks for decades. On the first evening of the strike, about 15,000 citizens rioted in Scollay Square, with extensive damage and widespread looting. Massachusetts Governor Calvin Coolidge activated the National Guard the following day, making his stamp on the history books with his cry that "there is no right to strike against the public safety by anybody, anywhere, anytime." The National Guard found, however, it could not contain the violence, which left four dead, and it took a total of 4,000 state guardsmen and 825 civilian volunteers to restore order after four days. The striking patrolmen voted to return to work, but the governor, labeling them deserters, ordered them dismissed. More than 1,100 striking officers were fired, and an almost entirely new force was created. The litigation extended over the next 20 years or so, but the dismissed workers were never restored.

Reaction throughout the nation was swift and strong. President Woodrow Wilson labeled the Boston action a "crime against civilization," equating a cop's role with that of a soldier. The Washington, D.C., Police Department echoed the common sentiment when it announced that it would fire any cop joining a police union. The AFL's revocation of all police charters killed the notion of police unions' affiliation with a national labor organization. Even the Fraternal Order of Police was stalled in its tracks. Management's resolve to resist stiffened, much as it was to stiffen many years later, when President Ronald Reagan fired illegally striking air traffic controllers. (Firemen, who had luckily escaped a similar holocaust simply because conditions had not produced such a crossroad, pursued their organizational goals, affiliated with the AFL, and emerged, decades later, far more closely tied to big labor and far better organized.)

As late as 1958 the International Association of Chiefs of Police was citing the Boston police strike to support its condemnation of police unions. It may not be too much to say that the chill that swept over organizing efforts generally in the 1920s and 1930s was at least made cooler by this fateful police action. And it helped gain Coolidge the Republican vice-presidential nomination, from which he ascended to the presidency. The cause of police unionism lay in ashes, and it would remain dormant for many decades.

Between the Wars

The hiatus between the world wars was, for America, a fairly somnolent time, despite some hi-jinks, a fling at self-absorption, and a searing economic experience. Although police unionism remained dormant during this period, subsequent developments may be placed in better perspective by briefly reviewing the state of American police between the wars. Reactive and reactionary, the police followed the nation's lead, assuming a posture of unexamined ease. Labor hunkered down, management got tougher, and police unionism lay buried in the rubble of the Boston fiasco.

The mysterious world of the cops remained isolated and unexplored. An understanding of the police is not possible without an appreciation of this unlikely insularity and mystery in a presumably wide open society. Dirty linen was not to be washed in public. We would look after our own. Informers were squealers. Brutality simply enabled you to get a tough job done, and what did the public know? A little graft simply redressed the obvious income deficiencies. A sense of brotherhood inspired affection, loyalty, a shared lore, and an uncritical acceptance of the value system. The process of acculturation, embedded in overpowering peer pressures, shaped everyone to the desired dimensions. This elite and secret society understood its power and saw itself as standing quite apart from the communities whose peace it oversaw.

Nationally, the tone of policing was set by the International Association of Chiefs of Police (IACP), an organization that included virtually every chief in the nation and that, under its one man-one vote system, was and continues to be controlled by the small town chiefs who constitute the vast majority of the membership. Under the guiding hand of an extremely conservative IACP[1] and the benign blandishments of an FBI director who was very comfortable with a complaisant arrangement that catered to his needs without cavil, any hope for significant progress or even enlightened discourse was bound to be dashed. Research in the police field was scandalously lacking. The few thinkers in the field were isolated voices, easily identified and labeled.

August Vollmer, a California police chief, made an impact with his progressivism on the 1905–32 period, which spanned the age of union growth and decline. Ironically, one of the exceptions to the axiom that the IACP was led by neanderthals, Vollmer spoke and wrote on and formally adopted a series of police innovations emphasizing training, education, progressive management techniques, and other contributions then flowing from a private sector hungry for progress. Vollmer influenced the few police administrators listening, notably William Parker, who went on to create a modern and efficient model of a police organization in Los Angeles, and Orlando W. Wilson, the author of one of the two basic texts in the field, *Police Administration*, and Mayor Richard Daley's Chicago police superintendent during the trying period of the mid-1960s. The Boston experience convinced Vollmer that affiliation with such labor organizations as the AFL was a mistake. He opted for a separate police labor organization on a national scale that would free the police of questionable entanglements with organized labor.

Also between the wars came incipient calls for turning law enforcement into a genuine profession. The prospect of such a coup would become a sort of Holy Grail adventure that would never get very far, despite consuming a lot of time and energy. Three police chiefs (Vollmer, Parker, and Wilson) and two textbooks (Wilson's *Municipal Police Administration* and *Police Administration*) were virtually all that the police world could boast about for more than 50 years of this century.

The 1920s and 1930s were a bleak time for the police for other reasons, too. Wages were low, benefits were scarce, and working conditions were awful. All these disabilities were justified on the basis that the cops enjoyed a job security other Americans envied. A steady job, in the 1930s, was a prize that few scorned. FDR's New Deal ushered in a period of great progress for the labor movement, with passage of laws protecting the workers' right to organize and to bargain collectively, but the public sector would not gain these rights until the 1950s — being held up by the members' own chariness at endangering job security, a resistance to the idea of organizing within the ranks, and legislators' reluctance to extend these rights to government employees.

During the 1920s and 1930s the leaders of police fraternal organizations befriended the powerful and cajoled, lobbied, coaxed, and begged for whatever concessions they might wrest from reluctant managers, with mixed results. At that time most cops entering the field could expect to function at the mercy of willful and unsympathetic managers, whose caprices would eventually be seen to have accelerated the process of unionization. The period between the Boston police strike and the outbreak of World War II was one of unarticulated desperation for the police (Juris and Feuille 1973), producing little ferment in the ranks. Police accepted the role of keeping radicals in their place, which only deepened the antipathy of the rank and file in law enforcement for the tactics and views of the early organizers. The police were the agents of peace in an age when the disrupters were those fighting, not always legally, for labor and other reforms those battles would produce.

Despite the labor disputes and demonstrations in the years between the wars, there were relatively few pressures on the police. America was not yet troubled by the insularity of the police. Although there were faint stirrings between the wars of what would ultimately capture police energies and suck them into the vortex of the activist 1960s, it was the onset of the Second World War that accelerated great social changes. Women entered the market in great numbers, unions expanded under the nurturing care of a sympathetic administration in Washington, and millions of men would return, hungry for the good things that a prosperous nation could bestow but that had had to be deferred.

THE POSTWAR YEARS

Following World War II, American labor progressed rapidly while police unionism lagged behind, still pulled by the wake of more powerful forces. It was not until the 1960s that the police would be directly touched by the forces of the preceding two decades, which only came to full flower in the 1970s. (Even then, however, it would remain true that the police world failed to produce a labor leader of any distinction.)

In the 1940s, the cops began a slow, barely perceptible, shift into a more militant posture, propelled by a number of factors: inadequate salaries, the declining status of law enforcers, the growing irrelevance of job security in a full employment economy, pressure to professionalize, changing job requirements, the democratization of the police — influenced by the return of veterans whose views of the world were not as accepting as they once had been, the politicization of the police, and growing stresses engendered by public pressure as the struggle with street crime intensified. Shortsighted and obdurate police managers' contributions to the growth of police militancy cannot, however, be minimized. For the police, as in other professions, the urgency for reform was directly related to the stubbornness and resistance of those whose duty it was to promote progress and understanding.

The American Federation of State, County and Municipal Employees (AFSCME) began a drive to organize the police in 1943, but the effort was vitiated when AFSCME quickly revoked the charter of an affiliate that struck. The message was clear that a worker's right to withhold his services would not be extended to government employees. The occurrence of the police strike on the heels of a severe national emergency greatly diminished the strikers' credibility and public acceptability. The fledgling AFSCME, only six years old at the time, was in no mood, or shape, for the struggle. The IACP could, in 1944, announce that unions had little appeal for the law enforcement community and that they could be banned, presumably with impunity (IACP 1977).

Nevertheless, police unions began to emerge, however fitfully, despite the law, court decisions, department policy, the semimilitary traditions of these organizations, and the cops' own sense of their inappropriateness working strongly against their growth. The International Conference of Police Associations emerged in 1953, but its requirement that its affiliates bargain locally and independently strengthened the centrifugal movement of these organizations. This effort would be mirrored in the early 1960s by the International Brotherhood of Police Officers and again in 1969 by John Cassesse's National Union of Police Officers.

The Teamsters, tempted by the prospect of even greater power, initiated in 1958 in New York City a romance with the idea of unionizing the police that would not, despite some serious reversals, abate even in the 1980s. The flirtation of the Teamsters had good and bad effects. Later we will see a dramatic example of the latter in the New Orleans strike of 1975. In 1958, however, in New York City, a nervous mayor quickly embraced the concept of collective bargaining with public employee unions, following the unsuccessful attempt that year by the Teamsters to organize the New York Police Department.

The New York experience may perhaps be illustrative of the twistings and turnings of the police labor movement. For 12 years Mayor Robert F. Wagner, the son of a senator who was an early champion of organized labor and who, perhaps rightly, saw the police as an unfathomable mystery capable of producing great and unwanted surprises, regularly produced what then appeared to be pretty generous wage increases for the police. In fact, in retrospect these can be labeled pretty paltry sums. The Patrolmen's Benevolent Association (PBA), under president John Carton, followed an amiably submissive path. It would not be until the troops had been radicalized by frustrations and anguish that they would turn to a man who symbolized their anger — John Cassesse.

The PBA, like practically all similar organizations, developed and grew as a result of local conditions, without much intervention from outside influences or controls. Each of these unions grew separately and at its own pace. It is one of the curiosities of the police world that police unions are varied and distinct, altogether lacking the stamp of uniformity that characterizes affiliates of national, centrally directed operations — and, indeed, lacking the stamp of uniformity that has for decades characterized police departments throughout America, despite their lack of communication with one another. Even the unions' names are different. What in New York is the Patrolmen's Benevolent Association is in Minneapolis the Police Officers' Federation.

The PBA in postwar New York City was able to identify various power centers. It operated in a complex world of fragmented authority. Locally the New York City Council, the city's legislative body, functioned largely as a rubber stamp to the strong mayoral government that characterized the city. Civil Service was a locus of concern over the protection of job rights. The Pension Board voted on granting disability pensions, a highly desirable perquisite that would ultimately be scandalously abused. The state legislature, which wielded crucial authority over legislation substantially affecting the police ranks, early became a focus of union interest. Accustomed to lobbyers, the representatives and senators welcomed the PBA as a source of campaign funds, support, and good times—for the cops learned how to entertain these fallible humans only too well. Dues checkoffs fueled the coffers.

Police management was never encouraged by its city hall superiors to enter the arena of legislative lobbying, leaving it to city hall operatives to counter the PBA thrusts. It was an unequal contest in which the mayor's representatives had little to offer and less expertise. The result was that even before the growth of the union's strength, the PBA was able to secure a firm grip on the legislative spigot in Albany. The advent of a tough police commissioner, Stephen P. Kennedy, in the mid-1950s speeded the process of union solidarity. A no-nonsense manager, he struck hard at a union that by today's standards was remarkably accommodating. Commissioner Kennedy resigned publicly from the PBA, having to tear up his card and then tape it together and tear it up again for the TV cameras, which had not captured the magical moment the first time.

Although during the Eisenhower era most of the police world remained a tranquil island in the turbulent sea of labor relations, this calm was beginning to be thrown off by the New York contingent, regularly exposed to the demonstrations of frustrated political exiles and a vigorous labor movement. A nascent but vibrant black rights movement and the vestigial traces of a still functioning group of leftist radicals offered a constant example of militancy, which proved an infectious model for the police in New York City. Midtown quarreled with the discordant shouts of Dominican, Cuban, and other exiles, Harlem resonated to the vitrolic cadences of Malcolm X, and other areas reverberated to the rhythms of unending lines of disaffected workers. Provoked by the abrasive style of an assertive police commissioner, the New York PBA members' largely unconscious and unarticulated resentments were given voice culminating in a clash between Stephen Kennedy and the union that was resolved by Mayor Wagner (notably sympathetic to labor) through the commissioner's departure. The militancy that overtook the New York City police would, generally speaking, take about a decade to catch on nationwide.

The 1960s

President John F. Kennedy's Executive Order 10,988, which took effect in 1960, extended recognition to public employee groups and authorized them to negotiate on behalf of their members. Many states followed suit, and the legal barriers to police unionization began to crumble, but slowly.

On September 1, 1967, comfortably close to Labor Day, the New York State legislature passed a law that would serve as a model of its kind and make the phrase "Taylor law" synonymous with a generous view toward public employee organizations. An outgrowth of a crippling two-week subway strike that began in New York City just after midnight on January 1, 1966, the Taylor law, actually the Public Employees Fair Employment Act, was the first such piece of legislation in the state. It forbade strikes and contained harsh punishments for such acts for both the unions and the leaders, but it also imposed an obligation on the employer to negotiate for a contract. This balanced what had been an unbalanced equation in which the workers ceded their right to strike and received nothing in return. The law permitted the securing of an injunction forbidding a strike and imposed the threat of fines or imprisonment. Management, in its turn, was required to demonstrate evidence of good faith negotiations and of efforts to settle a dispute and was ordered to refrain from interfering with the rights of employees. The Taylor law offered no alternative to the organization while requiring elections and the certification of a representative body that would not be affiliated with a national union. The law also had the very beneficial effect of launching an evolutionary process that sought to find better answers to thorny disputes. It led to such breakthroughs as grievance machinery and the submission of disputes to binding arbitrations. It would not, however, prove totally successful in precluding public employee strikes, as the subsequent history of the Transit Authority, and even the New York City Police Department, would demonstrate.

Much has been said and written about the restiveness of the 1960s, and 1968 probably is worth a book all by itself. Cops watched what they thought to be pampered kids churlishly scorning the privileges they would have fought to obtain, and angry, Afro-flaunting blacks invented "off the pig" as a salutation for America's police. As the ghettos stirred angrily, the cops were called in to put down the disorders — and to suffer the accusations of brutality. To paraphrase a prophet of the time, Malcolm X, the chickens were coming home to roost. Nineteen hundred and sixty-eight would be the year that would shake the nation in a way, for probably the first time, that intimately concerned the police. The country was undergoing dramatic and traumatic shifts in areas that were the province of the police, against the backdrop of the intense pressures generated by a rapidly rising wave of street crime and violence.

The country assigned its cops to put down the urban riots and to control the ghettos. Given the setting in which this occurred — in a nation that espoused freedom, constitutional rights, expression of ideas, and other democratic niceties — and given the cops' role to basically keep the underclass in its place, it should not be surprising that the normal frustrations of a job involving coping with people who are usually in disarray became much more psychologically painful for the dissonant message of oppression inherent in the assignment. It isn't easy being an army of occupation in a society that boasts of its freedoms. Furthermore, the efficacy of such muscle flexing as the police were called upon to contend with was not lost on the cops. It seemed to be working for students, blacks, labor, and others; why wouldn't it work for the cops? Not much had been asked of the police in earlier decades, but suddenly they were catapulted into the epicenter of society's bubbling and multifaceted cauldron.

The movement to unionize in the 1960s had to buck the by then commonly accepted objective of gaining the status of a profession – a dream that would never come close to being realized but that captured the police imagination for two-thirds of a century. The absence of altruism in union goals also ran counter to the concept of selfless service that at least theoretically guided soldiers, doctors, priests, lawyers, nurses, and cops. While the countervailing pressures were powerful, the movement to unionize nevertheless gained momentum, starting even before the social upheavals of 1968.

In the face of this momentum, in 1966, Mayor John V. Lindsay attempted to still minority concerns over police brutality by instituting a civilian review board in New York City. The union led an extraordinarily vigorous, ultimately successful, counterattack that merits description as an example of the early empowerment of police unions.

A fairly long-standing hostility between the police and the black community in New York City bubbled over in the early 1960s prior to Lindsay's administration when an off-duty white police lieutenant shot and killed a 15-year-old black youngster as a result of a fairly trivial water spraying incident into which the officer intruded, setting off shock waves of outrage and then riots in Harlem. The simmering resentment would linger for years, although the street disorders abated.

Those events prompted some liberal members of the city council in 1965 to sponsor not-very-hopeful legislation for the creation of a civilian review board, which quickly assumed coded significance. To most blacks, civilian review represented the promise of redressing long-standing grievances against the police. To most cops it represented submitting to the judgments of cop-hating militants. Sucked into the fray by the demands of its members, the PBA mustered 5,000 cops to picket city hall on June 29, 1965 (this tactic was used again in 1985 by police who claimed the city was failing to properly protect several officers who had been involved in a controversial shooting of an elderly black woman; see "Police Protest Indictments in Bronx Shooting" 1985; "When Police Revolt" 1985). The union also secured a half-million signatures protesting the passage of a civilian review law and had a bill introduced in the state legislature blocking the city's authority to initiate such legislation. Failing in its effort to block the legislation in court, the PBA then moved to place the issue on the ballot by referendum, with a half-million dollar budget and a high-powered public relations firm engaged to support the effort. Soon TV ads, billboards, leaflets, bumper stickers, speakers, and store fronts frightened the public with the image of a handcuffed police department.

John Cassesse, who had been catapulted to the New York City PBA presidency in 1958 over growing police disaffection with a host of problems (conveniently personalized in a tough commissioner), now moved smartly into the middle of the contest. The union now had not only recognition but a hefty treasury – thanks to the crucial benefit of having the dues deducted by the employer from the payroll checks. The civilian review issue would prove a useful primer in muscle flexing.

Lindsay inherited the civilian review controversy, but it was a comfortable enough fit to warrant the assertion that the man, the moment, and the issue all conveniently met in 1966. During Lindsay's first minute in office, 12:01 A.M., January 1, 1966, Michael J. Quill called a transit strike that paralyzed the city for two weeks and shocked and frightened a new mayor, tempering his relations with municipal unions for years to come. Lindsay's liberalism found ready expression in his relations with his police department. The new mayor had received enthusiastic campaign support from a black community that saw him as a champion of social and racial justice, and his conduct upon election reflected the mission that he had been elected to accomplish. Lindsay not only sought greater harmony between the government and black citizens but promoted the cause of social justice for such minorities as gays as well.

But it was in the area of the more traditional difficulties that he pressed hardest. He imported a Philadelphian to head the police force because the out-of-towner had "lived with a civilian review board" in the city of brotherly love, although what the phrase meant never got fully explained. Frustrated in his early attempts to create a review board through legal action, Lindsay constituted one through administrative fiat: Algernon Black, the Ethical Culture Society's leader and a respected citizen, was named to head the newly created body.

Despite notable gentleness by the board in dealing with the few cases it was asked to review,[2] the cops were furious. The upcoming election was seen as the denouement, and the union intensified its "Fear City" campaign. The PBA scored a resounding 3 to 2 victory on a referendum. The Civilian Review Board was dead, and the hopes of minorities were dashed. Canny bureaucrats, however, constructed a system of investigating allegations of police brutality that effectively eliminated systemic, widely accepted, and officially tolerated police excesses. It is not widely known that Lindsay was successful in eliminating the protections that wrongdoing cops had come to rely on. What was seen was the PBA victory, which enhanced the union's power and prestige enormously. Indeed, it became one of the crucial ironies of his mayoralty that Lindsay began by taking on the cops, on the brutality issue, and ended by taking them on again on the corruption question. Both proved bloody battles, but it might be fairly asserted that the luckless mayor actually won both— and they were the most intractable and difficult problems any one could confront in the police world.

The Late 1960s and the President's Report

Events proceeded rapidly for society and for the police throughout the nation as the decade was coming to a close. In the presidential contest of 1964, Senator Barry Goldwater struck hard at the issue of crime in the streets, and the response inspired the winner, Lyndon B. Johnson, to appoint the President's Commission on Law Enforcement and Administration of Justice (see Walker's chapter).

The commission's report (President's Commission 1968), providing a comprehensive analysis and suggesting a wide array of possible strategies, offered an unprecedented contribution to the field of literature on the police. However, it is a fascinating example of how far and fast police unions would move in the 1970s that this report fails to mention police labor organizations and can ignore their existence even in listing the possible obstacles to a series of daring reforms. We can now look back on the luxury of a time when such matters as precinct consolidation, name tags, one-person patrols, minority recruitment, women in policing, attacks on brutality and corruption, and a host of other sensitive subjects could be discussed – and a time when the necessary reforms could even be adopted – without reference to the unions that would soon make such issues their central concerns. The radicalization of the police seemed a very long way off in 1967. A decade and a half later the report would serve as a ghostly reminder of an innocent age, when the country thought that the challenge could be met with federal dollars and when the belief still prevailed that something might be done about the underlying social and economic conditions that spawned street criminals.

The report led in 1968 to the passage of the Safe Streets Act and the creation of the Law Enforcement Assistance Administration, whose expenditure of more than $7 billion over the next 12 years attracted scholars, researchers, and journalists to what had been a totally neglected police environment. The police themselves were encouraged to extend their education en masse. Under the impetus of public fear over a rising crime rate, the federal government had launched the police establishment on a giddy, if brief, adventure with forces that blew down the walls insulating the police world. While many plumbed the cornucopia for gadgets and toys, others saw the chance to promote studies, analyses, and experiments. Research and new findings brought the same sort of heady sense of progress that must have seized nineteenth-century medical practitioners as science began to lead them out of the wilderness of intuition in which they had wandered for centuries.

Fear of crime and the growing influence of the police led to such oddities as the election of a police lieutenant, Mario Biaggi, to Congress and the election of cops as mayors in Philadelphia and Los Angeles. But just as police managers were acquiring new stature by attaining important elective offices, rank-and-file cops were rapidly coalescing to find strength in union solidarity throughout the nation's urban centers. The lexicon of public employee labor relations was now enriched with such inventions as "blue flu" epidemics, "work-rule" slowdowns, "ticket blitzes," or, in opposite cases, "droughts." Detroit in 1967 experienced a ticket slowdown and an outbreak of blue flu. The New York Police Department followed the next year with its own version of blue flu, and Boston, half a century after its momentous strike, felt its way back to the ranks of labor militancy with the cops' refusal in 1969 to accept off-duty assignments. That same year the police in Vallejo, California, staged a four-day walkout, and Montreal's police struck with vandalism and disorder following.

The anguish of this troubled age had infected its keepers. Some jurisdictions stuck to the folly of forbidding unions, denying contracts, and criminalizing the bargaining process. Though public sector bargaining was still in its infancy in the late 1960s, it was not a movement that could be ignored with impunity—as we shall discover.

Within a comparatively few years union activities would embrace collective bargaining, pensions, hospitalization and insurance, workers' compensation, and grievance procedures and even delve into such arcana as governmental budgets and administrative, civil, and criminal law. Unions would reach to master such corridors as were occupied by the public, the political figures, the media, and other centers of power that impinged on their success or failure. The watchwords were expressed by a union official: "A union should delve into, and deal with, any area that concerns its members." If management thought of any province as containing its rights, it would have to move to protect the area or risk its loss.

The 1970s

As the 1960s ended, the police in about three-fourths of the cases were organized and in possession of the legal weapons needed to wage battle with management. A generation of cops, who grew up in the 1960s and bore that decade's stamp of impatience, was not ready to accept the hostility, the pressures to perform, the poor personnel practices, the long hours, the low status and pay, and management's arbitrary and capricious acts without a sharp reaction. The group's cohesiveness and the resentments engendered by witnessing the success of other militants fueled the process. Managment resistance—frequently obdurate, stupid, or insensitive—fanned the fire. It took a generation of haughty chiefs, imperiously asserting their will, to move the freer thinkers of the post-World War II era into the mood to resist. The quickest way to curb management's abuses was to curb management's power, and the handiest way to do this was through the elected union representatives, who presented the needed buffer to possible reprisals.

While organized labor in the private sector had to contend with a management pressured by such needs as costs, profits, stockholders, and scrutiny by a board of directors, police unions functioned in a managerial ambiance altogether lacking any familiarity with the business of the police. This critical knowledge vacuum among mayors and city managers made it easy for chiefs to collaborate with unions behind the scenes. The chiefs had at least two distinct incentives for such collusion: They rose through the ranks and could readily identify with the problems of the rank and file, and the unions could be handy allies if treated well or, if provoked, could make a lot of trouble for chiefs. (My private suspicion is that a chief's effectiveness, as a manager, is inversely proportionate to the praise heaped on him by the union's president.)

Any power relationship develops a dynamic that rapidly blurs limiting lines. It is natural for the struggle to transcend such questions as wages, benefits, or conditions of employment. Just as management's ascendancy once resulted in the suppression of progress for the worker on all fronts, the pendulum swing of power toward the police unions swept all manner of issues into the union's orbit. Frequently the unions were called on to defend members charged with wrongdoing. Perceiving the departmental disciplinary processes as unreasonable, unions moved in to play a role, just as they had intruded where management showed a willingness to share policymaking concerning such matters as the number of officers in a patrol car, shift and job assignments, and hiring, firing, promotion, and demotion. In a number of cities during the early 1970s (and as early as 1967 in New York City), unions were winning the battle with management for adoption of a bill of rights for police officers under departmental investigation.[3]

Union leaders in the 1970s were called on by their constituents to address not only internal affairs investigations but such image vacuums as were created by pusillanimous or cautious administrators who too often responded to the broadsides of minority leaders stridently charging brutality with such bromides as "I can't comment while the case is under investigation." The cops soon learned that the hot quotes made the headlines and soon looked to their union representatives to deliver the rejoinders.

A number of cities fell victim to union muscle flexing. Police in Pittsburgh in 1970 and in Milwaukee in 1971 exhibited their frustrations, the former in a sickout and the latter in a brief strike. In 1971 the NYPD staged a winter walkout that was mitigated by harsh weather and the continued performance of supervisors and detectives.[4] In the summer of 1974, the Baltimore police struck for five days with painful consequences for the rank and file, many of whom were fired.

The study of police labor relations in the 1970s is the study of how labor groups grew and filled power centers that had either been vacant or been defended without conviction. The experiences of two big cities, New York and Minneapolis, are instructive. Union outspokenness in New York City during the traumatic early 1970s illustrates the intrusion of police labor leaders into areas that had previously been the province of management. When the Knapp Commission's revelations, prompted by Frank Serpico's allegations, forced the NYPD in 1972 to attack the cancer of corruption within, Police Commissioner Patrick V. Murphy had to battle the PBA every step of the way. It was a sign of the times that the mayor's office, facing the prospect of a long, hot summer, had declined to push a tough investigation of police corruption because of the fear of alienating the cops. Everyone knew how the inquiry would be greeted. One of the key targets of the investigation was the head of a supervisor's union.

Even before the Knapp Commission was established, the PBA had shown no shyness about attacking management's attempts to clean house. When Commissioner Murphy, upon his appointment in the fall of 1970, moved quickly to remove the misfits and superannuated hacks that abounded at the upper ranks, the union president said Murphy was "destroying the department" and called on him to resign. And when the electrifying disclosures of the Knapp inquiry hit the public view two years later the union still felt justified in resisting administrative attempts to fight corruption. The PBA protested Murphy's use of "field associates" to spy on their colleagues and report serious cases of police wrongdoing. It labeled as entrapment and a violation of officers' civil rights the department's use of "integrity tests," such as surrendering a "found" wallet containing cash and no identity to police officers on patrol, to see how many turned the wallet in as required (only a few did, at first, and the others were disciplined for keeping the money). The union formally asked the prosecutor to get the police department to stop such integrity testing, but to no avail. The police labor leaders challenged the police commissioner's insistence that even anonymous complaints of police corruption or wrongdoing would be investigated. A curious echo of the outraged cries of these targets was heard years later when Congress and others bleated over the tactics employed by the FBI in its Abscam inquiry.

The New York experience illustrated the difficulty a determined and talented executive would encounter in trying to attack even systemic and widespread corruption. The brutality battle, fought half a decade earlier, had introduced the point. The PBA had become a reflexive apologist for its members and a vigorous defender of the position that inquiries into wrongdoing by its members not only had to be resisted but that it was, indeed, a union's duty to do so.

One of the more egregious illustrations of union overreaching during the 1970s comes from Minneapolis. The process there actually began at the end of the 1960s, and the damage was not fully apparent until the union's power was curbed during the early 1980s.

At the height of the national furor over crime in the streets in 1969, a spooked and divided public brought new meaning to the observation that, in a democracy, the people get the sort of government they deserve by electing the police union's president as mayor of Minneapolis. Charles Stenvig elevated his friends to high places and banished his foes. The latter turned to Al Hofstede, who, following two two-year terms by Stenvig, managed to unseat him in 1973. The outs were now in and the ins were now out. But then Stenvig upset Hofstede in 1975 and, over the next two years, transferred fully

45 percent of the force. The tables were turned once again in 1977. By then there had been a decade of the most corrosive politics imaginable within the police department, and the final months of Hofstede's term saw him having to cope with widespread allegations of corruption and political favoritism within the department, which forced the chief to resign. Sickened, exhausted, and frustrated, Mayor Hofstede, although still a young man, declined to seek reelection, and the cycle was broken with the election of Donald M. Fraser, a long-time congressman with no ties to the police department (see Fraser's chapter).

The decade of spoils system administration of the department resulted in organizational rewards and punishments based on political affiliation, in cover-ups, whitewashings, and protection of wrongdoing, in all two-person cars, in virtually no minority representation in the ranks, and in high wages and benefits but very low productivity. Such abuses resulted, for example, in a ratio of two supervisors for every three workers. The requirement of all two-person squads kept the department from fielding enough cars to answer all of the calls for help. The Minneapolis Police Department was left a divided shambles. Such commonly accepted innovations as 911 had to be ignored because of the energy-consuming internecine struggles. Name tags had been discarded early in the game. The organizational instability saw eight chiefs serving from 1969 through 1979, with the longest tenure being two years. Ironically, the age began with the ouster of Chief Don Dwyer and ended with his return, for a five-month go at cleaning up the mess. The effects of this decade of spoils were visible not only in the mayoralty, the chief's office, and the union's leadership but in such other areas as the Civil Service Commission (whose three overseers were appointed by the mayor) and similar governmental bodies.

Shortly after his election in 1980, Don Fraser undertook the cleaning of this Augean stable by appointing an outsider (myself) as the city's forty-eighth chief. The process faltered, however, when the union's presidency went to a young sergeant who, for the next two years, continued the confrontational tactics that represented the generalized anger over the interruption of this ten-year game. It was not until April 1982, when a moderate unionist became the head of the Police Officers' Federation, that it could be said that, in the mayor's office, the chief's, and the union president's, there had been a break with the past.

The two years of Fraser's first term saw court battles, arbitration proceedings, and endless strife, in the press and other forums, between a union that wanted to hang on to the management prerogatives it had usurped and an administration that attacked the issues. At stake were matters, some adverted to earlier, such as minority recruitment, discipline of wrongdoing officers, precinct consolidation, one-person patrols, name tags, enforcement policy (especially as it affected gay citizens), the creation of an investigator's position and elimination of the inspector's rank, promotional policy (the union insisted on adherence to a ruinously expensive plan that required frequent promotions, predictably sought in the name of "austerity"), the retention of the old guard, and contract language that froze firmly in place labor's control over administration of the enterprise. There was even an attempt to secure a provision that would have precluded any rule change that lacked the union's — and the chief's — approval. It was not hard to envision that the latter constituted a concession to facts that might later be ignored.[5]

Minneapolis, an unlikely candidate, had produced as egregious an example of the extremes to which the police union movement could be brought as could be found throughout the nation during the 1970s. But it was far from the only city that saw one of the more grotesque practical consquences of the burgeoning police union movement.

THREE POLICE STRIKES OF THE 1970s

The police unions that grew so rapidly in the 1970s have to be seen as vehicles for expressing the fears, frustrations, and ambitions of a police world increasingly radicalized by the social upheavals of the 1960s. Cops not only had been called on to serve as armies of occupation but were regularly exposed to the hostility and suspicion of a Warren Court that expounded defendants' rights seemingly more from a perceived need to control a police establishment running amok than from concern over such abstractions as constitutional issues. The student and civil rights movements caught up the cops and sucked them into the fray, and police came to be regarded by some as the agents of oppression in an increasingly tense class struggle that occasionally erupted into urban riots but more often surfaced as street crime. The average cop, imprisoned in a distinct and alien culture, experienced what came to be labeled "stress."

Set against this background, the fiscal woes of the decade provided the spark that kindled a number of labor walkouts. A review of how three of these police strikes unfolded during the middle and late 1970s will lay the basis for a number of subsequent observations concerning, among other matters, the causes of union militancy, the power of citizen sentiment in resolving strikes, the elusiveness of a definition of management and the difficulty of identifying who is authorized to bargain on its behalf, and the legacy left for the 1980s by the failure of labor and management to resolve disputes in ways that would facilitate constructive bargaining in the future.

San Francisco

Most of the San Francisco Police Department's 1,800 members belong to the Police Officers Association (POA), which was founded as a social organization in the 1940s. The organization grew more militant in the 1960s and became involved with the labor movement in the 1970s. The union's developing stridency was expressed by the election to the POA presidency in 1972 of a militant, Sergeant Gerald Crowley. The minority members of the department, sensing a divergence of purposes, had already formed their own Officers for Justice in 1968. The gulf between white and minority officers widened as the result of a civil rights suit in 1975, but the POA, consequently, became more aggressive and united.

In the absence of any collective bargaining law in 1975, the principals were simply enjoined by state law to meet and confer. This had not proved a problem in the past two decades, and indeed for 23 years the San Francisco police had received the maximum pay increase permitted by a generous city charter, which held only that salaries could not exceed those of the highest paid officers in any California city with more than 100,000 residents. But in the spring of 1975 the air was filled with rumors that this 23-year tradition would be broken. A harbinger came when the Board of Supervisors reached a compromise settlement with the deputy sheriffs. The cops were anticipating a 13 percent raise, but several other groups of municipal workers had settled for about 6.5 percent, precisely half the expected figure.[6] The San Francisco city fathers, along with the rest of the nation, were terrified by the specter of New York's collapse in 1975, after an epoch of largesse, as it laid off thousands of cops and teetered toward bankruptcy. In San Francisco, real estate taxes were an issue, and the pressures to economize that ultimately would blossom into Proposition 13 began to be seriously felt. The residence of 60 percent of the cops outside the city deprived the police of both political muscle and the sympathy of residents who felt stuck for the bills.

The city fathers held a hearing on the raises on August 7, and the union's expert, reflecting the growing sophistication of labor's approach, submitted a 53-page report to justify a 13 percent increase. The Board of Supervisors irked the cops by displaying inattentiveness. The POA polled its members on whether to strike, adopt a selective policy of responding to emergencies only, conduct a mass sick-in, or do nothing. Meetings were held on August 14, but suspiciously the poll's results were not announced. Management struck back with a poll of its own that indicated that only a few of the cops would walk out. Mayor Joseph Alioto threatened to fire any strikers, and the Board of Supervisors seemed genuinely unmoved by the threat of a strike. The union set about preparing for a walkout—printing literature, appointing picket captains, and issuing assignments.

A negotiating team was created by the city, but the union refused to meet with them since the legal authority for a settlement continued to rest with the Board of Supervisors, rather than the mayor. Nevertheless, Mayor Alioto, on the 18th, came out swinging, boasting that the city could win a strike. He vowed not to call in the National Guard, labeling them "amateurs." The climax was reached that afternoon at a meeting of the Board of Supervisors. With more than 200 cops in the chamber and another 200 outside, the board announced, on a 10 to 0 vote, a 6.5 percent pay increase. The offer was greeted with shouts of disapproval. POA President Crowley was denied the floor and stormed out. Within hours of the meeting, 90 percent of the cops surprised their chief by walking off the job. The chief had been assured that any job action would not be widespread, and no contingency plan of any consequence had been readied. The police administration would now be reduced to ad hoc responses.

The union approached the strike with enough confidence to advise its members to use no violence and to utter no criticism of the few cops and supervisors still working. On August 19, the city obtained a temporary restraining order requiring the workers to return. The other departments threatened to strike, and the mayor attempted a two-tiered policy of trying to mediate the dispute while threatening to fire the strikers. His lack of statutory authority over the wage negotiations was proving a crippling handicap. Emotions reached a fever pitch when reports came in that the mayor's house had been bombed. In fact the damage had been slight. Police cars and equipment were vandalized. Although the reports were sketchy (it has become one of the articles of faith in these tragedies that crime and other statistics that reflect the impact of such strikes are "impossible to compile"), crime, looting, and vandalism seemed to most observers to be up. The next day, August 20, the firefighters voted to strike. With 51.5 percent of the police department out for the third day, there was still no call for outside aid. The governor would not send the state's highway patrol to assist, absent the mayor's specific request for aid. At 6:00 P.M. 90 percent of the firefighters walked off their jobs.

On Thursday, August 21, the mayor reached an agreement with the police union for a 9.5 percent increase. The Board of Supervisors was furious over this illegal usurpation of its authority and, despite an overwhelming police vote of 800 to 50 to accept the pact, voted 9 to 0 to reject the agreement. The mayor stuck by his agreement and moved for a city charter change that would ratify his actions. The board denounced this as a "sellout." The resulting vote would serve as a referendum on citizen sentiment, and it proved to be pretty antiunion as the board's stiff stance was strongly supported. The mayor's views were rejected. The union was forced to accept the lesser package of 6.5 percent originally offered by the board. The POA leaders, sensing the power of citizen disapproval, returned to duty.

In January 1976 Charles Gain, a man with a reputation as a thinker and of a sociological bent, was appointed chief in San Francisco. The restiveness continued to bubble. Crime rose 32.6 percent in the first five months of 1976. The union and its president were fined $1,000 each for contempt of court. They had violated the court's temporary restraining order, secured on August 19, which prohibited a strike or mass picketing. The opinion seemed to drift to a consensus that the absence of legitimate avenues for the expression of grievances and the negotiation of contracts had led to union militancy. Nevertheless, rigid wage formulas were imposed, and the bitterness between the Board of Supervisors and the union continued. Chief Gain would be ousted in the wake of social unrest involving the dissatisfactions of the city's substantial gay community. A solid foundation was laid for an unhappy experience somewhere ahead. The lesson seemed to be that, for better or for worse, parties to these disputes should strive for definitive settlement.

Tucson

Festering sores do not tend to vanish through spontaneous remission. The Tucson, Arizona, scene illustrates the point. The city had been slow with raises for cops, and in 1969 it skipped them altogether. The result was not unified rank-and-file resistance but mass resignations, demonstrating the difference in approach that a few years can make. In December 1974, the Tucson officers, who belonged to the FOP, rejected a $50 per month raise. The mayor and the council also spurned the offer, but on the grounds that the city could not afford it. (In Tucson, the Civil Service Commission set the salary schedules, and the mayor and the council could only accept or reject the proposals.) The wage issue was submitted to an arbitrator, who recommended a 5 percent increase, effective January 1, 1976, a year hence.

The police and fire officers (who in 1971 had engaged in mass resignations as the police had two years earlier) sensed the need for greater strength and formed the Tucson Police and Firefighters Association. At a typically raucous meeting, the request for suggestions from the floor produced the predictable demand to strike. The leadership opted for a "blue flu" epidemic. The mayor refused a request for a closed meeting with the disaffected workers. After a 22-hour siege of "blue flu," during which most officers called in sick, negotiations were resumed. The media were sharply critical of the job action. The meandering course of the crisis was strengthened by the Civil Service Commission's six-week delay in reviewing the salary demands. Finally, in the fall of 1975, the workers, at a feverish late night meeting, favored a strike and threatened to walk out at 6:00 P.M., Monday, September 22.

Of the 510 officers on the Tucson force, 389 struck. Still the strikers continued to respond to some emergencies and offered their working colleagues backup on some calls. A temporary restraining order—the popular legal artifact of the age—was issued and defied. By the third day the city was threatening to fire the strikers and this, too, was ignored. The depleted force continued to patrol and respond to a reduced number of calls. Deputy sheriffs were on call but not used for normal policing operations. Two council members offered a 22 percent raise, and despite the questionable legal basis of the act, the anxious workers returned, at 10:30 P.M., on Sunday, September 28. The strike had lasted over six days, but the acrimony did not end with the return to duty. The city reneged on the unauthorized offer, and the exhausting, frustrating experience of the previous ten months soon had everyone looking to the November 4th election as a possible way out. A change in the charter would allow flexibility in such negotiations. Mayor Murphy was reelected. The unions were granted a 5 percent raise but sued to impose the 22 percent Memorandum of Understanding the council members had signed. The court ruled the latter agreement void. The police and firefighters were split when parity was broken, and a study recommended a 25 percent increase for the firefighters. The frustrations of this strike created another legacy of bitterness. Future developments would rest on who gained ascendancy over whom — and heaven help the weaker party.

New Orleans

The police, slow to react and shaped by conservative molds, were nevertheless moving intō more and more militant postures as the 1970s wore on, leaving their chiefs and city fathers in the dust in the race for power. Two back-to-back New Orleans strikes in 1979 illustrate the animosity and widening chasm of misunderstanding between cops and their employers.

The city of New Orleans has a population of two-thirds of a million and a force of 1,500 sworn personnel assigned to eight stations. The city's hallmark is pleasure, its emblem the Mardi Gras festival in February. Its mayor, Ernest Morial, is black, and the superintendent of police then was James C. Parsons, the product of a search that found him heading a department in Birmingham, Alabama. In 1978 the cops belonged to two unions: the FOP, an old-line and traditional outgrowth of the typical order, representing 650 members, and the Teamster-organized Policemen's Association of New Orleans (PANO), representing the swelling militancy of frustrated cops, who were then 710 in number. The connection to the Teamsters would be a storm warning to cities all over the nation, for it not only involved ties to a tainted and militant union but raised the large question of honoring picket lines and the train of issues swept along the path of affiliation with a national union. This was precisely the specter that Vollmer had warned against.

Such events rarely develop rapidly, and this one was no exception. By late summer of 1978 contract negotiations were going badly, and the threat of a strike was introduced into the discussions. The police superintendent suggested a pay hike, which the mayor ignored, while threatening to fire any striker. An unsatisfactory wage offer, seemingly generous at 15 percent but actually containing take-aways that ate up a lot of it, was quickly rejected by the officers. Playing an obvious game, the mayor recognized the FOP. PANO sought recognition and offered compromises on its demands. On February 8, 1979, 450 cops walked out, and the figure quickly swelled to 1,000 on the following day. The rank and file, radicalized by events and suspicious of a union (FOP) acceptable to hated management, opted for the militant course. The FOP abandoned negotiations as its support withered. A long meeting between PANO and the mayor resulted in a 2:00 A.M. agreement that extended recognition to PANO and granted benefits to the members. The walkout ended on February 10, after 30 hours.

There was no written agreement, and the parties now undertook the task of hammering out a written contract. PANO issued an ultimatum requiring a contract by February 16, but no agreement was reached, and by the evening of the 16th more than 1,000 of the city's 1,500 police officers struck. On February 17 the city was patrolled by the police supervisors who remained on duty, by the National Guard, summoned by the mayor, and by 250 state police officers. A few Mardi Gras events were cancelled, but for the most part preparations continued for the festival. Clearly this would be the event pressing on the city to reach an agreement, and the union played the card enthusiastically.

PANO's strident public statements fed a growing public resentment, as usual an unseen but critical impetus for a resolution of these disputes. The strikers rallied while the city council called for their return to work. The police superintendent, who had earlier been sympathetic to the workers' demands for a pay raise, now took a harder line and sided with the city government. His opposition turned bitter when a captain died at his desk, following 12-hour tours of duty. The superintendent blamed the strike for the officer's demise. The covert sympathy that police managers had felt for their striking brethren now abruptly ended.

Three court orders requiring a return to work were ignored by the strikers. The Mardi Gras lay dead under the ruins of the spreading controversy. But after another emotional rally on February 25, followed with an attack on the mayor's home, the union's euphoric momentum was rapidly ebbing, and a union meeting on March 2 turned chaotic and had to be adjourned. In disarray, and following threats of prosecution from the mayor and the police superintendent, all the strikers spontaneously returned to work the next day. Despite an ultimate union vote of 447 to 173 opposing resumption of work, the workers remained at their stations.

The strike was over, with no contract and no agreement. An angry city and an outraged mayor had prevailed. The courts imposed fines, and management withheld promotions. At the end there was still no law allowing collective bargaining, and future events were left to the tender mercies of these win/lose situations. Superintendent Parsons would soon be replaced, over a series of interracial cop-citizen shootings that exacerbated tensions between the police and the city's black community. The mayor, stung by the acrimony and the attack on his home, was reelected and remains in office. The bid by the Teamsters to organize the police suffered what many thought a fatal setback, not just in Louisiana but nationally. By overplaying its hand the union had provoked a sharp public recoil.

OBSERVATIONS ON THE STRIKES
AND ISSUES FOR THE 1980s

Half a century of relative quiet passed between the Boston police strike and the next major city work stoppage. Then came a rash, not only in the three cities described above but in Montreal, New York City, Oklahoma City, Las Cruces, Youngstown, and other locales. We can, in hindsight, observe the rising temperature of police militancy and would be wise to anticipate a logical progression. While all past serious job actions and strikes have had their roots in economic disputes, there is no reason to believe that the disaffection in other areas will not spill over into an overt response. The causes of the police strikes we have observed are rooted in such indirect factors as a cycle of recession/inflation and Propositions 13 and 2½, which seek to lower government's costs. Among the more direct causal factors we can include wages, the issue of parity with other city workers (a sore point with many cops), frustrations, stress and growing discontent among impatient and unaccommodating workers, poor communications between union officials and the city government, the absence of legal structures and mechanisms that could be used to resolve the disputes, lack of experience, proliferation of power centers and diffused authority that is frequently centered in unresponsive and obdurate bodies of government, the inhibiting influence of open meeting laws, the absence of continuity in a world where the central players are changed frequently, and the often encountered absence of trust.

Bargaining for a large, and largely unhappy membership is an economic, social, political and emotional process. The uneasy resolution of the disputes in San Francisco, Tucson, and New Orleans leave little confidence that festering discontent will not continue to be galvanized into unified, militant responses. Yet to be developed is an expertise that uses knowledge to avoid these crises.

Timing of Negotiations

Timing impinges both on the negotiations and their breakdown. There should be attempts to reach an agreement long in advance of the deadline, but the deadline should avoid such critical seasons as summer or the advent of important festivals like the Mardi Gras. If contract deadlines coincide with municipal elections they invite public posturing, and worse. Union elections are no better as contract deadlines. Timing also requires sensitivity to the crescendos of these events. Anticipating a surge of energy can facilitate a successful deflection and establish a momentum that inhibits further union adventures.

Developing Competent Managers

Police managers, notably absent either voluntarily or involuntarily in contract negotiations, must be involved. But for this police chiefs will need training in labor relations and perhaps even in the most rudimentary management skills. A sad constant in American policing is a general lack of preparation of chiefs to deal with the complex and demanding factors involved in trying to run a modern police department, which contrasts with the emphasis on executive development and training in many other fields. The annals of managerial America have not been filled with the exploits of police executives.

One factor in the general lack of managerial competence is that chiefs usually identify very closely with their charges and almost always have emerged from those ranks. Often police managers remain in the same bargaining unit as the rank and file, which undermines the prospects for their participation across the table. Management is gradually moving to propose legislation that distinguishes managerial levels from the rank and file and removes those levels from the bargaining unit. In a sense, this might help institutionalize the tradition of the supervisors working while the troops strike.

The role that police chiefs come to play in labor disputes will obviously depend to an important extent on the qualities of the individuals. Some, such as former Chief Frank Rizzo in Philadelphia, are paternalistic, possessive, and protective of their "boys." Such an executive might, on the one hand, see the union as a rival and treat its representatives harshly and, on the other hand, render the union superfluous by treating the rank and file well. Other chiefs, such as Charles Stenvig in Minneapolis, use the department as a political base. Friends get rewarded, enemies get punished, and a lot of the enterprise is subordinated to the pursuit of electoral muscle. Between the extremes represented by Rizzo and Stenvig can be found an unprepossessing population of police executives. Enlightened self-interest must impel the police executive to recognize that his troops seek direction, leadership, consistency, a sense of fair play, and a just internal environment. Achieving social justice in the complex world of modern policing requires a high degree of competence among police executives.

Defining Management

A critical issue remains in simply defining who is management for purposes of police labor negotiations. Private industry is not troubled by the question of who is management, but the government is. In negotiating a contract with a police union, we have the union on one side and any number of folks on the other. Sometimes the police administration is included, but this is a hit and miss proposition (and, again, one that is further complicated by the administrators' customary membership in the same or an allied bargaining unit and, hence, their opportunity to benefit from union gains). There are the budget folks, who must contend with the fiscal implications, and there are such city parents as mayors, councils, civil service commissions, and other bodies created for the purpose. The political entities grappling with these issues seem to be as many and as varied as the cities in which they take place. The variegated and colorful political mosaic of municipal America does not make comprehension easier.

Management must be defined because, despite its — and labor's — common needs to survive, remain on the payroll, avoid embarrassment, and such, different entities on the management side will be subject to different kinds of pressures. Most of the impelling factors are invisible and, where they are not previously made known to the proper players, are not likely to be discovered in the maelstrom of a public controversy. The mayor and other elected officials have more obvious strings pulling them this way and that, especially the money and muscle of a union in a close political race, but even such seemingly secure bodies as civil service or police commissions have elements of insecurity, and everybody has a constituency. This means that the arena of a police-labor controversy can shift — from city hall, to legislative halls, to the media, to the courts, and anywhere in between. The best advice for management under these circumstances is to be flexible and alert. The existence of trust among the adversaries is so central to the process that its importance cannot be overstated.

The question of who is management is further confused when unauthorized city officials purport to negotiate on behalf of the city, as happened in the three strike situations described above: in the mayor–Board of Supervisors clash in San Francisco, in the illegal 22 percent raise offered by two city council members in Tucson, and in the chief's suggested wage hike, repudiated by the mayor, in New Orleans. While the same kind of confusion about who is authorized to negotiate rarely afflicts the labor side of the process, training and sophistication are essential on both sides of the table, since an obdurate union leader may prove as troublesome as an ignorant chief. If union leaders are to be expected to function effectively, they should be freed for union activities, within sensible limits. In a department of some size this can be a wise long-term investment, as it ensures the immersion of an interested participant in this complex area.

Unions' Involvement in Selecting Police Chiefs

Occasionally, and with increasing frequency, police unions attempt to influence quite directly the outcome of the question of who is management — and not solely for purposes of identifying the parties to contract negotiations. Labor organizations can exercise their influence on the critical selection of police chiefs in a variety of ways, and their expertise grows as their coffers fill and political sophistication increases. The range of roles played by unions in chief selection can be illustrated by considering the appointments of several chiefs throughout the country in 1980 (see Potter and Blackmore 1980).

That year in Philadelphia the FOP followed the most common response to a candidate it found acceptable by adopting a wait-and-see attitude. Similarly, Chicago's choice of an insider, after Patrick V. Murphy's candidacy had been scuttled—due in part to union lobbying of city hall—was greeted noncommittally by the FOP. But San Francisco's POA really flexed its muscle, successfully ousting Charles Gain and resisting appointment of an outsider. An up-from-the-ranks choice proved acceptable. In several other cities during 1980 the unions succeeded in pressing for an insider as the new chief. In Cleveland, with the help of a 12-member committee that included, curiously enough, representatives from the city's three police associations, a popular insider was given the job. The danger of the choice may well have been signaled when the selection drew immediate praise from rank-and-file organizations. In Prince George's County, Maryland, the FOP forced the county executive to choose as chief of police an insider instead of a more controversial outsider.

The union in neighboring Montgomery County, Maryland, contributed a unique wrinkle to the face of union involvement in chief selection when it set up a "union watch" over their ousted chief, Robert diGrazia, who had previously held the superintendent's job in Boston. The union maintained a vigil over diGrazia's job searches and would contact sister organizations to alert them to battle his appointment hammer and tong. Not his first serious run-in with unions, diGrazia had also experienced deep problems with an entrenched union in Boston that, by way of illustrating the variety of its techniques, managed to get a state law passed banning the use of name tags on police uniforms just as Superintendent diGrazia was emerging from victory over the same union on the same issue in arbitration. He had won the arbitration but lost the war.

Unions did not have as much say in other chief selections during 1980, however. Although Dade County, Florida, opted for an insider, the union did not figure as either a negative or a positive force in the decision. Minneapolis was the only major city making a change in 1980 that named an outsider. There, the union's displeasure at going outside the department was overcome mainly by the public's disgust over the past decade's shenanigans. In some locales, the police labor movement was weak or splintered, preventing the rank and file from having much influence on the selection of a chief. In Houston, for example, the department was split by the existence of several unions. While the department received an insider as its head in 1980, two years later the new mayor was able to capitalize on the divided rank and file and appoint Atlanta's black public safety commissioner to head the force.

Union Efforts to Limit Management in the Contract

The validity of the earlier observation that "the only inherent rights of management are those labor does not bargain away from them" can be seen in a glance at the police contracts in most cities. As unions have enriched themselves and hired lawyers and labor experts, they have managed to get some pretty limiting language into the contracts. Anything that requires union approval—or that must be submitted to arbitration or to another third party for resolution—is not going to be ceded by labor without a price being exacted. Such contract terms as "past practices," by which changes in the status quo require prior union approval, lock management into a position of perpetuating past mistakes.

Management should fight to resist the adoption of such limiting language or strike it from preexisting contracts. One useful technique is a "management rights" clause, which acknowledges the obligations and rights of the administration to run the operation. Where contrary language already exists, such as a clause in a past Minneapolis contract requiring periodic promotions (further inflating a bloated bureaucracy of brass), its excision might be obtained in return for a pay raise. This issue was not resolved in Minneapolis until arbitration, but there the existence of the sweetening wage hike made the elimination of the promotion proviso palatable to the arbitrator, who, like most of his associates, mostly depended on the goodwill of labor for such assignments.

The strategy of trading wage hikes for the elimination of union incursions on management prerogatives might have been followed profitably during the 1982 New York City wage negotiations with its unions, when concessions from labor (on such issues as one-person patrol cars, shifts, and precinct consolidation) seemed possible. The moment was never seized because of the mayor's distraction with a gubernatorial campaign and his reluctance to offend powerful union lobbies that supported his candidacy.

Union Alliance with Other Municipal Employees

Another of the critical issues in the 1980s is the prospect of already powerful police unions increasing their clout geometrically by allying with other municipal employees, confronting the city manager or mayor with the prospect of a total shutdown of essential municipal services. The combining of police and fire personnel in one union, as occurred in Tucson, may increase not only the workers' muscle but their militancy—because of both the added strength and the firefighters' much stronger ties to organized labor. The fire unions grew under the umbrella of big labor and are today mostly affiliated with such giants as the AFL-CIO, through the International Association of Firefighters. The police lack such a national organization.

Even if police remain in an independent union, municipal leaders must appreciate the bearing of negotiations with other public employees on police adventurousness. The point was illustrated by the federal government's response to the air traffic controllers' strike. The dismissals of about 10,000 PATCO members greatly strengthened management's hand in dealing with government workers at all levels of government.

Addressing Grievances

Conditions that breed dissatisfactions must be addressed. Festering sores erupt, sooner or later. We saw how in Tucson police reacted to the lack of pay raises in 1969 by resigning but in 1975 by striking. What was missing in Tucson—and its absence has played a causal role in many strikes—was a meaningful grievance mechanism. If the worker is denied the right to withhold services, then alternate methods of pressure must be created, such as compulsory, binding arbitration.

Relations with the Media

Relations with the media, in the midst of tense negotiations, are both volatile and critical. Many of the participants are likely to be inexperienced, and nothing will jangle the emotions faster than a negative press report. The heat of media attention and a host of other pressures have combined in many of these crises to create a situation in which events have been allowed to get into the saddle and ride the participants. Asking, as one must, for cool heads under the pressure-cooker conditions of most police union negotiations is like asking someone to slowly walk a perfectly straight path across a stage while thousands in the audience look on expectantly for any flaws. It is not a difficult thing to do, but the psychological pressures suddenly add unexpected dimensions to the feat. The participants must understand that, as they conduct their negotiations in the public view, threats and insults can turn a personal reaction into a public catastrophe. The chances that labor-management negotiations will serve the public interest will be enhanced considerably if the opponents—for they are that—understand the centrality of chemistry in these controversies and treat one another with respect and at least a modicum of trust.

Management Planning for Contingencies

One of the clearer lessons of the police strikes—although it is hopelessly bromidic to say so—is that there must be management planning for the likelier contingencies. There is the perennial need for useful intelligence, coupled with the recognition that strikes can be surprising (as in San Francisco) and truly spontaneous acts. Before action impels everyone into uncontrollable motion, responses should be planned concerning such factors as tours to be worked, the invocation of mutual assistance pacts, calls for the National Guard, policy on leaves and recalls, priority levels of calls to be answered, security considerations for vulnerable points, and injunctions ordering the strikers back to work. Simple answers and emotional reactions do especially poorly in these circumstances, and when the system works well there are no clear victors or victims—everyone gets a little and gives a little. As we have seen, usually settlements result in the workers getting less than they demanded but more than management's last offer. San Francisco was an exception, where the union had to settle for precisely what the Board of Supervisors had offered prior to the strike.

Public Pressure for Resolution of Strikes

A pervasive but unseen presence is the public; public pressure has settled more than one strike, those in San Francisco and New Orleans being prime examples. San Franciscans felt little sympathy for the largely nonresident rank and file, who would not share the tax burden resulting from a salary hike. The New Orleans citizenry was furious with the police for ruining the Mardi Gras celebration and attacking the mayor's house. When the people slowly move to the development of a generally held view of the conflict, they can be counted on to make that feeling felt, over backyard fences, at bus stops, in letters to the editor, on call-in shows, and on the streets. This is more telling than any injunction. The media are the conduits for the messages, and they shape public reactions. This is not a very well-understood process, but unions that, unlike those in San Francisco and New Orleans, learn how to sell the public an idea reap the fruits of victory. Skillful manipulation of public opinion can produce surprising results. Informational vacuums, intelligently filled by labor publicists, can steal a march on management, against logic and heavy odds.

One example of union facility in manipulating public sentiment is the New York City PBA's campaign describing the parade of horribles that would have followed establishment of a civilian review board. Another example comes from Albuquerque's ten-day strike in July 1975, which illustrates how the public's reaction is formed by fleeting impressions, particularly when little information is forthcoming. The Albuquerque union energetically pursued a positive image through the media, promoting family shots of cops, in civilian clothes, graphically illustrating their needs. Violence was eschewed, and sympathy was actively wooed. The union's active media campaign, coupled with the city's reluctance to use the media, resulted in polls showing the citizens in support of the strike and even believing the cops were right to ignore an injunction—this despite the dangers and duration of the strike (Winfree and

Gehlen 1981). The public also was recorded as feeling that the police should not return to work before a settlement was reached. To be sure, the public sentiment varied across socioeconomic and other lines: Union members, blue-collar workers, women, and the less educated were found to be strongly supportive, while the better educated, male, executive types tended to be less sympathetic.

It is somewhat surprising to learn that the American public is about evenly split on the question of the police right to strike. One might have expected strong antistrike sentiment since police strikes inspire, in the average citizen, concern over personal safety, a fear of generalized lawlessness, worry over the impact on taxes, anxiety over police strike-related violence, and concern about the specter of police violating the law by striking. The surprise at realizing the amount of public sympathy for police strikes probably stems at least in part from the myth that cops are unpopular, a belief refuted by a series of polls, taken in the 1960s and 1970s, which consistently showed high levels of public support for the police.[7] Despite these findings, however, the police feel distinctly alienated, frustrated, and hostile. These feelings almost certainly affect the extent to which police union leaders are inclined to include a bid for public sympathy in their set of bargaining tactics.

Union President's Leadership and Representation of Rank and File

In all matters of consequence, the police union president must consider his constituents' preferences, for he has to be elected. It is important to understand that the union leader is frequently prodded by angry elements among the troops he represents. It is no accident that the brief accounts of police labor controversies presented earlier frequently feature steamy union halls, where stormy sessions become the rule. It is no wonder that the union leader finds himself occasionally leading his men into unwinnable battles. The union president is faced with the considerable obligation to be sufficiently militant to satisfy his restive followers yet reasonable enough to keep his adversaries at the table.

The union president's followers often comprise not only the most vocal and militant officers but also the most violent and those most prone to misbehave. The latter point needs to be explained. The unions have been sucked into the role, virtually across the land, of defending accused cops. Such cops, frequently the "thumpers" or sadists or crooks, desperately need the legal services and other protections the union can provide. They press for more and better defenses, in all forums, and they are driven by the desperate necessity of their plight. They spook their colleagues into supporting this posture by raising the specter of arbitrary disciplinary actions by management. Union newsletters, wonderful barometers of police rank-and-file sentiment, usually mirror this reality as they defend cops and attack the perceived enemies. The mayor of Cleveland, for example, was reported, on September 10, 1982, as being outraged by one such newsletter's reference to the killing of a suspect by a cop as "the extermination of another of society's maggots." This sort of language, by no means confined to Ohio's cities, reflects the mood of the elements prodding union leaders across the land.

A recent illustration of the unions' tendency to resist even deserved disciplinary processes, in response to militant elements in the rank and file, comes from my own city, Minneapolis. In the first part of 1983, Minneapolis's Police Officers' Federation attempted to secure a charter change that would reduce the chief's ability to discipline by making everything above a five-day suspension appealable to the Civil Service Commission, where a long-time union ally is highly placed. It added a rider to a bill that would have exempted cops from having to report to the Minneapolis Police Department that they had been arrested in another jurisdiction and tried to include language that severely restricted the operations of the department's internal affairs unit. In all cases the thrust was to limit the chief's disciplinary power over those accused of wrongdoing, and the union waged its campaign on quite a variety of battlefields. In one case the appeal went to the charter Commission, in another the city council was involved, and a third entailed a trip to the capital, demonstrating the symbiosis of police unions and state legislatures. Management's counterattack was to indeed seek a charter revision, but one granting the department head the right to dismiss an employee for cause. This initiative was pursued also with the Civil Service Commission. The bill in the legislature was killed by the city's legislative liaison. On another front the contract language was softened, to add an air of reasonableness to internal affairs processes.

In order to understand and therefore properly treat with the unions, it is vital that the forces impinging on union leaders be understood. Sometimes these men lead, and sometimes they are prodded. Simplistic responses can prove disastrous.

Tension Between Police Unions and Minorities

Rank and file leaders' responsiveness to the more militant and brutal cops—and the influence these leaders in turn have on more moderate officers—makes for a natural tension between police organizers and minority communities throughout America. This tension has not been eased, as some had hoped it would be, by widespread unionization and adoption of police officers' bills of rights. Both steps were expected by some to have a democratizing effect on the police or to make them more sensitive to the rights of others, including such currently unpopular minorities as gays. Even police who are not unionized become the focus of a good deal of resentment from a rapidly growing underclass, composed mostly of blacks and Hispanics, in whose restive ghetto neighborhoods the cops are frequently asked to serve as soldiers of occupation. This hostility is reflected in the frequent charges of police brutality hurled by black and Hispanic organizations. Violence in the ghetto, where unemployment reaches such unimaginable levels as 40 to 60 percent and where the leading cause of death of adult males is homicide, fuels the controversies.

The bitterness is transmitted to blacks and Hispanics who enter the police world as recruits and find themselves, in a sense, in the enemy's camp. The psychological dilemma is not helped by the white, male, and fairly insensitive leadership they encounter in their union halls; for the union leaders reflect their members, and the members have tended to be white males who are not anxious to surrender the chance to make room for their sons. The women, blacks, and Hispanics are seen as interlopers who are interrupting a chain of succession that has been in operation for decades. For instance, it was not mere churlishness that kept New York City's PBA from permitting women to join the union until compelled to do so by irresistibly powerful social and legal pressures. Blacks have faced similar resistance. The growth of such black organizations as the National Organization of Black Law Enforcement Executives (NOBLE) and the National Black Police Association (NBPA) is even starker proof of the dichotomy that has overtaken the ranks. These basically separatist groups have grown at precisely the time of the rapid expansion of police unionism, and they have done so at least partly out of the black officers' and executives' sense that black interests are not represented by the police unions. Union leaders, like police chiefs, are discovering, to their pain, that they are now functioning in a world that is far more complex and volatile than anything their predecessors had dreamed possible.

FISCAL CRISIS AND THE THREAT TO UNIONS

Perhaps the most difficult fact of life that police union leaders — and their bosses across the bargaining table — will need to cope with in the 1980s is the fiscal abyss into which most municipalities are plunging.

The Volunteer Movement and Police Auxiliaries

One of the public responses to shrinking police force size has been the volunteer movement. Increasingly afraid of street crime, Americans in recent years have reached out for such methods of protecting themselves and their property as neighborhood patrols, block clubs, and citizen self-help groups. The Guardian Angels group, mostly black and Hispanic "street kids" who voluntarily patrol and protect users of the New York subways and have recently established branches in other major cities, has become the symbolic centerpiece of the debate. This debate really centers on the contemporary citizen's bedevilling question: What is my role in assuring my own protection? Strangely, the chiefs say, "Leave it to us." Like Oliver Twist, however, they chant, "More, please sir, more." The unions, even more than the chiefs, heap scorn on such groups as the Guardian Angels, labeling them "untrained meddlers," "vigilantes," and so forth. Of course, the Angels, coming from the population that mostly produces our stereotype of the street criminal, constitute a convenient target. The resulting public scuffle, masterfully exploited by their public relations-wise leader, Curtis Sliwa, might, but for the deep and troubling question lying at the discussion's core, be dismissed as much ado about very little.

Police auxiliaries create a more difficult target. These selfless citizens don uniforms and perform an enormous variety of onerous tasks solely for the privilege of service. They might supplement a foot patrol operation, handle traffic at parades or sports events, or undertake any of a myriad of tasks that do not require a sworn, armed officer. The auxiliaries, sometimes called Police Reserves (as in the Los Angeles Sheriff's Department), inspire fear and loathing among the police rank and file. (The unions' reflexive opposition to auxiliary police provides another example of their readiness to participate in the resolution of issues that are more appropriately a management concern.)

Fears and Feelings Underlying the Controversies

As in many such controversies, the public discussion of volunteers and police aides tends to mask, rather than reflect, true feelings. The *New York Times*, on the front page of its September 8, 1982 issue, trumpeted the extension of an experiment that had uniformed police volunteers, members of New York's Auxiliary Police, patrolling in groups of about six the New York City subway system. It can easily be argued that this menacing underground environment needs all the help it can get, yet the union immediately labeled the effort "irresponsible." The articulated objections center on lack of professionalism, lack of preparation and training, and the jeopardy all this creates for the public. The cops talking among themselves, however, speak of the threat to their jobs created by these amateurs. While the latter is closer to the truth, nevertheless the real concern lies in the fact that the existence of citizens willing to do police work for nothing totally undercuts the unions' argument that they are out there risking their lives in a dangerous enterprise that no one would want to touch and therefore deserve better treatment from their employers.

It is absolutely vital to understand such deeper sources of concern if problems are to be attacked. A good deal of energy was wasted on the question of safety when women were introduced into the police trenches; in fact, a lot of the controversy actually arose from the concerns of police wives over the temptations their men would be subjected to when they were encased in steel, from midnight to 8:00 A.M., with a woman. It proved a very legitimate concern as the catalyst of sexuality ignited the intense chemistry of police partnership. The real problem with women in policing has turned out to be romance, not safety (FBI 1975).

Layoffs and Workload

The darkest fear prompted among unionists by the fiscal problems of the 1980s, of course, is the prospect of layoffs, a prospect that may present management with one of the greatest opportunities for retrieving its proper prerogatives during the 1980s. To explain this requires a brief note on boredom and the police. Police work has been characterized as long stretches of boredom punctuated by spikes of excitement. It might also be said that police activity is not a constant but fluctuates according to the neighborhood, the time of day, and the season of the year. Friday and Saturday summer nights in the ghetto jump. Many police chiefs want departments that are manned for these peaks, but this is not only wasteful but organizationally dangerous. Inactivity has been the source of many police scandals as well as such problems as sleeping on duty. Idleness is, indeed, the devil's workshop, and a world that offers as many temptations as a cop's does cannot stand additional incentives for mischief.

Instead of trading job security for resurrection of management prerogatives, it might pay for chiefs to step boldly into the face of the unions' worst fear and to shrink police forces to levels of maximum work and minimum boredom, allowing for the failures that will occur at the peaks of activity. Shifts should be adjusted accordingly. This could make for happier and more productive employees. The inverse of Parkinson's Law is that the labor force might be decreased to the point where the available work is such as to keep virtually everyone productively, and consistently, engaged. While heresy to the IACP, it might be profitable to urge the chiefs to call for less rather than more and to use the budget crises currently facing policing as excuses for reforms we have all been reluctant to pursue because of union resistance. Otherwise, storm clouds that loom on the horizon, such as private contracting for public services (on the growth of the private security industry, see Shanahan's chapter) may darken our skies before we have a chance to take proper precautions.

CONCLUSION

Police unions evolved, rather effortlessly, from their fraternal ancestors, lagging behind but picking up the gains. What was lost in time was compensated for in the absence of risk. Where the rare jurisdictional disputes arose they usually involved rival fraternities of varying militancy, and as we have seen, management could usually be relied on to act in a way that would drive the members into the most extreme ranks. Together with this, though, came an antipathy by the rank and file for national affiliation and an extension of the sense of exclusivity and locality that attends police work. To be sure, there were flirtations with national affiliation in 1929 and later with the Teamsters, but both of these resulted in scalded fingers and reinforced the sense that affiliation was both wrong and dangerous. Another peculiarity was the extreme solidarity. Cops belong to a brotherhood in blue of fierce intensity, and the police unions simply build on, and feed off, this cohesiveness.

The ebb and flow of union strength and aggressiveness that I have traced through the decades of this century led to a rising tide of militance beginning in the late 1960s. That militance was rooted in a complex tangle of factors that included resentment of the black and student groups the police frequently clashed with and a fairly widespread sympathy for white backlash political campaigns. The civil rights movement, the student revolts, a series of Supreme Court decisions that reflected a deep suspicion of the police, such questions as surrounded civilian review boards, increased violence toward the police, and a rising crime rate—all served to feed the self-pitying sense of frustration understandably experienced by groups asked to accomplish contradictory tasks, in isolation and amidst disapproval.

A police executive responsive to the sources of rank-and-file frustration will be able to more effectively assist the unions in playing their legitimate role in the police world and outside it. The competent manager will develop mechanisms that permit honorable and timely resolutions of conflicts with management. The question of role definition is critical. We might adopt one that has unions legitimately engaged in questions relating to wages, benefits, health, and welfare—and serving as protectors against the arbitrary and capricious acts of management. But the limits of the unions' role must also be respected, for the briefest look at police union history will alert management to the willingness of labor to make inappropriate incursions into management enclaves. As we have seen, police unions have become involved in such questions as the establishment of civilian review boards, the wearing of name tags, entrance and promotion standards, minority recruitment, the assignment of female officers, anticorruption strategies, the disciplinary process, one-person patrols, such items of equipment as Mace, bulletproof vests, types of guns and bullets, firearms discharge policies, the selection of the chief, the scheduling of shifts, whether to hire more cops, and residence policies. It is not too much to say that the unions have made the full scope of police operations their realm. Dealing with them requires all the skills of diplomacy, knowledge, and experience that negotiators for powerful adversaries must bring to their deliberations. Managers and unionists alike must recognize that management is not labor and labor is not management. We are still at a point in our development where counterproductive intrusions can be beaten back by determined managers. But the managers, too, must be prevented from poaching on labor's legitimate preserve.

In order to impose reforms, management must be seen as being willing to share the pain. The contemporary spectacle of layoffs at the bottom while promotions, or business as usual, continue at the top is precisely the sort of hypocrisy that sends cops scurrying to unionize or, once unionized, to take job actions. In ways and on matters that permit it, management should consult the union. While it cannot be denied that at this moment in history the unions are ascendant and the chiefs are playing catch-up, there is no need to swing the pendulum all the way back to the bad old days. Police unions are here to stay, and they have a crucial role to play in the law enforcement community and an important stake in a strong and well-managed department. As one prominent union leader recently put it, "I've been a cop a lot longer than I've been a union president." It was no accident that in Minneapolis in 1982 the union members opted for responsibility and voted in a cool, negotiating moderate over his firebrand rival.

We have seen that given the proper issues, the cops can be radicalized and galvanized to furious and effective actions. On these occasions the unions are roaring lions and ought to be treated very delicately. We have also seen that unions seek to intrude into management's realm and will do so if unopposed. Effective opposition, in which management utilizes the media to clearly outline its position as one adopted to make the department more efficient and effective public servants, will frequently reveal the unions to be paper tigers. By the same token, a willful and arbitrary management that has usurped the union's rightful role will very likely be driven back. Although the terrifying increase in crime America has experienced in recent decades may be symptomatic of a deeper socioeconomic problem, the police are, nevertheless, expected to cope with the results. In order to do so the institution must simply be managed better. And it will not make significant progress in this direction unless tough reforms can be initiated without having to face a gauntlet of obstacles created by police unions. When the roles of both labor and management are guided by their legitimate interests, when both parties treat labor relations as adversarial processes that can take place in an atmosphere of mutual trust, cooperation, and understanding, then managers and unions become much more formidable—and socially useful—combatants.

NOTES

1. It is a measure of the bedrock conservatism and even antiintellectualism of the IACP that as late as 1982 it could censure its most distinguished member, Patrick V. Murphy, then president of the Police Foundation and the former chief of police of Syracuse, New York City, Washington, D.C., and Detroit, for doing nothing more than uttering some mild criticisms calling

for introspection and reform. That the principal national police organization could bring itself to muzzle the legitimate, and perhaps only, heir to Vollmer, Parker, and Wilson was all the proof needed, if any were, of the deep-seated hostility to the urban, the intellectual, and the progressive elements within the police ranks.

2. In my view, the principal problem with such boards is that being inexperienced, they are easily gulled and co-opted by wrongdoing officers who should be punished (see Kerstetter's chapter).

3. Unfortunately, the extension of these procedural protections to police would not, in the main, ultimately fulfill the hopes of some of the proponents of the bills of rights that police would be sensitized to the need to respect the procedural rights of criminal suspects.

4. This latter point was not lost on wary observers of the municipal scene. It led to a move, well astir, to break supervisors out of the bargaining unit, labeling them "management." The creation of this division was seen as one way to continue functioning during a rank-and-file strike. The theory proved its worth repeatedly.

5. Each of these matters might deserve special treatment but two—the investigator's position and the elimination of the inspector's rank—ought to be explained more fully. Investigators in the Minneapolis Police Department were, almost exclusively, sergeants and lieutenants. Tasks performed by the lowest rank, police officer, in other cities were reserved for costly supervisors in Minneapolis. This arose from the unseated mayor's reluctance to return to the ranks as a "detective," so he changed all detectives to "lieutenants." The proposed reform was intended to thin out the bloated upper ranks, with emphasis on sergeants and lieutenants. Captains, though, would also be reduced, from 18 to 12. The inspector's rank, just above a captain's, would, as a symbol of austerity and to promote efficiency, be eliminated altogether, and the five incumbents would have to return to their lower permanent ranks. Their function, to ensure a high-ranking, uniformed presence on the streets of the city 24 hours a day, would be undertaken by captains. The decimation of the supervisory levels was seen as a way of making the department leaner.

6. Meanwhile other city workers were getting more. Many suspected they were being rewarded for political help. The sanitation union in New York City had long since discovered the advantages of helping someone into office. By the end of the decade sanitation workers were outearning cops in New York, though not in basic salary. The difference was concealed in such gimmicks as overtime, Sunday work, and a new one, "productivity savings."

7. A poll taken by the *Minneapolis Tribune* in May 1983 revealed that the police ranked first in public confidence among such institutions as the church, the Supreme Court, educational institutions, newspapers, the judiciary, the state legislature, and Congress.

24
The Chief and the Union:
May the Force Be with You

Robert B. Kliesmet

"Vandals! Visigoths! The beast kept at bay by the 'thin blue line'. . . . Rome forced into the arms of its men of arms. . . . The anguish of this troubled age infected its keepers. . . ." With this apocalyptic view of U.S. cities as background, Anthony Bouza attempts to allocate responsibility for the problems he sees in American policing. To be sure, he passes the blame around, both castigating the leadership of American policing and taking a broad swipe at the American police union movement. In my view, what he intends as an indictment of unions only underscores the dreadful state of police leadership in the United States. Moreover, as I shall argue, police unionism is really a source of stability in a police world of extraordinarily unstable and untalented leadership.

To understand Bouza's assessment of the current state of American policing, it is important to understand that his notion of police "professionalism" is police "reform" in the tradition of August Vollmer, William Parker, O. W. Wilson, and Patrick Murphy (compare the Skolnick-McCoy chapter, p. 112). In reform orthodoxy, you cannot spot the police "professionals" using the traditional scorecard. Traditionally, the professional is a practitioner of a discipline, trained in a university over an extended period, controlled not by bureaucratic supervision but primarily by internalized wisdom, knowledge, and skill as well as colleagues, and organized in an association that, supported by legislation, substantially controls entrance into the profession. By the term "professional," police reformers have meant instead strong bureaucratic command and control, legitimation by law, close supervision, rejection of the use of discretion by practitioners, and the creation of a professional elite—chiefs (see Klockars's chapter, p. 318 and Mayo's chapter, p. 399). This is not a semantic quibble; it is at the heart of my disagreement with Bouza's chapter.

For Bouza as well as his reform colleagues only chiefs can be professionals in the classical sense and belong to the so-called police professional associations: the International Association of Chiefs of Police or the Police Executive Research Forum. Both of these organizations specifically exclude practicing police officers from full membership. The folly of precluding rank-and-file participation in police policymaking processes (a point to which I will return later) was articulated well by Herman Goldstein (1977, p. 310) when he observed that, as "operating personnel," they are familiar "with the most important problems of the agency—those that arise in the actual delivery of service to the citizenry." An elitist model of professionalism—coupled with such managerial concepts as "efficiency" and "productivity," which the public sector has slavishly adopted from private sector administration—perhaps is what undergirds so troublesome a suggestion as that found at the end of Bouza's essay: "It might pay for chiefs to step boldly into the face of the unions' worst fear and to shrink police forces to levels of maximum work and minimum boredom, allowing for the failures that will occur at the peaks of activity."

This advice seems to ignore the implications of much of the contemporary police research about the multiplicity of police functions, the fear reduction potential of foot patrol, the service role of the police, the important roles police should be playing in assisting communities and neighborhoods to define their problems and seek solutions, and the importance of police officer discretion. The fact that police officers now spend a good portion of their time driving around bored in cars was not union doing. "Preventive patrol" has been part of the reform orthodoxy—only partly a means of delivering police services, it was developed by managers who were unable to devise meaningful forms of supervision and instead opted to keep police in cars and remote from citizens (see Cordner's chapter, p. 392).

If Bouza's conclusion concerning what to do about underutilized police resources gives me the feeling we've been watching different pictures, his recitation of the story of the 1919 Boston police strike, when rioters tore Boston apart and were only quelled by the military after days of unrest, brings to mind the classic Japanese film *Roshomon*. The story bears telling from another perspective.

During a period of rampant inflation, Boston police officers negotiated for a year and a half for a pay increase. An arbitration panel finally recommended an annual pay increase of $200. A police commissioner (who, it is generally conceded, was weak and ineffectual, especially when compared with earlier commissioners in Boston) and politicians ignored both the legitimate requests for pay increases and the arbitration recommendation. The police officers were caught in the middle as representatives of state and city interests struggled for control of the city (Boston police were under state control at that time). The appropriate image to describe the situation police officers found themselves in is not Bouza's observation that "battlers tumbling in the mud take their victories where they find them"; it is instead the African adage: "When elephants are fighting, the grass gets hurt." In an attempt to get hurt less, Boston police officers affiliated with organized labor (the AFL). Their leaders were fired. More than 1,100 of the approximately 1,500 officers went out on strike. The same commissioner, in collaboration with Governor Coolidge, refused to call for assistance at the initiation of the strike. Rioting ensued.

Never mind that this was not the first police strike (police had struck earlier, twice in London and once in Cincinnati, from which the Boston leadership should have drawn some lessons). Never mind that at the time the Boston Police Department was openly acknowledged to have the finest rank-and-file officers and to be one of the best and most honest police departments in the United States, if not the world (Scotland Yard officials had come to study its practices). Never mind that weak leadership threatened that pre-eminence and turned exemplary rank-and-file officers into frustrated and bitter union activists.

No, never mind all those things. Fire the strikers, destroy the finest police department in the United States, exalt the inept governor so he could become an inept vice-president and ultimately an inept president. Leave citizens to pick up the pieces. Leave the city with a rancorous labor-management tradition that plagues both officers and administrators to this day. Never mind that it was the political leadership of the state and city that gambled with the safety of Boston and the security of its citizens by humiliating union leaders and refusing to plan for the possibility of a strike.

Never mind all that. Use the story to perpetrate a myth: Strikes are irresponsible acts of police labor that threaten the very stability of society. Never mind that for every horror story of violence during a strike there are at least two untouted stories of skilled leadership that peacefully manages the strike period. Never mind that chiefs and politicians have parlayed the Boston horror story into negotiation and management styles that have retarded police salaries and the development of genuine professionalism while turning police departments into fiefdoms for chiefs who could hardly administer their way home let alone a large complex organization — fiefdoms in which talented, earnest, and idealistic young persons turn into cynical, bitter officers who start looking toward retirement when barely out of the academy.

The Boston police strike was an important milestone in police history. It exposed the abysmally low status of police officers, the willingness of politicians and chiefs to gamble with the safety of citizens for their own personal political gains, and the vulnerability of police organizations, even the best of them, to conniving or weak chiefs. Space does not allow me to go over some of the other horror stories Bouza presents, but almost all of them admit of similar retellings.

All of this does not mean that unions do not, or have not, made mistakes.

Of course we have. Blame for most of the problems of policing as we know it today does not belong to us, however. Unions were late on the scene and, given the complete dominance of politicians and police chiefs, we have had to play catch-up. Twenty years from now, we will claim some of the credit and accept our share of any blame for the shape of policing.

Today, as the officer on the street deals with troubled and anxious citizens he or she is virtually alone: unsupervised, with little or no policy guidance, and practically no relevant training. Most events police handle are so ambiguous and satisfactory outcomes so transitory that progressive management ideas such as efficiency and productivity are almost impossible to define in policing. Nevertheless, many police executives settle for slogans and gimmicks to impress politicians and citizens rather than genuinely educating them to just how complex it is on the street. They do this, in my view, at least partly because admitting the complexities would necessarily justify substantial police officer discretion, which in turn would reveal the focus of true professionalism in policing.

This belief leads me to an assertion I made earlier—that police unions are a source of stability in the police world. To discuss this I would note that Bouza seems a bit piqued and perplexed by the favorable response of the general public to police during strikes. Frankly, I'm not. He would attribute it to "union facility in manipulating public sentiment." In the Albuquerque example he gives, he points to a city government piously reluctant to use the press to further its point of view, although based on my involvement in a fair number of "job actions" it is hard for me to imagine that city representatives in any jurisdiction would sit on their hands—unless for some reason they believed it was in their best interests. Moreover, the fact that this support is not uniform across social classes is also of considerable interest, for the people who reportedly most support police are those who deal with police officers most often in their personal lives. They have seen us at our best and at our worst. Despite the fact that we cannot always help them, despite the occasional brutal officer, despite the mistakes the best of us make, and despite the attempts of administration to limit our contact with these citizens, we continue to provide almost every conceivable kind of service, and citizens realize that, for the most part, we do the best we can. And when police researchers— the Mannings, Muirs, Kellings, Rubensteins, Bittners, Van Mannens, and others of the world—observe us they find some fault but, for the most part, they have come to understand what a difficult task we have, how reasonable most of our actions are, and what little administrative and supervisory support we operate with on the street.[1]

The point is that although police chiefs come and go (their average tenure is less than three years) police services to communities remain fairly constant over the years. And it is the patrol officer on the street who is responsible for the quality of that service. The weakness and unevenness of police administration, supervision, training, and planning leave a vacuum in which the rank-and-file police officers and their unions in many respects provide more stability and continuity in policing than do chiefs.

Although police chiefs are not to blame for their lack of tenure, what is irksome is their general failure to draw on one of their best resources – the police officer – in an effort to make the most of their predictably short time at the helm. The elitism of chiefs, characterized as it is by general disregard for the contributions that the rank and file can make to police policy and strategies, has created a situation in which police officers have turned to their unions and associations for professional leadership as well as typical union "bread and butter" issues. In fact, police chiefs have behaved in ways that convince police officers that chiefs and their immediate aides believe that they alone have a corner on good ideas. Rank-and-file police officers simply have no meaningful input into matters of deep professional concern. I can hear chiefs saying, "Policy is an administrative prerogative." This misses the point. Even industry (most recently in response to the threat from Japanese ideas about how to manage effectively) has come to learn that workers perform at their best when they are consulted about production and performance issues – both jealously guarded in the past in industry as "management prerogatives." Police managers simply have not been willing to acknowledge that police officers themselves have good ideas that can improve policing. Instead, it has been more convenient for chiefs to label police officers and unions as opposed to innovation. This is untrue. Workers in any occupation want to be consulted regarding policy and strategic issues. As employees, we do not believe that we should have the final say. Involvement of police officers in such issues, however, is so alien to management that it is, for the most part, unheard of in policing.[2] Hopefully, for the sake of better community service, in the years ahead a more sensible balance will be struck between those who manage the police and the actual practitioners of the craft.

NOTES

1. Although there are many observational studies of patrol officers, with the exception of Louis Mayo's contribution to this volume I know of no similar observational studies of chiefs.

2. Police chiefs forget that even one of the most basic pieces of research in policing, the Kansas City Preventive Patrol Experiment (Kelling et al. 1974a), did not originate with Chief Clarence Kelley, or the Police Foundation, or even with the authors of the final report. It originated with members of a task force consisting primarily of patrol officers who were assigned by Chief Kelley to examine policing priorities in their district. (It will be recalled that the response of the IACP to the study was to propose that research be banned from police departments.)

25
Police Unions:
How They Look from
the Academic Side

James B. Jacobs

The emergence of public employee unions and the legitimation of public sector collective bargaining structures are crucial developments in the American system of government. As a consequence, public employees not only fulfill roles and implement policies designed by political leaders but they also help to shape those roles and determine the policies. Public agencies now must balance the interests of their employees with the pursuit of organizational goals.

It is important to remember that public employee unionism and collective bargaining are not unique to the police. Whatever the reason, the desire of public employees to organize and bargain collectively with their agencies proved irresistible in the 1960s, at least in those states with strong labor traditions. Perhaps this reflected a decline in salary and working conditions for public employees at a time when social and economic expectations were increasing. Perhaps it reflected some inexorable dynamic in American interest group politics such that Americans more and more came to make demands as groups. In any case, by the end of the 1960s many state and local governments faced serious political and administrative problems in managing the demands of public sector workers for higher compensation and reorganized working environments. The problem only became more acute in the face of severe fiscal difficulties.

Without diminishing the importance of the public employee movement toward formal labor relations and collective bargaining, it is also important to remember that a third of the states do not have collective bargaining laws (Schneider 1979; Edwards et al. 1979, pp. 259-60) and that among those that do the police are sometimes excluded or treated specially. On the one hand, police unions are sometimes barred from affiliating with nonpolice unions.

On the other hand, police unions often enjoy the advantage of interest arbitration.[1] The legal status of police associations or unions has critical implications. Without a formal collective bargaining law, there is no such thing as a police "union," or any other kind of public employee union, although, as Bouza shows, informal police organizations can at times organize limited protest actions. A collective bargaining law transforms an association with voluntary dues and membership and merely ad hoc means for "expressing" job concerns into a labor organization whose coffers are filled with money obtained by a dues check-off, and whose powers are infinitely strengthened by authorization to bargain over the terms and conditions of employment with the agency's leadership. Inevitably the first contract also brings a seniority clause and a grievance procedure, which also enhance the power of the union. A full-scale study of police unions would necessarily have to start with an analysis of formal and informal collective bargaining structures and the successes and failures of police to earn the same rights (or greater rights) than other public employees.

My research on prison guard unions suggests to me that during the 1960s, "management" was poorly prepared and off balance in negotiations with public sector unions. Many public administrators had no training in labor relations, dimly understood the process, and more or less convinced themselves that in time the "experiment" would go away. They approached the first contract negotiations with a cavalier attitude about "management prerogatives" and insufficient attention to details and strategy. Public employee unions sometimes enjoyed the assistance of those who had experience working in unionized organizations in the private sector before taking positions of public employment (Jacobs and Crotty 1978). In any case, my impression is that, in the corrections context, public employers were extremely defensive during the first few rounds of contract negotiations. The unions made demands; agency heads resisted as best they could. Many of the first contracts were extremely favorable to the unions (see Wynne 1978), not in small measure because negotiations were conducted by offices of employee relations rather than departments of correction. This meant that the personnel doing the negotiating frequently did not have much familiarity with prison practices and organizational constraints. They were often willing to make concessions on policies and administrative issues (for example, the way roles are organized) in exchange for moderation of wage demands. The same dynamics can probably be identified in the police context. Contract negotiations here, too, involve legislators and officials outside the police hierarchy. It stands to reason that interests other than those defined by police administrators will have weight.

Students of labor relations, American politics, and the criminal justice system should be extremely anxious to assess the impact of public sector collective bargaining on such public sector bureaucracies as courts, police, and prisons and jails. Unfortunately, the scholarship is skimpy.[2] Perhaps academia needs several decades to catch up with organizational developments in the real world, or perhaps this kind of development, as is so often the case, falls between the traditional academic stools. As I see it, there are four broad areas requiring analysis: the impact of collective bargaining on salaries and conditions of employment; the impact of collective bargaining on the administration of the agency; the impact of collective bargaining on agency policies; and the impact of collective bargaining on service delivery. A vast study and a book-length report would be required to assess these issues in the context of the American police. I can only indicate some of the questions and topic areas that I expect are important and, here and there, offer a hypothesis derived from my own research on the unionization of prison guards (Jacobs and Crotty 1978).

Whether public employee unionism has improved the salaries and fringe benefits of police is an issue I will leave to my economist colleagues.[3] Suffice it to say that there is a growing literature on this question (for an excellent, comprehensive review of these materials, see Ehrenberg and Schwarz 1984). One also would like to know whether unions have been able to increase the flow of nonsalary resources into their agencies. With police unions lobbying alongside police executives is there a greater chance of getting more police cars, better firearms, improved forensic laboratories, and so forth? In my view, the prison guard unions have missed a promising opportunity to improve their image and career opportunities for the rank and file by not being more creative in lobbying on behalf of corrections.

As Bouza vividly demonstrates, police unions potentially have an enormous impact on the administration of a police agency. It is worth hypothesizing that the very existence of a union and union leaders undermines the paramilitary chain of command on which all police organizations are constructed. The rank and file no longer have to look to the chief for all sorts of favors and benefits, and they no longer have as much to fear from the chief's disfavor. Employer-employee relations probably have become more formal and more adversarial. If true, this must have implications for morale, bureaucratic efficiency, and the quality of service delivery.

In a large metropolitan police department the union president or even a steward may have more de facto authority than lieutenants and captains. The union president will, for example, have greater access to the police chief and his top staff than many middle management personnel. The union may also have an immense impact on "command control." The seniority clause may limit the chief's capacity to assign his personnel as he thinks best.[4] Various disciplinary due process procedures may make it harder to reprimand, suspend, or dismiss a corrupt or poorly performing officer.[5] The union is certain to resist policies that its members oppose, such as one-person patrol cars (see, for example, Buder 1980). Beyond that, if the corrections experience is any guide, a police union may attempt to force the department to maintain certain patrol or staffing patterns on safety grounds. While it is possible that the tug and pull over such issues could improve employee morale and lead to more creative solutions to thorny deployment problems, it seems more likely that such issues will be defined as power struggles over who "really runs" the department.

Public sector unions typically push their bargaining demands beyond mere salary and fringe benefit issues. Teachers, for example, want to have a say in classroom size, teacher-student ratios, and curriculum (see, for example, *Pennsylvania Labor Relations Board* v. *State College Area School District* 1975). Prison guards want to have a say in building programs, vocational and educational programs, and inmate grievance procedures. There likely are parallels in the police context. Bouza points out that unions often want to have input in the selection of the chief and in other personnel matters; they also want to affect policy on civilian review boards and perhaps on using deadly force and choke holds. How much success they have in influencing the outcome of such issues is a matter for extended and comprehensive research.[6]

Obviously, strikes are the most dramatic and most frightening manifestation of police unionism. It is possible to have police "militancy," "job actions," and even walkouts without a union, and certainly without a formal collective bargaining structure. However, the organization of rank-and-file police officers in formal union structures increases the potential for concerted group action and the potential for success when group protests occur. Collective bargaining laws, of course, forbid strikes by public employees, especially "essential" employees such as police, but the history of public sector labor relations has shown that prohibitions and penalties have not prevented strikes by teachers, prison guards, firefighters, or police.

Of all public employees, inhibitions against striking are probably strongest within the ranks of the police, and public opposition to police strikes probably exceeds opposition to any other public employee strikes. Nevertheless, while there have not been many police strikes since 1970, they have occurred; certainly the police were more apt to strike in the 1970s than in the 1960s or 1950s. My impression is that, so far, although disruptive and cause for concern, these strikes have not been devastating. Supervisory personnel, nonstrikers, police from other jurisdictions, and National Guard forces have been able to ensure effectively public order. Perhaps the police themselves have been ready to compromise more readily than other unionized employees once they believed their point had been made. All of this is fertile ground for systematic investigation. It surely behooves the society to keep its finger on the pulse of police morale, militancy, and alienation. Frequent, protracted, and bitter police strikes would pose an enormous challenge to city governments.

The bottom line is whether the advent of public sector unionization and collective bargaining has improved or diminished the quality of police service. This is a very difficult question to answer because there is sharp debate over what constitutes good police service,[7] and there are probably insurmountable methodological difficulties in separating out the effects of unionism from all other variables that impact on the delivery of police services. Still, to the extent that unionization has fragmented the chain of command, put narrow self-interest over public interest, and produced all sorts of "inefficiencies," the results cannot be viewed with sanguinity. On the other hand, if police unions have improved morale by achieving better salaries, fairer procedures, and better lines of communication it is possible that a genuinely positive effect could be discerned.

NOTES

1. Interest arbitration, often an explicit substitute for the right to strike, is a procedure whereby an impasse in contract negotiations is submitted to a third party (for example, arbitrator) for resolution.

2. Studies of police unions include those of Juris and Feuille (1973), Levi (1977), and the very interesting study of unionism among British police by Reiner (1978). On police strikes, see International Association of Chiefs of Police (1979). Regarding prison guards, see Jacobs and Crotty (1978).

3. The definitive work is Ehrenberg and Schwarz (1984).

4. A seniority clause gives employees the right to bid for assignments, including posts and shifts. The bidder with the most seniority gets the open position even if the chief or other top administrator thinks it would be best to assign a different person to the job in question. This has been subject to enormous criticism by prison officials, who claim that their most experienced employees bid away from contact positions that are the most sensitive and demanding, thereby leaving the crucial posts in the facility to be covered by the least experienced officers.

5. Most collective bargaining agreements are able to achieve procedural and substantive rights greater than what exist in the civil service law; at least this is the case in corrections. This means that employees can only be suspended or fired for certain reasons (good cause), that various procedural steps have to be taken, and that union representation at all stages is assured. Sometimes there is a right to outside arbitration in such cases.

6. Such research on police unions should begin with some solid case studies on the impact of collective bargaining on the day-to-day operation of a police department—car, precinct, detail and shift assignments; internal investigations; disciplinary actions; relationships between the top ranking officials and the rank and file; and so on. It should also focus on the union's impact on major policies and procedures—one-person patrol cars, foot patrols, team policing, appointing the chief, purchasing bulletproof clothing, lethal force policies, arrest priorities, and so forth.

7. The controversy and ambiguity of the "police role" are treated in a most sophisticated way in Goldstein (1977, pp. 8–11).

PART 7

SUPPOSE WE WERE REALLY SERIOUS ABOUT USING THE POLICE FOR CRIME CONTROL?

Introduction

Americans *are* serious about using the police for crime control (by which I mean prevention of criminality, as well as detection, investigation, apprehension, and conviction of lawbreakers), but the proverbial visitor from another planet might be excused for occasionally misconstruing our intentions. What the alien is apt to see in the modern urban policeman is a soldier ill-equipped for his campaign: carrying ambiguous and in some ways irresponsibly ambitious orders, supplied with antiquated technology, and insufficiently briefed on his assigned area to distinguish friend from foe — or, if he can make the distinction, required to treat friends in ways not likely to elicit their cooperation in ferreting out and combating the enemy (see Morris and Hawkins 1970, 1977).

Clearly, the military analogy has its limitations as applied to policing (indeed, Carl Klockars's chapter in this section attributes many of policing's problems to the influence of the military model), but the analogy's relative simplicity helps to highlight the gulf that still remains in too many law enforcement agencies between their crime control mission and their methods of operation. The chapters in this section explore the opportunities that police leaders around the nation have and, in some cases, are currently using to deal aggressively and lawfully with epidemic levels of crime and fear of crime (also see the contributions to this volume by Lee Brown and Raymond Davis).

The contributors' point of departure is a tough-minded acceptance of the reality that, while much remains to be learned about police capacities, law enforcement agencies cannot do all that a crime-weary nation wants and misguidedly expects them to do. Moreover, the authors — three academics involved regularly in assisting police practitioners, two police chiefs, and three public housing officials — know that serious, if controversial, questions have been raised over the past decade about the usefulness of a number of traditional police techniques, including preventive patrol (Kelling et al. 1974a), police rapid response to calls for service (Pate et al. 1976), detective work (Greenwood and Petersilia 1975; see also Ward 1978), and crime labs (Peterson 1983). Such doubts shake the bedrock of police crime-fighting strategy. Under these circumstances, as one social observer noted, "If you're not confused, you're just not thinking clearly" (Peter 1977, p. 296). While some in policing and academia are less confused than others — in part because they do not accept the validity of many or all of these research findings — there is, nevertheless, wide agreement that, compared to America's feats of ingenuity on other fronts, we remain pretty much in the dark on how to avert serious crime. That they light candles rather than curse — or, worse, deny — this darkness is why the practitioners and scholars represented in the following pages have been asked to contribute to this volume. Happily, they have numerous counterparts nationwide.

The two issues the authors in this section have been asked to illuminate are the following: Does an increased emphasis on "order maintenance" (see Wilson and Kelling 1982 and the chapters in this book by Kerstetter, Mayo, Walker, and Pomeroy) inevitably lead to unconscionable use of force by police? And what are the sources of increased information to police for crime control, and how does one tap those sources? The first question is addressed candidly and lucidly in the George Kelling-Carl Klockars debate and in the reports by Hubert Williams and the Fort Lauderdale authors (Lindsey, Cochran, Quint, and Rivera) on their actual experiences in attempting to fight "clean but tough" against street crime. Wesley Skogan's chapter sheds important light on the second question by exploring the prospects for greater victim-witness cooperation with the police (see also Albert Alschuler's contribution); and the Fort Lauderdale report touches on the enormously important matter of expanded interagency collaborations — not just between the police and other primary criminal justice agencies such as the prosecutor's office and the corrections system but between the police and such secondary "social control" agencies as the public housing authority. The collaborative approach used in the oasis technique in Fort Lauderdale has important implications for better communication and cooperation between the police world and many others, including the public school, mental health, and public transit systems, zoning boards, the private security industry, and the business world (see Stewart's and Shanahan's chapters; see also Geller 1985).

Besides going to the core of modern policing's crisis and opportunity, inquiring about how to use the police effectively to secure freedom from fear for the residents of our beleaguered cities addresses in two ways this volume's theme of who runs and who should run the police. First, the question explores who sets law enforcement priorities, how, and why. Second, it examines the way in which the *idea* that the police exist primarily in order to control crime has, by creating public expectations about the police role, "run" the police over the years (see Douthit 1975). Thus the idea that the police should be able to control the level of crime has led the media and politicians to evaluate the "success" or "failure" of a city's police force mainly in light of the crime rates reported periodically in the FBI's *Uniform Crime Reports.*

The following five chapters, then, address the most pressing issue confronting this country's police leadership. The chapters cannot be expected to be comprehensive in their treatment of promising techniques. Hardly touched, for example, are such bright prospects as "differential police response" strategies that help free police to deal with solvable, significant crimes (Kelly 1984) and "crime classification systems" (Police Executive Research Forum 1982) that can supplement the *Uniform Crime Reports* in ways that help communities more accurately appraise the *seriousness* of crime — not just its quantity — and thus more effectively prioritize the use of scarce anticrime resources. Hardly noted, too, is the major opportunity for expanded foot patrol presented by the development of the personal, lightweight radio, worn on the officer's shoulder as part of his uniform. Such technological breakthroughs could help bring to life the cop who knows every resident on his beat — an image that some historians suggest has heretofore been mostly an apocrypha of Norman Rockwell's invention. The techniques the chapters in this section do address, however, have already begun to prove their worth in securing greater order — which Hegel called "the first requisite of liberty" — in Newark, Fort Lauderdale, Houston, and a number of other locales (also see the chapters in this book by Lee Brown and James Stewart). If these techniques could become more standard items in the police leader's tool kit, the rebuilding of America's urban centers could proceed apace.

26
Order Maintenance, the Quality of Urban Life, and Police: A Line of Argument

George L. Kelling

The reform era of policing is coming to a close. That era began during the early and mid-1900s, reached its peak during the late 1950s and 1960s, and began its decline during the 1970s. Police reform leaders, including August Vollmer, William H. Parker, and O. W. Wilson, reacted to a wide variety of forces: police corruption and inefficiency, political linkages between police and urban political machines, the Progressive movement, the Great Depression, the urban reform movement, Prohibition, Sunday liquor laws, and others. They moved to shape police in ways significantly different from the past. They changed the source of police legitimacy, police tactics and technology, police management, and the standards by which police were judged. Legitimacy derived from local political leaders and close ties to neighborhoods was rejected in favor of law, especially criminal law, and police professionalism. Foot patrol was replaced by preventive patrol in automobiles and rapid response to calls for service. Determination of beat structure on the basis of neighborhoods was replaced by mathematical formulas developed on the basis of calls for service and reported crime. Police administration moved from decentralized police units closely linked to neighborhoods and local political units to centralized patterns incorporating "scientific" management characteristics of the Progressive era: improved recruitment, supervision, training, management, record keeping, and methods of accountability. Informal means of judging police success were abandoned, and police impact on crime, measured by arrest statistics and the use of the FBI's *Uniform Crime Reports*, became the primary means of judging individual police officers and police organizations. Police behavior that did not lead to arrests (for example, counseling, teaching, cajoling, rousting, exhorting, or "jollying along") was neither organizationally recognized nor rewarded. Police actions were rarely seen as ends in themselves but instead were viewed as means to "process persons" into the justice system. (For a more extensive discussion of these matters, see Moore and Kelling 1983.)

The result was police as we know them today: generally focused on crime prevention, criminal apprehension, and arrests; mobilized in cars; remote from individual citizens, neighborhoods, and communities (both by design of management to reduce corruption and as a consequence of being sequestered in cars); oriented around enforcement of laws; reluctantly providing order maintenance and other public services but without managing them; surprisingly unaccountable to elected urban officials; and, increasingly, using management principles derived from the ideas inherent in scientific management.

Generally, even critics of the organizational strategy of reformers conceded that there were two important positive consequences of the reform movement in policing: It substantially reduced corruption, and it significantly improved the internal management of policing. However, this chapter argues that those improvements were largely offset by many of the unanticipated consequences of reform strategies. Chief among those, and central to this discussion, were the consequences of the decision to downgrade order maintenance activities of the police.

ORDER MAINTENANCE

For reformers, order maintenance was a sticky issue. (That it remains so will be apparent.) It was not always clear what disorder was. Although two forms of disorder, riot and serious crime, could be defined and identified with relative ease, the behavior contemplated by a whole range of other activities, such as minor crimes, vagrancy, disorderly conduct, and indecorous behavior, was unclear and ambiguous. Often it was only the individual police officer who could determine who was vagrant or what was disorderly. Indecorous behavior — hanging around, noisiness, panhandling, and the like — was even less well defined.

Implicit is a second point: The basis of authority to deal with these problems was unclear. For some forms of indecorous behavior, such as spitting on the sidewalk, the basis for intervention may have been health or other regulations, but often the sole justification was local traditions or policies, which only occasionally were codified. Because disorder was an ill-defined and ambiguous concept and authority to intervene was not always manifest, order maintenance activities had potential for serious abuse. Basic issues of liberty, equity, due process, individual self-expression, and privacy were involved. Reformers had ample evidence that the use of police discretion inherent in police order maintenance activities had at least created the circumstances in which corruption could take place and at most invited police corruption.

For reformers, concentrating on serious crimes that were clearly defined and for which there was a broad consensus that something should be done would avoid the potential for abuse that order maintenance activities presented. Enforcing criminal laws was seen as unambiguous, had a broad base of support, and was amenable to centralized management.

Several other factors convinced police of the wisdom of concentrating on even-handed enforcement of criminal laws. First, the increased willingness of courts to review, and define standards for, police handling of criminal events led the police to be more diligent about the individual rights of citizens. A consequence was that police began to approach noncriminal disorderly events with the same procedural standards required by serious criminal incidents. The wisdom of concentrating on criminal events was further confirmed by the police experience with the civil rights movement. Civil libertarians charged that the police were enforcing local and criminal laws in discriminatory ways. For the most part police could adequately defend themselves against allegations arising from their performance in handling serious crimes. Street crime was already an important concern of citizens and politicians. Counterarguments (whether valid or not) by reformers that concentration on street crimes rather than on white-collar crimes targeted police on minorities and also involved considerable police discretion were far too subtle to gain wide acceptance and seriously threaten the base of police legitimacy. But it was a different matter for the police to defend themselves against charges of discrimination in dealing with issues of disorder and public decorum. Critics could claim, and often with justification, that the order maintenance activities of the police were used to harass minorities, keep them out of neighborhoods, and, often, stifle political dissent. The "stickiness" of order maintenance for police executives was not a construct of their fancy; it was, and remains, a serious problem.

Notwithstanding that "stickiness," a variety of factors have lead critics to challenge the wisdom of downgrading order maintenance activities:

• Studies conducted during the 1960s and 1970s demonstrated that police continue to spend a major portion of their time in order maintenance activities. (The best summary of this literature is Wycoff 1982.)

• In spite of administrative attempts to reduce police discretion, it continues to characterize police operations at all levels (Wycoff 1982; Goldstein 1977).

• Studies of patrol effectiveness (preventive patrol and rapid response to calls for service) suggest that uncommitted patrol time has not been used productively. Despite the focus on law enforcement, there is little evidence that these strategies substantially reduce crime (Reiss 1971; Kelling et al. 1974a; Bieck 1977; Spelman and Brown 1982).

• Increasing the level or changing the style of automotive patrol is not recognized by citizens (Kelling et al. 1974a; Fowler and Mangione 1982).

- Citizens *do* recognize increases or decreases in levels of foot patrol (Police Foundation 1981; Trojanowicz 1982).

- Studies of citizen fear indicate that it is strongly related to disorder: youths hanging around, drunkenness, panhandling, gangs, and the like (Skogan and Maxfield 1981; Police Foundation 1981; Fowler and Mangione 1982).

- Citizen fear is reduced in areas where foot patrol is used (Police Foundation 1981; Trojanowicz 1982).

- Citizen calls for service are drastically reduced in areas where there is foot patrol (Trojanowicz 1982).

- Observations of foot patrol officers suggest that their primary activities consist of street management or regulation (Police Foundation 1981; Wilson and Kelling 1982; Trojanowicz 1982).

- Citizens' attitudes toward police are substantially improved in foot patrol areas (Police Foundation 1981; Trojanowicz 1982).

- There are suggestions in the empirical literature that police on foot patrol feel substantially less beleaguered than those on automotive patrol (Police Foundation 1981; Trojanowicz 1982).

The line of argument implicit in this sequence of findings challenges reform models of policing and suggests that improved police management of, and concentration on, order maintenance activities can substantially improve the quality of urban life. The argument is twofold: There are immediate benefits to be had from order maintenance activities, and order maintenance activities offer unique opportunities for crime control.

Immediate Benefits from Order Maintenance

Advocates of increased order maintenance suggest that police agencies, by properly managing and extending foot patrol and other order maintenance activities, can have an immediate impact on urban life, citing in support of their views the relationship of disorder and crime, the beneficial effects of foot patrol on citizen fear and attitudes, and the availability of unproductively used uncommitted patrol time. Proponents of order maintenance observe that fear reduction efforts can positively affect citizen use of public transportation systems (see Williams's chapter), neighborhood commercial and recreational facilities, and other private and public resources, thereby enhancing those systems and facilities. Moreover, the positive response of citizens to police order maintenance efforts will provide police with improved bases of community and political support, which in turn can be exploited to gain further cooperation from citizens in a wide variety of activities. Additionally, if, as early findings suggest, police officers will feel less beleaguered by organizing their work around the maintenance of public order, so much the better.

To those who dismiss fear reduction as little more than public relations (see discussions in Brown's and Williams's chapters), proponents of fear reduction strategies point to the current nonproductive use of patrol time and the terrible toll that fear itself has had on individuals and communities: abandonment of streets, neighborhoods, public transportation systems, and urban facilities. Thus fear reduction and other order maintenance techniques can be important first steps in addressing some of the immediate problems of urban life.

Impact of Order Maintenance on Crime

As to the long-term benefits, advocates of police order maintenance frankly admit to uncertainties in the argument that such activities can substantially improve the police record in dealing with serious crime. Nevertheless, there are empirical and theoretical reasons to believe that serious crime may be ameliorated by controlling disorder. The line of argument is as follows: Increased order maintenance activities affect crime in two ways—directly and indirectly. Directly, disorderly behaviors, left untended, often escalate into criminal events (Wilson and Kelling 1982). Street disputants, immediately controlled by the police, do not assault each other—at least not then and there and, in many cases, not later or elsewhere. A variety of other examples could be given. One that police report is panhandling by youths in subway stations. They describe a sequence: Youths panhandle; citizens give them money not only because of charitable motives but also because they are afraid not to; youths, sensing fear and emboldened by it, hassle and intimidate—citizens are "shaken down"; finally, a mugging occurs.

Disorder becomes serious criminality. Police, intervening early, can prevent this escalation. Moreover, it is not just police activities that can interrupt this sequence. Police activities to control disorder encourage normal self-defense activities of citizens. In situations such as described above, citizens, aware of the presence of police, and less fearful as a consequence, will be more difficult to intimidate and more willing to protect themselves and assist other citizens in distress. Police presence invites and channels the latent social control activities of citizens.

The second, indirect effect derives from the belief that increased concern for public disorder is important in the solution of crimes, an hypothesis based on research concerning both foot patrol and criminal investigation. Trojanowicz's (1982) research on foot patrol has demonstrated that in residential areas citizens are not only aware of the presence of foot patrol officers but many (37 percent) are familiar enough with foot patrol officers that they know them by name. This closeness probably explains the 41 percent drop in phone calls for service in areas with foot patrol; citizens make requests for service and give information directly to foot patrol officers. There is every reason to suspect that if neighborhood police officers actively encourage them, citizens will give the police other information, especially about criminal activities (see Skogan's chapter). Citizen crime information of this sort is central to crime solution by detectives (Pate et al. 1976; Greenwood and Petersilia 1975; Eck 1983). Increased police contact with citizens and the resultant goodwill should result in citizens' reporting more crimes and volunteering information valuable for criminal investigations and the prevention of future criminality. The familiarity of police with citizens and neighborhoods will allow police to make important judgments about the reliability of information and place it in meaningful contexts.

Proponents of better managed and increased order maintenance activities do not see such police work as competing with or precluding directed crime activities of special units. On the contrary, they see such programs as complementary. For example, if special units targeted particularly dangerous offenders, patrol officers would be in a strategic position to gather intelligence about the behavior of such offenders and share it with those units. The important point is that police order maintenance activities would have to be managed.

MANAGEMENT ISSUES

In advocating increased order maintenance activities, I am well aware that any shift of emphasis in that direction has the potential of raising serious problems. The two that immediately come to mind are controlling the performance of individual police officers and managing political input into policing.

Controlling Officer Performance

Academic critics of increased order maintenance are not alone in fearing that individual police officers might become involved in unwarranted intrusions into the lifestyle and privacy of citizens, especially minorities. Police administrators are equally concerned about this (see Pomeroy's chapter); equitable policing was a central concern of the reform movement. The proposal for expanded order maintenance activities is really nothing new or radical, however. Every study of police activity has shown that they continue a wide array of order maintenance activities. The point is to manage better and extend what police are regularly doing. Additionally, the internal managerial skills obtained during the reform era can be exploited to prevent undesirable side effects of such activities.

Nevertheless, even chiefs who strongly support the concept of policing directed at the maintenance of order remain troubled by its potential for causing some problems. The one mentioned most often is how individual officers will handle situations when disorderly citizens refuse to comply with a police request to stop or modify particular activities. In a chapter of this length, it is not possible to explore fully such an issue; nor would it be possible with unlimited space to say that there is a fully satisfactory answer. Yet some discussion is warranted.

It is true that if a disorderly person is set on tripping a showdown with an officer, he or she can do it. A variety of elements will shape the outcome: setting, style of the officer, behavior of the citizen, characteristics of the citizen, and many others. At the extremes, sometimes disorderly conduct statutes will be appropriately used to resolve the situation, and other times an officer, especially one who has not been sensitive to the setting or has used an overly aggressive style, may have to back down (admittedly an outcome to be avoided). But the most important point is that these events are extremely rare. Most citizens, even troublemakers, prefer not to confront the police. When they do, they are often drunk (not making them easier to handle, but often making use of disorderly statutes more appropriate). Even with the relatively low priority that is currently given to order maintenance activities, many thousands of events occur each day across America in which police ask or order citizens to do or stop doing something. In almost every case compliance is secured without incivilities occurring. When they do occur, few citizens are willing to go all the way and seriously challenge the police, and few police desire to use excessive force to settle the issue. The fact that problems can and, on rare occasions, do occur should not deter police from order maintenance.

But that response still does not deal with what happens when citizens do challenge the police. Although relatively rare occurrences compared to the generality of police-citizen contacts, nevertheless police can and do use force to manage citizens. When they do not, use of force by the police is always a latent threat, giving "teeth" to the police if citizens challenge them. This potential for use of force shapes every police-citizen contact (for an extensive discussion of this, see Bittner 1971). The following example raises the issue quite particularly.

Two white officers are on foot patrol on the streets of a large, aging eastern city noted for urban problems. The area being patrolled is the city center. It consists of businesses (many marginal), major transportation connections, and governmental agencies. Street people, mostly minorities, are conspicuous. One corner of the foot beat is *the* transportation nexus of the city. Although most streets become deserted after the 5 P.M. rush hour, this corner remains active as those who work late or change buses congregate there. Street people tend to stand close to the buildings; users of the transportation system, close to the street. There is little interaction. For some time police have enforced a street rule: no hassling or panhandling of people standing still (for example, waiting for a bus).

From half a block away one of the two patrolling officers sees something happening on the main intersection and breaks into a run. His partner follows.

A black pregnant woman, holding the hand of a three- to four-year-old girl is standing on the sidewalk, her back to the curb. A man, swaying slightly and gesturing animatedly, is talking to her. Both the woman and child exhibit fear: eyes wide and darting, backing away, the child staying close to the mother and trying to get even closer by turning her body into her mother's. The police officer runs up and asks the woman in a loud voice, "Do you know this man?" The woman shakes her head, implying no. The police officer takes the man by an arm, the first use of force, and turns the man away from the woman and tells him to walk away and not return. This officer's partner is now on the other side of the man, also holding an arm. They lead the man in the direction he has been instructed to walk. The man argues that he has done nothing wrong. Other street people, up to now watching without comment, now say, "Oh, oh, Joe wants to get arrested." They offer no other advice or comments.

The man continues to protest that he has done nothing wrong. He was just talking to the woman. The first police officer stops walking, physically stops the man, and turns him forcefully, but not roughly, to face him. The officer instructs him in a firm voice: "You are not to bother that woman. You are to walk away — and stay away for the rest of the night. You are to start walking now, and if you stop you're going to jail. Now *walk*!" The man takes three or four shuffling steps and then, with surprising speed, turns, dashes around the officers, and again approaches the woman saying, "I wasn't bothering you." The officers, only a step behind, forcefully grab the man and, somewhat roughly, wrestle him to the ground, with the first officer saying, "You god-damned fool — you really do want to get arrested." The miscreant's street companions chime in with similar comments, "Yup, he wanted to get arrested — fool."

One officer quickly handcuffs him; the other radios for a car. Several people start to form a circle, but the officers quickly disperse them with friendly comments. The man swears at the officers, the woman, and his own cronies. Nobody assists him or echoes his verbal abuse of the officers. A police car comes with two officers. The man is physically picked up and roughly thrown into the back seat. The officers joke among themselves. Finally, the officer who made the first move says, "Disorderly conduct — we'll be in in about an hour to write it up."

There are a variety of issues raised by this example. First, the police did something that needed to be done. A woman and child were being harassed and intimidated, although the "illegality" of the behavior would be hard to document. To everyone present, including this observer, the behavior of the officers appeared appropriate and restrained. Second, the need to intervene and the outcome stemmed from a combination of circumstances. A change in the composition of actors or bystanders could well have altered the outcome or judgments about the wisdom of the police response. Third, the officers capitalized on credits they had already developed on the street. What they did was seen as reasonable to bystanders because it was the result of street policies developed over months. The officers were not strangers to the actors and bystanders. Fourth, the officers kept giving the intoxicated person "outs." At no time did they structure the situation in ways that guaranteed that the drunk was bound to "lose" or get arrested. Finally, use of force was controlled and gradually escalated depending on the changing situation. At no time did the force exerted seem excessive.

As this example illustrates, police order maintenance activities, by their very nature, increase the contacts between police and citizens, thereby increasing the extent to which citizens can exert controls on officers. Foot patrol officers are not free to "crash in" on a scene, behave unpredictably, and then flee in their cars. They are much more vulnerable to the countercontrol mechanisms of citizens than their counterparts in cars.

Managing Political Influence

Most police administrators are extremely reluctant to move away from defining their legitimacy on the basis of criminal law and to give the community, at any level, real power in the process of setting police goals, priorities, and tactics (see discussions in Davis's and Brown's chapters). It should be remembered that early police management of political, or community, influences is generally not thought to be one of the glories of police history. In fact, police became the pawns of political and other vested interest groups. The litany of sins police perpetrated as a consequence includes tainting elections, serving and protecting special interests, and the garden-variety police corruption (Haller 1976; Levine 1971; Fogelson 1977). All of these embarrassments have been indelibly fixed on the collective consciousness and unconsciousness of the current generation of police leaders, and a good share of current police practices can be read as attempts to prevent their recurrence (Moore and Kelling 1983).

All the same, there are elements of exaggeration in this conventional characterization of early policing. The moral and political reformers (muckrakers, mugwámps, WASPs, and so on) had their own moral and political axes to grind and had real stakes in defining policing as they did. The picture was far more complex than many reformers would have us believe. Social work professionals were more than eager to portray police welfare practices in denigrating terms, not only to improve services but also to advance their own professional interests. The political machines of the period, with police as their adjuncts, served important interests of their constituencies in providing services and jobs. There were chiefs who could and did resist venality. Likewise, there were officers who resisted corruption and political indebtedness (Levine 1971). Moreover, during periods when crime was extremely low, enough was thought of police to attribute those circumstances to their activities.

To be sure, there were serious problems in policing. My point, however, is that the wholesale rejection of then-current sources of police legitimacy resulted in the abandonment and denigration of policing styles (for example, foot patrol) that had much to commend them and, most importantly, led to the inhibition of community influence on the police. As the reformers were aware, community influence on the police did create problems. But the solutions — reliance on criminal law, professionalization, and so forth — brought us to the point where it is widely considered to be exemplary if the police are unaccountable to local or elected officials. Although this state of affairs has increased the ability of police to define and shape their organizational strategies independently, the consequence has been a lack of responsiveness to communities — a fact increasingly recognized by politicians and citizens (see Hudnut's, Fraser's, and Andrews's chapters). There remains a strong reservoir of support for the police. But a public sense has developed that some structural or at least operational changes in policing must be made if we are to have the kind of police presence and peace and security we want.

Hopefully we can avoid a pendulum swing that simply repeats the mistakes of the reformers in mirror image. Where the reformers went wrong was that, in their concentration on the problems, they ignored the various benefits that arose from close integration of the police with communities. These included community support for police, active communication between police and citizens, police awareness of local community standards, police familiarity with such local institutions as churches and welfare agencies, a sense of police participation in the community, the development of trust between police and citizens that enabled informal solution of many problems, and a feeling of active police "presence" in a community. Finding a balance that both exploits the benefits of strong community influence and avoids the problems will not be a simple matter. Considerable experience will have to be gained in managing police relationships with the variety of institutional, corporate, political, neighborhood, and other interests that will escalate their demands on police to keep pace with the new receptivity. The first step should be abandonment of the idea that there is something inherently wise or prophylactic about keeping the police remote from the communities they serve. At the same time, police managers will have to develop considerable skill in managing their external environment, for the potential for abuse remains real. There are still neighborhoods that will attempt to use their closeness to the police to keep out individuals and groups (for example, minorities), corporations and businesses that will attempt to corner more than an appropriate share of police services (compare Shanahan's chapter), and politicians who will be tempted to use police for their own purposes. Striking the proper balance will be difficult, but the bureaucratization, unionization, and professionalization that characterize contemporary policing seem more than ample bulwarks against the inappropriate influence of any single neighborhood or interest.

IMPLICATIONS

There are a variety of steps police and communities can take to develop an organizational strategy focused on managing and exploiting order maintenance opportunities. This list of eight is preliminary. Accomplishing each will require complex sets of activities.

1. The broad base of real and potential support for police inherent in politics, traditions, regulations, and ordinances must be acknowledged and used. The idea must be abandoned that law and professional expertise are the primary bases of police legitimacy.

2. Police should be perceived and perceive themselves as an integral part of a network of community problem-solving resources that includes other city agencies, private sector agencies, corporations, voluntary organizations, interest groups, and a host of others. Problems, whether disorder, crime, or other, are the responsibility of all citizens and organizations. (Goldstein [1977, 1979, 1981, 1982c] has best described this orientation and process.)

3. Priority should be given in the allocation of police to those areas essential to city life: transportation hubs, small business areas, schools and recreation facilities, entertainment areas, and neighborhoods particularly threatened by disorder that could turn into serious crime. Determination of allocation patterns and beat structures primarily on the basis of reported crime and calls for service ignores problems of disorder and other important issues. Moreover, such an allocation scheme makes no attempt to identify neighborhood strengths, weaknesses, and resources. Indicators of such problems and resources often will not be quantifiable, and new approaches to beat construction will have to be developed.

4. For the patrol division of a police department, the most important goal should be to increase the quantity and improve the quality of police-citizen contacts. Where population density of an area allows it, patrol officers should be on foot. Where it does not, police should use automobiles to go to population centers and then walk. (This does not preclude the use of vehicles for other directed activities by other units. Likewise, there may be times when even patrol units should use automobiles extensively. But the primary model of patrol should be a police officer on the street dealing with citizens.)

5. Officers at all levels must perceive themselves as resources through which neighborhoods and communities maintain social control. Officers should develop the consulting skills required to work effectively with street, neighborhood, and community leaders.

6. "Rapid response" to calls for service must be deemphasized because,

without providing offsetting benefits in crime control, it imposes the costly requirement that a substantial part of the police force be held in reserve to be available. Even though local community preferences should be influential in setting policing priorities, police leadership has the responsibility of disabusing the public of false, ingrained notions that underlie their desire for rapid response.

7. Emphasis must be given to gathering information from citizens and disseminating it beat to beat, watch to watch, and among patrol, special units, and detectives. Officers who share information should be rewarded; those who do not should be reprimanded. With rare exceptions, arrests should be viewed as a group achievement and rewarded as such (see Reiss's chapter).

8. It should be recognized that current indicators of police success—crime levels and arrests—are of extremely limited value as measures of police performance. Other easily quantifiable measures are not available. Developing them will be a long and complex and essential task.

Just as this chapter argues that there are theoretical and empirically based implications for what police *should* do, there are also implications for what they should *not* do. The increased concern for improved order maintenance services in cities currently emanating from citizens, politicians, and decision makers has created pressure for police administrators to "do something." The temptation will be to use reform model methods—preventive patrol, tactical units, and other such remote "stranger" policing strategies—buttressed by resurrected disorderly conduct statutes to "sweep up," intimidate, arrest, "roust," and "move on" persons presenting problems of disorder. Such approaches will appear to have advantages. They are congruent with the current orientation and practices of police agencies and easy to initiate. Nevertheless, these are short-term, unwise, and potentially dangerous approaches. They continue to rely on remote professional and centralized political authority. Moreover, they fail to recognize the inherent normative pluralism of communities and neighborhoods and will likely be perceived as police acting against, rather than on behalf of, localities. Such activities put a premium on arrest rather than counseling, instruction, teaching, and negotiation. Officers' activities are not seen as peacemaking and civility-inducing ends in themselves but rather as the initial processing of "offenders."

These activities jeopardize the working relations that neighborhood police officers develop with communities. Many citizens will be quick to interpret such activities as a return to police work that targets racial, ethnic, or lifestyle characteristics. In addition, such activities communicate organizational double messages: Neighborhood cops are there to pacify and do a public relations job in a community; the real cops—aggressive tactical unit police—do real police work (that is, making arrests). Regardless of whether the arrests are made by patrol or tactical units, a good share of the crime-reducing potential of increased order maintenance activities is shattered. The trust that develops from police and citizens working together to maintain social control is lost, crime control and order maintenance remain police tasks rather than shared responsibilities, information sharing ceases, and the anticrime potential of maintaining public order is likely lost. Order maintenance activities will not "tack on" to current reform era strategies without creating serious problems.

CONCLUSION

The organizational strategy of the police during the reform era has not produced the results that were desired and hoped for by reformers and police administrators. Fear and crime appear to be unresponsive to the technologies developed during this era. Community support for police has waned. Police feel beleaguered. Managing and exploiting order maintenance activities can provide immediate gains for the community and police by reducing fear, improving community support, and reducing the police sense of isolation from the public. In addition, there are theoretical and empirical reasons to believe that such activities can be of genuine use in preventing and solving crime.

27

Order Maintenance, the Quality of Urban Life, and Police: A Different Line of Argument

Carl B. Klockars

In his contribution to this volume and in an earlier essay, "Broken Windows," with James Q. Wilson (Wilson and Kelling 1982), George Kelling has proposed a dramatic enlargement of the police role in what he and Wilson before him (1968) call order maintenance. What order maintenance means is police assumption of an active role in the suppression of a whole range of citizen behaviors that community respectables find disruptive, annoying, or offensive even though those behaviors violate no laws. To one degree or another police everywhere engage in activity of this type, but in order to give it the priority he believes it deserves, Kelling advises police agencies to take a series of steps to encourage it. These steps include adopting foot patrol wherever population density permits it, deemphasizing police response to telephone requests for service, abandoning law and professional expertise as the primary bases for the legitimacy of police action, and substituting in their place "the broad base of real and potential support for police inherent in politics, traditions, regulations, and ordinances . . . " (see Kelling's chapter).

In arguing for the enlargement of the police role in order maintenance, Kelling maintains that he and Wilson are proposing "nothing new or radical." In the very limited sense that what he is asking police to do is only more of what, to one degree or other, they do already, Kelling is most certainly correct. However, for police to give order maintenance the priority Wilson and Kelling suggest it should be given and to control and manage it effectively require changes that are wholly without precedent in the history of American policing and nothing short of radical in terms of the structural changes in police organization that would be required to maintain them. Moreover, absent such fundamental changes, the position promoted in "Broken Windows" is destined to deteriorate into window dressing and on its way to doing so is likely to cause great pains (see Walker 1984).

THE POLITICAL ECOLOGY OF PATROL

In order to understand what the Kelling order maintenance proposal means in context, what the obstacles are that stand in the way of its enactment, and why they are not likely to yield without radical change, it is necessary to say a few things about the origins of uniformed police patrol. Specifically, I should like to show what patrol as a way of policing meant on the eve of its invention, how it grew into the form in which we find it in most police agencies today, and why its future in that form is none too certain.

The Origins of Patrol and the War on Crime

Uniformed patrol as we know it today in the United States is a direct descendant of the form of patrol that was instituted in London in 1829 and imported into this country between the middle and the end of the nineteenth century. Patrol was, of course, used in other countries before the nineteenth century, but there is no evidence that those countries' use of patrol exerted any influence whatsoever on the American or British decisions to adopt patrol as the major means of getting policework done.

What is of cardinal importance to remember about patrol is that in both England and the United States it was *created primarily as a means of controlling police abuses*. In London, feared abuses were political. The New Police, as they were called, were created at a time of massive middle- and working-class protest, which expressed itself in a fear that the New Police would be used as an instrument of aristocratic government repression. The English needed only to look across the Channel to France to find the kind of non-uniformed, investigative, political police they feared. Uniformed patrol assuaged their fears by in its very structure promising that except when called inside the police would be confined to the street; police would not be used as spies and would be clearly identifiable so when people furnished information they would know it was a constable they were giving it to; and anyone who gave information to a constable would be likely to be noticed doing so. Moreover, it was understood that patrol would confine constables to two relatively apolitical types of interventions: situations in which they were called on for help by citizens who approached them on the street, and situations that, from the street, they could see required their attention. This second type of intervention, it was assumed, would be much rarer than the first because most people would not be so foolish as to commit an offense where, from the street, a highly visible patrolling constable could see them. These structural safeguards that patrol tendered were far from perfect guarantees of political neutrality, but they were meaningful enough to the English to inhibit for nearly 50 years the organization of the Metropolitan Criminal Investigation Division (CID) and until that time hold down the size of their nonuniformed detective division to less than 16 officers in a police force of 3,000.

For the creators and shapers of police patrol in the United States, the fear that American police would be used as a repressive tool of aristocratic government was groundless, not only because an American aristocracy anything like the English tradition did not exist but also because policing in virtually every major city in the United States was tied to the lowest levels of municipal government. If you wanted to become a policeman in New York (Miller 1977; Richardson 1970) or Chicago (Haller 1976) in the late nineteenth century, the person to see was your alderman or ward leader. And although it was not always necessary to do so, it was advisable to come with some money in your pocket and leave with it in his. Thus, while the political problem for the creators of the New Police of London was to demonstrate that they would be as nearly as possible politically neutral, the political problem for police administrators in Chicago, New York, and most other American cities was running a police department in which every day-to-day decision could be reversed by some local politician.

In this context, uniformed patrol allowed early police administrators to set an extraordinarily minimal standard for job performance: Be in uniform on your beat. In the earliest days of American policing compliance with this order could be checked by setting up "straight beats" laid out so that a patrol sergeant could look down a long street to see whether or not his patrolman was where he was supposed to be. Later, such systems were replaced by checkpoints and electric pullboxes, all of which served to keep patrolmen on the street and out of saloons, whorehouses, gambling joints, their own homes, and the homes of friends where they could find things other than policework to occupy their time (Rubenstein 1973).

To anyone familiar with the origins of patrol it is nothing short of astounding to realize that what was once clearly understood as a means of controlling police could grow to acquire a front-line role in a war on crime. In order to appreciate how a distinctly uniformed, predictably patrolling constable or later a much larger and even more distinctly marked patrol vehicle, both of which can be easily seen and avoided, could come to be appreciated as weapons in an all-out assault on crime requires that we understand them in relation to two profound movements in the history of American policing. The first is policing's militarization; the second, its professionalization.

Militarization

The chief task of American police administrators during the first half century of policing can be simply stated: Wrest from the hands of local politicians the administrative means necessary to run the department. Without control over these means—hiring, firing, promotion, demotion—no administrator can control any organization and particularly not one as difficult to manage as the police. To the extent that early chiefs managed to gain control over these fundamental administrative tools, they did so by persuading the public and its politicians to see the work of the police in terms of what Fogelson (1977) has called "the military analogy." Like all great strokes of political rhetoric the military analogy was simple and powerful in its message and profound in its consequences. The message was that police were, in effect, society's domestic army in a war on crime. The idea of a "war" on crime conveyed a sense of urgency and emergency. Moreover, insofar as police could be seen as soldiers in that war and their chiefs the generals, the analogy associated them with the victories and the heroes of the military rather than the back rooms of municipal politics. More important, though, the military analogy allowed early police chiefs to argue that their relationship to local politicians should be much the same as that which characterized military-political relations at the national level. The politicians, of course, retained the right to decide whether or not a given war should be fought, but the day-to-day fighting and the administration of the army should be left to the generals.

Eventually, in ways historians of major metropolitan police agencies will someday be able to describe in detail, the early chiefs won control of the administrative means necessary to run their departments. However, the spoils of that early battle were not limited to those means alone. Because the early chiefs had pushed the war on crime analogy so hard as a way of getting the traditional generals' privileges, they were stuck with the crime-fighting image and expectations the analogy had promised. So strong was that image in fact that virtually every purchase of equipment, every request for additional personnel, and every change in operational procedure had to be promoted or defended in terms of its role in fighting crime. Uniformed patrol, the motorcycles, the large and powerful cars, the radios, the communications center, the new computer, and all else the chiefs wanted or needed were requested, demanded, funded, and deployed with the promise that they would play an essential role in the war on crime. In a manner wholly consistent with this tradition, George Kelling is obliged to tout the crime control benefits of order maintenance in the face of evidence from his own study (Police Foundation 1981) that it had no measurable effect on crime control at all.

The spoils of the early chiefs' victories also included a quasi-military administrative structure. Once heralded as a model of efficiency by chiefs who sought to use its punitive potential to weed out of police ranks the lazy, the stupid, the brutal, and the corrupt, many if not most chiefs now realize that it, too, was an innovation of dubious benefit. Organizationally primitive, the quasi-military administrative model suffers from two main defects. First, it works, to the extent it works, largely by setting hundreds and sometimes even thousands of rules and regulations covering everything from haircuts to shoeshines and punishing even trivial deviations from those rules and regulations severely. Unfortunately, the success of this type of administrative structure depends on the unwarranted assumption that policemen will not discover that the surest way to avoid doing anything wrong in such an organizational environment is to do as little as possible—out of sheer self-defense. The "cover your ass" syndrome and the injunction never to snitch on a fellow police officer, the "blue curtain"—both of which are rampant in the occupational culture of modern American police departments—are the direct product of this punitiveness.

The second feature of the quasi-military administrative model that undermines administrative aspirations has to do with the fact that in any agency whose major management tool is punishment, punishment must not only control malpractice but induce productivity. To encourage productivity in this way a department must set clear levels of expected performance and identify and punish those who fall short of these levels. The problem is that the nature of police work, and particularly that kind of police work called order maintenance, is such that setting clear levels for its expected performance is almost impossible. Most police work takes place out of sight of supervisors and before witnesses who cannot be regarded as reliable evaluators of its quality. An arrest sometimes is a measure of good police work and sometimes is a measure of bad. The paper an officer generates is sometimes an indicator of what he or she actually did in responding to a complaint, but often it is not. Consequently, the expectations a police department sets for its employees must be both crude and minimal—crude because they cannot measure whether or not good work has actually been done; minimal because they must represent the level of performance below which a supervisor can justify imposing punishment on an officer.

Professionalization

Like militarization, the movement for what police administrators were inclined to call their "professionalization" also sought to eliminate the influence of partisan politics on police executives. And, like militarization, professionalization partook of an analogy. The professional analogy held that, like doctors, lawyers, engineers, and other professionals, the police possessed a body of special skills that were necessary to do and to understand the work required of them. Hence, it would be no more appropriate for a politician to instruct a police officer on how to do police work than it would be for the politician to instruct a doctor on how to remove an appendix or an engineer on how to build a bridge. It followed also that to do the work of professional policing, police administrators would require not only the highly sophisticated technological tools of professional police work but employees of intelligence and education to use them. Only in a police agency free from political interference, staffed with officers of such caliber, and equipped in this way could a police administrator be expected to create the kind of centralized administrative structure that would ensure the delivery of modern, professional police service.

To be sure, the professional analogy was attractive and successful as a device for gaining not only some college-educated police officers and some sophisticated police hardware but also some added administrative autonomy. However, the success of the analogy rested entirely on the extent to which the work of policing could be construed as a plausible political equivalent of removing an appendix or building a bridge. Doing so involved selling widely the idea that the work of police consisted, by and large, of enforcing "the law."

The "law enforcement" image of what police work was had a number of advantages. It fostered the impression that police action was largely dictated by the provisions of the written law and was ultimately supervised and reviewed by the courts. Both of these notions proved highly compatible with what many Americans thought the police of a democratic society should be. Moreover, the law enforcement conception gave would-be professional police administrators a powerful argument against political attempts to influence their work: If policing consisted predominantly of enforcing the law, what reason could there be for political interference in that task, except the protection of violators?

The essential problem with the law enforcement image of police work was that it was just plain wrong. Most of what police were called on to do involved not the enforcement of any laws but help with some form of personal or interpersonal problem (Cumming, Cumming, and Edell 1965). In fact, the modal tour of police duty, even in the high-crime areas of some of the nation's largest cities, does not involve even one arrest (Reiss 1971). The idea that the courts supervise police behavior or even review anything but the small fraction of it that the police, after prosecutorial screening, decide to present to them was completely untrue. In fact, if a visitor from another planet, anxious to learn our ways, asked us to explain how our police behave, perhaps the most *un*helpful response we could make would be to point to our legal code and say, "Our police enforce these laws." This response ignores the enormous range of duties the police are called on to perform and the very considerable discretion that, far more than legal codes, shapes the way they perform them.

MILITARIZATION, PROFESSIONALIZATION, AND ORDER MAINTENANCE

I have said this much about the evolution of American policing in order to describe the context within which Kelling's order maintenance proposal must survive and against which the wisdom of proposing it must be evaluated.

The heritage of that history leaves contemporary American policing with four distinctive features each of which is likely to pervert or undermine any attempt to raise order maintenance to the position of priority Kelling argues it deserves. Those four features are the crime-fighting mandate and self-image, the quasi-military administrative structure, "the law" as the basis for the legitimacy of police action, and the peculiar politics of police power.

Order Maintenance and the Crime-Fighting Mandate and Self-Image of American Police

The history of American police has left them with an extraordinarily strong crime-fighting mandate, which they have accepted as the prime purpose of their work, adopted as a public self-image, and exploited to gain resources and personnel. In line with this heritage, order maintenance proposals will be introduced and promoted with a promise that they will reduce crime, even though it is most unlikely they will do so. The reason they will fail to do so is that the causes of crime — the age structure of the population, the condition of the economy, political and social freedoms, the architecture of modern cities, cultural changes that weaken societal norms, and practices in the social welfare and criminal justice systems — are matters over which police have no control whatsoever. The police might get lucky, and the crime rate might go down in the company of order maintenance as a matter of happy coincidence, but there is no reason to believe that any of that welcome change, should it occur, will occur as the result of their actions.

If order maintenance, sold to the public as a device for fighting crime, runs a substantial risk of failing to deliver what it promises, is it possible to promote it on some other basis, albeit one new to the history of American policing? There are very few selling points as attractive and compelling to Americans as a reduction in serious crime, but there is at least one other that is uniformly compelling: cost. If it could be promised that order maintenance could be provided at a cost less than or equal to what it now costs taxpayers to have police sit or drive around in cars doing nothing of consequence, order maintenance and the foot patrols needed to carry it out could, I think, sell like hotcakes.

The problem, though, is that foot patrol does cost more than motor patrol. And it is highly unlikely to be welcomed by the average city dweller if its adoption is purchased, as Kelling implies it might be, at the price of a reduction in response to telephone calls for police service. An alternative might be to appeal to those in high population density areas of cities, who stand to gain the most from foot patrol and order maintenance, and get them to support it through voluntary, tax-deductible contributions. I have in mind particularly merchants and other members of the business community whose customers and employees depend on orderly streets for access to their shops and businesses. It is no secret that such persons have long purchased additional police services and attention by attracting patrol officers to their places of business with police discounts, free gifts, and other rewards. They could achieve the same effect above the table, tax-deductible, and possibly even at lower cost with a contribution to a foot patrol fund. Other salutary effects of making a virtue of a long-standing historical vice in this way are self-evident.

The flaw in this option, however, is that the best research data available to date show that commercial respondents are singularly unimpressed with foot patrol. The Newark Foot Patrol Experiment found that commercial respondents in its impact survey perceived "a deterioration in their neighborhoods: more activity on the street, more crime-related problems, reduced safety, more victimizations, poorer police service, and greater use of protective devices" (Police Foundation 1981, p. 88).

Order Maintenance and the Quasi-Military Administrative Structure of American Policing

Modern police executives, owing to historical events over which they have had no control, operate with an administrative structure that discourages their employees, generates hostility to administrative action, prevents them from demanding from officers much more than crude and minimal performance of their duties, and nurtures a "cover-your-ass" and "you-cover-my-ass-and-I'll-cover-your's" rank-and-file mentality. Any attempt to bring that type of administrative apparatus to focus on order maintenance, particularly insofar as doing so involves attempts to develop "easily quantifiable" measures of its success (Kelling's chapter), ultimately will mean bringing the same destructive management and attitudes to order maintenance that currently infect and undermine most other parts of police work (see Kliesmet's and Bouza's chapters).

The most direct way this situation might be handled would be to restructure radically the quasi-military police administrative apparatus. For many reasons, some of which will be noted in the two sections below, this is unlikely to happen. The alternative is to do nothing: to continue to allow police order maintenance to occupy the largely invisible, unmeasured, unsupervised, unpromoted, latent role it does at present. It is precisely this do-nothing, say-nothing position vis-à-vis order maintenance that I would like to offer as an alternative to the Kelling argument for its enlargement and its priority.

This is not to say that police ought not to engage in order maintenance policing. They should, and, as Kelling notes, they do. In fact, with the probable exception of doing nothing or contending with the paper demands of the quasi-military police administrative structure, order maintenance is what American police spend most of their time doing (Cumming, Cumming, and

Edell 1965; Webster 1970; Black 1980; Rubenstein 1973; Muir 1977; Kelling et al. 1974a). Moreover, to the extent they do it well, and there is some evidence to suggest that they do, it is at least partly because, unrecognized by crude, minimal, and punitive administrative controls, it does not demand the paperwork, the quotas, or the defensive approach to a tangle of regulatory restrictions that other police work does.

In arguing for the considered continuation of a police policy of nonpromotion, nonrecognition, and nonregulation of order maintenance police work, it is appropriate to identify what forces presently regulate how order maintenance policing is done in the absence of administrative controls. The best evidence we have suggests that at least four factors influence police order maintenance decisions. The first is what Bittner (1971) has termed the police officer's grasp of "the dictates of situational exigencies"—the police officer's sense of what a particular order maintenance situation requires in light of the nature of the problem, the particular people involved, and the options available to him for handling the situation. Second, there is considerable evidence that an enormous influence is exerted on police decisions by what citizens involved in such situations express a preference for police to do. For example, Black (1971, p. 1095) found that in situations in which police could have made an arrest of a suspect but in which citizens expressed a preference that no arrest be made, police made arrests in only one-tenth of the cases. In situations where citizen complainants expressed a preference for an arrest, police made arrests in three-fourths of the cases. Third, police order maintenance decisions are significantly influenced by the demeanor of suspects. Antagonism and incivility toward police produce higher rates of arrest than does civil and compliant behavior (Pilavin and Briar 1964; Black and Reiss 1970; Reiss 1971).

Finally, police are generally inclined to look for ways to solve problems that minimize the likelihood of complaints, especially complaints that may force the officer to return to the scene for the same or a related problem and complaints that may provoke disciplinary action or other trouble for the officers. To be sure, some complaints carry far more weight than others, from which it follows that if one wants order maintenance policing to proceed with fairness to the poor, the politically powerless, and the socially unpopular, one must see to it that such persons in particular are accorded fair and ready access to impartial grievance and complaint procedures. If one wants to improve the quality of order maintenance policing, it is, I suggest, by opening channels for complaints to those with limited access to them rather than by developing "easily quantifiable" measures of success that improvements will come about. Goldstein (1977, p. 140) has written that "the real test of a police force in a democracy is the degree to which it responds to the legitimate demands of minorities, whether the minorities be racial, religious, political, geographical, or even criminal."

Order Maintenance and "The Law" as the Basis
for the Legitimacy of Police Action

Because the rhetoric of police professionalism once demanded it, because they could not comfortably divulge the sources that controlled their exercise of discretion, because it was easier to police under the pretense that they did not make "the law" but merely enforced it, and because it was compatible with popular, stork-story beliefs about how law in democratic societies was supposed to operate, American police claim "the law" as the basis for their authority to do what they do. Order maintenance policing is policing that involves overenforcing, underenforcing, and selectively enforcing laws, as well as taking actions wholly without legal basis or authority for purposes unrecognized by written codes of law. Hence, Kelling is at least half right when he says that to promote order maintenance "[t]he idea must be abandoned that law and professional expertise are the primary bases of police legitimacy" (see his chapter).

To make the Kelling quote completely correct all one has to do is understand "professional" in the very special sense that police administrators always intended when they used it. To them it meant tighter administrative control, a more heavily centralized administrative structure, and more extensive regulation of officer discretion. What is peculiar about this sense of "professional" is that it is almost exactly the opposite of what "professional" means when it is applied to all other occupations. In all other occupations—law, medicine, engineering, teaching, and even such "professions" as hair dressing—what "professional" implies is that a broad range of discretion will be accorded to the professional, who will be entrusted with handling situations in an atmosphere marked by a lack of supervision (see Kliesmet's chapter).

It is this genuine sense of "professional," rather than the perverted sense of it that has long been promoted by police administrators, that order maintenance policing requires. Genuine professionalism is required because the police officer is entrusted with a substantial and highly consequential right—the right to use and to threaten to use coercive force in an almost infinite variety of situations. Choices about exercising that right will regularly be made out of sight of supervisors and other reliable evaluators. Moreover, while there is no doubt that "the law" bears some relationship to what the police officer does, it is better understood as a tool he may see fit to use when he believes a situation calls for it than a guide or set of instructions for how he ought to behave (see Kerstetter's chapter).

All of these reasons police must occupy a truly professional role are in the nature of police work. In reality, as Reiss (1971) pointed out more than a decade ago, police officers already have a genuinely professional role and the obligations and responsibilities that go along with it; what they lack is the education, status, and organizational environment that recognize that fact. Policing has long been a real profession whose identification and acceptance as a profession have been prevented by a series of historical accidents. If policing is indeed an unacknowledged professional task, it may be asked why it should not be allowed to continue in the unrecognized role it currently occupies.

There are at least three answers to this question, all of which bear directly on the Kelling order maintenance proposal. First, policing has not been able to draw either at line levels or for administrative positions persons with the kind of talent, ability, imagination, and leadership that police administration requires. Order maintenance policing in particular cannot tolerate crudeness, either in those who do it or in those who superintend the ways in which it is done.

Second, to work well, order maintenance policing requires a professional administrative structure. This means an atmosphere of collegial exchange and criticism in which officers may learn from others and have their work evaluated by them. It means open dialogue with organizational superiors, communication upward as well as orders coming down. It means extending to officers with talent, intelligence, and leadership ability an opportunity to market their talents outside the agency they joined as recruits — a virtual impossibility given the way police agencies operate in the United States today. No other genuine profession would dream of dooming its most talented members to spending their entire professional lives within a single organization or having to start their careers over again at the bottom if they should decide to move.

Third, professional status — the deference, honor, and respect a genuine profession commands — is unquestionably helpful to the work of order maintenance policing. This is so for one quite simple and practical reason: It is better to have people respond to police order maintenance decisions out of deference and respect for police authority than from fear of coercive force. Police can gain compliance with their demands for order by "kicking ass," a practice Wilson and Kelling (1982) cite approvingly, but endorsement of such behavior must rest on the view that people whom police seek to control in that way do not deserve or cannot comprehend better treatment. That line of reasoning is barely plausible when the vision of those who get their asses kicked is confined to derelicts, winos, street prostitutes, panhandlers, and juvenile gangs. But it is patently offensive when we realize that the order maintenance tasks of modern police officers require them to direct, control, and discipline persons from all walks of life — including *us*. "Fear," says Egon Bittner (1971), "may prevent me from protesting the traffic patrolman's vulgarity but it will not inspire my trust in him as a public official."

Order Maintenance and the Peculiar Politics of Police Power

The history of American policing from the turn of the century to the present day can be described as a series of battles between police administrators and local politicians for control over local policing. The considerable autonomy police administrators won in those battles was won at the price of an unrealistic and unrealizable crime-fighting image and mandate, a crude and destructive police administrative structure, and a fundamental misrepresentation of police work as a mere ministerial enforcing of "the law." Under such conditions order maintenance is best left an unpromoted, latent part of police work.

Is there reason to believe that this configuration of structure, aspirations, and beliefs will change in ways that will permit and advise the promotion of order maintenance to the position of priority Kelling has argued it deserves? The answer to that question must, I think, be an unhappy "no," because each of the players in the politics of police power has a substantial stake in keeping things as they are. Although the police are miscast in the crime-fighting role, we in the audience insist that they play the part. In the face of nearly a century of false hopes and false promises the need and desire of the public and its press to believe that police can fight crime remain strong. That need and desire appeal as much to line officers and police administrators as to politicians and researchers, all of whom will continue to promote all things police with the promise that they will aid in the fight against crime.

Insofar as fighting crime remains the mandate and priority of American police, the crude, minimal, and punitive police administrative apparatus need not change. To a public that does not understand its consequences, this apparatus tenders an image of snappy discipline and control. To politicians it offers a well-groomed and presentable appearance of efficiency. And to police administrators it offers the power to punish on occasions of gross brutality and corruption. Line officers have made considerable progress in thwarting some of the more outrageous violations of employee rights that working under such an administrative structure once meant, but they and their unions recognize that with few exceptions such organizations are the only game in town.

Finally, almost everyone appears to have a substantial stake in the belief that what police do and are supposed to do is enforce "the law" (see Pomeroy's chapter). To citizens, particularly middle-class citizens, this notion reinforces the civics book portrait of how law in a democracy is supposed to operate. To poor people, and particularly those of color, it offers at least an illusion of protection from illegal and extralegal discriminatory police practice. Neither group is likely to willingly forego its belief in "the law" as the basis for the legitimacy of police action. Likewise, the pose of merely enforcing "the law" has served and will continue to serve the needs of line police officers and police administrators alike. It relieves line police officers of the need to disclose the sources and forces that structure their discretion and lends apparent credence to the assertion by police administrators that they really exercise very little discretion. This administrative pose continues to be useful in fending off attempts by politicians or citizen groups to control or influence police executive decisions. Confronted with these dynamics, the path of choice for police leadership in America seems, for the foreseeable future, to be the one on which order maintenance activities are not a highly visible part of the landscape.

28

The Oasis Technique: A Method of Controlling Crime and Improving the Quality of Life

William H. Lindsey, Ronald Cochran, Bruce Quint, and Mario Rivera

Can the police control crime? This question can be answered in any number of ways, depending on one's definition of the words "control" and "crime." If control means to reduce crime in a high-crime area, one set of police actions is called for; if control means to hold the line on crime in a low-crime area, an entirely different set of police actions is in order; and if control means virtually to stop the incidence of crime in any area, yet another set of police actions is required.

If crime is perceived as a violation of any law, the police are faced with an almost impossible enforcement task. But if crime is perceived as lawbreaking activities that negatively impact a community's quality of life, then the ability of the police to control crime becomes more manageable, and, in the minds of many, more relevant to what the role of the police should be. (On the role of the police, see Moore and Kelling [1983] and Smith and Visher [1981].) That role, in our view, should consist primarily of purposeful efforts to produce measurable community gains by controlling the crimes that most dramatically affect people and their neighborhoods. A community's failure adequately to define crime is problematic. The observation was made a decade ago that

> words like crime have become rhetorical talismans to be dangled in arguments about the condition and future of cities. As a result, the words and the human problems they refer to have become vague and abstract. They have lost the ability to convey the meaning of daily life on the sidewalks. (Yates 1974)

When that meaning is lost, so-called crime control efforts become expensive hoaxes on the public. As Wilson and Kelling (1982) have pointed out, crime statistics and victimization surveys in recent years have contributed to shifting our attention from communal losses, which they do not measure, to individual losses, which they do. These scholars argue forcefully that police must return to the long-abandoned goal of protecting communities as well as individuals.

The question of central importance, then, is not whether the police can control crime, but whether they can control crime to the extent that our neighborhoods become better places to live. While not every community can answer this question affirmatively, during the past few years a variety of federal, state, and local officials and a cross-section of private businesspeople, community leaders, and local citizens have had an opportunity to see Fort Lauderdale, Florida's, attempt to provide an affirmative response. The effort is an 11-year-old, ongoing experiment that is taking place in this town's inner-city neighborhoods. The purpose of the experiment, called the Oasis Technique, is to demonstrate a program that revitalizes slum and blighted neighborhoods, reduces crime, and improves the quality of life.

These goals obviously are quite ambitious. Nevertheless, public officials and private citizens who have seen the Oasis Technique firsthand have noted dramatic results. National media have called the program an effective solution to problems affecting our nation's cities (Kuralt 1982). Moreover, exposure of local reporters to the effort has enhanced the way the media have viewed police work in target neighborhoods (see, for example, Dawkins 1982a, 1982b; Jones 1982; cf. Skolnick and McCoy's chapter). Others around the nation who have not seen this program personally often respond with skepticism to descriptions of what it can accomplish. This is understandable because the results contradict conventional wisdom concerning the poor, crime, and the ability of governments to work effectively at the local level. Comments such as "the poor will always be with us" or "the police can't be effective in *those* parts of town" are heard so often that many have come to accept their validity without examining the context in which they are made. The Oasis Technique does not attempt to refute such conventional thinking. Instead, it modifies the context of these thoughts and, in so doing, creates a whole new range of possibilities. In our Fort Lauderdale experiment, the serious problems of crime, police-community relations, and citizens' rights have become more manageable because diverse elements of the community have been provided common agendas on which they can all agree.

Before the results and methods of this experiment are examined, a brief description of its genesis and its relation to law enforcement is important. In 1972, one of the authors, Bill Lindsey, came to Fort Lauderdale as a VISTA (Volunteers in Service to America) worker in order to assist low-income, minority residents in their battle against slumlords. His work was well received and led the Fort Lauderdale Housing Authority to make him its executive director in the hope that he could improve the quality of public housing in the city. Lindsey approached the job with the belief that, regardless of the physical improvements that could be achieved, both public and private housing in deteriorating neighborhoods would remain bad places to live so long as residents felt unsafe in their homes and so long as surrounding neighborhoods were characterized by slum and blight. He developed the Oasis Technique in an attempt to establish a method that would allow physical improvements to be made *and* sustained in neighborhoods. In broad outline, the elements of the approach were that the police would regain control of the streets and that private citizens and public agencies would share the responsibility of finding solutions to the problems of slum and blight.

The logistical problem was how to work cooperatively with the police so that crime and the fear of crime could be reduced to the extent that residents would feel safe in their homes and their neighborhoods. Fear of crime was a major concern; as most police officers know this fear is one of the more pernicious by-products of criminal activity.[1] Rye (1980, p. 1) observes, "Its consequences are more pervasive than the effects of any actual crime. It is an intangible whose cost cannot be allocated to each crime committed, yet its overall cost can be seen in the decline and deterioration of any community." Further compounding the problem is the fact that residents of low-income neighborhoods often perceive the police as an invading force (see Roncek 1981; Bell and Fancik 1981). For their part, the police perceive the residents of these neighborhoods as hostile and combative, an attitude that creates a great deal of stress for both the residents and the police. This stress increases the estrangement of the police from the community and decreases the potential for police and residents to work together to solve common problems (Hagan and Albonetti 1982).

The Oasis Technique, then, was created to enable the responsible residents — those who are concerned about safety, law, and order — of a bad neighborhood to treat the police as allies. What we mean by bad neighborhood is indicated by the decision to apply the Oasis Technique only in sections of Fort Lauderdale with the highest crime rates, most unemployment, most substandard housing, and highest concentration of low-income and, coincidentally, minority families. This effort was also undertaken to combat current trends in the criminal justice system and federal housing programs that support the rights of criminals and those who destroy neighborhoods over the rights of those who want to live better (see Symposium on Judicial Reform 1982; Bok 1983; Specter and Michel 1982). In Florida, this phenomenon was underscored when the courts mandated that inmates be released from prisons because of overcrowded conditions.[2] Yet the authors (Lindsey and Quint) were involved in their official capacity in numerous situations in which Florida judges would only evict public housing residents for nonpayment of rent. Even when housing residents used their apartment for gambling and drugs, when an apartment was overcrowded, or when residents vandalized their unit, we found that the courts were reluctant to sustain evictions. It appeared inconsistent that the courts would enforce housing codes on behalf of criminals who resided in prison but not on behalf of noncriminals who resided in government housing. Some judges privately confessed that evicting a family and putting them on the street was a drastic action to be used only as a last resort. The result, however, was that neighborhoods would be ruined because people who violated housing laws would not be held accountable for their destructive behavior.

It was decided that to make headway in the face of this relative lack of judicial support, the key agencies involved in the implementation of the Oasis Technique would be the police and the housing authority. In attempting to revitalize a neighborhood, housing is critical because it makes the most visual statement about the quality of life in a neighborhood. Police activities are critical, too, because if neighborhood residents are victims of crime or have a heightened fear of crime, they will want to leave their neighborhood regardless of how nice the housing may be.

The program's task, then, was to establish a methodology that would link police activities to housing activities in such a way that one complemented the other. The effort would be made to break the traditional pattern, by which police arrest individuals for street crimes such as drug use, breaking and entering, assault, or illegal possession of weapons, only to see them quickly return to the areas where they were arrested. In most instances, these criminals return to a specific area because the physical environment supports their behavior. The street criminals hang out around houses or businesses that are dirty and rundown. (Rarely does this criminal element venture into parts of town where their presence would not be tolerated.) Thus, despite the statistical efficiency of the Fort Lauderdale police (they made an appropriate number of arrests), local neighborhoods were retaining their negative crime profile.[3] Like the police, housing officials would perform their role and make physical improvements in these high-crime areas, but the improvements were short-lived, and the negative environment persisted. Thus, despite considerable resources devoted to these neighborhoods, both the police and housing officials were ineffective.

Ironically, the relatively high profile of police in slum neighborhoods may reinforce the vicious cycle of negative perceptions and attitudes. Too often police are left to be the problem solvers. When civil unrest and violence erupt, the police are society's first line of defense. If neighborhood problems persist, the police are blamed by both politicians and neighborhood residents. This scapegoating is unfortunate. Police departments often are placed in the position of having to be "all things to all people," whereas their proper role should be to serve as the arm of government most immediately involved in the restoration of order. Even in situations where police action may increase the tension in a crisis environment, the police department is the agency mandated to quell unlawful action. The context in which police enter a neighborhood is, therefore, critically important.

The Oasis Technique attempts to alter the role of the police in a neighborhood. The police and housing officials form a team to select the locations where criminal activity and housing problems are clearly related. Then both departments coordinate their resources so that the police apply direct pressure to the criminal element with increased patrol and increased use of court-sanctioned raids, while the housing officials step up housing modernization, rehabilitation, and other physical improvements to the law-abiding citizens. In essence, the Oasis Technique establishes a system that analyzes the strengths and weaknesses of a neighborhood so that a wide range of government and private sector services can be used to reinforce the strengths and minimize or eliminate the weaknesses. The program's aim is to turn bad areas good and give responsible residents the opportunity to play an active role in keeping their neighborhoods good.

In the terms used in our program, the revitalized area is called an oasis. The coalition in this area among police, housing officials, and local residents creates a basis for a rise in property values. This rise triggers reinvestment by the private sector, which offsets the need for more government investment. Through continued support by the police and housing officials, this oasis area sets an example of what can be accomplished; thus, over time it creates a natural ripple effect that triggers positive change in an ever-expanding area.

No area is designated for oasis treatment until analysis reveals that it contains "good people" — people who routinely maintain their rent or mortgage payments, maintain their property, respect their neighbors' right to peace, privacy, and quiet, and are willing to assist police and housing officials.[4] In this manner the Oasis Technique builds on the positive social structure that already exists in a neighborhood, as well as on its physical structure; and the police are able to serve and protect good citizens, who become "real" people to officers on the beat rather than faces in a crowd. According to Detective Ronald Range, a Fort Lauderdale undercover officer who is deeply involved in the program:

> Citizens became very active in supporting police efforts to gain control and maintain law and order. Tips, information, and open support for the police department increased manyfold. We became so backed up acting on citizens' tips regarding day-to-day criminal activity that we virtually had to put people on a waiting list. Officers who before would not have considered working in ghetto areas put in for transfers. They wanted to become part of the new, exciting, rewarding police style.
>
> The community began to welcome the presence of the police, and officers, feeling a part of the community, no longer took an "us-versus-them" approach. There was a new spirit of cooperation rather than competition between the police and community. Violent confrontations no longer were

the norm between the police and residents. Officers received help from citizens in locating and apprehending criminals, who were no longer welcome in the community. Officers saw meaning in the arrests they made and felt a real sense of accomplishment in performing their tasks. They no longer were reluctant, half-hearted maintainers of law and order, but proactive, service-oriented law enforcement officers. (Range 1983)

To explore the effectiveness of the Oasis Technique, a police department/housing authority cooperative data analysis project was carried out in Fort Lauderdale. The authors of this chapter, along with officers in the police department's district command, public information, and data analysis sections, studied crime information using a department computer and data base. We focused on changes in crime statistics between 1982 and 1983 because prior to this period crime data were not retrievable with the computer system.

Neighborhoods were examined according to general income level, as indicated by census data, and most prevalent type of crime, as reflected in the 96 crime categories the police department uses on its daily report forms. As expected, upper-, middle-, and low-income areas displayed progressively greater crime rates. For example, during the 1982–83 study period, the police received 489 disorderly conduct calls in the selected upper-income areas, 663 such calls in the selected middle-income areas, and 2,429 in the selected lower-income areas. Although we analyzed the 96 crime categories, our prime interest was in "quality-of-life" crimes — those crimes that we and police officers reviewing the data considered most likely to lead residents to leave their neighborhoods. Thirty-three crimes were listed as quality-of-life crimes. For example, disorderly conduct, drug-related street crime, breaking and entering, assault, robbery, and the like were included because they can easily spill over and affect any resident, and are so perceived. On the other hand, crimes such as kidnapping or forgery did not receive priority attention because their incidence and threat level do not trigger departure from a neighborhood.

We then examined over time the frequency of quality-of-life crimes in the low-income, high-crime areas (the only areas where the Oasis Technique was applied). This examination revealed that while the crime rate remained relatively constant in the low-income areas generally, there were substantially fewer quality-of-life crimes in the oasis sites as compared with the other low-income neighborhoods of Fort Lauderdale. Moreover, crime rates in the low-income oasis areas compared well with those of upper-income neighborhoods.

This study was not intended to be a formal, academic examination. The Oasis Technique evolved over time and was the outgrowth of the authors' (Lindsey and Quint) attempt to revitalize slum and blighted neighborhoods. Since our energies were fully taxed attempting to make change rather than study it, as yet there have been no ongoing studies with hypotheses being tested in a structured way. A great portion of the results discussed here are drawn from the informal, personal statements of numerous police officers and residents who lived through the neighborhood changes. Nevertheless, when the crime data are combined with the personal testimony of police and residents who work and live in Fort Lauderdale's low-income areas, the results are extremely encouraging.

In light of these results, the question naturally arises, How would the Oasis Technique work in ghettos in the Bronx, Chicago, Los Angeles, Detroit, or elsewhere? Sometimes this question is premised on the notion that Fort Lauderdale was an easy challenge, that "it ain't hard to be nice in paradise." The assumption that our community's slums are tame is simply uninformed, however. Admittedly, the size of the slums is a distinguishing factor, but large slum areas such as the South Bronx, Roxbury, or Watts are, in actuality, geographic constructs that only appear on maps. In human terms, these areas consist of many neighborhoods sharing common problems.[5] Within these neighborhoods are problems of differing scale for which different institutions, government agencies, and individuals have varying degrees of responsibility. The program we have developed would not tackle the entire slum areas in New York, Boston, Los Angeles, or elsewhere as a monolithic problem; instead, it would identify and address the critical problems that exist within specific areas of specific neighborhoods. The strengths and weaknesses of these areas would be analyzed, together with the human, governmental, and corporate resources that are available, with plans of action following from this analysis. As specific neighborhood areas improve, taking the form of oases, local government retains the option of applying the technique in other areas.

In addition, it is often asked, How expensive is it to implement the Oasis Technique? The reality is that this approach to improving neighborhood safety and vitality often saves money. The program does not call for substantial new expenditures. It provides a method that leverages private and public resources by pinpointing the opportunities to use those funds on projects that maximize a given neighborhood's strengths and minimize its weaknesses. The Oasis Technique enables police and other public officials to redirect existing resources to activities that are more relevant to improving the community, so that economies are realized as waste and mismanagement are reduced.

The greatest roadblock to the implementation of the Oasis Technique has been the public officials and individuals who are locked into the old ways of thinking and those who believe that significant and sustained change is not possible. In Fort Lauderdale the greatest problems centered around efforts to overcome bureaucratic inertia and stereotypes concerning what can be accomplished working with poor people in bad neighborhoods.

In most cities, the working relationship between police and the housing authority or other city agencies is tenuous. Such relationships usually develop because of "turf guarding" or interdepartmental directives that often work at cross-purposes. While these conditions existed in Fort Lauderdale in the early development stages of the Oasis Technique, the visual improvement of the target neighborhoods reduced the "nasty" atmosphere that prevailed. The police felt more comfortable patrolling these neighborhoods, and the potential benefits of an interagency and citizen participatory effort became clearly evident. Once the police joined the oasis process, a self-sustaining dynamic of cooperation ensued. Police found themselves welcome in formerly hostile and perilous neighborhoods, and a police-resident alliance replaced the usual adversarial relationship.

Today police-resident programs, established in the context of the Oasis Technique, go far beyond traditional Crimewatch and Crimestoppers projects. The programs, in fact, encompass these techniques and others in an unyielding anticrime campaign. These cooperative programs have created an atmosphere of safety so that there is greater incentive to support lawful behavior. As a result, many of Fort Lauderdale's formerly high-crime areas have become relatively crime-free and safe, as attested to by our computer analysis of crime data and by testimony of officers and residents.

The cornerstone of police-resident cooperation is joint crime fighting, maintenance of order, and sustained two-way communication. Crime fighting and order maintenance are facilitated by deploying the police in target neighborhoods so that they may support good residents who are working to improve their living conditions. Before the Oasis Technique, police were deployed generally to patrol the target area. Under our program, depending on the extent of the problems revealed in the analysis of neighborhood strengths and weaknesses, varying numbers of police were directed to patrol the most strategically important sites in the oasis area. Communication is encouraged by holding meetings at police headquarters every two months among community residents, city and private sector agency representatives, and police.[6] A typical roster of groups in attendance, in addition to residents, includes the police department, housing authority, City Department of Community Affairs, NAACP, the local business association, code enforcement personnel, landlords, and property owners. These meetings allow residents to identify problems they consider pressing and to suggest solutions. City and police officials in attendance help delineate options and form action plans. Task forces made up of police and resident members deal with specific problems, such as code enforcement and trash dumping, as well as specific problem sites, such as violations being committed by a particular liquor store or apartment complex.

The residents make wide-ranging contributions at these meetings. Participants from target neighborhoods have identified specific sites where prostitution, drug dealing, illegal trash dumping, trespassing, loitering, and other illicit activities occur. While many problems are known to the police, residents present concerns they find particularly urgent, such as prostitution and drug dealing in a school yard or a park frequented by their children.

While a most common complaint about the police, in particular, and government in general, is that they are unresponsive, the Oasis Technique has created an atmosphere of trust and cooperation. The program is a method of neighborhood analysis and action that potentially can be useful to police, housing and other government agencies, and residents in any city because it takes unique features of the locality into account. One basic precondition to employment of the Oasis Technique is the genuine commitment of local leaders to change policies and procedures that have proved ineffective in overcoming the problems associated with slum and blight.

In summary, the Oasis Technique is a method of controlling crime and improving the quality of life in neighborhoods that have been deteriorating. While it was originally developed as a housing and community development tool to combat slum and blight, it has developed into an effective police tool. Analysis suggests that with this approach police can return control of the streets to the good residents of inner-city neighborhoods; create an atmosphere of trust and cooperation between police and neighborhood residents; remove themselves from the scapegoat role for the social problems of the inner city; improve media perception of the police in inner-city neighborhoods; reduce the incidence of street level crime; and establish policies and procedures that provide more cost-effective police services to minority and low-income neighborhoods.

In the past few years, the Oasis Technique has received national attention. It has been lauded by the president of the United States, the governor of Florida, the federal Department of Housing and Urban Development, and television and print journalists (see, for example, Michelmore 1984; Friedrich 1985). It was endorsed and recommended by the International Association of Chiefs of Police.[7] Several cities are currently considering use of the Oasis Technique, and we anticipate that many other jurisdictions will perceive a need to use such a program in neighborhoods that are deteriorating and are plagued by crime and fear of crime. As some of these cities begin implementation of the technique, we will have the opportunity to study its impact in a more controlled manner than we did in Fort Lauderdale. Objectives that can be measured over a specific time period will be established. Moreover, we will have the opportunity to gain new, useful insight into the factors bearing on the transferability of the Oasis Technique to other communities. If our experience in formerly blighted neighborhoods of Fort Lauderdale is any indication, such communities will find the program an important component of their overall efforts to turn the tide of urban decay and malaise.

NOTES

1. Fear of crime has become a more topical subject. The National Institute of Justice, in 1983, funded fear reduction experiments and studies in Newark, New Jersey, and Houston, Texas. The results from these studies should help clarify the relationship between fear of crime and actual crime.

2. See *Costello* v. *Wainwright* (1976). But compare *Mitchell* v. *Untreiner* (1975) and *Miller* v. *Carson* (1977).

3. The appropriateness of the arrest rates and the negative crime profile of the neighborhood were determined through both a review of police records and informed discussions with the police department's assigned shift commanders.

4. The analysis to determine the presence of "good" people is conducted by the agency selected to implement the Oasis Technique. In Fort Lauderdale it was the housing authority, but in other communities it could be the police/and or community development agencies. The analysis includes a specialized survey of the physical, economic, and social components of a target neighborhood. The federal Department of Housing and Urban Development provided funding to the Fort Lauderdale Housing Authority to produce a handbook on the Oasis Technique, which should be completed by mid-1985 and will fully explain the methods of analysis, site selection, and neighborhood strategies.

5. For the purposes of this chapter, "neighborhood" is defined as a geographic area in a community that is determined by the perceptions of the residents and workers who interact within that area. While the boundaries of a neighborhood may be variable due to different perspectives, the neighborhood core is identifiable and is the nexus for day-to-day activity.

6. Such periodic meetings were also a key part of the "team policing" concept (see Sherman et al. 1973).

7. The IACP passed the following resolution on March 12, 1983 at its annual convention: "Now, THEREFORE, BE IT RESOLVED, that the Board of Officers of the International Association of Chiefs of Police endorses, and encourages the implementation of, the Oasis Technique as a valuable method for improving housing conditions and the quality of life, and thereby promoting safer neighborhoods and improved community relationships between police, private citizens and governmental agencies."

29
Making Better Use of Victims and Witnesses

Wesley G. Skogan

Commissioning a series of essays on policing focusing on "getting serious about crime control" might imply that the principal route to that end is through law enforcement. This could be true, but not if new energies are simply appended to the usual modes of policing. Rather, even at the heart of the traditional police function—solving crimes and apprehending criminals—the most cost-effective innovations must necessarily encourage more citizen involvement in keeping the peace. This is because citizens hold a virtual monopoly over the key item necessary to succeed in combatting crime: information. Understanding how much and what kind of information is out there and organizing to gather and use it more effectively could be the key to making significant gains in real police productivity.

One reason for concern about solving crimes and making arrests is that by some important measures the police are not doing these things very well. The picture is particularly bleak when we examine the most frequently cited indicator of their performance, the clearance rate. Clearance rates never have been high for many types of crime, a fact that thus far has eluded the police. Opinion studies indicate that people consistently overestimate the success the police have in making arrests, perhaps due to the steady diet of masterful detective work they see on television. The reality is that the police clear in one fashion or another only about one-quarter of the robberies that come to their attention and only about 15 percent of burglaries and thefts. In big cities clearance rates are even lower. Those figures appear worse if more re-

Work on this chapter was supported in part by Grant Number 81-IJ-CX-0069 awarded by the National Institute of Justice, U.S. Department of Justice. Points of view or opinions stated in this chapter are those of the author and do not necessarily represent the official position or policies of the U.S. Department of Justice.

fined measures of success are employed. One study in New York City looked carefully at clearances, including the credibility of "multiple" clearances (attributing many crimes to one felon) and the veracity of "administrative" clearances (wiping crimes off the books for technical, organizational, or policy reasons). It concluded that only about 4 percent of burglaries and larcenies, 8 percent of auto thefts, and 13 percent of robberies were definitely "solved." Studies of other cities have come up with similar figures (Greenwood et al. 1975; Reiss 1971).

Worse, another way of looking at the rate at which crimes are solved is to compare them not with "crimes known to the police" (the official count) but with a better estimate of the true number of crimes that have been committed. Because a great number of incidents go unreported by victims or unrecorded by the police, victimization surveys have been used to make independent measurements of their frequency. When these estimates of the total of personal, household, and commercial crimes are compared to arrests, the true "solution rates" for robbery, rape, and assault are further reduced by a factor of more than 3 (Skogan and Antunes 1979). Finally, clearance rates look bad because they are declining. For example, in Illinois, clearances for murder have dropped from 90 to 77 percent and from 21 to 17 percent for burglary since 1972.[1]

Of course, there is great interest in devising better ways of apprehending criminals. Some reforms in this area involve hardware, some software, and some more or better trained patrol officers. One of the most innovative ideas in crime control has been that of "co-production." The notion is a simple one: To a large extent the police are dependent on the cooperation of citizens to produce a safe environment. Most of the attention given to co-production has been devoted to community crime prevention, including such programs as BlockWatch, OperationID, and other self-help measures. These are neighborhood-based volunteer activities, often assisted by police community service officers (Podolefsky and DuBow 1981). These efforts are the wave of the future because they are "off-budget." They promise to have some effect in reducing crime without significant expenditure on the part of the government. Such prevention programs have a demonstrable effect for the better on fear of crime and public morale. They may reduce the unrealistic expectations people have about the role of the police in preventing crime by making clear their own responsibilities. Thus they are good politics because they get people involved and give them a sense of confidence without costing or (perhaps) promising too much.

However, not all co-production is confined to prevention activities. There are also important roles for citizens to play in the traditional police domain of solving crimes and catching criminals. While some of what the police do is self-initiated, the vast majority of serious crimes with victims are brought to their attention by the public, and (other than traffic) a similarly large proportion of all encounters between the police and individual citizens are initiated by the latter (Reiss 1971). One of the most important aspects of those transactions is that information changes hands. In their roles as victims and witnesses, citizens have a virtual monopoly over information about who did what, and this tight control extends over almost all Index and most non-Index crimes. Probably the most critical aspect of policing is how effectively the authorities gain access to this information, and much of what the police do and how they are organized reflect implicit theories about the best way of doing this. For example, one of the central features of police departments is that they are organized to minimize response time. Their almost exclusive reliance on squad cars, the placement of those cars on beats rather than near station houses and under the 'eye of sergeants, work-load-based personnel allocations across shifts, and massive capital investments in communication dispatch systems — all reflect the assumption that the key to identifying offenders is getting to crime scenes fast. The fact that this is untrue in almost every circumstance is only now worming itself into the field (Van Kirk 1977). But the possibility of gathering more information in other, better, ways remains the greatest hope for dramatic improvements in the success of police departments in clearing criminal cases.

STUDIES OF INFORMATION

Some of the most controversial evaluations of police work have concerned how effectively they manage the task of acquiring and using information. Examinations of detective operations by the Rand Corporation, the Stanford Research Institute, and the Urban Institute dramatized the matter by claiming they do it very poorly (Greenwood et al. 1975; Greenberg, Yu, and Lang 1973; Bloch and Bell 1976). Those evaluations emphasized the critical role of information gathered immediately after the crime by responding patrol officers and, in particular, the importance of clear and specific suspect identifications by victims and witnesses.

> The single most important determinant of whether or not a case will be solved is the information the victim supplies to the immediately responding patrol officer. If information that uniquely identifies the perpetrator is not presented at the time the crime is reported, the perpetrator, by and large, will not be subsequently identified. (Greenwood et al. 1975, p. ix)

The Washington, D.C., "supercops" study conducted by INSLAW looked at another problem but came to a complementary finding (Forst, Lucianovic, and Cox 1977). The investigation was concerned with why some D.C. patrol officers were so much more effective than others at making arrests — and making them stick. A study of department records indicated a few officers were making most D.C. felony arrests, and the evaluation was to find out why. The answer seemed to be that these so-called supercops took information seriously. They devoted a great deal of attention to rounding up bystanders at crime scenes and attempting to convert them to witnesses. They carefully questioned bystanders and victims and kept them apart from suspects if they were still around. (Among other things this tactic diminishes the common problem that bystanders, afraid of retaliation, give the police false names and addresses [Cannavale and Falcon 1977].) Moreover, these officers kept in contact with witnesses to find out what they had heard and to keep them committed to the case and willing to appear (perhaps several times) in court. This is also extremely important. Analyses of court records indicate the availability of nonpolice witnesses leads to much higher rates of conviction and that witness noncooperation is the leading cause of evidentiary problems in the prosecutor's office (Forst, Lucianovic, and Cox 1977; see also McDonald's chapter and McNamara's response). Supercops did not drive to crime scenes any faster. Rather, they were very "people-oriented" in their investigation and paid attention to what witnesses and victims had to say.

Other research indicates there are a lot of people around crime scenes who potentially have something to tell the police. This can be seen in the findings of the National Crime Survey (NCS), a continuing survey conducted by the Census Bureau for an arm of the Justice Department.[2] This survey reveals that most victims of personal crimes know a substantial amount about "whodunit," and under many circumstances there are also other people around (beside victims and predators) who potentially could be tapped for information as well.

As part of the crime survey, victims are quizzed in some detail about the characteristics of the perpetrators of offenses. The most striking fact about the resulting data is the great gulf between personal and property crimes in the amount of information that victims have to offer. In the case of burglaries and thefts, victims are willing to hazard few guesses about offenders, for fewer than 5 percent witnessed the crime or saw the getaway. On the other hand, most personal crime victims know a substantial amount about their attackers. Overall, about 50 percent had seen them before, and almost 40 percent were at least casually acquainted with the miscreant. This positive identification is critical, for it is very unlikely the police will clear a crime by making an arrest unless someone identifies the perpetrator and has a good idea about where he or she can be found. In the Rand Corporation study of detective productivity (Greenwood et al. 1975), the most important of the "solvability factors" the researchers could isolate was the ability of responding officers (not detectives, for they could not add much) to get a name and location of a suspect from those on the scene.[3] The possibility of positive identification was higher for victims of assault and rape than for victims of other personal crimes. Virtually none of those struck by a purse snatcher or pickpocket knew much about the identity of the offender, although some could describe the culprit in general terms. Overall, only 8 percent of personal crime victims could not remember the race of offenders, and 17 percent were unwilling to hazard a guess about age. Much of that confusion was confined to multiple-offender cases, and the percentage of victims able to describe the age of their attacker was more than 97 percent in one-offender cases.

Another issue on which the NCS sheds some light is the frequency with which there are, at least potentially, witnesses to personal crimes. This is indicated very indirectly by victims' responses to the question, Were you the only person there besides the offender(s)? In a surprisingly large number of cases they were not. Between 1973 and 1979, "other people" appear to have been around in 25 percent of rapes, 38 percent of robberies, 63 percent of assaults, 51 percent of purse snatchings, and 67 percent of pickpocket cases. Although this finding only crudely indicates the extent to which these by-standers actually witnessed the crime, the figures do belie somewhat the stereotype that danger is confined to empty streets. Some studies of police files have reached a similar conclusion (for example, one in California found that other people were described as being "nearby" in 50 percent of robberies). On the other hand, an investigation of the same issue using the files of six local police agencies in New York found witnesses were present in less than 10 percent of reported burglaries and thefts (Feeney and Weir 1973; Pope 1977).

The NCS also asked about the reporting of crimes to the police. According to the survey very few burglaries were reported by persons who were not members of the victimized household, and many of those incidents were reported long after the event. Further, even witnesses to personal crimes do not do much that is constructive about things they see. Persons other than the victim or a member of his or her household are involved in reporting only a fraction of all personal crimes. Of the crimes reported, other witnesses did so in 20 percent of assaults, 16 percent of rapes, robberies, and purse snatchings, and only 6 percent of pickpocket cases. The gap between other persons "being there" and being the ones who report crimes is considerable.

Finally, the NCS, which was conducted in part because it was apparent large numbers of offenses were going unreported, documents that in major crime categories victims and witnesses report only about half of all incidents, except in some important categories where that percentage is even lower. For example, police are informed about half of the rapes, assaults, and purse snatches and about 55 percent of robberies but about only 25 percent of all simple property thefts. These levels of nonreporting have several significant consequences for policing. Large numbers of offenses are hidden from official view. They do not enter the planning or allocation calculations made by police departments. Their perpetrators are largely immune from police action. There are so many unreported crimes that the actual rate at which they are solved by arrest is unlikely to have much deterrent effect on desperate adults or adventure-seeking young males, whose chances of being apprehended for any particular offense must be extremely low. Finally, the existence of this large pool of unreported incidents threatens the evaluation of innovation in police work. One of the first things that happens when effective, citizen-oriented crime prevention programs are mounted is that the official crime rate soars (Schneider 1976). While this is in reality a consequence of increased crime reporting and new confidence in the police, it can be hard to explain to city councils.

IMPLICATIONS

All of this suggests there is a great deal of untapped information about crime and criminals in the hands of victims and witnesses. More people are apparently around than are taking an active role in reporting crimes, and victims of personal crimes have a fair amount of detailed information to contribute about offenders. Significant increases in the certainty of arrest of those committing crimes may be gained by extending the arm of the law more deeply into this pool of currently unidentified offenders. The issue from the point of view of the police is how to gather and utilize information better and how to encourage citizens to play a more active role in assisting in that effort.

The "supercops" study pointed to a number of specifics that seemed to enhance the effectiveness of patrol officers in doing their part. The Police Foundation's response time study in Kansas City examined the relationship between how fast the police arrived on the scene and the presence of bystanders, on the presumption that they will quickly drift away after the excitement dies down (Van Kirk 1977). This study found that response times have to be unrealistically short to have much effect. Other research on police management has focused on the opposite problem, how to identify and shunt aside quickly the inevitably large number of cases that are essentially devoid of useful information. The Police Executive Research Forum, the Stanford Research Institute, and other organizations have conducted "burglary investigation" studies to specify decision rules for guiding police investigators in doing this (Eck 1979; Greenberg 1977). As indicated above, the NCS suggests that this is a good idea, as the incidence of "don't know" responses is very high for questions about the details of burglaries and simple thefts. Presumably, by shedding the lead of unproductive cases, more resources can be directed toward those that promise to be solvable — which is largely a question of how much information is available about them.

Another area of improvement would involve recognizing the importance of patrol officers in clearing crimes. Currently they are expected to give cases only perfunctory attention and then return to "active duty." Cases are followed up later by detectives, who turn over the same ground and usually add little useful information to the case file. Experiments with "full service" policing by patrol officers, teaming detectives with uniformed personnel, and other forms of organization that encourage officers first on the scene to pursue the case as long as it seems to pay off have led to substantial increases in arrest productivity (Bloch and Bell 1976).

The problem of how to get more bystanders to step forward is a difficult one. Most scholarly research on bystanders in emergency situations has focused on their personal intervention in those emergencies. There is a great deal of evidence that citizens are relatively willing to step into cases involving less serious offenses (for example, delinquencies) and that such intervention enhances the effectiveness of the informal system of social control in their neighborhood. When serious crimes involving older offenders occur, however, intervening can be a risky move.

One of the presumptions behind renewed interest in foot patrol is that the easy interaction between police and citizens it presumably fosters will encourage more communication about persons and events in the neighborhood (Police Foundation 1981; Wilson and Kelling 1982; see also Kelling's "order maintenance" chapter). A great deal of useful information that currently somehow does not seem appropriate for the emergency number could flow from that exchange. This is congruent with academic experiments on the reporting of staged crimes in real settings, like supermarkets. Shoppers who have been encouraged even in subtle ways to report crimes when they see them are much more likely to do so, and they are also more likely to report to clerks with whom they already have had a pleasant encounter (Bickman 1975).

There may be a significant role for public education concerning the importance of good witness-like behavior. People should be reminded of the importance of noting the appearance of suspicious parties and unique ways of identifying them (such as license plate numbers and who else was around at the moment). There already have been many (unevaluated) campaigns encouraging bystanders to call the police when they witness crimes or even suspicious circumstances. Community crime prevention programs always stress the importance of prompt and thorough reporting and can have strong effects on the reporting rate for an area. Opinion surveys indicate that there is a great deal of public interest in crime prevention and that great masses of people can be reached effectively with simple messages about possible actions they can take. A recent evaluation of the "McGruff" crime prevention dog ad campaign indicates that he is recognized by 50 percent of adults, and most of those can recall at least one specific about the message he bears (Mendelsohn and O'Keefe 1981). New rounds of the McGruff campaign will be featuring police-community relations and crime reporting, which may stimulate more positive action on the part of witnesses to crime.

If the large number of persons who are apparently around when crimes occur were to become more involved as bystanders, the implications for crime control would also be considerable. One of the fundamental tenets of prevention theory is that "surveillance" activities and "territorial" reactions to illegitimate activity will stop crimes from being committed in the first place. Thus encouraging a greater role for citizens in solving crime and apprehending offenders may, in the long run, have actual prevention effects as well.

NOTES

1. These figures were supplied by the Statistical Analysis Center, Illinois Law Enforcement Commission.

2. The analyses reported here were conducted by the author. A general description of the National Crime Survey can be found in Garofalo and Hindelang (1977).

3. The extent to which victims can make such an identification is, of course, only an imperfect indication of how many crimes could be solved in that way.

30
Retrenchment, the Constitution, and Policing

Hubert Williams

There can be no question that the most important missions of the police are crime control and the maintenance of order. Their success in achieving those missions is dependent on two factors: the willingness of the public to finance police operations, and the degree to which they are willing to give up certain liberties. In the former instance, the public has spoken quite loudly in recent years. The ability of municipalities to finance their operations has been severely limited by federal, state, and local cutbacks in funding. At the same time, escalating costs have forced many municipalities into a position of reducing the size of their police forces, despite rises in crime and increasing demands for police services. This push-pull phenomenon has resulted in ever-increasing calls to "unhandcuff the police." Unfortunately, the public generally fail to perceive the reality of such a prospect or, if they do, assume it will be solely at the expense of the "other guy."

The Bill of Rights' constraints on the state and its agents provide the language and values that we use to negotiate the trade-off between individual freedoms and public safety when we attempt to increase police effectiveness in the control of crime. Extreme caution must be exercised in any move toward increased order maintenance (Wilson and Kelling 1982; see also Kelling's chapter on order maintenance) to ensure we do not sacrifice constitutional rights. To be sure, the precise meaning of most of the constitutional rights bearing on police work is far from clear (see Kerstetter's chapters) and is altered constantly by numerous, sometimes conflicting, legislative, judicial, and administrative decisions. Let there be no doubt that the police, given the opportunity and the zeal to accomplish their mission, will strain to the limit whatever powers we give them. So the difficult question arises: Is it possible to use the police for effective crime control without sacrificing constitutional freedoms, and, if so, how?

I believe it is possible, providing that those people in positions to effect change are willing and innovative enough to strike some sensible balances between competing values. When I was Police Director in Newark, we introduced several order maintenance programs that do not breech constitutional rights and yet achieve a reasonable degree of success. One program, the Newark Truancy Task Force, has garnered national interest and acclaim. Started in early 1982, this program was designed to deal with children staying out of school and roaming the streets. We, in the police department, recognized that many of these children were the very ones getting into trouble. Complaints were streaming in from all quarters of the community about this problem. The dilemma, of course, was what to do about the youth, short of arresting them for truancy.

In our analysis of the problem, we came to the conclusion that resorting to the arrest option would have had several drawbacks: There would be little or no selectivity of enforcement — many good kids, out on a childish lark, would feel the full negative impact of the system; pushing these youth into the police and court systems would be a poor long-range solution; and, in any event, the police department did not have the resources to mount the kind of large-scale arrest program that would be essential for a significant impact. Fortunately, at the same time we were wrestling with the problem, a new superintendent of schools arrived in Newark. He, too, recognized the problem and accepted the challenge of getting these children back into the schools. This became the basis of a unique partnership between the police and the school system in which both organizations combined resources in an attack against truancy. Five teams, each consisting of school attendance officers and a police officer, scoured the city looking for truants. Kids caught playing hooky were gathered up and transported to one designated school where board of education officials began a process of notifications, youth and parent counseling, and follow-up checks. In this program, arrests were made only as a last resort.

Newark's program achieved remarkable results: More than 7,000 children were picked up in one year, less than 7.5 percent of whom were picked up as repeaters, and truancy in Newark was reduced by 10 percent. From the police department's point of view, success took the form of dramatically reduced complaints from the public during school hours — a result that may reflect both a reduction in crime and a reduction in the public's fear of crime. In some areas of the city, daytime burglaries were also reduced. This program is an excellent example of two agencies collaborating to address a problem that neither could deal with effectively alone. It is also important to note that while the program is clearly an order maintenance effort, it is so in the least offensive way, since arrests were made only as a last resort. That is not generally the case with order maintenance programs; arrests are, in fact, an essential element of most successful efforts. This is true of our Selective Area Field Enforcement (SAFE) program, initiated on April 12, 1982.

The SAFE program was designed from its inception to focus on the problem of large crowds of people loitering at particular locations and generating a wide variety of complaints from area residents. Many of these complaints traditionally would have been classified as so-called nuisance complaints and assigned a low response priority by hard-pressed urban police departments, ours included. Public drinking, excessive noise, and obscene language complaints must often give way to other more serious complaints flooding into communications centers. Radio cars would be sent whenever possible, or radio cars cruising by known trouble locations would attempt to move these loiterers from the locations, but their attempts were generally ineffective. The Newark ordinance on loitering (C.O. 17:2-14), along with court rulings, mandated that the police order such groups to disperse prior to initiating any arrest. The result was that people would disperse on being ordered to do so, only to return immediately after the police left the scene.

Designed to deal with this problem, the SAFE effort began by having each district commander compile a list of problem locations within the city based on his experiences within the community. He would then select a date and time at which a sweep would be made. The program was coordinated so that each of the four districts would conduct its sweep on a different date. This was necessary since personnel would be drawn from other commands to conduct the operation. At the appointed date and time, one radio team would be drawn from each district and would respond to the command conducting the sweep. The commanding officer of the district, along with a superior officer from his command and the four radio teams would then assemble and be given the target locations for the sweep. One team would be assigned to drive a large prisoner van, while another team (usually the home district team) would be assigned to make the required dispersal notifications. In all, each SAFE operation involved a "spotter" unit (an unmarked vehicle that monitors the target area prior to or immediately following an operation), a "lead" unit (described below), a prisoner van, field units, support units (tactical and patrol officers stationed at the perimeter of the target area), supervisory unit(s), and "processing" and record bureau personnel (to facilitate processing of interrogation or arrest subjects).

To commence an operation, all relevant personnel and units would respond to a predesignated assembly point, near the day's first target location but out of view. Once everyone was in place, the notification (or lead) team would proceed to the location with its emergency lights activated and, using the vehicle's public address system, announce "that a SAFE operation will be undertaken in that area and that persons engaged in criminal or suspicious activity, or loitering with no legitimate purpose, may be subjected to the arrest or interrogation process" (Newark Police Department 1982). The lead team would also carefully note those people who had been ordered to leave the location. Once the people had left, this team would depart and return to the assembly point. After a 15-minute wait, the entire caravan of police units would proceed to the scene, and those persons who could be identified as having returned after the order to disperse would be arrested. This procedure would be repeated until the van was full or all locations targeted for the day were exhausted.

This program proved to be a considerable success. The word went out throughout the city that the police meant business. Public reaction was highly favorable since the areas chosen were well-known trouble spots, and the arrests were confined to those who were previously warned. Another significant benefit was that after the program had been in operation for several weeks, it was much easier for regular patrol units to disperse loiterers at problem locations and keep those areas clear. (Over the nine-month period from August 1983 through April 1984, on 29 of 34 separate occasions on which the SAFE strategy was employed, the targeted groups dispersed in response to the lead car's announcement — without the need for arrests and questioning by the full panoply of units [Williams 1984, p. 8].) Loiterers were not prone to return since they had no way of knowing if the police would reappear shortly to make arrests. Importantly, we did not fall into the trap of confusing displacement of disorder with maintenance of order within our city. Many of the loiterers who were out-of-town narcotics dealers simply left Newark rather than switch to another street corner. And, as indicated, we continued to work with the schools to develop alternatives to the street corners for Newark's youngsters.

Finally, it is important to note that legal requirements were carefully observed. While some libertarians might complain that a program such as SAFE is oppressive, I would argue that by specifically addressing the signs of lawlessness and disorder prevalent within particular neighborhoods the police can help prevent deterioration of the quality of living for the residents in and around problem areas. Also, such actions are necessary both to maintain public confidence in the police and ensure the general public's right to be free from such nuisances.

A hallmark of our approach to policing during my tenure in Newark, exemplified by this program, is that we elicited the community's attitudes toward major police initiatives and obtained *prior* community support for new programs, particularly if they involved actions that could be seen as unwarranted intrusions on community privacy. Thus both of the cited order maintenance programs were instituted in response to serious public complaints. The programs that we designed to address these complaints were crafted to achieve our goals within legal and constitutional constraints and to use scarce personnel resources effectively. Our approach takes legitimate advantage of the reality, by now well established, that police officers and police agencies must exercise very considerable discretion in light of legislative tendencies to make criminal nearly everything that is objectionable. As Morris and Hawkins

(1977, p. 45) observed cogently: "[T]he existence of a broad charter of discretion, although it affords opportunities for abusive discrimination, equally permits the exercise of choice in a socially advantageous fashion. It means that the police are in a position to deploy their resources in such a way as to make them more responsive to the prime needs of their communities."

Two other programs in the same vein as the SAFE program have, like that effort, been studied as part of the federally funded Fear Reduction project that also has focused on police-community programs in Houston (see Brown's and Stewart's chapters). These two Newark programs (not funded out of the federal grant, which only covers the research on the various policing strategies) are Roadcheck and a bus inspection effort called BUS'T Crime (Williams 1984, pp. 8-9).

The Roadcheck program, in order to demonstrate police presence and control in Newark neighborhoods, establishes checkpoints on busy roads and, consistent with case law (*Delaware* v. *Prouse* [1979]; *U.S.* v. *Prichard* [1981]; *State* v. *Coccomo* [1981]; and *People* v. *John BB* [1982]), stops every fifth vehicle for driver and/or vehicle examination. During the nine-month period following the program's inception in June 1983, 7,805 vehicles passed through the checkpoints, 1,701 were stopped, and police issued 487 summonses and made 24 arrests. The number of infractions discovered and penalized, of course, is of secondary importance compared to the clear establishment of police presence — and the consequent reduction of destabilizing fear of crime.

Those same goal priorities also govern the bus inspection program, which nevertheless has yielded some impressive statistics. During the first nine months of this effort, which involves patrol officers randomly stopping public transportation vehicles and boarding them to inspect for passengers engaged in disruptive or disorderly behavior (smoking, drinking, loud playing of radios, and the like), bus crime dropped by 40 percent, and bus ridership increased by 7 percent in Newark (Williams 1984, p. 9; NOBLE 1984; Woody 1984; Pezzino 1984). The bus crime reduction in Newark, accomplished through 1,719 inspections during the nine-month study period, compares, according to the New Jersey Transit Authority, with a statewide 23 percent reduction of bus crime (Pezzino 1984). Officers involved in this program reported that it was not unusual for the senior citizens and other passengers on the buses to applaud when the police ejected a disorderly person from the bus (ejection rather than arrest was the prime technique).

Not all police efforts to stem the rising tide of community fear are as successful, of course. Sometimes the weakness of an anticrime or order maintenance program is attributable to police insensitivity to community preferences and needs. With a reasonable amount of inquiry, a police leader ought to be able to assess whether a potential program will be acceptable to his service population. For example, several years ago, faced with an emotionally charged community reaction to the killing of a six-month-old baby in a public housing project in Newark, my impulse was to establish a strong police presence in the project and to control strictly all movement within it. I dropped my plans to "occupy" the buildings, however, after detecting opposition to the idea from both the community and my top command staff. In my view, while the police chief must exercise leadership, he must do so with sensitivity to, and genuine respect for, the community's own definition of good police service (see Davis's chapter).

That definition seems to be an ever-expanding one. Ever since Sir Robert Peel formed the first modern police department (in England) in 1829, the police have been given a continually increasing regulatory role over public and private conduct. Additionally, they have taken on a host of other duties that bear little relationship to their most important missions of crime control and order maintenance. Such sundry duties as traffic enforcement, sanitary code enforcement, dog licensing, staffing courts with security personnel, operating detention facilities, providing escort services, and even operating ambulance and towing services sap the resources of the police at the expense of their crime and order control missions. There is a tendency for legislators to use the police as the agency of last resort whenever faced with a problem that does not squarely fit within the province of another agency. This practice has routinely dissipated much needed resources in the effort to reduce crime and maintain order.

If we, as a nation, were really serious about using the police for effective crime control, we would reexamine their role in light of their resource and skill limitations and strip from them those responsibilities that interfere with their redefined role and mission. Those duties that interfere with their mission would be reassigned to other agencies or new agencies. Cost analysis alone would dictate such a move, for rather than simply shifting the expenses to another city agency, this would eliminate current duplications of effort. It is not unusual for a single officer to cost a municipality $30,000 per year when salary and benefits are calculated. It boggles the mind that such sums are spent to keep one officer on a traffic post, directing traffic or performing other mundane chores. (The argument that his or her visible presence helps to maintain order in the general vicinity appears to be flawed predicated on research findings and also because the public, so far as I can tell, sees traffic police as not wanting or unable to leave their posts to deal with matters other than traffic control.) Until such time as government becomes cost-effective, it is unlikely we will make any serious inroads in effectively controlling crime.

We have now come full circle in this discussion and must return to the issue of public financing. Any serious effort to revamp our police system for more effective crime control must address this issue. In order to preserve local control over the police, our nation relies on a system of local funding. As I pointed out earlier, the public, recoiling from the spiral of ever-increasing taxes, has seriously hampered the ability of state and local governments to raise revenues. In California, voters adopted Proposition 13, and in New Jersey the citizens imposed a state "CAP" law. Both of these laws, together with similar legislation in many other states, seriously limit the adequacy of funding for police departments across the nation.

The phenomenon of police layoffs, unheard of a decade ago, has swept the country and is now commonplace. There has been a general failure of the public and legislators to recognize that the preservation of public order hinges on their willingness to finance the police operation. Local governments cannot preserve the peace, maintain public order, or control crime without an adequately funded police agency. Order maintenance programs, such as those outlined earlier, only serve as temporary measures to address a growing dilemma faced by police administrators. Confronted by constantly shrinking resources, they must continually search for new and innovative ways to do more with less. One of the techniques we adopted in Newark as a stopgap strategy is a resource allocation model that uses auxiliary and support personnel one day per month to perform general patrol and service delivery duties as part of the patrol operation. The benefits are twofold: First, a valuable resource pool becomes available for fear reduction and crime reduction operations (nearly 10,000 man-hours over eight months was diverted from support/auxiliary to patrol with no discernible impact on the former functions). Second, the capabilities of both the support/auxiliary personnel and the regular patrol personnel are enhanced by commingling officers who are not accustomed to field work and officers unfamiliar with the needs of police officials assigned to the department's "inside" tasks (Williams 1984, pp.7-8). Despite police administrators' best efforts to make do with what we have, however, I am convinced that we have reached a critical juncture in our society. Somehow, we must find a method to fund our police system adequately.

Failing that, there is a growing danger that calls to "unhandcuff the police" will pressure both Congress and the courts to react in ways that diminish our freedoms. It is a threat that expands as the police struggle to meet public demands. In 1984, on the day following Independence Day, the Supreme Court, which had been chipping away somewhat gingerly at the exclusionary rule for some time, took a chunk out of that evidentiary device for controlling illegal searches and seizures (*U.S.* v. *Leon* [1984]; and *Massachusetts* v. *Sheppard* [1984]). Although the "good faith" exception enunciated by the Court was only explicitly applied to warrant cases, many observers see the eventual application of the exception to all searches and seizures as a virtual certainty. Other recent Supreme Court excavations include carving out an "inevitable discovery" exception to the exclusionary rule in cases involving confessions and seizures of tangible objects (*Nix* v. *Williams* [1984]) and creating a "public safety" exception to the *Miranda* rule (*New York* v. *Quarles* [1984]). Many other examples could be cited; they are easily gathered by perusing the increasingly vehement and, I fear, quixotic dissents of Supreme Court Justices William Brennan and Thurgood Marshall.

It is not the expansion of police power or the tapping of new information sources (see Skogan's chapter) that, in my view, will greatly improve policing. It is, rather, the redefinition of the police mission to exclude sundry tasks and duplicative agency efforts. And the funding issue must be squarely addressed. A new method to finance adequately police operations might be based on the English system of funding local police operations. In England, 50 percent of the cost of maintaining police departments is carried by the central government through the office of the Home Secretary. The only restrictions are regular audits by a central agency, Her Majesty's Inspectors of the Constabulary, to ensure the efficiency of operations. The remaining monies are raised locally, through taxes. Such a method ensures adequate budgetary support while maintaining both autonomy and local control. It also lifts the burden of total financing of the police operation from municipalities caught in a constantly closing vise.

There are no panaceas that we know of that can alleviate the burden of crime in our society. Yet it is my view that local police, acting in concert with the citizenry they serve, can make a difference. This objective will not be easily attained. It will require a reprioritization of resources, a redefinition of roles, and a more frank, honest, and open assessment of the issues than has existed in the past. The toughest challenge of police leadership in cities that are experiencing fiscal crisis (not all cities are) is to make creative, intelligent, innovative, and constitutional use of existing resources. The preservation of peace in our society cannot and should not be achieved at the expense of hard-won freedoms. Thus my prescription is a stringent one, but I believe it represents this nation's best chance to make a truly serious effort at controlling crime.

PART 8

WHITHER PROFESSIONALISM?

Introduction

The 11 papers in this section explore the state of police "professionalism," a concept whose definition and implications remain caught in a tug of war between different factions in the law enforcement community. (Besides the discussions here, see Robert Kliesmet's, Anthony Bouza's, and Carl Klockars's chapters; see also Farris 1982.) Some commentators will not apply the term "profession" to policing. Bittner (1984), for example, says police work is treated by its practitioners more like an adventure than a craft; Etzioni (1961) is a bit more lenient, calling law enforcment a "semiprofession."

Clearly, the label applied is less important than the quality of police work; but traditional concepts of professionalism are of some use in assessing the quality of policing. The landscape surveyed in this section is hardly virgin turf, as Samuel Walker and other contributors make clear, yet these surveyors' eyes are keen, their instruments modern, and their vantage point strong. Most importantly, the terrain they are exploring has undergone some dramatic changes over the years and merits a fresh look. The contributors assess the professionalism of police administration by focusing on several key issues, a number of which bear on the matter of who runs the police and who should.

One such issue, addressed by Walker, is policing's receptivity to professional standard setting. Given the general expectation that a profession is supposed to develop and police its own rules, Walker discusses several important efforts to articulate law enforcement standards and goals over the past several decades, some of which were dominated by police, others of which were not.

Another measure of an occupation's professionalism is said to be its use of research as a tool to improve its performance. In that regard, James Stewart's elegant exhortation to police chiefs is to "work smarter, not harder."

Gary Cordner concurs and adds the caution that elaborate statistical presentations can support, but should rarely supplant, commonsense propositions. The failure of many researchers to effectively explain counterintuitive (and critical) findings has clearly contributed historically to giving research a bad name in the police world—and elsewhere. Many in policing would embrace the definition of research as "a straight line from the tangent of a well-known assumption to the center of a foregone conclusion" (Neville 1979). Underscoring such cynicism toward academic inquiry is the practical realization by many police managers that the researcher's acquisition of significant knowledge about their agencies presents the risk of altering the existing balance of power between the chief and the researcher (see Goldstein 1977, chap. 11; Eisenberg 1975). If, however, the police insist that research which saps agency resources provide some tangible law enforcement benefit and if they seize the opportunity to expand their own research skills during their exposure to the researcher (see Morris and Hawkins 1970, p. 107), the experience can be mutually beneficial.

While both Stewart and Cordner highlight the value of research for planning purposes, Louis Mayo takes a close look at the accuracy of police leaders' information about their agencies' current performance. Although he sees opportunities for progress, Mayo captures a major element of policing's present crisis in his appraisal that many chiefs are "leading blindly." "And if the blind lead the blind," the Bible counsels (Matthew 15:14), "both shall fall into the ditch."

One way of averting that fate may be by greater, more effective experimentation with police operational programs. Since the Kansas City Preventive Patrol Experiment (Kelling et al. 1974a) was conducted more than a decade ago, the police world has hosted several other important experiments, concerning, for example, the relevance of foot patrol to crime reduction and fear reduction (Police Foundation 1981; IACP 1982), the impact on domestic violence of different mode of police response (Sherman and Berk 1984), and the usefulness of the "differential police response" strategy—in which nonemergency calls are handled in some way other than the immediate dispatch of a squad car—for improving service while reducing costs (Farmer 1981; Cohen and McEwen 1984; Kelly 1984). Taking the view that a profession ought to consider not only the legality but the morality of its behavior, several chapters in this section explore the ethics of such experimentation. Both practitioners' and academics' viewpoints are reflected in John Shapard's chapter and in the responses to it by Bergstrom, Rice, Elliston, and Kelling.

Experimentation in law enforcement, which may come more easily to small departments than large ones (Goldstein 1977, p. 321), also bears on this volume's theme of who runs the police, in two ways. First, as some of the authors argue, without program experimentation, chiefs will not acquire the kind of information they need in order to discover what their officers are doing and how well they are doing it—and, as suggested above, such information is power. Second, because program experiments involve alterations in the provision of police service, they sometimes engender opposition from officer unions, politicians, and community groups and thus become tests of the chief's authority.

Police chiefs' professionalism is gauged by Michael Shanahan on another dimension: their willingness and capacity to forge creative collaborations with the business world and particularly with the burgeoning private security industry. This public-private marriage is seen not as an option but as an historical imperative if public policing is to emerge with some modicum of strength from the fiscal crisis afflicting most of urban America. The failure of public law enforcement to "hold its audience" against the incursions of private security is viewed as a grave prospect in a recent consideration of the future of policing, which worried that people without the means to hire private police would receive poorer and poorer policing as wealthier elements in society lost their incentive to "support municipal police services" (Panel on the Future of Policing 1984).

Lawrence Sherman's chapter completes this book by reminding the reader about both the virtues and the vices that can be practiced in the name of police professionalism. In my view, his call for police chiefs to transcend parochialism and become urban statesmen is increasingly being heeded; and in that lies enormous hope that American police leadership will overcome many of the problems articulated throughout this volume.

31
Setting the Standards: The Efforts and Impact of Blue-Ribbon Commissions on the Police

Samuel Walker

The blue-ribbon commission is an established part of American public life. In this process, an appointed panel of recognized experts studies a particular subject and makes recommendations for change and improvement. Many blue-ribbon commissions are a form of crisis management, created in the wake of an emergency such as a riot. Others are part of the longer range process of professionalization through which members of an occupational group define minimum standards of professional competence. Commissions are either "public," in the sense of being created by government officials, or "private," in the sense of being creatures of nonpublic professional or civic groups.

In American policing, blue-ribbon commissions have played an important role in the effort to bring about reform. In the ten years between 1963 and 1973 three major commissions studied the police, each producing a report with specific "black-letter" recommendations (President's Commission on Law Enforcement and Administration of Justice 1968; American Bar Association 1973, 1980; National Advisory Commission on Criminal Justice Standards and Goals 1973a). These three reports continue to serve as basic reference points for discussions of police reform. More recently, the Commission on Accreditation for Law Enforcement Agencies (CALEA) has published its set of minimum standards (CALEA 1983a), and the Panel on the Future of Policing has completed a report with recommendations (Panel 1984).

These recent reports on the police have historical antecedents and are supplemented by observations concerning the police in reports on other problems. The Wickersham Commission published the first national survey of American policing in 1931. One volume focuses exclusively on police misconduct (the "third degree") and another defines general standards for police management (National Commission on Law Observance and Enforcement

354

1931a, 1931b). The Wickersham Commission was preceded by several state and local commissions (see Cleveland Foundation 1922; Missouri Association for Criminal Justice 1926; Illinois Association for Criminal Justice 1929). Meanwhile, there is a long tradition of "riot commissions" convened following racial disturbances in the twentieth century. The first of these was created after the 1919 Chicago race riot (Chicago Commission on Race Relations 1922), and the most recent is the National Advisory Commission on Civil Disorders (1968), known popularly as the Kerner Commission. Since the police were, in most cases, directly involved in the incidents precipitating the riot, all of the reports make recommendations for changes in policing.

Despite their prominence, whether the various commissions and their reports are a significant factor in changing American law enforcement is a matter of some debate.[1] Testifying before the Kerner Commission, noted psychologist Kenneth B. Clark stated the best case for a skeptical view:

> I read that report . . . of the 1919 riot in Chicago, and it is as if I were reading the report of the investigating committee on the Harlem riot of '35, the report of the investigating committee on the Harlem riot of '43, the report of the McCone Commission on the Watts riot.*** I must again in candor say to you members of this Commission—it is a kind of Alice in Wonderland, with the same moving picture re-shown over and over again, the same analysis, the same recommendations, and the same inaction. (National Advisory Commission on Civil Disorders 1968, p. 483)

May the same indictment be made of the reports of the major police commissions? Do they, too, repeat the same analyses, make the same old recommendations, and produce no results?

The pages that follow will focus primarily on the three major reports that cover the mid-1960s to mid-1970s era: the report of the President's Commission on Law Enforcement and Administration of Justice (1967a, 1967b), the American Bar Association's *Standards Relating to the Urban Police Function* (1973, 1980), and the work of the National Advisory Commission on Criminal Justice Standards and Goals (1973a). It is too early to assess the impact of the recently published CALEA standards, but discussion of the three earlier reports may suggest the prospects for this accreditation effort. In considering the three principal blue-ribbon commissions and their reports, I will touch on the origins and composition of the commissions, the context in which they worked, and the substance and impact of their recommendations.

ORIGINS

The three commissions originated in an era of extreme political controversy over the issues of crime and criminal justice. Although the last to be published, the ABA's *Standards Relating to the Urban Police Function* was the first to be conceived. It started with a proposal by Walter E. Craig, president-elect of the ABA, in May 1963, to develop a set of minimum standards for the entire criminal process. Eventually, 17 separate reports were issued, the *Urban Police Function* volume being the last. In the words of one participant, Supreme Court Justice Tom Clark, "The standards were born in a climate of deep concern over the burgeoning problems of crime and the correlative crisis in our courts occasioned by overwhelming caseloads, recidivism, and a seeming incapacity of the system to respond to the challenges of the Sixties" (Jameson 1974, p. 256; Symposium 1974, 1975).

The "challenges of the Sixties" included several historic social and political developments (see Bouza's chapter). The first was the growing momentum of the civil rights movement in the late 1950s and early 1960s. The demand for full and equal participation in American society on the part of black Americans challenged traditional practices in criminal justice, most notably police behavior in black neighborhoods. At the same time, the U.S. Supreme Court undertook a sweeping redefinition of the meaning of due process and, in a series of landmark decisions, wrote new rules for police, trial courts, juvenile courts, and correctional institutions (see Cox 1968). Meanwhile, the dramatic increase in crime between 1963 and 1973 (which interrupted nearly a century of decreasing rates of violence in America) provoked heightened public fear of crime, with a potent though somewhat delayed political impact.[2] Finally, the urban riots and militant protests against the Vietnam War sparked a political backlash that further fueled the "law and order" mood in the country.

These developments not only provided the impetus for reform, and thus the perceived need for recommended standards, but they polarized the country over the issues of crime and justice. Key Supreme Court decisions, such as the right-to-counsel ruling in *Miranda*, were the symbolic battleground for those who wanted more restraints on official criminal justice agencies and those who wanted to give them even greater latitude in fighting crime. In short, the three major commissions were launched in the context of a broad consensus on the need for reform and a sharp polarity over the direction reform should take.

The President's Commission on Law Enforcement and Administration of Justice, established by President Lyndon Johnson in early 1965, was even more directly inspired by political events. Crime had not been a major national political issue until Republican presidential candidate Barry Goldwater railed against "crime in the streets" during the 1964 election campaign. Johnson was determined to preempt the issue and created the presidential Commission and the Office of Law Enforcement Assistance (OLEA) within the Justice Department to support innovation in the field of criminal justice (Cronin et al. 1981). OLEA later became the Law Enforcement Assistance Administration (LEAA), which in turn was divided into a battery of Justice

Department offices, including the National Institute of Justice. NIJ continues to fund research on police and other criminal justice topics.

The National Advisory Commission on Criminal Justice Standards and Goals (NAC) was initiated with a $1.7 million LEAA grant in late 1971, four years after the President's Commission had published its reports and while the ABA was still wrestling with its standards for the police. The NAC sought to develop a comprehensive set of standards for the entire criminal justice system but took a somewhat different approach than the ABA project. The latter devoted most of its volume to critical "decision-points" in the criminal justice process (pretrial release, guilty pleas, sentencing, and so on). The NAC produced seven large volumes. Three dealt in a comprehensive fashion with the components of the criminal justice system (police, courts, corrections), and a fourth summarized the entire system (NAC 1973a, 1973b, 1973c, 1973d). Two others were essentially recommendations for broader criminal justice policy (NAC 1973e, 1973f), and a final volume was devoted to the proceedings of a national conference based on the other documents (NAC 1973g).

In certain respects the National Advisory Commission project was no less a partisan political effort than Johnson's Commission on Law Enforcement and Administration of Justice. The NAC was one part of the Nixon administration's LEAA-based showcase for a tough approach to crime control. The NAC's summary volume, *A National Strategy to Reduce Crime*, promised a 50 percent reduction in "high-fear" crimes within ten years.[3]

COMPOSITION

The three commissions differed somewhat in terms of their composition, that is, the occupations of their participants. The ABA project was dominated by lawyers. At least ten of the twelve members of the Advisory Committee on the Police Function[4] were attorneys, while the chair of that committee and both of the reporters, who did much of the actual drafting of the standards, were law school professors. The Advisory Committee contained only one former top police official and one police legal adviser (compared with three judges). Although police officials did not have a strong direct voice in drafting the *Urban Police Function* standards, the ABA committee did establish a close working relationship with an advisory committee from the International Association of Chiefs of Police. At least two participants in the project have argued that this linkage with the IACP — apparently the first formal working arrangement between the bar and police officials — was extremely important, particularly in terms of influencing the IACP in the direction of professionalization (Nichols 1974; Goldstein 1983).

The President's Commission drew on a much wider range of advisers and consultants. Participants included some of the most respected academic experts on the police, a number of law enforcement officials, members of the bar, and past or present elected officials. The National Advisory Commission was far more heavily dominated by police officials than either of the other two commissions. Not only was its Police Task Force chaired by a police chief (Edward M. Davis, of Los Angeles), but five of the other fourteen Task Force members were police chief executives. Meanwhile, the vice-chair of the National Advisory Commission itself was a sheriff, and four of the remaining twenty commission members were police chiefs.

SUBSTANTIVE RECOMMENDATIONS

The President's Commission produced a final report, *The Challenge of Crime in a Free Society* (1968), that contained 48 "black-letter" recommendations for the police (34 in the chapter on the police, 2 in the chapter on juvenile delinquency, and 12 in the chapter on science and technology). In addition, the commission produced accompanying volumes entitled *Task Force Report: The Police* (1967b), which provided much of the supporting evidence for the police recommendations, and *Task Force Report: Science and Technology* (1967c), which contained important material on policing.

Of the three commissions under review in this essay, the work of the President's Commission is unique in two major respects. It was most obviously shaped by the crisis atmosphere of the mid-1960s. The commission began and completed its work during the period of urban racial violence that swept the country from 1964 to 1968. The commission's recommendations are evidently skewed in the direction of attempting to address the immediate police-community relations crisis. At the same time, the commission is responsible for launching a "research revolution" in American policing. The commission itself sponsored some of the most important early field research on police activity (Reiss 1971; Black 1980). The impact of this continuing research revolution has been enormous (Walker 1983a, chaps. 1, 13; see also Bouza's chapter). The most significant recent addition to the police literature, for example, is the essay, "Broken Windows," by James Q. Wilson and George L. Kelling (1982). Their controversial effort to rethink the nature of the police role draws its inspiration from the major contributions of the research revolution.

The sequence of the President's Commission's recommendations about the police reveals the effect of the prevailing crisis atmosphere. The recommendations begin with the area of community relations, move to personnel matters, and conclude with organization and management. This represents a reversal of the sequence found in the standard police texts, wherein considerations of organizational structure precede and dominate all others and where community relations is virtually an afterthought (see, for example, Wilson and McLaren 1977). The crisis provoked by Supreme Court decisions of the preceding few years also weighs heavily on the commission's report. The chapter on the police begins with a discussion of the legal authority underlying police work, and the very first recommendation concerns the then-unresolved question of the legality of "stop and frisk" practices.

To address community relations problems, the commission recommended that police departments create formal Police Community Relations (PCR) units, develop citizens' advisory committees in minority group neighborhoods, recruit and promote more minority group officers, and establish formal procedures for handling citizen complaints (President's Commission 1968, pp. 255–65). Two of the most novel and controversial recommendations were also inspired by police-community relations considerations. The commission recommended experiments with the then-new concept of "team policing" and proposed dividing police functions into three distinct roles, each with its own entry requirements and career tracks. The "Police Agent" would concentrate primarily on criminal investigation, the "Police Officer" would carry out routine patrol, and the "Community Service Officer" (CSO) would handle many of the less critical police tasks. The CSO position was presented as a way of facilitating recruitment of minority group officers (many of whom, it was assumed, would subsequently move up into one of the other two career tracks) (President's Commission 1968, pp. 274–75, 298).

The President's Commission reiterated many of the traditional items on the police professionalization agenda, recommendations that can be traced back through the works of O. W. Wilson, the Wickersham Commission, and the very early work of August Vollmer and Raymond Fosdick (Fogelson 1977; Walker 1977).[5] In doing so, however, the commission confronted a serious dilemma: Many if not most of these recommendations conflicted with the new concern with community relations.[6] The commission recommended higher educational standards for police officers but acknowledged that this would bar many racial minorities from police employment (President's Commission 1968, p. 274). The three-tiered entry system was designed to resolve this conflict. The commission recommended further centralization of command and control within police departments, yet this conflicted with the simultaneous endorsement of team policing, a community relations-oriented decentralization of police operations. This tension between the conflicting demands of centralized command and control and community-oriented flexibility remains an important though unresolved issue in American policing (see Schwartz and Clarren 1977, p. 7).

Other major recommendations of the blue-ribbon panels included a variety of old standards and novel items. The NAC recommended the pooling and/or consolidation of services among small departments and departments in metropolitan areas. This proposal had been a standard item in public administration circles for nearly four decades (Merriam et al. 1933; Norrgard 1969; President's Commission 1968; see Ostrom, Parks, and Whitaker 1978 for a critique of the proposal). At the same time, both the President's Commission and the NAC recommended the development of state-level agencies that would establish minimum standards for police agencies within each state. New York and California had pioneered with this concept (with respect to training standards only) in 1959. Reflecting a growing awareness of the importance of discretion in policing, both the President's Commission and the NAC recommended that departments develop guidelines for the exercise of discretion. The President's Commission offered a separate, more specific recommendation for guidelines on the use of deadly force.

The ABA standards and the NAC report are both more comprehensive than the work of the President's Commission in their coverage of policing, in large measure because they followed the presidential commission's report by six years and drew on the rapidly accumulating literature on policing that the earlier commission helped to spawn. Both documents, unlike the President's Commission report, seek to offer a complete and rationally organized set of minimum standards. Moreover, neither seems to be as directly influenced by a crisis atmosphere as was the President's Commission.

The ABA's *Urban Police Function* report is particularly interesting because it resulted from two failed attempts to draft standards for the police. The story of these initial failures is important because it reveals the rapidly changing currents of thought among police experts. The Police Advisory Committee to the ABA's Standing Committee on Association Standards for Criminal Justice began by drafting a set of recommendations on management issues that police chiefs regularly encounter (for example, height requirements for recruits). This effort was abandoned as being beyond the scope of expertise of members of the legal profession. In a second effort, the committee set out to draft standards relating to issues of traditional concern to lawyers, primarily constitutional standards for police activity. This approach was abandoned when it was recognized that the standards would be essentially negative in thrust – that is, they would set forth guidelines on what the police should not do but say little about what the police *should* do (Remington 1975).

At this point, the Police Advisory Committee seriously considered abandoning the project altogether. But at the urging of Chief Justice Warren Burger, a third attempt was made (Remington 1975, pp. 461–62). This ultimately successful effort bears the strong imprint of Herman Goldstein, who served as the initial reporter for the committee (from 1969 through December 1970) and who has been one of the most thoughtful and original thinkers in the police field for the past two decades. Goldstein's contribution to the *Urban Police Function* report was to cast it in terms of a fundamental rethinking of the police role – the issue to which he has devoted the bulk of his professional writings (see Goldstein 1977, 1979, 1981, 1982a, 1982b, 1982c).

The Goldstein view begins with the principle that the police role involves "complex and multiple tasks." While the police are formally an agency of criminal justice, they undertake a wide range of public order maintenance tasks and, in fact, rarely invoke the criminal process. This view reflected the emerging consensus of police scholars in the 1960s and is today part of the conventional wisdom. In the words of other scholars, the police are essentially "peacekeepers" rather than law enforcers and routinely act as "philosopher, guide, and friend" (Cumming, Cumming, and Edell 1965; see also Banton 1964). The peacekeeping view of the police contrasts sharply with the conventional crimefighter image. Goldstein's point is that meaningful police reform must begin with a recognition of what the police actually do, not with the false image that both the media and the police themselves project. Traditional police reform had been organized around the idea of enhancing the crime-fighting effectiveness of the police (Goldstein 1977, chaps. 1, 2).

Because it begins with such a radically different premise, *The Urban Police Function* is the most innovative of the three reports under consideration. This is not immediately apparent, as many of the specific standards it recommends are fairly conventional. The needs for improved personnel standards, for effective internal management controls, and for research and planning, for example, are extremely conventional proposals that few would challenge. The ABA standards contain nothing as seemingly novel as the President's Commission's recommendations of team policing and the three-tiered entry/career track system. However, the idea that the police should conceptualize their role in terms of non-law enforcement activities and organize their resources accordingly is a far more radical proposal than anything found in the President's Commission report. Toward this end, *The Urban Police Function* recommended that the police employ "methods other than arrest and prosecution to deal with the variety of behavioral and social problems which they confront" (Standard 3.3).

The Urban Police Function also broke new ground in its last section on "Evaluation." It rejected as inappropriate the traditional crime control-oriented measures of police performance: arrests, clearance rates, crime rates (Standard 10.1). And it proposed the development of alternative measures that would adequately reflect the broad range of responsibilities of the police.[7] The report also gave strong endorsement to a wide range of mechanisms for the control of police activities, including the still-controversial exclusionary rule, tort liability for individual officials and governmental units, and injunctive relief (Standards 5.1–5.5). These external mechanisms of accountability, it was urged, should be supplemented by internal mechanisms, including a comprehensive set of guidelines governing all police activities. Finally, the report acknowledged that punitive sanctions were not sufficient and that positive rewards for good performance were also necessary.

In light of the relative prominence of police officials on the NAC's drafting committee, it is not surprising that the NAC's report covers police management issues in much more detail than is true of either of the other two commissions. For example, the NAC volume offers specific recommendations relating to physical fitness and police uniforms. Somewhat surprisingly for a management-oriented document, the report endorses the right of police officers to form unions (Standard 18.3). This could be interpreted as a concession to reality. Unions had not even been mentioned in the President's Commission report, but between 1967 and 1973 unionism swept American policing and became an established fact of life (Walker 1983a, chaps. 12, 13; see also Bouza's chapter).

The NAC recommendations on the police role are rather similar to the ABA standards (more so than one might have expected, given the disparate composition of the two groups). While not going quite as far as the ABA standards, the NAC report begins with the recommendation that police departments should develop explicit policy statements concerning their role (Standard 1.1). Although the report clearly defines the police role primarily in terms of crime control, it recognizes the need for flexibility in carrying out that role. Thus the first three standards call on police departments to develop their own "mission" statements (implying that different agencies might have different roles and priorities) and policies limiting the misuse of authority and formally recognizing police discretion (Standards 1.1, 1.2, 1.3). According to the NAC, formal recognition of discretion would involve seeking legislative authority for the exercise of discretion and developing internal policies to govern its exercise.

These recommendations further testify to the rapidly changing currents of thought in police circles. Only a few years before, it would have been unthinkable for the chiefs of major police departments to discuss openly the complexity of the police role, to endorse formal limits on police authority, to admit that police misused that authority, or to acknowledge that the police routinely exercise discretion.

The National Advisory Commission also endorsed two novel concepts originally proferred by the President's Commission: experiments with team policing (NAC Standards 6.1, 6.2) and development of expanded career opportunities within particular job and rank classifications (Standard 14.2). But whereas the President's Commission attempted to deal with the issue of job enrichment through its three-tiered entry/career track proposal, the NAC suggested that officers have an opportunity to obtain advancement (in the form of salary increments and specialist designation) within a particular rank or assignment. Both commissions' proposals were attempts to deal with the widely recognized problem of career stagnation and low morale among rank-and-file police officers.

ASSESSING THE IMPACT

Even the principal participants in the three major blue-ribbon commissions find it extremely difficult to evaluate the impact of their recommendations. In large part, the problem is assigning causality. It would be relatively easy, for example, to devise a checklist for each of the three reports and then, either through a national survey or selected case studies, determine the extent of compliance. Thus we could determine how many departments experimented with team policing or developed the recommended policy on deadly force or raised their minimum educational requirements. But this would not necessarily tell us whether any of the three reports had played a role in influencing that change. One could argue, for example, that recent changes in deadly force policy have been a result of political pressure and/or court rulings (see Geller 1982, pp. 151-77). In this context, the specific recommendation of the President's Commission may have been irrelevant. Conversely, some of the most important changes in policing clearly were not impelled by blue-ribbon commissions. For example, unionism, which has completely altered the landscape of police management since the late 1960s, took hold years before the ABA and NAC standards recommended its acceptance, even then as a concession to an inescapable reality. As indicated, the President's Commission did not even mention unionism, much less endorse it. Not all change, in other words, is planned change, and it is difficult to isolate the impact of planning documents — the blue-ribbon commission reports under review here — in the larger context of a continually changing police. Nonetheless, on a number of important issues — personnel standards, minority recruitment, the control of discretion — the various commission reports have served to frame the context of public debate and, in that respect, stimulated and shaped the direction of police reform.

An inherent problem with all blue-ribbon commissions is the absence of any enforcement mechanism and the consequent reliance on voluntary compliance. The extent of that voluntary effort is highly questionable. The American Bar Association developed an elaborate implementation process, involving wide dissemination of the published reports and planned meetings in local communities with bar association leaders, public officials, and other civic activists (Nichols 1974). For the most part, blue-ribbon commissions have not addressed the problems of implementation. One critic pointed out that the NAC's report on *Corrections* was "virtually silent" on the question of implementation (Vanagunas 1976, p. 237). Even if a realistic implementation plan were outlined, powerful obstacles would stand in the way. Vanagunas argues that the NAC's corrections standards threaten established bureaucratic interests and impose considerable fiscal demands. Cole and Neubauer (1976), meanwhile, fault the NAC's court standards for overemphasizing structural change and ignoring the social and political dynamics of court operations and, thereby, simply missing the point on the courts and their problems. The same argument can be made with respect to most of the reports on the police.

Moreover, some recommendations are more easily implemented than others. The ABA seems to have a good track record of implementing standards that can be adopted or imposed through decisions by appellate courts or through court-promulgated rules of criminal procedure. By 1974, various ABA standards had been cited in an estimated 2,000 appellate court opinions (Nichols 1974, p. 269), and over the ensuing decade the number of citations has grown to approximately 12,000 (Lynch 1984). It has made less progress, however, with standards, such as the police recommendations, whose adoption would be the primary responsibility of the executive and legislative branches of government (Wilson 1974).

Despite general concerns about establishing causation, some cautious views may be offered regarding the impact of the recommendations of the three reports. For these purposes, the recommendations may be divided into three general categories. On one level certain aspects of the reports have had an indirect but nonetheless pervasive and important influence on American policing. On another level, certain recommendations have in fact been implemented, in some cases successfully and in others unsuccessfully. Finally, there are certain recommendations that fell on deaf ears and have had no impact whatsoever on American policing.

The most important impact of the three reports has been in the first category, the conceptual arena. Together, they have given authoritative endorsement and publicity to new ideas about policing. Goldstein (1983) observes that the notion that police have a complex and multidimensional role today pervades the literature. Similarly, it is now generally recognized that police officers routinely exercise discretion and that these decisions constitute the making of social policy. There is also a general (though not unanimous) opinion that the exercise of discretion should be guided through an explicit planning and policymaking process. These were bold, radical ideas 20 years ago. Today, they are (or are rapidly becoming) the conventional wisdom (see Cordner's chapter).

One of the ways in which it seems clear that the blue-ribbon bodies fundamentally affected concepts of policing is indirectly through research sponsored and inspired by the President's Commission. Besides funding some of the earliest and most important observational studies of police work (Reiss 1971; Black 1980), the commission inspired, directly or indirectly, three of the most important subsequent pieces of research: the Kansas City Preventive Patrol Experiment (Kelling et al. 1974a), the Rand study of the criminal investigation process (Greenwood et al. 1975), and the studies of police response time (U.S. Department of Justice 1978b). Evidence from this research has lent support to a reconceptualization of policing, particularly a downgrading of the importance of the crime-fighting role (Walker 1983a, chap. 13; Wilson and Kelling 1982).

A number of recommendations fall into the category of those adopted with varying degrees of success. On the one hand, virtually all departments have increased the length of recruit training and introduced new subjects (particularly in the area of race relations and human relations) into the curriculum

(Walker 1983a, pp. 265–68). On the other hand, few departments have raised the minimum entry-level requirement for educational achievement. A high school diploma suffices in more than 90 percent of all departments. Despite this low minimum requirement, however, the overall level of educational attainment has risen significantly (U.S. Department of Justice 1978a). This is a result of both the selection of recruits with more than a high school education and the continued educational pursuits of sworn officers (facilitated in large part by LEAA's Law Enforcement Education Program [LEEP] in the 1970s).

A mixed pattern of recommendation adoption is reflected, too, in the recruitment of minority group police officers. Despite the exhortations of the three major commissions, and virtually every other expert in the field, voluntary affirmative action efforts have been the exception rather than the rule. Progress in equal employment opportunity has often been the result of litigation and court-ordered hiring plans (Walker 1983c).

Administrative controls over police discretion have grown, but it is difficult to assess this situation with precision. A large and detailed procedure manual is currently the norm in American policing, at least among the large (300 + officers) departments. Yet these manuals tend to overemphasize internal regulations (wearing of hats while on duty or protocol for addressing superior officers) rather than practices relating to police-citizen contacts. The most notable progress has occurred with respect to deadly force policy (Geller 1982; Geller and Karales 1981a, 1981b; Milton et al. 1977). But there has been only spotty progress in terms of controlling officer discretion in general arrest situations.[8]

With respect to police-community relations, most big city police departments did follow the President's Commission's recommendation and create a special PCR unit. But in the view of police experts, these units generally have low status and are peripheral to basic police operations and hence have little direct impact on an agency's relationship with racial minority group communities (U.S. Department of Justice 1973). Moreover, many PCR units or programs have been eliminated or downgraded as a result of the fiscal constraints of the late 1970s and early 1980s (Malcolm 1975).

A large number of departments adopted the recommendation of both the President's Commission and the NAC to experiment with team policing. The idea emerged as one of the more popular fads of the early 1970s. The early experiments did not fulfill their proponents' expectations, however, and team policing soon lost most of its glamour. The concept survives in name,[9] but it is questionable whether programs currently bearing that label contain many of the key elements of the original concept. Indeed, there is serious doubt that the concept ever received a true test, given the problems and compromises involved in the experiments that did occur (Sherman, Milton, and Kelly 1973; Schwartz and Clarren 1977; U.S. Department of Justice 1977; cf. Hastings 1984).

There has been a small but noticeable trend in the direction of consolidation of small police departments (with the disappearance of about 1,000 agencies in the past few years), but this development remains marginal to the mainstream of American policing (U.S. Department of Justice 1980, p. 6). The development of state law enforcement commissions and state-required training for all sworn officers has been far more significant. More than 30 states now require training for all officers. The impact of this development has been felt most strongly on small police departments.

A number of major recommendations by the three commissions have had little if any impact on American policing. If the idea that the police have a complex role to play has gained wide acceptance, it is difficult to discern where it has had any practical impact on policing. Meanwhile, the ABA's suggestion that alternative measures of police effectiveness be developed has prompted some discussion (U.S. Department of Justice 1982) but produced few results. Nor are there more than a few isolated experiments with either the President's Commission's proposal for Community Service Officers or the NAC's expanded career track concept.

In the end, the impact of blue-ribbon commissions on American policing remains ambiguous. The recommendations of these commissions clearly have an important indirect influence on the halting progress of police reform. But they may not have a direct effect, and one cannot assert confidently that they are immediately responsible for effecting change. Rather, the reports of these blue-ribbon commissions should be regarded as major chapters in the history of police reform. They are occasions for the articulation of the received wisdom concerning minimum standards and, in varying degrees, the vehicles for disseminating and endorsing new and controversial ideas. Whatever their direct impact, these standards-setting efforts clearly have played a significant role in stimulating and shaping police reform efforts.

SOME THOUGHTS ON ACCREDITATION

In mid-1983 the Commission on Accreditation for Law Enforcement Agencies (CALEA) published its *Standards* manual, containing well over 100 specific standards, and began the formal process of reviewing agencies for accreditation. Although a definitive judgment on this project would be premature, my review of the three blue-ribbon commissions may offer some useful perspectives.

The idea of law enforcement accreditation grew out of the work of these blue-ribbon commissions. The National Advisory Commission (1973a, p. vii) noted the absence of "a document to which a police administrator can go to establish and maintain an effective police agency." In 1970 and 1976 the IACP submitted proposals to LEAA requesting funds to develop a comprehensive set of standards. Both requests were denied. The present Commission on Accreditation was established by a 1979 LEAA grant to the IACP and three other organizations: the National Organization of Black Law Enforcement Executives (NOBLE), the National Sheriffs' Association (NSA), and the Police Executive Research Forum (PERF) (U.S. Department of Justice 1979, p. 1). The composition of the group is significant. Not only does it deny the IACP an exclusive jurisdiction over accreditation but it includes two groups – PERF and NOBLE – that, in different ways, have been critical of the IACP. Indeed, PERF was founded, at least in part, as an alternative to the IACP for research-oriented police executives (see the Skolnick-McCoy chapter). Inclusion of NOBLE, moreover, lends significant visibility to an organization representing black police officials.

Three and one-half years were devoted to launching the accreditation process. The initial phases involved drafting and revising standards for particular aspects of policing and then field-testing these standards on selected agencies. CALEA began accepting applications from agencies seeking accreditation on October 1, 1983. In the first month, 33 applications were submitted (CALEA 1983b) and, within a year, 175 agencies had applied (Dodenhoff 1984, p. 11; see also CALEA 1984). On May 25, 1984, the 24-member Mt. Dora, Florida, Police Department became the first law enforcement agency to be accredited by CALEA (Washington Crime News Services 1984a, pp. 8-9), and on November 2, 1984, accreditation was voted for four more: the Baltimore County, Maryland, Police Department, the Arlington County, Virginia, Police Department, the North Providence, Rhode Island, Police Department, and the Elkhart, Indiana Sheriff's Department (O'Connell 1984; see also Dodenhoff 1984). By May 1985 the number of accredited agencies had grown to 12.

The accreditation process is purely voluntary. While many departments may opt for undergoing the review process, there is no direct penalty for not doing so. In this respect the accreditation effort faces the same problem of voluntarism as did the recommendations of the three blue-ribbon commissions. Two comparisons illustrate the inherent weakness of the voluntary approach. Accreditation in higher education is also voluntary, but with a difference. For the most part, federal monies (especially for student aid) are unavailable to students enrolled in unaccredited institutions. Thus the potent muscle of federal financial assistance undergirds the nominally voluntary accreditation process (Finkin 1973). British law enforcement presents an equally instructive contrast. In England, local police agencies receive half of their annual budget from the national government if they pass a formal, nationally administered inspection (Critchley 1972, pp. 190-94). Thus a government subsidy is the stick by which minimum standards are enforced. No such compulsory mechanism exists in the present American accreditation movement.

Another obstacle facing the CALEA effort is the opposition of some state and local professional law enforcement groups to the idea of national standards (concerning objections by California and New York police chiefs, see Washington Crime News Services 1984b, p. 1; Dodenhoff 1984). Under pressure from such police executive associations, the IACP in 1984 retreated from its initial strong support for CALEA, deleting from its original resolution favoring the concept of accreditation any specific mention of CALEA (Dodenhoff 1984). A third and perhaps even more serious question concerns the content and likely impact of the standards themselves. Here, again, comparison with the field of education is illuminating. By their very nature, written standards relate to measurable phenomena and not necessarily to the actual quality of the service that is to be delivered. In education, for example, it is quite possible for an institution to meet the minimal standards (number of volumes in the library, existence of science laboratories, and the like) and yet simply have no academic standards whatsoever. Even the standards that come closest to controlling the quality of those delivering the service will not necessarily achieve that end. The fact that a certain percentage of the faculty at one college have doctorates does not ensure that those people are conscientious and competent teachers or researchers.

A preliminary review of the content of the recently published CALEA standards reveals a mixed pattern, ranging from strong, progressive requirements to a deafening silence on critical issues. For example, on the one hand, the deadly force standard is fairly progressive (it falls short of the "defense-of-life" approach but is stricter than the policies employed by many police departments) (CALEA 1983a). On the other hand, the standards contain only a general statement with respect to the broader question of discretion. Standard 1.2.2 requires departments to have "a written directive [that] governs the use of discretion by sworn officers." The standards contain nothing more specific about discretion in making arrests, despite the widespread attention that such matters have been receiving within the police community, particularly on such matters as domestic violence arrests (see Loving 1980; Sherman and Berk 1984). Presumably a police department could achieve accreditation merely by having a written policy on the subject of discretion, regardless of the policy's content.

Traditionally, accreditation has been a process for weeding out the absolute worst, for example, the school with no library at all (on accreditation, generally, see Simpson 1979). Similarly, the police accreditation standards are likely to be a prod for reform in the most deficient departments. Perhaps this expectation will be surpassed, and the CALEA effort will encourage further improvement in better departments. Standard 1.1.1, for example, requires "the formulation, annual updating, and distribution to all personnel of written goals and objectives for the agency and for each organizational component within the agency." For the most part, even the more competent American police agencies do not think about their goals and objectives and rarely if ever put such thoughts down on paper. The accreditation movement, by providing local actors with a useful frame of reference, may cause police agencies to take the first important step down the road to thoughtful planning and analysis.

One unresolved issue concerning the long-term impact of accreditation involves the relationship of accreditation standards to litigation. It is entirely possible that an agency could use its "accredited" status to defeat lawsuits challenging its present policies or practices. There are undoubtedly many courts — and insurance companies — that would be receptive to the argument that the agency meets accepted professional standards by virtue of accreditation (see Dodenhoff 1984, pp. 11, 14). In this respect, however, accreditation raises the danger of establishing an inadequate "floor." It is still too early in the accreditation process to make a final judgment on this matter.

The road to police improvement is a long and tortuous one indeed. Accreditation standards, like the recommendations of the three blue-ribbon commissions reviewed here, may be important milestones on that road. The historical record seems to suggest that we can conclude on a note of cautious optimism. Previous blue-ribbon commissions have not, by any means, transformed American policing. But they have made significant contributions to police reform. Even in the absence of any enforcement mechanism, simply by virtue of "setting the standards" they have shaped the thinking and the efforts of all those individuals and groups who have pursued the goal of a professional police in a free society.

NOTES

1. There is very little literature on the impact of the three commissions under review. On the President's Commission, generally, see Wilson (1967) and Walker (1978, pp. 1–12), and with reference to the police, see Walker (1983a, chap. 13). On the National Advisory Commission, see Cole and Neubauer (1976, pp. 293–99); Singer (1977a, 1977b); and Vanagunas (1976). And see, generally, Skoler (1977), Walker (1983b), Newman and Sweeney (1970), and Goldstein (1977, chap. 12).

2. The most useful compendium of data on both criminal activity and public opinion is U.S. Department of Justice (annual). These volumes provide the appropriate references to the original sources of data.

3. The NAC was created by LEAA Director Jerris Leonard, who felt that the agency's primary mission was crime reduction. He was succeeded in 1973 by Donald Santarelli, who defined LEAA's goals in terms of "system improvement," a subtle but important distinction (Cronin et al. 1981, p. 137).

4. This group should not be confused with the American Bar Association's Standing Committee on Association Standards for Criminal Justice, of which the Advisory Committee was a part.

5. Fosdick, who subsequently became the president of the Rockefeller Foundation, wrote the pioneering 1920 survey, *American Police Systems*. August Vollmer served as chief of police in Berkeley, California, from 1909 until 1932. He did more than any other person to promote police professionalization in the first three decades of this century. O. W. Wilson was Vollmer's most notable protégé. After working under Vollmer for a few years, he became chief of police

in Wichita, Kansas (1928-39), dean of the School of Criminology at the University of California, and then superintendent of the Chicago police (1960-67). He was also author of an enormously influential textbook, the most recent edition of which is Wilson and McLaren (1977).

6. This dilemma was most explicitly noted by the Kerner Commission: "Indeed, many of the serious disturbances took place in cities whose police are among the best led, best organized, best trained and most professional in the country" (National Advisory Commission on Civil Disorders 1968, p. 301).

7. Developing alternative measures of police performance has proven to be an awesome undertaking. Not only do the police perform many different tasks (crime fighting, order maintenance, service) but there is no consensus on the proper criteria for evaluating any of these tasks. The values of effectiveness, efficiency, equity, and accountability make their separate and at times competing claims. For a thorough review of this extremely complex subject, see U.S. Department of Justice (1982).

8. The recent trend toward specific policies with respect to arrest in domestic violence situations is the exception that proves the rule (see Loving 1980; Sherman and Berk 1984).

9. Nineteen of the 50 police departments responding to a 1977 survey of police administrative practices (Heaphy 1978) indicated that they maintained team policing.

32
Research and the
Police Administrator:
Working Smarter, Not Harder

James K. Stewart

Throughout history, societies have formed governments to protect themselves against invaders from without and predators within. Maintaining public order so that all of us can go about our lives in reasonable security is a fundamental obligation of our own government. Americans traditionally have looked to the police to provide the security guaranteed them in our Constitution. Today, however, there are signs that the traditional authority of police may be slipping away. Fiscal stringencies and management decisions to cut back services are having unintended consequences. Continuing public concern over crime, fueled by the individual's fear of becoming a victim, has, almost imperceptibly, chipped away at confidence in law enforcement and led many to seek ways to bolster their self-protection. Their decisions suggest a changing public view of the role of police.

A growing number of police executives recognize that we are at a crossroads. Many of us concerned with the future of law enforcement sense that pressures are building that will force a fundamental reassessment of policing as we approach the twenty-first century. This chapter discusses some of the trends that brought police to this point and notes some consequences likely to flow from these trends. It reflects the perspective of one who has spent many years in police administration and now sees law enforcement from a different vantage point: as director of a national research program. My experience tells me that the future of police as an institution that exercises leadership rests with police executives and the decisions they make in the next few years. If they invest in developing knowledge now—through research and experimentation—they will be in a much stronger position to make their voices heard and emerge as principal managers of public safety in the next decades.

PRESSURES FOR CHANGE

Beginning in the mid-1960s, American anxiety about public safety mounted as crime spiralled upward (Gallup 1982). As high crime rates continued, people turned to the experts – police, judges, academia, government officials – for answers. But what they heard was anything but reassuring. Those in authority began to retreat from accountability for controlling crime. Even in police circles, the rhetoric spoke of how little direct effect police had on crime (Wilson 1975). Such remarks were intended to convey the complexity of the crime problem, but they sent other signals to the public that suggested official abdication of responsibility for controlling crime.

It is plausible to assume that this apparent lack of accountability coupled with a continuing perception of risk has contributed to waning public confidence in police. A 1981 poll found that half those surveyed had little or no confidence the police could protect them from crime ("The Plague of Violent Crime" 1981). And, despite decreases in reported crime during the past three years, the perception of crime and the need to do something about it remains extraordinarily high. A 1984 Roper survey shows that crime and drug abuse top the list of American worries, exceeding concerns about the economy and other national issues ("Our Worries: Crime, Drugs Top Economy" 1984).

Diminishing Resources and Fragmented Jurisdiction

Despite their concern, however, the public seems unwilling to invest additional resources in public law enforcement. After some 25 years of increasing investment in police protection (Jacob and Lineberry 1982), departments faced shrinking budgets. By 1981, 44 percent of police executives and sheriffs surveyed reported the same or fewer personnel in 1981 than in 1976 (Cunningham and Taylor 1984). Measures to restore funds and maintain levels of services cut in so-called taxpayer revolts have met with mixed results at the polls. In California, for example, voters approved special police taxes in two jurisdictions but rejected such measures in cities like Oakland, Los Angeles, and Pasadena (Stellwagen and Gettinger 1984).

The resource crunch has forced police to make tough decisions about services. Police managers have, with increasing regularity, divested some of their jurisdictional authority to other autonomous public agencies. In cities across the nation, the number of special jurisdiction police has been growing. Public housing projects, parks, public schools, stadiums, transit authorities, and even harbors and highways have their own police organization, authority, and jurisdictions. This trend suggests a desire for specialized police services and a perception that these services can best be delivered by specialists operating separately from traditional police.

The question arises, however, whether decisions to cede chunks of jurisdictional authority may be shortsighted. The public is paying for these services, but it is unclear whether such specialization is a prudent investment of public resources. These agencies promulgate their own policies, establish their own rules of conduct, and decide which cases they ought to present for prosecution. Generally there is little formal coordination or routine cooperation on interjurisdictional crime problems.

Private Security Growth

Taxpayer resistance to government spending does not reflect indifference to the need for protection against crime. On the contrary, public perception of the staggering costs of crime — not just direct losses but such indirect "crime taxes" as decreased property values and dwindling business — has generated even more demand. But the public has increasingly turned to private and collective safety substitutes to enhance basic levels of police protection.

As certain assignments — foot patrols, watchman duties, responding to alarms — have been reduced by economy-minded police, private security has been increasingly available to step in and fill the gaps. By 1982, private security personnel outnumbered publicly sworn officers by about two to one, according to National Institute of Justice research. In stark contrast to police administrators, private security directors reported substantial budget increases during 1977-81. Half reported annual revenue increases of more than 15 percent — this during a period of general recession. The study also projected that security revenues would soon reach $15 to $20 billion annually. And the future looks bright: One market research estimate predicts revenues of $53 billion in 1995 (Cunningham and Taylor 1984).

Private security is expanding in scope as well (see Shanahan's chapter). In addition to their traditional loss prevention duties, private security personnel in some areas have taken on, with the initial blessing of police officials, duties usually carried out by publicly sworn officers. In New York City, for example, security personnel in some of the major department stores make arrests, file reports, maintain records, assign NYPD arrest numbers, and transport suspects in their own private paddy wagons to city jails.

Private protection is no longer reserved for business and industry. Neighborhood groups and condominium dwellers have pooled resources to hire private security guards to patrol their streets and buildings. Burglar alarms, ranging from expensive electronic systems to inexpensive intrusion alarms, have become police surrogates for many Americans. One National Institute study found that 40 percent of those surveyed in ten major cities had installed some kind of security device — alarms, special locks, window bars, and so forth — in their homes (Jacob and Lineberry 1982).

Citizen Activism

In addition to buying protection, many people are investing their own time and energy in functions performed by police. Rather than leaving crime solely to the "experts," they have increasingly taken steps to reduce their vulnerability and fear by watching, patrolling, and gathering information on crimes and suspects in their neighborhood. Efforts such as Home Alert, Neighborhood Watch, Apartment Watch, Crimestoppers, and other grassroots organizations have spread across the country. They have sprung up not only in middle-class or suburban areas but in inner-city neighborhoods as well (Lavrakas 1981).

Police have recognized the potential of such groups in supplementing their limited resources and improving communication with the communities they serve. Some 90 percent of police and sheriffs departments have established formal crime prevention programs (Cunningham and Taylor 1984), and a number of chiefs have cited citizen involvement as a positive force in recent declines in crime.

MODELS FOR THE FUTURE

These trends in public safety place new demands on police executives. They come in the wake of two decades of significant reforms that altered police policies on arrest, search and seizure, use of force, civil disorder management, patrol practices, and hiring and promotions. Unlike those largely inward-looking reforms, today's pressures require police to grapple with more fundamental questions about their role in public safety. Will police be leaders, partners, or cogs in the public safety apparatus? In thinking about the future of the police, there appear to be several different alternatives, each with its own set of implications for those concerned with policing.

Status Quo

This future represents a business-as-usual stance. Police would remain essentially reactive to the market forces outlined above. The orientation would be toward efficiency rather than fundamental change. Police would patrol the streets and respond to citizens' calls, attempting to provide more or less traditional services within the confines of limited resources. There would be little in the way of crime analysis or directed patrol. But resources are likely to be even more constrained as demand continues to rise. A new survey reveals a 20 percent average increase in calls for service from 1976 to 1981 (Levine 1984).

Who would fill the resulting vacuum? Given the competitive fiscal climate, one might see other "blue" forces that have arisen from specific jurisdictional authority delegated away from police — regional park police or county sheriffs, for example — step in with a different level or combination of services that might be more appealing to the community. The private security industry could be expected to vie for a larger share of the market. And citizens might well expand their neighborhood and community prevention activities.

Thus a status quo future could change the existing "authority ratios." Further encroachment on police territory might relegate chiefs to fighting to maintain budgets and basic functions, responding to serious street crime in some neighborhoods while allowing other less crime-ridden areas to search for alternative protection. If the perceived loss and fragmentation of authority by police were sufficient, public confidence could be further undermined, with the attendant risks of more aggressive citizen activism and even vigilantism. Serious questions of equity could arise as more affluent neighborhoods were able to garner greater protection from nonpublic sources than those without such assets.

Free Market

Another possibility for the future would see the growth of a "free market" approach to the delivery of police service. As the number of alternative agencies capable of providing safety services increases, some local governments — particularly those under severe fiscal stress — might look to them to deliver services such as preventive patrol in business or residential communities.

Changes are already taking place in the way certain services are delivered in some jurisdictions. They range from user fees to "privatization" of functions. A number of public services have been turned over to private enterprise, including operation and management of hospitals, ambulance services, and solid waste collection and disposal (Shulman 1982). Another possibility is that services shift to other levels of government — a county assumes responsibility for a city jail. Still another is that selected services are discontinued entirely.

It is unlikely that essential police services would be discontinued, but cities are not obligated to maintain a traditional approach to their delivery. The reason that privatization has not encroached on law enforcement to a significant degree may be because no one is promoting it as a viable option — yet. If alternative services become available at lower cost, however, police involvement in certain functions might well be seen as an expensive anachronism. Disengagement of police from providing certain peripheral services — policing private establishments and events, transporting VIPs, licensing bicycles — would be welcomed by many police administrators. The issue, however, is not really services but authority and who exercises it.

In the extreme, public police leadership might be isolated from decisions concerning the functions to be shifted and the staff to be cut. Privatization also raises questions about where liability would rest for those empowered to use force to make an arrest, how the courts would deal with evidentiary issues, and whether existing case law on search and seizure would apply under these new circumstances. For the public, concerns over justice and fairness, the right to privacy, and equitable and reliable distribution of services could be expected.

Regionalization

A third possibility would combine increased contracting out for specific public safety services, expansion of cooperative arrangements, and perhaps reorganization on a regional basis. Many smaller departments have already turned to the first two methods as ways of saving or sharing costs. Police regularly purchase such services as vehicle and communications equipment maintenance, data processing, parking enforcement, traffic control, training, crime prevention, and dispatching. Pooling of resources to enjoy scale economies in certain functions such as forensics, communications, or training is increasingly common.

Although financially attractive, consolidation or regionalization of agencies has met with less acceptance (Skoler 1980). Many local governments and police chiefs view it as a threat to local control and independence. Others argue that consolidated agencies are no more effective or cost-efficient than smaller departments.

Consolidation is workable but not necessarily superior to today's organization. The issue of local control might be resolved through creation of a formal advisory board or committee on which local agencies represent local concerns and review service accomplishments or disagreements (Koepsell and Girard 1979). British police have moved toward the regional model, consolidating 100 individual departments into 43 agencies. The smallest of these commands several thousand officers. The central government funds 50 to 70 percent of agency expenditures, with the remaining funds drawn from local revenues. Each community is represented on local police authorities that review policies in consultation with the central government (Home Office 1984).

Consolidation can provide a greater range of service at a lower cost and has the potential to improve coordination in dealing with regional crime problems. Bigger is not always better, of course. Some research on police agency structure suggests that smaller departments perform patrol activities more efficiently than larger departments and can have closer ties with the community. On the other hand, large departments rank higher in specialized services, such as sophisticated criminal investigation units (Whitaker 1983). Thus creation of larger regional agencies could put police in a position to mount more sophisticated efforts to cope with the growing complexity of lawlessness, such as computer crime, drug trafficking, terrorism, organized crime, and white-collar crime.

Whether regionalization could ever take hold in America, given our strong traditions of localism in law enforcement, is an open question. However, issues of crime control effectiveness and economic considerations are increasing pressure for improved management. Regionalization is no panacea, but expanded arrangements for sharing responsibilities and costs may be an option police can no longer afford to ignore.

Obviously, movement toward regionalism would have to proceed incrementally in full recognition of the political accommodations required. Concerns over policy in areas of enforcement, staffing, services, and use of force need to be addressed. Questions of how to allocate costs and issues related to personnel are crucial. The often-cited problem of "too many chiefs" is an obstacle (Koepsell and Girard 1979) but may be resolved by such means as creating an overall public safety director and permitting existing chiefs to retain their rank and salary. The experience of those involved in such efforts — policing of regional transit systems like BART (Bay Area Rapid Transit) and Metro (serving the Washington, D.C. area) are examples that come to mind — would be valuable in thinking about ways to make the regional approach more palatable to local agencies.

Resource Managers

There is another possible model for policing evolving over the next decade. It calls for a different way of thinking about delivery of protection services. It necessitates greater analytical effort by police to assess what the community wants and needs in the way of services and how those services can be delivered more effectively and efficiently. The result would be a reconceptualization of the police as not only providers of protection services but also brokers who enlist other organizations and groups within a community or region in coordinated efforts to meet protection needs.

Inherent in this approach would be much greater coordination between public and private police (see Shanahan's chapter). Despite its increasing size and scope, the private security industry remains unregulated. Measures to set standards and license security personnel have been recommended for a number of years (National Advisory Commission on Criminal Justice Standards and Goals 1976; Cunningham and Taylor 1984). Currently, however, private security is developing substantially in isolation, with the market making decisions that impinge on public safety.

Private security, by definition, is responsible to those who purchase its services and has a jurisdiction specific to a building or area. There is growing recognition, however, that a corporation's or a development's security concerns are not just confined to a building or complex but extend to the surrounding areas as well. Citizens must venture beyond privately policed safe zones to carry out their daily routine. Thus exclusive reliance on private security may not repay the substantial investment involved if the result is further erosion of the ability of public police to assure the kind of safety the public seeks in choosing areas to work or shop (Reiss 1984).

There are alternatives to public-private safety separation. Perception of fear of crime is a key reason for cooperation and centralized resource management. Police, real estate developers, and local businesses joined forces in Oakland, California, to improve police services in the downtown area and make revitalization efforts pay off. Under an agreement with the city, the private sector is providing financial resources to pay for enhanced police services for the area. The commitment is long term, ten years, with annual contributions between $300,000 and $400,000.

The Oakland experience suggests that private enterprise is recognizing the value of a proper mix of protection services and centralized management. Public police have long experience in diagnosing crime problems in an area and are sensitive to issues of equity both in enforcing laws and delivering services. Private forces cannot be expected to have the same attributes. Making public police the centerpiece of security efforts appears to be working in Oakland. Fear of crime is down in the central city, and the area is thriving (Reiss 1984).

The obvious question, however, is whether police will take up the challenge of such public-private partnerships. Will they invest in the search for knowledge they need to guide efficient allocation of protection resources? Do they have the expertise to assume responsibility for licensing and inspecting security services and setting physical and training standards? Can police complement the "bottom line" perspective of private security with their own public-oriented perspective (see Shanahan's chapter)?

If the quality of their knowledge is superior and their policies effective, then police can begin to assume this kind of leadership role as managers of multiple public safety resources. Research is a key instrument for building such knowledge. With a better understanding of crime and the effects of police response, police chiefs are in a position to guide socially productive change in public safety.

THE ROLE OF RESEARCH

The National Institute of Justice is now committed to research that can help answer some of the critical issues facing police over the next decade and a half. Some of these are touched on in this essay—the need for new management strategies in an era of cutbacks, ways to capitalize on private and community resources that can supplement leaner police operations, how to conserve valuable police resources, and how to define better the police role and citizen expectations.

How should research priorities be structured to help police meet these and other challenges they face? In a broad sense, research should capitalize on the dramatic advances in technology that permit economical collection, analysis, and transmittal of information. More specifically, research should influence the kinds of information sought by police, show how to synthesize it into forms useful for decision making, and demonstrate the value of information to the shaping of police responses and the attainment of public objectives (see Reiss's chapter).

Shaping Police Responses

Police are awash in information, but they have lagged far behind advances in the management of information. Now, with powerful microcomputers available at relatively low cost, most departments should be able to afford to acquire rudimentary computing capability, even in these fiscally hard-pressed times. With such technology police agencies can sift through the masses of data available and determine what is useful and what is not, and pinpoint gaps that hinder effective management.

Research now under way is testing a system that gathers and analyzes the full range of information and social factors relating to a criminal incident. Crime analysis then becomes a broad-based information tool for solving problems and charting effective responses — whether they be specific police responses or ones that call on other agencies of local government, community groups, or the private sector.

With more sophisticated analysis of information, police managers can better anticipate issues that deserve priority attention. Fear of crime, for example, was previously not considered to be of direct concern to police. But with growing apprehension about the potentially debilitating effect of fear on the social and economic health of neighborhoods, helping to alleviate those fears is now seen as an important police responsibility (Sherman 1982). Some suspect that not only crime but the signs of disorder — graffiti, vandalism, incivilities, unruly youth, derelicts — cause people to withdraw into their homes, venturing out only when necessary. And this climate may create more opportunities for crime to flourish (Wilson and Kelling 1982).

Institute-funded experiments now under way in Houston and Newark put police in the vanguard of efforts to reduce these feelings of insecurity (Police Foundation 1983). The aim is to unify citizens and local government in restoring the vitality of inner-city areas (see the chapter by Lindsey et al.). The results will give police chiefs and elected officials authoritative new information on how to build and maintain cohesive community action and which steps appear to lessen the fear of crime. Other useful ideas for managing productive community action are expected to emerge from evaluations of popular prevention programs like Neighborhood Watch and Crimestoppers.

Expanded analytic capability will enable police to evaluate both services and existing methods of service delivery. Research has shown, for example, that the "standard" police response of immediate dispatch of a patrol unit to all calls wastes valuable resources (Farmer 1981). Police have consequently made strides in analyzing calls for service, setting priorities for the timing and method of response (McEwen and Cohen 1984). Other studies, which have recommended much greater selectivity in deciding which cases should receive investigative priority (Greenwood et al. 1975; Cawley et al. 1977), have improved the management of investigative resources. More recent research indicates that, as a result of previous advances, even more improvements — such as targeted investigations against career criminals — are now possible (Eck 1983, 1984).

The spirit of experimentalism that fostered these advances can help police confront new priorities, such as the career criminal. Research has found that career criminals are responsible for much of the serious crime (Greenwood 1982; Chaiken and Chaiken 1982) and thus represent a continuing drain on police resources. This knowledge calls for increased sophistication in devising apprehension and investigation strategies to cope with the serious, repeat offender. A few police programs exist for monitoring activities of known felons (for example, those in Washington, D.C., New York City, and Minneapolis), and research that examines the theory, practice, and results of such programs can make a contribution to police effectiveness.

Valuable new information is also emerging on the drug-crime link. Research shows that drug-abusing offenders commit large amounts of crime, including violent crime (Chaiken and Chaiken 1982). If we can accurately identify addicts at the time of arrest, this information can be useful to police in carrying out investigations and essential to courts in deciding whom to release before trial and under what conditions. Removing dangerous offenders from the community pending trial means that police will not have to use valuable resources confronting the same offender over and over again. In the District of Columbia, where preventive detention is authorized by law and arrestees have routinely been tested for drug use, research is now exploring the value of sophisticated new urinalysis technology for detecting heroin and other drugs in arrested defendants. The study also is evaluating the benefits of treatment versus surveillance in helping to curb pretrial crime (Toborg 1984).

With continuing fiscal stress, pressures for accountability from mayors, city managers, business and community groups, and the media are not likely to abate. The costs as well as the benefits of specific services need to be understood. Research in progress will help determine costs of such specific functions as making an arrest or answering a call for help. Research on the general concerns of performance and productivity measurement will help agency managers and their oversight bodies assess client demands and maximize efficiency.

Shaping Research

The experience of the past 15 years suggests that police have in general been receptive to research and experimentation, but perhaps slow to change. Where resistance to change exists, some of it may stem from the quality or relevance of the research itself. Many early studies were simply descriptive or merely scratched the surface of an issue. Some early innovations are now found to have drawbacks as well as benefits. Mobile response is not overwhelmingly superior to older methods such as foot patrol. Team policing may promote unhealthy competition within a department.

If research is to play a meaningful role for the future, then greater collaboration between police administrators and researchers is essential. Where researchers and police work hand in hand in an atmosphere of professionalism, new information gains greater acceptance and use. A case in point is the recent effort in Minneapolis where police and researchers from the Police Foundation, under National Institute of Justice auspices, conducted a controlled experiment in the handling of domestic assaults (Sherman and Berk 1984). Police interest in the findings from this research has been extremely high. In 1984, the Institute convened a meeting of the researchers with police officials from major cities to review the policy implications of the research and to discuss the design of a proposed replication of the Minneapolis experiment.

The National Institute of Justice is committed to bringing about stronger partnerships between police executives and researchers. This does not mean pandering to parochial concerns or unimportant issues. It does mean constructing research that can help police evolve with the demands of the changing market for public safety.

CONCLUSION

By law and tradition, police have had a "corner" on the public safety market. Today there are serious challenges to that traditional monopoly. Through thousands of small decisions, citizens are moving away from their traditional reliance on public police. The cumulative effect of these decisions could erode the position and authority of police in our society.

The future can be different. Police can be an influential force in the twenty-first century and managers of a multiplicity of resources to protect the public. To survive as leaders in public safety, they will need to reestablish their credibility and update their craft. Although yesterday's police leaders toiled in earnest and in good faith to provide quality public services, tomorrow's will find that one of the secrets to success is better use of applied research. In short, the prescription is to work smarter, not harder.

33
Police Research and Police Policy: Some Propositions about the Production and Use of Knowledge

Gary W. Cordner

The quantity of what we term police research has grown tremendously in the past 15 to 20 years. Although the work of the police was once of little interest to academics, today it "may well be, next to the work of politicians, the most thoroughly studied occupation in the United States" (Wilson 1980, p. 146). This heightened interest has not been solely American, and in fact there is now an International Panel on Police Research with formal representation from six countries (Farmer 1981, p. 86).

At this juncture, with the relatively recent demise of LEAA and the emergence of the National Institute of Justice (see Stewart's chapter) and with some turmoil in the field of criminal justice education (Sherman and National Advisory Commission on Higher Education for Police Officers 1978; Diamond 1981), we might profitably inquire about the effects of the police "research revolution" (Farmer 1978). The preponderance of testimonial evidence seems to support the view that all this research has affected the police world, and probably beneficially. James Q. Wilson (1978a, pp. viii, ix) has observed that "there is in some communities a sense of innovation and experimentation in police management" due in part to the "flood of books, articles, commission reports, seminars, conferences, and public debates about policing that have appeared since the mid-1960s" (see also Walker's chapter). Sherman (1979, p. 58) has argued that research has "caused the police field to rethink basic policies and procedures," while Farmer (1981, p. 23) states flatly that "research on police can make, and is making, a difference." Patrick V. Murphy opines that police research has fostered "dramatic" change (Allin-

An earlier version of this essay was presented at the 1981 annual meeting of the American Society of Criminology, Washington, D.C. Comments by Derral Cheatwood on the first draft of this chapter are gratefully acknowledged.

son 1981, p. 55). I, too, hopped aboard the bandwagon, having forecast that "many of the major findings of the patrol research studies will find their way into the intellectual marketplace" and "will almost certainly wittingly or unwittingly" be used (Cordner 1980a, p. 20).

Even the doubters are inclined to ascribe some positive effects to the outpouring of police research. Gerald Caplan, for example, thinks that what we have learned about reducing crime from our police research has been very limited and mostly in the "what doesn't work" category (Allinson 1981, p. 56). Herman Goldstein finds only minimal impact so far from police research findings but indicates that this may be a natural stage in the development of the field (Allinson 1981). And Wilson (1980, p. 146) concludes that "most of this research has had little immediate practical value, and some of it has not even had much intellectual value, but its cumulative effect should not be underestimated."

Police research and its effects have been systematically treated in several recent publications (Sherman 1974; Manning 1979a, 1979b; Cordner 1980a; Wilson 1980; Farmer 1981). Here, I will consider several key propositions about research and its relationship to policy as they apply to the police field. My thesis is that we harbor some overly simplistic ideas and naively optimistic expectations with respect to both the production of knowledge and its use in policymaking. We have underestimated the political features of what we think we know and of how we go about using it to make choices. We have accepted a highly consensual model of how we do and should analyze and solve our social problems. Overall, much of the discussion of research and its role in policymaking seems to embrace a rational model of both science and government, either to describe the present situation or to specify how things ought to work. This rational model downplays the role of partisan interests and minimizes the importance of common, ordinary knowledge, while ascribing supreme authority to research, science, and other forms of expertise.

In order to examine critically these prevailing ideas and expectations about research and policy, I will discuss a number of propositions that run counter to the rational, consensual model. The propositions are drawn from an important recent essay on social science and social problem solving (Lindblom and Cohen 1979) and from a recent empirical study of the use of expert forecasting (Ascher 1978). The propositions may be summarized as follows:

1. Research refines ordinary knowledge more than it creates new, previously unformulated knowledge.
2. Occasionally research adds an increment of knowledge sufficient to carry a proposition across the line of disbelief; in rare circumstances, it issues an outright challenge to a substantial body of established belief.
3. It may be that, without achieving conclusiveness or authoritativeness, re-

search is nevertheless capable of clarifying our understanding of the social world.

4. The usual effect of research is to raise new issues, stimulate new debate, and multiply the complexities of the social problem at hand.
5. Research may, as a condition of making some of its most significant contributions, be required to accept substantial lags and indirections in achieving an influence.
6. Reporting (description) may represent a contribution by research to social problem solving more significant than what has been achieved through the pursuit of authoritative scientific generalization.
7. Despite the accepted convention that researchers are engaged in the pursuit of conclusive fact and proof, they are instead engaged in producing inconclusive evidence and argument.
8. Research is to a degree incapacitated in contributing to social problem solving because of its own metaphysics, fashions, traditions, and taboos.
9. Much of "research utilization" involves selecting research that confirms our ordinary knowledge, construing it as authoritative, and acting on it.
10. Use of research is partisan in that it serves to advance the interests of persons playing roles in an interactive process.
11. Regard for research is strongly influenced by regard for the institution conducting or sponsoring it.
12. The acceptability of research is enhanced to the extent that the situation in which it would be used is characterized by a high level of perceived goal consensus.
13. Research with clear policy implications, which, however, does not force policy choice, is most likely to be accepted.
14. Researchers may not understand that although democracy has been interpreted to be a device to bring reason to bear on policy, it is also a device to frustrate it.[1]

PRODUCTION OF KNOWLEDGE

The first two propositions hold that research only rarely creates new knowledge or directly challenges substantial, established beliefs. Most often it "merely" refines ordinary knowledge, and occasionally it adds the critical increment of knowledge that carries an idea across the line of disbelief.

The police response time studies (Pate et al. 1976) provide a good example of research that refines ordinary knowledge. Most people believed that rapid police response to calls for service would result in desirable outcomes, and society invested heavily in command and control systems, allocation models, and other technology to minimize the time it took the police to respond. From the response time research, however, we have learned that police response time is already negligible when compared to prior delays in reporting crimes to the police. That is, considerable time elapses after the commission of most crimes before the police are notified. Our ordinary knowledge, in refined form, now is that rapid police response to true "hot calls" may lead to more desirable outcomes. This represents not a brand new idea but rather a more careful and refined statement of our original notion.

The Kansas City Preventive Patrol Experiment (Kelling et al. 1974a) may represent the case of research adding an increment of knowledge sufficient to carry an idea across the line of disbelief. The ordinary knowledge in question here is the belief that routine patrol prevents crime. While patrol has traditionally been considered the backbone of any police department, it has also been common to find preventive patrol characterized as "doing nothing" and as "waiting for something to happen." Cawley (1978) reports chiefs describing preventive patrol as "smoothing the cobblestones," "random riding," and "air pollution." Preceding the Kansas City experiment, many jurisdictions had experienced crime increases, hired more police, observed no effect, and begun to question the productivity of the principal police strategy. Thus the widely publicized and uncommonly authoritative findings of the Kansas City study may have come along at an opportune moment and functioned as the critical increment of knowledge.

Are these the common kinds of contributions to knowledge that result from police research? One is certainly hard-pressed to think of police research that has created "new, previously unformulated knowledge." Perhaps the closest is the accumulation of police patrol work load studies, reviewed in Cordner (1979), that had the effect of destroying the common view of the police as "crimefighters." The public, in particular, having drawn their ordinary knowledge from the popular media, might regard research evidence that police work involves mainly order maintenance or social service functions as brand new knowledge. The public seems not to have been persuaded (or informed), though, while the police themselves may have accepted the research findings as the critical increment in altering their own, more informed, views of their work (Wilson 1980, p. x). To complicate the issue further, however, serious doubts about the validity and interpretation of this new knowledge have been raised (Goldstein 1977, pp. 24–29; Shearing and Leon 1977; Cordner 1979).

Obviously, to some extent our acceptance of these propositions hinges on the meaning of key terms, especially "ordinary knowledge." Lindblom and Cohen (1979, p. 12) provide this definition:

> By "ordinary knowledge," we mean knowledge that does not owe its origin, testing, degree of verification, truth status, or currency to distinctive . . . [research] techniques but rather to common sense, casual empiricism, or thoughtful speculation and analysis. It is highly fallible, but we shall call it knowledge even if it is false. As in the case of scientific knowledge, whether it is true or false, knowledge is knowledge to anyone who takes it as a basis for some commitment or action.[2]

In general, Lindblom and Cohen (1979, p. 12) argue, researchers "greatly overestimate the amount and distinctiveness of the information and analysis they offer." Their argument is that the stock and flow of ordinary knowledge is considerable, while the contributions of research are very limited. His review of criminal justice research in the 1970s led Peter Manning (1979a, p. 721) to a similar conclusion: "[R]esearch, by and large, follows public opinion and amplifies aspects of conventional wisdom. It seldom sets questions independently."

ENLIGHTENMENT

Propositions 3, 4, and 5 pertain to the indirect and often unanticipated consequences of research. They suggest that the absence of authoritativeness does not necessarily make research useless, that research may lead to divergence rather than convergence of thinking about a problem, and that the effects of research are sometimes delayed and circuitous.

Lindblom and Cohen (1979) argue forcefully that research is rarely scientifically conclusive (clearly answering a question) and even more rarely authoritative (accepted as the basis for action). Nevertheless, research can have important, albeit indirect, effects on our thinking and action by altering the conceptual or intellectual frameworks that guide us in understanding and interpreting our world. Though policymakers rarely base their decisions explicitly on research, "they may take the whole organizing framework or perspective for their work from academic social science" (Lindblom and Cohen 1979, p. 79). More generally, Myrdal (1953, p. 221) suggests that when we shift our attention from day-to-day activity to more long-range considerations, we find that research and science are "the sources of the ideas out of which social change comes."

This sort of indirect effect of research can already be seen in the police field, despite the recency of most of the research. Manning (1979a, p. 721), focusing largely on the police, reports: "The facticity of the criminal justice system — what the practitioners think they are doing, how and for what societal benefits and ends, and what the public is willing to grant them — is being altered by research. The reflexivity of thought, what people think other people think about their thoughts and actions, is slowly bringing about change." Wilson (1978a, pp. ix, x; 1980, pp. 146–52), in a similar vein, argues that as a consequence of work load and effectiveness research the police now perceive what they do very differently. Responding to suggestions that police work is only partly concerned with crime-related business, that the police provide a variety of social services, or that the effect of the police on crime is limited, the police are now likely to say that "everyone knows that." Everyone did not know that a decade ago, however.

Some recent research on directed patrol (Cordner 1981) may help illustrate the third proposition. The research was intended as an evaluation of the patrol strategy and was funded by a police agency. Because experimental conditions could not be established, however, conclusive evidence of the effects of the directed patrol strategy vis-à-vis alternative strategies could not be collected. Evidence was developed, though, about the effects of different levels of the strategy (the "treatment") and also more generally about the effects of aggressive patrol. The results of the research have not been and may never be used instrumentally by the police agency that paid for them or by any other policymakers. Despite this lack of conclusiveness and authoritativeness, the research contributes to the growing view among social scientists that "the police, by variations in their styles and tactics, can make a difference in the rates of certain kinds of common street crimes" (Wilson 1978a, p. xi). A small parcel of information is added to our understanding of the social world, even as the research failed to fulfill a more direct role in the shaping of police policy.

The fourth proposition maintains that research often raises more questions than it answers. Cohen and Garet (1975, p. 42) note that "research does not necessarily reduce disagreement. Instead, it calls attention to the existence of conflicting positions, sometimes elaborates them, and sometimes generates new issues altogether." Consider the Kansas City Preventive Patrol Experiment (Kelling et al. 1974a; Kelling's chapter on experimentation in policing), for example. No more elaborate, skillful, or expensive piece of research is to be found in the police field. It was a seemingly straightforward test of the effects of three levels of preventive patrol. And yet it has stirred a heated debate, its findings have been variously interpreted, and many new questions have surfaced. To what extent are the findings only valid for Kansas City? Do the findings apply only to motorized patrol? What exactly was the "preventive patrol" that had so little effect in Kansas City? These questions have stimulated further research, such as that on the effects of foot patrol (Police Foundation 1981), which in turn promises to stir debate and raise new questions.

The fifth proposition, related to the preceding two, holds that research effects, such as they are, are often lagged and indirect. Lindblom and Cohen (1979, pp. 79–81) point, for example, to the situation in economics, in which Keynesian, macro, and international trade theories gained popularity long after their initial development and arguably long after their relevance to current conditions had passed. In a more optimistic vein, Myrdal (1953, p. 221) speaks of the "long-range intellectual leadership" provided by social scientists, while Cohen and Garet (1975, p. 36) argue that research has "its effect mostly on loose systems of knowledge and belief," but perhaps through an "undisciplined process by which inquiry has intermittent and often unforeseeable effects." The picture that emerges is clearly one characterized by considerable chance and uncertainty, in which research may or may not have much of an effect on public policy, and in which such effects as do eventuate may or may not be as intended.

REPORTING

Proposition 6 holds that research that "merely" describes the present state of affairs often makes a greater contribution than more sophisticated, more inferential, or more theoretically inclined research. Reviewing social research and its effects on public policy, for example, Rivlin (1971) found that much had been learned about the extent and locus of problems but not about why they persisted or how to solve them. She noted that "considerable progress has been made in identifying and measuring social problems in our society" and that "this knowledge itself has helped clarify policy choices" (p. 7). She also found some progress toward identifying the initial costs and benefits of alternative programs but little gain in understanding the long-range consequences of alternatives or in devising more effective policies and programs.

This nearly 15-year-old assessment of social research seems exactly on the mark for police research today. We understand much more clearly than in the past what the police do, how much crime there is, how different crimes are perpetrated, and so forth. We also have better information about the immediate effects of different operational strategies, administrative arrangements, and policies. About the more direct and long-range consequences of police alternatives, however, we know much less. And we seem decidedly ignorant when it comes to generating more effective means for accomplishing our purposes. One key reason why research that "merely" reports or describes might seem more useful to policymakers is discussed later in connection with the thirteenth proposition.

RESEARCH AS ACTION

The preceding discussion has covered much of propositions 7 and 8. One important point to be made, though, is that research should not be perceived only as a thinking exercise. Lindblom and Cohen (1979, p. 81) argue that despite the common view that researchers "are engaged in the pursuit of conclusive fact and proof, they are instead engaged in producing inconclusive evidence and argument." Cohen and Garet (1975, p. 42) make the similar point that "research resembles a discourse about social reality." This is all partly due to the inevitable inconclusiveness of research, which mandates that findings be regarded as evidence rather than proof. It is also due to the fact that research is a social act, undertaken by fallible people with varying motives. In addition, research products are not immutable things, but rather are what they are communicated and interpreted to be. As Bolan (1980, p. 273) has noted with respect to planning: "Technique is not the dominant feature of professional activity." Rather, the complete research episode involves "creating an authentic professional performance in a social setting with other constituent actors."

More will be said in the next section on the social act of research use. The important point here is that such research processes as the selection of phenomena to study, the choice of research design and data analysis methods, the specification of a theoretical framework, and the interpretation and communication of findings are all also social acts. They are frequently carried out among a group, with an audience in mind. Practical realities, such as funding considerations, commonly intrude, as do more mundane matters such as whether or not the researchers know how to use a computer. The social dynamics of doing research are not completely prescribed by the scientific method.

The argument of the eighth proposition is that researchers constitute a social or cultural group that has its own norms, traditions, and taboos, and that these characteristics limit the contributions of research to problem solving. Certainly the employment of many researchers in universities, with the accompanying pressure to publish large numbers of works with little regard for quality, is one example of such a norm. (On this dimension police should have little difficulty empathizing with the usually alien academic, whose work product suffers from publication quotas much as the cop's work product suffers from arrest and ticket quotas.) The tradition of empirical, logical-positivist research strongly influences many academics and much of police research. As heavily quantitative analysis has become more fashionable (along with behaviorism), more and more researchers have adapted to its style (see Mayo's chapter, pp. 412-13).

Police research is particularly susceptible to the problem of taboos, mixed up as policing is with emotional and ethical issues. For example, police work frequently puts its practitioners in positions of having to decide whether to employ illegal and/or immoral means in order to achieve good ends (Klockars 1980; see also Kerstetter's and Klockars's chapters and Kelling's "order maintenance" chapter). A suspect may refuse to divulge information that could save another's life. An officer may know that unless he embellishes his testimony, a surely guilty defendant will go free. An officer may be convinced that unless he carries a drunken tenant out of the apartment building and then arrests him for public intoxication, a serious assault will be committed against the tenant by his neighbors and landlord. Despite the prevalence and salience of incidents like these in police work, however, apparently they have been the subject of no research (Klockars 1980). The issue is regularly exploited in fiction but is virtually taboo in the halls of academe.

RESEARCH AND THE PLAY OF POWER

Probably the key notion underlying propositions 9, 10, and 11 is that when research is used, it is used by people playing particular roles in an interactive process. How they interpret and use the research depends in part on how it relates to their ordinary knowledge, in part on their role, in part on the implications of the research for the advancement of their own interests, and in part on their regard for those who sponsored and/or conducted the research.

Policy is and will be made, with or without research. Policymakers pursue some combination of personal, organizational, and public interests and draw on a wealth of ordinary knowledge in devising strategies for attaining these interests. Lindblom and Cohen (1979) argue that when research is used in policymaking, it is commonly because of its dependent authoritativeness — because it supports the policymaker's stock of ordinary knowledge. Policymakers thus select that research which is consistent with their ordinary knowledge, promote it as authoritative, and then use it as the basis for action.

Waller (1979, p. 204) reports this kind of behavior in criminal justice policymaking. He argues that practitioners draw on "highly persuasive," ordinary, "firsthand knowledge" of their particular agency to interpret and use legislation, social indicators, and research. Previously acquired personal ideologies also influence criminal justice policymakers' interpretation and use of research, leading sometimes to divergent views. The inconclusiveness of most research and this tendency toward divergence rather than convergence of research-generated knowledge make it easy for the policymaker to use research as support for ordinary knowledge, while making it difficult to establish any "objective" interpretation of the "facts."

The policymaking process is perhaps best understood as a play of power, in which various actors carry out partisan roles in an interactive process (Lindblom 1980). Information, analysis, and research are among the ammunition and currency used to exercise influence in the process, but so are money, votes, and reciprocal support. When research is "used," it may not be in a disinterested fashion but rather in the pursuit of partisan interests. This does not imply that all policymaking is narrow-minded and self-interested but only that even broad-minded statesmen are guided by a "partisanship embodied in their very conception of the public interest" (Lindblom and Cohen 1979, p. 63).

A fine illustration of this characterization of research use is provided by current police programs based on the Rand study of criminal investigations (Greenwood and Petersilia 1975), the Kansas City Preventive Patrol Experiment (Kelling et al. 1974a), and the response time studies (Pate et al. 1976). The combined effect of these studies has been to throw into serious question the value of the three basic components of modern police work — follow-up investigations by detectives, preventive patrol, and rapid response to calls for assistance. The principal form in which the studies have been used in the police field has been as evidence of the need for stricter managerial control over the activities of police personnel (Anderson 1978; Krajick 1978; Cordner 1980a). Clearly, certain actors in the policymaking process (police managers) have used the research to gain influence over other actors (police patrol officers, detectives, and police unions). Their use of the research has been partisan, in support of their own personal and bureaucratic interests (see Kliesmet's chapter, p. 282). Their claim, of course, is that their actions are in the public interest, and they can point to several major federal initiatives and evidence of reasoned support (Cawley and Miron 1977; Cawley et al. 1977; Grassie and Crowe 1978). Their claim may be valid, but their actions and their use of the research are nevertheless partisan. Similarly ambiguous or clearly disingenuous claims of serving some higher value can be seen in some of the police practitioners' objections to proposed program experiments on the ground that the experiments would violate certain rights of human subjects (see Shapard's and Bergstrom's chapters; see also Kelling's chapter on experimentation in policing).

But just as research may be used to fuel partisan battles, it may be used to reduce the appearance, if not the reality, of partisan policymaking, as Lindblom and Cohen (1979, p. 65) note:

> In social problem solving, partisans ordinarily find it too costly to fight to the death over their differences. Hence, they develop rules and procedures, explicit or tacit, that damp the conflict. These procedures range from the formality of voting, to the subtleties of reciprocal obligations: "You let me win this time, and I'll owe you one."
>
> It appears that, in certain circumstances common especially in the bureaucracy, a tacit agreement comes into play according to which the victory goes to the superficial "winner" of the debate. We do not mean that those who concede are persuaded by the debate. But they in effect follow a tacit rule that declares that better evidence (especially better numbers) carries the day. As a result, . . . [research] becomes a principal weapons maker in the struggle.[3]

Especially in these constrained financial times, this role for research may be observed in government budget deliberations. In a world increasingly driven by the cost-benefit calculus, the government agency having "better numbers" than its competitors will often be the one to maintain or increase its resources. As becomes immediately clear to those within the system who must play this numbers game on behalf of their agency, the figures are used as weapons in a struggle, not as neutral information in a rational decision process (Wildavsky 1974; Hudzik et al. 1981, pp. 180–208; Greene, Bynum, and Cordner 1981).

The evidence in support of the proposition that regard for research is influenced by regard for who did it or sponsored it is so strong as to need little discussion. Some police administrators dismiss any research associated with the Police Foundation or PERF, while others would doubt the validity of anything coming out of the IACP (see, generally, Goldstein 1977, pp. 323–24, 327–28). Some would seriously consider research produced by Michigan State but reject anything out of Berkeley. That a piece of research was funded by the federal government might impress some but alienate others. Now that "solvability factors" have been independently validated by police departments (Eck 1979), they certainly are held in higher regard by administrators than when they were only supported by university-affiliated research (Greenberg et al. 1977).

POLICY CHOICES

Proposition 12 holds that research is more likely to be accepted and used when the policy setting is characterized by goal consensus rather than goal conflict. Ascher reports that, because of this feature, research more often has direct and unambiguous impact in the corporate context (where the clear goal is profit) than in the governmental context (where the goals are multiple and ambiguous). Addressing the use of expert forecasts, he observes: "It is hard to imagine that a believable forecast would be deliberately disregarded by corporate decision-makers. Governmental decision-makers may have quite good reasons for disregarding believable forecasts that conflict with their goal priorities" (1978, p. 20). This lack of goal consensus is endemic to government agencies and policies. Wilson (1978b, p. 204) notes that "we turn to government in part precisely because we wish to attain vague, complex, controversial, hard-to-produce objectives." With respect to criminal justice in particular, Waller (1979) also points out that the services provided are unclear, and the policy issues are often quite emotional.

What we are facing here is another element of the relationship between means and ends. When ends are clear, attention is focused on selecting efficient means, and research can be a very helpful aid in decision making. When ends are not clear, however, the choice among means resembles a debate more than analysis, as it is the ends that are really at issue, if only implicitly. This is partly why research on the relative effectiveness of different models of body armor or patrol vehicles is more easily accepted and used than research on, say, aggressive patrol versus community-oriented patrol.[4] This also suggests that police research might more easily be used in more homogeneous communities, where there is general agreement about what the police function is, than in heterogeneous communities.

394 / POLICE LEADERSHIP IN AMERICA

The thirteenth proposition is an intriguing one, perhaps less obvious than some of the others. It, too, comes from Ascher's (1978) study of forecasting. He found that policymakers ordinarily desired information but resisted studies or advice that would reduce their flexibility in policy choice. Policymakers liked research that enlarged their range of options or that helped them predict the likely consequences of different alternatives, as long as the research did not predetermine their choice. Thus "forecasts with clear policy implications, which, however, do not force policy choice, are most likely to be accepted" (p. 37).

Much of the initial opposition to the Kansas City Preventive Patrol Experiment may have resulted from fear by police administrators that the research would force certain policy choices (see Kelling's chapter on experimentation in policing). Some early interpretations, for example, were that the study proved we had more police than we needed or that preventive patrol was a complete waste and should be eliminated. When it was later realized that the study could be interpreted as supporting greater flexibility in police resource allocation and use, the research suddenly became much more popular among police administrators. The response time (Pate et al. 1976) and investigative (Greenwood and Petersilia 1975) studies have been interpreted in a similar fashion and similarly have become popular among police policymakers.

One clear example of inquiry that meets the requirements of proposition 13 is purely descriptive research that simply reports on current conditions. It provides background information and may have policy implications, but the policymaker's autonomy is not imperiled. Hence, as noted earlier, descriptive research reportedly is seen as very useful by practitioners.

LIMITS OF REASON

The final proposition indicates simply that the role of research in public policymaking is *supposed* to be limited. The authority to make decisions and policies is diffused, all sorts of interests are given an opportunity to participate, and many problems are dealt with through interaction rather than by analysis. If a principal characteristic of our policymaking system is the fragmentation of power, a result is that "no small group, not even one that may think it knows what needs to be done, can achieve a greatly disproportionate influence on policy" (Lindblom and Cohen 1979, p. 70). Elsewhere, Lindblom (1980, p. 124) has referred to this as the cruel joke of democracy — "It gives some power to the citizen, but it also gives power to all other citizens. For any one person, consequently, most of his fellow citizens constitute barriers to having his own way."

In addition to these characteristics of democratic policymaking that limit the role of research, there is also an important philosophical issue involved.

It is generally accepted that an "ought" cannot be derived from an "is," which translates that research, analysis, theory, science, or facts cannot tell us what we should do. Stated more elegantly, "Practical discourse directed toward political action cannot be reduced to technical control or the technical application of theoretical knowledge, for this distorts human social life and the medium of communicative action" (Bernstein 1976, p. 219). Put yet another way, scientists and researchers have an important advisory role to play in public policymaking, but their counsel must be limited to informing rather than replacing what are, inherently and properly, *political* choices.

A ready illustration of this notion in the police field is provided by job analysis (Cordner 1980b). Job analysis is a technique used to measure the content of a job, to translate that content into required worker capabilities, and to design instruments for selecting applicants who possess the needed capabilities. Properly employed, it is a very useful aid in personnel decision making. It is frequently the case, however, that job analysis information is allowed to dominate personnel *policymaking*. In policing, this has meant that instead of deliberating about the kinds of people we think should be employed to do police work, we have let personnel technicians set our policy on the basis of what present role incumbents say it takes to do the work as they have construed it (Goldstein 1977, p. 262). We have abdicated our policymaking and political responsibilities, with the effect, in this instance, that the status quo has been deified. That might not matter much if we were talking about bricklayers or airline pilots, but the social reality of police work is tremendously subjective. We should no more let the police define that social reality as the basis for personnel selection than for deadly force policies, but with rare exceptions we do.

The job analysis example illustrates that when research exceeds its proper role in policymaking, it may be due more to policymaker irresponsibility than to researcher overbearance. Particularly in the absence of goal consensus, or in the face of controversial issues, policymakers may prefer to at least give the appearance that their choices were mandated by "hard research." It may be the case that the research actually serves as an after-the-fact rationalization, or policymakers may truly rely on it in order to avoid their political responsibilities. It has been suggested that a feature of our contemporary civilization is a withering away of our practical, political faculties, such that we allow science and technology to intrude improperly in the normative realm of public policymaking, to our detriment (Habermas 1973).

CONCLUSION

When we inquire into the use of research in police policymaking or speculate about enhancing such use we need to avoid uncritical acceptance of some overly simplistic ideas. We need to remember that research-based knowledge is but one form of knowledge, and perhaps a minor one at that. We need to recognize that research rarely produces conclusive or authoritative evidence. Without abandoning the effort to be as objective as possible, we need to admit the subjectivity of research and its products. We also must realize that policy is and should be made on the basis of a variety of considerations, of which research-based knowledge is only one. And in the policymaking process, when research is used, we must accept that it is ordinarily on behalf of some partisan interest (which the researcher may or may not regard as the public interest). Finally, the greatest impact of research may often go unnoticed, as it sifts, indirectly and with delays and detours, into the stock of conventional wisdom, altering our understanding of how the world works and how to change it (see Walker's chapter). The conceptual framework in the policymaker's head, the assumptions that set the boundaries of the policy debate, may owe much to long-forgotten research, even as the policymaker dismisses the practical utility of research.

NOTES

1. These propositions are closely paraphrased from the two works cited. The only real changes are in the use of the term "research." Propositions 1-10 and 14, from Lindblom and Cohen (1979), refer in the original form to professional social inquiry. Propositions 11-13, from Ascher (1978), pertain in his work to forecasting. No claim is made here that these authors would agree with the alteration of their propositions. Rather, it is my intention to consider whether the propositions make sense in the context of police research and its use.

2. The term "research" is inserted for the phrase "professional social inquiry" in the quote. See note 1.

3. Again, the term "research" is inserted for the phrase "professional social inquiry" in the quote. See note 1.

4. The IACP is reported to have "cited development of better equipment techniques as the major benefit of police research" (Allinson 1981, p. 56). Certainly this kind of research is the easiest used and least controversial.

34

Leading Blindly: An Assessment of Chiefs' Information about Police Operations

Louis A. Mayo

There is nothing more difficult to take in hand, more perilous to conduct, or more uncertain in its success, than to take the lead in the introduction of a new order of things.

— Machiavelli, *The Prince*

Lack of professionalism contributes to the extensive misinformation and information voids that permeate and impede police administration today. In everyday usage, professionalism means "professional quality and status"; professional means "characterized by or conforming to the technical and ethical standards of a profession"; and profession means "a calling requiring specialized knowledge and often long and intensive academic training" (Gove 1967). The occupation of police chief in the United States does not meet the test of any of these definitions. It should satisfy all of them.

The literature of police administration consistently describes the role of the police chief as one of the most demanding, challenging, and important executive functions anywhere in public administration (Fosdick 1920; Vollmer 1931; Kelly 1975; Saunders 1970; Goldstein 1977; Bopp 1984; Cohen 1984a, 1984b, 1984c). The wide chasm between this stated need for professionalism and the realities of police management in America today has undesirable ripple effects throughout the administration and operations of a police department.[1] In particular, this deficiency fundamentally affects notions about what kinds of information should be compiled, analyzed, and reported by subordinates to police chiefs and by chiefs to other officials and the public.

This paper was prepared independent of the author's employment with the National Institute of Justice. Views expressed are those of the author and not necessarily those of the Institute.

Knowledge about the role of the police chief is very limited. The body of research on chiefs is miniscule in comparison with studies on the line police officer. There are some autobiographies by chiefs, such as Jenkins (1970), Ahern (1972), Davis (1978), and Murphy and Plate (1977), which have made substantial contributions; however, a search of the literature from 1900 to 1960 revealed no book-length research on chiefs. In the ensuing two dozen years, only five such inquiries were discovered, including my study (Germann 1962; Grosman 1975; National Advisory Commission 1976; Bussom et al. 1981; and Mayo 1983). The general management literature indicates that the role of any chief executive is unique; it is not simply middle management operating at a higher level (Barnard 1938; Holden, Fish, and Smith 1951; Holden, Pederson, and Germane 1968; Burger 1978; Klein and Murphy 1979). The essential function of the chief executive is, through leadership, to provide a sense of purpose, ethical content, and direction for all others in the organization to follow. The management of change is the touchstone of chief executive competence and probably the most difficult of all management tasks, according to Drucker (1973) (see also Couper 1983). Yet Goldstein (1977) found only six articles in all the police literature that dealt with managing change. Bennis and Namus (1984) distinguished the role of the chief executive in that he is responsible for doing the right things, whereas all lower managers are responsible for doing things right.

Davis (1973, p. 41) argues that deciding on "the right things" requires an underlying philosophy:

> The problem of greatest importance in the field of management is . . . philosophy of management. A philosophy is a system of thought. It is based on some orderly, logical statements of objectives, principles, policies and general methods of approach to the solution of some set of problems. . . . Industrial leaders without such a philosophy are business mechanics rather than professional executives.

Bopp (1977, p. vii) states this need in the police context:

> Central to this definition are certain fundamental questions which have not been satisfactorily answered: To whom are the police directly responsible? What constitutes police work? How should officers be evaluated? Which level of government should control them? To what extent should individual liberty be surrendered in return for police protection?

Couper (1983, p. 13) adds a chief's perspective:

> The ability of a police agency to perform its function adequately is based upon its ability to define and understand its proper objectives, to translate these objectives into precise policies and operational procedures, and to

employ qualified professionals to carry out these objectives. While this may sound like a simple notion, it is actually very difficult.

Ahern (1972), Goldstein (1977), and others agree on both the essential need for and the lack of a philosophy of policing to guide police chiefs (see also Kenney 1975; Cizanckas and Hanna 1977; Murphy and Plate 1977; National Commission on Productivity 1973). This void seriously impedes police administration (Davis 1978; Ahern 1972; Goldstein 1977; Manning 1978). Information systems to inform a police chief how well he is achieving the objectives that would arise from such a philosophy of policing cannot exist when the philosophical foundation does not exist. It is difficult to measure progress toward an unclear goal, and problem analysis requires an understanding of the sense of purpose or "why" of the goal. Once this is accomplished, it is crucially important that management information systems be related to organizational goals (Brightman 1971). Otherwise, the result will be confusion and conflict in both the implementation and monitoring of agency activities.

Perhaps more detrimental than lack of a clear sense of direction for police chiefs is the misdirection that has occurred under the guise of professionalism, especially in the past 50 years. This has created police "misinformation" systems that provide distortion and distraction for the police chief. O. W. Wilson is referred to as the primary leader for professional police (Bopp 1977). His concepts were a major improvement over the violence, incompetency, and corruption that typified the police about 1930, as described by the Wickersham Commission (1931); almost any change would have been an improvement. Unfortunately, until recently in its evolution, policing has been frozen in the era of this Wilsonian professionalism model. This model embodies the antithesis of professionalism, as defined in almost every dimension, except for advocating college education and integrity (see Kliesmet's chapter). O. W. Wilson's militaristic bureaucracy is described by Bopp (1977, pp. 5, 6, 134, 136):

> He unswervingly subscribed to the notions of narrow spans of control, a rigid chain of command, the sanctity of written pronouncements on a wide variety of subjects, specialization of tasks, carefully controlled delegation of authority and responsibility, and the close supervision of the troops in the field. . . . Within this framework, police officers would ultimately reach the pinnacle of professionalization by doing precisely what they were told to do by their commanding officers. . . . It is narrow in the extreme, and has actually retarded professionalization by fostering an administrative attitude that the rank and file police officers are not to be trusted; they must be closely watched, the subjects of massive policy pronouncements limiting their discretion, and consistently threatened with punishment to forestall misbehavior. . . . *** He may have also contributed to the task-centered approach to law enforcement in which police officers, blindly following orders, functioned as an army of occupation in a community, rather than a social

service agency.*** Another Wilsonian inclination was to simplify the nature of crime and the causes of community conflict which, to him, could be solved by aggressive police action and firm courts. Within this context, then, Wilson never truly understood the dynamics of community behavior. He tended to see the police department as an apparatus and the community as the field in which it operated. . . . *** O. W. Wilson's conception of police excellence was quite narrow. It involved more changes in form than in substance. . . . Yet, a beautiful-looking police department is not necessarily a professional one.

This antiprofessionalism design, coupled with a major change in police perspectives from order maintenance and service to enforcing laws and increased preoccupation with firearms by the police, occurred about the same time—the mid-1930s (Walker 1977). This new perspective of the 1930s was dubbed the legalistic form of policing by James Q. Wilson (1970). The legalistic style persists as the primary form of policing in the United States today in spite of a number of major voices that have been raised in praise of other courses: the 1967 *Police* report of the President's Commission on Law Enforcement and Administration of Justice, which emphasized the preeminence of police service and order activities over enforcement of laws; the 1973 *Police* report of the National Advisory Commission on Criminal Justice Standards and Goals, which touted the concept of neighborhood team policing; and the writings of many subsequent authors, particularly Goldstein (1977), which underscore how inappropriate and even destructive this legalistic model is to the effectiveness of policing. The model governs the recruitment, training, organization, and management of police, as well as the information reported to the police chief and the information he in turn reports to the government and citizens. To the extent that a chief prefers a different style of policing and a different organization structure, such as Wilson's (1970) service style, embodied in neighborhood team policing, his efforts to introduce the new mode in his agency will be like "bending granite," as Guyot (1979) so artfully depicted the task of attempting to change the military rank structure of police agencies. The typical policy reinforcement and statistical systems of most police departments are designed in accordance with the O. W. Wilsonian model, resulting in a flow of information to the police chief that distracts from the need for major changes by reinforcing past practices.

Fyfe (1981) analogized such a crime enforcement–oriented police department to a fire department that is organized and managed—and that reports information—with an almost exclusive focus on arson. Any activities outside arson would be considered as "other" and of minor importance, notwithstanding that almost all of the activities were "other." The fire chief would receive a constant barrage of staff papers and briefings and statistics on arson but little else. This closely describes many police departments, which have an average "Mayo Crime Index" rate of 1.4.[2]

There are those who advocate the abolition of police professionalism because it is inappropriate and unsuccessful, as Misner and (Jerry) Wilson urged in testimony before the President's Violence Commission (1968), pointing out that crime rates had not been reduced. But true police professionalism has not been tried to any extent. Crime rates are of little value in judging the police; they are primarily a product of police reporting policies rather than a measure of police effectiveness (Manning 1978). Moreover, customary forms of reporting crime rates do not adequately describe the nature and seriousness of events (Thomas 1983). Even if we had accurate and descriptive crime rates, they would be inappropriate measures of the quality of policing, according to Couper (1983). He feels much the same about other common indices of police effectiveness, including community feelings of safety, police morale, appearance, programs, and technology. He asserts: "[N]one of these standards provides an accurate measure of how good or bad a police agency is; none of them can tell us how effectively a police agency is dealing with problems of public safety and public order" (1983, p. 3). Although not normally considered when discussing police evaluation criteria, I would suggest that one should include indicators of how safe the citizens are from unlawful acts against them *by* the police or lawful police acts that are performed with unfair discrimination against certain groups. As the state of the art stands today, police managers' evaluation systems are burdened by misinformation and information voids, due in large measure to the so-called professional police model. Couper (1983, p. 4) emphasizes:

> Lacking the information they need to make rational judgments, people have to rate police on the basis of their own perceptions of what a police agency should do, and they tend to use crime, arrest and clearance rates. . . . Those measures, in turn, give rise to a number of myths about what makes a good police agency.

O. W. Wilson's primary emphasis on form over substance is no more likely to produce quality policing than dressing mud wrestlers in leotards and tutus is likely to make them ballet dancers. Neither does the finest dance training help if the trainees are subsequently put to work as mud wrestlers in an emporium that is designed, operated, and evaluated for the quality of its mud wrestling. Indeed, those who would attempt ballet steps in the mud would quickly be thrown out. Rush (1975) found that police middle managers in California could not utilize skills learned in university management seminars because the traditional military bureaucracy of their agencies was incompatible with the teachings of modern management.

The service model of policing, with its emphasis on responsiveness to the community and participatory management, and its acknowledgment of police discretion, is virtually the antithesis of the legalistic model and has the potential to evolve into a genuinely professional model. Unfortunately, there is no orderly, efficient progression from the legalistic to the service model. Several police agencies have tried, but successes are rare. For police departments evolving in this direction, the transition period may be lengthy, possibly more than a century. I believe that several generations of police officers must pass to overcome all of the vested interests and other impediments. During the interim transitional period these agencies will be "schizophrenic" in staffing, operations, policy, and related monitoring systems designed to inform the police chief. There may be no clear indication which style of policing is controlling a given function at any time or place. The result is confusion and conflict both within the police department and in its interaction with other government agencies and the public. The road to professionalism is rough and hazardous.

Despite the assertion for more than 50 years by national commissions and prominent authors that the police chief is the key to effecting needed improvements, the critical role of the police chief is frequently misperceived by both the general public and the appointing authorities to be that of a minor or ministerial function and not as an executive policymaker (President's Commission 1967b; see also Andrews's chapter). The position has been staffed accordingly in many cases. Generally, the police chiefs (along with directors of public works and finance) have a lower level of education than other heads of municipal departments (Municipal Manpower Commission 1962). Management training is not deemed to be very important for police chiefs, except in the far western parts of the United States, where a survey revealed 30 percent were college graduates in contrast to 12 percent nationwide (National Advisory Commission 1976).

RESEARCH ON THE ROLE OF THE POLICE CHIEF

Against this historical and management background, I was interested in observational study to understand better the role of the police chief. There are little data about how and why police chiefs utilize their most scarce and nonrenewable resource—their time—to develop and implement policy, assess the need for change, perform other duties, and provide leadership for needed improvements—all within the context of a political environment rich with misperception concerning the chief's role and fraught with other impediments to proper executive performance. Similarly, the effect of notions of professionalism on these issues is not fully understood.

During the four years from 1978 to 1982 I developed and implemented a methodology for comprehensive analytical study of the role of the police chief in a particular department. The goal was not only substantive inquiry but the testing of a new research approach that could be replicated efficiently in other departments so as to broaden the initial knowledge resulting from this study. I conducted three in-depth case studies of nationally prominent police chiefs who served suburban populations of 150,000 to 550,000. Henry Mintzberg's (1973, Appendix O) structured direct observation technique was enhanced to assess the time utilization of police chiefs. Instruments were developed on which minute-by-minute detailed observations were continuously recorded by codes for several categories of data for one week in each case. James Q. Wilson's (1970) categorization of three types of police departments provided the basis for developing an instrument for the analysis of the police chiefs' departmental records, policies, and goals in comparison with actual practices in the three agencies.

The primary focus of the study was the impact of time utilization, policies, and practices on the role of the police chief in effecting change. This was one of the first empirical studies of police chiefs, and it was exploratory, as is any other initial research. The three suburban police chiefs I studied would be considered superior by many of their peers. Presumably, the problems discovered in these three cases would be more severe for "average" police chiefs and possibly would be more severe in large urban departments.

Time Utilization

It has been effectively argued that the police chief should not manage his department's current activities but should ensure that the department is well managed by competent subordinates (Ahern 1972; Davis 1978). This provides time for the police chief to concentrate on long-range planning for needed change and other broad issues. Such an approach to management was not practiced by the three police chiefs whose time utilization was monitored for this study. More than 50 percent of the police chiefs' time was spent on activities of less than ten minutes' duration, such as signing documents, brief telephone conversations, or meetings. This rapid change of issues did not allow for much in-depth examination of many issues. Only 5 percent of total time was spent on activities of more than 60 minutes, such as formal meetings inside or outside the police department, conferences with the county executive, or legislative hearings.

Incoming and outgoing documents handled by the police chiefs averaged 370 per week. Few of these documents were originated by the chiefs, and many incoming documents were routine in nature and would never reach the chief executive's desk in a private organization. Laws and regulations frequently required the personal signature of the police chief, and therefore the signing could not be delegated to subordinates in some cases. Examples included small purchase order contracts and individual certification that each police officer in the department had completed mandated in-service training. There were some variations among the three police chiefs, who handled 261, 377, and 467 documents in a week, respectively.

The chiefs averaged 17 scheduled meetings (20, 19, and 14) and 50 unscheduled meetings (43, 62, and 37) in a week. Mintzberg (1973) notes that the mix of planned and impromptu meetings will vary with the size of the organization. Generally, he found, the smaller organizations are more informal, and their chief executive has more unscheduled meetings and fewer scheduled meetings, as do lower level managers in larger organizations. Public administrators generally are more informal than their private counterparts. This profile of lack of time-use control was reinforced by tabulation of initiators of unscheduled meetings and telephone calls. Fifty percent of the sessions and calls were initiated by persons other than the police chief. The police chief, it has been urged, should be accessible without appointments, but, except for emergencies, this free accessibility should be limited to a specific time of day, such as the end of the day (Davis 1978), rather than permit continual interruptions.

The time-use profiles and associated problems of these police chiefs are similar in some ways to the time-use profiles of both the chief executives and midlevel managers of medium to large organizations that Mintzberg (1973) studied.[3] There is support in the police administration literature for the finding that police chiefs perform as lower level managers, Ahern (1972), Goldstein (1977), and Murphy and Plate (1977) attributing the phenomenon in many cases to the chief's inability to delegate daily operations responsibilities due to a lack of competence or lack of support for policy on the part of subordinate staff. Ambivalence concerning the chief's policies may be particularly evident if the chief is hired from outside the department (see Murphy's chapter), which was true of two of the chiefs who participated in this study.

Purpose of Activities

The purposes for which the chiefs used their time in this study were particularly revealing. The police chiefs spent more than 50 percent of their time on current issues with relevance of from zero to two weeks, such as daily operations reports. They spent less than 20 percent of their time on long-range issues with relevance over one year, such as future budgets or other long-range planning. By contrast, Mintzberg's chief executives spent only 4 percent of their time on current issues and 50 percent on long-range issues. Police chiefs spent more than 10 percent of their time as "disturbance handlers," whereas Mintzberg's chief executives spent only 4 percent of their time in this way. Disturbance handling included civil suits in active litigation, allegations of misconduct by police, urgent inquiries from the county executive or legislature, and major crimes or other crises.

To be sure, long-range perspectives by police chiefs are impeded by their lack of tenure and an average term in office of about four years (National Advisory Commission 1976). Police chief executive preoccupation with current matters is also partly explained by a lack of information relevant for long-range planning. Another important factor is lack of professionalism in chiefs' subordinates, which other observers have also noted (Ahern 1972; Goldstein 1977; Murphy and Plate 1977). This weakness was particularly acute in the two departments I studied that had "outside" chiefs. In those agencies, staff opposition to the top executives' policies was evident, and, despite frequent recommendations to the contrary (for example, Holden, Fish, and Smith 1951), there were no long-term management development programs to assure quality in senior management.

Although the emphasis of the three chiefs I observed was on current issues, they did spend 13 percent of their time on management of innovation. Most of this time, however, was devoted to work related to current innovative projects, including initiating new opportunities for outside training and conference attendance, zero-based budgeting, civilian professional staff, management development programs, task force management, and decentralization of the organization. Mintzberg's executives devoted only 6 percent of their time to innovation, and much of this time arguably should be placed in a category other than "innovation," as it was devoted to refinements such as a new method for serving school lunches, replacing a weak executive, and acquisition of a computer system.

All of the chiefs in this study spent time in activities related to professional organizations, including writing professional articles, serving on committees, and/or speaking at conferences. This type of activity probably enhanced the opportunity for the chiefs to develop new ideas and concepts for their departments.

Policy Formation/Implementation

Policy formation/implementation was analyzed in the framework of Wilson's (1970) typology of three types of police departments: watchman, legalistic, and service. I made the assumption that legalistic and service police orientations are inherently conflicting in terms of the policies and activities they generate. The high level of discretionary arrest rates and police autonomy from the community that Wilson describes as the legalistic style of policing appear to be incompatible with the low arrest rates and community involvement of the service style of policing. Such variations in activities reflect conflicting characterizations of the police as an occupying army or public servants.

The three police chiefs studied all stated that they wanted their departments to operate in the (J. Q.) Wilsonian service style of policing, with strong community involvement. However, in response to my request that the chiefs list factors they considered indicators of achievement of their departmental goals, they cited a mix of legalistic and service indicators. The responses of one chief were primarily legalistic, and those of another were primarily service; the third was in between. All cited some goals and indicators that Wilson considered to be legalistic, including arrests and citations.

The officer performance evaluation systems provided little reinforcement for officers who achieved the stated service-oriented goals of the department. Ratings were based primarily on legalistic issues or neutral factors. One police chief was sensitive to this issue and had instructed his staff to design an officer performance evaluation system that would reinforce the desired service orientation for the department.[4] As of the time I studied these three departments, however, performance evaluation information received by the police chiefs was inconsistent with their information need for assessing their stated goals. Accordingly, to an important extent the chiefs were leading blindly, without the benefit of relevant performance evaluations. Actual practices, as indicated by discretionary arrest statistics, also indicated a mixture of legalistic and service profiles in terms of Wilson's descriptors. These included high rates of traffic citations and larceny and assault arrests in two departments and high juvenile arrest rates in one department (see Table 1).

None of the three police chiefs had issued a directive setting forth their philosophy to guide policy formulation. (One chief prepared such a statement of philosophy after discussions with me during this research.) This type of void presents impediments to development of a coherent set of policies and contributes to conflicts between agency policies and practices. The impact is felt by both the police chief and lower level managers, who are responsible for translating policies into practices.

The policing literature indicates that a clear goal structure, based on a coherent philosophy of policing, is important to guide all organizational activities toward stated objectives and consistent practices (David 1978; Goldstein 1977; Couper 1983; American Bar Association 1980). Such clarity of purpose is especially important for consistent direction when major changes are occurring in the police department. The departments under study did not appear to me to have this clarity of purpose, although this can hardly be surprising, since it is generally agreed that a fully developed philosophy of policing does not exist (Davis 1978; Goldstein 1977). Such a clear statement of principles would have the added virtue of facilitating community interaction with the police chief in setting policy through democratic processes (Ahern 1972; American Bar Association 1980). Such interaction, in turn, could result in an increase in community understanding, involvement, and cooperation with the police. At present, public involvement in any form of police policy formation is largely absent, aside from its major manifestation in the selection of a police chief (Eisenberg and Lawrence 1980; Wilson 1970).

Even assuming that emerging professionalism results in a coherent philosophy, a consistent goal structure, and comprehensive and reinforcing policies, and recruitment, selection, promotion, organization, and management are all tied to the goal structure, an essential ingredient is still missing for the governance of a police department — accountability (Murphy and Plate 1977).

TABLE 1. Arrest/Discretion Statistics for Three Police Agencies and Wilson Taxonomy/Data for Eight Cities

I. Police-Invoked Law Enforcement – Traffic Citation Rates
    3 Agencies

BCA
72–78

11.4	16.4	61.0	97.8	109.1	247.7

| Wilson's 8 Agencies | Watchman | Service | | Legalistic | |

II. Citizen-Invoked Law Enforcement – Larceny Arrest Rates
    3 Agencies

A B C
5.5.1–7.1

0.9	1.6	2.0	8.9

| Wilson's 8 Agencies | Watchman | Service | Legalistic |

III. Police-Invoked Order Maintenance – Drunk/Disorderly Arrest Rates
     3 Agencies

C	A	B
1.8	4.9	6.1

9.1	45.0

| Wilson's 8 Agencies | Watchman – (Service?)* | Legalistic |

IV. Citizen-Invoked Order Maintenance – Assault Arrest Rates
    3 Agencies

C		A	B
1.8		4.9	6.1

1.2	4.0

| Wilson's 8 Agencies | Watchman – (Service?)* | Legalistic |

V. Key Discretion Indicator – Juvenile Arrest Rates
    3 Agencies

B	A	C
5.5	5.7	9.5

0.1	1.3	12.0

| Wilson's 8 Agencies | Watchman | Service | Legalistic |

*Wilson's data sets are incomplete. Extensive computation and extrapolation from his data and text were required to get comparable data for the three types of police agencies. In some cases this was not possible and estimates are indicated by a question mark.

Regardless of who should "run" the police department, policies may not be translated into practices unless those responsible for implementation can be held accountable for costs, procedures, and results. Otherwise, philosophies and goals, no matter how well designed, are only paper tigers. In all three departments, the accountability powers of the police chief were very limited. All subordinates had civil service tenure. Despite the resulting limitations on the chiefs' legal powers, however, if the position of police chief had high professional status (an element of professionalism), the chief would have sufficient *informal* influence to impose some accountability on their subordinates.

Tenure/Appointment

Each of the three police chiefs studied stated that he had civil service tenure. (The courts later ruled otherwise after one of the chiefs was dismissed.) Two of the chiefs, who were appointed from outside their departments, had been in office from 18 months to 3 years at the time of the study. All had initiated major changes soon after their appointment. In one case, the new policies met strong employee resistance, ending in a "no-confidence" vote by the police union. This chief was dismissed three days after a new county executive took office. Another chief resigned after four years in office, and the third remained in office but was promoted to director of public safety. The policies of the third chief continued after he was promoted, but many of the policies of the other two executives were discontinued after their departure and replacement by more traditional police chiefs.

Part of the reason the lineage of blind police leadership persists is that, as the policing literature emphasizes, in addition to the many other barriers to accomplishment, there are few rewards and many risks for police chiefs who initiate change (Vollmer 1931; Kenney 1975; Goldstein 1977; International City Management Association 1977; Grosman 1975). The perils of being a reformer were verified in this study. I saw no evidence of any rewards provided to these three police chiefs for implementing new concepts. In fact, the one of the three police chiefs who was dismissed when a new appointing authority was elected met his downfall at least partly because of his innovative policies. Another chief resigned voluntarily, but newspaper publicity had emphasized problems he incurred from the employees as a result of his innovative policies.

In a truly professional environment, peer review and recognition for outstanding performance are basic elements. This is not generally the way things work for police chiefs, though; indeed, peer condemnation may be the "reward" for those who upset the status quo, as in the case of the International Association of Chiefs of Police vote to censure Patrick Murphy (Herbers 1982). Unfortunately, this criticism does not apply only to police chiefs.

Emanuel Velikovsky was blackballed only a few years ago by the scientific community for his concepts on the nature of our planets—this notwithstanding that recent deep space research by NASA has proved that Velikovsky was correct. If new concepts are correct, then old concepts may be wrong, and the establishment in any field does not like to admit that it is wrong.

Those chiefs who nevertheless attempt significant changes will find that five years or more can be needed to institutionalize fully major new program directions (National Advisory Commission 1976; Goldstein 1977) and that that period exceeds the average tenure of police chiefs by about a year (National Advisory Commission 1976). Most chiefs lack the permanent tenure or fixed contracts that could ensure sufficient time to phase in their ideas on long-range planning and implementation (see Andrews's chapter). Police chiefs who are appointed from outside their departments are especially vulnerable to employee opposition to change (Grosman 1975; Murphy and Plate 1977; Goldstein 1977). However, appointment from outside is the best way to infuse new ideas into a department (Grosman 1975; National Commission on Productivity 1973). These conflicting dynamics present a "catch-22" situation for police improvement and are sufficient to drive any responsible police executive into a blind rage.

Organizational Development

In any case, even under the best of circumstances, managing change is difficult in an organization and more difficult in a centralized bureaucracy such as most police agencies. Police chiefs need a comprehension of effective change management technologies, particularly organizational development (Whisenand and Ferguson 1973; More 1975; Roberg 1979). These techniques include open communication, participative management, and general applications of the social sciences to management. I observed three particular problem areas. First, although all three chiefs practiced some of the principles of organizational development, such as task forces for problem solving and planning, they lacked a thorough understanding of these concepts and an awareness of their importance for facilitating change in their organizations. Second, all three departments were organized along the military bureaucracy style, which inhibits applying modern management concepts, including organizational development, and conflicts with the basic requirements of policing (More 1975; Manning 1978; Goldstein 1977; see Klockars's chapter). Third, the rapidity with which the two outside chiefs attempted to make change is contrary both to the principles of organizational development and to the review/change/stability cycles discussed in the general management literature (Mintzberg 1973). Thus, in spite of ad hoc adherence to some principles of organizational development, these police chiefs found their efforts impeded by the lack of a more structured and comprehensive approach.

Education

One police chief in this study held a bachelor's degree and had two years of graduate study. Another chief held a bachelor's degree with no graduate study, and the third chief (who was promoted from within the department) did not hold a college degree but had completed extensive management training courses. It appeared to me that the police chief who lacked a college degree had a more coherent set of policies and policy reinforcements than the other two chiefs.

No statistical conclusions can be drawn about the effects of educational levels on the performance of police chiefs due to the limited sample in this exploratory study, but an observation of potential importance emerged from the research. I found that the two police departments where the police chiefs held college degrees had high educational standards for officers and financial incentives for continued college education. In both departments recruits were required to have two years of college, more than 35 percent of the officers held bachelor's degrees, and 10 to 20 percent held graduate degrees. But the department where the police chief did not hold a college degree required no college attendance for entrance and had no educational incentive pay; moreover, only 16 percent of its officers held bachelor's degrees, and just one member of the department had a graduate degree. (These departments had 380, 950, and 133 employees.)

The implications of this finding for larger departments in urban environments are not clear, but the literature provides some hints. College-educated police officers are more open to progressive changes than less educated officers (Cohen 1963; Goldstein 1977). College-educated police officers also are frequently penalized in performance evaluations by their less educated supervisors (Cohen 1963; Sherman and National Advisory Commission on Higher Education for Police Officers 1978), which seems consistent with Sherman's (1978) finding that police chiefs who have not been to college feel threatened by college-educated employees. Many police departments have effectively subverted any beneficial impact of education on facilitating change of the status quo, despite outward support of college education. Sherman noted that these problems should subside as older and less educated chiefs are replaced by younger and more educated chiefs. He emphasized also that police departments must make major changes, including their policies and organizational form, before education will yield benefits. I did not observe such fundamental changes in any of the three departments I studied.

RESEARCH CONCLUSIONS AND IMPLICATIONS

The major voids and conflicts concerning the stated goals of the three police chiefs and the realities in their departments are reflections of voids in aspects of police professionalism. The concept of professionalism, which embodies an established philosophy of policing derived from formalized ethical and educational standards, is almost the opposite of what is frequently meant by professional policing in the police literature. The absence of a well-articulated philosophy of policing leaves chiefs without substantive guidance in policy formation, priority setting, and program implementation. The result is operational and management problems that were manifested in the chiefs' time-use profiles (attention more to current operational matters than long-term planning) and in misinformation or gaps in information for the police chief.

The two observed departments that were experiencing major policy redirection encountered two types of impediments to successful innovation. First, the chiefs and their key subordinates did not comprehend the principles of organizational development. Indeed, in both departments, which had chiefs appointed from the outside, subordinates opposed the chiefs' policies in some cases and thwarted implementation by artful filtering of information to and from the chief executives. Second, the innovation process was extremely fast-paced, possibly a result of the chiefs' awareness that the average tenure of people in their jobs is quite short.

The methodology developed for this research can be efficiently replicated to validate these initial findings on the role of the police chief. As indicated earlier, since these three police chiefs enjoyed well-deserved national stature, my expectation is that the problems discovered in this research would turn out to be more severe for most other American police chiefs.

In light of these conclusions, what can we say about the questions, Who runs the police? and, Who should? Those questions prompt another — Who should *not* run the police? — and require a definition of "run." If "run" refers to directing daily operations, two things are clear: that police chiefs perform this function, and that they should not. As indicated, such a focus, which frequently is necessitated by incompetence and/or disloyalty in subordinates (Ahern 1972; Goldstein 1977; Murphy 1977; Grosman 1975), distracts chiefs from their need to provide leadership on broad, long-term issues (Ahern 1972; Davis 1978).

If "run" means to set policies, priorities, and mechanisms to ensure both achievement and accountability, there are major voids. That is, *no one* runs the police. The process is more informal than structured (Wilson 1970). Setting policies and assuring their implementation are two different and separable issues, and converting ideas into reality can be very difficult. I have adverted to several issues in policy setting that have implications for professionalism. First, we lack an adequate philosophy of policing to serve as a foundation that gives ethical content to public or management discussions and resulting policy formation in police agencies. Second, there is a dearth of standards for police chief selection that could help identify applicants qualified to undertake one of the most demanding, complex, and responsible positions anywhere in public administration. Such standards, if they demanded the highest qualifications, would afford police executives professional status and thereby enhance their leadership and influence and consequent ability to convert policies into realities.

What is filling these voids in running the police department? They are filled to a great degree by tradition – by the ghost of O. W. Wilson, prevailing on modern police executives from their earliest recruit training to maintain militaristic bureaucracies with legalistic orientations. "To a great extent, the police are prisoners of the past" (Walker 1983a, p. 2). This ghost must be exorcised by a very strong force – true professionalism. The exorcism will entail, among other things, fully appreciating how deficient the information available to us – and chiefs – is concerning police operations. It is no accident that James Q. Wilson's (1970) indicators for the various styles of policing are all legalistic (arrest rates and citations), even for the service style of policing. This is because police departments, for the most part, do not keep statistics on levels and quality of service to their community, even when, like each of the chiefs I studied, the chief sincerely desires a style for his department that embodies the service and order maintenance approaches, in the context of community cooperation. The nearly exclusive reporting of legalistic measures is evident in almost every police annual report that I have seen over many years, including those of the three departments studied in this research. To redirect police management and information systems will require coming to grips with a set of constituencies who are ignorant of or hostile to the needed changes. It is as if the chiefs and other forces for progress are trying to design an efficient jet plane at a time when almost all the pilots and support personnel are trained on propeller planes and are skeptical of or morally opposed to jets and when the public is uneducated about the benefits of jet transportation. In such an environment, the information that flows to police chiefs will continue to be management misinformation concerning needs, problems, directions, and solutions.

In the extensive research that will be required to enlighten and professionalize both the understanding and the practice of the police chief, the focus should be on thinking rather than counting. The current emphasis on data analysis in criminal justice research detracts from the fundamental need for selecting, defining, and understanding the question before attempting the answer. University courses in "research methodology" aggravate this problem, with emphasis on calculating the answer frequently overriding emphasis on defining the question (Brown 1982, p. 12). In many cases, sophisticated mathematics camouflage foggy thinking and yield highly precise misinformation. Computers have compounded this problem by facilitating complex analysis of doubtful data about misleading questions. Precision without perception is counterproductive to meaningful research, but precision is easier to achieve than perception, and there is a strong tendency to take the easy path in any endeavor (see Cordner's chapter). The destruction wrought by believing in false precision is similar to the problems created in organizations where process triumphs over purpose (Goldstein 1979). In his biography of researcher Peter Drucker, Tarrant (1976, p. 12) cites the reaction by Chris Argyris of Harvard that has application to the topic at hand:

> Some social scientists may fault Peter for not being more of an empirical researcher. I do not, for if he were, I wonder if he could have made the conceptual path-clearing contributions that he has made. If I were to fault Peter, it would be that he never seemed to realize that in his "nonscientific" consulting-based methods of inquiry were the seeds of a new methodology for social science — one that it needs desperately if it is to become generally applicable.

Although exploration of some basic questions will benefit from quantitative analysis, many basic questions about the police in general, and the police chief in particular, involve ethical and political questions that are difficult, if not impossible, to quantify. For example, Friedrich (1980, p. 83) notes: "[I]f, as . . . Reiss . . . says, 'at law, the police in modern democracies such as the United States possess a virtual monopoly on the *legitimate* use of force over civilians,' then it is clear that to examine the police use of force is to examine an activity at the core of politics and society."

The paucity of research concerning the police chief is both a problem and a benefit. The problem has been discussed at some length already. The benefit is that the subject area is not overloaded with poor research, so a fresh start is possible without having to override or contradict large amounts of existing "learning." Writing on a relatively clean slate, however, does not reduce the complexity of the assignment: a total rethinking, reorientation, and reorganization of the police (see Ahern 1972; Goldstein 1977; Manning 1978; Sherman and National Advisory Commission on Higher Education for Police Officers 1978). But how does one replace the coal burners on a ship with a nuclear engine without putting the ship in dry dock? Such interruption of police services is not viable, and the sudden mass substitution of nuclear engineers for coal shovelers is not possible; nevertheless, methods must be found to accomplish these fundamental and drastic changes.

Most police and their chiefs, who have had this militaristic, bureaucratic legalism imbedded in them since their first day in basic training, find change is very difficult. Citizens and city councils, who have never heard of any alternatives, cannot conceive of hiring a police chief of any other persuasion.

Most of the literature cited in this chapter expresses great urgency but little hope about correcting these problems in the near future. If one were to seek the ideal police chief today, with all the indicated attributes of professionalism, it would be an impossible dream. It would approximate the quixotic search for the ideal superintendent of schools, described by Argyris and Schon (1974, p. 145):

First, the profession cannot be counted on to reform itself since it is too much the prisoner of its own world, which may include its own pecuniary interests. But the professional school is hardly the place to initiate reform since it tends to be divorced from the real world of professional practice. Second, if the professional schools could begin to turn out a completely new kind of professional, how would that person fare in a professional establishment made up of professionals of the old type? Third, professional education must be reformed in order to produce the new professionals capable of initiating professional reform; but where are the professionals who will reform professional education? And where is the theory and the competence for the practice of reform?

From this lament about the obstacles to improvement of the acknowledged profession of teaching, it is obvious that professionalism alone is not enough to ensure that workers in a given occupation will function effectively in light of current societal needs. To be sure, professionalism on the part of police chiefs and their subordinates will not solve all of the problems of the police and the citizens they should serve. However, without a significant movement closer to the goals, structure, and substance of professionalism, I see little hope for realization of the improvements desperately needed in American law enforcement, which have been advocated by leading authorities and national commissions for more than 50 years. There remains little doubt today that the quality of policing is primarily dependent on the quality of its personnel (Saunders 1970), particularly its leadership (Ahern 1972; Murphy and Plate 1977; Goldstein 1977; Couper 1983).

A number of benefits will follow the professionalization of police executive work. Four come to mind. First is a full realization by police chiefs of the need for fundamental changes in policing, based on their acquiring the widespread knowledge that already exists. Second is an understanding of the kinds of modifications that are essential and the change-management techniques for enhancing success. Third is improved stature for the police chief, resulting from his professional obligation to provide information and leadership to the community and government concerning the basic reforms that are required for enhancement of the quality of life and justice. Fourth is a foundation for developing a management information system (in the broadest context, not just computers) that will provide valid guidance to the police chief on progress and problems and will facilitate the translation of the ideas into reality.

Mecum (1979) describes the evolution over decades of a profession from an occupation. The evolution has seven phases, all of which are to be continually enhanced: need recognition, behavior definition, body of knowledge, expected behavior (two phases), entry restriction, control, and code of ethics. In the development of police chiefs' professionalism, we are only at phase two or three. There is a long and difficult road ahead, but progress must continue. Essential steps are to recognize that the role of the police chief is unique and distinctive from the roles of all subordinate police managers and to develop a body of knowledge bearing on the chief's job, including his unique information needs. Perhaps a helpful way to begin this hazardous journey is to recognize and implement the nine principles of policing articulated by Peel, Rowan, and Mayne (Reith 1952). Actual use of these principles would advance police practices in the United States to the state of knowledge that existed in 1829. These principles embody the concept that the police are effective only to the degree that they have the cooperation and support of the public for crime control, order maintenance, social service, or any other function. In my opinion, no other approach can be successful, and no other approach is possible in a democracy (see Brown's, Davis's, and Reiss's chapters).

There are those who assert that many of the described problems of police chiefs are found commonly elsewhere in public administration and corporate management. They are correct. Left unsaid, but nonetheless true, is the unhappy reality that the distinctive role of the chief executive has been largely neglected in research and writing. The recently published *Taking Charge*, by Bennis and Namus (1984), is one of the few management books on the chief executive to be published since Barnard's *The Functions of the Executive* in 1938. The police field, unfortunately, is not alone in its failure to professionalize its chief executives. Public administration and corporate management have much in common (Peters and Waterman 1983; Drucker 1973; Shinn 1978).

What Deal and Kennedy say in *Corporate Cultures* (1982, pp. 21, 31) is no less true for the police:

> Values are the bedrock of any corporate culture. As the essence of a company's philosophy for achieving success, values provide a sense of common direction for all employees and guidelines for their day-to-day behavior. These formulas for success determine (and occasionally arise from) the types of corporate heroes, and the myths, rituals, and ceremonies of the culture. . . . *** They suggest what kind of information is taken most seriously for decision-making purposes. . . . They define what kind of people are most respected. . . .

Deal and Kennedy also note that the organization's culture is strongly driven by these normally informal and unwritten value systems and that these strong values run the risk, as they become obsolete, of inhibiting change. They emphasize that differences between the rhetoric and performance of the chief executive can be very confusing to the organization. Their book, although written for a different arena, has substantial relevance to policing and to questions of the legalistic versus service orientation and the militaristic, bureaucratic versus participative management orientation of American law enforcement. Deal and Kennedy continue (p. 38):

> The management ethic has to do with order, procedure, and fitting square pegs into square holes. Heroes defy order in pursuing their vision. And this violates the management canon: You don't do anything unless you can figure out whether it makes sense. So, while business certainly needs managers to make the trains run on time, it more desperately needs heroes to get the engine going.

Although widespread research, discussion, and study are needed for improved performance by chief executives in many fields, if a triage system were used to prioritize those chief executives needing most immediate attention, police chiefs would be at the front of the line. As the literature cited earlier amply demonstrates, the police chief's role is complex and important; few positions anywhere in public or private management are as difficult. Virtually no other chief executive holds such a public trust, where performance under his command so directly affects each citizen's life, liberty, peace, and ability to pursue happiness. Proper performance of this role and fulfillment of this trust require the highest capabilities and professionalism for the police chief, as well as a maximum effort by researchers and others to support and assist the emerging, professional police chief. Hopefully, my own research and the other contributions in this book are steps in this direction.

In a 1983 speech at the FBI Academy, Alvin Toffler (1982), author of such books as *Future Shock* and *Third Wave*, expressed concern that the historical and current use of police as agents of control, employed and deployed to retain the status quo, would cause a social explosion. He depicted today's society as becoming more diverse and pluralistic, reversing prior trends toward uniformity. If the police try to continue to enforce the monolithic lifestyles of the past, Toffler asserted, the resulting social pressures will destroy our democracy and leave in its place a totalitarian government. In this view, then, appropriate performance by the police is vital not only to individual liberty in particular situations but to the very survival of our democratic system of government. The police chief must take the lead in improving police performance, but he can succeed only with much greater realization of the elements of professionalism.

Who should run the police? Ahern (1972, p. 248) provides an answer: "Above all, it means people who are willing to 'support your local police' by turning police departments upside down and making the police on whom they depend the kind of professionals who can do their jobs within strictly defined limits of legal and ethical practice." The public — and police chiefs — will be at a serious disadvantage in any attempts to turn things "upside down" until chiefs and researchers can begin to create a philosophical basis of policing. With this foundation, we could start developing a coherent goal structure and a better sense of what information police executives need about their operations and how they can best acquire and use it. All of this requires a full appreciation of James Q. Wilson's (1970) assertion that the most important manifestation of a political culture is the selection of a police chief and the National Advisory Commission's (1973b, p. 42) perception that "the most enduring problems in criminal justice are neither technical or financial—they are political."

NOTES

1. This discussion is limited to the United States. Writers have contrasted the low standards for U.S. police chiefs with the high standards for police chiefs in Europe since the beginning of the twentieth century (see, for example, Fuld 1909; Fosdick 1920).

2. The "Mayo Crime Index" measures the FBI's Uniform Crime Reports "Part I" calls for service per patrol officer per week for a city. For all U.S. cities over 50,000 population, regardless of demographics or police/population ratio, the index is almost a constant with about 90 percent of all these cities having an index rate between 1.0 and 1.9 (Mayo 1983, p. 7).

3. Direct comparison between police chiefs and Mintzberg's chief executives must be attempted cautiously because most of Mintzberg's executives were in the private sector. The five chief executives he studied headed a consulting firm, an engineering research company, a hospital, a consumer goods manufacturer, and a public school system. All five organizations were large, with budgets in the $15 million to $100 million range and were in that sense comparable to the three police departments I examined.

4. The resulting performance evaluation criteria included such factors as quality of work, quantity of work, work habits, attitude, people relationships, personal appearance, dependability, judgment, initiative, knowledge, and progress potential.

35
The Ethics of Experimentation in Law Enforcement

John E. Shapard

Some years ago a halfway house program was mounted in California in an effort to break the vicious cycle in which ex-drug addicts paroled from prison, finding themselves unable to secure employment, return to drugs and the crime necessary to support their drug habits and soon return to prison to repeat the cycle. The idea was that the halfway house, through firm control over its residents, would preclude their return to drug use while helping them find employment, housing, and, in general, a place in the mainstream of society. Realizing that not all ideas that are promising in concept turn out to be effective in practice, California authorities undertook to test this program by a rigorous experiment (Fisher 1965). From among the population of parole-ready inmates thought suitable for the program, some were randomly chosen for parole to the halfway house and the others were granted conventional parole. Comparison of the subsequent recidivism, employment, and other successes or failures of the two groups was to reveal the effectiveness (if any) of the program.

From the point of view of research methodology this was an admirable undertaking. The dangers of false inference about program effects arising from the garden-variety try-it-and-see-what-happens experiment are legion. One need look no further than medicine, where the truth of beliefs about treatment effectiveness is of obviously great importance, to be appalled at the mistakes that have arisen from inadequate experimentation. One specific example is a surgical treatment used as a prophylactic against bleeding of esophageal varices that was performed routinely for many years before a controlled experiment revealed that the risks of the surgery exceeded the risks presented by the condition the surgery sought to correct (Strauss 1973).

From the point of view of law and ethics, however, the halfway house experiment does not pass muster so easily. It presents a number of questions.

First, recognizing that this experiment was conducted by the parole board and involved the incarceration of inmates in the halfway house, one must ask whether the parole board had any legal authority to do that. Second, if it did have the legal authority, was it a proper exercise of the board's discretion — was it, in the general sense of the word, *ethical* for the board to place parole-eligible inmates in the more confined environment of the halfway house? After all, the act of conducting an experiment is an admission that the parole board was not convinced the halfway house would do any good. If, on the other hand, the board was confident about the effectiveness of the halfway house, what justification can there be for randomly depriving some parolees of that treatment?

My purpose in this chapter is not to argue that it is wrong to conduct an experiment of the kind I have just illustrated. Quite the contrary, my purpose is to illustrate how it may be quite proper, perhaps even necessary, that experiments of this kind be conducted, despite the difficult issues they may sometimes present. In particular, my intention is to outline the conclusions that the Federal Judicial Center's Advisory Committee on Experimentation in the Law — a group of distinguished judges, lawyers, and scholars, convened by the Chief Justice of the U.S. Supreme Court — reached concerning the ethics of conducting justice system experiments (Federal Judicial Center 1981).[1] My hope is that others, more knowledgeable than I about policing, will be able to weigh the suitability of these conclusions for guiding decision making in the law enforcement arena.

ETHICAL QUESTIONS AND PROGRAM EXPERIMENTS: AN OVERVIEW

At the outset I should make clear that neither this discussion nor the committee report that it summarizes offers a checklist of dos and don'ts that allows one to determine whether a given experiment should or should not be done. At best, these efforts will only tell a police chief or other major policymaker what things to consider in reaching his decision and assist him in weighing competing considerations. Since ethical questions almost never admit of clear-cut answers, it is no failure of judgment that a decision that has had to grapple with competing ethical principles turns out, in retrospect, to have been the wrong decision, provided that the right ingredients went into the choice. A decision that fails to take account of the relevant issues, however, represents a failure of responsibility even if it turns out in retrospect to be right decision.

This chapter is limited in scope to "program" experiments, which involve alteration in the actual operation of the justice system, as distinguished from "simulation" or "laboratory" experiments. For instance, a classroom experiment testing student witnesses' ability to describe the perpetrator of a surprise but mock offense committed in the classroom is not a program experiment. Nor is it a program experiment when psychologists evaluate the recollection of real witnesses about real crimes but not in a manner that purposefully influences the solution of the crimes or the prosecution of the perpetrator. But an experiment comparing different methods of witness interrogation to see how those methods influence the police or prosecution function, involving real witnesses and real crimes, would be a program experiment.

The extent of official or governmental involvement differs considerably in program experiments and laboratory/simulation experiments, as the three preceding examples attest. There is no police involvement in the classroom experiment involving a mock crime. Moreover, police need not be involved in the experiment where psychologists use real witnesses beyond helping the psychologists secure the witnesses' cooperation. But in the program experiment, it is the police themselves who conduct the test, and this is so whether or not expert researchers are involved — who may think *they* are conducting the experiment. The point is that program experiments in the justice system are authorized and conducted only by the official(s) responsible for the operational component of the justice system that is being manipulated for experimental purposes.

The fact that it is the police department, and ultimately the police chief, that conducts a program experiment in police operations is central to the difference between the guidance provided by the Advisory Committee's report and accepted but inapposite ethical guidelines common to such disciplines as medicine and psychology.[2] This point may be illustrated by considering the divergent contexts in which a psychologist and a police chief would reach a decision whether to conduct similar psychological experiments. The psychologist, interested in the experiment for the contribution it might make to the general body of psychological knowledge, has two choices. He can proceed with the experiment, provided he can obtain the necessary cooperation from the intended subjects and he is not otherwise precluded by lack of resources, his own professional ethical principles, or laws prohibiting what he proposes to do. Alternatively, he can choose to forego the experiment and do nothing. He is not under any basic moral obligation to discover the information the experiment promises to reveal. The police chief, in contrast, being obliged to administer his agency, cannot simply decline to address a personnel or other problem he believes exists in his department. Because a proposed innovation promises to address a specific agency need, the police chief has three choices. He can adopt the suggested innovation, forego it, or conduct an experiment to resolve uncertainties that preclude an acceptable choice between the first two options. In seeking the best balance of advantages and disadvantages, the police chief cannot properly decline to experiment after considering only the problems associated with the experiment; he must also consider the problems associated with the other alternatives. As problematic as an experiment may be, it may nonetheless be preferable to retaining the status quo or adopting the innovation without knowing whether it will succeed or whether it will produce worse problems than those it is intended to correct.

The context in which justice system administrators must evaluate the wisdom of particular experiments is viewed as enormously important by the Advisory Committee's report. The overriding theme of the committee's guidance is that decisions about program experiments are inextricably bound into the fabric of decisions that justice system administrators must make about how their institutions ought to function; the ethical considerations bearing on such experimentation therefore must derive in large measure from the ethical considerations that guide all judgments justice system administrators must make about the operation of their institutions. Placing ethical standards for experimentation outside the context in which the results of the experiment will be put to use deprives experiments of any basis for justification and deprives the justice system of any recourse other than shots in the dark when hard choices must be made.

Implicit in this central theme is another key recommendation: When an experiment to improve the operation of the justice system is needed, it may well be wrong not to experiment, so long as the effort is properly designed to provide the required information. Concomitantly, a program experiment should be undertaken only if it is really needed. If a satisfactory choice can be made without experimentation, or if the results of the experiment are unlikely to influence a future decision to alter the operation of the justice system (for example, because the proposed innovation is fiscally or politically infeasible), then it will probably be wrong to conduct the experiment.

QUESTIONS TO GUIDE THE ETHICAL ASSESSMENT

More specifically, the Advisory Committee (Federal Judicial Center 1981, p. 7) proposed four sequential questions to guide justice system administrators in evaluating the necessity for program experimentation:

1. Do the circumstances justify consideration of a program experiment?
2. What experimental designs will be adequate to produce the required information?
3. What ethical problems might these experimental designs present, and how can they be resolved?
4. What authority and procedures are necessary for undertaking the experiment?

The first question in turn requires reflection on four "threshold conditions":

First, the status quo must in fact warrant substantial improvement or be of doubtful effectiveness. Second, there must be significant uncertainty

about the value or effectiveness of the innovation. Third, information needed to clarify the uncertainty must be feasibly obtainable by program experimentation, but not readily obtainable by other means. And fourth, the information sought must pertain directly to the decision whether or not to
adopt the proposed innovation on a general, nonexperimental basis.

It should perhaps be emphasized that the fourth threshold condition has the
corollary that experimentation for experiment's sake has no place in the justice
system. If psychologists want to know how traffic offenders given warnings
differ in response from those given summonses, but the police department
has no need for that information to decide how it should deal with traffic
offenders, the psychologists will simply have to look to something other than
an experiment involving actual manipulation of police response to traffic
offenders.

The second question requires the police chief or other justice system administrator to have expertise or access to expertise in research methodology
in order to identify the kinds of experiments that "may, or may not, yield
sufficiently precise and unambiguous results.*** [S]uch an understanding
reveals that experimental design is not merely the technical concern of researchers, but is a crucial ethical consideration in the decision to undertake
a program experiment" (Federal Judicial Center 1981, p. 7).

The third question demanded the bulk of the committee's attention in
its report:

> Two [basic ethical] principles, equal treatment and respect for persons, are
> recognized as having paramount importance in evaluating experiments in
> the justice system. To the extent that experimental practices encroach upon
> these principles, they harm the interests of individuals, and must therefore
> carry a commensurate burden of justification.
>
> The necessary basis for justifying infliction of harm is the benefit likely
> to be achieved. In weighing harms against benefits, one must recognize the
> varying significance attached to different kinds of harm or benefit. The
> crucial decisions about program experiments involve weighing harms to par-
> ticular individuals against benefits to some larger group or to the general
> public.*** The balance of harms and benefits associated with a proposed
> program experiment must always be evaluated in light of the harms and
> benefits that may ensue from alternative courses of action—retaining the
> status quo or innovating without prior experiment. (pp. 1-8)

The committee's approach was not strictly utilitarian (a point on which I will
say more later), as it recognized that some harms were unacceptable regardless
of the benefits.

Among the specific kinds of harm that the third question envisions the
justice administrator having to weigh in considering program experiments are

mandatoriness (that is, use of subjects in ways to which they do not consent), disparate treatment, infringement of subjects' privacy, and concealment from subjects of the purpose or fact of the experiment. Mandatoriness includes involuntary imposition of the experimental treatment, unilateral denial of the experimental innovation to persons in the control or comparison group, and nonconsensual use of persons merely as means for experimentation. Disparate treatment is measured according to a number of variables, including the extent and significance of the difference in treatment, whether the disparity is mandatorily or voluntarily imposed, and the not entirely metaphysical issue of whether the disparity involves a differential provision of benefit or a differential imposition of harm.

Sometimes the last issue is argued in a manner I regard as disingenuous, such as the suggestion that disparate provision of a beneficial treatment (for example, early parole) is not an imposition of harm but a mere denial of benefit. But that is true only when the practical alternative to experimentation is maintenance of the status quo. If the only acceptable alternatives are adoption of the beneficial innovation across the board without experiment or conducting an experiment involving disparate provision of that treatment, then we must face the fact that, for the sake of experimentation, some subjects will receive a more onerous treatment than they otherwise would. There is rarely a rational basis to distinguish between the half-full glass and the half-empty glass. Responsible decisions to undertake problematic experiments demand that we admit when the experiment poses troublesome ethical issues and offer our arguments in justification, not that we pretend there are no problems and thus no need for justification.

When individual subjects' privacy is at stake, the experimenter is obliged to protect their "confidentiality and, where possible . . . anonymity." The Advisory Committee took the position on the fourth harm it identified that "even if the research process might be strengthened by concealing from the subjects that they are involved in an experiment, . . . or the nature of the experiment, concealment is a doubtful course and imposes a special burden of justification" (p. 9).

The report wrestles with the bases for justifying experimentation in the face of obvious harms not by proposing "black-letter" decision rules but by offering examples to show how the factors it has identified might be weighed against one another in reaching a decision (pp. 49–66). As a general, commonsense proposition, one will need strong justification for imposing significant harm for the sake of experimentation. At the same time, however, if there are both substantial uncertainties about the effectiveness of the proposed innovation and serious problems with the status quo, the case for experimentation is strong. The Kansas City preventive patrol experiment (Kelling et al. 1974a) might be a good example, in the sense that the status quo of preventive patrol was of uncertain value and problematic because of the drain it placed on police personnel, whereas the alternative of reducing or eliminating preventive patrol raised the serious question whether it would lead to an increase in crime. I do not mean to suggest that justifying an experiment in such circumstances will be a simple matter, but I do suggest that it is quite possible. There are, I would think, many more instances where questionable innovations ought to have been tested by program experimentation before they were implemented than there are experiments that ought not to have been conducted.

Some experiments, as adverted to earlier, ought not be conducted regardless of their possible social utility. The committee recognized certain absolute limits, such as the obvious constraint that we cannot experiment with programs that are beyond our legal or constitutional authority to implement on a nonexperimental basis. No matter how promising it is as a crime control technique, for instance, I take it the police cannot experiment with on-the-spot delivery of corporal punishment to offenders caught in the act of crime. One-stop shopping for criminal justice is not what the founding fathers had in mind for the American experiment. Even where the Constitution and law could permit a given treatment, however, there are limits to experimentation. Capital punishment presents a case in point. Assuming that there are grounds for uncertainty about the efficacy of capital punishment and that there are feasible ways of resolving the uncertainty by experiment, I take it that such an experiment simply could not be justified. In some areas, we must proceed, if at all, in the face of uncertainty.

WHY INFORMED CONSENT IS NOT NECESSARILY REQUIRED

Because informed consent is a concept of such paramount importance in the ethics of research involving human subjects, it will not do to leave my earlier remark that consent "does not make sense" in the justice system context as the only argument in support of the committee's acceptance of non-consensual use of persons as experimental subjects. I should make it clear, however, that I am going to offer my own argument. While it builds on the report's observation that "[e]xperiments within the justice system will often unavoidably involve compulsory participation on the part of individuals because the justice system has many compulsory aspects" (p. 4), my reasoning is not presented as that of the committee.

In my view informed consent is not an *absolute* requirement in any area of research, including medicine and psychology.[3] I believe it makes no sense to talk about the ethics of research as a set of principles that exist independently of principles governing the concrete activities that constitute a particular experiment. To characterize an activity as research is to make a statement about the state of mind of some person involved in that activity (the researcher). Describing an activity involving human subjects as "research" describes nothing at all about the influence of that activity on the human subjects. At least in modern Western societies, moral concepts of rights and obligations have to do with how individuals (and other entities such as governments) may and may not influence one another. I submit that one cannot discern what moral principles pertain to me and to my relationship with another person without knowing something more than the bare fact that I regard that relationship as one in which I am a researcher and the other is a subject.

It is certainly true that if my proposed use of a person as a research subject involves doing something that I cannot otherwise do without his consent, then I must have that consent to conduct the experiment. But it seems to me that if the intended subject has no general moral privilege to preclude me from doing what I propose to do, then I am not obliged to secure his consent when I propose to do it as "research." So if someone chooses to take a stroll in Central Park, I am not obliged to secure his consent before I observe the strolling, whether or not my observation is in the context of research, press coverage, casual curiosity, or perverse fantasy. There are, of course, things that one person may be privileged to do to another under specific conditions, but those conditions are not satisfied merely because the one person is doing research. Police officers are privileged to arrest persons under certain circumstances, but they are not privileged to arrest persons merely because they are doing research that would be furthered by making the arrest. On the other hand, if conditions warrant an arrest, the subject's consent is not necessarily required merely because the arrest will be used in furtherance of research.

I think the general presumption that informed consent is required in all research involving human subjects has had unfortunate results, interfering with responsible research and sometimes making a mockery of the endeavor to ensure that research is not conducted in an unethical manner. Where the consent requirement has been perceived to be too burdensome, the effort has not been to reexamine the requirement but instead to look for exceptions. The exceptions, however, tend to be based on considerations of convenience, which are not satisfying as bases for justifying moral wrongs. It is not ordinarily agreed that larceny is justified provided that the theft is petty and the need is great. Similarly, I cannot see how, if the subject's consent is required, we can be justified in using the subject without consent, merely because we regard the ends as important and the harm as slight. I think it would be far more defensible to acknowledge that consent is not always required and to maintain a firm ethical stance in those circumstances where it is required.

APPLYING THE SUGGESTED ANALYSIS
TO A HYPOTHETICAL POLICE EXPERIMENT

To illustrate more concretely some of the recommendations of the Advisory Committee's report, I will attempt to apply them to a hypothetical police experiment intended to provide information that will aid the chief in improving the department's response to cases of spouse abuse.[4] The police in this jursidiction have at their disposal three responses they can make in an instance of spouse abuse: arrest, referral to a public agency for counseling by a social worker, or issuance of a warning. The proposed experiment would employ random choices among three alternatives in order to provide a basis for evaluating which response is most effective in what circumstances.

The threshold conditions for considering a program experiment are easily satisfied. First, the status quo is seriously inadequate for a number of reasons, including a high incidence of assault on officers who attempt arrests in spouse abuse cases, serious harm to victims and drain on police resources resulting from repeated problems in the same households, and a serious morale problem among officers who confront these situations with little guidance on how to respond. Second, there is significant uncertainty about the value and effectiveness of all three possible responses. It is noteworthy that because all three responses have for some time been employed at the discretion of individual officers, there is no obvious "innovative" program subject to experiment. Instead, it is the intention of the proposed experiment to discover ways of deploying existing treatments in a more effective manner. There is some confidence that each of the three available treatments is most appropriate in some circumstances, but there is very little confidence that those circumstances are well understood for any of the three treatments. Third, information that might resolve these uncertainties cannot be obtained other than through a program experiment. Efforts have already been made to assign treatments in accordance with guidelines suggested by experts and to draw inferences about the treatments through comparative analysis of cases in which officers followed these guidelines and cases in which they picked treatments using their own discretion. None of these efforts has proved helpful. Fourth, the information sought pertains directly to decisions about deployment of the treatments to be tested by the experiment.

The second task posed in the committee report, which is beyond the scope of this paper (see Federal Judicial Center 1981, pp. 15–24, 81–122), is a detailed examination of what experimental designs will be adequate to produce the required information. Suffice it to say that, due to the history of failed research efforts, there is no hope of obtaining reliable information other than by random assignment of spouse abuse cases to the three different treatments. Even so, a likely weakness of this experiment is that we cannot be especially confident that the results will lead to improvements. It is possible that we simply cannot find a basis for distinguishing between cases where one treatment rather than another tends to have the best results. So the justification for the proposed experiment will be that it is our only present hope for mitigating a serious problem.

The third prerequisite to experimentation is identification of the ethical difficulties created by the various experimental designs and a determination whether any of those designs is justified in light of competing considerations. Here is where this hypothetical experiment will present the most difficult issues. I assume that when an officer is presented with a spouse abuse situation, he or she is confronted with a number of conflicting responsibilities and may experience varying degrees of uncertainty about how to respond. I also assume that ordinarily there will be significant room for exercise of the officer's judgment. In the range of possible circumstances encountered, there will be occasions when the officer finds that one of the three available responses — arrest, referral to social work, or warning — is an obvious best or only choice. There will be other circumstances where the officer is quite uncertain which alternative to choose. Two basic alternatives for the proposed experiment are that all spouse abuse cases are to be included in the random assignment scheme, even when the officer feels confident that a particular treatment is best, and, at another extreme, that the only cases subject to random assignment are those where the officer personally feels unable to make a choice among the three alternatives. There are various possible approaches between these extremes.

As a general matter, there will be less difficulty in justifying an experiment in which only cases involving the greatest uncertainty are subject to random assignment.[5] It will be very difficult to justify an experiment calling for random assignment of all cases, including those that seem clearly to call for one particular treatment. Specifically, it will be nearly impossible to justify random assignment in a case where arrest seems clearly necessary to protect the safety of family members. And it will be difficult (but perhaps not as difficult) to justify arrest of a person where, in the absence of the experiment, that person clearly would not be arrested.

One argument that is sometimes advanced in support of this type of experiment was specifically disapproved by the Advisory Committee. The argument is that random assignment of (in this instance) spouse abuse cases can be fully justified on the ground that the results obtained by exercise of various standards of judgment are indistinguishable from those ensuing from random decisions. There are two things wrong with this argument. One is the simple logical fallacy that trying and failing is the same thing as just not trying. Although in some circumstances that may be true, there are other circumstances, including those where one has a responsibility to try, where it clearly is not true. The committee report identifies an obligation of individualized treatment by justice system operatives, an obligation perhaps most apparent in the judge at sentencing, who cannot justify flipping a coin because he is uncertain. I would suppose there exists a similar obligation in law enforcement. The second fallacy in equating apparently random results with intentionally random decisions is an empirical fallacy, that what our best efforts at analysis suggest is no better than randomness is in fact randomness. I am not suggesting here that the hypothetical experiment is foreclosed by ethical considerations; merely that the apparent randomness of current decisions does not, by itself, justify foregoing the attempt at rational decisions. More is needed to justify random assignment. In this hypothetical experiment, it is very likely that random assignment of some *subset* of the class of all spouse abuse cases can be justified in light of the potential benefit of knowledge that may improve decision making in the future.

A FINAL NOTE ON THE IMPORTANCE OF EXPERIMENTATION

In undertaking, as I have done here and as the Federal Judicial Center's Advisory Committee has done in its report, to analyze the objections that may be made to a particular practice, it is easy to be misunderstood as creating hurdles rather than clearing paths. It is important to understand that the report is not intended to discourage experimentation but to facilitate it — to "foster responsible experimentation within the justice system." It challenges two patterns of thought that have stood in the way of needed experimentation. First, it says quite clearly that ill-conceived experiments — tryouts that cannot feasibly provide adequate information about the success or failure of an innovation — are worse than no experiment at all. The choices that may properly be available to a police administrator are to accept an innovation without experimentation, to forego the innovation, or to conduct a well-conceived experiment, one that has been designed to provide information that will help resolve significant uncertainties. Second, the report cuts down to size two arguments that have often stood in the way of adequate police experimentation: the argument that random assignment is barred as an unethical deprivation of benefit or imposition of harm, and the argument that experimental subjects must consent. These are concerns that demand examination in reaching a decision about undertaking an experiment, but they are not absolute barriers. Judiciously weighing these and other ethical issues that bear on police innovation is among the toughest and most important challenges that will confront police leadership in the decades ahead.

NOTES

1. My primary focus in this chapter — and the primary focus of the Federal Judicial Center's committee, on which I served as staff director — is ethical considerations. Space does not permit discussion of the legal, constitutional, political, fiscal, and programmatic issues frequently raised by police experimentation (see Federal Judicial Center 1981, p. 6).

2. When the Federal Judicial Center's committee turned to existing literature about the ethics of research involving human subjects for help in resolving such dilemmas as the clash between random assignment of experimental program participants and provision of innovative services

to all in the service population, the guidance we found seemed quite inapposite to our immediate concern with testing court innovations. To mention only the most obvious example, a cardinal principle of traditional human research ethics is that one must have the informed consent of the experimental subjects. Because judges do not need the consent of the arrestee before such decisions as setting bail or other terms of pretrial release, it did not seem to make sense that consent should be required merely because that decision would constitute an element of an experiment.

3. This view flies in the face of the prevailing notion that informed consent is an absolute prerequisite to research involving human subjects. In the medical context, a patient's consent to his physician's probings is generally assumed and not expressly solicited, which has made it easy for the physician to overlook the sometimes fuzzy distinction between experimentation and accepted practice. Although I do not see informed consent as an absolute moral imperative, nevertheless I have no objection to an absolute requirement for informed consent as part of the ethical canons of research of some professional group. The American Psychological Association, for example, might reasonably include the informed consent requirement as part of its "code of professional ethics," not because of an ethical imperative but because it is thought to be an effective means of protecting the reputation of the profession or of providing a margin of safety against research that might overstep basic moral obligations.

4. Although real experiments of this sort have been conducted, my comments are not about any actual research efforts.

5. Although justification may be easier in such an instance, gathering a sufficient number of cases to do research could present serious practical problems since police officers are professionally socialized to be decisive even when harboring some doubt about the proper treatment of an incident. This is not said in denigration of police officers. They are men and women of action, deployed by society to "get involved" in circumstances that most of the rest of us would rather avoid. Police leadership and the community at large would need to convey clear support for police officers' admissions of doubt concerning proper disposition of spouse abuse cases before this hypothetical experiment could be expected to sufficiently overcome police officers' "face" of self-confidence (see Kerstetter's chapter).

36
Justifying the Moral Propriety of Experimentation: A Case Study

George L. Kelling

In 1971 a group of consultants visited the command staff of the Kansas City Police Department at the request of Chief Clarence Kelley and the Police Foundation to assist the department in patrol planning. The impetus for this interest was that 320 new officers were to be added to the patrol bureau, and Chief Kelley wanted to deploy them to increase the effectiveness of patrol.

At that time in the United States, police patrol tactics were dominated by two pieces of conventional wisdom: Moving police cars rapidly through city streets created a feeling of police omnipresence and prevented crime, and rapid police response to all calls for service resulted in increased arrests of criminal violators. In addition, most police believed that these tactics decreased citizen fear and increased citizen satisfaction with police.

Proposals originating inside the police department at that time to improve the effectiveness of patrol in Kansas City generally took one of three forms: Modify the existing beat structure to increase the amount of patrol time available for preventive patrol and reduce response time, use new personnel to provide more intensive patrol at given times or places, and increase plainclothes or undercover patrol. A standoff resulted among adherents of these three positions. At a consultant's suggestion, Chief Kelley created task forces in each of the patrol districts to recommend, with the aid of a Police Foundation consultant, means to improve patrol. Each innovation would be evaluated, a process I was retained to facilitate by advising each task force as it came close to devising a plan.

The task force in the South Patrol District quickly arrived at its own standoff: Task force members agreed that the most serious problems in the area were created by juveniles. Some members of the task force wanted to plan special tactics that focused new patrol resources on youth. Others believed strongly that use of officers to enhance preventive patrol and rapid response to calls for service was so basic to community safety that diversion of personnel, even new personnel, to tasks other than patrol would be inconceivable. A new debate emerged in the task force: the efficacy of preventive patrol. (Rapid response to calls for service was another matter; challenges to the ideas inherent in rapid response would come later in Kansas City, but from some of the same personnel [see Bieck 1977; Spelman and Brown 1982].) Some officers argued vigorously that preventive patrol was the "thin blue line" between order and chaos. Others asserted, equally vigorously, that preventive patrol was a waste of time. The task force decided to evaluate preventive patrol as a first step in the process of determining future patrol strategies. Chief Kelley gave tentative approval to the idea.

THE EXPERIMENT

The design selected to evaluate preventive patrol was experimental. In five beats the level of preventive patrol was substantially increased, in five beats it was held at the level it was prior to the experiment, and in five beats preventive patrol was reduced as far as possible — South District patrol cars would only go into those areas when responding to calls for service. The independent variable was the amount of time police spent patrolling an area. The dependent variables were victimization, recorded crime, citizen fear, arrests, and citizen satisfaction with police. We deliberately did not change any police services other than preventive patrol (see Kelling et al. 1974b).

During the experiment's one-year duration, approximately 50,000 citizens lived with substantially reduced levels of preventive patrol in their neighborhoods. It turns out that they did not know it, suffered no significant increases in recorded crime or victimization, and lost no confidence in police as a result. Another 50,000 citizens lived with substantially increased levels of preventive patrol. They did not know it either. Fear, crime, victimization, and levels of confidence in the police were not affected (Kelling et al. 1974a).

ETHICAL CONSIDERATIONS

This discussion will concentrate on the ethical propriety of the Kansas City Preventive Patrol Experiment to provide an actual case study against which the reader may consider John Shapard's chapter in this volume and the report on which it draws (Federal Judicial Center 1981). Unlike much of the experimentation Shapard contemplates, but like the hypothetical spouse abuse study he discusses, the program experiment in Kansas City tested the status quo rather than exploring an alternative to it. Experimenting with the status quo accentuated the problems of ethical justification, for even the President's Commission on Law Enforcement and Administration of Justice (1967a), which looked critically at so many elements of the criminal justice system, reaffirmed the conventional wisdom of police that preventive patrol was the necessary heart of policing. The question in the police field at that time was not whether or not preventive patrol was effective but how it could be expanded. Few chiefs of police hesitated to assert before their city councils that crime would be reduced if only more police were provided and used in preventive patrol. Its unpopularity in minority communities, acknowledged by the President's Commission, was to be dealt with by community relations programs — often little more than attempts to convince citizens of the wisdom of then-current modes of policing.

Outside the realm of police administration, however, and despite the President's Commission, inchoate questions about the value of preventive patrol were mounting from those few researchers in the police area. Black (1968) and Reiss (1971) questioned the arrest productivity of proactive police patrol. Press (1971) attempted to evaluate increased patrol in New York City, but the findings were inconclusive. An evaluation of the Indianapolis Fleet Car Plan (Fisk 1970) — an attempt to increase the sense of police presence by having police officers take their patrol cars home and use them privately — also produced unclear results (see Hudnut's chapter, p. 25). Researchers increasingly called for more systematic and powerful evaluation of preventive patrol (Kakalik and Wildhorn 1971; Larson 1972).

It was in the context of this polarity over the efficacy of preventive patrol that the experiment was initiated in Kansas City. The burden of justifying the experiment in Kansas City at first fell on consultants and the evaluation team. Later, the burden was shared by the South Patrol task force. The issue, of course, was the safety of the citizens in those areas where the time police officers spent patrolling was to be reduced to the lowest level possible. (Nobody expressed concern about those areas where police presence was to be increased, admittedly a possible function of the absence in these discussions of certain community interests.) In the areas patrol was reduced, which we called "reactive," patrol officers were only to respond to calls for service. Upon completion of response activity, police were to leave the beat and go to those areas where preventive patrol levels were increased ("proactive" areas).

The ethical propriety of reducing patrol presence came up in the South Patrol task force as soon as the design was suggested. Many officers sincerely believed that criminals would "run away with the place." When the methodologists suggested that we needed as many beats as possible in each experimental condition — not, as task force members hoped, one beat in each condition — this concern became even more acute.

Our justification to the task force for experimentation was twofold. First, we argued that there were substantial reasons to doubt the efficacy of preventive patrol: They had their own doubts about its value, the empirical literature cast some doubt about its effectiveness, and despite increases in preventive patrol over the years crime was continuing to rise. Second, we promised to establish procedures for constant monitoring of crime reports and assured the task force that if reported crime did show any signs of significantly increasing in reactive areas and those signs persisted, we would recommend that the experiment be aborted. Fed by its own doubts about the value of preventive patrol and reassured by the prospect of an ongoing monitoring system, the task force agreed to recommend the experiment to the various levels of command.

Indeed, the task force joined the consultants and evaluators in presenting the justification for the experiment in turn to the district commander, the command staff, and the chief, none of whom had spent the time the task force had considering the pros and cons of the experiment or had the task force's pride of authorship in the proposal. Most of the administrators, relatively unimpressed by the doubts of patrol officers about the efficacy of patrol and minimally impressed by the empirical literature, nevertheless found two factors presented by the group persuasive: the willingness of the district commander to conduct the experiment in his district and the existence of a monitoring system that would provide weekly feedback about reported crime. The final persuasive factor was that Chief Kelley subtly communicated some willingness to conduct the experiment, even before his administrators formally recommended that the experiment proceed. The command staff recommended implementation of the experiment, Chief Kelley approved, and steps were taken to initiate the experiment.

The issue of propriety arose again after the experiment was authorized and the assignment of beats to conditions was to be decided. The researchers wanted to assign beats to experimental conditions in a two-step process. First, the fifteen beats would be grouped into five sets of three beats each by matching them on crime and demographic variables. Then beats would be assigned randomly from each group to each condition: proactive, reactive, and control. At this point the task force balked. They were concerned about a variety of issues: If we selected randomly, the reactive beats might cluster and thus affect response time; really "bad" beats should not be without patrol; a particular shopping center just could not be without protection; and several others.

The researchers responded, with limited persuasiveness, by attempting to sell the importance of randomness. Finally we selected several random patterns and identified them in the order they were drawn. We strongly advocated that the task force select the first one, which, from our point of view, was *the* random sample. We also suggested that they consider the others and, as a group, attempt to devise a pattern with which they could all be happy. Not surprisingly, *every* alternative was unsatisfactory to somebody, an impasse that lead the group finally to select the random sample we had been advocating all along.

Predictably, concern for the safety of citizens in reactive beats did not dissipate. Indeed, it was such an issue to so many police officers that the experiment had a false start. Not appreciating just how strong the officers' drive would be to get into their beats, we had made provision for patrol officers to enter their reactive beats to serve warrants. We were not worried because we were aware of how rarely officers serve warrants. Once the experiment started, however, officers set all-time records for the quantity and pace of warrant service. In fact, many officers spent a good share of their time doing little else. The experiment was stopped, the ground rules changed, the officers convened, the importance of the experiment and the provisions for monitoring the beats reiterated, and the importance of entering beats only in accordance with experimental guidelines emphasized. Chief Kelley also added this note: The relevant officers were ordered to stay out of their beats, and a midlevel manager was given an assignment that generally was thought to be disciplinary.

What became apparent during this interlude was a problem that we had noted throughout the planning phase: The issue of the ethical propriety of experimentation was a genuine one and had to be rigorously addressed, but it also was a powerful rallying point for those who for other reasons wanted to block or subvert the experiment. As such, it was a clever ploy. Walter Lippmann's statement "There is nothing so bad but it can masquerade as moral" probably is a little too strong in this context, but it certainly can be said that there was not a single basis of opposition to the experiment — opposition to outsiders working in the department, opposition to the chief, reluctance to change working patterns, antiintellectualism, resistance to systematic program evaluation, and so on — that was not, at one time or another, masked as concern about the moral propriety of experimentation. As Reiss (1979, p. 93) warned, "Social institutions and organizations can be protected from dangerous knowledge in the guise of protecting others."

Differentiating between legitimate moral concerns and other resistances to experimentation and responding appropriately to each was difficult. Those resisting in this way often get the moral high ground. If deeply committed they can threaten or use publicity to destroy the experiment. The trouble is, they often can only be dealt with through administrative use of authority. They are like acting-out children who, when told to do something, respond by saying, "Just give me one good reason why I should do that." Such a response appeals to our sense of fairness and reason. And it may be a good faith question. Often, however, the question is not a request for information. When information is given, the response is, "That's not a good reason" — over and over to each additional bit of information. Once into such a dialogue, the trapped adult usually responds with, "Well, you're going to do it because I told you to." The child walks away victoriously, "Why didn't you say that in the first place?" As a matter of fact, in Kansas City the questions were not asked in good faith; they were a challenge to authority. In that setting, there could be no good reasons. Ultimately, as was the case in Kansas City at that time, such episodes have to be dealt with on the basis of authority but in ways that do not jeopardize any particular experiment with various audiences.

CONCLUSION

In Kansas City, a group of police officers, consultants, and researchers experimented with the status quo of policing. We experimented with it because those who had installed it as a police tactic never tested it in the first place. The burden fell on us to justify the experiment, as approximately 50,000 residents would be left without a police service conventional wisdom asserted was essential to their safety, feeling of security, and confidence in the police. Informed consent was out of the question. The conventional wisdom of policing was so pervasive that telling citizens they would be without preventive patrol services would have resulted in widespread fear. It also might have encouraged criminals to be active in the area. If preventive patrol had the effect that police said it did, its absence or presence alone should be recognizable by citizens and a measurable impact result. Publicity about the experiment or gaining community consent would have negated the experiment.

We justified the experiment to multiple groups on the basis of the literature and some police doubt about the effectiveness of patrol. Our own confidence was buttressed by theories of crime and social control that did not posit the police as central to crime control and prevention. To avoid doing harm to citizens, we monitored reported crime statistics on a weekly basis and were prepared, if crime had reached levels significantly different from anticipated trends for a predetermined period of time, to scrap the experiment. Although concern for the moral propriety of the effort enabled its opponents to delay and threaten the inquiry, such hurdles are probably unavoidable — and perhaps useful — parts of conducting police experiments in a democratic setting.

37
Rights and Risks: The Ethics of Experimentation in Law Enforcement

Frederick A. Elliston

When should experimentation be undertaken by the police? The report of the Federal Judicial Center's Advisory Committee on Experimentation in the Law (1981), as ably summarized in this volume by John Shapard, attempts to provide a systematic answer to this question. Though I am in substantial agreement with many of the conditions set forth, I disagree on two points: the threshold test of the need for improvement and the waiver of consent.

THE NEED FOR IMPROVEMENT

The Advisory Committee's position that current practices must be in substantial need of improvement before experimentation is warranted can easily prove too restrictive. For example, if the current practice is of dubious effectiveness because no reliable evaluative evidence is available, experimentation can and should be undertaken (assuming the other conditions are satisfied). The well-known Kansas City Preventive Patrol Experiment was conducted not because preventive patrol was not working but because no one knew whether or not it was effective in deterring crime, as popular wisdom held.

Moreover, even if present practices are working, when current but incomplete data suggest the prospects for improvement are sufficiently great, an experiment to test the proposed innovation may be warranted. In my view, the appropriate calculation is the improvement of the proposed change over the current practice less the costs of the experiment measured in both monetary and moral terms. What is critical is the improvement to be accomplished by the implementation of an experimental innovation, not simply the acceptability or unacceptability of the current practice.

One difficulty, I concede, is that costs and benefits cannot be easily or precisely determined. But neither can the degree of acceptability of the present practice. It is not at all clear, for example, who should judge the need for improvement and against what standard. Do we simply count the number of people who find the status quo acceptable? As a question about engaging the machinery of change, the answer provided by the Advisory Committee is plausible: The adequacy of present practices should be judged by the administrator in charge of the program. Yet how should he or she make such judgments? Citing with approval a decision to experiment with alternative programs designed to reduce juvenile recidivism, the committee states that the "apparent inadequacy of the status quo [arose] from the judges' serious doubt about how best to use the two programs — not from mere lack of strong or scientific evidence." This statement is one of the most troublesome in the book for me, for two reasons.

First, the adjective "mere" connotes a disparaging, antiquated attitude toward social scientists. Indeed, various critics have suggested that it is the failure of criminal justice practitioners to appreciate and integrate the work of social scientists that has made such a mess of the system (compare Stewart's, Cordner's, and Mayo's chapters), especially the judiciary, where disparate treatment of "clientele" has persisted as a serious and almost intractable problem. Second, and equally importantly, the word "mere" gets the problem backwards. It is precisely the lack of evidence — nothing more and nothing less — that provides the sole legitimate basis for the judges' doubts. Such scientific evidence, carefully gathered and cautiously evaluated, rather than personal predilections or political pressures, should serve as the driving force for innovation and change in the criminal justice system.

THE PROBLEM OF CONSENT

The committee takes a radical stance on the requirement of informed, voluntary consent by research subjects — a pervasive and strong restriction on human experimentation. Shapard attempts to explain why this requirement can be supplanted by the discretion of a criminal justice system administrator, who has standing authority to coerce people in certain ways. Does this substitute suffice? Before attempting to answer this question, let me pose a logically prior one: Who are the subjects?

When a doctor injects placebo into a patient, the subject of the experiment is obviously the person who receives the injection. When a student fills out a questionnaire on employment, again it is obvious who the subject is. But in the case of organizational research, the subject is more difficult to identify. And when the organization is a courtroom or police department, it is not nearly so obvious who the subject is. The biomedical model of experimenter-subject breaks down as too simplistic for the complexities of organizational research.

In the case of the policing, one could take the individual department as the subject. But the boundaries of a police organization are difficult to determine. They would seem to encompass at least the police administrators and officers. But what about those detained and accused by the police, the members of the public served by the police, and the agencies to whom the police department reports? If the department in some meaningful sense includes all of these elements, then the consent of each would be required. If it includes only some, then what is the principle of demarcation and its rationale?

In Shapard's elaboration of the consent problem, he asserts that consent is required if I am doing something to someone that I cannot do without his consent — that is, something that I am not authorized to do. Accordingly, if a judge has the authority to sentence someone to jail or put him on probation, then he does not need his consent to test an experimental probationary program. The implications of this position for the police raise some concerns. Shapard's deference to authority must be balanced by a recognition of its limits. Though judges have the authority to sentence offenders, they can only impose a sentence that falls within the limits of the law. Similarly police authority is limited by the rights of citizens generally and the rights of individuals in various roles, such as the accused, convicted, or incarcerated. Police executives' authority is also limited by the rights of various criminal justice system operatives, such as police officers, sergeants, district attorneys, and judges.

Will the authority of a police chief serve as an adequate substitute for the consent of those affected by an experiment, as the Advisory Committee and Shapard suggest? I think not, for two basic reasons, one practical, one principled. First, if a police chief relies exclusively on his authority and makes no effort to obtain the consent of officers, he may very well alienate or demoralize them. His ability to lead and administer the department — and to run an experiment — may be undermined by overreliance on authority in place of consultation, consideration, and goodwill. Police officers can subvert an experiment they believe will be harmful to the community or the department, and the process of securing their consent serves to elicit the support that is vital to sound experiments.

Second, in opposition to the authority of police administrators, I would place the principle that people — individuals and the public at large — should not be placed at risk, even an unknown risk, without obtaining their knowing consent in some fashion. This principle is a corollary of the Kantian dictum to demonstrate respect for persons.

Admittedly, this consent cannot always be secured in advance without undermining the experimental design. For that reason the public's consent was not obtained in the Kansas City Preventive Patrol Experiment, a decision with which Shapard and the committee would concur. In that experiment and in others it was critical that the public's attitudes and beliefs not be altered and therefore that they not be informed immediately and directly. Assuming this need in a given experiment, it seems to me that the consent of the public's representative could nevertheless be obtained. Members of the jurisdiction's city council meeting in camera could provide "proxy consent" on behalf of the community or refuse it. They could also perform some of the functions of an institutional review board by maintaining a disinterested and watchful eye that checks any misplaced enthusiasm of police administrators and social scientists. Alternatively, one could insist on a debriefing so that citizens are informed, at least retrospectively. If they find the experiment objectionable, they can restrict the authority of those who implemented it, throw them out of office, or impose safeguards to mitigate their concerns.

By appealing to the compulsory aspects of the criminal justice system that deprive many subjects of a choice, Shapard and the committee have in mind those arrested, incarcerated, or convicted. These citizens are under the jurisdiction of the courts, and their freedoms are thereby curtailed. Though I would not challenge the general principle that such citizens have less choice, I would question its implications and applications. First, it does not follow that such citizens have no rights. From both a legal and a moral point of view, even detained and incarcerated citizens have rights that any experimental design must respect. While the practical difficulties in requiring their consent are serious, I have yet to be convinced that they are unsurmountable. Second, police departments are unlike the courts in that their officers deal far more extensively with the public at large. Such members of the community are unlike prisoners and detainees who arguably have diminished rights. Consequently, the public's consent should be obtained before experiments are conducted that may adversely harm them. This consent could be obtained directly through town meetings or open sessions of city council. It could be obtained indirectly through closed meetings with their representatives. Or it could be obtained retrospectively through debriefing sessions that allow citizens to voice concern and hold administrators accountable for their exercise of authority.

CONCLUSION

It is difficult today to decide what works in criminal justice. According to some critics, nothing works, and we would do well to scrap the entire system and start over again. Others such as John Shapard and the other authors of the Advisory Committee's report favor a piecemeal approach that targets areas in need of reform and enlists the services of social scientists to develop alternatives that will bring about improvements. Despite my criticisms, I support the spirit of the report. It is a bold document that offers the prospect of fruitful collaboration between the police administrator and the social scientist to improve police services.

38
The Quest for Certainty: Ethical Concerns in Police Experiments

Fred Rice, Jr.

In thinking about what circumstances justify a program experiment, I found myself in sympathy with both Elliston's and Shapard's chapters for this volume, even though the former emphasizes the potential for significant benefit from experimentation and the latter emphasizes the need for caution and reminds us of the potential for negative consequences. As a chief executive, I want both of these perspectives when deciding whether to approve a proposed experiment.

Along with Keith Bergstrom, I am less inclined to support the concept of experimentation for its own sake, to which Elliston seems favorably disposed. Such an approach to experimentation, in my opinion, increases the potential for abuse. Moreover, it can strain already tight police budgets. I favor a policy that encourages "laboratory" experimentation, where possible, to justify proposed program experiments. By laboratory experimentation, I mean, as Shapard says, an experiment that does not involve alteration in the actual operation of an on-line program.

I agree with the contention that the pursuit of knowledge is an important aspect of managing professional police agencies. But when we do experiment, I consider it essential that the experiment meet the threshold conditions identified by Shapard and the committee with which he worked.

On the other hand, I find troublesome Shapard's suggestion that the medical profession is under no moral obligation to contribute to medical knowledge, even though he denies any intent to extend this reasoning to the police. In my view, if doctors have an obligation to cure, then they also have a moral and perhaps a legal responsibility to cure as effectively as possible. But they cannot do so, as medical malpractice suits and the profession's code of ethics imply, unless they constantly strive for better palliatives. Having said this, however, I should respond also to the notion that there is a moral imperative to experiment. Some proponents of this position—not Shapard—believe that one need only identify an organizational deficiency to create that imperative, a perspective that ignores the organizational and societal costs that may be imposed by a poorly conceived experiment.

Although Kelling makes an eloquent defense of the moral justifiability of the Kansas City Preventive Patrol Experiment, I am left with some doubts, which I offer as observations rather than criticisms. (As a public figure I am acutely aware of how easy it is to be a Monday morning quarterback or an angel in paradise.) One concern I have is that the informed consent of the Kansas City population most likely would have been impossible. An informed population probably would not have permitted the experiment or, at the very least, would have contaminated it. It appears that the problem was resolved by disregarding the issue of consent altogether. I wonder, too, whether the "informed cooperation" of the police officers was sought. Kelling points out that Chief Kelley had to "order his men to stay out of their beats." It is obvious that the patrol force in Kansas City had at the very least some lingering faith in the "prevailing wisdom" of preventive patrol. Would additional strategizing about the police officers' reactions to this experiment have been more advisable? Bear in mind that if the preventive patrol officers had such a negative reaction to the experiment, other personnel who were *not* restricted from the area—such as traffic, gang crimes, and detective units—may have taken up some of the "preventive patrol" slack. If this did occur, how did it affect the experiment? Did the absence of "informed cooperation" cause any personnel problems for the Kansas City Police Department? I would be interested in a follow-up study analyzing the impact of the experiment on that organization.

My concern about the officers' reactions heightens my interest in Elliston's question, "Who are the subjects?" In experiments like the one conducted in Kansas City, are not police officers also subjects? If so, do we need to grapple with the issue of how we can obtain their informed consent? And what do we do when they will not give their consent? Anyone who has served in the armed forces will be familiar with the military system of securing "volunteers," but is that desirable in this setting?

The problem of obtaining consent from those operating and being "operated upon" by a paramilitary organization is not easily resolved. One approach may be to seek resolution through legislation or executive decree. I think that "proxy consent," one of Elliston's proposals, deserves further examination. We discovered in the early history of our nation that true democracy became more difficult as populations increased. The mechanism we developed to deal with this problem is a form of democracy once removed, or "representative democracy." The "representative consent" or proxy consent that Elliston suggests may be the closest we can come to a plausible solution. Like most police chiefs, I hope such a solution will be tried soon—in any city other than my own! An obvious problem with proxy consent would be the undermining activities (media leaks and the like) of those within the representative body who oppose either a particular experiment or an incumbent city administration.

I do not, however, support the concept, also advanced by Elliston, of "retrospective consent." "Consent" implies compliance with something proposed, not completed, and requires an act of will. Although I acknowledge the existence of retrospective consent whenever my wife comes home with some new dresses, as a professional matter my view is that retrospective consent is impossible.

I consider the quest for certainty about which Elliston writes a call to action. Because it is adventuresome it carries with it both the potential for dynamic and productive improvement in operations and the potential for disruption. Current police operations have developed incrementally, and many have been the result of true democratic compromise. Accordingly, I recommend that we move cautiously in our quest. Few administrators vigorously oppose the concept of zero-based budgeting. But fewer still would permit us to eliminate all programs we cannot immediately justify. Reengineering the police function should proceed slowly and cautiously.

Innovation and experimentation in the police field have been comparatively rare. For every experiment we carried out in the past, I suspect, along with Shapard, that ten appropriate and necessary experiments were not conducted. Casual examination of this situation would encourage the uninitiated to draw some standard conclusions about partisan politics or lazy public officials. But the real problem is that experimentation has been discouraged by a number of factors. One has been a genuine, although unarticulated, concern over ethical issues. This concern may nevertheless have found voice in the insistence by a number of police managers asked to approve program experiments over the years that any experimental population be given the full benefit of the constitutional rights normally applicable in criminal cases. (This insistence may help account for the "accidental compliance" of many previous experiments with the constraints Shapard recommends.) Another factor that has discouraged experimentation has been the absence until now of intelligent, well-researched ethical guidelines geared to the particularities of the police world.

Some experiments have had to proceed, just as other aspects of policing must proceed, in the absence of apparently useful guidance. I can relate one example of unguided experimentation from my own agency's experience. Early in 1982 the Chicago Police Department was asked to participate with a local charitable organization in a program experiment to ensure that the benefits offered by the new Illinois Domestic Violence Act were extended to persons experiencing domestic violence. The program sought to have police officers provide the charitable organization with the identity of people whose involvement in domestic violence has resulted in a call to the police. We agreed to participate in the program on a pilot basis in two police districts.

Without an extended discussion, I think I can establish that the threshold conditions Shapard mentions were met, although we had no familiarity with them at the time. First, current practice, we were willing to admit, was of doubtful effectiveness. Second, there was significant uncertainty about the value of the proposed referral program. Third, there were no other practical means besides experimentation to resolve uncertainties about the usefulness of the proposal. And fourth, the experiment was intended to assist in a future choice between retaining current practices or implementing the innovation.

Early in the planning stages, questions were raised about the need to secure informed consent for the referral from the citizens involved in domestic violence. After lengthy discussion with our research and legal staff, we were advised that notifications by police officers to the social service agency should be made only if a victim was willing to grant permission for a referral and sign a permission section on the referral card. Our compliance with this advice seriously hampered the entire program for two reasons: Victims who initially were willing to have their situation referred were reluctant to sign their name to a referral card, and in other cases officers did not attempt to secure the victim's signature and otherwise complete the referral cards, probably owing to a pervasive police distaste for paperwork.

In January 1984, after the program had been in operation for five months, the issue of consent was again raised, and additional legal research failed to uncover an appropriate legal reason for obtaining the victim's consent. We decided, as Shapard puts it, that the victim lacked any "privilege" to prevent the referral. We then instructed our officers to complete the referral card in all cases and not to seek the victim's signature. Despite persistent discomfort by some of our personnel about nonconsensual referrals, the increase in notifications has been dramatic.

I do not know whether the decisions we made in planning and modifying this pilot project would have been different if we had known about these experimentation guidelines at the time. But I am sure that we would have been much more comfortable with those decisions because, as Chief Bergstrom observes, we would have dealt *explicitly* with immensely important issues that tend to get lost in relatively informal considerations. Since that time, to enhance the department's research design expertise and to help us assess the difficult issues raised by research proposals, I have established an ongoing departmental "research advisory committee," which includes internationally respected police and legal scholars, all of whom serve at no expense to the agency.

In closing, it occurs to me, in contributing to a volume whose hallmark is the mixture of practitioners and academics, that the issue of experimentation in law enforcement raises precisely the kinds of questions on which police managers and scholars can productively join forces. Together, perhaps, we can make greater strides in pursuit of solutions to the difficult problems of providing better policing to the public.

39
Police Experimentation with Civilian Subjects: Formalizing the Informal

Keith R. Bergstrom

In considering the issues raised by my co-contributors concerning police experiments in which civilians rather than officers are the intended subjects, I will direct my comments to three areas: the utilitarian justification for the potential harms that may be involved in program experiments; some policy issues such experiments may generate; and the value that program experiments can bring to police agencies by forcing management to formally consider several ethical issues that are currently at best informally evaluated, at worst deliberately ignored.

UTILITARIAN JUSTIFICATION

Despite Shapard's recognition that some absolute limits must be imposed on the tolerable harms produced by experimentation, I am uneasy that, in the pragmatic world of policing and city government, most of the key decisions will nevertheless be guided by the harm-benefit calculus of classic utilitarianism. These decisions include whether the status quo should be changed; if so, whether a program experiment is needed and can be justified; and the resolution of issues in the conduct of program experiments (for example, when the principles of equal treatment and respect for persons may be violated and when the experimenter may choose not to obtain the subjects' consent because doing so might affect experimental conditions or stop the experiment) (also see Kelling's chapter). I am afraid that too often the answer in all these instances will turn on whether the benefits outweigh the harms.

For me, this prospect raises some hard questions. For example, who

---

The subtitle of this chapter is taken gratefully from Goldstein (1977, p. 82).

defines — and in what way — the harms and benefits that are fed into the calculus? How do we trade off short- and long-term harms and benefits? How do we measure individual, let alone societal, gains and losses in areas like privacy, disparate treatment, or respect for persons? Who sets the basic rules, through what process, to absolutely limit what can be justified?

Although the mechanisms of applying utilitarianism, or most other philosophical systems, are imperfect, for me the hardest part is swallowing the ethical implications of resolving police experimentation questions by resort to utilitarian values. My difficulty is that, as Rawls (1971, pp. 24–26) argued, the principle of utility does not necessarily serve the ends of "justice" as that notion has come to be embraced in this nation. The utilitarian objective of maximizing the net balance of societal satisfaction does not preclude violating the "liberty of a few" in exchange for creating a "greater good shared by many." In short, I do not believe we can justify the possible inequities in program experiments by calling upon a philosophical rationale that fosters rather than corrects those same inequities.

Further, and equally important, we must be careful not to mislead ourselves into believing that we have solved the ethical questions surrounding program experiments simply because we have elevated them to the higher ground of moral philosophy. All we have done is to put those questions at one remove conceptually.

PUBLIC POLICY ISSUES

Program experiments such as those described in some of the other chapters in this volume (see, for example, Brown's, Davis's, Stewart's, and Williams's chapters) raise several public policy issues, six of which I will touch on here. First, I have some concern that, in considering the need for experimentation at the "micro level" of a specific community, we may judge a police practice as deficient from an aggregate, "macro" — or national — perspective. For example, just because preventive patrol has generated police-community friction in some communities in America, are we justified in mounting a test of its efficacy, with the attendant risks, in a community where it is *not* an issue?

Second, like Shapard and Rice, I am skeptical about experiments for experimentation's sake alone. Although street policing is certainly a school in what is best and worst in our society, it is not a university. Our fundamental task is to provide law enforcement and various social services to society. Our mission is not to generate knowledge (unless it is a by-product of an effort to improve our services) but to apply knowledge. If the social harms are very low and, in this era of cutback budgeting, the economic costs are minimal, modest experimentation for the sake of knowledge may be both justified and feasible. However, such experimentation cannot expect a high priority.

Third, beyond the ethical and legal issues associated with the random assignment of treatment alternatives that frequently would be desirable in police program experiments, there is a major practical issue. Shapard refers (hypothetically) to the Police Foundation–sponsored spouse abuse experiment in Minneapolis, which included different treatments that police were to apply randomly (Sherman and Berk 1984). My judgment is that a police officer should not be put in a position of being forced to use a particular treatment regardless of his or her evaluation of the circumstances surrounding that case. Exigent circumstances, whether they be subtle or patently obvious, will cause the officer to feel the need to take a particular action. Randomization will be, as it should be, ignored. If the officer believes that an arrest has to be made or he will likely come back in a few hours to find that one or the other spouse is no longer among the living, he will act as he sees fit, not as a researcher sees fit.

This should not be an insurmountable obstacle to such an experiment because if officers are encouraged to use their independent judgment under exigent circumstances — and to report their decisions — then those data can be separated from the rest of the data and analyzed in their own right. If, as managers, we were to apply great administrative pressure on the officers *not* to exercise judgment, the experienced, *good* officers would still take the action the situation seemed to require, management's orders notwithstanding. Impelled by the survival instinct, however, some of these officers might attempt to disguise what actually was done. The result is officers disenchanted with research and further alienated from their managers and distorted data that invalidate the researcher's findings.

Fourth, as a practitioner I am concerned about how we will guarantee that a specific level of harm will trigger the modification or cancellation of a major program experiment. As was done in Kelling's Kansas City Preventive Patrol Experiment, the harm level should be clearly specified in advance with a commitment in writing by the researchers to report the danger and by the police administrator to act. Otherwise, the psychological momentum that develops in major programs may carry the parties too far. There will be a natural tendency for the people who have a stake in a program to keep it going: the officers who have been persuaded to commit to it, the researchers whose prestige and funding depend on it, and the chief who has promised beneficial results to his mayor and council. Ethically, the decision to cancel an experiment may be one of the most important and hardest decisions to make. I have often wondered how many times Kelling awoke out of a nightmare with spectral visions of crime statistics inexorably moving upward. Chiefs of police have been known to have these recurrent nightmares but for reasons unrelated to program experiments.

Fifth, in terms of policy implementation, I believe that the internal politics associated with the implementation of a program experiment in a police agency will generate far more intractable problems than will the experimental design itself. There is a substantial body of literature dealing with the problems of implementing change in organizations and some literature specific to major change efforts in police agencies (see, for example, Wycoff and Kelling 1978). A program experiment, particularly a major one, represents procedural, logistical, and other changes in the host agency and will be faced with whatever problems traditionally attend organizational change. Moreover, a program experiment is played out on an organizational stage, with a cast of police personnel who are, more often than not, characterized by fierce intra-organizational conflict. Line and management personnel alike will try, sometimes forgetting the distinction between fact and fantasy, to read what implications the substance of the experiment holds for them and what opportunities it may provide for goring their enemies.

Sixth, Superintendent Rice commented on obtaining the consent of the police officers who may be involved in or affected by a program experiment. It would go without saying, were it not so often overlooked by both the public and police managers, that police officers are human beings, entitled as any of us are to have their rights, privileges, and dignity respected. From a pragmatic point of view, if a police chief and experimenter do not gain the consent of both participating and observing officers, there may be no program experiment, or at any rate none that produces reliable results. Kelling (1984) summed it up nicely with the felicitous comment that "managing resistance masked as morality is extremely important to researchers and administrators hosting experiments." If the police officers and the brass wall (middle management) are not somehow brought aboard the experiment, they can destroy or sabotage it, sometimes with minimal effort. In the case of the Kansas City Preventive Patrol Experiment, all it would have taken was an officer of any rank who had the ear of a friendly reporter on the *Kansas City Star* and a "hot dime." (Of course, that was in the days when telephones responded to dimes.)

Understanding the importance of rank-and-file consent provides a practical perspective on the question of who has the authority to authorize a program experiment. Although we know from Weber's dictum that authority is legitimated power, we must also remember that authority and power are not necessarily coextensive. The chief has the authority to propose, but the troops often have the power to dispose. Hence, program efficacy alone requires not only the consent of civilian subjects — whether it be informed or by proxy or retroactively — but the consent of the police themselves (see Elliston's chapter).

FORMALIZING THE INFORMAL

Finally, with respect to the issues of both consent and the introduction of change into a service delivery organization, I would note that police agencies frequently alter practices that affect the public without asking or even thinking about asking for citizen consent. Accordingly, to the extent that program experiments make us confront the issue of consent, even if by proxy or retroactively, I think the citizens benefit rather than lose. Further, police agencies, sometimes systematically and knowingly and sometimes not, routinely provide disparate services to the public. The motives may range from necessity to sheer discrimination. Therefore, to engage in a program that provides differential treatment that is planned, systematic, articulated, and for motives clearly stated varies from *current* practice in police agencies in its formality but not necessarily in its intent or disparate impact. To deal explicity with issues previously hidden or ignored, such as consent and disparate treatment, I think is a gain, not a loss. Having said this, I recognize that formalizing the informal does not expiate the sins of deception, coercion, disparate treatment, and disrespect for persons. The point is, and this may be somewhat of a harsh commentary on my own field, that we commit these sins *now* from time to time; but program experiments, by their very protocol, at least make us confront our deeds and our accountability for them.

In conclusion, I think program experiments often can be justified, even if I have serious reservations about using the utilitarian approach. Program experiments have the pragmatic merit of producing potentially valid data for decision making, and they have the ethical value of formally addressing key democratic principles. In this sense, such experiments have an intrinsic value of their own, despite the questions they raise.

40

Private Enterprise and the Public Police: The Professionalizing Effects of a New Partnership

Michael G. Shanahan

THE IMPERATIVE OF PRIVATE-PUBLIC SECTOR COOPERATION

In the last decade, much has changed beneath the surface waters of American policing that will fundamentally influence U.S. law enforcement over the next several decades. Federal, state, county, and local agency heads are now just beginning to feel the effects of the burgeoning private sector response to crimes against corporations. In the past 15 years the private security industry has leapfrogged public law enforcement in number of personnel. An estimated total private security employment in 1969 of less than 300,000 persons today has grown to 1.1 million, more than double the number of sworn law enforcement officers at the state and local levels. Moreover, private security industry revenues were approximately $2.5 billion in 1969 and will be closer to the $12 billion to $15 billion mark by the end of 1985. Overall private policing has grown at the rate of 12 to 15 percent per year (Cunningham and Taylor 1985). The preferences of public law enforcement officials are no longer a controlling factor in these developments. Private corporate interests, economically and politically, dwarf anything that could be assembled within the present American police family.

The corporate victimization that has prompted this topsy-like growth in the private security industry has been acute. The annual corporate loss due to employee theft — which is underwritten, of course, by the American consumer — is said to run somewhere between $40 billion and $100 billion ("Stealing from the Boss" 1983). (The imprecision of this expert estimate suggests how little is known about the bottom line of corporate losses.) Additionally, the U.S. Chamber of Commerce has disclosed that "more than 30 percent of all business failures are caused by internal theft" ("Stealing from the Boss" 1983).

Nevertheless, corporations have been deterred from criminally prosecuting their employees by the prospects of bad publicity, unsympathetic juries, counter lawsuits, and other real and perceived problems. Instead, employers frequently settle for the offender's dismissal or resignation. The current reluctance of the business world to fight its internal crime wave with a joint private-public offensive cannot last forever, however. The entrance of the high-tech white-collar criminal, whose skillful predations can prove disastrous for a corporation, will likely be the most significant catalyst bringing the private sector and the various components of the criminal justice system together for mutual assistance. Just as large urban public and private universities learned during the 1960s and 1970s that they no longer could operate without the benefit of fully trained police forces, during the 1980s and 1990s the business community will need to formalize its working relationships with the public criminal justice system.

The impending collaboration of private enterprise and public law enforcement can have far-reaching national consequences, not the least of which is enhanced police professionalism. The magnetism attracting these two great forces to one another, the need of each for survival in the political economy, is reminiscent of another historical imperative that Winston Churchill proclaimed before the British Parliament in August 1940. He challenged the deep opposition of many of his countrymen to the idea of leasing any territories to the United States for use as military bases.

> Presently we learned that anxiety was also felt in the United States about the air and naval defence of their Atlantic seaboard, and President Roosevelt has recently made it clear that he would like to discuss with us, and with the Dominion of Canada and with Newfoundland, the development of American naval and air facilities in Newfoundland and in the West Indies. There is, of course, no question of any transference of sovereignty — that has never been suggested — or of any action being taken without the consent or against the wishes of the various Colonies concerned, but for our part His Majesty's Government are entirely willing to accord defence facilities to the United States on a ninety-nine years' lease-hold basis, and we feel sure that our interests no less than theirs, and the interests of the Colonies themselves and of Canada and Newfoundland, will be served thereby. These are important steps. Undoubtedly this process means that these two great organizations of the English-speaking democracies, the British Empire and the United States, will have to be somewhat mixed up together in some of their affairs for mutual and general advantage. For my own part, looking out upon the future, I do not view the process with any misgivings. I could not stop it if I wished; no one can stop it. Like the Mississippi, it just keeps rolling along. Let it roll. Let it roll on — full flood, inexorable, irresistible, benignant, to broader lands and better days. (Churchill 1949, pp. 408-09)

How is the grand alliance between America's corporate and law enforcement communities evolving? What manner of courtship will be conducive to a long and happy marriage? What will be the consequences for law enforcement as we know it today? This chapter will briefly address these and a few other key issues raised by the growing interplay between corporate America and the public police.

At the outset, it must be acknowledged that the present array of policing issues confronting public agency heads will persist well into the future. The vast numbers of Americans who live in neighborhoods, who organize themselves into local political action groups, and who direct the American governmental bureaucracy will remain very much in evidence. But the inevitable focus of police executives on such issues as use of deadly force, vicarious liability, freedom of information, the imposition of law enforcement standards, and preservation of local control will be diverted somewhat as the business community learns that it, too, can influence police leaders and their agencies.

Some observers of the political scene may argue that there is nothing new about the entry of business interests into the arena of local law enforcement policy setting. Reflection on the late 1960s and early 1970s reminds us of minority neighborhood and antiwar groups stridently asserting how, for too long, city fathers had allowed business interests disproportionate influence in setting police service priorities. Whether those perceptions were valid is now immaterial. The national attitude about the corporate community in the last few years has become much more supportive of business needs. Americans no longer divorce corporate well-being from the strength of the national or local economy or from their own fate or the fate of their children. In fact, sustained media focus on the national economy has given the average citizen a mini-course in basic economics. Never before have so many Americans understood what the balance of payments, the strength of the dollar, interest rates, a federal deficit, and the money supply mean for personal life goals. Hence the stage is set for national and local acceptance of a larger role for the private sector in the world of public safety.

THE NEED TO MANAGE KEY DIFFERENCES IN OPERATING STYLES

A greater popular and police acceptance of corporate interests does not, however, suggest that our nation will be spared some of the difficult questions that inevitably arise when major powers explore ways of collaborating to mutual advantage. For example, one of the issues that immediately surfaces and permeates public-private sector communications is the matter of turf. It is the first item needing resolution before any meaningful progress can be made by the involved parties. When that issue is put to rest, however, the need of mutual aid becomes strikingly apparent. For decades, public law enforcement and private security officials have traveled essentially parallel courses, communicating mostly through appreciation luncheons. To be sure, their courses have converged occasionally, typically in cases of labor unrest, industrial accidents, and specific violent crimes occurring on corporate property.

Beyond their need to overcome turf jealousies, the parties to this emerging public-private alliance must recognize and learn to manage the reality that corporate security and public policing differ in important ways. For example, generally a corporate security manager is employed by a firm whose interests cross not only city, county, and state lines but international borders as well. The security manager often cannot form policy that would dramatically affect overall corporate operations, nor does he have direct access to the chief executive officer or the senior executive vice-president. In the main, security policy changes.must pass through a variety of corporate staff reviews.

In contrast, the law enforcement executive's principal sphere of concern is the comparatively small geographic area whose safety he must superintend; he also enjoys both relative autonomy from and reasonable access to his jurisdiction's senior public officials. Additionally, the law enforcement manager works openly with civic groups and the media on a broad range of community issues. Bureaucrats who want to affect the public safety agency, as in the case of budget decisions, cannot make unilateral incursions but must follow a typically well-publicized budget hearing process.

These differences help explain why, over the years, it has been difficult for law enforcement officials to establish common protocols to be followed throughout the business community. Achievement of this and other important goals in light of these variations in operating styles will require a number of changes. Among them must be demonstrable support by the public and the news media for corporations that prosecute offending employees. Boards of directors must openly insulate chief executive officers from unfair criticism for pursuing aggressive, punitive policies in the area of business fraud. Corporate executives will also need to adopt an attitude that such measures in the long run can only increase company profitability and strengthen the firm. Although the independence of the American worker may never permit a level of organizational commitment rivaling the corporate loyalty of the Japanese and other competitors, still our businesses — especially retailers who make major strides in internal security — may discover that, as in the case of good manufacturing, advertising, marketing, and distribution, proper attention to security can improve their relative position in the marketplace.

If the profit margin is not a sufficient incentive for the private sector to seek greater assistance from the police on internal security, then corporate concern about public image may provide the needed stimulus. A 1983 Gallup poll revealed that 64 percent of Americans believe that "at least half of all big-company executives cheat on their taxes," 74 percent of the public "think that at least half of the business people pad their expense accounts," and a surprising 28 percent hold the opinion that "half or more of the business people in their own communities give bribes or favors to the police" (Ricklefs 1983). What is doubly troubling about these views is that they may lead employees to legitimize their own misdeeds based on the real or perceived example set by their bosses. A related consequence of these public opinions may be that corporate security managers eventually will play significantly greater roles in forming personnel policy, not only as it affects the question of security but as it affects the development of ethical standards bearing on all aspects and levels of corporate life.

Effective management of the different operating modes of the business and police worlds will necessitate changes on the law enforcement side, too. Police executives must learn to think across multijurisdictional lines in terms of corporate decision making. They will need to be highly sensitive to their own agency's management of corporate fraud and theft cases if they are to earn and enlarge the confidence of the private firm with which they are working. Furthermore, police managers and their subordinates will need to remain understanding of the differences between the various parties. The tough drama of the precinct station would be anathema in the corporate boardroom, which obviously has its own distinct brand of toughness. Police executives need to create an awareness in their agencies that injudicious triggering of bad publicity on the evening news could cause the restructuring of a corporate board, unfairly decimate a company's senior staff, and set off a damaging selling spree by stockholders.

NATIONAL ASSOCIATION AND GOVERNMENTAL INTEREST

There never has been a better time for a public-private "merger" of sorts. Several national agencies and associations seem to be simultaneously considering the private sector's role in law enforcement, which in part explains the rapid growth in membership of the American Society for Industrial Security — from 10,566 in 1977 to 20,573 in 1983 (Sherwood 1984). This group of professional security managers and involved supporters has long recognized the basic problems of public-private sector interface. However, in recent years groups such as the International Association of Chiefs of Police (IACP) and the National Sheriffs' Association have formed their own private security committees. Now combinations of sheriffs, police chiefs, federal agency administrators, and corporate security managers, through interassociation contact, are becoming professionally and personally more comfortable with one another. Efforts are also bearing fruit within the IACP's Division of State Associations of Chiefs of Police (SACOP).

Additionally, projects sponsored by the National Institute of Justice and other elements of the federal government (see, for example, Stellwagen and Gettinger 1984) are finally providing the needed research backdrop against which an informed sense of urgency can evolve. Law enforcement and business executives are rapidly coming to appreciate their pressing need to learn to cross-communicate and operate jointly through a series of carefully written and researched operational standards, so that the public sees a well-coordinated offensive to reduce corporate victimization. Citizens—as consumers, taxpayers, and stockholders—will be watching with growing interest.

DISMANTLING OLD MYTHS AND BUILDING SECURITY

Meaningful public-private collaboration will require not only resolution of the jurisdictional jealousies mentioned earlier but the debunking of some old myths. One of the most prominent and most easily exploded is the charge that individual corporate executives who work with law enforcement would somehow expect special treatment for themselves if they became caught up in the criminal justice process. The strongest defense against this is the growing independence of line law enforcement personnel as individual practitioners, a development that has been considerably enhanced over the last score of years by the emergence of strong police unions and collective bargaining. As a result, any reasonably sophisticated corporate executive would know that name dropping or influence pushing with the trooper, sheriff's deputy, police officer, or detective could land him on the front pages of the evening newspaper. Agency heads, the media, and even the public have learned that discretion in law enforcement increases as you go down the chain of command. Line personnel can respond very harshly to "do-you-know-who-you-are-talking-to?" proposals. Probably even harsher would be the response of the corporate power structure, since corporations are extremely sensitive about their community image and any negative public exposure of their senior officials.

A related myth is that particular private companies that do "favors" for the police will receive more than their rightful share of police resources. Again, the laws of the marketplace provide a reassuring barrier against such inequities. Police executives and private sector managers alike recognize that, as is true when dealing with political officials, the news media, and neighborhood and other groups, there exist a multiplicity of interests in the corporate world who would scream foul at any signs of favoritism on the part of law enforcement officials. Companies constitute substantial taxpaying groups and would object to a "good-old-boy network" that might unfairly benefit their competitors. Moreover, corporations, like individuals, are citizens both for legal purposes and in terms of their moral obligation to improve their communities. Promoting corruption within the local police department hardly satisfies the imperative of good citizenship.

Police chiefs who may be dubious that entrepreneurs can ever see past their profit-loss tables would find interesting a conversation between a corporate official and a police executive reported in a publication on fund-raising techniques for police (Criminal Justice Center 1983, p. 12):

> [T]he vice president of a prestigious bank in the Northeast found out at a recent social gathering that the local police chief had to pass up the opportunity to send several officers to a particularly good management program because of budget constraints. When he asked why nobody had come to the bank to ask for a donation to help pay for the training, the police chief said he was afraid that if he accepted money from the bank, its officers would try to influence his decisions in future situations involving the bank. The vice president stared at the chief in disbelief. "You mean to tell me," he said, "that I can buy the whole damned police department for a few thousand bucks?"

Myths concerning improper relationships are most easily discredited when they are openly discussed early on, especially in the group setting of the various trade and professional associations.

MUTUAL ADVANTAGES

This interaction will probably produce different benefits for each participant, including enhanced professionalization of public law enforcement. Corporate people eventually will learn to operate more comfortably with some of the openness and public accessibility required of criminal justice agencies. Private sector executives will also learn to interact with people who are action-oriented, who show a great deal of initiative, and whose freshness in attacking problems is devoid of some of the intrigue and subtleties that frequently are found in the corporate bureaucracy.

On the other side, law enforcement officials will be exposed to a higher degree of organizational sophistication. They will learn to view corporate problems through the eyes of chief executive officers, upwardly mobile corporate managers, and stockholders (see "Spotlight" 1984, p. 21). They will learn, too, that realistic planning and effective marketing are basic to survival.[1] The police managers also will become sensitized to the fact that corporate entities, unlike police agencies, must measure up to competing firms or go out of business. When one hears police executives assert that they possess the same managerial talents as major CEOs, one wonders at the sudden metamorphosis these police leaders might undergo if they were taken off the tax rolls and had to compete for consumer patronage in their own jurisdiction with several other law enforcement agencies, with "sales" of services determining whether their department could meet the next payroll.

As more and more law enforcement administrators and staff work closely with their corporate counterparts, the police will see the practical application of concepts, such as strategic planning,[2] management by objectives, and employee performance appraisal that previously seemed to be luxuries, if not useless abstractions. One could also expect the closer working relationships to lead corporations to assign temporarily their own experts to "loaned executive teams" for general use in the police community, much as the Xerox and IBM corporations have been doing for nonprofit organizations for some years (see Criminal Justice Center 1983, p. 13) and as President Franklin D. Roosevelt's administration urged the nation's private sector to do under the "dollar-a-year-man" program. The Baltimore County Police Department currently enjoys the benefits of a loaned executive program, in which local business executives are donated by their companies one or more days per week, sometimes for months on end. These private sector managers have helped this agency revamp its administrative procedures, incorporate computer technology into daily operations, assess departmental needs, and prepare budget requests accordingly.

Another intriguing prospect is that corporations will open their senior in-service management schools to police leadership. This is already happening in the state of Washington, as a result of the joint adoption by police and private interests of the "law enforcement executive forum" concept. The Washington Law Enforcement Executive Forum (WLEEF)[3] has assembled on a statewide basis well-defined task groups of senior corporate officials and law enforcement administrators who work cooperatively for enhanced public safety. As active members of WLEEF, the Boeing Company, the Weyerhaeuser Company, and Pacific Northwest Bell Telephone have been leaders in making their executives and training programs available to police managers. The years ahead will likely see reciprocity from law enforcement, which might take the form of providing police experts to assist corporate personnel administrators in managing such company problems as drug and alcohol abuse, traffic safety, and personal protection.

In the area of legislative action (where police administrators traditionally have not been strong), WLEEF members have been active in jointly drafting and lobbying for legislation dealing with such matters as computer crime and the right of corporations to access the conviction records (on a job-related basis) of prospective or current employees. The forum concept is an expanding, grass-roots idea that provides trade association officials, corporate executives, and law enforcement officials with a reasonable opportunity for group discussion, statewide planning, and implementation of coordinated public-private sector strategies in support of common legislative, operational, and professional goals. Developed four years ago in Seattle, the WLEEF concept currently is spreading, through the IACP's SACOP division, to the states of Oregon, Connecticut, and Kansas.

A forum in a particular state, while intended to serve its own region's interests in light of local economic, political, and cultural conditions, will benefit greatly from expertise developed by other state forums, by national law enforcement, security, and business associations, and by the federal government. The time is at hand for the federal government to serve as a facilitator of these state-level collaborations by developing a series of model policies to guide law enforcement and corporations in day-to-day joint operations. Such choreography will be critical if working relationships are to move out of chiefs' offices and corporate suites down to police fraud and corporate security units. Among the other partners in the development of guidelines for forums should be the American Society for Industrial Security, the International Association of Chiefs of Police, the National Sheriffs' Association, the National Institute of Justice, the U.S. Department of Commerce, and the various trade associations headquartered in Washington, D.C.

The success of the forum concept will require something of an ecumenical spirit among the participants. That means the inclusion of leaders from law enforcement agencies at all levels of government, as well as a genuine cross section of the corporate community. It will be important, too, for participating public officials to adopt an attitude that corporate interface will heighten both their agencies' operational effectiveness and their own professionalism.

ADAPTING TO THE NEW CORPORATE PARTNERSHIP

American policing is now meeting a business community that has undergone a philosophical change concerning its self-protection. Today, many corporate security units far exceed most law enforcement agencies in investigative and technical sophistication. But American policing should be able to adjust to this development because, as James Q. Wilson noted more than a decade ago, the decentralized system of law enforcement that characterizes our country has facilitated adaptation and innovation. Wilson (1972) observed:

It is impossible in Great Britain or in France, or the countries with essentially centralized or nationalized police services, to find anybody willing to really stick his neck out — to try something really new. I can't imagine that the family crisis intervention unit which was pioneered in New York City would have been pioneered in other countries because it was such a change from the normal way of doing things that the Home Office, the national forces, the Ministry of the Interior or whatever would have said, "Well, let's don't do it" or "Let's do it slowly" or "Let's discourage people who want to do it." I think a lot of the other changes you find going on now in many of the most productive American police departments are the ones you are not going to find going on in other countries where the degree of local control is less. This is one of the advantages of localism.

The day of the corporate "rent-a-cop" is gone forever (see "Spotlight" 1984, pp. 15, 20). One can only hope that all involved parties will discover soon how much they need one another. The discovery process may not be easy. At times, it may resemble the rocky road to friendship traveled by Virgil Tibbs, the black homicide detective from Philadelphia, and Bill Gillespie, the white police chief from a small southern town, portrayed masterfully by Sidney Poitier and Rod Steiger in the movie *In the Heat of the Night*. As the film draws to a close and Poitier boards the train for Philadelphia, Steiger speaks his first civil words to the detective: "Virgil, you take care, ya hear." In the silence that follows, the men for the first time exchange professional respect and acknowledge their interdependence; they at least begin to forget the unfair stereotypes they had built up about each other's "kind" over the years. The moment is at hand for corporate interests and public law enforcement to make a similar gesture and forge a professional bond. Its creation would serve the welfare of all citizens by producing far-reaching benefits for American policing.

NOTES

1. Interaction will afford law enforcement executives excellent opportunities to improve their own agencies by adapting the techniques used successfully by business in reaching corporate decisions. Where corporations must think in a proactive way and expend limited risk capital as they move into new product areas, law enforcement has until recently remained in a more reactive posture. Now, cutback management and the fixed resources of local governments are making the governmental budget planning process much more refined and predictable.

2. It will be interesting to see whether the impending corporate-police marriage fundamentally affects the attitude of police toward such matters as applied research. One police executive (see Cordner's chapter) has argued that goal consensus (profitability) in the private sector gives considerable stature to well-conducted policy research, whereas goal uncertainty or a multiplicity of goals in the police-government world makes it far easier for administrators to dismiss as irrelevant and unhelpful even high-quality research.

3. The *Strategic Plan* of the Washington Law Enforcement Executive Forum is available through the Washington Association of Sheriffs and Police Chiefs, in Olympia, Washington. The document was prepared by the WLEEF Strategic Planning Committee April 20, 1982, under the chairmanship of Gerald S. Rees, corporate security director, Weyerhauser Company.

41
The Police Executive as Statesman

Lawrence W. Sherman

There is much to be gained from the professionalization of American police management. But those managers who rise to become chief police executives must temper their professionalism with values and politics. The improvement of American policing will be better served by police executives who perceive themselves as statesmen first and professionals second.[1] This chapter suggests a strategy for improving American policing, shows how the current dysfunctions of police executives inhibit the attainment of that strategy, and notes the uses and limits of professionalization of executives.

A STRATEGY FOR IMPROVED POLICING

The police mandate includes many goals (Goldstein 1977), but many communities would be delighted if police could simply reduce crime and fear and maintain a more orderly level of public behavior. Few police executives would reject these goals for their departments. Yet few have been able to accomplish them. The failures of the police to cope with crime and disorder may have two different explanations. One is that the magnitude and complex causes of the problem are beyond the reach of any police agency and that nothing can be done. The other explanation is that while more effective police strategies are possible, they simply have not yet been tested. Some may not even have been thought of. Since the first explanation offers no hope for improvement, the second seems to be a better premise for action. And proposals for better police strategies are not hard to find (although they may be very hard to test).

Diagnosis

Any plan for improving policing depends on a diagnosis of the "failures" of the currently prevailing approaches. Neither the diagnosis nor the plan can be conclusive without rigorous empirical testing. But all tests should be premised on a theory about why some strategies work and others do not.

My own diagnosis of American policing is premised on several assumptions. One is that more can be gained by *prevention* than through intervention after the fact. In crime control as in disease control, lifestyle and daily activities of the general population make more difference than emergency responses by experts. Just as diet and exercise have more impact than coronary bypass surgery on heart disease, individual and neighborhood crime prevention can have more impact on burglary than police dusting for fingerprints.

Another premise is that the police must be concerned with the needs of the entire community, and not just those people who call on the phone to ask for help. When police are occupied responding to minor requests for service, they are diverted from other activities that could contribute toward lower levels of crime, fear, and disorder for the whole community. Serving one citizen may be a disservice to most citizens.

A third premise is that information about social life and human relationships is the raw material of police work. Without that information, police will be unable to solve crimes, maintain order, or alleviate public fear. They can make serious mistakes in mediating potentially violent disputes, just like a doctor giving an injection without knowing the patient's allergies.

A final premise is that police actions in citizen encounters can be guided by a scientific body of knowledge. The effects of police actions on the immediate, short-term and long-term behavior of victims, complainants, and suspects can all be measured through experimentation (see the chapters on experimentation in this volume). Armed with hundreds or thousands of experiments, police could be far more effective in dealing with people, just as medical practice has been greatly improved by research.

These premises suggest several failures of current police organization and methods. American policing devotes almost all of its resources to reaction rather than prevention. Police officers stay in their cars waiting for emergencies to occur rather than developing citizen practices that can help prevent emergencies. They devote most of their time to servicing people who ask for help and rarely seek out the views of the "silent majority" who never call the police. They make little systematic effort to gather information about the communities they serve; what information some officers do collect is rarely shared with other officers (see Reiss's chapter, p. 64 and Kelling's chapter, p. 307). And while the police have been extraordinarily open to experimentation, not nearly enough funding has been available to pursue even basic questions about the effects of police actions.

Strategy

This diagnosis suggests a new strategy of policing that might be worth testing. The strategy would be closely focused on the accomplishment of short-term tactical objectives (other than answering calls for service) as a means of accomplishing longer term goals. Reducing panhandling on a certain street corner, reducing muggings near a certain bar, taking an inventory of all the parolees in a neighborhood — these and other specific tasks would be the main job of the day, and not just whatever comes over the air. Only the most serious calls for service would be allowed to interfere with the accomplishment of an officer's daily objectives. Other calls would be delayed or refused.

This proactive approach to police work would emphasize frequent contacts with area residents and businesspeople. The purpose of the contacts would be to educate[2] the public for better crime prevention and to gather information about human relationships and possible criminal activities. A more formal structure for police-citizen contact at the beat or neighborhood level might even be developed to determine local police policies and priorities.

The information obtained from citizens would be the basis of regular meetings of all officers working on a beat. The meetings would exchange and analyze the information. With a growing body of scientific evidence about police encounters, the discussions could plan how to use the information to prevent or respond to certain problems.

Most important, this strategy of policing would emphasize the preservation of certain values in policing: the primacy of protecting life over all else, the need for legality and constitutionality in police procedures, and equal treatment regardless of race or ethnicity.

THE DYSFUNCTIONS OF THE POLICE EXECUTIVE

Whatever the merits of this strategy for improving policing, it is unlikely to be implemented in the near future. A radical shift in police strategy away from the "dial-a-cop" system — in which "911 runs the police department," to quote one senior police manager — would have to overcome massive resistance from both police and the public. It could only occur with gifted leadership, and then only under the right historical conditions. But most police agencies lack that kind of leadership.

Much has been written on the functions of the executive since Barnard's classic 1938 treatise. His vision of the executive infusing an organization with value and moral purpose was elaborated by Selznick's (1957) conception of the executive making the critical or strategic decisions for an organization. Wilson (1978b, p. 163) has reformulated the executive's responsibility as the "maintenance" of the organization: "generally assuring that the organization obtains the essential resources — money, personnel, clients, goodwill, political support — necessary for it to prosper as well as to survive."

What many police executives appear to have done is to replace "prosperity" with "survival." If prosperity means increasing success at accomplishing organizational goals, few police executives have achieved it. Nor have they decided to try. Many police executives have either avoided the big strategic decisions or have decided de facto to continue the current strategy with all its limitations. The road to personal survival of the police executive, if not the success of the organization, does seem to lie with current strategies of policing. But personal survival is not the primary function of the executive.

Some police executives are extremely capable of performing the functions Barnard identified. But a few of them choose to infuse their organizations with the "wrong" values: disregard for civil liberties, racial equality, and the preservation of life. The impact of their value messages on police behavior seems to be substantial. One study in 17 cities found a strong correlation between the police chiefs' (and mayors') attitudes towards blacks and the level of aggressiveness police used in black communities (Rossi, Berk, and Eidson 1975, pp. 150–204). Another study found that a strong value message from police executives in three cities (accompanied by minor policy changes) drastically reduced the frequency of police shootings (Sherman 1983).

Other police executives hold the right values but pursue a strategy they know is bad for the public because it reduces complaints. One police executive interviewed by Wilson (1968, pp. 70–71) acknowledged that stable beat assignments were more effective for police work in general, but because they increased citizen complaints about response time he chose to emphasize highly mobile patrols. Some executives firmly believe rapid response to calls is the primary goal of policing, despite extensive evidence (Spelman and Brown 1982) that the speed of police response makes little difference in the quality of police service. There are other failings of police management as well. One is a widespread tendency to respond to the most recent stimulus (phone call, visit, inbox item) rather than pursuing larger strategic goals (see Mayo's chapter). Police executives (like managers in other organizations) tend to be as reactive as the officers they lead. Another failing is uncritical use of available performance measures, such as arrests and clearances, without enough attention to the qualitative issues underlying those numbers.

The Need for Statesmanship

These managerial failures of police executives must be distinguished from their failures as statesmen, or rather, their failures to become statesmen. By "statesman" I mean a leader of a democracy, someone who can transcend the current values of the day and lead both police and the public into accepting a better set of values and strategies for policing.

The notion of an unelected bureaucrat serving as a political leader may give some people pause, but it has its precedents. In policing, William Parker, J. Edgar Hoover, and O. W. Wilson fit the definition. While one may criticize in retrospect the values and strategies they stood for, their decisions led to definite improvements over earlier values and strategies for the Los Angeles Police Department, the FBI, and the Chicago police. Achieving the new approaches to police work required great skills of statesmanship that are quite different from day-to-day managerial skills: public speaking, closed-door negotiations with the press and business elites, close liaison with elected officials, and a keen sense of public opinion and dramaturgy. Few police executives today have these skills. Those who do are rarely willing to take the risk of incurring their superiors' wrath by using their skills (see Davis's chapter).

THE USES OF PROFESSIONALIZATION

If statesmanship is quite different from management, why professionalize management? The question presumes a definition of a "professional," since the term has been used to mean so many things (see Kliesmet's, Klockars's, and Mayo's chapters). One leading student of the professions, Everett C. Hughes (1965, p. 2), concluded that expertise is the basic claim of a professional, from which other consequences, privileges, and responsibilities flow: "Professionals . . . profess to know better than others the nature of certain matters, and to know better than their clients what ails them or their affairs. This is the essence of the professional idea and the professional claim."

The general field of management has claimed technical expertise at what it does for most of this century. The last two decades have witnessed increasing claims to professionalism by specialized managerial groups, such as hospital and university administrators, trade association executives, and YMCA executives. The general management professionals claim a technical ability to run any kind of organization, doing any kind of work. The specialized management professionals claim a technical expertise at running one type of organization, an expertise that is closely linked to the unique nature of the organization's work. Since people of general management backgrounds are generally barred from appointment to police management ranks, professionalization of police managers would necessarily be specialized in nature.

The specialized professionalization of police management would have several uses for accomplishing the police improvement strategy outlined earlier. Assume that a police management profession would have these features (analogous to, say, the city managers): a membership association restricted to managers, but not just executives; codification of knowledge and periodical literature on management techniques; national standards for various aspects and policies of police management, enforced through accreditation; testing and certification of police managers, with continuing education; national academies or graduate school programs in police management that would be virtual prerequisites for appointment to police executive positions; and a portable pension plan.

If those features succeeded in resocializing the police superior officer into an identification with a national *profession* stronger than the officers' identification with the local *department*, then professionalization could foster a great deal more innovation. If police managers judged themselves by the opinion of a national peer group rather than a local one, then they might be more willing to confront risks of local opposition to change. If the police managers conscientiously read reports of new developments and kept learning how better to manage people and policing, they might be better able to break with whatever local traditions bind a department's outdated management practices. If police managers all the way down to sergeant's level were trained in and evaluated by their ability to manage for objectives, then patrol work itself might become much more proactive and goal-directed. And if all police managers were better trained in crime analysis and integration of information provided by the community, police tactical planning for crime control might become much more effective.

Perhaps the most important use of police managerial professionalism would be the symbolic power of national standards for police practices that could be invoked in debates over police policies and resources. Any attempt to lead a community and a police agency away from a strongly held value (like rapid response or preventive patrol) could be greatly aided by a national professional association's standard supporting the move.

Other long-term consequences might flow from the professionalization of police management. The prestige of such work might be increased, attracting more talented people into police ranks. Professional police managers could lobby for laws permitting lateral entry at superior ranks, which would enhance the available talent pool to fill vacant jobs, increase the mobility of police managers, attract more cosmopolitan individuals to that line of work, and break down the parochialism that afflicts many agencies.

FROM MANAGERS TO STATESMEN: THE LIMITS OF PROFESSIONALIZATION

While the uses of professionalism could be substantial, one must acknowledge both its limits and its costs. The limits lie at the door of the police executive's office. While the chief executive's performance may be enhanced by a highly professionalized managerial staff, his own performance cannot be governed by any fixed set of professional approaches. There is no codifiable body of expertise that tells a police executive how to act. Just as the performance of U.S. presidents, actors, and criminal lawyers cannot be "professionalized," the art of statesmanship in a police executive's office probably depends much more on instinct and personality than it does on professional training. Winston Churchill was a professionally trained soldier, but he was a born statesman.

This does not mean that improving police performance is a matter of finding people "born" to be great police executives. Rather, it means that the professionalization of police management should be accomplished in a way that attracts and develops people with innate leadership abilities. One of the uses of professionalization may be that it can attract people with more interest in and ability for bold, creative leadership. If that is true, then the pool of police managers should be able to produce a higher portion of police executives capable of statesmanship.

The danger of professionalization is that it may stifle creativity by making peer group judgments too important and creating too many fads. Some Harvard Business School faculty, for example, have blamed America's economic woes on the professionalization of business management. By making chief executives (in particular) overly conscious of strategic decision making, professionalization (through M.B.A. educations and analytic skills) has prompted the wave of corporate takeovers and deflected resources from developing new products and increasing productivity. Some argue that something similar has already happened to policing in its first stages of professionalization: The fads of rapid response and motorized preventive patrol, with civil service systems blocking minority hiring, led to poor community relations and contributed to race riots (Fogelson 1977).

Another potential cost of professionalization is increasing the value placed on managerial autonomy at the expense of democratic accountability and public control. Wilson (1978b) argues that autonomy is the major goal of public administrators. A reasonable amount of freedom for daily operations is certainly justified. But major strategic or policy decisions merit public participation. One highly mobile police manager exemplified the danger of autonomy when he asked at an IACP seminar, "What business does the public have in influencing our professional decisions about when to shoot people?"

These potential costs of professionalization can be controlled by a statesman police executive, one whose keen political instincts and sense of values can make the police department both professional and accountable. But where statesmanship is lacking, as it has been recently in some police agencies where the executive has civil service tenure, the dangers of professionalization are ever-present. Any movement for professionalizing police management needs a constant dialectic between expertise and accountability, between professional standards for research and public demands. Professionals are very good at adapting their practices to the examples of a few statesmanlike leaders. But without that leadership, it is unlikely that policing can be substantially improved.

NOTES

1. The use of archaic terms entails a risk of sexism. My preference for the more elegant word "statesman" over the more cumbersome "statesperson" does not diminish the relevance of the comments to women police managers and executives.

2. Some of the leading voices in policing are using a much stronger word than "educate"; they call on the police to *organize* their communities (see, for example, Brown's and Davis's chapters).

References

Abrams v. *United States*. 1919. 250 U.S. 616 (Holmes dissenting).

Ahern, James F. 1972. *Police in Trouble*. New York: Hawthorne.

Allinson, Richard S. 1981. "The Uncertain Future of Police Research." *Police Magazine*, July, pp. 55–56.

American Bar Association. 1980. *Standards Relating to the Urban Police Function*. 2nd ed. Boston: Little, Brown.

———. 1973. *Standards Relating to the Urban Police Function*. New York: Institute of Judicial Administration.

Americans for Effective Law Enforcement. Monthly. *AELE Legal Liability Reporter*. South San Francisco, Calif.

———. 1974. *Survey of Police Misconduct Litigation 1967–1971*. South San Francisco, Calif.

Anderson, David C. 1978. "Management Moves In on the Detective." *Police Magazine*, March, pp. 4–13.

Angel, John E. 1971. "Towards an Alternative to the Classic Police Organizational Arrangements: A Democratic Model." *Criminology* 9 (2, 3): 185–206.

Antieau, Chester. 1980. *Federal Civil Rights Acts*. 2nd ed. Rochester, N.Y.: Lawyers Cooperative Publishing.

Arcuri, Alan F. 1973. "Police Perception of Plea Bargaining: A Preliminary Inquiry." *Journal of Police Science and Administration* 1: 93–101.

Argyris, Chris, and Donald A. Schon. 1974. *Theory in Practice*. San Francisco: Jossey-Bass.

Arons, Stephen, and Ethan Katsh. 1977. "TV Cops and Their Assault on Justice." *Student Lawyer*, May, pp. 39–43, 50.

Ascher, William. 1978. *Forecasting: An Appraisal for Policy-makers and Planners*. Baltimore: Johns Hopkins University Press.

Baker, Duane. 1976. "A Model Firearms Policy for California Law Enforcement." *Journal of California Law Enforcement* 10(1): 5.

Baker, Mary Holland, Barbara C. Nienstedt, Ronald S. Everett, and Richard McCleary. 1983. "The Impact of a Crime Wave: Perceptions, Fear, and Confidence in Police." *Law and Society Review* 17: 319–35.

Banton, Michael. 1964. *The Policeman in the Community*. New York: Basic Books.

Bard, Morton, and Dawn Sangrey. 1979. *The Crime Victim's Book*. New York: Basic Books.

Bardach, Eugene, and Robert Kagan. 1982. *Going by the Book*. New York: Twentieth Century Fund.

Barnard, Chester I. 1938. *The Functions of the Executive*. Cambridge, Mass.: Harvard University Press; reprint ed., Cambridge, Mass.: Harvard University Press, 1968.

Barry, Dave. 1983. "So What's News? A Visit to *THE* 9 O'Clock Eyewitness News Center Studios." *Chicago Tribune Magazine*, December 4, p. 34.

Basler, Barbara. 1980. "Serious Crimes Nearing Record in New York." *New York Times*, November 18, p. B1.

Battelle Memorial Institute. 1977. *Forcible Rape: A National Survey of the Response by the Police*. Washington, D.C.: U.S. Government Printing Office.

Bell, Ralph, and Jeffrey M. A. Fancik. 1981. "Housing Projects and Crime: Testing a Proximate Hypothesis." *Social Problems* 29 (2): 151–66.

Bennis, Warren, and Bert Namus. 1984. *Taking Charge*. New York: Harper & Row.

Berkely, George F. 1969. *The Democratic Policeman*. Boston: Beacon Press.

Bernstein, Richard J. 1976. *The Restructuring of Social and Political Theory*. New York: Harcourt Brace Jovanovich.

Bickman, L. 1975. "Bystander Intervention in a Crime." Paper presented at the First International Advanced Study Institute on Victimology, Bellagio, Italy.

Bieck, William. 1977. *Response Time Analysis*. Kansas City, Mo.: Kansas City Police Department.

Bittner, Egon. 1984. "The Broken Badge: Reuss-Ianni and the Culture of Policing." *American Bar Foundation Research Journal* 1984: 206–13.

_____. 1970. *The Functions of the Police in Modern Society*. Washington, D.C.: U.S. Government Printing Office.

_____. 1968. "Police Encounters and Social Organization." Ph.D. Dissertation, University of Michigan.

_____. 1967. "Police Discretion in Emergency Apprehension of Mentally Ill Persons." *Social Problems* 14: 278–92.

Black, Donald J. 1980. *The Manners and Customs of the Police*. New York: Academic Press.

_____. 1971. "The Social Organization of Arrest." *Stanford Law Review* 23 (June): 1087–111.

Black, Donald, and Albert J. Reiss, Jr. 1970. "Police Control of Juveniles." *American Sociological Review* 35 (February): 63–77.

Blasi, Vincent. 1977. "The Checking Value in First Amendment Theory." *American Bar Foundation Research Journal* 3: 521–649.

Bloch, P., and J. Bell. 1976. *Managing Investigations: The Rochester System*. Washington, D.C.: Police Foundation.

Blodgett, Nancy. 1985. "People v. Police: More Suits Invoke Rights Act." *American Bar Association Journal* 71 (February), p. 36.

Bok, Derek C. 1983. "A Flawed System." *Harvard Magazine* 85 (5): 38–45, 70–71.

Bolan, Richard S. 1980. "The Practitioner as Theorist: The Phenomenology of the Professional Episode." *American Planning Association Journal* (July): 261–74.

Bonsignore v. *City of New York*. 1981. 521 F. Supp. 394 (S.D.N.Y.): aff'd., 683 F.2d 685 (2d Cir.).

Bopp, William J. 1984. *Crises in Police Administration*. Springfield, Ill.: Charles C Thomas.

_____. 1977. *O. W. Wilson and the Search for a Police Profession*. Port Washington, N.Y.: Kennikat Press.

Borsage, Betty B. 1982. "Case Study in Leadership: How Chicago's Superintendent Kept a Cop-Killer in Prison." *Crime Control Digest*, September 27, pp. 2–6.

Bouza, Anthony V. 1983. Remarks at the Conference on Review of Police Misconduct Allegations sponsored by the Department of Criminal Justice of the Univ. of Illinois at Chicago and the Community Relations Service of the U.S. Dept.

of Justice, Chicago, June.

Boydstun, John E., and Michael E. Sherry. 1975. *San Diego Community Profile: Final Report*. Washington, D.C.: Police Foundation.

Brake, Mike. 1978. "Establishing a Public Information Office." *FBI Law Enforcement Bulletin*, October, p. 23.

Brightman, Richard W. 1971. *Information Systems for Modern Management*. New York: Macmillan.

Brosi, Kathleen. 1979. *A Cross-City Comparison of Felony Case Processing*. Washington, D.C.: U.S. Government Printing Office.

Brown, Gary E. 1984. "The Metamorphosis of a Police Executive: How to Climb to the Top and Not Fall Off." *Police Chief*, November, pp. 28–32.

Brown, Lee P. 1979. *Atlanta Bureau of Police Services Plan of Improvement*. Atlanta: Department of Public Safety (December 3).

———. 1973. "The Death of Police Community Relations." Howard University, Institute for Urban Affairs and Research, Occasional Paper Ser. 1 (October).

Brown, Michael K. 1981. *Working the Street*. New York: Russell Sage Foundation.

Brown, Stephen E. 1982. "Research Methods and Criminal Justice Curricula: Surmounting the Obstacles." *Criminal Justice Review* 7 (1): 11–16.

Buckner, Hubbard T. 1967. "The Police: The Culture of a Social Control Agency." Ph.D. dissertation, University of California, Berkeley.

Buder, Leonard. 1980. "McGuire Suspending Police Patrol Duty in One-Officer Cars." *New York Times*, January 30, p. 1.

Burger, Chester, ed. 1978. *The Chief Executive*. Boston: CBI Publishing.

Burnham, David. 1974. "How Police Corruption Is Built into the System — And a Few Ideas for What to Do about It." In *Police Corruption: A Sociological Perspective*, edited by Lawrence W. Sherman. Garden City, N.Y.: Anchor Books.

Bussom, Robert S.; Laris L. Larson; William M. Vicars; and James J. Ness. 1981. "The Nature of Police Executives' Work." Washington, D.C.: National Institute of Justice. Mimeographed.

California Police Officers' Association. 1978. *CPOA News*, March.

Campbell, Angus, and Howard Schuman. 1969. "Racial Attitudes in Fifteen American Cities" (supplemental study for the National Advisory Commission on Civil Disorders). Washington, D.C.: U.S. Government Printing Office.

Cancilla, Robert C. 1977. "Handling Citizen Complaints at the San Mateo County Sheriff's Office: A Manual of Policy and Procedures." Master's thesis, San Jose State University.

Cannavale, Frank, and William Falcon. 1978. *Witness Cooperation*. Lexington, Mass.: Heath.

———. 1977. *Improving Witness Cooperation*. Washington, D.C.: National Institute of Law Enforcement and Criminal Justice.

Carden, Gerald E., ed. 1983a. *International Handbook of the Ombudsman: Evolution and Present Function*. Westport, Conn.: Greenwood Press.

———. 1983b. *International Handbook of the Ombudsman: Country Survey*. Westport, Conn.: Greenwood Press.

Caruso, Philip, and Adam Walinsky. 1984. "Spotlight on the Police Corps." *National Centurion*, August, pp. 15–22, 45–48, 60–61.

Cawley, Donald F. 1978. "Viewpoint: The Patrol Question." *Police Magazine*, March, pp. 31–32.

Cawley, Donald F., and H. Jerome Miron. 1977. *Managing Patrol Operations: Manual*. Washington, D.C.: U.S. Government Printing Office.

Cawley, Donald F.; H. Jerome Miron; William J. Araujo; Robert Wasserman; Timothy A. Mannello; and Yale Huffman. 1977. *Managing Criminal Investigations: Manual*. Washington, D.C.: University Research Corporation.

Center for the Study of Democratic Institutions. 1973. "Broadcasting and the First Amendment: Report on a Center Conference." *Center Magazine*, May–June, p. 24.

Chabotar, Kent John. 1982. *Measuring the Costs of Police Services*. Washington, D.C.: National Institute of Justice.

Chaiken, Jan M., and Marcia R. Chaiken. 1982. *Varieties of Criminal Behavior*. Santa Monica, Calif.: Rand Corporation.

Chambliss, William J. 1976. "The State and Criminal Law." In *Whose Law? What Order?* edited by William J. Chambliss and Milton Mankoff. New York: Wiley.

Chevigny, Paul. 1969. *Police Power*. New York: Pantheon Books.

Chicago Commission on Race Relations. 1922. *The Negro in Chicago: A Study of Race Relations and a Race Riot*. Chicago: University of Chicago Press.

Chicago Daily News. 1969. *Chicago Daily News*, March 6, p. 8.

Chicago Police Department. 1976. *Statistical Summary for 1976*. Chicago.

Chicago Tribune. 1969. *Chicago Tribune*, March 6, p. 2.

"Chrysler Corp. Elects Union's Bieber to Board." 1984. *Wall Street Journal*, October 5, p. 17.

Churchill, Winston S. 1949. *The Second World War: Their Finest Hour*. Cambridge, Mass.: Houghton Mifflin.

Cizanckas, Victor I., and Donald G. Hanna. 1977. *Modern Police Management and Organization*. Englewood Cliffs, N.J.: Prentice-Hall.

Clark, John P. 1969. "Isolation of the Police: A Comparison of the British and American Systems." In *Crime and Justice in Society*, edited by Richard Quinney. Boston: Little, Brown.

Clark, Kenneth R. 1984. "The Power of TV to Right a Nation's Wrongs." *Chicago Tribune*, October 29, Sec. 4, pp. 1, 3.

Cleveland Foundation, ed. 1922. *Criminal Justice in Cleveland*. Reprinted, Montclair, N.J.: Patterson Smith, 1968.

Cohen, Bernard. 1963. "Leadership Styles of Commanders in the New York City Police Department." *Journal of Police Science and Administration* 8 (2): 125–38.

Cohen, David K., and Michael S. Garet. 1975. "Reforming Educational Policy with Applied Social Research." *Harvard Educational Review* 45 (1): 17–43.

Cohen, Jerry. 1984a. "Police Chief: Pressure Is Unrelenting." *L.A. Times*, November 11, pp. 1,20,21.

_____. 1984b. "Chief's Job: His Troops Come First." *L.A. Times*, November 12, pp. 1,3,14.

_____. 1984c. "Police Chief: It's No Job for Timid." *L.A. Times*, November 13, pp. 1,3,16,17.

Cohen, Marcia, and J. Thomas McEwen. 1984. "Handling Calls for Service: Alternatives to Traditional Policing." *NIJ Reports*, September, pp. 4–8.

Cole, George F., and David W. Neubauer. 1976. "The Living Courtroom." *Judicature* 59, January, pp. 293–99.

Commission on Accreditation for Law Enforcement Agencies (CALEA). 1984. "Applicant Agencies Top 100." *Commission Update* 28 (Spring).

_____. 1983a. *Standards for Law Enforcement Agencies*. Fairfax, Va.

_____. 1983b. *Commission Update* 26 (October).

"Complaint Review Boards in Florida: Who's Complaining?" 1983. *Nova Law Journal* 7: 353.

Connie Francis v. *Howard Johnson, Inc.* 1976. 419 F. Supp. 1210 (E.D.N.Y.) (not appealed).

Conte v. *Horscher*. 1977. 365 N.E. 2d 567 (Ill. App.).

Cordner, Gary W. 1981. "The Effects of Directed Patrol: A Natural Quasi-Experiment in Pontiac." In *Critical Issues in Law Enforcement*, edited by James J. Fyfe. Beverly Hills, Calif.: Sage.

_____. 1980a. "Police Patrol Research and Its Utilization." *Police Studies* 2 (4): 12–21.

_____. 1980b. "Job Analysis and the Police: Benefits and Limitations." *Journal of Police Science and Administration* 8 (3): 355–62.

_____. 1979. "Police Patrol Workload Studies: A Review and Critique." *Police Studies* 2 (2): 50–60.

Costello v. *Wainwright*. 1976. 525 F.2d 1239, rehearing 539 F.2d 547 (1976); 489 F. Supp. 110 (1980).

Couper, David C. 1983. *How to Rate Your Local Police*. Washington, D.C.: Police Executive Research Forum.

Cox, Archibald. 1968. *The Warren Court*. Cambridge, Mass.: Harvard University Press.

Criminal Justice Center, John Jay School of Criminal Justice. 1983. *Private Funding for Police Training*. New York.

Critchley, Thomas A. 1972. *A History of Police in England and Wales*. 2nd ed. Montclair, N.J.: Patterson Smith.

Cronin, Thomas E.; Tania Z. Chronin; and Michael E. Milakovich. 1981. *U.S. v. Crime in the Streets*. Bloomington: Indiana University Press.

Cumming, Elaine; Ian Cumming; and Laura Edell. 1965. "Policeman as Philosopher, Guide, and Friend." *Social Problems* 12 (3): 276–86.

Cummings, Geanne. 1979. "70% Cases Decided Before Trial." *Columbia (Md.) Times*, September 5, p. 4A.

Cunningham, William C., and Todd H. Taylor. 1985. *The Hallcrest Report: Private Security and Police in America*. Portland, Ore.: Chancellor Press.

_____. 1984. "The Growing Role of Private Security." *Research in Brief*. Washington, D.C.: National Institute of Justice.

Dade-Miami Criminal Justice Council. 1981. *Evaluation: Metropolitan Dade County Independent Review Panel*. Miami, Fla.

Davis, Edward M. 1978. *Staff One: A Perspective on Effective Police Management*. Englewood Cliffs, N.J.: Prentice-Hall.

_____. 1977. "Testimony." In U.S. Congress, House. Select Committee on Narcotic Abuse and Control. *Hearings*, 90th Cong., 1st Sess., p. 82.

Davis, Kenneth Culp. 1975. *Police Discretion*. St. Paul, Minn.: West.

_____. 1973. *Discretionary Justice*. 2nd ed. Chicago: University of Illinois Press.

_____. 1969. *Discretionary Justice: A Preliminary Inquiry*. Baton Rouge: Louisiana University Press.

Davis, R. C. 1973. "Research Management During the '50s." In *Concepts in Organizational Guidance*, edited by Walter H. Klein and David C. Murphy. Boston: Little, Brown.

Dawkins, R. E. 1982a. "To Create Oasis Amid the Blight Is Goal of Police, Housing Officials." *Miami Herald*, August 19.

————. 1982b. "Officers Change Image of Police." *Miami Herald*, October 12, p. BR1.

Deal, Terrence E., and Allan A. Kennedy. 1982. *Corporate Cultures*. Reading, Mass.: Addison-Wesley.

Delaware v. *Prouse*. 1979. 440 U.S. 648.

Dent, Edward H. v. *City of New Orleans*. 1980. (E.D. LA.) (case settled).

Diamond, E. 1981. "Panel Rips 'Haphazard' Growth of CJ Education, Issuing Voluntary Set of Minimum Standards." *Law Enforcement News*, September 7, pp. 1, 4.

Dodenhoff, Peter. 1985. "Interview: Robert B. Kliesmet." *Law Enforcement News*, January 21, pp. 9–11.

————. 1984. "Accreditation's Embryonic Empire: Interview with James V. Cotter." *Law Enforcement News*, December 10, pp. 11–14.

————. 1983. "Policing a Municipal Melting Pot: An Interview with Raymond C. Davis." *Law Enforcement News*, September 12, pp. 8–10.

Dominick, Joseph R. 1978. "Crime and Law Enforcement in the Media." In *Deviance and Mass Behavior*, edited by C. Winnick. Beverly Hills, Calif.: Sage.

Douthit, Nathan. 1975. "Police Professionalism and the War Against Crime in the United States, 1920s–30s." In *Police Forces in History*, edited by George L. Mosse, pp. 317–33. Beverly Hills, Calif.: Sage.

Drucker, Peter F. 1973. *Management: Tasks, Responsibilities, Practices*. New York: Harper & Row.

Eck, John. 1984. "Research in Action: Solving Crimes." *NIJ Reports*, March, pp. 1–8.

————. 1983. *Solving Crimes: The Investigation of Burglary and Robbery*. Washington, D.C.: Police Executive Research Forum.

————. 1979. *Managing Case Assignments: The Burglary Investigation Decision Model Replication*. Washington, D.C.: Police Executive Research Forum.

Edwards, Harry T.; R. Theodore Clark, Jr.; and Charles B. Craver. 1979. *Labor Relations Law in the Public Sector*. New York: Bobbs-Merrill.

Ehrenberg, Ronald, and Josh Schwarz. 1984. "Public Sector Labor Markets." In *Handbook of Labor Economics*, edited by Orley Ashenfelter and Richard Layard. New York: North-Holland Press.

Eisenberg, Terry. 1975. *Collaboration Between Law Enforcement Executives and Social Scientists*. San Jose, Calif.: National Conference of Christians and Jews.

Eisenberg, Terry, and Sharon Lawrence. 1980. "Citizen/Police Relations in Police Policy Setting." Los Gatos, Calif.: Institute for Social Analysis. Mimeographed.

Ellis, Havelock. 1922. "Introduction" to *Against the Grain*, by Joris-K. Huysmans (translated by John Howard), reprint ed. New York: Lieber & Lewis.

English, Myra, and Steven L. Fowler. 1983. *Fear Reduction Plan*. Houston, Tex.: Houston Police Department (May).

Etzioni, Amitai. 1961. *A Comparative Analysis of Complex Organizations*. New York: Free Press.

Farmer, David J. 1981. "Thinking About Research: The Contribution of Social Science Research to Contemporary Policing." *Police Studies* 3 (4): 22–40.

————. 1978. "The Research Revolution." *Police Magazine*, November, pp. 64–65.

Farmer, Michael T. 1981. *Differential Police Response Strategies*. Washington, D.C.: Police Executive Research Forum.

Farris, Edward A. 1982. "The Path to Professionalism: Five Decades of American

Policing – 1932-1982." *Police Chief*, November, pp. 30-36.

FBI. 1975. "Women in Policing." *FBI Bulletin*, September.

"FBI Launches Probe of Slaying on Circle." 1981. *Indianapolis Star*, November 21, pp. 1, 4.

Federal Judicial Center. 1981. *Experimentation in the Law: Report of the Federal Judicial Center Advisory Committee on Experimentation in the Law*. Washington, D.C.

Feeney, F., and A. Weir. 1973. *The Prevention and Control of Robbery*. Davis, Calif.: Center on Administration of Criminal Justice, University of California-Davis.

Finkin, Matthew W. 1973. "Federal Reliance on Voluntary Accreditation: The Power to Recognize as the Power to Regulate." *Journal of Law and Education* 2: 339-75.

Fisher, S. 1965. "The Rehabilitative Effectiveness of a Community Correctional Residence for Narcotics Users." *Journal of Criminal Law, Criminology, and Police Science* 56: 190.

Fisk, Donald, Jr. 1970. *The Indianapolis Fleet Car Plan*. Washington, D.C.: Urban Institute.

Fogelson, Robert M. 1977. *Big-City Police*. Cambridge, Mass.: Harvard University Press.

Forst, Brian; Frank Leahy, Jr.; Jean Shirhall; Herbert Tayson; Eric Wish; and John Bartolomeo. 1982. *Arrest Convictability as a Measure of Police Performance*. Washington, D.C.: National Institute of Justice.

Forst, Brian; Judith Lucianovic; and Sarah H. Cox. 1977. *What Happens After Arrest? A Court Perspective of Police Operations in the District of Columbia*. Washington, D.C.: Institute for Law and Social Research.

Fosdick, Raymond B. 1920. *American Police Systems*. New York: Century; reprinted, Montclair, N.J.: Patterson Smith, 1969.

Fowler, Jr., Floyd J., and Thomas W. Mangione. 1982. *Neighborhood Crime, Fear, and Social Control: A Second Look at the Hartford Program*. Washington, D.C.: U.S. Department of Justice.

Fowler, Jr., Floyd J.; Thomas W. Mangione; and Frederick E. Pratter. 1977. *Gambling Law Enforcement in Major American Cities: Executive Summary*. Washington, D.C.: U.S. Government Printing Office.

Friedrich, Otto. 1985. "Man of the Year: Seven Who Succeeded." *Time*, January 7, pp. 43-44.

Friedrich, Robert J. 1983. "Police Use of Force: Individuals, Situations, and Organizations." In *Thinking About Police: Contemporary Readings*, edited by Carl B. Klockars, pp. 302-13. New York: McGraw-Hill.

_____. 1980. "Police Use of Force: Individuals, Situations, and Organizations." *Annals of the American Academy of Political and Social Science* 452 (November): 82-97.

Fuld, Leonard F. 1909. *Police Administration*. New York: Putnam's; reprinted, Montclair, N.J.: Patterson Smith, 1971.

Fuller, Hugh. 1931. *Criminal Justice in Virginia*. New York: Century.

Fyfe, James J. 1981. Personal interview. Washington, D.C. (June).

_____. 1979. "Administrative Interventions on Police Shooting Discretion." *Journal of Criminal Justice* 7: 313-35.

_____. 1978. "Reducing the Use of Deadly Force: The New York Experience." In *Police Use of Deadly Force: A Workshop Conducted by the Community Relations Service at the 1978 Annual Conference of the National Association of Hu-*

man Rights Workers, edited by Bertram Levine, pp. 28–40. Washington, D.C.: U.S. Government Printing Office.

Gallup. 1982. *Gallup Report No. 200*, May 1982. Princeton, N.J.

Gans, Herbert. 1979. *Deciding What's News*. New York: Pantheon.

Garner, Gerald W. 1984. *The Police Meet the Press*. Springfield, Ill.: Charles C Thomas.

Garofalo, J., and Michael J. Hindelang. 1977. *An Introduction to the National Crime Survey*. Washington, D.C.: Bureau of Justice Statistics, U.S. Department of Justice.

Geller, William A. 1985. *Chicago Community Trust Criminal Justice Commission: A Planning Report*. Chicago: American Bar Foundation.

_____. 1985 forthcoming. "The Ecology of Police Shootings: Environmental and Organizational Correlates of Police Shootings in Chicago Police Districts."

_____. 1982. "Deadly Force: What We Know." *Journal of Police Science and Administration* 10 (2): 151–77.

Geller, William A., and Kevin Karales. 1981a. "Shootings of and by Chicago Police: Uncommon Crises." *Journal of Criminal Law and Criminology* 72 (4): 1813–866.

_____. 1981b. *Split-Second Decisions: Shootings of and by Chicago Police*. Chicago: Chicago Law Enforcement Study Group.

Gellhorn, Walter. 1967. *Ombudsmen and Others*. Cambridge, Mass.: Harvard University Press.

_____. 1966. *When Americans Complain*. Cambridge, Mass.: Harvard University Press.

Germann, A. C. 1962. *Police Executive Development*. Springfield, Ill.: Charles C Thomas.

Gerth, Hans, and C. Wright Mills, eds. 1948. *From Max Weber: Essays in Sociology*. New York: Oxford University Press.

Gitlin, Todd. 1980. *The Whole World Is Watching: Mass Media in the Making and Unmaking of the New Left*. Berkeley: University of California Press.

Gold, Todd. 1983. "Extracurricular Cops: The Part-time Deputies of the L.A. Sheriff's Department Risk Their Lives for Only $1 a Year (77¢ After Taxes)." *California Living*, May 22, pp. 14–17.

Goldstein, Herman. 1983. Interview (October).

_____. 1982a. "The Drinking Driver in Madison: A Study of the Problem and the Community Response." Vol. II. Madison: University of Wisconsin Law School, July. Mimeographed.

_____. 1982b. "The Repeat Sexual Offender in Madison: A Memorandum on the Problem and the Community's Response." Vol. III. Madison: University of Wisconsin Law School, July. Mimeographed.

_____. 1982c. "Experimenting with the Problem-Oriented Approach to Improving Police Service: A Report and Some Reflections on Two Case Studies." Vol. IV. Madison: University of Wisconsin Law School, July. Mimeographed.

_____. 1981. "The Problem-Oriented Approach to Improving Police Service: A Description of the Project and an Elaboration of the Concept." Vol. I. Madison: University of Wisconsin Law School, March. Mimeographed.

_____. 1979. "Improving Policing: A Problem-Oriented Approach." *Crime and Delinquency* 25 (April): 236–58.

_____. 1977. *Policing a Free Society*. Cambridge, Mass.: Ballinger.

_____. 1960. "Police Discretion Not to Invoke the Criminal Process: Low-Visibility

Decisions in the Administration of Justice." *Yale Law Journal* 69: 543.

Gove, Philip B., ed. 1967. *Webster's Seventh New Collegiate Dictionary*. Springfield, Mass.: G. & C. Merriam Co.

Graber, Doris A. 1980. *Crime News and the Public*. New York: Harper & Row.

Grassie, Richard G., and Timothy D. Crowe. 1978. *Integrated Criminal Apprehension Program: Program Implementation Guide*. Washington, D.C.: Law Enforcement Assistance Administration.

Greenberg, B. 1977. *Felony Investigation Decision Model: An Analysis of Investigative Elements of Information*. Menlo Park, Calif.: Stanford Research Institute.

Greenberg, B.; O. Yu; and K. Lang. 1973. *Enhancement of the Investigative Function*. Vol. I. *Analysis and Conclusions*. Menlo Park, Calif.: Stanford Research Institute.

Greenberg, Bernard; C. V. Elliot; L. P. Kraft; and H. S. Procter. 1977. *Felony Investigation Decision Model: An Analysis of Investigative Elements of Information*. Washington, D.C.: U.S. Government Printing Office.

Greene, Jack R.; Tim S. Bynum; and Gary W. Cordner. 1981. "Dividing Up the Pie in Criminal Justice: Planning and the Play of Power." East Lansing: Michigan State University. Mimeographed.

Greenwood, Peter W., with Alan Abrahams. 1982. *Selective Incapacitation*. Santa Monica, Calif.: Rand Corporation.

Greenwood, Peter W.; Jan M. Chaiken; Joan Petersilia; and L. Prushoff. 1975. *The Criminal Investigation Process*. Vol. III. *Observations and Analysis*. Santa Monica, Calif.: Rand Corporation.

Greenwood, Peter W., and Joan Petersilia. 1975. *The Criminal Investigation Process*. Vol. I. *Summary and Policy Implications*. Santa Monica, Calif.: Rand Corporation.

Grosman, Brian A. 1975. *Police Command*. Toronto: Macmillan.

Gross, Avrum. 1978. "Remarks." Presentation to the Special National Conference on Plea Bargaining, June 14–17, French Lick, Ind.

Guyot, Dorothy. 1979. "Bending Granite: Attempts to Change the Rank Structure of American Police Departments." *Journal of Police Science and Administration* 7 (3): 253–84.

Habermas, Jurgen. 1973. *Theory and Practice*. Boston: Beacon.

Hacker, Andrew. 1983. *A Statistical Portrait of the American People*. New York: Viking.

Hagan, John, and Celesta Albonetti. 1982. "Race, Class and the Perception of Criminal Injustice in America." *American Journal of Sociology* 88 (September): 329–55.

Haller, Mark. 1976. "Historical Roots of Police Behavior: Chicago, 1890–1925." *Law and Society Review* 10: 303–23.

Harris, Richard W. 1973. *The Police Academy*. New York: Wiley.

Harvard Law Review. 1984. "Developments in the Law—Public Employment." *Harvard Law Review* 97: 1611–800.

Hastings, Thomas F. 1984. "Team Policing Still Works Well." *Law Enforcement News*, February 27, p. 10 passim.

Heaphy, John F. 1978. *Police Practices: The General Administrative Survey*. Washington, D.C.: Police Foundation.

Herbers, John. 1982. "Murphy Is Accused by Police Chiefs." *New York Times*, July 8, pp. A1, B15.

Hillenbrand, Susan W. 1984. "Protecting Crime Victims and Witnesses." *American Bar Association Journal*, November, p. 146.

Holdaway, Simon, ed. 1979. *The British Police*. Beverly Hills, Calif.: Sage.

Holden, Paul E.; Carlton A. Pederson; and Payton E. Germane. 1968. *Top Management*. New York: McGraw-Hill.

Holden, Paul E.; Lounsbury S. Fish; and Hubert L. Smith. 1951. *Top-Management Organization and Control*. New York: McGraw-Hill.

Home Office. 1984. Personal communication between William Saulsbury, National Institute of Justice, and members of the Home Office staff. London (July).

Hudson, James P. 1972. "Organizational Aspects of Internal and External Review of the Police." *Journal of Criminal Law, Criminology, and Police Science* 63: 427–33.

Hudzik, John K.; Tim S. Bynum; Jack R. Greene; Gary W. Cordner; Kenneth E. Christian; and Steven M. Edwards. 1981. *Criminal Justice Manpower Planning: An Overview*. Washington, D.C.: U.S. Government Printing Office.

Hughes, Everett C. 1965. "Professions." In *Professions in America*, edited by Kenneth S. Lynn. Boston: Beacon.

Illinois Association for Criminal Justice. 1929. *The Illinois Crime Survey*. Reprinted, Montclair, N.J.: Patterson Smith, 1968.

INSLAW (Institute for Law and Social Research). Undated. *Application Software Package: Technical Description*. Washington, D. C.

International Association of Chiefs of Police. 1982. "M.S.U. to Establish National Foot Patrol Center." *IACP Newsletter*, August, pp. 3–4.

———. 1979. *Police Strikes: Causes and Prevention*. Gaithersburg, Md.

———. 1977. *Critical Issues in Police Labor Relations*. Gaithersburg, Md.

International City Management Association. 1982. *Local Government Police Management*, 2d edition. Washington, D.C.

———. 1977. *Local Government Police Management*. Washington, D.C.

Jacob, Herbert, and Robert Lineberry, with Anne M. Heinz, Janice A. Beecher, Jack Moran, and Duane H. Swank. 1982. *Governmental Responses to Crime: Crime on Urban Agendas*. Washington, D.C.: National Institute of Justice.

Jacobs, James B., and Norma Meacham Crotty. 1978. *Guard Unions and the Future of the Prisons*. Ithaca, N.Y.: Cornell Labor Relations Press.

Jacoby, Joan E. 1981. "Police and Prosecutor Responses to the Standard Case Set." Presentation to the Conference on Research Approaches to Police-Prosecutor Coordination, December 14, National Institute of Justice, Washington, D.C.

———. 1977. *The Prosecutor's Charging Decisions: A Policy Perspective*. Washington, D.C.: U.S. Government Printing Office.

Jacoby, Joan E.; Lenard R. Mellon; Edward C. Ratledge; and Stanley S. Turner. 1982. *Prosecutorial Decisionmaking*. Washington, D.C.: National Institute of Justice.

Jameson, William J. 1974. "The Beginning: Background and Development of the ABA Standards for Criminal Justice." *American Criminal Law Review* 12 (Fall): 255–61.

Jencks, Christopher. 1983. "How We Live Now." *New York Times Book Review*, April 10, p. 7.

Jenkins, Herbert. 1970. *Keeping the Peace*. New York: Harper & Row.

Johnson, Thomas A.; Gordon Misner; and Lee P. Brown. 1981. *The Police and Society: An Environment for Collaboration and Confrontation.* Englewood Cliffs, N.J.: Prentice-Hall.

Johnston, David. 1983. "The Cop Watch." *Columbia Journalism Review* 22 (Winter), pp. 51–54.

_____. 1982. "Burglar Alarms — False Reports Drain Police Resources." *Los Angeles Times,* August 9, Pt. 2, pp. 1–3.

Jones, Linda. 1982. "Police Seek Black Residents' Input, Help in Stopping Crime." *Fort Lauderdale Sun-Sentinel,* August 19.

Juris, Hervey A., and Peter Feuille. 1973. *Police Unionism.* Lexington, Mass.: Heath.

Kakalik, James S., and Sorrel Wildhorn. 1971. *Aids to Decision-making in Police Patrol.* New York: Rand Corporation.

Kelling, George L. 1984. "Remarks on Experimentation in Policing." Presentation at the annual meeting of the Academy of Criminal Justice Sciences, March 28, Chicago.

Kelling, George L.; Tony Pate; Duane Dieckman; and Charles E. Brown. 1974a. *The Kansas City Preventive Patrol Experiment: A Summary Report.* Washington, D.C.: Police Foundation.

_____. 1974b. *The Kansas City Preventive Patrol Experiment: Technical Report.* Washington, D.C.: Police Foundation.

Kelly, Joseph A. 1984. *Differential Police Response: Participant's Resource Manual.* Washington, D.C.: National Institute of Justice.

Kelly, Michael J. 1975. *Police Chief Selection: A Handbook for Local Government.* Washington, D.C.: Police Foundation.

Kenney, John P. 1975. *Police Administration.* 3rd ed. Springfield, Ill.: Charles C Thomas.

Kerstetter, Wayne A. 1981a. "Police Participation in Structured Plea Negotiations." *Law and Policy Quarterly* 3: 95–119.

_____. 1981b. "Police Perceptions of Influence in the Criminal Case Disposition Process." *Journal of Criminal Justice* 9: 151–64.

_____. 1979. "Peer Review as the Primary Control Mechanism in Police Agencies." *Criminal Justice Review* 4 (2): 113–20.

_____. 1970. *Citizen Review of Police Misconduct: Or Who Will Watch the Watchman.* Chicago: Center for Studies in Criminal Justice, University of Chicago.

Klein, Walter H., and David C. Murphy, eds. 1979. *Policy: Concepts in Organizational Guidance.* Boston: Little, Brown.

Klockars, Carl B. 1983. *Thinking About Police: Contemporary Readings.* New York: McGraw-Hill.

_____. 1980. "The Dirty Harry Problem." *Annals of the American Academy of Political and Social Science* 452 (November): 33–47.

_____. 1979. "Dirty Hands and Deviant Subjects." In *Deviance and Decency: The Ethics of Research with Human Subjects,* edited by Carl B. Klockars and Finbarr W. O'Connor, pp. 261–82. Beverly Hills, Calif.: Sage.

Knapp Commission. 1972. *The Knapp Commission Report on Police Corruption.* New York: George Braziller.

Knight, Athelia. 1980. "D.C. Police at Court: $1.4 Million Mostly for Waiting." *Washington Post,* September 29, p. B1.

Knutson, Jeanne N. 1980. "The Terrorists' Dilemmas: Some Implicit Rules of the Game." *Terrorism: An International Journal* 4: 125–221.
Koepsell, Terry W., and Charles M. Girard. 1979. *Small Police Agency Consolidation: Suggested Approaches.* Washington, D.C.: National Institute of Justice.
Krajick, Kevin. 1978. "Does Patrol Prevent Crime?" *Police Magazine*, September, pp. 5–16.
Kuh, Richard H. 1975. "Plea Bargaining: Guidelines in the Manhattan District Attorney's Office." *Criminal Law Bulletin* 11: 48–61.
Kuralt, Charles. 1982. "Slumbuster." A report appearing on the weekly television series "CBS Sunday Morning," October.
Lane, Roger. 1967. *Policing the City: Boston 1822–1885.* Cambridge, Mass.: Harvard University Press.
Larson, Richard C. 1972. *Urban Patrol Analysis.* Cambridge, Mass.: MIT Press.
Lavrakas, Paul; with Janice Normoyle; Wesley G. Skogan; Elicia Herz; Greta Salem; and Dan A. Lewis. 1981. *Factors Related to Citizen Involvement in Personal, Household, and Neighborhood Anti-Crime Measures.* Washington, D.C.: National Institute of Justice.
Lee, W. L. Melville. 1901. *A History of the Police in England.* London: Methusen; reprinted, Montclair, N.J.: Patterson Smith, 1971.
Levi, Margaret. 1977. *Bureaucratic Insurgency: The Case of Police Unions.* Lexington, Mass.: Heath.
Levine, Charles. 1984. *Fiscal Stress and Police Services: A Strategic Perspective.* Washington, D.C.: National Institute of Justice.
Levine, Jerald Elliot. 1971. "Police, Parties, and Polity." Ph.D. dissertation, University of Wisconsin.
Lindblom, Charles E. 1980. *The Policy Making Process.* 2nd ed. Englewood Cliffs, N.J.: Prentice-Hall.
Lindblom, Charles E., and David K. Cohen. 1979. *Usable Knowledge: Social Science and Social Problem Solving.* New Haven, Conn.: Yale University Press.
Linn, Amy; Andrew Ross; and Scott Winokur. 1983. "With the Authority of Law: Police Violence in Richmond." *San Francisco Examiner*, June 19 (five-part series).
Littlejohn, E. J. 1981. "Civilian Police Commission: Deterrent to Police Misconduct." *University of Detroit Journal of Urban Law* 5: 59.
Logan v. *Shealy.* 1981. 660 F.2d 1007 (4th Cir.).
Lohman, Joseph D., and Gorden E. Misner. 1966. "The Police and the Community: The Dynamics of Their Relationship in a Changing Society, Volume II." Background paper for the President's Commission on Law Enforcement and Administration of Justice. Washington, D.C.: U.S. Government Printing Office.
Loving, Nancy. 1980. *Responding to Spouse Abuse and Wife Beating: A Guide for Police.* Washington, D.C.: Police Foundation.
Lynch, Richard P. 1984. Personal communication with director of American Bar Association Standing Committee on Association Standards for Criminal Justice, November.
McDonald, William F. 1984. *Plea Bargaining: Critical Issues and Common Practices.* Washington, D.C.: U.S. Government Printing Office.
_____. 1979. "The Prosecutor's Domain." In *The Prosecutor*, edited by William F. McDonald. Beverly Hills, Calif.: Sage.

McDonald, William F.; Henry Rossman; and James Cramer. 1981. "Police-Prosecutor Relations in the United States." Washington, D.C.: National Institute of Justice.

_____. 1979. "The Prosecutor's Plea Bargaining Decisions." In *The Prosecutor*, edited by William F. McDonald. Beverly Hills, Calif.: Sage.

McEwen, J. Thomas, and Marcia Cohen. 1984. "Handling Calls for Service: Alternatives to Traditional Policing." *NIJ Reports*, September 1984.

McIntyre, Donald. 1975. "Impediments to Effective Police-Prosecution Relationships." *American Criminal Law Review* 13: 201-34.

McIntyre, Donald, and Raymond T. Nimmer. 1972. *Survey and Evaluation of Illinois State's Attorneys Association Comprehensive Project*. Hinsdale: Illinois State's Attorneys Association.

Malcolm, Andrew H. 1975. "Civilian Boards on Wane as Watchdogs of Police." *New York Times*, February 10, p. 1.

Mankiewicz, Frank. 1983. Remarks to the Law Day dinner of Business and Professional People for the Public Interest, May 2, at the Drake Hotel, Chicago, Ill.

Manning, Peter K. 1979a. "The Reflexivity and Facticity of Knowledge: Criminal Justice Research in the 1970s." *American Behavioral Scientist* 22 (6): 697-732.

_____. 1979b. "Crime and Technology: The Role of Scientific Research and Technology in Crime Control." East Lansing: Michigan State University. Mimeographed.

_____. 1978. "The Police: Mandate, Strategies and Appearances." In *Policing: A View from the Street*, edited by Peter K. Manning, and John Van Maanen. Santa Monica, Calif.: Goodyear Publishing Co.

Massachusetts v. *Sheppard*. 1984. – U.S. – , 82 L. Ed.2d 737.

Mayo, Louis A. 1983. "Analysis of the Role of the Police Chief Executive." Ph.D. dissertation, American University.

"Mayor Names 25 to Study Police Deadly-Force Use." 1980. *Indianapolis Star*, November 27, p. 33.

Mecum, Richard V. 1979. "Police Professionalism: A New Look at an Old Topic." *The Police Chief* 46 (8): 46-49.

Meiklejohn, Alexander. 1965. *Political Freedom*. Cambridge: Oxford University Press.

_____. 1948. *Free Speech and Its Relation to Self-Government*. New York: Harper & Brothers.

Mendelsohn, H., and G. O'Keefe. 1981. *A Mass Communications Strategy for Generating Citizen Action Against Crime*. Denver, Colo.: Center for Mass Communications Research and Policy, University of Denver (grant report to the National Institute of Justice, U.S. Department of Justice).

Merriam, Charles E.; S. D. Parratt; and A. Lepawsky. 1933. *The Government of the Metropolitan Region of Chicago*. Chicago: University of Chicago Press.

Metropolitan Dade County Independent Review Panel. 1983. *The Independent Review Panel: The First Three Years*. Miami, Fla.

Michelmore, Peter. 1984. "Saga of a Slum Buster." *Reader's Digest*, October, pp. 1-6.

Miller, Arthur. 1963. "Remarks at the University of Michigan's Annual Hopwood Literary Awards Ceremony," May.

Miller, Wilbur R. 1977. *Cops and Bobbies: Police Authority in New York and London, 1830-1870*. Chicago: University of Chicago Press.

Miller v. *Carson*. 1977. 563 F.2d 741.

Milton, Catherine; Jeanne Halleck; James Lardner; and Gary Albrecht. 1977. *Police Use of Deadly Force*. Washington, D.C.: Police Foundation.

Mintzberg, Henry. 1973. *The Nature of Managerial Work*. New York: Harper & Row.

Missouri Association for Criminal Justice. 1926. *The Missouri Crime Survey*; reprinted, Montclair, N.J.: Patterson Smith, 1968.

Mitchell v. *Untreiner*. 1975. 421 F. Supp. 886.

Monell v. *Department of Social Services*. 1978. 436 U.S. 658.

Monroe v. *Pape*. 1961. 365 U.S. 167.

Moore, Mark H., and George L. Kelling. 1983. "To Serve and Protect: Learning from Police History." *The Public Interest* 70 (Winter), pp. 49–65.

More, Jr., Harry W. 1975. *Effective Police Administration: A Behavioral Approach*. San Jose, Calif.: Justice Systems Development.

Morris, James E. 1983. *Victim Aftershock: How to Get Results from the Criminal Justice System*. New York: Franklin Watts.

Morris, Norval, and Gordon Hawkins. 1977. *Letter to the President on Crime Control*. Chicago: University of Chicago Press.

_____. 1970. *The Honest Politician's Guide to Crime Control*. Chicago: University of Chicago Press.

Muir, Jr., William Ker. 1980. "Power Attracts Violence." *Annals of the American Academy of Political and Social Science* 452 (November): 48–52.

_____. 1977. *Police: Streetcorner Politicians*. Chicago: University of Chicago Press.

Municipal Manpower Commission. 1962. *Governmental Power for Tomorrow's Cities*. New York: McGraw-Hill.

Munro, James L. 1974. *Administrative Behavior and Police Organizations*. Cincinnati: W. H. Anderson.

Murphy, Cornelius P. 1984. "Memorandum." San Francisco: Office of the Chief, San Francisco Police Department. May 2.

Murphy, Patrick V., and Thomas Plate. 1977. *Commissioner*. New York: Simon and Schuster.

Myrdal, Gunnar. 1953. "The Relation Between Social Theory and Social Policy." *British Journal of Sociology* 4: 210–42.

Nader, Ralph, and William B. Schultz. 1985. "Public Interest Law with Bread on the Table." *American Bar Association Journal* 71 (February), pp. 74–77.

National Advisory Commission on Civil Disorders. 1968. *Report*. New York: Bantam.

National Advisory Commission on Criminal Justice Standards and Goals (NAC). 1976. *Police Chief Executive: Report of the Police Chief Executive Committee of the International Association of Chiefs of Police*. Washington, D.C.: U.S. Government Printing Office.

_____. 1973a. *Police*. Washington, D.C.: U.S. Government Printing Office.

_____. 1973b. *Courts*. Washington, D.C.: U.S. Government Printing Office.

_____. 1973c. *Corrections*. Washington, D.C.: U.S. Government Printing Office.

_____. 1973d. *Criminal Justice System*. Washington, D.C.: U.S. Government Printing Office.

_____. 1973e. *A National Strategy to Reduce Crime*. Washington, D.C.: U.S. Government Printing Office.

_____. 1973f. *Community Crime Prevention*. Washington, D.C.: U.S. Government Printing Office.

_____. 1973g. *Proceedings of the National Conference on Criminal Justice.* Washington, D.C.: U.S. Government Printing Office.

National Commission on the Causes and Prevention of Violence. 1968. *Rights in Conflict.* Washington, D.C.: U.S. Government Printing Office.

National Commission on Law Observance and Enforcement. 1931a. *Report on Lawlessness in Law Enforcement.* Washington, D.C.: U.S. Government Printing Office.

_____. 1931b. *Report on Police.* Washington, D.C.: U.S. Government Printing Office.

National Commission on Marihuana and Drug Abuse. 1972. *Marihuana: A Signal of Misunderstanding.* Washington, D.C.: U.S. Government Printing Office.

National Commission on Productivity. 1973. *Opportunities for Improving Productivity in Police Services.* Washington, D.C.

National District Attorneys' Association. 1977. *National Prosecution Standards.* Chicago.

National Institute of Law Enforcement and Criminal Justice. 1978. *Exemplary Projects.* Washington, D.C.

National Lawyers Guild. 1981. *Police Misconduct Litigation,* edited by Michael Avery and David Rudovsky. New York: Clark-Boardman.

Neiderhoffer, Arthur. 1967. *Behind the Shield: The Police in Urban Society.* New York: Doubleday.

Neville. 1979. "Neville's Conclusion." In *1,001 Logical Laws, Accurate Axioms, Profound Principles, Trusty Truisms, Homey Homilies, Colorful Corollaries, Quotable Quotes, and Rambunctious Ruminations for All Walks of Life,* compiled by John Peers, p. 45. Garden City, N.Y.: Doubleday.

Newark Police Department. 1982. "Memorandum Number 82-68: Implementation of Selected Area Field Enforcement (SAFE) Program." Newark, N.J.

Newman, Bruce L., and John J. Sweeney. 1970. "Catalysts for Criminal Justice Reform: The Cleveland Experience." *The Urban Lawyer* 2 (4): 518–31.

New York v. *Quarles.* 1984. – U.S. – , 81 L. Ed.2d 550.

New York State Crime Commission. 1927. *Report to the Commission of the Subcommittee on Statistics.* Albany, N.Y.

New York Times v. *Sullivan.* 1964. 376 U.S. 254.

Nichols, Louis B. 1974. "Placing the ABA Standards in the Marketplace: The Implementation Process." *American Criminal Law Review* 12: 263–75.

Nix v. *Williams.* 1984. – U.S. – , 81 L. Ed.2d 377.

NOBLE (National Organization of Black Law Enforcement Executives). 1984. "Experiments in Fear Reduction." *NOBLE Actions,* July. Landover, Md. Mimeographed.

Nolan v. *Police Com'r of Boston.* 1981. 420 N.E. 2d 335 (MA).

Nonet, Phillipe. 1980. "The Legitimation of Purposive Decisions." *California Law Review* 68: 263.

Nonet, Phillipe, and Phillip Selznick. 1978. *Law and Society in Transition: Toward Responsive Law.* New York: Harper Colophon.

Norrgard, David L. 1969. *Regional Law Enforcement.* Chicago: Publication Administration Service.

O'Connell, Richard J. 1984. "Accreditation Commission Approves Four More Agencies." *Crime Control Digest* 18 (46), November 19, pp. 1,7.

Ostrom, Elinor; Roger B. Parks; and Gordon P. Whitaker. 1978. *Patterns of Metropolitan Policing.* Cambridge, Mass.: Ballinger.

"Our Worries: Crime, Drugs Top Economy." 1984. *USA Today*, August 27, 1984 (source: Roper Reports).

Owen v. *City of Independence*. 1980. 445 U.S. 622.

Panel on the Future of Policing. 1984. *The Future of Policing*. Seattle: William O. Douglas Institute.

Pate, Tony; Robert A. Bowers; and Ron Parks. 1976. *Three Approaches to Criminal Apprehension in Kansas City: An Evaluation Report*. Washington, D.C.: Police Foundation.

Pate, Tony; Amy Ferrara; Robert A. Bowers; and Jon Lorence. 1976. *Police Response Time: Its Determinants and Effects*. Washington, D.C.: Police Foundation.

Payton v. *New York*. 1980. 445 U.S. 573.

Pennsylvania Labor Relations Board v. *State College Area School District*. 1975. 337 A. 2d 262 (PA).

People v. *John BB*. 1982. 438 N.E. 2d 864 (N.Y.).

Perez, Douglas. 1978. "Police Accountability: A Question of Balance." Ph.D. dissertation, University of California, Berkeley.

Peter, Laurence J., ed. 1977. *Peter's Quotations: Ideas for Our Time*. New York: Bantam Books.

Peters, J. Thomas, and Robert H. Waterman. 1983. *In Search of Excellence*. New York: Harper & Row.

Peterson, Joseph L. 1983. "The Crime Lab." In *Thinking About Police: Contemporary Readings*, edited by Carl B. Klockars, pp. 184–98. New York: McGraw-Hill.

Pezzino, Angelo. 1984. Letter from Chief of Security of New Jersey Transit Bus Operations, Inc., to Newark Police Director Hubert Williams, April 23 (on file at Newark Police Department).

Pilavin, Irving, and Scott Briar. 1964. "Police Encounters with Juveniles." *American Journal of Sociology* 70 (September): 206–14.

"The Plague of Violent Crime." 1981. *Newsweek*, March 23.

Podolefsky, A., and Fred L. DuBow. 1981. *Strategies for Community Crime Prevention*. Springfield, Ill.: Charles C Thomas.

Police Act (British), 1976. *Halsbury's Laws of England, Annual Abridgment 1976*, edited by F. M. Walter and K. H. Mugford, pp. 451–52, para. 1923. London: Butterworth & Co. Ltd.

Police Complaints Board. 1983. *Police Complaints Board Triennial Review Reports, 1983*. CMNO 8853. London: Her Majesty's Stationery Office.

Police Executive Research Forum. 1982. *Summary Report on the Crime Classification System for the City of Colorado Springs, CO*. Washington, D.C.

Police Foundation. 1983. "Experiments in Fear Reduction: Program and Evaluation Plans" (report on file at the National Institute of Justice, Washington, D.C.).

————. 1981. *The Newark Foot Patrol Experiment*. Washington, D.C.

Pope, C. 1977. *Crime Specific Analysis: An Examination of Burglary*. Report No. SD-AR-11. Washington, D.C.: National Criminal Justice Information and Statistics Service, U.S. Department of Justice.

Potter, Joan, and John Blackmore. 1980. "Rising to the Top: The New Chiefs and How They Got There." *Police Magazine*, May, pp. 40–46.

President's Commission on Law Enforcement and Administration of Justice. 1968. *The Challenge of Crime in a Free Society*. New York: Avon.

_____. 1967a. *The Challenge of Crime in a Free Society*. Washington, D.C.: U.S. Government Printing Office.

_____. 1967b. *Task Force Report: The Police*. Washington, D.C.: U.S. Government Printing Office.

_____. 1967c. *Task Force Report: Science and Technology*. Washington, D.C.: U.S. Government Printing Office.

President's Violence Commission. 1968. *Transcript of Proceedings*. Washington, D.C.: U.S. Government Printing Office.

Press, James S. 1971. *Some Effects of an Increase in Police Manpower in the 20th Precinct of New York City*. New York: Rand Corporation.

Public Broadcasting System. 1984. "Forces of Order" (one-hour TV documentary), September-October.

Range, Ronald. 1983. "The Police and the Oasis Technique." A presentation at the annual convention of the International Association of Chiefs of Police, October.

Rawls, John. 1971. *A Theory of Justice*. Cambridge, Mass.: Belknap-Harvard University Press.

Reiner, Robert. 1978. *The Blue Coated Worker: A Sociological Study of Police Unionism*. Cambridge, Mass.: Cambridge University Press.

Reiss, Jr., Albert J. 1984. *Policing a City's Central District: The Oakland Story*. Washington, D.C.: National Institute of Justice.

_____. 1982. "Forecasting the Role of the Police and the Role of the Police in Social Forecasting." In *The Maintenance of Order in Society*, edited by Rita Donelan, pp. 132-52. Canada: Minister of Supply and Services (Canadian Police College).

_____. 1979. "Governmental Regulation of Scientific Inquiry: Some Paradoxical Consequences." In *Deviance and Decency*, edited by Carl B. Klockars and Finbarr W. O'Connor, pp. 61-95. Beverly Hills, Calif.: Sage.

_____. 1971. *The Police and the Public*. New Haven, Conn.: Yale University Press.

_____. 1967. "Career Orientations, Job Satisfaction, and the Assessment of Law Enforcement Problems by Police Officers." In *Studies in Crime and Law Enforcement in Major Metropolitan Areas: Field Surveys III*. Vol. II. Background paper for the President's Commission on Law Enforcement and Administration of Justice. Washington, D.C.: U.S. Government Printing Office.

Reith, Charles. 1952. *Blind Eye of History*. London: Faber & Faber; reprinted, Montclair, N.J.: Patterson Smith, 1975.

Remington, Frank. 1975. "The Standards Relating to the Urban Police Function." *American Criminal Law Review* 12 (Winter): 459-68.

"Report of the Tanselle-Adams Commission to the Honorable William H. Hudnut, III, Mayor of Indianapolis, as Recommended by Majority Vote of That Commission on May 14, 1981." 1981. Indianapolis.

Richardson, James F. 1970. *The New York Police: Colonial Times to 1901*. New York: Oxford University Press.

Ricklefs, Roger. 1983. "Public Gives Executives Low Marks for Honesty and Ethical Standards." *Wall Street Journal*, November 2, p. II-29.

Rivlin, Alice M. 1971. *Systematic Thinking for Social Action*. Washington, D.C.: Brookings Institution.

Roberg, Roy J. 1979. *Police Management and Organizational Behavior: A Contingency Approach*. St. Paul, Minn.: West.

Robinson, Cyril. 1975. "The Mayor and the Police: The Political Role of the Police in Society." In *Police Forces in History*, edited by George Mosse, pp. 277–315. Beverly Hills, Calif.: Sage.

Roncek, Dennis W. 1981. "Dangerous Places: Crime and Residential Environment." *Social Forces* 60 (September): 74–96.

Rossi, Peter; Richard Berk; and Bettye K. Eidson. 1975. *The Roots of Urban Discontent*. New York: Wiley.

Royko, Mike. 1982a. "A Forceful Cop." *Chicago Sun-Times*, December 5, p. 2.

––––––. 1982b. "Justice on the Rocks: 'Critics' the Brutal Ones." *Chicago Sun-Times*, August 8, p. 2.

Rubenstein, Jonathan. 1973. *City Police*. New York: Farrar, Straus and Giroux.

Ruchelman, Leonard, ed. 1973. *Who Rules the Police?* New York: New York University Press.

Rush, George E. 1975. "An Evaluation of Police Middle Management Training in California." Ph.D. dissertation, Claremont University.

Rye, John G. 1980. "Neighborhood Involvement." *FBI Law Enforcement Bulletin*, February, pp. 1–5.

Rynecki, Steven B., and Michael J. Morse. 1981. *Police Collective Bargaining Agreements: A National Management Survey*, rev. and expanded ed. Washington, D.C.: National League of Cities and Police Executive Research Forum.

Saffold, Howard. 1984. Remarks to the Black Law Students' Forum, Northwestern University School of Law, Chicago, Ill., February 21.

San Francisco Examiner. 1981. July 10, p. A4.

––––––. 1982. November 3, p. B11.

San Francisco Police Department. 1981. "Status Report on the Implementation of the Measures Adopted by the Police Commission to Improve the Internal Affairs Process," October 28.

Saunders, Jr., Charles B. 1970. *Upgrading American Police*. Washington, D.C.: Brookings Institution.

Savitz, Leonard A. 1975. "Early Rejection of Flawed arrests from the Criminal Justice System: A Case Study." In *Criminal Justice Research*, edited by Emilio Viano. Lexington, Mass.: Heath.

Schneider, A. L. 1976. "Victimization Surveys and Criminal Justice System Evaluation." In *Sample Surveys of the Victims of Crime*, edited by Wesley G. Skogan, pp. 135–50. Cambridge, Mass.: Ballinger.

Schneider, Betty. 1979. "Public Sector Labor Legislation and Evolutionary Analysis." In *Public Sector Bargaining*, edited by Aaron Benjamin. Washington, D.C.: Bureau of National Affairs.

Schuck, Peter H. 1983. "Organization Theory and the Teaching of Administrative Law." *Journal of Legal Education* 33: 13.

Schwartz, Alfred J., and Sumner N. Clarren. 1977. *The Cincinnati Team Policing Experiment*. Washington, D.C.: Urban Institute and Police Foundation.

Selensky v. *City of Dubuque*. 1979. Case #42264, Iowa District Court, Dubuque County; filed September 28; settled out of court.

Selznick, Phillip. 1957. *Leadership in Administration: A Sociological Interpretation*. New York: Harper & Row.

Shapiro, Nat, ed. 1984. *Whatever It Is, I'm Against It*. New York: Simon & Schuster.

Shearing, Clifford D., and Jeffrey S. Leon. 1977. "Reconsidering the Police Role: A Challenge to a Challenge of a Popular Conception." *Canadian Journal of Criminology and Corrections* 19 (4): 331–45.

Shelden, Randall. 1982. *Criminal Justice in America*. Boston: Little, Brown.

Sherman, Lawrence W. 1983. "Reducing Police Gun Use." In *Control of the Police Organization*, edited by Maurice Punch. Cambridge, Mass.: MIT Press.

_____. 1982. "Research Design Report: Experiments in Fear Reduction." Report submitted to the National Institute of Justice, Washington, D.C.

_____. 1979. "A Case for the Research Police Department." *Police Magazine*, November, pp. 58–59.

_____. 1974. "How Police Corruption Is Built into the System — And a Few Ideas for What to Do About It." In *Police Corruption: A Sociological Perspective*, edited by Lawrence W. Sherman. Garden City, N.Y.: Anchor Books.

_____. 1974. "The Sociology and the Social Reform of the American Police: 1950–1973." *Journal of Police Science and Administration* 2 (3): 255–62.

Sherman, Lawrence W., and Richard A. Berk. 1984. "The Minneapolis Domestic Violence Experiment," *Police Foundation Reports* 1 (April): 1–8.

Sherman, Lawrence W.; Catherine H. Milton; and Thomas V. Kelly. 1973. *Team Policing*. Washington, D.C.: Police Foundation.

Sherman, Lawrence W., and National Advisory Commission on Higher Education for Police Officers. 1978. *The Quality of Police Education*. San Francisco: Jossey-Bass.

Sherwood, Darlene. 1984. Phone conversation with Ms. Sherwood, President, American Society for Industrial Security, September 12.

Shinn, Richard R. 1978. "Managing Change in a Corporation." In *The Chief Executive*, edited by Chester Burger. Boston: CBI.

Shulman, Martha A. 1982. "Alternative Approaches for Delivering Public Services." *Urban Data Reports* 14 (10) (October). (published by International City Management Association).

Silberman, Charles E. 1978. *Criminal Violence, Criminal Justice*. New York: Random House.

Simon, Roger. 1982. "Cop Brutality — In Eye of Beholder." *Chicago Sun-Times*, March 4, p. 7.

Simpson, Antony E. 1979. *Accreditation and Its Significance for Programs of Higher Education in Criminology and Criminal Justice: A Review of the Literature*. Chicago: Joint Commission on Criminology and Criminal Justice Education and Standards.

Singer, Neil. 1977a. "Economic Implications of Standards for Correctional Institutions." *Crime and Delinquency* 23 (January): 293–99.

_____. 1977b. "Economic Implications of Standards Affecting Correctional Programs." *Crime and Delinquency* 23 (April): 180–95.

Singer, Robert. 1984. *The Bad Guys' Quote Book*. New York: Avon.

Skogan, Wesley G., and G. E. Antunes. 1979. "Information, Apprehension and Deterrence: Exploring the Limits of Police Productivity." *Journal of Criminal Justice* 7: 217–41.

Skogan, Wesley G., and Michael G. Maxfield. 1981. *Coping with Crime*. Beverly Hills, Calif.: Sage.

Skoler, Daniel. 1980. "Police Consolidation and Coordination." In *Progress in Polic-ing: Essays on Change*, edited by Richard Stauffenberger. Cambridge, Mass.: Ballinger.

———. 1977. *Organizing the Non-System*. Lexington, Mass.: Lexington Books.

Skolnick, Jerome. 1966. *Justice Without Trial: Law Enforcement in a Democratic Society*. New York: Wiley.

Smith, Alexander B., and Bernard Lock. 1971. "Problems in Arrests and Prosecu-tions for Obscenity and Pornography." In *Societal Control Mechanisms: Techni-cal Report*. Vol. V. Background paper for the Commission on Obscenity and Por-nography. Washington, D.C.: U.S. Government Printing Office.

Smith, Douglas A., and Christy A. Visher. 1981. "Street Level Justice: Situational Determinants of Police Arrest Decisions." *Social Problems* 29 (2): 167-77.

Specter, Arlene, and Paul R. Michel. 1982. "The Need for a New Federalism in Crim-inal Justice." *Annals of the American Academy of Political and Social Science* 462 (July): 59-71.

Spelman, William, and Dale K. Brown. 1982. *Calling the Police*. Washington, D.C.: Police Executive Research Forum.

"Spotlight: Bob McGuire." 1984. *National Centurion*, July, pp. 15-22.

"Star Wins Pulitzer Prize for Police Probe." 1975. *Indianapolis Star*, May 6, pp. 1, 3.

State v. Coccomo. 1981. 427 A.2d 131 (N.J.).

"Stealing from the Boss." 1983. *Newsweek*, December 26, p. 78.

Steckler, Craig T. 1984. Unsolicited letter to Americans for Effective Law Enforce-ment. AELE Reference File #4511. June 13.

Steiner, Eric. 1979. "Steiner's Statements." In *1,001 Logical Laws, Accurate Axioms, Profound Principles, Trusty Truisms, Homey Homilies, Colorful Corollaries, Quotable Quotes, and Rambunctious Ruminations for All Walks of Life*, com-piled by John Peers, p. 134. Garden City, N.Y.: Doubleday.

Stellwagen, Lindsay, and Stephen Gettinger. 1984. *Strategies for Supplementing the Police Budget*. Washington, D.C.: National Institute of Justice.

Stenning, Philip C. 1981. "The Role of Police Boards and Commissions as Institu-tions of Municipal Police Governance." In *Organizational Police Deviance: Its Structure and Control*, edited by Clifford D. Shearing, pp. 161-208. Toronto: Butterworth.

Strauss, M. B. 1973. "Ethics of Experimental Therapeutics." *New England Journal of Medicine* 288: 1183.

Symposium. 1975. "The American Bar Association Standards Relating to the Ad-ministration of Criminal Justice, Part II." *American Criminal Law Review* (Win-ter).

———. 1974. "The American Bar Association Standards Relating to the Administra-tion of Criminal Justice, Part I." *American Criminal Law Review* (Fall).

"Symposium on Judicial Reform." 1982. *Policy Studies Review* 10 (June): 663-707.

Tarrant, John J. 1976. *Drucker: The Man Who Invented the Corporate Society*. Boston: Cahners.

Taylor, Ian; Paul Walton; and Jock Young. 1973. *The New Criminology*. New York: Harper & Row.

Thomas, Gregory. 1983. "Crime Classification System." Speech at FBI Academy, Quantico, Va. June.

Thompson, E. P. 1966. *The Making of the English Working Class*. New York: Random House.

Toborg, Mary. 1984. "Drug Use and Pretrial Crime in the District of Columbia." *Research in Brief*, National Institute of Justice, Washington, D.C.

Toch, Hans, Douglas Grant, and Raymond T. Galvin. 1975. *Agents of Change*. New York: Wiley.

Toffler, Alvin. 1982. Speech at the FBI Academy, Quantico, Va. August.

Trojanowicz, Robert. 1982. *An Evaluation of the Neighborhood Foot Patrol Program in Flint, Michigan*. East Lansing: Michigan State University.

Tuchman, Gaye. 1978. *Making News*. New York: Free Press.

"U.A.W. President on Chrysler Board." 1984. *New York Times*, October 5, p. 34.

U.S. Commission on Civil Rights. 1981. *Who Is Guarding the Guardians?* Washington, D.C.

_____. 1972. *A Report of the Wisconsin State Committee to the U.S. Commission on Civil Rights*. Washington, D.C.

U.S. Department of Justice. Annual. *Sourcebook of Criminal Justice Statistics*. Washington, D.C.: U.S. Government Printing Office.

_____. 1982. *Basic Issues in Police Performance*. Washington, D.C.: U.S. Government Printing Office.

_____. 1980. *Justice Agencies in the United States: Summary Report—1980*. Washington, D.C.: U.S. Government Printing Office.

_____. 1979. *LEAA Newsletter* 8 (November).

_____. 1978a. *National Manpower Survey of the Criminal Justice System*. Vol. 2. *Law Enforcement*. Washington, D.C.: U.S. Government Printing Office.

_____. 1978b. *Response Time Analysis: Executive Summary*. Washington, D.C.: U.S. Government Printing Office.

_____. 1977. *Neighborhood Team Policing*. Washington, D.C.: U.S. Government Printing Office.

_____. 1973. *Improving Police/Community Relations*. Washington, D.C.: U.S. Government Printing Office.

U.S. v. Leon. 1984. – U.S. – , 82 L. Ed.2d 677.

U.S. v. Prichard. 1981. 645 F.2d 854 (10th Cir.).

Vanagunas, Stanley. 1976. "National Standards and Goals on Corrections: Some Issues of Implementation." *Criminology* 14 (August): 233–40.

Van Kirk, M. L. 1977. *Response Time Analysis*. Kansas City, Mo.: Kansas City Police Department.

Van Maanen, John. 1980. "Street Justice." In *Police Behavior*, edited by Richard J. Landman, pp. 296–311. New York: Oxford University Press.

_____. 1974. "Working the Street: A Developmental View of Police Behavior." In *The Potential for Reform of Criminal Justice*, edited by Herbert Jacob, pp. 83–130. Beverly Hills, Calif.: Sage.

Vaughan, Bill. 1977. "Law." In *Peter's Quotations: Ideas for Our Times*, edited by Laurence J. Peter, p. 288. New York: Bantam Books.

Vera Institute of Justice. 1981. *Felony Arrests: Their Prosecution and Disposition in New York City's Courts*, rev. ed. New York: Longman.

_____. 1977. *Felony Arrests: Their Prosecution and Disposition in New York City's Courts*. New York.

Vollmer, August. 1931. "The Police Executive." In *Wickersham Commission (National Commission on Law Observance) Reports, No. 14: Report on Police*, pp. 17–52. Washington, D.C.: U.S. Government Printing Office; reprinted, Montclair, N.J.: Patterson Smith, 1968.

Walker, Samuel. 1984. "'Broken Windows' and Fractured History: The Use and Misuse of History in Recent Police Patrol Analysis." *Justice Quarterly* 1 (1): 75–90.

_____. 1983a. *The Police in America: An Introduction*. New York: McGraw-Hill.

_____. 1983b. "Reform as History: The Dynamics of the Change Process in Criminal Justice." Paper read at a conference on the Impact of Reform, November 2–3, San Francisco.

_____. 1983c. "Employment of Black and Hispanic Police: Trends in the 50 Largest Cities." *Review of Applied Urban Research* (October).

_____. 1978. "Reexamining the President's Crime Commission: *The Challenge of Crime in a Free Society* After Ten Years." *Crime and Delinquency* 24 (January): 1–12.

_____. 1977. *A Critical History of Police Reform: The Emergence of Professionalism*. Lexington, Mass.: Lexington Books.

Waller, Irwin. 1979. "Organizing Research to Improve Criminal Justice Policy: A Perspective from Canada." *Journal of Research in Crime and Delinquency* (July): 196–217.

Ward, Richard H. 1978. "Viewpoint: Defending Detectives." *Police Magazine*, May, p. 55.

Washington Crime News Services. 1984a. "Mt. Dora, Florida, Police Dept. Wins First Accreditation." *Crime Control Digest* 18 (22), June 4.

_____. 1984b. "Accreditation and Operation Identification Developing Rifts in State Chiefs' Associations." *Crime Control Digest* 18 (30), July 30.

_____. 1984c. "Dade-Miami Criminal Justice Assessment Center International Conference Planned for March." *Crime Control Digest*, October 29, pp. 9–10.

_____. 1984d. "Publishing the Names of Victims and Witnesses: What Can Police and Prosecutors Do to Stop It?" *Criminal Justice Journal*, February, pp. 1, 8–12.

Weber, Max. 1957. *The Theory of Social and Economic Organizations*. Glencoe, Ill.: Free Press.

Webster, John A. 1970. "Police Task and Time Study." *Journal of Criminal Law, Criminology, and Police Science* 61: 94–100.

Weiser, Benjamin L., and Athelia Knight. 1983. "Street Cops." *Washington Post*, July 17 (seven-part series).

Westley, William A. 1970. *Violence and the Police*. Cambridge, Mass.: MIT Press.

Wheeler, Russell, and Howard Whitcomb, eds. 1977. *Judicial Administration*. Englewood Cliffs, N.J.: Prentice-Hall.

"When Police Revolt." 1985. *New York Times*, February 10, p. EY22.

Whisenand, Paul M., and R. Fred Ferguson. 1973. *The Managing of Police Organizations*. Englewood Cliffs, N.J.: Prentice-Hall.

Whitaker, Gordon P. 1983. "Police Department Size and the Quality and Cost of Police Services." In *Political Science of Criminal Justice, 1983*, edited by Stuart Nagel et al., pp. 185–96. Springfield, Ill.: Charles C Thomas.

Whitney v. California. 1927. 274 U.S. 357.

Wickersham Commission (National Commission on Law Observance). 1931. *Wickersham Commission Reports, No. 14: Report on Police.* Washington, D.C.: U.S. Government Printing Office; reprinted, Montclair, N.J.: Patterson Smith, 1968.

Wildavsky, Aaron. 1974. *The Politics of the Budgetary Process.* 2nd ed. Boston: Little, Brown.

Williams, Hubert. 1984. "Newark Fear Reduction Program." Report to the National Institute of Justice and the National Organization of Black Law Enforcement Executives, May 24. Mimeographed.

Wilson, James Q. 1980. "Police Research and Experimentation." In *Progress in Policing: Essays on Change,* edited by Richard A. Staufenberger, pp. 129–52. Cambridge, Mass.: Ballinger.

_____. 1978a. *Varieties of Police Behavior: The Management of Law and Order in Eight Communities.* Cambridge, Mass.: Harvard University Press.

_____. 1978b. *The Investigators: Managing FBI and Narcotics Agents.* New York: Basic Books.

_____. 1972. "Police in Politics." Remarks at the FBI National Academy, Quantico, Va. May.

_____. 1970. *Varieties of Police Behavior.* New York: Atheneum.

_____. 1968. *Varieties of Police Behavior.* Cambridge, Mass.: Harvard University Press.

_____. 1967. "A Reader's Guide to the Crime Commission Reports." *Public Interest* 9 (Fall), pp. 64–82.

Wilson, James Q., and George L. Kelling. 1982. "Police and Neighborhood Safety: Broken Windows." *Atlantic Monthly* 249 (March), pp. 29–38.

Wilson, Jerry. 1975. *Police Report: A View of Law Enforcement.* Boston: Little, Brown.

Wilson, Orlando W. 1950. *Police Administration.* New York: McGraw-Hill. Current edition: O. W. Wilson, and Roy C. McLaren. 1977. *Police Administration.* 4th ed. New York: McGraw-Hill.

_____. 1938. *Municipal Police Administration.* Chicago: Institute for Training in Municipal Administration. Current (7th) edition: 1971. Washington, D.C.: International City Management Association.

Wilson, Orlando W., and Roy C. McLaren. 1977. *Police Administration.* 4th ed. New York: McGraw-Hill.

Wilson, Paul E. 1974. "Implementation by Court Rule of the Criminal Justice Standards." *American Criminal Law Review* 12 (Fall): 348–49.

Winfree, L. Thomas, and Frieda Gehlen. 1981. "Police Strike: Public Support and Dissonance Reduction During a Strike by Police." *Journal of Police Science and Administration* 9 (4): 451–62.

Woody, Kenneth. 1984. "Bus Crimes Cut 40% by Police Checks." *Newark Star-Ledger,* May 6.

Wycoff, Mary Ann. 1982. "The Role of Municipal Police." Washington, D.C.: Police Foundation. Mimeographed.

Wycoff, Mary Ann, and George L. Kelling. 1978. *The Dallas Experience: Organizational Reform.* Washington, D.C.: Police Foundation.

Wynne, John M. 1978. *Prison Employee Unionism*. Washington, D.C.: National Institute of Law Enforcement and Criminal Justice.

Yates, Douglas. 1974. *City Hall and the Neighborhoods: A Street Level View of Urban Problems*. Santa Monica, Calif.: Rand Corporation (March).

Zeisel, Hans. 1982. *The Limits of Law Enforcement*. Chicago: University of Chicago Press.

Name Index

Subject Index

About the Editor and the Contributors

WILLIAM A. GELLER is a project director at the American Bar Foundation, Chicago, IL. Prior to 1981 he served as law clerk to Illinois Supreme Court Justice Walter V. Schaefer and then as research and executive director of the Chicago Law Enforcement Study Group. Mr. Geller has consulted and published widely on policing and criminal justice, focusing particularly on the causes and prevention of police-involved shootings. His articles have appeared in numerous books, professional and academic journals, and newspapers. He co-authored *Split-Second Decisions: Shootings Of and By Chicago Police*, cited by the U.S. Supreme Court in its landmark March 1985 "fleeing felon" decision in *Tennessee* v. *Garner*. He was awarded the Chicago Police Department's Medal of Honor for his co-chairmanship of a fund-drive that raised $1.5 million to equip all 12,500 officers of that agency with bullet-proof vests. Mr. Geller holds a B.S. from the State University of New York at Buffalo and a J. D. from the University of Chicago Law School.

ALBERT W. ALSCHULER is Professor of Law at the University of Chicago and has written extensively on a variety of criminal justice topics. He holds a B.A. from Harvard University and an LL.B. from Harvard Law School.

ALLEN H. ANDREWS, JR. is Director of Public Safety, Peoria, IL. He has lectured and written on public safety matters. He holds an A.B. in political science from the University of Illinois and an M.S. in law enforcement and public safety administration from Michigan State University.

KEITH R. BERGSTROM is Chief of Police, Oak Park, IL. He holds an M.A. in politics and urban affairs from the University of Miami and an M.A. in political science from the University of Wisconsin-Madison. He has completed all but his dissertation for a Ph.D. in political science at the University of Wisconsin-Madison.

ANTHONY V. BOUZA is Chief of Police, Minneapolis, MN, former Bronx Commander, New York City Police Department, and former Deputy Chief, New York City Transit Police. He has written several books and numerous articles on policing and police administration, including *Police Administration, Organization and Performance* and *Police Intelligence*. He holds a B.B.A. and M.P.A. from the City University of New York.

513

LEE P. BROWN is Chief of Police, Houston, TX, and Vice President, International Association of Chiefs of Police. He is former Director of Public Safety, Atlanta, GA, and former Director of Public Safety, Multnomah County, OR. His extensive writings include the book *The Police and Society: An Environment for Collaboration and Confrontation*. He holds a B.S. from Fresno State University, an M.S. in sociology from San Jose State University, and a master's and doctorate in criminology from the University of California, Berkeley.

RICHARD J. BRZECZEK is a practicing attorney and former Superintendent of Police, Chicago, IL. He has written and lectured extensively on a wide range of public administration and criminal justice issues. He holds a B.S. from Loyola University-Chicago, an M.P.A. from the Illinois Institute of Technology, and a J.D. from John Marshall Law School.

RONALD COCHRAN is Chief of Police, Fort Lauderdale, FL. He lectures periodically at St. Thomas Villanova University in Miami on police administration. He holds a B.A. in public administration from Biscayne College, Miami.

GARY W. CORDNER is Chief of Police, St. Michaels, MD. Until 1984 he was Assistant Professor and Graduate Program Director, Criminal Justice Department, University of Baltimore. He holds a B.S. in criminal justice from Northeastern University, Boston, and an M.S. in criminal justice and a Ph.D. in social science from Michigan State University.

RAYMOND C. DAVIS is Chief of Police, Santa Ana, CA. He has lectured and written extensively on police-community collaboration for public safety. He holds a B.S. from California State University at Long Beach and an M.P.A. from Golden Gate College, San Francisco.

FREDERICK A. ELLISTON is Visiting Professor, Department of Philosophy, University of Hawaii. He has written widely on police and professional ethics including two co-edited books, *Moral Issues in Police Work* and *Ethics, Public Policy and Criminal Justice*. He holds a B.A. from Trinity College, Toronto, and a Ph.D. in philosophy from the University of Toronto.

DONALD M. FRASER is Mayor, Minneapolis, MN. He served in the House of Representatives and is a former congressman and Minnesota state senator. He holds a B.A. and an LL.B. from the University of Minnesota.

JACK W. FULLER is Editorial Page Editor, Chicago *Tribune*. He served as special assistant to U.S. Attorney General Edward Levi. He has written extensively on a wide spectrum of public policy matters. He holds a B.S. from Northwestern University and a J.D. from Yale Law School.

WILLIAM H. HUDNUT III is Mayor, Indianapolis, IN. He is Past-President of the National League of Cities, a former congressman, and a third generation Presbyterian minister. He is a member of President Reagan's Advisory Counsel on Intergovernmental Relations, chairman of the Transit Committee, member of the board of the Roosevelt Center for American Policy Study, and co-chairman of the Federal Deficit Task Force. He holds a B.A. from Princeton University and a divinity degree from Union Theological Seminary.

JAMES B. JACOBS is Professor and Director of the Center for Research in Crime and Justice at New York University School of Law. He has written widely on criminal justice issues, especially prisons, including *Stateville: The Penitentiary in Mass Society* (1977), *Guard Unions and the Future of the Prisons* (1978), and *New Perspectives on Prisons and Imprisonment* (1983). He holds a B.A. from Johns Hopkins University, a J.D. and a Ph.D. from the University of Chicago.

GEORGE L. KELLING is Research Fellow and Executive Director of the John F. Kennedy School of Government, Program in Criminal Justice Policy and Management, Harvard University. His publications include reports on the landmark Kansas City Preventive Patrol Experiment and the Newark Foot Patrol Experiment and his widely discussed article coauthored with James Q. Wilson, "The Police and Neighborhood Safety: Broken Windows." He holds a B.A. from St. Olaf College and a Ph.D. in social welfare from the University of Wisconsin-Madison.

WAYNE A. KERSTETTER is Associate Professor, Dept. of Criminal Justice, University of Illinois at Chicago and a project director at the American Bar Foundation, Chicago, IL. He is former Superintendent, Illinois Bureau of Investigation and former Assistant First Deputy Commissioner, New York City Police Department. He has written extensively on a wide range of criminal justice topics. He holds a B.A. and J.D. from the University of Chicago.

ROBERT B. KLIESMET is President, International Union of Police Associations, AFL-CIO, and former President, Milwaukee Police Association. Among his many appointments, he served on the Panel on the Future of Policing convened by the William O. Douglas Institute for the Study of Contemporary Social Problems. He has delivered guest lectures at the University of Wisconsin Law School and the Kennedy School of Government, Harvard University.

CARL B. KLOCKARS is Associate Professor of Criminal Justice at the University of Delaware. He has written extensively on professional crime, police, criminal investigation, research ethics and criminological theory. His books include *The Professional Fence, Deviance and Decency: The Ethics of Research with Human Subjects* (coedited), *Thinking About Police: Contemporary Readings*, and *The Idea of Police*. He holds a B.A. in sociology from the University of Rhode Island and an M.A. and a Ph.D. in sociology from the University of Pennsylvania.

WILLIAM H. LINDSEY is Executive Director, The Housing Authority of Fort Lauderdale, FL. Prior to that he was a VISTA worker focusing on housing problems in Fort Lauderdale. His "slumbusting" successes have received wide media coverage, including in *Reader's Digest* and on the *60 Minutes* television show. He was honored in *Time* Magazine's 1984 Man-of-the-Year issue as one of seven Americans who exemplify the spirit of inventiveness and courage needed to improve the quality of life in the nation. He holds a B.A. in chemistry and an M.A. in systems theory from East Carolina University.

LOUIS A. MAYO is Director, Training and Testing Division, National Institute of Justice. He has taught and consulted widely on criminal justice matters. He holds a B.A. in criminology from California State University, Fresno and an M.A. and Ph.D in public administration from the American University, Washington, D.C.

CANDACE MCCOY is a member of the Ohio Bar and is currently Attorney General Research Fellow with the California Department of Justice. She holds a B.A. from Hiram College and a J.D. from the University of Cincinnati. She is a candidate for a Ph.D. in jurisprudence and social policy at the University of California, Berkeley.

WILLIAM F. MCDONALD is Associate Professor of Sociology and Deputy Director of the Institute of Criminal Law and Procedure, Georgetown University. He has written extensively on prosecutors and other criminal justice matters. He holds an A.B. from the University of Notre Dame, an M.Ed. from Boston College, and a Ph.D. in criminology from the University of California, Berkeley.

JOSEPH D. MCNAMARA is Chief of Police, San Jose, CA, and former Chief of Police, Kansas City, MO. Before that he rose from patrolman to deputy inspector in the New York City Police Department. Among his many publications are two recent books, *Safe and Sane* and *The First Direc-*

tive. He holds a B.S. from John Jay College and a Ph.D. in public administration from Harvard University.

NORVAL MORRIS is Julius Kreeger Professor of Law, University of Chicago Law School and a member of the Chicago Police Board. He is a widely respected criminologist and lawyer, having served on blue-ribbon criminal justice commissions throughout the world. Among his many posts, he served as director of the United Nations Asia and Far East Institute. His many books on criminological, correctional, and criminal law problems include *The Honest Politician's Guide to Crime Control, The Future of Imprisonment, Letter to the President on Crime Control,* and *Madness and the Criminal Law.* He holds an LL.B. and LL.M. from the University of Melbourne and a Ph.D. from London University.

PATRICK V. MURPHY is Past-President of the Police Foundation, Washington, D.C. He has held the positions of Commissioner, New York City Police Department, Commissioner, Detroit Police Department, Public Safety Director, Washington, D.C., Chief, Syracuse Police Department, and Administrator, Law Enforcement Assistance Administration, U.S. Department of Justice. He has written extensively on policing and served on innumerable blue-ribbon panels throughout the world on improving the administration of justice. He holds a B.A. from St. John's University and an M.P.A. from the City College of New York.

GEORGE NAPPER is Commissioner of the Department of Public Safety, Atlanta, Georgia. He holds a B.S., an M.A. and a Ph.D. in criminology from the University of California, Berkeley.

WESLEY A. CARROLL POMEROY is Executive Director, Independent Review Panel of Dade County, FL. He is former Executive Secretary, Detroit Board of Police Commissioners and former Chief of Police, Berkeley, CA. He holds a J.D. from San Francisco Law School.

BRUCE QUINT is Director of Planning and Development, The Housing Authority of Fort Lauderdale, FL. He holds a B.A. in psychology and an M.S. in rehabilitation counseling from Hunter College-New York and a Ph.D. in rehabilitation education from New York University.

ALBERT J. REISS, JR. is William Graham Sumner Professor of Sociology and Lecturer in Law, Yale University. He is immediate Past-President of the American Society of Criminology and an internationally respected scholar. Among his many books are *The Police and the Public* and *Cities and*

Society. He holds a Ph.B. in philosophy from Marquette University and a Ph.D. in sociology from the University of Chicago.

FRED RICE, JR. is Superintendent of Police, Chicago, IL. He serves on the executive committee of the International Association of Chiefs of Police and is a founding member of the National Organization of Black Law Enforcement Executives. He holds a B.S. and an M.S. in public administration from Roosevelt University.

MARIO A. RIVERA is Consulting Analyst, Housing Authority and Oasis Institute, Fort Lauderdale, FL. He holds a B.A. in social relations from Harvard and an M.A. in theology and social ethics and a Ph.D. in government and international studies from the University of Notre Dame.

WAYNE W. SCHMIDT is Executive Director, Americans for Effective Law Enforcement. AELE is a non-profit, tax-exempt educational organization that publishes several periodicals and research documents relating to police liability and sponsors periodic seminars on that topic throughout the country. He has written, lectured, and consulted extensively on legal issues affecting American policing. He holds an LL.M. from Northwestern University and a J.D. from Oklahoma City University.

AMITAI SCHWARTZ is Staff Counsel, American Civil Liberties Union of Northern California and former director of the Northern California Police Practices Project of the ACLU. He has written on legal questions concerning the police and civil rights. He holds a B.A. in economics from Brandeis University and a J.D. from the University of California, Berkeley.

MICHAEL G. SHANAHAN is Chief of Police, University of Washington. He is Past-General Chairman, International Association of Chiefs of Police, Division of State Associations of Chiefs of Police, Past-President, Washington Association of Sheriffs and Police Chiefs, and founding chairman, Washington Law Enforcement Executive Forum. He has written widely on public and private policing and police administration. He holds a B.A. from Stanford University.

JOHN E. SHAPARD is on the professional staff of the Federal Judicial Center, Washington, D.C. He has written widely on judicial matters and on the ethics of experimentation in law. He holds a B.A. from Pomona College and a J.D. from the U.C.L.A. School of Law.

LAWRENCE W. SHERMAN is Director of the Center for Crime Control and Professor of Criminology at the University of Maryland. He has written extensively on a wide range of police and criminal justice matters. His books include *Scandal and Reform* and *Ethics and Criminal Justice Education*. He holds an M.A. and a Ph.D. in sociology from Yale University.

WESLEY G. SKOGAN is Professor of Political Science and Urban Affairs at Northwestern University. He has written extensively on criminal justice and evaluation techniques. He holds a B.A. in political science from Indiana University and a Ph.D. in political science from Northwestern University.

JEROME H. SKOLNICK is Professor of Law (Jurisprudence and Social Policy) and former Chairman, Center for the Study of Law and Society, University of California, Berkeley. His extensive writings on policing, domestic relations, criminal law, and jurisprudence include the books *Justice Without Trial: Law Enforcement in Democratic Society, The Politics of Protest*, and *House of Cards: Legalization and Control of Casino Gambling*. He holds a B.B.A. from City College of New York and a Ph.D. in sociology from Yale University.

CARL STERN is Law Correspondent for NBC-TV News. He has served on many blue-ribbon panels aimed at improving the practice of journalism. He holds an M.S. from Columbia University and a J.D. from Cleveland State University.

JAMES K. STEWART is Director, National Institute of Justice, U.S. Department of Justice, appointed by President Reagan in 1982. Formerly he was special assistant to Attorney General William French Smith, a White House Fellow, and Commander of Criminal Investigations, Oakland Police Department. He has written and lectured throughout the world on the administration of justice. He holds an M.P.A. from California State University.

SAMUEL WALKER is Professor, Dept. of Criminal Justice, University of Nebraska, Omaha. He has written widely on criminal justice and police reform, including the books *A Critical History of Police Reform: The Emergence of Professionalism, The Police in America: An Introduction*, and *Sense and Nonsense about Crime*. He holds a B.A. in American culture from the University of Michigan, an M.A. in American history from the University of Nebraska, Omaha and a Ph.D. in American history from Ohio State University.

HUBERT WILLIAMS is President of the Police Foundation, Washington, D.C., and former Police Director, Newark, N.J. He has served on numerous national panels assessing the prospects for improved criminal justice. As Police Director, he hosted a number of nationally significant research experiments in Newark, including the Foot Patrol Experiment and a recent inquiry on fear reduction. He holds a B.S. from John Jay College of Criminal Justice and a J.D. from Rutgers University School of Law. He held a Fellowship at Harvard Law School.